Philosophy of Action

BLACKWELL PHILOSOPHY ANTHOLOGIES

Each volume in this outstanding series provides an authoritative and comprehensive collection of the essential primary readings from philosophy's main fields of study. Designed to complement the *Blackwell Companions to Philosophy* series, each volume represents an unparalleled resource in its own right, and will provide the ideal platform for course use.

Philosophy of Action

An Anthology

Edited by

Jonathan Dancy and Constantine Sandis

WILEY Blackwell

Fred Dretske and Jonathan Lowe died while this volume was in preparation.
It is dedicated to them.

Contents

Preface

Though all the great philosophers since Plato have included accounts of action in their philosophical systems, the philosophy of action only began to be conceived of as a discrete topic in philosophy towards the end of the last century. It is only recently that we have begun to find graduate classes devoted entirely to philosophy of action. The work of Wittgenstein has been seminal in this change, and with that in mind we have placed some especially influential passages from this work in Chapter 1, outside the six parts that follow. With this exception, the material in the volume is divided thematically rather than chronologically (though the various parts have been ordered chronologically where doing so makes sense).

While appreciating that readers often dip into anthologies with very specific purposes, we have grouped the papers we reprint here (all except John McDowell's chapter are already in print) into six parts. These are to some extent artificial, and certainly could have been done differently, but our aim was to offer a structure that might help in the design and development of a course on recent philosophy of action. That structure itself has led to some classic papers failing to find a place; most of them are mentioned in the Further Reading at the end of the introduction to each part.

Each part has an introduction designed to give students an overview of the material it contains that will help them navigate through it. The philosophy of action is a fast-growing field that cuts across a large number of philosophical and scientific discourses. We have tried to give a taste of some of the latest research

without prioritizing this over the work that has made the subject what it is.

A number of acknowledgments are due: many thanks to several anonymous referees for helping us with the selection and organization of the material included here. We also received sage advice on these matters from Maria Alvarez and John Hyman; Erasmus Mayr gave us timely and perceptive feedback on all of our introductions.

In addition, we are very grateful to John McDowell for allowing us to include a new recension of some of his recent work on intention. For correspondence and permission to make minor editorial changes to their work we should also like to thank Maria Alvarez and John Hyman (again), Michael Bratman, Fred Dretske, Jennifer Hornsby, E. J. Lowe, Joseph Raz, and Michael Smith.

At Wiley-Blackwell we should like to thank Nick Bellorini for commissioning the volume, as well as Lindsay Bourgeois, Jennifer Bray, Liam Cooper, Jeff Dean, and Allison Kostka for their invaluable help and patience throughout. Particular thanks are owed to Christopher Feeney for his meticulous copy-editing and to Joanna Pyke for overseeing everything.

Finally, we owe thanks to our research assistants Robert Vinten and István Zárdai for helping out with the first and last stages of the work. We should not have been able to fund them without generous support from Oxford Brookes University's Central Research Fund and the Darrell K. Royal Fund at the University of Texas at Austin.

JD & CS
Oxford

Source Acknowledgments

The editors and publisher gratefully acknowledge the permission granted to reproduce the copyright material in this book:

Wittgenstein, L. (2009), *Philosophical Investigations* §§611–628 (omitting 626), 4th edn., ed. P. M. S. Hacker and Joachim Schulte (Oxford: Wiley-Blackwell). © 2009 by Blackwell Publishing. Reprinted with permission of John Wiley & Sons Ltd.

Davidson, D. (1971), "Agency," in R. Binkley, R. Bronaugh, and A. Marras (eds.), *Agent, Action, and Reason* (Toronto: University of Toronto Press), 3–25. Reprinted with permission of the publisher.

Bennett, J. (1973), "Shooting, Killing and Dying," *Canadian Journal of Philosophy* 2 (3), 315–323. Published by University of Calgary Press. © Jonathan Bennett. Reprinted with kind permission of the author.

Frankfurt, H. G. (1978), "The Problem of Action," *American Philosophical Quarterly* 15 (2), 157–162. Reprinted with permission.

Alvarez, M., and Hyman, J. (1998), "Agents and their Actions," *Philosophy* 73 (2), 219–245. Published by Cambridge Journals, Cambridge. © Royal Institute of Philosophy 1996. Reproduced with permission.

Hornsby, J. (2004), "Agency and Actions," in J. Hyman and H. Steward (eds.), *Agency and Action* (Cambridge: Cambridge University Press), 1–23. © Royal Institute of Philosophy and the contributors 2004. Published by Cambridge University Press. Reproduced with permission.

Prichard, H. A. (1945), "Acting, Willing, Desiring," in *Moral Obligation* (Oxford: Oxford University Press, 1949), 272–281. Reprinted with permission of Oxford University Press.

Ryle, G. (1949), "The Will," in *The Concept of Mind*, 60th anniversary edn. (Abingdon: Routledge, 2009), 62–74. Reprinted with permission of Taylor & Francis Books.

Hornsby, J. (1980), "Acting and Trying to Act," in *Actions* (London: Routledge and Kegan Paul), 33–45. Reprinted with permission of Taylor & Francis Books.

Lowe, E. J. (1996), "Action and Volition," in *Subjects of Experience* (Cambridge: Cambridge University Press), 140–156. Copyright © Cambridge University Press 1996. Reproduced with permission.

Anscombe, G. E. M. (1957), *Intention* §§1–9 (omitting 2 and parts of 8) (Cambridge, Mass.: Harvard University Press), 1–16. Copyright © 1957, 1963 by G. E. M. Anscombe. Reprinted by permission of the publisher.

Donnellan, K. S. (1963), "Knowing What I Am Doing," *Journal of Philosophy* 60 (14), 401–409. Reprinted with permission of The Journal of Philosophy.

Davidson, D. (1978), "Intending," in Y. Yovel and D. Reidel (eds.), *Philosophy of History and Action* (Jerusalem: The Magnes Press, The Hebrew University), 41–60. First published by D. Reidel. Reprinted with permission of Springer.

Bratman, M. (1984), "Two Faces of Intention," *Philosophical Review* 93 (3), 375–405. Copyright © 1984 Cornell University. All rights reserved. Republished by permission of the copyright holder and current publisher Duke University Press, www.dukeupress.edu.

McDowell, J. (2009), "Acting As One Intends." This chapter was prepared by Jonathan Dancy from McDowell's Hägerström Lectures, given at Uppsala University in 2005. © John McDowell. Reprinted with kind permission of the author.

Knobe, J. (2003), "Intentional Action and Side Effects in Ordinary Language," *Analysis* 63 (3), 190–194. Reprinted with permission of Oxford University Press.

Kavka, G. S. (1983), "The Toxin Puzzle," *Analysis* 43 (1), 33–36. Published by Oxford Journals, Oxford University Press, Oxford. Reprinted with permission of Oxford University Press.

Stoutland, F. (2008), "The Ontology of Social Agency," *Analyse & Kritik* 30, 533–551.

Davidson, D. (1963), "Actions, Reasons, and Causes," *Journal of Philosophy* 60 (23), 685–700. Reprinted with permission of The Journal of Philosophy.

Dancy, J. (2000), "How to Act for a Good Reason," excerpts from *Practical Reality* (Oxford: Oxford University Press), chs. 5 and 6. Reprinted with permission of Oxford University Press.

Korsgaard, C. (2008), "Acting for a Reason," in *The Constitution of Agency* (Oxford: Oxford University Press), 207–229. © C. Korsgaard 2008. Reprinted with permission of Oxford University Press.

Hursthouse, R. (1981), "Arational Actions," *Journal of Philosophy* 88 (2), 57–68. Reprinted with permission of Rosalind Hursthouse and The Journal of Philosophy.

Raz, J. (2001), "Agency, Reason, and the Good," in *Engaging Reason* (Oxford: Oxford University Press), 22–45. Reprinted with permission of Oxford University Press.

Watson, G. (1977), "Skepticism about Weakness of Will," *Philosophical Review* 86 (3), 316–339. Copyright © 1977 Cornell University. All rights reserved. Republished by permission of the copyright holder and the present publisher, Duke University Press, www.dukeupress.edu.

Hempel, C. G. (1963), "Explanation in Science and in History §§1–3," in Robert G. Colodny (ed.), *Frontiers of Science and Philosophy* (Pittsburgh, Pa.: University of Pittsburgh Press), 276–284. Reprinted with permission of University of Pittsburgh Press.

Dray, W. (1957), "The Rationale of Actions," in *Laws and Explanation in History* (Oxford: Oxford University Press), 118–137. Reprinted with permission of Oxford University Press.

Hempel, C. G. (1963), "Explanation in Science and in History §§4–7," in Robert G. Colodny (ed.), *Frontiers of Science and Philosophy* (Pittsburgh, Pa.: University of Pittsburgh Press), 284–296. Reprinted with permission of University of Pittsburgh Press.

Smith, M. (2009), "The Explanatory Role of Being Rational," in D. Sobel and S. Wall (eds.), *Reasons for Action* (Cambridge: Cambridge University Press), 58–80. © Cambridge University Press 2009. Reprinted with permission.

Malcolm, N. (1968), "The Conceivability of Mechanism," *Philosophical Review* 77 (1), 45–72 (omitting final section). *Philosophical Review* is published by Duke University Press, Durham, N.C.

Collins, A. W. (1984), "Action, Causality, and Teleological Explanation," *Midwest Studies in Philosophy* 9 (1), 345–369. Reprinted with permission of John Wiley & Sons, Ltd.

Dretske, F. (2004), "Psychological vs. Biological Explanations of Behavior," *Behavior and Philosophy* 32 (1), 167–177. *Behavior and Philosophy* is published by the Cambridge Center for Behavioral Studies. Reprinted with permission.

Chisholm, R. (1964), "Human Freedom and the Self," in *The Lindley Lectures* (Lawrence, Kans.: University of Kansas), 3–15. Reprinted with permission of The University of Kansas.

Frankfurt, H. G. (1969), "Alternate Possibilities and Moral Responsibility," *Journal of Philosophy* 66 (23), 829–839. Reprinted with permission of Harry Frankfurt and The Journal of Philosophy.

Fischer, J. M. (1997), "Responsibility, Control, and Omissions," *Journal of Ethics* 1 (1), 45–64. Reprinted with permission of Springer.

Strawson, G. (2011), "The Impossibility of Ultimate Responsibility?," in R. Swinburne (ed.), *Free Will and Modern Science* (Oxford: Oxford University Press), 126–140. Reprinted with permission of Oxford University Press.

Steward, H. (2011), "Moral Responsibility and the Concept of Agency," in R. Swinburne (ed.), *Free Will and Modern Science* (Oxford: Oxford University Press), 141–157. Reprinted with permission of Oxford University Press.

Mele, A. R. (2011), "Free Will and Science," in R. Kane (ed.), *The Oxford Handbook of Free Will*, 2nd edn. (Oxford: Oxford University Press), 499–514. Reprinted with permission of Oxford University Press.

Every effort has been made to trace copyright holders and to obtain their permission for the use of copyright material. The publisher apologizes for any errors or omissions in the above list and would be grateful if notified of any corrections that should be incorporated in future reprints or editions of this book.

1

Philosophical Investigations §§611–628

Ludwig Wittgenstein

611. "Willing – wanting – too is merely an experience," one would like to say (the 'will' too only 'idea'). It comes when it comes, and I cannot bring it about.

Not bring it about? – Like *what*? What can I bring about, then? What am I comparing it with when I say this?

612. I wouldn't say of the movement of my arm, for example, that it comes when it comes, and so on. And this is the domain in which it makes sense to say that something doesn't simply happen to us, but that we *do* it. "I don't need to wait for my arm to rise – I can raise it." And here I am making a contrast between the movement of my arm and, say, the fact that the violent thudding of my heart will subside.

613. In the sense in which I can ever bring about anything (such as stomach-ache through overeating), I can also bring about wanting. In this sense, I bring about wanting to swim by jumping into the water. I suppose I was trying to say: I can't want to want; that is, it makes no sense to speak of wanting to want. "Wanting" is not the name of an action, and so not of a voluntary one either. And my use of a wrong expression came from the fact that one is inclined to think of

Wittgenstein, L. (2009), *Philosophical Investigations* §§611–628 (omitting 626), 4th edn., ed. P. M. S. Hacker and Joachim Schulte (Oxford: Wiley-Blackwell). © 2009 by Blackwell Publishing. Reprinted with permission of John Wiley & Sons Ltd.

wanting as an immediate non-causal bringing about. But a misleading analogy lies at the root of this idea; the causal nexus seems to be established by a mechanism connecting two parts of a machine. The connection may be disrupted if the mechanism malfunctions. (One thinks only of the normal ways in which a mechanism goes wrong, not, say, of cog-wheels suddenly going soft, or penetrating each other, and so on.)

614. When I raise my arm 'voluntarily', I don't make use of any means to bring the movement about. My wish is not such a means either.

615. "Willing, if it is not to be a sort of wishing, must be the action itself. It mustn't stop anywhere short of the action." If it is the action, then it is so in the ordinary sense of the word; so it is speaking, writing, walking, lifting a thing, imagining something. But it is also striving, trying, making an effort – to speak, to write, to lift a thing, to imagine something, and so on.

616. When I raise my arm, I have *not* wished it to rise. The voluntary action excludes this wish. It is, however, possible to say: "I hope I shall draw the circle faultlessly." And that is to express a wish that one's hand should move in such-and-such a way.

617. If we cross our fingers in a special way, we are sometimes unable to move a particular finger when someone tells us to do so, if he only *points* to the

Philosophy of Action: An Anthology, First Edition. Edited by Jonathan Dancy and Constantine Sandis.
© 2015 John Wiley & Sons, Inc. Published 2015 by John Wiley & Sons, Inc.

finger – merely shows it to the eye. However, if he touches it, we *can* move it. One would like to describe this experience as follows: we are unable to *will* to move the finger. The case is quite different from that in which we are not able to move the finger because someone is, say, holding it. One is now inclined to describe the former case by saying: one can't find any point of application for the will until the finger is touched. Only when one feels the finger can the will know where it is to engage. – But this way of putting it is misleading. One would like to say: "How am I to know where I am to catch hold with the will, if the feeling does not indicate the place?" But then how do I know to what point I am to direct the will when the feeling *is* there?

It is experience that shows that in this case the finger is, as it were, paralysed until we feel a touch on it; it could not have been known a priori.

618.　One imagines the willing subject here as something without any mass (without any inertia), as a motor which has no inertia in itself to overcome. And so it is only mover, not moved. That is: one can say "I will, but my body does not obey me" – but not: "My will does not obey me." (Augustine)

But in the sense in which I can't fail to will, I can't try to will either.

619.　And one might say: "It is only inasmuch as I can never try to will that I can always will."

620.　*Doing* itself seems not to have any experiential volume. It seems like an extensionless point, the point of a needle. This point seems to be the real agent – and what happens in the realm of appearances merely consequences of this doing. "I *do*" seems to have a definite sense, independently of any experience.

621.　But there is one thing we shouldn't overlook: when 'I raise my arm', my arm rises. And now a problem emerges: what is left over if I subtract the fact that my arm rises from the fact that I raise my arm?

((Are the kinaesthetic sensations my willing?))

622.　When I raise my arm, I don't usually *try* to raise it.

623.　"I want to get to that house at all costs." – But if there is no difficulty about it, *can* I strive at all costs to get to the house?

624.　In the laboratory, when subjected to an electric current, for example, someone with his eyes shut says "I am moving my arm up and down" – though his arm is not moving. "So", we say, "he has the special feeling of making that movement." – Move your arm to and fro with your eyes shut. And now try, while you do so, to talk yourself into the idea that your arm is staying still and that you are only having certain strange feelings in your muscles and joints!

625.　"How do you know that you've raised your arm?" – "I feel it." So what you recognize is the feeling? And are you certain that you recognize it right? – You're certain that you've raised your arm; isn't this the criterion, the measure, of recognizing?

[…]

627.　Consider the following description of a voluntary action: "I form the decision to pull the bell at 5 o'clock; and when it strikes 5, my arm makes this movement." – Is that the correct description, and not *this* one: "… and when it strikes 5, I raise my arm"? — One would like to supplement the first description: "And lo and behold! my arm goes up when it strikes 5." And this "lo and behold!" is precisely what doesn't belong here. I do *not* say "Look, my arm is going up!" when I raise it.

628.　So one might say: voluntary movement is marked by the absence of surprise. And now I don't mean you to ask "But *why* isn't one surprised here?"

Part I

Action and Agency

Introduction to Part I

1.

Although accounts of action have been central to most philosophical systems from Plato to Kant, it is only in recent years (following the writings of Wittgenstein and Anscombe, Chapters 1 and 11) that philosophy of action has come to be seen as a subject in its own right. We begin this volume with enquiries into what we might call the most basic question in this area of study: what is action?

One obvious suggestion is that action is bodily motion. But not all bodily motion is action; when you jog my arm, the motion of my arm is not an action of mine – I haven't moved my arm – and it isn't an action of yours, either. So what is the difference between those bodily motions that are actions and those that are not? The most popular strategy is to adopt a causal theory, whereby the distinction between actions and other forms of behavior lies in their causal origins; a sneeze, for instance, is typically not going to count as an action, because it has the wrong sort of cause. So which causes are of the right sort? Davidson's influential answer to this question identifies the causes of action with (the onset of) beliefs and pro-attitudes (such as desires, preferences, and values) that *rationalize* the action, that is, show how the action that is their effect made sense to the agent, and so can be thought of as the agent's reasons for doing what he did (see Chapter 19). Most sneezes are not actions, because they are not caused by rationalizing beliefs and desires, but by such things as tickles. Davidson saw this account as an improvement on earlier views which identified the causes in question with inner acts of will. His view is a form of event-causalism (since the action is an event and its causes are events, too), and due to its prominence in the literature is frequently also referred to as 'the standard view'.

Event-causalism faces two general challenges. The first, recognized by Davidson himself, is that the right sort of cause (viz. a 'rationalizing' one) can bring about an action in the wrong sort of way (i.e. not in virtue of its rationalizing power). So we don't just need things of the right sort to do the causing, we need them to do their causing in the right sort of way. Davidson (Chapter 2) gives the now famous example of a climber who wants to rid himself of the weight and danger of holding another man on a rope, and who knows that the way to do this is to let go of the rope; but if this belief and desire together so unnerve him that his grip relaxes and the rope slips through his fingers, the loosening of the grip is something that happens to him rather than something that he does; so it is not an action of his even though it is caused by a rationalizing belief-desire combination (Davidson 1973). This has come to be known as the problem of deviant causes (addressed by Smith in Chapter 28).

Philosophy of Action: An Anthology, First Edition. Edited by Jonathan Dancy and Constantine Sandis.

The second challenge to event-causalism relates to the lack of any causal role played by agents themselves in all this. If actions are events caused by (the onset of) prior mental states and/or neural processes, we arguably lose sight of what, if any, role *we* play in all this. If we are not ourselves actively involved, are we really the agents of our own actions or are we mere vehicles for them? It seems insufficient for agency that the causes in question occur inside us. Our digestive processes, for example, are alien to our agency in a way in which our actions had better not be. This worry has come to be known as the problem of 'the disappearing agent'; it affects any account that, like Davidson's, understands actions as a species of events, viz. ones with a cause that is not identified with the agent. This problem is the focus of Hornsby's contribution in this part (Chapter 6). (There are other challenges to the details of Davidson's view, which are discussed in Parts IV and V.)

So an alternative strategy that is not event-causalist – and is sometimes even misleadingly described as non-causalist – identifies the cause with the agent himself (Chisholm 1964; Reid 1969; O'Connor 2000) rather than with some event. This idea, known as agent-causation, is thought to avoid the two problems discussed above. Agent-causalists disagree over whether the agent causes her action or whether the action consists in her causing a certain result (the latter is argued by Alvarez and Hyman in Chapter 5). But either way, there is the further question of whether an agent's causing something should itself be understood as an event, and if so, what, if anything, brings about that event. (Ruben 2003 denies that there are such events as the causing of things by agents; O'Connor 2000 denies that they need further causes.)

Not everybody agrees that action is bodily motion with a particular kind of cause. For instance Frankfurt (Chapter 4) defends the non-causalist view that what makes a bodily motion of yours an action is that you are embracing it as your own and that it occurs under your guidance. On this account there can be actions that do not involve the causation of bodily motion at all, so long they are embraced by the agent in the relevant way. Examples of such actions might be pressing one's hand against a door to keep it closed, refraining from apologizing, and

omitting to send a card. In addition, some 'volitionist' philosophers identify actions not with bodily motions, however caused, but with the inner causes of those motions, which they take to be acts of will or volitions. Other volitionists take actions to be complex events composed of volitions followed (causally or otherwise) by bodily movements; on this view neither the volition nor the bodily motion is itself an action. These and other related views will be considered in more detail in the introduction to Part II.

Whatever the causes of action may be, most of the above views seem to identify actions themselves with events of some sort. But some thinkers identify actions with processes rather than events. The precise difference between the two characterizations is contentious, but it is generally agreed that – unlike events – processes need not occur throughout or across a temporal stretch (Mourelatos 1978). Dretske (1988) argues that an action is the causal process of a mental/neural event causing a bodily event. More recent process-theorists inspired by Aristotle (e.g. Stout 1997) prefer to think of actions as non-causal processes. These are teleological processes defined by an end or goal that need not be achieved in order for it to be true that the process has taken place. One may, for example, be in the process of baking a cake without ever succeeding in baking one, or crossing the road without ever making it to the other side. So understood, there can be cake-baking or road-crossing processes without there having been a cake-baking or road-crossing event.

Whether actions are events or processes, it may seem that they are at least occurrences or happenings. In Anscombe's terms, "I do what happens … there is no distinction between my doing and the things happening" (1957: §29). On this outlook, the problem of action we have been dealing with is that of offering a way of distinguishing the doings of an agent from what 'merely' happens to him (see the chapter by Frankfurt in this part). But even this framework can be, and has been, rejected. Some philosophers take actions to be instances of relations (e.g. Hyman 2001). Others remind us that to act is to do something (e.g. bring about *x*) and then proceed to distinguish between the thing done (the deed?) and the event of one's doing it (Macmurray 1938; Hornsby 1980; Ricœur 1986). This distinction is often compared to that between the thing thought and one's thinking it, or between the thing said and one's saying it.

2.

The term 'basic action' was first introduced by Danto, in his 1963 paper "What We Can Do." Danto's goal was to identify the point at which agency begins (and arguably freedom and moral responsibility with it, but see the discussion of these issues in our introduction to Part VI). Danto's governing thought is that no matter how complex the action I am doing, there must always be a basic element to it, viz. something by doing which I do everything else that I am doing. But the notion of the basic needs careful handing everywhere in philosophy, not least in the case of basic action. Baier (1971) has raised the worry that there are at least eight kinds of basicness, some of which are a matter of degree rather than kind: causally basic, instrumentally basic, conventionally basic, ontologically basic, logically basic, genetically basic, ease basic, and isolation basic. If so, we need to be sure which one of these we are talking about. Danto's own example of a paradigmatic basic action is that of moving an arm "without having to do anything to cause it to move" (so pushing it with the other arm won't count). Volitionists, by contrast, maintain that such an action as moving one's arm is the effect of a volition; this volition is the basic action and its effect, the moving of the arm, is another action (done by means of the basic action of willing).

Chisholm has offered an alternative, teleological, definition of basic action intended to be neutral on these issues of causality: "'A is performed by the agent as a basic act' could be defined as: the agent succeeds in making A happen, and there is no B, other than A, which he undertook to make happen with an end to making A happen" (Chisholm 1964: 617, n.7). But it seems odd to talk of succeeding in making one's own actions happen. In later works Danto himself replaces all talk of causal or temporal basicness with the notion of *mediation*: "Actions we do but not *through* any distinct thing which we also do … I shall call basic, and mediated ones are accordingly non-basic" (Danto 1973).

A remaining and persistent difficulty with any non-teleological view of basicness is that in order to locate those actions that are basic, we need a principle of action individuation. Anscombe (in §26 of *Intention*) and Davidson (in numerous works, including "Agency") famously argued that the basicness of an action is sensitive to our description of it. This account falls out of the more general position that actions are events with an indefinite number of descriptions, each of which will highlight some psychological and/or physical feature(s) of the event in question.

For example, suppose that Donald poisons the inhabitants by replenishing the water supply, and that he does the latter by operating the pump, which in turn he does by moving his arm in a particular way. Arguably, what we have here is not four actions but one action with four different descriptions, viz. those of poisoning, replenishing, pumping, and moving. (It is not equally plausible that all by-relations operate in this way; if I win an award by performing well in a contest, my performing well is not my winning.) One of these descriptions is the most basic description of the action, and the 'by-relation' may tell us which it is. Donald poisoned by pumping, he did not pump by poisoning.

So how many actions has Donald performed, four or one? As we have seen, Anscombe and Davidson argued that what we have here is not so much four actions as four different descriptions of one action. According to this 'reductionist' view, being basic is a matter of description. Davidson accordingly maintains that *all* actions are basic or 'primitive' under some description, since, strictly speaking, "we never do more than move our bodies: the rest is up to nature" ("Agency", p. 18 in this volume). By contrast, 'pluralists' or 'multipliers' such as Goldman (1970) and Thomson (1971) argue that each of the above descriptions picks out a different action, and that only one of them (at most) is basic. Hornsby (1979) rejects the labels 'unifiers' and 'multipliers' in favor of 'identifiers' and 'differentiators' on the grounds that the former pair serves to conflate identity criteria with *counting* questions that do not obviously apply to action.

3.

A related debate focuses not on the number of actions performed but on their spatio-temporal location. Suppose that Bob Marley shot the sheriff at time t^1, but that the sheriff only died at a later time t^3, before which – at time t^2 – Marley recorded his famous song. Did Marley kill the sheriff before or after recording his song (he certainly didn't do it while singing)? It seems as implausible to claim (with the differentiators) that Marley did not kill the sheriff until t^3 – after he had left the scene of the crime – as it would be to follow identifiers in maintaining that he killed the sheriff at t^1 – before the sheriff died. It is often objected (for instance by Bennett, Chapter 3) that the implausibility of the latter claim is not (genuinely) ontological but (merely) a linguistic oddity. We do not call a woman a mother before she has any children, yet we may, after the birth or adoption of her first child, legitimately speak of what this 'mother' did before she had any children. By the same token (or so the argument goes), while we cannot at t^1 (while the sheriff was still alive) truthfully *say* that Marley killed the sheriff, at t^3 (when the sheriff is dead) it becomes perfectly acceptable to talk of Marley 'killing' him at t^1 (before he died).

A different strategy is to distinguish between the *cause* of the sheriff's death, namely the shooting, from the logically related (yet distinct) *causing* of his death, namely the killing. While it is arguably acceptable to conceive of both these things as 'events' of people acting, it would be problematic to think of the causing of an event as something which could itself be brought about. Finally, it has been argued (e.g. by Dretske 1988) that while causings can be located in time and space, we cannot always do so in a fine-grained manner. To *insist* on a more precise temporal location is as silly as insisting that the killing must have also had a spatial location which is smaller than, say, that of a tin of soup. If Marley shot the sheriff in March 1973 (before recording his song about it in April 1973), and if the sheriff (unlike the deputy) did not die until November 1973 (after the hit record was released), then we can truthfully (and informatively) say that Marley killed the sheriff in 1973, though we cannot be any more specific than that. Finally, the temporal location of any given event at a certain time does not imply that it must have been occurring continuously throughout that period (consider chess matches, for example).

References

Anscombe, G. E. M. (1957), *Intention* (Oxford: Blackwell).

Baier, A. (1971), "The Search for Basic Actions," *American Philosophical Quarterly* 8 (2), 161–170.

Chisholm, R. M. (1964), "The Descriptive Element in the Concept of Action," *Journal of Philosophy* 61 (20), 613–624.

Danto, A. C. (1963), "What We Can Do," *Journal of Philosophy* 60 (15), 435–445.

Danto, A. C. (1973), *Analytical Philosophy of Action* (Cambridge: Cambridge University Press).

Davidson, D. (1973), "Freedom to Act"; reprinted in *Essays on Actions and Events* (Oxford: Clarendon Press, 1980), 63–82.

Dretske, F. (1988), *Explaining Behavior: Reasons in a World of Causes* (Cambridge, Mass.: MIT Press).

Goldman, A. I. (1970), *A Theory of Human Action* (Princeton, N.J.: Princeton University Press).

Hornsby, J. (1979), "Actions and Identities," *Analysis* 39 (4), 195–201.

Hornsby, J. (1980), *Actions* (London: Routledge).

Hyman, J. (2001), "-Ings and -ers," *Ratio* 14 (4), 298–317.

Macmurray, J. (1938), "What is Action?," *Proceedings of the Aristotelian Society* Supplementary Volume 17, 69–85.

Mourelatos, A. P. D. (1978), "Events, States, and Processes," *Linguistics and Philosophy* 2 (3), 415–434.

O'Connor, T. (2000), *Persons and Causes: The Metaphysics of Free Will* (Oxford: Oxford University Press).

Reid, T. (1969), *Essays on the Active Powers of the Human Mind*, ed. B. A. Brody (Cambridge, Mass.: MIT Press).

Ricœur, P. (1986/1991), *From Text to Action*, trans. K. Blamey and J. B. Thompson (London: The Athlone Press).

Ruben, D.-H. (2003), *Action and its Explanation* (Oxford: Oxford University Press).

Stout, R. (1997), "Processes," *Philosophy* 72 (279) (Jan.), 19–27.

Thomson, J. J. (1971), "The Time of a Killing," *Journal of Philosophy* 68 (5), 115–132.

Further Reading

Danto, A. C. (1965), "Basic Actions," *American Philosophical Quarterly* 2 (2), 141–148.

Davidson, D. (1969), "The Individuation of Events"; reprinted in his *Essays on Actions and Events* (Oxford: Clarendon Press, 1980), 163–180.

Mayr, E. (2011), *Understanding Human Agency* (Oxford: Oxford University Press).

Thompson, M. (2008), *Life and Action* (Cambridge, Mass.: Harvard University Press).

von Wright, G. H. (1963), *Norm and Action* (London: Routledge & Kegan Paul).

2

Agency

Donald Davidson

What events in the life of a person reveal agency; what are his deeds and his doings in contrast to mere happenings in his history; what is the mark that distinguishes his actions?

This morning I was awakened by the sound of someone practising the violin. I dozed a bit, then got up, washed, shaved, dressed, and went downstairs, turning off a light in the hall as I passed. I poured myself some coffee, stumbled on the edge of the dining room rug, and spilled a bit of coffee fumbling for the *New York Times*.

Some of these items record things I did; others, things that befell me, things that happened to me on the way to the dining room. Among the things I did were get up, wash, shave, go downstairs, and spill a bit of coffee. Among the things that happened to me were being awakened and stumbling on the edge of the rug. A borderline case, perhaps, is dozing. Doubts could be kindled about other cases by embroidering on the story. Stumbling can be deliberate, and when so counts as a thing done. I might have turned off the light by inadvertently brushing against the switch; would it then have been my deed, or even something that I did?

Many examples can be settled out of hand, and this encourages the hope that there is an interesting principle at work, a principle which, if made explicit, might help explain why the difficult cases are difficult. On the other side a host of cases raise difficulties. The question itself seems to go out of focus when we start putting pressure on such phrases as "what he did," "his actions," "what happened to him," and it often matters to the appropriateness of the answer what form we give the question. (Waking up is something I did, perhaps, but not an action.) We should maintain a lively sense of the possibility that the question with which we began is, as Austin suggested, a misguided one.[1]

In this essay, however, I once more try the positive assumption, that the question is a good one, that there is a fairly definite subclass of events which are actions. The costs are the usual ones: oversimplification, the setting aside of large classes of exceptions, the neglect of distinctions hinted by grammar and common sense, recourse to disguised linguistic legislation. With luck we learn something from such methods. There may, after all, be important and general truths in this area, and if there are how else will we discover them?

Philosophers often seem to think that there must be some simple grammatical litmus of agency, but none has been discovered. I drugged the sentry, I contracted malaria, I danced, I swooned, Jones was kicked by me, Smith was outlived by me: this is a series of examples designed to show that a person named as subject in sentences in the active, whether

Davidson, D. (1971), "Agency," in R. Binkley, R. Bronaugh, and A. Marras (eds.), *Agent, Action, and Reason* (Toronto: University of Toronto Press), 3–25. Reprinted with permission of the publisher.

Philosophy of Action: An Anthology, First Edition. Edited by Jonathan Dancy and Constantine Sandis.
© 2015 John Wiley & Sons, Inc. Published 2015 by John Wiley & Sons, Inc.

or not the verb is transitive, or as object in the passive, may or may not be the agent of the event recorded.[2]

Another common error is to think verbs may be listed according to whether they do or do not impute agency to a subject or object. What invites the error is that this is true of some verbs. To say of a person that he blundered, insulted his uncle, or sank the *Bismark* is automatically to convict him of being the author of those events; and to mention someone in the subject position in a sentence with the verb in the passive tense is, so far as I can see, to ensure that he is not the agent. But for a host of cases, a sentence can record an episode in the life of the agent and leave us in the dark as to whether it was an action. Here are some examples: he blinked, rolled out of bed, turned on the light, coughed, squinted, sweated, spilled the coffee, and tripped over the rug. We know whether these events are actions only after we know more than the verb provides. By considering the additional information that would settle the matter, we may find an answer to the question of what makes a bit of biography an action.

One hint was given in my opening fragmentary diary. Tripping over a rug is normally not an action; but it is if done intentionally. Perhaps, then, being intentional is the relevant distinguishing mark. If it were, it would help explain why some verbs imply agency, for some verbs describe actions that cannot be anything but intentional; asserting, cheating, taking a square root, and lying are examples.

This mark will not work, however, for although intention implies agency, the converse does not hold. Thus spilling the coffee, sinking the *Bismark*, and insulting someone are all things that may or may not be done intentionally, but even when not intentional, they are normally actions. If, for example, I intentionally spill the contents of my cup, mistakenly thinking it is tea when it is coffee, then spilling the coffee is something I do, it is an action of mine, though I do not do it intentionally. On the other hand, if I spill the coffee because you jiggle my hand, I cannot be called the agent. Yet while I may hasten to add my excuse, it is not incorrect, even in this case, to say I spilled the coffee. Thus we must distinguish three situations in which it is correct to say I spilled the coffee: in the first, I do it intentionally; in the second I do not do it intentionally but it is my

action (I thought it was tea); in the third it is not my action at all (you jiggle my hand).[3]

Certain kinds of mistake are particularly interesting: misreading a sign, misinterpreting an order, underestimating a weight, or miscalculating a sum. These are things that strictly speaking cannot be done intentionally. One can pretend to misread a sign, one can underestimate a weight through sloth or inattention, or deliberately write down what one knows to be a wrong answer to an addition; but none of these is an intentional flubbing. To make a mistake of one of the mentioned kinds is to fail to do what one intends, and one cannot, Freudian paradox aside, intend to fail. These mistakes are not intentional, then; nevertheless, they are actions. To see this we need only notice that making a mistake must in each case be doing something else intentionally. A misreading must be a reading, albeit one that falls short of what was wanted; misinterpreting an order is a case of interpreting it (and with the intention of getting it right); underestimating is estimating; and a miscalculation is a calculation (though one that founders).

Can we now say what element is common to the cases of agency? We know that intentional acts are included, and that the place to look to find what such acts share with the others is at the coffee spillings and such where we can distinguish spillings that involve agency from those that do not. I am the agent if I spill the coffee meaning to spill the tea, but not if you jiggle my hand. What is the difference? The difference seems to lie in the fact that in one case, but not in the other, I am intentionally doing *something*. My spilling the contents of my cup was intentional; as it happens, this very same act can be redescribed as my spilling the coffee. Of course, thus redescribed the action is no longer intentional; but this fact is apparently irrelevant to the question of agency.

And so I think we have one correct answer to our problem: a man is the agent of an act if what he does can be described under an aspect that makes it intentional.

The possibility of this answer turns on the semantic opacity, or intensionality, of attributions of intention. Hamlet intentionally kills the man behind the arras, but he does not intentionally kill Polonius. Yet Polonius is the man behind the arras, and so Hamlet's killing of the man behind the arras is identical with his killing of Polonius. It is a mistake to suppose there is a class of intentional actions: if we took this tack, we should be compelled to say that one and the same action was both intentional and not intentional. As a first step toward straightening things out, we may try talking not of actions but of sentences and descriptions of actions instead. In the case of agency, my proposal might then be put: a person is the agent of an event if and only if there is a description of what he did that makes true a sentence that says he did it intentionally. This formulation, with its quantification over linguistic entities, cannot be considered entirely satisfactory. But to do better would require a semantic analysis of sentences about propositional attitudes.[4]

Setting aside the need for further refinement, the proposed criterion of actions seems to fit the examples we have discussed. Suppose an officer aims a torpedo at a ship he thinks is the *Tirpitz* and actually sinks the *Bismark*. Then sinking the *Bismark* is his action, for that action is identical with his attempt to sink the ship he took to be the *Tirpitz*, which is intentional. Similarly, spilling the coffee is the act of a person who does it by intentionally spilling the contents of his cup. It is now clearer, too, why mistakes are actions, for making a mistake must be doing something with the intention of achieving a result that is not forthcoming.

If we can say, as I am urging, that a person does, as agent, whatever he does intentionally under some description, then, although the criterion of agency is, in the semantic sense, *intensional*, the expression of agency is itself purely *extensional*. The relation that holds between a person and an event when the event is an action performed by the person holds regardless of how the terms are described; and we can without confusion speak of the class of events that are actions, which we cannot do with intentional actions.

Perhaps it is sometimes thought that the concept of an action is hopelessly indistinct because we cannot decide whether knocking over a policeman, say, or falling down stairs, or deflating someone's ego is or is not an action. But if being an action is a trait which particular events have independently of how they are described, there is no reason to expect in general to be able to tell, merely by knowing some trait of an event (that it is a case of knocking over a policeman, say), whether or not it is an action.

Is our criterion so broad that it will include under actions many events that no one would normally count as actions? For example, isn't tripping over the edge of the rug just part of my intentional progress into the dining room? I think not. An intentional movement of mine did cause me to trip, and so I did trip myself: this was an action, though not an intentional one. But "I tripped" and "I tripped myself" do not report the same event. The first sentence is entailed by the second, because to trip myself is to do something that results in my tripping; but of course doing something that results in my tripping is not identical with what it causes.

The extensionality of the expression of agency suggests that the concept of agency is simpler or more basic than that of intention, but unfortunately the route we have travelled does not show how to exploit the hint, for all we have seen is how to pick out cases of agency by appeal to the notion of intention. This is to analyze the obscure by appeal to the more obscure – not as pointless a process as often thought, but still disappointing. We should try to see if we can find a mark of agency that does not use the concept of intention.

The notion of cause may provide the clue. With respect to causation, there is a certain rough symmetry between intention and agency. If I say that Smith set the house on fire in order to collect the insurance, I explain his action, in part, by giving one of its causes, namely Smith's desire to collect the insurance. If I say that Smith burned down the house by setting fire to the bedding, then I explain the conflagration by giving a cause, namely Smith's action. In both cases, causal explanation takes the form of fuller description of an action, either in terms of a cause or of an effect. To describe an action as one that had a certain purpose or intended outcome is to describe it as an effect; to describe it as an action that had a certain outcome is to describe it as a cause. Attributions of intention are typically excuses and justifications; attributions of agency are typically accusations or assignments of responsibility. Of course the two kinds of attribution do not rule one another out, since to give the intention with which an act was done is also, and necessarily, to attribute agency. If Brutus murdered Caesar with the intention of removing a tyrant, then a cause of his action was a desire to remove a tyrant and an effect was the death of Caesar. If the officer sank the

Bismark with the intention of sinking the *Tirpitz*, then an action of his was caused by his desire to sink the *Tirpitz* and had the consequence that the *Bismark* sank.[5]

These examples and others suggest that, in every instance of action, the agent made happen or brought about or produced or authored the event of which he was the agent, and these phrases in turn seem rendered by the idea of cause. Can we then say that to be the author or agent of an event is to cause it? This view, or something apparently much like it, has been proposed or assumed by a number of recent authors.[6] So we should consider whether the introduction of the notion of causation in this way can improve our understanding of the concept of agency.

Clearly it can, at least up to a point. For an important way of justifying an attribution of agency is by showing that some event was caused by something the agent did. If I poison someone's morning grapefruit with the intention of killing him, and I succeed, then I caused his death by putting poison in his food, and that is why I am the agent in his murder. When I manage to hurt someone's feelings by denigrating his necktie, I cause the hurt, but it is another event, my saying something mean, that is the cause of the hurt.

The notion of cause appealed to here is ordinary event-causality, the relation, whatever it is, that holds between two events when one is cause of the other. For although we say the agent caused the death of the victim, that is, that he killed him, this is an elliptical way of saying that some act of the agent – something he did, such as put poison in the grapefruit – caused the death of the victim.

Not every event we attribute to an agent can be explained as caused by another event of which he is agent: some acts must be primitive in the sense that they cannot be analyzed in terms of their causal relations to acts of the same agent. But then event-causality cannot in this way be used to explain the relation between an agent and a primitive action. Event-causality can spread responsibility for an action to the consequences of the action, but it cannot help explicate the first attribution of agency on which the rest depend.[7]

If we interpret the idea of a bodily movement generously, a case can be made for saying that all primitive actions are bodily movements. The generosity must be open-handed enough to encompass such "movements" as standing fast, and mental acts like deciding and computing. I do not plan to discuss these difficult examples now; if I am wrong about the precise scope of primitive actions, it will not affect my main argument. It is important, however, to show that in such ordinary actions as pointing one's finger or tying one's shoelaces the primitive action is a bodily movement.

I can imagine at least two objections to this claim. First, it may be said that, in order to point my finger, I do something that causes the finger to move, namely contract certain muscles; and perhaps this requires that I make certain events take place in my brain. But these events do not sound like ordinary bodily movements. I think that the premises of this argument may be true, but that the conclusion does not follow. It may be true that I cause my finger to move by contracting certain muscles, and possibly I cause the muscles to contract by making an event occur in my brain. But this does not show that pointing my finger is not a primitive action, for it does not show that I must do something else that causes it. Doing something that causes my finger to move does not cause me to move my finger; it *is* moving my finger.

In discussing examples like this one, Chisholm has suggested that, although an agent may be said to make certain cerebral events happen when it is these events that cause his finger to move, making the cerebral events happen cannot be called something that he does. Chisholm also thinks that many things an agent causes to happen, in the sense that they are events caused by things he does, are not events of which he is the agent. Thus if moving his finger is something a man does, and this movement causes some molecules of air to move, then although the man may be said to have caused the molecules to move, and hence to have moved the molecules, this is not something he did.[8]

It does not seem to me that this is a clear or useful distinction : all of Chisholm's cases of making something happen are, so far as my intuition goes, cases of agency, situations in which we may, and do, allow that the person did something. When a person makes an event occur in his brain, he does not normally know that he is doing this, and Chisholm seems to suggest that for this reason we cannot say it is something that he does. But a man may even be doing something intentionally and not know that he is; so of course he can be doing it without knowing that he is. (A man may be making ten carbon copies as he writes, and this may be intentional; yet he may not know that he is; all he knows is that he is trying.)

Action does require that what the agent does is intentional under some description, and this in turn requires, I think, that what the agent does is known to him under some description. But this condition is met by our examples. A man who raises his arm both intends to do with his body whatever is needed to make his arm go up and knows that he is doing so. And of course the cerebral events and movements of the muscles are just what is needed. So, though the agent may not know the names or locations of the relevant muscles, nor even know he has a brain, what he makes happen in his brain and muscles when he moves his arm is, under one natural description, something he intends and knows about.

The second objection to the claim that primitive actions are bodily movements comes from the opposite direction: it is that some primitive actions involve more than a movement of the body. When I tie my shoelaces, there is on the one hand the movement of my fingers, and on the other the movement of the laces. But is it possible to separate these events by calling the first alone my action? What makes the separation a problem is that I do not seem able to describe or think how I move my fingers, apart from moving the laces. I do not move my fingers in the attempt to cause my shoes to be tied, nor am I capable of moving my fingers in the appropriate way when no laces are present (this is a trick I might learn). Similarly, it might be argued that when they utter words most people do not know what muscles to move or how to hold their mouths in order to produce the words they want; so here again it seems that a primitive action must include more than a bodily movement, namely a motion of the air.

The objection founders for the same reason as the last one. Everything depends on whether or not there is an appropriate description of the action. It is correctly assumed that unless the agent himself is aware of what he is doing with his body alone, unless he can conceive his movements as an event physically separate from whatever else takes place, his bodily movements cannot be his action. But it is wrongly supposed that such

awareness and conception are impossible in the case of speaking or of tying one's shoelaces. For an agent always knows how he moves his body when, in acting intentionally, he moves his body, in the sense that there is *some* description of the movement under which he knows that he makes it. Such descriptions are, to be sure, apt to be trivial and unrevealing; this is what ensures their existence. So, if I tie my shoelaces, here is a description of my movements: I move my body in just the way required to tie my shoelaces. Similarly, when I utter words, it is true that I am unable to describe what my tongue and mouth do, or to name the muscles I move. But I do not need the terminology of the speech therapist: what I do is move my mouth and muscles, as I know how to do, in just the way needed to produce the words I have in mind.

So there is after all no trouble in producing familiar and correct descriptions of my bodily movements, and these are the events that cause such further events as my shoelaces' being tied or the air's vibrating with my words. Of course, the describing trick has been turned by describing the actions as the movements with the right effects; but this does not show the trick has not been turned. What was needed was not a description that did not mention the effects, but a description that fitted the cause. There is, I conclude, nothing standing in the way of saying that our primitive actions, at least if we set aside such troublesome cases as mental acts, are bodily movements.

To return to the question whether the concept of action may be analyzed in terms of the concept of causality: what our discussion has shown is that we may concentrate on primitive actions. The ordinary notion of event-causality is useful in explaining how agency can spread from primitive actions to actions described in further ways, but it cannot in the same way explain the basic sense of agency. What we must ask, then, is whether there is another kind of causality, one that does not reduce to event-causality, an appeal to which will help us understand agency. We may call this kind of causality (following Thalberg) *agent-causality*.

Restricting ourselves, for the reason just given, to primitive actions, how well does the idea of agent-causality account for the relation between an agent and his action? There is this dilemma: either the causing by an agent of a primitive action is an event discrete from the primitive action, in which case we have problems about acts of the will or worse, or it is not a discrete event, in which case there seems no difference between saying someone caused a primitive action and saying he was the agent.

To take the first horn: suppose that causing a primitive action (in the sense of agent-causality) does introduce an event separate from, and presumably prior to, the action. This prior event in turn must either be an action, or not. If an action, then the action we began with was not, contrary to our assumption, primitive. If not an action, then we have tried to explain agency by appeal to an even more obscure notion, that of a causing that is not a doing.

One is impaled on the second horn of the dilemma if one supposes that agent-causation does *not* introduce an event in addition to the primitive action. For then what more have we said when we say the agent caused the action than when we say he was the agent of the action? The concept of *cause* seems to play no role. We may fail to detect the vacuity of this suggestion because causality does, as we have noticed, enter conspicuously into accounts of agency; but where it does it is the garden-variety of causality, which sheds no light on the relation between the agent and his primitive actions.

We explain a broken window by saying that a brick broke it; what explanatory power the remark has derives from the fact that we may first expand the account of the cause to embrace an event, the movement of the brick, and we can then summon up evidence for the existence of a law connecting such events as motions of medium-sized rigid objects and the breaking of windows. The ordinary notion of cause is inseparable from this elementary form of explanation. But the concept of agent-causation lacks these features entirely. What distinguishes agent-causation from ordinary causation is that no expansion into a tale of two events is possible, and no law lurks. By the same token, nothing is explained. There seems no good reason, therefore, for using such expressions as "cause," "bring about," "make the case" to *illuminate* the relation between an agent and his act. I do not mean that there is anything wrong with such expressions – there are times when they come naturally in talk of agency. But I do not think that by introducing them we make any progress towards understanding agency and action.

Causality is central to the concept of agency, but it is ordinary causality between events that is relevant, and it concerns the effects and not the causes of actions (discounting, as before, the possibility of analyzing intention in terms of causality). One way to bring this out is by describing what Joel Feinberg calls the "accordion effect,"[9] which is an important feature of the language we use to describe actions. A man moves his finger, let us say intentionally, thus flicking the switch, causing a light to come on, the room to be illuminated, and a prowler to be alerted. This statement has the following entailments: the man flicked the switch, turned on the light, illuminated the room, and alerted the prowler. Some of these things he did intentionally, some not; beyond the finger movement, intention is irrelevant to the inferences, and even there it is required only in the sense that the movement must be intentional under some description. In brief, once he has done one thing (move a finger), each consequence presents us with a deed; an agent causes what his actions cause.[10]

The accordion effect will not reveal in what respect an act is intentional. If someone moves his mouth in such a way as to produce the words "your bat is on backwards," thus causing offence to his companion, the accordion effect applies, for we may say both that he spoke those words and that he offended his companion. Yet it is possible that he did not intend to move his mouth so as to produce those words, nor to produce them, nor to offend his companion. But the accordion effect is not applicable if there is no intention present. If the officer presses a button thinking it will ring a bell that summons a steward to bring him a cup of tea, but in fact it fires a torpedo that sinks the *Bismark*, then the officer sank the *Bismark*; but if he fell against the button because a wave upset his balance, then, though the consequences are the same, we will not count him as the agent.

The accordion effect is limited to agents. If Jones intentionally swings a bat that strikes a ball that hits and breaks a window, then Jones not only struck the ball but also broke the window. But we do not say that the bat, or even its movement, broke the window, though of course the movement of the bat caused the breakage. We do indeed allow that inanimate objects cause or bring about various things – in our example, the ball did break the window. However, this is not the accordion effect of agency, but only the ellipsis of event-causality. The ball broke the window – that is to say, its motion caused the breakage.

It seems therefore that we may take the accordion effect as a mark of agency. It is a way of inquiring whether an event is a case of agency to ask whether we can attribute its effects to a person. And on the other hand, whenever we say a person has done something where what we mention is clearly not a bodily movement, we have made him the agent not only of the mentioned event, but of some bodily movement that brought it about. In the case of bodily movements we sometimes have a brief way of mentioning a person and an event and yet of leaving open the question of whether he was the agent, as: Smith fell down.

The accordion effect is interesting because it shows that we treat the consequences of actions differently from the way in which we treat the consequences of other events. This shows that there is, after all, a fairly simple linguistic test that sometimes reveals that we take an event to be an action. But as a criterion it can hardly be counted as satisfactory: it works for some cases only, and of course it gives no clue as to what makes a primitive action an action.

At this point I abandon the search for an analysis of the concept of agency that does not appeal to intention, and turn to a related question that has come to the fore in the discussion of agent-causality and the accordion effect. The new question is what relation an agent has to those of his actions that are not primitive, those actions in describing which we go beyond mere movements of the body and dwell on the consequences, on what the agent has wrought in the world beyond his skin. Assuming that we understand agency in the case of primitive actions, how exactly are such actions related to the rest? The question I now raise may seem already to have been settled, but in fact it has not. What *is* clear is the relation between a primitive action, say moving one's finger in a certain way, and a consequence such as one's shoelaces being tied: it is the relation of event-causality. But this does not give a clear answer to the question of how the movement of the hands is related to the action of tying one's shoelaces, nor for that matter, to the question of how the action of tying one's shoelaces is related to one's shoelaces being tied. Or, to

alter the example, if Brutus killed Caesar by stabbing him, what is the relation between these two actions, the relation expressed by the "by"? No doubt it is true that Brutus killed Caesar because the stabbing resulted in Caesar's death; but we still have that third event whose relations to the others are unclear, namely the killing itself.

It is natural to assume that the action whose mention includes mention of an outcome itself somehow includes that outcome. Thus Feinberg says that a man's action may be "squeezed down to a minimum or else stretched out" by the accordion effect. "He turned the key, he opened the door, he startled Smith, he killed Smith – all of these are things we might say that Jones *did* with one identical set of bodily movements," Feinberg tells us. It is just this relation of "doing with" or "doing by" in which we are interested. Feinberg continues: "We can, if we wish, puff out an action to include an effect."[11] Puffing out, squeezing down, stretching out sound like operations performed on one and the same event; yet if, as seems clear, these operations change the time span of the event, then it cannot be one and the same event: on Feinberg's theory, the action of opening the door cannot be identical with the action of startling Smith. That this is Feinberg's view comes out more clearly in his distinction between simple and causally complex acts. Simple acts are those which require us to do nothing else (we have been calling these primitive actions); causally complex acts, such as opening or shutting a door, or startling, or killing someone, require us to do *something else* first, as a means.[12] Thus Feinberg says, "In order to open a door, we must first do something else which will *cause* the door to open; but to move one's finger one simply moves it – no prior causal activity is required."[13] He also talks of "causally connected sequences of acts."

The idea that opening a door requires prior causal activity, a movement that causes the door to open, is not Feinberg's alone. He quotes J. L. Austin in the same vein: "… a single term descriptive of what he did may be made to cover either a smaller or a larger stretch of events, those excluded by the narrower description being then called 'consequences' or 'results' or 'effects' or the like of his act."[14] Arthur Danto has drawn the distinction, in several articles, between "basic acts," such as moving a hand, and other acts that are caused by the basic acts, such as moving a stone.[15]

It seems to me that this conception of actions and their consequences contains several closely related but quite fundamental confusions. It is a mistake to think that when I close the door of my own free will *anyone* normally causes me to do it, even myself, or that any prior or other action of mine causes me to close the door. What my action causes is the closing of the door. So the second error is to confuse what my action of moving my hand does cause – the closing of the door – with something utterly different – my action of closing the door. And the third mistake, which is forced by the others, is to suppose that when I close the door by moving my hand, I perform two numerically distinct actions (as I would have to if one were needed to cause the other). In the rest of this paper I develop these points.[16]

There is more than a hint of conflict between two incompatible ideas in Austin and Feinberg. As we noticed before, Feinberg shows some inclination to treat moving one's hand and opening the door (and startling Smith, etc.) as one and the same action, which is somehow stretched out or contracted; but he also says things that seem to contradict this, especially when he claims that one must first do something else to cause the door to open in order to open the door. The same strain is noticeable in Austin's pronouncement, for he speaks of different terms descriptive of *what the man did* – apparently one and the same thing – but the terms "cover" smaller or larger stretches of events. Events that cover different stretches cannot be identical.[17]

There are, I think, insuperable difficulties that stand in the way of considering these various actions, the primitive actions like moving a hand, and the actions in describing which we refer to the consequences, as numerically distinct.

It is evident that the relation between the queen's moving her hand in such a way as to pour poison in the king's ear, and her killing him, cannot be the relation of event-causality. If it were, we would have to say the queen caused herself to kill the king. This is not the same as saying the queen brought it about, or made it the case, that she killed the king; these locutions, while strained, do not seem clearly wrong, for it is not

clear that they mean anything more than that the queen brought herself to kill the king. But then the locutions cannot be causal in the required sense. For suppose that by moving her hand the queen caused herself to kill the king. Then we could ask how she did this causing. The only answer I can imagine is that she did it by moving her hand in that way. But this movement was by itself enough to cause the death of the king – there was no point to a further action on the part of the queen. Nor is there any reason (unless we add to the story in an irrelevant way) why the queen should have wanted to cause herself to kill the king. What she wanted to do was kill the king – that is, do something that would cause his death. Is it not absurd to suppose that, after the queen has moved her hand in such a way as to cause the king's death, any deed remains for her to do or to complete? She has done her work; it only remains for the poison to do its.

It will not help to think of killing as an action that begins when the movement of the hand takes place but ends later. For once again, when we inquire into the relation between these events, the answer must be that the killing consists of the hand movement and one of its consequences. We can put them together this way because the movement of the hand caused the death. But then, in moving her hand, the queen was doing something that caused the death of the king. These are two descriptions of the same event – the queen moved her hand in that way; she did something that caused the death of the king. (Or to put it, as I would rather, in terms of a definite description: The moving of her hand by the queen on that occasion was identical with her doing something that caused the death of the king.) Doing something that causes a death is identical with causing a death. But there is no distinction to be made between causing the death of a person and killing him.[18] It follows that what we thought was a more attenuated event – the killing – took no more time, and did not differ from, the movement of the hand.

The idea that under the assumed circumstances killing a person differs from moving one's hand in a certain way springs from a confusion between a feature of the description of an event and a feature of the event itself. The mistake consists in thinking that when the description of an event is made to include reference to a consequence, then the consequence itself is included in the described event. The accordion, which remains the same through the squeezing and stretching, is the action; the changes are in aspects described, or descriptions of the event. There are, in fact, a great many tunes we can play on the accordion. We could start with "The queen moved her hand" and pull to the right by adding "thus causing the vial to empty into the king's ear"; and now another tug, "thus causing the poison to enter the body of the king"; and finally (if we have had enough – for the possibilities for expansion are without clear limit), "thus causing the king to die." This expression can be shortened in many ways, into the centre, the left, or the right components, or any combination. For some examples: "The queen moved her hand thus causing the death of the king" (the two ends); or, "The queen killed the king" (collapse to the right); or "The queen emptied the vial into the king's ear" (the centre). There is another way to pull the instrument out, too: we could *start* with "The queen killed the king," adding "by pouring poison in his ear," and so on – addition to the left. Many of these expressions are equivalent: for example, "The queen killed the king by pouring poison in his ear" and "The queen poured poison in the king's ear thus causing his death." And obviously the longer descriptions entail many of the shorter ones.

But this welter of related descriptions corresponds to a single descriptum – this is the conclusion on which our considerations all converge.[19] When we infer that he stopped his car from the fact that by pressing a pedal a man caused his automobile to come to a stop, we do not transfer agency from one event to another, or infer that the man was agent not only of one action but of two. We may indeed extend responsibility or liability for an action to responsibility or liability for its consequences, but this we do, not by saddling the agent with a new action, but by pointing out that his original action had those results.

We must conclude, perhaps with a shock of surprise, that our primitive actions, the ones we do not do by doing something else, mere movements of the body – these are all the actions there are. We never do more than move our bodies: the rest is up to nature.

This doctrine, while not quite as bad as the bad old doctrine that all we ever do is will things to happen,

or set ourselves to act, may seem to share some of the same disadvantages. Let me briefly indicate why I do not think that this is so.

First, it will be said that some actions require that we do others in order to bring them off, and so cannot be primitive: for example, before I can hit the bull's eye, I must load and raise my gun, then aim and pull the trigger. Of course I do not deny we must prepare the way for some actions by performing others. The criticism holds only if this shows some actions are not primitive. In the present example, the challenge is to demonstrate that hitting the bull's eye is a primitive action. And this it is, according to the argument I have given; for hitting the bull's eye is no more than doing something that causes the bull's eye to be hit, and this, given the right conditions, including a weapon, I can do by holding my arms in a certain position and moving my trigger finger.

Second, it is often said that primitive actions are distinguished by the fact that we know, perhaps without need of observation or evidence, that we are performing them, while this is not a feature of such further events as hitting a bull's eye. But of course we can know that a certain event is taking place when it is described in one way and not know that it is taking place when described in another. Even when we are doing something intentionally, we may not know that we are doing it; this is even more obviously true of actions when described in terms of their unintended begettings.

Finally, it may seem a difficulty that primitive actions do not accommodate the concept of trying, for primitive actions are ones we just do – nothing can stand in the way, so to speak. But surely, the critic will say, there are some things we must strive to do (like hit the bull's eye). Once more the same sort of answer serves. Trying to do one thing may be simply doing another. I try to turn on the light by flicking the switch, but I simply flick the switch. Or perhaps even that is, on occasion, an attempt. Still, the attempt consists of something I can do without trying; just move my hand, perhaps.

The same fact underlies the last two answers: being attempted and being known to occur are not characteristics of events, but of events as described or conceived in one way or another. It is this fact too that explains why we may be limited, in our actions, to mere movements of our bodies, and yet may be capable, for better or for worse, of building dams, stemming floods, murdering one another, or, from time to time, hitting the bull's eye.

We may now return to the question of the relation between an agent and his action. The negative result we have reached is this: the notion of cause has nothing directly to do with this relation. Knowledge that an action *a* has a certain upshot allows us to describe the agent as the cause of that upshot, but this is merely a convenient way of redescribing *a*, and of *it*, as we have seen, there is no point in saying that he is the cause. Causality allows us to redescribe actions in ways we cannot redescribe other events; this fact is a mark of actions, but yields no analysis of agency.

To say that all actions are primitive actions is merely to acknowledge, perhaps in a misleading way, the fact that the concept of being primitive, like the concept of being intentional, is intensional, and so

cannot mark out a *class* of actions. If an event is an action, then under some description(s) it is primitive, and under some description(s) it is intentional. This explains why we were frustrated in the attempt to assume a basic concept of agency as applied to primitive actions and extend it to further actions defined in terms of the consequences of primitive actions: the attempt fails because there are no further actions, only further descriptions.

The collapse of all actions into the primitive, which is marked in syntax by the accordion effect, leads to a vast simplification of the problem of agency, for it shows that there is a relation between a person and an event, when it is his action, that is independent of how the terms of the relation are described. On the other hand, we have discovered no analysis of this relation that does not appeal to the concept of intention. Whether intention can be understood in terms of more basic or simpler ideas is a question with which I have not tried to cope in this paper.

Notes

1. See J. L. Austin, "A Plea for Excuses," in *Philosophical Papers* (Oxford: The Clarendon Press, 1961), pp. 126–127.
2. The point is developed in Irving Thalberg's "Verbs, Deeds and What Happens to Us," *Theoria*, 33 (1967), 259–260.
3. This threefold division should not be confused with Austin's subtle work on the differences among purpose, intention, and deliberation in "Three Ways of Spilling Ink," *Philosophical Review*, 75 (1966), 427–440.
4. For an attempt at such a theory, see my "On Saying That," *Synthèse*, 19 (1968–69), 130–146.
5. In "Actions, Reasons, and Causes," reprinted in this volume as Chapter 19, I developed the theme that to give a reason or intention with which an action is performed is, among other things, to describe the action in terms of a cause. In this essay I explore how the effects of actions enter into our descriptions of them.
6. For example, Roderick Chisholm, "Freedom and Action," in *Freedom and Determinism*, edited by Keith Lehrer (New York: Random House, 1966); Daniel Bennett, "Action, Reason and Purpose," *The Journal of Philosophy*, 62 (1965), 85–96; Anthony Kenny, *Action, Emotion and Will* (London: Routledge & Kegan Paul, 1963); Georg Henrick von Wright, *Norm and Action*

(London: Routledge & Kegan Paul, 1963); Richard Taylor, *Action and Purpose* (Englewood Cliffs, NJ: Prentice-Hall, 1966). Previous criticism of this kind of causal analysis of agency can be found in my "The Logical Form of Action Sentences," in *The Logic of Decision and Action*, edited by Nicholas Rescher (Pittsburgh: University of Pittsburgh Press, 1967) and Irving Thalberg, "Do We Cause our Own Actions?" *Analysis*, 27 (1967), 196–201.
7. Here, and in what follows, I assume that we have set aside an analysis of agency that begins by analyzing the concept of intention, or of acting with an intention, or of a reason in acting. These concepts can be analyzed, at least in part, in terms of event-causality. In the article mentioned in footnote 5, I try to show that although beliefs and desires (and similar mental states) are not events, we can properly say that they are causes of intentional actions, and when we say this we draw upon the concept of ordinary event-causality ("Actions, Reasons, and Causes," pages 183, 192).
8. Chisholm, "Freedom and Action."
9. Joel Feinberg, "Action and Responsibility," in *Philosophy in America*, edited by Max Black (Ithaca, NY: Cornell University Press, 1965).

10. The formulation in this sentence is more accurate than some of my examples. Suppose Jones intentionally causes Smith intentionally to shoot Clifford to death. We certainly won't conclude that Jones shot Clifford, and we may or may not say that Jones killed Clifford. Still, my formulation is correct provided we can go from "Jones's action caused Clifford's death" to "Jones caused Clifford's death." There will, of course, be a conflict if we deny that both Jones and Smith (in our story) could be said to have caused Clifford's death, and at the same time affirm the transitivity of causality. We could, however, preserve the formula in the face of a denial that under the circumstances Jones could be said to have caused Clifford's death by saying that under the circumstances the transitivity of causality also breaks down. For further discussion of the issue, see H. L. A. Hart and A. M. Honoré, *Causation in the Law* (Oxford: The Clarendon Press, 1959); Joel Feinberg, "Causing Voluntary Actions," in *Metaphysics and Explanation*, edited by W. H. Capitan and D. D. Merrill (Pittsburgh: University of Pittsburgh Press, 1965); and J. E. Atwell, "The Accordion-Effect Thesis," *The Philosophical Quarterly*, 19 (1969), 337–342.

11. Feinberg, "Action and Responsibility," p. 146. I am concerned with an issue that is not central in Feinberg's excellent paper. Even if my *caveats* are justified, his thesis is not seriously affected.

12. *Ibid.*, p. 145.

13. *Ibid.*, p. 147.

14. Austin, "A Plea for Excuses," p. 145.

15. Arthur Danto, "What We Can Do," *Journal of Philosophy*, 60 (1963), 435–445; "Basic Actions," *American Philosophical Quarterly*, 2 (1965), 141–148; "Freedom and Forbearance," in *Freedom and Determinism*. Chisholm endorses the distinction in "Freedom and Action," p. 39.

16. Danto's view that if I close the door by moving my hand, my action of closing the door is caused by my moving my hand, has been ably criticized by Myles Brand, "Danto on Basic Actions," *Noûs*, 2 (1968), 187–190; Frederick Stoutland, "Basic Actions and Causality," *Journal of Philosophy*, 65 (1968), 467–475; Wilfrid Sellars, "Metaphysics and the Concept of a Person," in *The Logical Way of Doing Things*, edited by Karel Lambert (New Haven: Yale University Press, 1969).

My target is more general: I want to oppose any view that implies that if I do *A* by doing *B* then my doing *A* and my doing *B* must be numerically distinct.

17. There is further discussion of these issues in my "The Individuation of Events," in *Essays in Honor of Carl G. Hempel*, edited by Nicholas Rescher *et al.* (Dordrecht: D. Reidel, 1970).

18. See footnote 10. The argument goes through if the claim of this sentence is weakened by adding "in the case where a person is killed by doing something that causes his death."

19. This conclusion is not new. It was clearly stated by G. E. M. Anscombe, *Intention* (Oxford: Blackwell, 1959), §§23–26. I followed suit in "Actions, Reasons, and Causes."

3

Shooting, Killing and Dying

Jonathan Bennett

I

There was a duel at dawn between A and B. A shot B, who lingered on until dusk of that day, and then died of his bullet-wound. Certain background conditions are satisfied (it doesn't matter now what they are) which make it right to say not just that A caused B's death but that he killed him. So, A shot B and killed him. This seems to be structurally different from "A shot B and he kicked him," but what is this structural difference? How does the shooting relate to the killing?

Conflicting answers to this question are plausible.

On the one hand, at noon on the fatal day B is still alive; so he has not yet been killed; but he has already been shot; and so his being shot is distinct from his being killed, and therefore A's shooting of him is distinct from his killing of him.

On the other hand, it seems wrong to say that A performed two distinct actions with regard to B – shooting him and killing him. If A dropped dead (with a bullet from B's pistol in his heart) just as his bullet entered B's body, it would be clearly wrong to say that later in the day A *did* anything to B; and yet we could still argue that by noon B has not yet been killed although by dusk he has been.

Bennett, J. (1973), "Shooting, Killing and Dying," *Canadian Journal of Philosophy* 2 (3), 315–323. Published by University of Calgary Press. © Jonathan Bennett. Reprinted with kind permission of the author.

There is a small tangle here. In the fine presentation of the problem by Judith Jarvis Thomson, all the materials for a definitive solution are presented.[1] Indeed, Mrs. Thomson actually states the view which, I shall argue, solves the problem; but unfortunately she introduces it with the operator "It would be merely fanciful to say that …".[2] I shall argue that it is not fanciful at all.

The solution I shall defend is as follows. A performed only one action with regard to B; at dawn, when it was performed, the action was a shooting; and it became a killing at dusk, when B died.

Mrs. Thomson is surely right in saying that there is no short, fully satisfactory answer to the question "Precisely when on the fatal day did A kill B?"[3] The answer "At dawn" suggests that B died at dawn; the answer "At dusk" suggests that A did something at dusk; and no other short answer is even a starter. But that does not imply that our notion of the time of a killing is rendered loose or hazy by the time-lag between the initial action and the resulting death. Nor do I infer – as Mrs. Thomson seems to – that in answering the above question we must present the facts in terms of movements and causes, not using "kill" or any of its cognates. We may answer in that way, but we do not have to. For we can instead say: "A performed at dawn an action which at dusk became the killing of B."

Of the proffered short answers to the question "When on the fatal day did A kill B?," the better one is "At dawn"; but it is not fully satisfactory because it

Philosophy of Action: An Anthology, First Edition. Edited by Jonathan Dancy and Constantine Sandis.
© 2015 John Wiley & Sons, Inc. Published 2015 by John Wiley & Sons, Inc.

can be taken to mean that at dawn A performed an action which was *then* a killing of B. To the slightly different question "When on the fatal day did the killing of B occur?," the answer "At dawn" might be less misleading and could be absolutely correct. It may be that the questioner knows that there was an action which has come, by the time of his asking the question, to qualify as a killing of B; he has the action in his ontology under that description; and he is asking when *that action* occurred. In that case, the right answer is "At dawn." Of course, if one thinks that the questioner may not know that B took hours to die, and one wishes to guard him against error about this, further explanation may be needed. I don't contend that the answer "At dawn" could not mislead; only that it might not mislead and would sometimes be correct.

What was the situation at noon? Well, B was alive, and so he had not yet been killed. But it does not follow that the killing of B had not yet occurred. In fact, the action in question – the one we refer to as "the killing of B" – had occurred, but was not yet a killing. This mops up both difficulties: on the one hand, at noon B was still alive; on the other, at noon nothing remained to be *done*.

II

On this theory, the action acquires a new characteristic long after it has been completed. I distinguish (a) an action's *immediate* characteristics, which it has at the time when it occurs, from (b) its *delayed* characteristics, which it acquires at some later time.

One might wonder how an action or event could have delayed characteristics. Once it has occurred or been performed, it is all over and done with; it no longer exists, is no longer part of the world's furniture; and so – one might think – it is too late now for there to be any change in its characteristics. But that argument would be clearly wrong, as can be seen by noticing how *objects* can acquire characteristics after they have ceased to exist – as when a man becomes notorious after his death. This is possible because notoriety is a relational characteristic, which an object can acquire purely through alterations in other things (people). Similarly, to call an action a "killing of B" is

to say, in part, that it causes B's dying; this is a relational property of it, which it may acquire long after the action has been performed and in that sense after it has ceased to exist.

Furthermore, there are some uncontroversial examples of events having delayed characteristics. The composer of *Parsifal* was born in 1813; so in 1813 someone gave birth to the composer of *Parsifal*; but that act of giving-birth did not merit that description until about 1880 when *Parsifal* was composed. We know about the event, and know that it did eventually qualify as the birth of the composer of *Parsifal,* and so we can properly refer to it through that description. But it didn't merit that description when it occurred; and this could be made explicit if the need arose.

III

Sometimes we have a description D of a particular event E, attributing to E certain characteristics of which some were immediate and some delayed. (Any characteristic's status as "delayed" may result from D's meaning, or be a matter of fact about E, or be borderline between those two. It doesn't matter.) If D does not explicitly separate the immediate from the delayed amongst the characteristics it attributes to E, we can replace it by a description D* which does explicitly make this separation. In doing this, I shall say, we *split* the description D.

So D* must attribute to E exactly the characteristics attributed to it by D. If the two descriptions differ in logical force, it is because D* implies of some attribute of E that it was delayed, while D merely implies that E did have that attribute at some time. And the two may have exactly the same logical force, differing only in that D *implies* whereas D* *explicitly states* that a certain characteristic of E was a delayed one.

There is sometimes a certain indeterminacy in the notion of "the time when the event occurred"; and even when something clearly is a delayed characteristic of an event, the delay may be so brief as not to merit attention in any normal context. But I am merely explaining how to perform a split in cases where there are delayed characteristics and one *does* want to say explicitly what they are.

IV

Here is a simple example. At a certain time, Smith was (D) *submitting the winning entry* in the poetry competition. If the competition was not corrupt, we can split this by saying that Smith was (D*) *submitting the entry which later became winning;* and this can be modified to yield the more idiomatic "… which later became the winning one" or "… which later won the competition." In this example the split goes especially smoothly, because D has the form "Verbing the Adjective Noun," with the adjective expressing all and only the delayed characteristics; so that the split can be performed simply by substituting (D*) "Verbing the Noun which later became Adjective," and then rewording slightly to keep it colloquial.

Splits can be more complicated than that. For example, (D) "giving birth to the composer of *Parsifal*" splits into (D*) "giving birth to the child who [or: something which] later became the composer of *Parsifal*." Here, D does not contain an adjective expressing all and only the delayed characteristics of the event. Still, things are not too bad; for there is a noun phrase which expresses the delayed characteristics and no others, and so we can split (D) "Verbing the Noun-phrase" into (D*) "Verbing the Noun-phrase* which later became Noun-phrase," leaving the verb untouched. We shall come to still trickier cases in a moment.

In both those examples, an event acquires a characteristic because it involves an enduring object (a poem, a person) which acquires a characteristic. This is not the only way it can happen, however. For example, (D) *uttering a famous insult* will ordinarily be (D*) *uttering an insult which later becomes famous*. In such a case, what becomes famous is not an object (the sentence) but rather an action (the insulting, the uttering of the sentence in certain circumstances). Incidentally, I see no significance, for present purposes, in the fact that that example involves an indefinite rather than the definite article.

V

I am now placed to slide quickly from my examples back to my main topic. A *famous insult* is relevantly like a *fatal shooting* which in turn is relevantly like a *killing*.

Just as an insult becomes famous through becoming widely known and talked about, so a shooting can become fatal through a death's arising from it; and so someone's performing (D) *a fatal shooting* can be his performing (D*) *a shooting which later became fatal*. This may sound slightly odd or strained; but I contend that there is no error in it, and that it shows how the occurrence at dawn of a fatal shooting can involve the world at dusk as well as at dawn.

Now consider the description "a killing," as applied to the case described at the start of this paper. Here the split is even less mechanical and straightforward, because the elements we want to separate – the immediate part pertaining to dawn and the delayed part which became true of the action only at dusk – are embedded in the single word "kill." But here again the split can be made accurately and helpfully, even if with some violence to colloquial naturalness.

It won't do to replace (D) *a killing* by (D*) *a killing of someone who later died*. That, among other defects, does not give a clean split – it masks the fact that "kill" itself pertains to dusk as well as to dawn. We could replace D by (D*) *a shooting of someone who later died*. That splits cleanly and in the right place, and it fits the facts of the case as presented. But it does so by eliminating "kill" and its cognates entirely, whereas we want to make the split while keeping "kill" at work. Also, although in our example A did kill B by shooting him, we are trying to devise a split of (D) *a killing,* not of the more specific *a killing by shooting*. It must be remembered that D* is to attribute to the event only characteristics which D attributes to it, differing at most in what it implies about *when* certain characteristics came to apply to the event. So we cannot allow a D* which implies that B was shot, when D does not imply this.

The right way to split (D) *a killing,* as applied to our original case, is to replace it by (D*) *an action which later became a killing*.

This is not fanciful. It is perhaps a little strained; but I have tried to show that this is a kind of strain which is present in lesser degree in other, less controversial cases of splitting. The aim of the examples is to create a presumption that the unnaturalness of "an action which later became a killing" results from superficial and accidental features of our language, and that it is not evidence that that splitting of "a killing" is incorrect.

We might well have had, instead of the substantive "killing," only the noun-phrase "killing action," this being grammatically like "fatal shooting." Then we could, with no strain or unnaturalness, split (D) "a killing action" into (D*) "an action which later became killing."

Davidson has argued persuasively that statements about actions and events have an underlying form expressible in quantifications over events.[4] For example, "Brutus stabbed Caesar with a knife" is argued to have the form "(∃ x)(x was a stabbing & x was by Brutus & x was of Caesar & x was with a knife)." If this view is correct, as I suspect it is, then splitting becomes boringly simple in all cases. For example, (∃ x)(x was by A & x was of B & x occurred at dawn & x became a killing at dusk).

VI

Mrs. Thomson says that the "fanciful" view here defended "would be a misleading fancy in any case, ... for while A is shooting B he is killing him."[5] I contend that if as A is shooting B someone says "A is killing B," and in fact B does not die until several hours later, then what the speaker says is false. As we look back on the situation, with the aid of hindsight, we may not be struck by the falsity of the comment that as A was shooting B he was killing him, because we know that what A was doing did eventually become a killing of B. This is like our acceptance of "As the French fleet approached, Nelson was sending his famous signal," even though we know that at that time the signal was not famous.

The briefer the delay between the shooting and the dying, the feebler will be our sense of the falsity of the comment that as A was shooting B he was killing him. If the delay is brief enough, the comment becomes not merely passable but true; for otherwise we should be trapped in a present in which nothing could happen because it had no duration. For example, by strict enough standards we can say that A's trigger-pulling *became* a B-shooting, this being a delayed characteristic of it, and that while the bullet was in the air A had shot at B but had not yet shot him. But this delay is too short to be worth mentioning in most normal contexts, and some delays are too short to be worth mentioning in any normal context.

As well as the brevity of the delay between shooting and dying there is a related parameter, namely the degree of inevitability, at the time of the shooting, that B will die as a result of being shot. In proportion as one is confident that B will die of being shot, one is likely to tolerate "A is killing B"; and it may be that if one is entitled to complete confidence (i.e. if it is by ordinary standards inevitable) that B will die as a result of being shot, then the comment "A is killing B" will be not just tolerable but actually true. Similarly, as Mrs. Thomson has pointed out to me, a wound can be "fatal" at the time it occurs, if it is certain to lead to the victim's death; and the same may be true of a shooting's being "fatal," despite my previous implication to the contrary.

But mere inevitability-of-upshot, without brevity-of-delay, will not make it true (and to many ears will not even make it tolerable) to say that as soon as A has shot B he "has killed him." This is because we have no firm obstacle to the move from "A has killed B" to "B has been killed" and thence to "B is dead." There is, admittedly, a rather florid usage in which one may say something of the form "A has killed B" although one knows that B is still alive. Mrs. Thomson calls this "the 'Hollywood' use of language";[6] and I have found examples of it in a bad poem by Browning and (used in a moment of high excitement by one of the characters) in a fine chapter by Tolstoy.[7] I agree with Mrs. Thomson that the usage in question is an extravagance: while B is alive it cannot be strictly true that anyone has killed him.

If A shoots B at 8 a.m., and B is certain to die as a result at some time between 8:02 and 8:03 a.m., then it may be literally true that as A is shooting B he is killing him. And if in this case we ask about the situation at 8:01 a.m. we have the sort of difficulty to which Mrs. Thomson has called attention: we want to say both that A has killed B (because he was killing him and has finished) and yet that B has not yet been killed (because he is still alive). This is a situation for which we are not fully conceptually fore-armed; but, as usual when we are not fore-armed, this is because we haven't much need to be. Just because the interval between the shooting and the dying is brief, there will usually be no occasion for seeking correct descriptions during that interval;

and only philosophers will care much, later, about the question of what description would have been correct between the shooting and the dying.

VII

I have just three more remarks to offer.

(1) Mrs. Thomson discusses the question of when the killing of B ended. I say that it ended when the shooting of him ended, whenever that was. Similarly, the (obstetrical) delivering of the composer of *Parsifal* ended whenever the delivering of young R. Wagner ended, on a day in 1813; and not, of course, in 1880.

(2) Davidson says: "Hamlet, in killing the king, avenges, among other murders, his own."[8] This seems right. The king did murder Hamlet, and he didn't get away with it: vengeance was exacted, and Hamlet exacted it. But Davidson goes on: "This he could not do if he had not already been murdered." I agree with Mrs. Thomson in being reluctant to swallow the idea that Hamlet fought a whole sword-fight after being murdered.[9] What, then, are we to say about this case? I say that Hamlet avenged several actions by the king, including one which was already an attempted murder

and which would later become a murder of Hamlet. So the action was available as a possible object of vengeance, and yet Hamlet had not yet been murdered and so could be the avenger. If we must pin it down very hard, then at the time of Hamlet's stabbing the king, Hamlet's murder had occurred but Hamlet had not yet been murdered; but of course this sounds most peculiar, and it would be absurd to offer it without an accompanying explanation – namely that an action had occurred which would later become the murder of Hamlet.

(3) Legal procedures confirm my account. A shoots B and is charged with assault; then B dies and the charge is altered to one of homicide. This is because what A did has become homicide. There is a law against a certain class of actions which is partly defined by the relational property of causing-a-death; and A's action, although completed before even the first charge was laid, has acquired that relational property and thus come to fall under that law. The fundamental logic of this is the same as in a case where I am charged first with keeping an animal which is a nuisance, and then – under a different law – with keeping a dangerous animal, because my dog's character has deteriorated: it was a nuisance but has become a danger. Similarly, what A did was an assault, and has become a killing.

Notes

1. Judith Jarvis Thomson, "The Time of a Killing," *The Journal of Philosophy*, LXVIII, 5 (March 1971): 115–132. I have been helped by Mrs. Thomson's comments on an earlier version of the present paper.
2. *Ibid.*, p. 132.
3. *Ibid.*, pp. 122–123.
4. Donald Davidson, "The Logical Form of Action Sentences," in N. Rescher (ed.), *The Logic of Decision and Action* (Pittsburgh, 1967); and several other papers. [Added in 1990: I no longer find that work of Davidson's "persuasive". It is refuted in Jonathan Bennett, *Events and their Names* (Indianapolis, 1988), chapter 11.]
5. Judith Jarvis Thomson, *op. cit.*, p. 132.
6. *Ibid.*, p. 120.
7. R. Browning, "Incident of the French Camp," last stanza. L. Tolstoy, *War and Peace*, Book IV, chapter 5.
8. Donald Davidson, "The Individuation of Events," in N. Rescher *et al.* (eds.), *Essays in Honor of Carl G. Hempel* (New York, 1970), note 16.
9. Judith Jarvis Thomson, *op. cit.*, p. 120.

4

The Problem of Action

Harry G. Frankfurt

I

THE problem of action is to explicate the contrast between what an agent does and what merely happens to him, or between the bodily movements that he makes and those that occur without his making them. According to causal theories of the nature of action, which currently represent the most widely followed approach to the understanding of this contrast, the essential difference between events of the two types is to be found in their prior causal histories: a bodily movement is an action if and only if it results from antecedents of a certain kind. Different versions of the causal approach may provide differing accounts of the sorts of events or states which must figure causally in the production of actions. The tenet they characteristically share is that it is both necessary and sufficient, in order to determine whether an event is an action, to consider how it was brought about.

Despite its popularity, I believe that the causal approach is inherently implausible and that it cannot provide a satisfactory analysis of the nature of action. I do not mean to suggest that actions have no causes; they are as likely to have causes, I suppose, as other events are. My claim is rather that it is no part of the nature of an action to have a prior causal history of any particular kind. From the fact that an event is an

Frankfurt, H. G. (1978), "The Problem of Action," *American Philosophical Quarterly* 15 (2), 157–162. Reprinted with permission.

action, in my view, it does not follow even that it has a cause or causes at all, much less that it has causal antecedents of any specific type.

In asserting that the essential difference between actions and mere happenings lies in their prior causal histories, causal theories imply that actions and mere happenings do not differ essentially in themselves at all. These theories hold that the causal sequences producing actions are necessarily of a different type than those producing mere happenings, but that the effects produced by sequences of the two types are inherently indistinguishable. They are therefore committed to supposing that a person who knows he is in the midst of performing an action cannot have derived this knowledge from any awareness of what is currently happening, but that he must have derived it instead from his understanding of how what is happening was caused to happen by certain earlier conditions. It is integral to the causal approach to regard actions and mere happenings as being differentiated by nothing that exists or that is going on at the time those events occur, but by something quite extrinsic to them – a difference at an earlier time among another set of events entirely.

This is what makes causal theories implausible. They direct attention exclusively away from the events whose natures are at issue, and away from the times at which they occur. The result is that it is beyond their scope to stipulate that a person must be in some particular relation to the movements of his

Philosophy of Action: An Anthology, First Edition. Edited by Jonathan Dancy and Constantine Sandis.
© 2015 John Wiley & Sons, Inc. Published 2015 by John Wiley & Sons, Inc.

body *during* the period of time in which he is presumed to be performing an action. The only conditions they insist upon as distinctively constitutive of action may cease to obtain, for all the causal accounts demand, at precisely the moment when the agent commences to act. They require nothing of an agent, once the specified causal antecedents of his performing an action have occurred, except that his body move as their effect.

It is no wonder that such theories characteristically run up against counterexamples of a well-known type. For example: a man at a party intends to spill what is in his glass because he wants to signal his confederates to begin a robbery and he believes, in virtue of their prearrangements, that spilling what is in his glass will accomplish that; but all this leads the man to be very anxious, his anxiety makes his hand tremble, and so his glass spills. No matter what kinds of causal antecedents are designated as necessary and sufficient for the occurrence of an action, it is easy to show that causal antecedents of that kind may have as their effect an event that is manifestly not an action but a mere bodily movement. The spilling in the example given has among its causes a desire and a belief, which rationalise the man's spilling what is in his glass, but the spilling as it occurs is not an action. That example makes trouble particularly for a causal theory in which actions are construed as essentially movements whose causes are desires and beliefs by which they are rationalised. Similar counterexamples can readily be generated to make similar trouble for other variants of the causal approach.

I shall not examine the various maneuvers by means of which causal theorists have attempted to cope with these counterexamples.[1] In my judgment causal theories are unavoidably vulnerable to such counterexamples, because they locate the distinctively essential features of action exclusively in states of affairs which may be past by the time the action is supposed to occur. This makes it impossible for them to give any account whatever of the most salient differentiating characteristic of action: during the time a person is performing an action he is necessarily in touch with the movements of his body in a certain way, whereas he is necessarily not in touch with them in that way when movements of his body are occurring without his making them. A theory that is limited to describing causes prior to the occurrences of actions and of mere bodily movements cannot possibly include an analysis of these two ways in which a person may be related to the movements of his body. It must inevitably leave open the possibility that a person, whatever his involvement in the events from which his action arises, loses all connection with the movements of his body at the moment when his action begins.

II

In order to develop a more promising way of thinking about action, let us consider the notion that actions and mere happenings are indistinguishable in themselves. This notion is an important element in the motivation for causal theories. If it were thought that actions and mere happenings differ inherently, then it would be obvious that the way to explicate how they differ would be by identifying this inherent difference between them. It is because causal theorists think that there is no other way to differentiate between actions and mere happenings that they seek a differentiating difference among the events that precede them.

David Pears, who believes that desires play an essential causal role in the production of actions, makes this explicit:

> We simply do not possess the general ability to distinguish between those bodily movements which are actions and those which are mere bodily movements without using as a criterion the presence or absence of the relevant desire.... It is true that there are various intrinsic characteristics of bodily movements which do give some indication of their classification. For example, a very complicated movement was probably produced by a desire. But ... the simplicity of a movement does not even make it probable that it was not produced by a desire.

Because we cannot find any inherent characteristic of action which permits us to distinguish it reliably from mere bodily movement, we must therefore, in Pears' view, "classify some bodily movements as actions solely by virtue of their origins."[2]

Pears observes correctly that the movements of a person's body do not definitively reveal whether he is performing an action : the very same movements may occur when an action is being performed or when a mere happening is occurring. It does not follow from this, however, that the only way to discover whether or not a person is acting is by considering what was going on *before* his movements began – that is, by considering the causes from which they originated. In fact, the state of affairs *while* the movements are occurring is far more pertinent. What is not merely pertinent but decisive, indeed, is to consider whether or not the movements as they occur are *under the person's guidance*. It is this that determines whether he is performing an action. Moreover, the question of whether or not movements occur under a person's guidance is not a matter of their antecedents. Events are caused to occur by preceding states of affairs, but an event cannot be guided through the course of its occurrence at a temporal distance.

It is worth noticing that Pears is mistaken when he concedes that very complicated movements, though they may possibly be mere happenings, are probably to be classified as actions. The complicated movements of a pianist's hands and fingers do, to be sure, compellingly suggest that they are not mere happenings. Sometimes, however, complexity may quite as compellingly suggest the likelihood of mere bodily movement. The thrashings about of a person's body during an epileptic seizure, for example, are very complicated movements. But their complexity is of a kind which makes it appear unlikely to us that the person is performing an action.

When does complexity of movement suggest action, and when does it suggest its absence? This depends, roughly speaking, upon whether the movements in question cohere in creating a pattern which strikes us as meaningful. When they do, as in the case of the pianist, we find it difficult to imagine that the movements would have occurred, in just those complicated ways required by the meaningful pattern they have created, unless the pianist had been guiding his hands and fingers as they moved. In the epileptic's case, on the other hand, we find it unlikely that a person would have created such an incoherently complicated pattern if he had been guiding his body through its movements. A person's simple movements, as Pears notes, generally suggest neither an action nor a mere happening. This is because their patterns do not ordinarily strike us as being in themselves either meaningful or incoherent. They do not present us on their faces with any indication of whether or not they are being guided by the person as they occur.

Complexity of body movement suggests action only when it leads us to think that the body, during the course of its movement, is under the agent's guidance. The performance of an action is accordingly a complex event, which is comprised by a bodily movement and by whatever state of affairs or activity constitutes the agent's guidance of it. Given a bodily movement which occurs under a person's guidance, the person is performing an action regardless of what features of his prior causal history account for the fact that this is occurring. He is performing an action even if its occurrence is due to chance. And he is not performing an action if the movements are not under his guidance as they proceed, even if he himself provided the antecedent causes – in the form of beliefs, desires, intentions, decisions, volitions, or whatever – from which the movement has resulted.

III

When we act, our movements are purposive. This is merely another way of saying that their course is guided. Many instances of purposive movement are not, of course, instances of action. The dilation of the pupils of a person's eyes when the light fades, for example, is a purposive movement; there are mechanisms which guide its course. But the occurrence of this movement does not mark the performance of an action by the person; his pupils dilate, but he does not dilate them. This is because the course of the movement is not under *his* guidance. The guidance in this case is attributable only to the operation of some mechanism with which he cannot be identified.

Let us employ the term "intentional" for referring to instances of purposive movement in which the guidance is provided by the agent. We may say, then, that action is intentional movement. The notion of intentional movement must not be confused with that of intentional action. The term "intentional action" may be used, or rather mis-used, simply to convey that an action is necessarily a movement whose course is under an agent's guidance. When it is used in this way, the term is pleonastic. In a more appropriate usage, it refers to actions which are undertaken more or less deliberately or self-consciously – that is, to actions which the agent intends to perform. In this sense, actions are not necessarily intentional.

When a person intends to perform an action, what he intends is that certain intentional movements of his body should occur. When these movements do occur, the person is performing an intentional action. It might be said that he is then guiding the movements of his body in a certain way (thus, he is acting), and that in doing so he is guided by and fulfilling his intention to do just that (thus, he is acting intentionally). There appears to be nothing in the notion of an intentional movement which implies that its occurrence must be intended by the agent, either by way of forethought or by way of self-conscious assent. If this is correct, then actions (i.e., intentional movements) may be performed either intentionally or not.

Since action is intentional movement, or behavior whose course is under the guidance of an agent, an explication of the nature of action must deal with two distinct problems. One is to explain the notion of guided behavior. The other is to specify when the guidance of behavior is attributable to an agent and not simply, as when a person's pupils dilate because the light fades, to some local process going on within the agent's body. The first problem concerns the conditions under which behavior is purposive, while the second concerns the conditions under which purposive behavior is intentional.

The driver of an automobile guides the movement of his vehicle by acting: he turns the steering wheel, he depresses the accelerator, he applies the brakes, and so on. Our guidance of our movements, while we are acting, does not similarly require that we perform various actions. We are not at the controls of our bodies in the way a driver is at the controls of his automobile. Otherwise action could not be conceived, upon pain of generating an infinite regress, as a matter of the occurrence of movements which are under an agent's guidance. The fact that our movements when we are acting are purposive is not the effect of something we do. It is a characteristic of the operation at that time of the systems we are.

Behavior is purposive when its course is subject to adjustments which compensate for the effects of forces which would otherwise interfere with the course of the behavior, and when the occurrence of these adjustments is not explainable by what explains the state of affairs that elicits them. The behavior is in that case under the guidance of an independent causal mechanism, whose readiness to bring about compensatory adjustments tends to ensure that the behavior is accomplished.[3] The activity of such a mechanism is normally not, of course, guided by us. Rather it *is*, when we are performing an action, our guidance of our behavior. Our sense of our own agency when we act is nothing more than the way it feels to us when we are somehow in touch with the operation of mechanisms of this kind, by which our movements are guided and their course guaranteed.

Explaining purposive behavior in terms of causal mechanisms is not tantamount to propounding a causal theory of action. For one thing, the pertinent activity of these mechanisms is not prior to but concurrent with the movements they guide. But in any case it is not essential to the purposiveness of a movement that it actually be causally affected by the mechanism under whose guidance the movement proceeds. A driver whose automobile is coasting downhill in virtue of gravitational forces alone may be entirely satisfied with its speed and direction, and so he may never intervene to adjust its movement in any way. This would not show that the movement of the automobile did not occur under his guidance. What counts is that he was prepared to intervene if necessary, and that he was in a position to do so more or less effectively. Similarly, the causal mechanisms which stand ready to affect the course of a bodily movement may never have occasion to do so; for no negative feedback of the sort that would trigger their compensatory activity may occur. The behavior is purposive not because it results from causes of a certain kind, but because it would be affected by certain causes if the accomplishment of its course were to be jeopardised.

IV

Since the fact that certain causes originate an action is distinct from the considerations in virtue of which it is an action, there is no reason in principle why a person may not be caused in a variety of different ways to perform the same action. This is important in the analysis of freedom. It is widely accepted that a person acts freely only if he could have acted otherwise. Apparent counterexamples to this principle – "the principle of alternate possibilities" – are provided, however, by cases that involve a certain kind of overdetermination. In these cases a person performs an action entirely for his own reasons, which inclines us to regard him as having performed it freely; but he would otherwise have been caused to perform it by forces alien to his will, so that he cannot actually avoid acting as he does.[4]

Thus, suppose a man takes heroin because he enjoys its effects and considers them to be beneficial. But suppose further that he is unknowingly addicted to the drug, and hence that he will be driven to take it in any event, even if he is not led to do so by his own beliefs and attitudes. Then it seems that he takes the drug freely, that he could not have done otherwise than to take it, and that the principle of alternate possibilities is therefore false.

Donald Davidson argues to the contrary that whereas a person does intentionally what he does for his own reasons, he does not do intentionally what alien forces cause him to do. While the movements of his body may be the same in both cases, Davidson maintains that the person is not performing an action when the movements occur apart from pertinent attitudes and beliefs. Someone who has acted freely might have done the same thing even if he had not been moved on his own to do it, but only in the sense that his body might have made the same movements: "he would not have acted intentionally had the attitudinal conditions been absent." Even in the "overdetermined" cases, then, something rests with the agent: "not … what he does (when described in a way that leaves open whether it was intentional), but whether he does it intentionally."[5]

The issue here is not, as Davidson suggests at one point, whether a person's *action* can be intentional when alien forces rather than his own attitudes account for what he does. It is whether his *behavior* can be intentional in those circumstances. Now the behavior of the unknowing addict is plainly as intentional when he is caused to take the drug by the compulsive force of his addiction, as it is when

he takes it as a matter of free choice. His movements are not mere happenings, when he takes the drug because he cannot help himself. He is then performing the very same action that he would have performed had he taken the drug freely and with the illusion that he might have done otherwise.

This example is not designed to show that Davidson is mistaken in insisting that there can be no action without intentionality, or in the absence of pertinent attitudinal conditions. Even when the addict is driven to do what he does, after all, his behavior is presumably affected both by his craving for the drug and by his belief that the procedure he follows in taking it will bring him relief. His movements, as he sticks the syringe into his arm and pushes the plunger, are certainly intentional. However, the relevant problem is not whether an action can occur apart from attitudinal conditions. It is whether it is possible that an action should be caused by alien forces alone.

This will seem to be impossible only if it is thought that an action must have attitudinal conditions among its causes. But it is not essential to an action that it have an antecedent causal history of any particular kind. Even if there can be no action in the absence of certain attitudinal conditions, therefore, it is not as prior causes that these conditions are essential. The example bears upon the point that is actually at issue, by illustrating how an action (including, of course, any requisite attitudinal constituents) may have no causes other than non-attitudinal or alien ones. Thus it confirms the falsity of the principle of alternate possibilities, by showing that a person may be caused by alien forces alone to perform an action which he might also perform on his own.

The example also suggests, by the way, that the attitudinal conditions of a person's action may themselves be alien to him. There is no reason to assume that an addict who succumbs unwillingly to his craving finally adopts as his own the desire he has tried to resist. He may in the end merely submit to it with resignation, like a man who knows he is beaten and who therefore despairingly accepts the consequences defeat must bring him, rather than like someone who decides to join with or to incorporate forces which he had formerly opposed. There are also obsessional and delusional beliefs – e.g., "If I step on a crack it will break my mother's back" – which a person may know to be false but whose influence he cannot escape. So even if it were true (which it is not) that every action necessarily has attitudinal conditions among its antecedent causes, it might nonetheless be alien forces alone which bring it about that a person performs an action.

The assertion that someone has performed an action entails that his movements occurred under his guidance, but not that he was able to keep himself from guiding his movements as he did. There are occasions when we act against or independently of our wills. On other occasions, the guiding principle of our movements is one to which we are not merely resigned; rather, we have embraced it as our own. In such cases, we will ordinarily have a reason for embracing it. Perhaps, as certain philosophers would claim, our having a reason for acting may sometimes cause it to be the case that movements of our bodies are guided by us in a manner which reflects that reason. It is indisputable that a person's beliefs and attitudes often have an important bearing upon how what he is doing is to be interpreted and understood; and it may be that they also figure at times in the causal explanations of his actions. The facts that we are rational and self-conscious substantially affect the character of our behavior and the ways in which our actions are integrated into our lives.

V

The significance to *our* actions of states and events which depend upon the exercise of our higher capacities should not lead us, however, to exaggerate the peculiarity of what human beings do. We are far from being unique either in the purposiveness of our behavior or in its intentionality. There is a tendency among philosophers to discuss the nature of action as though agency presupposes characteristics which cannot plausibly be attributed to members of species other than our own. But in fact the contrast between actions and mere happenings can readily be discerned elsewhere than in the lives of people. There are numerous agents besides ourselves, who may be active as well as passive with respect to the movements of their bodies.

Consider the difference between what goes on when a spider moves its legs in making its way along the ground, and what goes on when its legs move in similar patterns and with similar effect because they are manipulated by a boy who has managed to tie strings to them. In the first case the movements are not simply purposive, as the spider's digestive processes doubtless are. They are also attributable to the spider, who makes them. In the second case the same movements occur but they are not made by the spider, to whom they merely happen.

This contrast between two sorts of events in the lives of spiders, which can be observed in the histories of creatures even more benighted, parallels the more familiar contrast between the sort of event that occurs when a person raises his arm and the sort that occurs when his arm goes up without his raising it. Indeed, the two contrasts are the same. The differences they respectively distinguish are alike; and they have, as it were, the same point. Each contrasts instances in which purposive behavior is attributable to a creature as agent and instances in which this is not the case.

This generic contrast cannot be explicated in terms of any of the distinctive higher faculties which characteristically come into play when a person acts. The conditions for attributing the guidance of bodily movements to a whole creature, rather than only to some local mechanism within a creature, evidently obtain outside of human life. Hence they cannot be satisfactorily understood by relying upon concepts which are inapplicable to spiders and their ilk. This does not mean that it must be illegitimate for an analysis of human agency to invoke concepts of more limited scope. While the general conditions of agency are unclear, it may well be that the satisfaction of these conditions by human beings depends upon the occurrence of events or states which do not occur in the histories of other creatures. But we must be careful that the ways in which we construe agency and define its nature do not conceal a parochial bias, which causes us to neglect the extent to which the concept of human action is no more than a special case of another concept whose range is much wider.

Notes

1. For discussion of the problem by adherents to the causal approach, cf. Alvin Goldman, *A Theory of Human Action* (Princeton, 1970), pp. 61–63; Donald Davidson, "Freedom to Act," in T. Honderich (ed.), *Essays on Freedom of Action* (London, 1973), pp. 153–154; Richard Foley, "Deliberate Action," *The Philosophical Review*, vol. 86 (1977), pp. 58–69. Goldman and Davidson evidently believe that the problem of avoiding the counterexamples is an empirical one, which is appropriately to be passed on to scientists. Foley's "solution" renounces the obligation to provide suitable analysis in another way: he specifies conditions for acting and, when he recognises that they may be met by spasms and twitches, he simply declares that such movements are nonetheless actions if they satisfy his conditions.

2. David Pears, "Two Problems about Reasons for Actions," in R. Binkley, R. Bronaugh, A. Marras (eds.), *Agent, Action and Reason* (Oxford, 1971), pp. 136–137, 139.

3. A useful discussion of this way of understanding purposive behavior is provided by Ernest Nagel, "Goal-directed Processes in Biology," *The Journal of Philosophy*, vol. 74 (1977), pp. 271 ff. The details of the mechanisms in virtue of which some item of behavior is purposive can be discovered, of course, only by empirical investigation. But specifying the conditions which any such mechanism must meet is a philosophical problem, belonging to the analysis of the notion of purposive behavior.

4. Cf. my "Alternate Possibilities and Moral Responsibilities," *The Journal of Philosophy*, vol. 66 (1969), pp. 829–839; and "Freedom of the Will and the Concept of a Person," *The Journal of Philosophy*, vol. 68 (1971), pp. 5–20.

5. *Op. cit.*, pp. 149–150.

5

Agents and their Actions

Maria Alvarez and John Hyman

In the past thirty years or so, the doctrine that actions are events has become an essential, and sometimes unargued, part of the received view in the philosophy of action, despite the efforts of a few philosophers to undermine the consensus.[1] For example, the entry for *Agency* in a recently published reference guide to the philosophy of mind begins with the following sentence:

> A central task in the philosophy of action is that of spelling out the differences between events in general and those events that fall squarely into the category of human action.[2]

There is no consensus about what events are. But it is generally agreed that, whatever events may prove to be, actions are a species or a class of events.

We believe that the received view is mistaken: actions are not events. We concede that for most purposes, the kind of categorial refinement which is involved in either affirming or denying that actions are events is frankly otiose. Our common idiom does not stress the difference between actions and events, at least not in general terms, because it has no need to. Perhaps it sounds a little odd to say that some events are performed; but if we balked at describing, say, the

abdication of Edward VIII as one of the politically significant events in Britain in 1936, it could not be for metaphysical reasons. And since actions, like events, are datable — though often, as we shall see, only imprecisely — actions are said to take place and to occur. But an important class of actions consist in moving something; indeed, according to many philosophers, every action consists in moving something. And when we consider actions of this sort from a theoretical point of view it becomes imperative to distinguish between actions and events. Or so we shall argue.

So, in what follows, we shall defend the negative doctrine that actions are not events, criticize a number of related claims about the nature of agency and actions, and make some positive proposals of our own. Several of the points we shall be urging are not new; but we hope that by bringing them together, and organizing them properly in relation to one another, the received view may appear in a new and less favourable light. These points include the following: that agents do not cause their actions; that saying that an agent caused an event is not an elliptical way of saying that one event caused another; that if an agent ϕs by ψing, his ϕing and his ψing are not typically one and the same action; that failing to ϕ and refraining from ψing may be intentional, but are not actions; that some human actions are not intentional, regardless of how they are described; that there are inanimate agents; and that actions are not events.

Alvarez, M., and Hyman, J. (1998), "Agents and their Actions," *Philosophy* 73 (2), 219–245. Published by Cambridge Journals, Cambridge. © Royal Institute of Philosophy 1996. Reproduced with permission.

Most of these points, perhaps all of them, have been defended at one time or another; but there has been no attempt, so far as we are aware, to combine them in a single and coherent conception of agency. We hope to adumbrate such a conception, as well as undermining the received view; although we cannot pretend that we have painted it in exhaustive detail.

We shall begin, in section 1, by introducing the concept of agent causation. We shall argue that the concept of agency involves the notion of an agent's causing an event. But we shall examine and reject a view traditionally associated with the concept of agent causation, namely, that agents cause their *actions*; in our view, agents cause the *results* of their actions. In sections 2 and 3, we shall examine various considerations which have been thought to support the doctrine that actions in general and bodily movements in particular are events. In sections 4, 5 and 6, we shall say what we think actions are, and something about the significance that our view has for some other issues in the philosophy of action.

Two doctrines which we do not seek to defend can be noted at this early stage. One is the doctrine that the concept of agent causation is in some sense more fundamental than the concept of event causation. The other is the doctrine that when the verb 'cause' appears between a term for an agent and a term for an event, it has a different meaning from the meaning it has when it appears between two expressions which denote events. The first doctrine, as it stands, is too vague for serious consideration, and we shall not attempt to sharpen it. Regarding the second, we believe that 'cause' expresses the same idea in both cases – as Anscombe put it, the idea of 'derivativeness'.[3]

1. Agent Causation

Without prejudice to the results of philosophical analysis, we can describe an agent as something or someone that makes things happen. And we can add that to make something happen is to cause an event of some kind, that is, to exercise the power to cause an event of that kind to occur. Our pre-theoretical talk of agency extends to animals and plants, and also to inanimate things. We say, for example, that

beavers build dams, or that oxygen rusts iron. Indeed, inanimate substances are often described as agents of one sort or another: cleaning agents, analgesic agents, etc. The pre-theoretical view of what it is to be an agent that this sort of talk implies acknowledges that inanimate substances and living creatures incapable of acting voluntarily or intentionally can be agents. But it is common nowadays to find that philosophical discussions of agency are conducted on the assumption that it is only when an agent acts intentionally that we have a genuine instance of agency. An action by an inanimate agent is, according to this view, an *ersatz* action with an *ersatz* agent.

The view that genuine agency is invariably intentional has given rise to a variety of proposals for 'spelling out the differences between events in general [and actions in particular]'. But the deepest division among philosophers on this matter is between those who claim that genuine agency can be understood in terms of causal relations between *events*, and those others – so-called agent causalists – who deny this. Philosophers who belong in the former category may, for example, hold that actions are movements of parts of the agent's body which were caused in a particular way by events involving the agent's intentions, beliefs and desires. Whereas the agent causalists will tend to argue that if an agent freely or intentionally caused an event, we cannot 'reduce it to the case of an event being a cause';[4] and hence, that the correct account of our concept of agency is one which preserves for the *agent* the rôle of an action's cause. So on the one hand we have the view, roughly, that actions are events caused by intentions; and on the other the view, roughly, that they are events intentionally caused by agents.

Ironically, the attempts made by agent causalists to preserve a concept of agent causation which cannot be dissolved by analysis have generally involved a controversial doctrine which has contributed to making the very concept of agent causation appear unsound, namely, the doctrine that agents cause their actions. Richard Taylor puts it thus: 'for anything to count as an act there must be an essential reference to an agent as the cause of that act.'[5] Chisholm's view is more complex; but it is founded on the same idea.[6] We shall argue that the concept of agent causation, although widely disparaged, can be rehabilitated, by detaching it from the doctrines that agents cause their actions and that actions are events.

The traditional conception of agent causation is founded on the idea that actions are events caused by agents. But this idea is now widely thought to be untenable, and with good reason. For if an action is an event caused by an agent, then the question can be posed, whether causing *this* event is itself an action or not. If it is, then *ex hypothesi* it is an event caused by the agent, and we can ask again, whether causing this event is an action or not. If, as the question is repeatedly reiterated, the answer at every step is that the causing is an action, then an agent who performs one action performs an infinite series of actions: he causes his action; he causes the causing of his action; he causes the causing of the causing of his action; as so on. But this is absurd. On the other hand, if a causing of an event need not be an action, what principle can an advocate of the traditional conception of agent causation invoke, to distinguish between those causings of events which are actions and those which are not? Not the principle that a causing is not an action unless it is intentional, or free, or voluntary, since this does not halt the regress. For if the causing of an event was not intentional, then the event caused was not caused intentionally; but if actions are events caused by agents, then an intentional action is surely one that was intentionally caused. Hence, if an event was an action, and therefore *ex hypothesi* intentional, its causing must also have been intentional, and therefore *ex hypothesi* an action; and the regress is not avoided. But no other principle recommends itself, or has been recommended. It is therefore safe to conclude – at least *pro tem.* – that the doctrine that actions are events caused by agents is false.[7] An agent who acts causes an event; but actions are not events that agents cause.

The doctrine that actions are events caused by agents may appear especially convincing if we consider those actions which consist in moving parts of our bodies. It is clear that many actions are bodily movements. For example, A may raise his arms, wiggle his toes or flutter his eyelids; and if he does any of these things, he has performed an action. But it is equally clear that not every bodily movement is an action, because A's toes may wiggle without A wiggling them and his eyelids may flutter because he has a tic. Hence, to say that A moved part of his body,

implies more than just that part of A's body moved; for it implies that A made it move, that A caused that bodily movement to occur. And hence – one may want to argue – what distinguishes those of A's bodily movements which are his actions from those which are not, is that he causes the first sort, but not the second. But if A causes the bodily movements which are his actions, it follows that he causes his actions.

So one might think. But as several philosophers have shown, arguments involving the term 'bodily movement' sometimes involve a fallacy of equivocation, because they disregard an ambiguity which affects the use of the term 'bodily movement' (or 'bodily motion', as some authors prefer).[8] The root of the ambiguity lies in the verb 'move', which has a transitive and an intransitive form.[9] Thus, in 'A moved B' it occurs transitively (e.g. 'The curate moved the lectern', 'The Commissioners moved the boundary', etc.); whereas in 'B moved' it almost always occurs intransitively ('The lectern moved', 'The boundary moved', etc.). Consequently, the phrase 'a movement of B' may either signify an action which consisted in making B move, in which case it will correspond to the transitive form of the verb; or it may signify B's moving, and correspond to the intransitive form. For example, 'a movement of B's finger' may signify an action which consisted in moving B's finger, or it may signify the result of such an action, that is, B's finger's moving. But if these two uses of such a phrase are not carefully distinguished, it is easy to arrive at the conclusion that agents cause their actions. For if A moves his finger, then he does indeed cause *a movement of his finger*; and his action certainly is *a movement of his finger*; and it is therefore easy to conclude that he causes his action. But if we bear the distinction in mind, it is evident that this argument is fallacious; for the movement of A's finger which he causes is not his action, since it does not correspond to the transitive form of the verb 'move': it is the result of his action, which corresponds to its intransitive form.[10] (We shall return to this subject in section 3.)

Does it follow that the concept of agent causation is unsustainable? We do not think so. What appears to be unsustainable is the doctrine that actions are events caused by agents. But it is possible to detach the concept of agent causation from this doctrine, for the claim that there is a defensible conception of agent causation implies only that an action is a causing of an event by an agent: there is no need to suppose, in addition, that this event is the agent's action, or that an action is itself an event.[11] In fact, as we shall argue below (section 4), the event in question is not the agent's action, but its result. But before we begin to discuss the nature of actions in positive terms, we shall examine the view that actions are events.

2. Actions and Events

Although the doctrine that actions are events is widely accepted, it is not evidently true, and we do not know of a convincing argument in its favour. The reader may be inclined to believe that Davidson's influential arguments about the logical form of action sentences strongly support the doctrine that actions are events. But in fact, what these arguments show, if they are sound, is that our talk about actions implies that there are events: they do not support the doctrine that actions are events. Davidson argues that we cannot transform action sentences into logical notation without quantifying over events; but he *assumes* that the events we need quantify over are the actions that these sentences report.[12]

The article about the logical form of action sentences does, however, include an independent and explicit argument to the effect that actions are events. Davidson argues as follows:

> If I fall down, this is an event whether I do it intentionally or not. If you thought my falling was an accident and later discovered I did it on purpose, you would not be tempted to withdraw your claim that you had witnessed an event.[13]

But this argument fails on two counts. First, Davidson assumes that falling is something that can be done intentionally, or on purpose; but this is false. Pretending to fall is something that *must* be intentional, and making or letting oneself fall is something that *can* be intentional; but neither of these is the same as falling. If I fall, this cannot be intentional, since it is not something I do, but something that happens to me. Hence, 'I fell intentionally' can be true only if it is elliptical for 'I made (or let) myself fall intentionally.'

Secondly, Davidson argues that unless intentional actions are events, one can witness a fall that was not

an accident without witnessing an event. But again this is false. It is undeniable that if you saw me fall, then you witnessed an event, whether my falling was an accident or not. But this is entirely consistent with the view that making or letting myself fall is not an event. If I made or let myself fall then I fell; and since that is an event, you witnessed an event if you saw it happen – whether or not it transpires that I made or let it happen intentionally.[14]

Perhaps some philosophers would argue that actions are events on the grounds that although an agent can legitimately be described as the cause – or, strictly, the causer – of an event, 'we understand this only when we can reduce it to the case of an event being a cause'.[15] For if this is true, sentences like 'John killed Jim' and 'Sam caused a stir' can be rescued from obscurity only by a paraphrase which says explicitly that such and such an event caused Jim's death or caused a stir. And since a plausible paraphrase will need to preserve the implication that John and Sam were responsible for the events they caused, 'John's action caused Jim's death' and 'Sam's action caused a stir' are the most conspicuous candidates. But deeming them satisfactory carries the implication that actions are events.

We doubt whether there is any reasonable prospect of explaining the concept of agency in terms of the concept of a causal relation between events. If we are right about this, the enthusiasm for this sort of paraphrase is unfounded and frankly specious. But in any case, it does not provide any rational support for the doctrine that actions are events.[16] On the contrary, one would need to assume that actions are events in order to accept that 'Sam's action caused a stir' is a sentence in which an event is described as a cause. Indeed, far from supporting the doctrine that actions are events, reductionism about agency is sometimes implicitly founded on the assumption that the doctrine is true. For example, when Davidson claims that the concept of causation we make use of when we say that the author or agent of an event caused it is 'the relation, whatever it is, that holds between two events when one is the cause of the other', he supports the claim with the following argument:

> For although we say that the agent caused the death of the victim, that is, that he killed him, this is an elliptical

way of saying that some act of the agent – something he did, such as put poison in the grapefruit – caused the death of the victim.[17]

This argument is surely very weak. First, Davidson does not explain why we should accept that saying that John killed Jim is an elliptical way of saying that some act of John's – such as putting poison in the grapefruit – caused Jim's death; or why we should not prefer the view that saying that some act of John's caused Jim's death is an elliptical way of saying that John killed Jim by doing something – such as putting poison in the grapefruit. Secondly, even if it were true that saying that John killed Jim is an elliptical way of saying that some act of John's caused Jim's death, it would not follow that it is an elliptical way of saying that one event caused another, *unless* an act of John's is an event. Hence, if we assume that actions are events, the ellipsis Davidson claims to diagnose makes it plausible that the concept we make use of when we say that John killed Jim or that Sam caused a stir is the concept of a causal relation between two events. But the assumption that actions are events needs an independent argument to support it.

The reductionist doctrine would, of course, be a legitimate one if only events can cause events; but we are not aware of an argument which shows that this is true. There is a more plausible principle which is implied by the principle that only events can cause events, but does not imply it – namely, that every event that has a cause is caused by another event. And perhaps this is true. But whether it is true or false, it does not imply that actions are events. It does imply that if an agent causes an event e_2, there is another event e_1 that causes e_2; but it does not follow that e_1 is the agent's action. And nor does the weaker principle imply that if an agent is described as the causer of an event, 'we understand this only when we can reduce it to the case of an event being a cause'. 'John caused Jim's death' and 'Sam caused a stir' appear to be perfectly comprehensible, regardless of whether we can provide them with a paraphrase which says that one event caused another; and the weaker principle does not imply that this appearance is deceptive.

We mention the weaker principle because the stronger one is sometimes confused with it. For example, J. D. Velleman appears to confuse the two in the following passage:

> our scientific view of the world regards all events and states of affairs as caused, and hence explained, by other events and states, or by nothing at all. And this view would seem to leave no room for agents in the explanatory order.[18]

Velleman does not say why he regards this as a scientific rather than a philosophical view. But in any case, if it is true that 'our scientific view of the world regards all events and states of affairs as caused, and hence explained, by other events and states, or by nothing at all', it does not follow that there is 'no room for agents in the explanatory order'. As we have seen, if all events are caused by other events and states, or by nothing at all, some events may also be caused by agents. It is the view that only events can cause events which seems to leave no room for agents, and which certainly implies that any talk which makes use of the concepts of an agent or of agent causation can be deemed significant only to the extent that it can be paraphrased by talk about events and their causal relations. But if this view leaves no room for agents, then by the same token, it leaves no room for actions either. Such a view of the world would be an incomplete one; but it is not, so far as we are aware, a view that is implied by any plausible theory in the natural sciences.

3. Bodily Movements

Although philosophers have failed to argue convincingly that actions are events, they have not failed to explain what kinds of events they believe actions to be. Many have claimed that actions, or an important class of them, are bodily movements. But as we argued above (p. 35), the term 'bodily movement' is ambiguous, since it can correspond either to the transitive or to the intransitive form of the verb 'move'. We now propose to argue, first, that the claim that bodily movements are an important class of actions is true only if the term 'bodily movement' corresponds to the transitive form of the verb; and secondly, that the term is used to refer to an event only if it corresponds to the intransitive form of the verb. For the sake of convenience, following Hornsby, we shall use the subscripts '$_T$' and '$_I$' to indicate whether a phrase should be understood as corresponding to the transitive or intransitive form of a verb. Thus, we shall argue that bodily movements$_I$ are not actions; and that bodily movements$_T$ are not events. We shall take it to be uncontroversial that bodily movements$_T$ are actions; that bodily movements$_I$ are events; that *if* bodily movements$_I$ are actions, they are the same actions as the corresponding bodily movements$_T$; and that *if* bodily movements$_T$ are events, then either they are the same events as the corresponding bodily movements$_I$, or their causes. For example, if A raises his arm, A's raising his arm is an action; A's arm's rising is an event; if A's arm's rising is an action, it is the same action as A's raising his arm; and if A's raising his arm is an event, then either it is the same event as A's arm's rising or its cause.

Davidson is one philosopher who claims that, in some cases, 'my raising my arm and my arm rising are one and the same event.'[19] But my raising my arm is my causing my arm to rise. Hence, if my raising my arm is an event, it is the same event as my causing my arm to rise. And hence, if my raising my arm and my arm's rising are one and the same event, then my causing my arm to rise and my arm's rising are one and the same event. But it cannot be plausible that causing an event to occur is not merely an event itself, but the very same event as the event caused. Davidson himself insists that 'To trip myself is … not identical with what it causes [*sc.* my tripping].'[20] But this is precisely because my tripping myself is my causing my tripping, and my causing an event is not identical with the event caused, any more than my making or breaking a pot is identical with the pot I make or break.[21] Hence, if my raising my arm is an event, it is not the same event as my arm's rising: bodily movements$_T$ are not identical with bodily movements$_I$. But since bodily movements$_I$ are not actions unless they are the same actions as the corresponding bodily movements$_T$, bodily movements$_I$ are not actions.

In the last fifteen years or so, considerations of this sort have made Davidson's view lose popularity in favour of the view that bodily movements$_T$ are events which cause bodily movements$_I$.[22] Perhaps we should find this surprising. For we might expect the doctrine that actions are events to lose its allure, once it is conceded that A's raising his arm is not identical with A's arm's rising. For the concession is presumably the result of realizing that A's raising his arm is A's *causing* his arm's rising, and this fact surely has no tendency to suggest that A's raising his arm is an event. It is, after all, far from obvious that a causing, like the event caused, is itself an event.

Be that as it may, if bodily movements$_T$ are events which cause bodily movements$_I$, then either bodily movements$_T$ are events, perhaps neural events, which occur inside the agent's body, as for example Hornsby maintains in her book *Actions*;[23] or they are events of another sort, which do not – presumably events which have no location at all, if there are such events. The first alternative implies that bodily movements$_T$, unlike their effects, are not normally perceptible without a special apparatus.[24] The second implies that bodily movements$_I$ are caused both by neural events and by events of another sort, and therefore raises the difficult question of how these two sorts of events are related. It also implies that bodily movements$_T$ can never be perceived, whatever sort of apparatus we are equipped with. But we can and do see people and animals moving their limbs without making use of any sort of apparatus; and seeing a person or an animal moving its limbs is seeing a bodily movement$_T$. Hence neither alternative is tenable; and it follows that bodily movements$_T$ are not events which cause bodily movements$_I$. We do not wish to deny that when an agent causes a bodily movement$_I$, an event – perhaps in the agent's nervous system – causes the same bodily movement$_I$; but the agent's action is not identical with this event. (We shall say more about events of this kind in section 5.)

In fact Hornsby considers the objection that if bodily movements$_T$ are events which occur inside the agent's body, they are normally imperceptible. In her book *Actions*, she writes as follows:

> … the objector thinks that we see actions themselves, and I am inclined to agree. But he says 'If actions are inside the body, then we cannot see them.' Some doubt is cast on his conditional when we remember that to say that actions take place inside the body is not to deny that they take place in larger portions of space … Perhaps then we see actions in virtue of seeing *some* place where they occur when they occur; perhaps we see actions in virtue simply of seeing the people whose actions they are at the time of their happening. Or again, perhaps we see actions in seeing their effects.[25]

Hornsby does not appear to decide which of these alternatives she wishes to endorse. Instead, she argues that the objection owes part of its force to the assumption that actions are bodily movements₁, and the rest, to a mistaken hypothesis about what we can and cannot see. But in fact no such assumption and no such hypothesis are needed in order to show that none of the alternatives mooted is satisfactory. For, first, I do not see an event in someone's nervous system in virtue of seeing some place where this event occurs when it occurs – such as Hyde Park or Washington Square. Secondly, I do not see an event in someone's nervous system in virtue simply of seeing him when the event occurs; any more than I see a door open inside a house in virtue simply of seeing the house when the door opens. And thirdly, I do not see an event in someone's nervous system in seeing its effects; any more than I see the piston of an engine move in seeing the car accelerate along a highway.

More recently, Hornsby has retracted the claim that actions are events which occur inside the agent's body, although she continues to maintain that 'the relation between an action of someone's moving her body and her body's moving is a causal one'.[26] But she has also argued that actions may after all be invisible; and that a theory of action can safely ignore the question of whether it implies that they are:

> … nothing of moment has to revolve around the specific question of whether, among [the events which occur when there is an action], actions are visible. And it is arguable that we have no firm intuition on this specific question which is not dependent on some prior view of what actions are.[27]

But if, as Hornsby explicitly acknowledges, 'people see one another doing things', then the proposition that actions are visible is not merely an intuition: it is a fact.[28] For if A sees B salute an officer, then A sees a salute; and a salute is an action. If A sees B dive into a pool, then A sees a dive; and a dive is an action. And so on, for the myriad of actions which can have eye-witnesses – whether or not actions are among the events which occur when there is an action. Seeing a person doing something need not amount to witnessing an action, because there are things we can do, such as trip or fall, which are not actions. But if what

A does is to perform an action of some kind, then seeing A do it is seeing an action.

Since bodily movements_T are not identical with bodily movements₁, and they are not events which cause bodily movements₁ either, we conclude that they are not events.[29] But an objection might be raised at this point, which could be put as follows: You have argued that an event, for example A's arm's rising, can be caused both by an agent and by another event, such as an event in the agent's nervous system. But does this not raise precisely the difficulty that you raised in connection with the thought that bodily movements₁ can be caused both by neural events and by events of another sort, or at any rate an equally intractable one, viz. the difficulty of explaining how these two sorts of causes are related?

The answer to the objection is that the difficulty is not intractable precisely because the causes (strictly, the cause and the causer) are an event and an agent. We hold that if A's arm rose because A raised his arm, then A's arm's rising was caused by A. But we can explain why an agent like A is able to raise his arm to the extent that we can say what sorts of events cause A's arm to rise when A raises his arm, that is, to the extent that we can describe what Strawson nicely calls 'the micro-mechanisms of production'.[30] Just as we can explain why an acid has the power to corrode metal to the extent that we can say what sorts of events occur when it does so. (These events will be ones which involve other kinds of substance with their particular causal powers, which can be explained in their turn.) Hence, the explanations of an event which we give when we identify the agent that caused it and the events that caused it are not competing explanations, but complementary ones.

4. What Actions Are

We have not denied that actions are events because we propose to revive the doctrine that verbs of action are relational expressions, comparable to 'is taller than', 'is above' or 'is the father of'. We are happy to follow Aristotle in assigning actions to a category *sui generis*; although we also believe that a sentence which reports an action entails that an agent and an event stand in the relation 'is the causer of'. For example, 'Brutus killed Caesar' entails that Brutus was the causer of Caesar's death, and 'The sun bleached the curtain' entails that the sun was the causer of the curtain's bleaching. Our view is that to act is to exercise a causal power – to cause, bring about or effect an event. But the exercise of a causal power is neither an event, nor the relation between agent and event that it entails.[31] Sometimes it is more convenient to say that the agent brought about a state of affairs, or that he brought an object into existence, than to say that he caused an event. For example, parking one's car is bringing it about that one's car is parked, and throwing a pot (on a potter's wheel) is, portentous as it may sound, bringing a pot into being. But in such cases, the inception of the state of affairs and the object's coming into being are events which the agent caused.

An agent does not normally cause his actions: he causes the *results* and at least some of the *consequences* of his actions. The idea that actions have results and consequences is familiar from our everyday talk about agency; but, following von Wright, we shall use the terms 'result' and 'consequence' in a technical sense.[32] An action, although the phrase is a clumsy one, is a causing of an event by an agent; the result of an action is that very event; and its consequences are effects of its result.[33] Thus, a killing is a causing of a death; the result of a killing is the death caused; and its consequences are effects of that death. Similarly, the result of the sun's melting the chocolate is the chocolate's melting, and its consequences are effects of the chocolate's melting, e.g. the tablecloth's becoming stained. Hence, an action is of such and such a kind if and only if its *result* is of the corresponding kind: an action is a killing if and only if its result is a death, a raising of an arm if and only if its result is a rising of an arm, a melting$_T$ of a piece of chocolate if and only if its result is a piece of chocolate's melting$_I$, and so on.

The result of one action may be a consequence of another. For example, if Jessica opens a trap by pulling a lever, the trap's opening is caused by the lever's motion. The trap's opening is therefore the result of Jessica's opening the trap and a consequence of her pulling the lever. But the result and consequences of a single action must be distinct events. Suppose, for example, that Mary makes Fred blush. If Fred is the Secretary of State, then Fred's blushing and the Secretary of State's blushing are one and the same event; Mary's making Fred blush and Mary's making the Secretary of State blush are one and the same action; and the Secretary of State's blushing is the result, not the consequence, of Mary's making Fred blush.

The distinction between these two kinds of cases – that is, between cases which involve two descriptions of the same action, and cases which involve descriptions of two actions, the result of one of which is the consequence of the other – is often marked in our common idiom with the prepositions 'in' and 'by'. Thus, Jessica opened the trap *by* pulling the lever; but *in* making Fred blush Mary made the Secretary of State blush. But there are also many instances, some of which involve legal, social or ad hoc conventions, in which idiom alone does not record whether two events, and therefore two actions, are involved, or only one. For example, we would normally say that Jean gave the signal *by* opening$_T$ the window, even if the window's opening$_I$ *is* the signal, and hence Jean's opening$_T$ the window and Jean's giving the signal are one and the same action.

These examples make implicit use of a criterion of identity for actions, which can be formulated explicitly as follows. Let 'A_1' and 'A_2' be two expressions each of which refers to an action: A_1 is the same action as A_2 if, and only if, the result of A_1 is the same event as the result of A_2. This contradicts the popular view that whenever an agent ϕs by ψing, his ϕing is the same action as his ψing, but we do not regard that as a defect in the proposal. We hold that when an agent ϕs by ψing, his ϕing *may* be the same action as his ψing, as it is in the last example mentioned in the last paragraph; but that when the result of an agent's ϕing is the effect of the result of his ψing, as it is if he opens a trap by pulling a lever, then his ϕing and his ψing are distinct actions because they have distinct results.[34] Davidson and others, who have denied this, were right to reject the view that if Jessica opens a trap by pulling a lever, her opening the trap and her pulling the lever are related either as cause and effect or as whole and part.[35] But they were wrong to infer that these actions must therefore be identical.

(We mention, in parenthesis, that the popular view – the view that if an agent ϕs by ψing, his ϕing is the same action as his ψing – is likely to appear especially tempting if one believes that agency is invariably intentional. For if Jessica opens a trap by pulling a lever, she may intend to pull the lever without intending to open the trap. Hence, if we want to insist that her opening the trap was an intentional action – at least *qua* action of some kind or other – one, and perhaps the only, way of doing so is to claim that if an agent ϕs by ψing, his ϕing and his ψing are the same action, which may be intentional *qua* ψing and unintentional *qua* ϕing. We shall argue in due course that agency is not invariably intentional. In the meantime, we simply note that it is perfectly consistent to deny that if an agent ϕs by ψing, his ϕing and his ψing are the same action, whilst acknowledging that a single action, such as one man's causing another man's death, may be intentional *qua* killing and unintentional *qua* parricide.)

Davidson argues that if an agent ϕs by ψing, his ϕing is the same action as his ψing with the following example. Suppose that the queen moves her hand in such a way as to pour poison in the king's ear:

> The moving of her hand by the queen on that occasion was identical with her doing something that caused the death of the king. Doing something that causes a death is identical with causing a death. But there is no distinction to be made [in this sort of case] between causing the death of a person and killing him.

It follows, Davidson argues, that 'the killing ... did not differ from the movement of the hand.'[36] Davidson also asks, rhetorically:

> Is it not absurd to suppose that, after the queen has moved her hand in such a way as to cause the king's death, any deed remains for her to do or complete?[37]

Neither the argument nor the question proves its point.[38] The argument is a *petitio*, because the question, whether doing something that causes a death is identical with causing a death, is precisely what is at issue. If the queen does something that causes a death, then, to be sure, she causes a death, and *vice versa*; but this logical equivalence does not imply that her doing what she does – in this case, her moving her hand – is *identical* with her causing a death. It is, and remains, natural to suppose that causing one event is as distinct from causing another event as one event is from another.

But, one might protest, there is surely a difference between the case where the result of one action (a death) is the consequence of another (a movement of a hand), and the case where two actions (a killing and a movement of a hand) have nothing to do with each other. Surely, the second case is the one in which there really are distinct actions – the case, one might say, in which the agent was *busier*. The answer to this objection is that we do indeed want to mark the difference between the two cases, but the difference is simply this: only in the first case was the result of one action the consequence of the other. As Davidson suggests, we leave it to nature to unfold the consequences of our actions, and can busy ourselves with other matters while it does so. But it does not follow that the two sentences 'The queen moved her hand' and 'The queen killed the king' describe the same action if nature ensures that the result of the second ensues upon the result of the first.

As for the question, 'Is it not absurd ...', it simply fails to prove that the killing 'did not differ from the movement of the hand'. There was nothing more for the queen to do, because she killed the king by moving her hand, and not by moving her hand and then doing something else, say, flaring her nostrils. But this is no reason to believe that her moving her hand and her killing the king were one and the same action. If we consider events instead of actions, the weakness of the argument is just as plain. If one event – say, the white ball's striking the red ball with a certain force – is all that needs to happen for another event – the red ball's beginning to move – to happen, it does not follow that only one event occurred.

5. Basic Actions

The preposition 'by' has been used to single out a class of actions which is thought by many philosophers to deserve special attention, namely 'basic' or 'primitive' actions – 'the ones we do not do by doing something else', as Davidson puts it.[39] The queen killed the king by pouring poison into his ear, and she poured poison into his ear by moving her hand in the right way at the right moment. But did she move her hand by doing something else, or was her moving her hand a basic action?

Perhaps the question of which actions, if any, are basic is an interesting one in its own right; but there is little doubt that it has attracted as much interest as it has, for a quarter of a century or more, because the doctrines that actions are events and that if an agent ϕs by ψing, his ϕing and his ψing are one and the same action, together invest the question with a singular and fundamental importance. If these two doctrines were true, and if, for example, it transpired that our basic actions – 'the ones we do not do by doing something else' – are events which occur in our nervous system, it would follow that *every* action is an event in the agent's nervous system, and a significant part of the task of 'spelling out the differences between events in general and those events that fall squarely into the category of human action' would have been accomplished.[40] Obviously, we do not believe that the question of which actions are basic has *this* significance, for we deny that actions are events, and we deny that if an agent ϕs by ψing, his ϕing and his ψing are one and the same action. However, the question can be put. And, Wittgenstein assures us, when a question can be put, so can its answer.

We propose that an action be described as basic if, and only if, its result is not the consequence of – that is, the effect of the result of – another action by the same agent. Which actions are these? Among those who assume that the class of basic actions can be neatly circumscribed, the most popular candidate is a subclass of bodily movements$_T$. We shall argue that some bodily movements$_T$ are indeed basic actions; and we shall comment inconclusively on the question of whether all basic actions are bodily movements$_T$.

It is indisputable, and not disputed, that not all bodily movements$_T$ are basic actions, because it is possible to move one part of one's body by moving another. As we have often been reminded, one can raise one's left arm with one's right arm. But if an agent raises an arm directly, is this a basic action, or is it the consequence of another action by the same agent?

Against the view that actions of this sort are basic actions, one can object that we move our limbs by doing other things, for example, by causing certain events to occur in our brains, which cause our limbs to move. If these events in our brains are results of our actions, then movements$_I$ of our limbs are consequences of other actions we perform, and movements$_T$ of our limbs are therefore not basic actions.

But is the objection convincing? Davidson dismisses it, arguing that 'doing something that causes my finger to move ... *is* moving my finger.'[41] We have denied that this is true; but be that as it may, it is a poor reason for Davidson to give, for as we have seen, he also argues, on exactly the same grounds, that in the example he gives, the queen's moving her hand *is* the queen's killing the king. But he does not deny that killing the king is something that the queen does by doing something else, namely, moving her hand.

This much is certain: if A raises his arm directly, events of certain kinds occur in A's brain and nervous system, which cause A's arm to rise. But it does not follow immediately that if A raises his arm directly, this is not a basic action. For this conclusion to follow, we need an additional premise, namely, that if A raises his arm directly, he causes these events to occur in his brain and nervous system.

The question of whether this premise is true turns on where we divide the agency of complex agents and the agency of their parts, and in particular, the agency of human beings and the agency of parts of their bodies. As Harré and Madden point out, it is the business of science to explain the powers and liabilities of things and substances, including human beings and other living things, partly by reference to their structure, and partly by reference to the powers and liabilities of their constituent parts.[42] But philosophy too sometimes needs to ensure that the powers and actions of agents are not confused with the powers and actions of their parts. Hence, if we want to maintain that when an agent moves a limb directly, its motion is not the consequence of another action of his, we shall need to argue that the events in his brain and nervous system which cause his limb to move are not caused by the agent himself, but by parts of his body.

It would certainly be a mistake to suppose that one *cannot* cause events to occur in one's brain. One can – by passing one's hand in front of one's eyes, for example, or by biting one's tongue. But these events will be ones which were caused by, and not causes of, the motion of one's hand or the pressure of one's teeth. (If one's body is in good working order, every bodily movement$_I$ will cause events to occur in one's brain, and so every bodily movement$_T$ will number such events among its consequences.) So these examples do not support the view that if I raise my arm directly, I cause the events which cause my arm to rise.

Suppose, however, that – in the course of an experiment, for example – A raised his arm because he wanted events of these kinds (whatever they may be) to occur, and they did. Does it follow that he caused them to occur? If so, raising his arm was not, on this occasion, a basic action, and it will be difficult to maintain that it ever is. For even if there are some kinds of events one cannot cause unless one wants to the kinds of events which occur in one's brain are not among them. But the only pertinent difference between this case and the case where A raises his arm to reach a shelf or hail a taxi is in his reason. Hence, if A caused the events which caused his arm to rise during the experiment, it is reasonable to infer that he causes the corresponding events whenever he raises his arm directly, and hence that raising one's arm directly is not a basic action.

But in fact, if A raised his arm because he wanted events of these kinds to occur, and they did, it does not appear to follow that he caused them to occur. It follows that had he not wanted events of these kinds to occur, he would not have raised his arm, or at any rate, not for the same reason. And it follows that he ensured, or made certain, that events of these kinds had occurred, by raising his arm. But notice: 'had', not 'would'. I can ensure that such and such a kind of event *will* occur by performing an action of which it is sure to be a consequence; and I can ensure that such and such a kind of event *has* occurred either by performing an action of which it is the result, or by discovering that it is sure that it has occurred, or – as in the present case – by performing an action whose result is sure to be an effect of an event of that kind. But unless it can be shown that the third way is a variant of the first, there is no reason to accept that A caused the events which caused his arm to rise.

For these reasons, we doubt whether we ourselves, as opposed to parts of our bodies, cause the events in our brains which cause our limbs to move, when we move our limbs directly. But if we are right about this, where exactly does the boundary lie between those events which should be attributed to the agency of human beings, and those which should be attributed to the agency of parts of their bodies? Contractions$_1$ of

our muscles seem to be as close to the boundary as it is possible to get, but on which side do they lie? We feel unsure, perhaps because the boundary is a vague one. But in any event, contractions$_1$ of our muscles are movements$_1$ of parts of our bodies, so we see no reason to deny that some basic actions are bodily movements$_T$.

Are all basic actions by human beings bodily movements$_T$? If an action is a causing of an event by an agent, then it may seem possible to argue that they are not, as follows.

Consider so-called 'negative acts' or acts of omission. As we have seen, one can open a trap by pulling a lever or poison a king by moving one's hand; but one can also burn a sauce by failing to take it off the hob, improve one's health by desisting from smoking, or damage it by fasting. If, as we have argued, to act is to cause or bring about an event, then we can comfortably acquiesce in the simple-minded view that not doing something is not doing something. More precisely: acts of omission are not actions. For although the fact that A failed to ϕ may explain the fact that such and such an event occurred or failed to occur, failing to cause, or refraining from causing, an event of some kind is not an instance of causing an event to occur.

But if acts of omission are not actions, it may appear to follow that not all basic actions are bodily movements$_T$. For if A burnt a sauce because he forgot to take it off the hob, A's burning the sauce appears to have been a basic action – an action whose result was not the consequence of another action by the same agent – since forgetting to do something is not an action, and since A need not have burnt the sauce by doing anything other than forgetting to take it off the hob. But since burning a sauce is not a bodily movement$_T$, it follows that not all basic actions are bodily movements$_T$.

If this argument is sound, then basic actions by human beings form a heterogeneous class, of which a subclass of bodily movements$_T$ is merely an important subclass. But it is far from obvious that the argument is sound, for it is surely possible to object that if A's failing to cause, or refraining from causing, an event are not actions, then neither are A's letting the sauce burn, or allowing it to burn. For letting an event occur, or allowing it to occur, is nothing other than failing to prevent it or, perhaps, failing to do anything to prevent it. It would not follow that letting or allowing are not themselves things we do, sometimes intentionally, and for which we can be held to account, deemed culpable or deserve credit. But it would follow that the kind of examples we have been considering are not counter-examples to the doctrine that all basic actions are bodily movements$_T$.

The objection is unconvincing as it stands. For if A's failing to cause, or refraining from causing, an event are not actions, it does not follow immediately that A's failing to prevent an event is not either. For 'A failed to cause B's death' does not entail that an event of any particular sort occurred, and hence it cannot entail that A caused an event to occur. If the same is true of 'A failed to prevent B's death', as it certainly is of 'A failed to do anything to prevent B's death', then it does not describe an action. But arguably, 'A failed to prevent B's death' entails that B died; and if it does, then we can certainly ask whether it also entails that A caused B's death. And we can, in any case, ask whether 'A failed to prevent B's death and B died' entails that A caused B's death.

One plausible answer is that it does, but only in conjunction with some other premise or premises, concerning A's duties or obligations. For example, we may be willing to say that A caused B's death if B died because A failed – whether intentionally or not – to fulfil a duty of care towards her. But it is also plausible to argue that in these circumstances, although A let B die, he did not cause her death. For we can concede that A's letting B die was something A did, and that he may have done it intentionally, and that he is certainly (*prima facie*) culpable, without conceding that it was an action.[43]

There are, to be sure, subtle questions to be answered here. But they are not our subject. What does concern us, is that however these matters should be treated, the question of how we should decide the scope of basic human actions turns in part on whether the concept of agency should be deemed to embrace all or some instances of 'negative' as well as 'positive' causal responsibility for events. The doctrine that an action is a causing of an event does not imply any particular conclusion in this matter. But it does imply that any indeterminacy in the application of the verb 'cause' will be matched by a corresponding indeterminacy

in the concept of agency; and that if, in certain circumstances, A's letting someone or something die is tantamount to A's causing their death, then, in those circumstances, it is an action of A's. And if not, not.

6. Actions and Locations

If actions are causings of events by agents, where and when do they take place? The doctrine that actions are events gives rise to a familiar quandary about the temporal and spatial location of actions. If all actions are bodily movements$_T$, then a murder may already have taken place a month before the victim dies, and in a place where he has never set foot; but if the victim's death is part of a murder, a murderer may die a month before he has killed his victim, and part of his action may occur where he has never been.[44] But although we avoid this quandary by abandoning the doctrine that actions are events, do we not also commit ourselves to the implausible view that actions take place nowhere and at no time?

It is undeniable that many actions are performed at times and in places which we can readily identify as precisely as we normally identify the place where a substance is to be found, or the time at which an event occurred. For example, A may pour a glass of water at three-fifteen, in the kitchen, by the sink. But if A ϕd by ψing, and if the results of these two actions occur in different places or at different times, then the only direct answer to the question, where A ϕd, which is dictated by the nature of the case, will be one which is sufficiently imprecise to embrace both events – the results of A's ϕing and of his ψing. (The qualification 'which is dictated by the nature of the case' is needed because legal arrangements may sometimes require a more precise answer than they are strictly entitled to. If they do, then where possible we gerrymander: perforcedly, and therefore with a clear philosophic conscience, since neither logic nor metaphysics can avail.[45])

For example, if the queen poisoned the king last Tuesday in Elsinore and the king died last Thursday in Horsholm, then the queen killed the king last week in Denmark. This is a *direct* answer. But we can always answer the question, where and when an agent performed an action, indirectly: that is, by locating one or more events and one or more other actions by the same agent. Thus: 'Where and when did the queen kill the king?' 'She poisoned him last Tuesday in Elsinore; and he died last Thursday in Horsholm.' This answer provides more precise information than the direct one; but although it implies that the queen killed the king last week in Denmark, it does not say explicitly where or when the killing took place.

In short, the doctrine that an action is a causing of an event by an agent does not imply that actions have no spatial or temporal location. It implies that their location will often be imprecise, and that if an action was performed at such and such a time and in such and such a place, then its result occurred at the same time and in the same place.
[…][46]

Notes

1. The dissenting voices include G. H. von Wright, *Norm and Action* (London: Routledge & Kegan Paul, 1963); K. Bach, 'Actions are not Events', *Mind* 89 (1980); R. Stoecker, 'Reasons, Actions and their Relationship', in Stoecker (ed.), *Reflecting Davidson* (Berlin: Walter de Gruyter, 1993).

2. S. Guttenplan (ed.), *A Companion to the Philosophy of Mind* (Oxford: Basil Blackwell, 1994), 121. Cf. J. Kim and E. Sosa (eds), *A Companion to Metaphysics* (Oxford: Basil Blackwell, 1995), 3.

3. G. E. M. Anscombe, 'Causality and Determination', repr. in Anscombe, *Metaphysics and the Philosophy of Mind* (Oxford: Basil Blackwell, 1981), 136. Since our concern is with the question of whether actions are events, we shall also ignore the question of whether states, states of affairs or facts are causes.

4. D. Davidson, 'The Logical Form of Action Sentences: Criticism, Comment and Defence', in Davidson, *Essays on Actions and Events* (Oxford University Press, 1980), 128.

5. R. Taylor, *Action and Purpose* (Englewood Cliffs, N.J.: Prentice-Hall, 1966), 115. Cf. T. Reid, *Essays on the Active Powers of Man* (Edinburgh: John Bell, 1788), I.v.50: 'the notion of efficiency … is a relation between the cause and the effect, similar to that which is between us and our voluntary actions.'

6. R. M. Chisholm, *Person and Object* (London: Allen & Unwin, 1976); Chisholm, 'The Agent as Cause', in M. Brand and D. Walton (eds), *Action Theory* (Dordrecht: D. Reidel, 1976).

7. Cf. D. Davidson, 'Agency', Chapter 2 in this volume, 15, Davidson, 'Problems in the Explanation of Action', in P. Pettit, R. Silvan and J. Norman (eds), *Metaphysics and Morality: Essays in honour of J. J. C. Smart* (Oxford: Basil Blackwell, 1987), 36; J. Hornsby, *Actions* (London: Routledge & Kegan Paul, 1980), 101.

8. Bach, op. cit., 114–15; Hornsby, *Actions*, ch. 1; D. W. D. Owen, 'Actions and Bodily Movements: Another Move', *Analysis* 40 (1980), 33.

9. The transitive verb (or form of the verb) 'move' is what grammarians call a causative, because 'A moved B' implies 'A caused B to move', where 'move' is the corresponding intransitive verb (or form).

10. Taylor, op. cit., 122 f. commits this fallacy; and Chisholm appears to commit a similar fallacy in 'Human Freedom and the Self', repr. in G. Watson (ed.), *Free Will* (Oxford University Press, 1982), 30, as follows:

    whenever a man does something A, then (by 'immanent causation') he makes a cerebral event happen, and this cerebral event (by 'transeunt causation') makes A happen.

    In its first appearance 'A' seems to signify an action, for example, a movement (transitive) of a part of the man's body; whereas in its second appearance, 'A' seems to signify the action's result, for example, a movement (intransitive) of a part of the man's body.

11. Bishop and O'Connor also reject the doctrine that agents cause their actions; but they retain the doctrine that actions are events. J. Bishop, 'Agent Causation', *Mind* 92 (1983), 77; T. O'Connor, 'Agent Causation', in O'Connor (ed.), *Agents, Causes and Events* (New York: Oxford University Press, 1995), 181.

12. See, for example, Davidson, 'The Logical Form of Action Sentences: Criticism, Comment and Defence', loc. cit., 147. An argument by Hornsby is open to similar objections: see Hornsby, *Actions*, 3–4 & 133–35. These matters are examined in detail in M. Alvarez, 'Actions and Events: Some Semantical Considerations', *Ratio* 12 (1999), 213–39, where it is argued that the events we need to quantify over in order to formalize action sentences are the results of actions, and not actions themselves.

13. Davidson, 'The Logical Form of Action Sentences', repr. in *Essays on Actions and Events*, 113.

14. See also Bach, op. cit., 115.

15. Davidson, 'The Logical Form of Action Sentences: Criticism, Comment and Defence', loc. cit., 128. Davidson writes there: 'I see no objection to saying that agents are causes'; but we prefer to circumscribe the use of the noun 'cause' in a manner which accords more closely with idiomatic English. Since this excludes using the noun 'cause' in every case of agency, we prefer the less common, but unimpeachable, 'causer'.

16. Not every philosopher who argues that the concept of causation we make use of in attributions of agency is the concept of event causation also argues that actions are events. For example, Bach (op. cit., 114) denies that actions are events but still maintains that 'the relation essential to action is analysed in terms of relations between events', and describes the concept of agent causation as 'controversial'.

17. Davidson, 'Agency', loc. cit., 13. Since agents do not do events, what an agent does is not an event. We shall assume that Davidson meant to say that an agent's *doing* what he does is an event.

18. J. D. Velleman, 'What Happens when Someone Acts?', *Mind* 101 (1992), 467.

19. Davidson, 'Problems in the Explanation of Action', loc. cit., 37; see also 'The Logical Form of Action Sentences: Criticism, Comment and Defence', loc. cit., 124 & 128. We write, 'in some cases', because Davidson only defends this doctrine in relation to what he calls 'primitive actions, the ones we do not do by doing something else.' Davidson, 'Agency', loc. cit., 18. For arguments against Davidson's view, see J. Montmarquet, 'Actions and Bodily Movements', *Analysis* 38 (1978); Bach, op. cit.; Hornsby, *Actions*, ch. 1.

20. Davidson, 'Agency', loc. cit., 12.

21. It has been argued by David Lewis that an event may be a part of a larger event that it causes, e.g. a battle which starts a war. See D. Lewis, 'Causation', repr. in Lewis, *Collected Papers*, vol. 2 (New York: Oxford University Press, 1986), 173. But this has no tendency to support the claim that causing an event can be identical with the event caused.

22. E.g., Hornsby, *Actions*; O'Connor, op. cit.

23. Hornsby (*Actions*, 14) claims that 'all actions occur inside the body'. Later in the same essay (106), she claims that as we trace our way back along the sequence of events which led to a bodily movement$_I$, 'there is a point in the neurophysiological sequence at which … we no longer find events that the agent made happen, because at that point we find the action.' Hornsby (ibid., 45) also claims that 'actions are tryings

to move$_T$ the body or bring about bodily movements$_I$', but we do not propose to discuss this claim here.

24. For an interesting discussion of this and related matters, see the exchange between Lowe and Hornsby published in *Analysis*: E. J. Lowe, 'All Actions Occur inside the Body', 41 (1981); Hornsby, 'Reply to Lowe on Actions', 42 (1982); Lowe, 'Reply to Hornsby on Actions', 43 (1983); Hornsby, 'Events that are Causings: A Response to Lowe', 43 (1983); Lowe, 'A Note on a Response of Hornsby's', 44 (1984).

25. Hornsby, *Actions*, 103.

26. Hornsby, *Simple Mindedness* (Cambridge, Mass.: Harvard University Press, 1997), 232 n. 1 and 94.

27. Ibid., 99.

28. Ibid., 97.

29. This conclusion does depend on the assumption that if bodily movements$_T$ are events, then either they are the same events as the corresponding bodily movements$_I$, or their causes. We said that we would take this to be uncontroversial. But in fact there have recently been attempts to defend the idea that a bodily movement$_T$ is a larger event of which the corresponding bodily movement$_I$ and a mental or neural event which causes it are parts. The influence of these ideas has been limited, and we shall not discuss them here. But we note that they imply that bodily movements$_T$ are partly perceptible and partly imperceptible (Hornsby (*Actions*, 103) rightly observes that if her own theory of action implies that actions are invisible, theories of this sort imply that actions are not events which 'take place in their entirety "strictly before our very eyes".') Cf. O'Connor op. cit.

30. P. F. Strawson, 'Causation and Explanation', in B. Vermazen and M. B. Hintikka (eds), *Essays on Davidson: Actions and Events* (Oxford University Press, 1985), 122.

31. Cf. Bach, op. cit., 119; Bishop, op. cit., 71 f.

32. von Wright, op. cit., 39. The distinction between the result and the consequences of an action is similar to one Reid draws between the immediate and more remote effects of a power, except that Reid's distinction is explicitly restricted to 'the effects of human power': Reid, op. cit., I.vii.61.

33. Strictly, an action is a causing of an event by one or more agents. More than one agent can jointly perform a single action, for more than one agent can jointly cause a single event. We shall ignore this complication, since as far as we can tell, it does not materially affect the argument.

34. Ontologically parsimonious philosophers need not be alarmed: as indicated above (n. 12), we also believe that

the most effective formalization of action sentences requires quantification over events, but not over actions themselves.

35. Davidson, 'Agency', loc. cit., 16ff. Danto argues that they are related as cause and effect, while Austin and Ginet argue that they are related as whole and part. See A. Danto, 'Basic Actions', repr. in A. White (ed.), *The Philosophy of Action* (Oxford University Press, 1968), 50f.; J. L. Austin, 'A Plea for Excuses', repr. in Austin, *Philosophical Papers* (Oxford University Press, 1961), 149; C. Ginet, *On Action* (Cambridge University Press, 1990), ch. 3.

36. Davidson, 'Agency', loc. cit., 17.

37. Ibid., 17. See also G. E. M. Anscombe, 'Under a Description', repr. in Anscombe, op. cit. note 3, 215f.

38. Similar points to the ones which follow are made in Ginet, op. cit., 59ff.

39. Davidson, 'Agency', loc. cit., 18.

40. See above, n. 2.

41. Davidson, 'Agency', loc. cit., 13.

42. R. Harré and E. H. Madden, *Causal Powers* (Oxford: Basil Blackwell, 1975), 105.

43. Someone's doing something intentionally need not be an action, for refraining from causing a stir is something one can do intentionally. Cf. Davidson 'Agency', loc. cit., 12 (our emphasis): 'a person does, *as agent*, whatever he does intentionally under some description.'

44. We do not propose to discuss these problems, or the various attempts in the literature to make one of the alternatives appear plausible: Bach, op. cit., 116f. and Ginet, op. cit., ch. 3 include useful summaries.

45. An interesting letter on this subject from Stephen Kobrin appears under the heading 'Taxation and Location', in *The Economist*, 21–27 June, 1997. Kobrin asks: 'Does an Indian programmer's repair of software on a computer in London (via a satellite link) take place in Bangalore or London? The answer [he says] is that the question is no longer relevant. The very idea of geographical jurisdiction may therefore no longer be meaningful.' And he notes that 'Property is becoming increasingly intangible and consumption difficult to locate precisely (even if consumers are not).'

46. A section on inanimate agency has been omitted here.

6

Agency and Actions

Jennifer Hornsby

Among philosophical questions about human agency, one can distinguish in a rough and ready way between those that arise in philosophy of mind and those that arise in ethics. In philosophy of mind, one central aim has been to account for the place of agents in a world whose operations are supposedly 'physical'. In ethics, one central aim has been to account for the connexion between ethical species of normativity and the distinctive deliberative and practical capacities of human beings. Ethics then is involved with questions of moral psychology whose answers admit a kind of richness in the life of human beings from which the philosophy of mind may ordinarily prescind. Philosophy of mind, insofar as it treats the phenomenon of agency as one facet of the phenomenon of mentality, has been more concerned with how there can be 'mental causation' than with any details of a story of human motivation or of the place of evaluative commitments within such a story.

This little account of the different agenda of two philosophical approaches to human agency is intended only to speak to the state of play as we have it, and it is certainly somewhat artificial. I offer it here as a way to make sense of attitudes to what has come to be

known as the *standard story of action*. The standard story is assumed to be the orthodoxy on which philosophers of mind, who deal with the broad metaphysical questions, have converged, but it is held to be deficient when it comes to specifically ethical questions. Michael Smith, for instance, asks: 'How do we turn the standard story of action into the story of orthonomous action?', where orthonomous action is action 'under the rule of the right as opposed to the wrong'.[1] Smith is not alone in thinking that the standard story is correct as far as it goes but lacks resources needed to accommodate genuinely ethical beings. Michael Bratman is another philosopher who has this thought; and I shall pick on Bratman's treatment of human agency in due course.

The standard story is sometimes encapsulated in the slogan: 'Beliefs and desires cause actions'. In the version of Smith's that I shall consider here, it says:

> Actions are bodily movements that are caused and rationalized by an agent's desire for an end and a belief that moving her body in the relevant way will bring that end about.

Smith's unpacking of the slogan shows how reason is supposed to enter the story: the word 'rationalize' is used in conveying that that which causes an action constitutes the agent's reason for it.[2] For the purposes of the present paper, it need not matter very much exactly how the story is formulated. My objection to

Hornsby, J. (2004), "Agency and Actions," in J. Hyman and H. Steward (eds.), *Agency and Action* (Cambridge: Cambridge University Press), 1–23. © Royal Institute of Philosophy and the contributors 2004. Published by Cambridge University Press. Reproduced with permission.

Philosophy of Action: An Anthology, First Edition. Edited by Jonathan Dancy and Constantine Sandis.
© 2015 John Wiley & Sons, Inc. Published 2015 by John Wiley & Sons, Inc.

the standard story will be that – despite the fact that the word 'agent' appears in definitions like Smith's – *the story leaves agents out*. Human beings are ineliminable from any account of their agency, and, in any of its versions, the standard story is not a story of agency at all.

The claim I intend by saying that the story leaves agents out is not answered by adding states of mind of different sorts from beliefs and desires to the causes of bodily movements. For what concerns me is the fact, as I see it, that 'belief-desire psychology' as it is understood in the standard story can cover none of the ground where human agency is found, and cannot do so even when it is supplemented with further mental states.[3] The popularity of the standard story then seems very unfortunate. It is not merely that that which supplements it inherits its crucial flaw. It is worse than that. For when the standard story is the base line for questions in moral psychology, a shape is imposed on those questions that they should never have been allowed to take on. Meanwhile the orthodoxy in philosophy of mind is silently reinforced.

Before I criticize Bratman's attempt to supplement the standard story (§3), I want to draw attention to what I shall call its *events-based character*, and to explain how and why that is a source of trouble (§1). Events-based accounts introduce a conception of the causal order in which agents have no place (§2). The causal role that agents actually occupy disappears in an account, which is events-based (§4).

1

There are some ideas in the background of the standard causal story which I should start by spelling out. The basic idea is that there is a category of particulars called 'events', and that some of the things in this category – spatiotemporal things that can happen only once – merit the title actions. Thus any of the following may on occasion apply to an event: 'a mosquito's biting me', 'the chocolate's melting', 'Don's falling from the cliff', 'Jones's stealing the jewels', 'Helen's waving her right arm'. And, very likely, the last two phrases here – but (*human* action being implicitly understood) only these two – apply to events that are actions. As we have seen, *bodily movements* (some of them) are said to be actions in the standard story. That is because such things as stealing the jewels are things that people do by moving their bodies; and if Jones stole the jewels by moving his body thus and so, then his stealing the jewels is (the same event as) his moving his body thus and so. 'His stealing the jewels' describes a bodily event by allusion to an effect that it had.[4]

Some of this is already controversial. And I need to set some controversies aside now in order to move on. There are philosophers who object to the whole idea that actions are events. I think that their objection will be easier to understand when some of its sources have emerged. (Without defending the idea that actions are events in the present paper, I would suggest that its innocence may be manifest when it is freed from everything with which it has so often and so readily been wrongly associated. Much of the opposition to the idea is explained [I believe] by the alacrity with which philosophers whose outlook is 'naturalistic' have moved from this idea to events-based accounts of agency: see §§4 and 5 *infra*.) Again, there are philosophers who allow that actions are events, but who draw upon a conception of events different from the standard story's own. I hope that it will come to be evident that errors I find in the standard story are not a product of its conception of events as such (see n.14 below). Then again, there are those who allow that an action can be an event of someone's moving their body but who don't believe that such an event is a movement. They refuse to equate (say) *a*'s moving her leg with *a*'s leg's movement. Here I agree, but leave expression of my own disbelief for much later because I want to avoid muddying the waters for the present. For the time being, then, let us simply follow the standard story in speaking as if bodily movements were the events which are redescribed in terms of effects or results they have – redescribed so as to reveal interesting things done by someone who moved their body in some way.

An account of action which is *events-based*, as I shall mean this, assumes more than that actions are such redescribable bodily movements. It also assumes that the phenomenon of human agency, and not just a category of events, is delimited when it is said which events are actions. And it takes it that the causal truths about agency can be formulated as claims about causation of, or by, an action – as claims about particulars.

(See Smith's version quoted above in which both of these assumptions are implicit.) An events-based account thus accords a very central role to events, having recourse to them both in marking out the phenomenon of agency, and in a causal depiction of it.

The events-based character of the standard story is what I shall criticize to begin with. One way to see the error of its first assumption is to think about failures to act (in a certain sense). One way to see the error of its second assumption is to think about how action-explanation works. I take each of these in turn now.

1.1 The key notion in much theory of action has been that of doing something *intentionally*. This is evidently the notion that has informed the standard story, which takes 'believe', 'desire' and 'do intentionally' to form a sort of conceptual trio. Behind the use of 'intentionally' is the thought that one keeps track of what is significant in someone's life as an agent if one attends to what they *intentionally do*. That was one of Davidson's principal claims in his paper 'Agency'.[5]

But someone can do something intentionally without there being any *action* that is their doing the thing. Consider A who decides she shouldn't take a chocolate, and refrains from moving her arm towards the box; or B who doesn't want to be disturbed by answering calls, and lets the telephone carry on ringing; or C who, being irritated by someone, pays that person no attention. Imagining that each of these things is intentionally done ensures that we have examples of agency in a sense that Davidson's claim brought out. But since in these cases, A, B and C don't move their bodies, we have examples which the standard story doesn't speak to.

It might be thought that the standard story needs to take the emphasis off *bodily movements*. And certainly it seems that the story would encompass more than it does if actions weren't defined by reference to the body and its movements.[6] If D's temptation to take a chocolate was so powerful that she had to tense her muscles in order to hold herself back, then arguably 'her refraining from taking a chocolate' would apply to an event even though her body did not move: it would apply to D's tensing her muscles, perhaps. Still to adapt the standard story in order to let in an example such as this would not address the real point here,

which is that in cases like the three imagined, there simply is no event – no particular – which is the person's intentionally doing the relevant thing. In the cases of A, B and C, that which ensures that something is done intentionally is not a matter of the occurrence of an event at all. Of course there will be plenty of events in the region of these agents at the time at which they do their things. But as the cases are imagined, none of these events is someone's doing something intentionally. One might put the point by saying that 'there is no positive performance' on the part of A or B or C, and that when actions are taken to be events, they are 'positive performances'.

Notice that one cannot put the point by saying that there are 'negative actions' on the parts of A, B and C. Of course not: where 'action' is taken in the standard story's sense, there could not be any such thing as a negative action.[7] It is true that philosophers who are interested in categories such as *omitting, refraining, letting happen* sometimes speak of these as categories of 'negative actions'. But then they don't use the word 'action' as having application to events. It may put a strain on those who raise questions about 'negative actions' to use the word as the standard story does – so that it is denied application as soon as there is no event which can be identified as an action. (This is why speaking of 'a positive performance' can help to make the point about the examples.) Still the strain is something that one has to put up with if one adopts the terminology of the standard story in order to evaluate it. The bodily movements of which the story speaks are spatiotemporal particulars. And in any of its versions, the standard story finds actions among such particulars – among events. To that extent, it fails to deal with examples where there is (in its own sense) no action. If such examples appeared to have been included in the story, perhaps that is because it is so easy to forget that 'action' is used there in a semi-technical, philosophers' sense.

1.2 If it were a matter of its preferring one conception of agency to another, then the standard story could not be faulted for leaving out cases where there is no 'positive performance'. And one can imagine someone thinking that there are reasons to hold on to a relatively narrow conception of agency, which treats the territory of agency as defined by the domain of the events which are actions. (It might, for instance, be thought that certain questions in metaphysics receive a particularly sharp formulation by reference to this domain.) Still the problem with the standard story's narrow conception is not that it serves only certain purposes: it doesn't even serve its own.

The reason why the standard story doesn't serve its own purposes is that it purports to work with a rather general conception of agency, deriving from a model of action-explanation. We saw that proponents of the standard story take the notion of being *intentionally* done to provide a hallmark of agency. This is thought to provide a hallmark because of its connexion with 'reason-explanation' – explanation which speaks about agents' beliefs and desires. A's, B's and C's cases count as agency on this reckoning, because one can construct tales of what each of them believed and desired which will appropriately explain their doing their things – not moving, letting the 'phone ring, not paying attention to X. So the standard story locates examples in a certain explanatory setting in order to characterize them as examples of agency, yet, by treating actions as events in accordance with the standard story, it ensures that there are cases that belong in that setting but don't have a place in the story.

Well, a proponent of the standard story might acknowledge that there are more explanations in the 'belief-desire' style than there are events (sc. 'positive performances') about which his story could be told, but respond by suggesting that action-explanation comes in two sorts. The suggestion would be that there are explanations in which the occurrence of an event – of a bodily movement – is explained and the standard story can straightforwardly be told; and there are, in addition, explanations in which the standard story cannot be told, although some other, related story, which also mentions 'beliefs and desires', no doubt can. But the suggestion is actually not at all plausible. For when we ask why someone did something, expecting to learn about what they thought or wanted, we don't always need to consider whether or not there was a positive performance on their part; explanation can carry on in the same vein, whether there was or not. One might discover that it was because she wanted to wreak revenge on the producer that she spoiled the show, and it not matter very much whether, for example, she put a sleeping tablet into the principal performer's drink (so that her spoiling the show was an event that was her putting …) or she simply failed to turn up (so that there was no *event*, or at least no bodily movement of hers, that was her spoiling the show). Either way, we say that she spoiled the show because she wanted to wreak revenge; and it makes no odds here whether the case is of such a sort that we can construct a statement 'Her wanting to wreak revenge caused [an event which was whatever bodily movement was] her Φ-ing'.

In the version of Smith's that we looked at, the standard story contains such causal statements as: 'Her desiring … and her believing … caused and rationalized a bodily movement'. Simplifying a bit, we can say that the standard story's causal statements are on the following style and pattern:[8]

(SS) Her desire … caused [an event which was] her bodily movement.

What we have just seen is that it is sometimes impossible to find a statement in this style, and implausible that we should be looking for statements in two different styles. That surely suggests that our focus should be on the sort of causal claim which comes naturally and which applies in every case:

(⋆) She did such and such because she desired… .

Causal statements like this hardly need defence: they are statements of a kind that we commonly recognize to be true.[9]

One may wonder now why causal claims like (SS), which are part of the standard story, should ever have been made. For even where there is an event of the agent's doing something, its occurrence is surely not what gets explained. An action-explanation tells one about the agent: one learns something about her that makes it understandable that she should have done what she did. We don't want to know (for example) why there was an event of X's offering aspirins to Y, nor why there was the actual event of X's offering aspirins to Y that there was. What we want to know is why X did the thing she did – offer aspirins to Y, or whatever.[10] When we are told that she did it because she wanted to help in relieving Y's headache, we learn what we wanted to know.

Now the standard story's proponents say that 'Actions are caused by a desire and a belief of the agent'. So they not only take the occurrence of a particular to be causally explained when an action-explanation is given, they also assume that items in a realm of particulars are what do the explaining. Hence their recurrent talk of 'belief-desire pairs' as causes, and of beliefs and desires as 'token' states. This is not the place to issue a challenge to the very idea of token states as they figure in the philosophical orthodoxy.[11] But we can notice that those who treat a state of mind a person was in – wanting to help, as it might be – as if it were a particular inside that person, appear to confuse two quite different uses of 'state'. And it is surely the events-based character of the standard story which gives rise to the idea that action-explanations record truths about causally-related particulars. Only when events are on the scene would there be any incentive to move from (*) to (SS). (*) gives the form of some action-explanations as normally understood; (SS) purports to see particulars standing in a relation of 'cause'.[12]

It will have to suffice here to have questioned the conception of action-explanation that an events-based account characteristically leads to. First, a causal explanation of why someone did something could not always be the explanation of an event's occurrence (for want sometimes of a 'positive performance'). Secondly, an action-explanation doesn't ever seem to be focused on saying why an event occurred. Once these points are appreciated, perhaps the habit of thinking that action-explanations mention items which combine with one another in the production of an event will start to be undermined.[13]

2

The foregoing is meant to indicate that agency is misconceived in an events-based account of it. Examples where there is no 'positive performance' suggest that the account leaves things out, and they point towards the impossibility of accommodating agency to its view about the operation of causality. Perhaps that view – of causality operating through items linked in causal chains – is the correct view of causal truths in some areas. But the truths that make up the phenomenon of agency seem not to belong in a world in which causality operates only in such a manner.[14]

I come now to a more direct way of showing that agency cannot be captured if one takes this view of causality's operation. I suggest that if one attempts to locate agency within the confines of such a view, one fails.

Consider Hume on the subject of bodily movements' production:

> We learn from anatomy, that the immediate object of power in voluntary motion, is not the member itself which is moved, but certain muscles, and nerves, and animal spirits, and, perhaps, something still more minute and more unknown, through which the motion is successively propagated, ere it reach the member itself whose motion is the immediate object of volition. [T]he power, by which this whole operation is performed is, to the last degree, mysterious and unintelligible. … [W]e have no power [to move our limbs]; but only that to move certain animal spirits, which, though they produce at last the motion of our limbs, yet operate in such a manner as is wholly beyond our comprehension.[15]

Hume's account of how limb movements come about provides one way of filling out one part of the standard story. But it is impossible to believe that Hume has succeeded in offering any part of any story of human agency. The lesson from anatomy, supposedly, is that the only effects we can produce are events in our brains, and thus, as Hume himself puts it, 'totally different from' the effects that we intend. But it is undeniable that among the effects we produce when we do something intentionally, there are some that we intend – whether bodily movements, or events in the region beyond our bodies. And if we do produce intended effects, then we can produce them. It is true, of course, that advances in neurophysiology have made the production of limb movements less incomprehensible than Hume took it to be. But the present point is not that Hume could not comprehend how our limbs come to move, but that, with an events-based account as his only resource, he finds himself saying that we *cannot* ('have no power to') move them.[16]

In Hume's story of agency, there is no place for beings who can move their bodies. Thomas Nagel has said that 'There seems no room for agency in a world of neural impulses, chemical reactions, and bone and muscle movements'. When he presented 'his problem of autonomy', Nagel adopted an external perspective from which 'the agent and everything about him seems to be swallowed up by the circumstances of action; nothing of him is left to intervene in those circumstances'. If you try to imagine your actions as part of the flux of events, then you won't succeed, Nagel said. 'The essential source of the problem is a view of … the order of nature. That conception, if pressed, leads to the feeling that we are not agents at all.'[17]

Some commentators share Nagel's anxiety. Not everyone has gone along with it, however. Those who have got used to thinking that someone's doing something intentionally is constituted by states and events see no difficulty about discovering examples of human agency in the picture on show from Nagel's external perspective. But perhaps one can appreciate the source of some of Nagel's anxiety by thinking about where Hume was led by his assumption that instances of agency consist of items – volitions, and then movements of muscles, nerves, animal spirits and, eventually, limbs – linked on causal pathways. It is surely because there seems to be no place for a sort of being that can move itself in his account that Hume is led to the conclusion that we cannot move our limbs. Where Hume plumps for a manifestly false conclusion, Nagel tells us that we find problems.[18]

The problem now would seem to be that agency cannot be portrayed in a picture containing only psychological states and occurrences and no agent making any difference to anything. It is no wonder that some of those who share Nagel's worry take it to be a problem for the standard story of action.[19]

3

Michael Bratman, so far from sharing Nagel's worry, thinks that it is obvious that an account of our agency had best be 'embedded in the event causal order'. He recognizes that 'in some cases we suppose … that the agent … is not merely the locus of a series of happenings, of causal pushes and pulls'. And he is led to seek a fuller account of actions' aetiology than the standard story provides. In a series of recent articles, Bratman builds upon that story, adding further states to its

beliefs and desires.[20] I look at his account now in order to illustrate the direction in which philosophers are led if they think that treating distinctively human forms of agency is a matter of bolstering the standard story.

Bratman is right, of course, to think that the standard story is conceptually inadequate insofar as it mentions only beliefs and desires. Everyone agrees that a life-like account of human agency will include states of mind of many more sorts than these. And Bratman himself has done more than anyone else to show that agents' intentions cannot be reduced to their beliefs and desires.[21] But to agree to this is not to accept the strictures of what Bratman calls a 'broadly naturalistic psychology', wherein phenomena are all to be seen as 'consisting in some, perhaps, complex, causal structure involving, events, states and processes'.[22] These strictures, rather than its simple shortage of mental states, are what lead Bratman to think that the way to treat agency is to add further pieces of psychological machinery to the standard story's states.

In Bratman's account a distinction falls between action determined or governed by an agent – confined to adult human beings, and '(merely) motivated behaviour' – found for instance among children who have beliefs and desires but do not yet have the conceptual resources for normative deliberation. The question what makes someone a *full-blown agent* of X is a question about the type of psychological functioning – beyond what is found where behaviour is motivated merely – from which X issues.[23] Bratman postulates that where agency is full-blown, actions are caused by higher-order reflexive policies. Any such policy has a content of this sort: Treat desired end E as providing reasons in one's motivationally effective deliberation, and treat it so as a result of having this policy.[24] The proposal is that when action is the upshot of such a policy, there is a strong form of agency, so that 'the *agent* is the source of, determines, directs, governs the action, and is not merely the locus of … causal pushes and pulls'.

Well, there doesn't seem to be any ordinary evidence that people regularly operate with second-order, reflexive policies of Bratman's kind. The fact that people show consistency in exhibiting one or another virtue certainly doesn't seem to provide evidence. When you call someone 'considerate', for example, it doesn't seem that you say that their actions are caused by the presence of a policy to treat respect for others' feelings as providing reasons in their motivationally effective deliberation and so to treat it as a result of having the policy. (If it really were as a result of a policy that someone showed consideration, then its content most probably would be 'Be considerate'.) It is not clear what could persuade us that anyone pursues policies of Bratman's kind. Certainly it seems very unlikely that many people would readily assent to possessing them. And it will be doubtful that many of us would be prepared to settle for a definite list of ends to encompass all of what we do as self-determined agents. At the very least, then, it is implausible that many adult human beings will be revealed as fullblown agents on Bratman's account of the matter. Yet presumably few adult human beings only ever go in for what Bratman calls '(merely) motivated behaviour'.

Suppose, however, for the sake of argument, that we go along with Bratman's policies. Suppose that we can define the ends we desire, and that we have the relevant policies in respect of each of them, and that such policies sometimes account for what we do. Even so, we surely should not want to say that someone is self-determined only insofar as the presence of such a policy actually explains what they do at some time. Consider a segment of someone's life history – a day's worth, say. Even allowing that, within this segment, policies with a second-order reflexive content sometimes cause actions, we shall not think that this shows that the person's self-determination is sometimes switched on. Much of what is done by a self-determined agent is not at all remarkable, so that most likely very many of the examples of agency found in such a segment will be quite mundane, and lack any distinctly rational or ethical deliberative history. The property of being a self-determined agent surely does not derive from particular occasions when some distinctive sort of state of mind – a special kind of policy or whatever it might be – kicks in to produce an action.

There are two sorts of objection to Bratman in the foregoing. Firstly, he postulates states of mind which are not plausibly states of ordinary people. Secondly, he assumes that we have to consider what it is for an *action* to be of an especially high-grade sort in order to

come to understand particular forms of *agency*. (This assumption is also present in Smith, when he raises the question what it is for an action to be orthonomous.) The assumption flows from allegiance to the standard story. The story tells us how the events that are actions are caused. And Bratman (like Smith) thinks that we have to find a particularly high-grade sort of cause for the actions of a self-determined (or orthonomous) agent.

Life would be tough if pursuing second-order reflexive policies were the only option for a genuinely ethical agent. Pursuing them would be cognitively taxing and interfere with exercising more ordinary capacities – capacities to react appropriately to the particularities of the various situations in which one may find oneself. These other capacities can be taken for granted if one rejects the assumption that characterizing self-determined agency is a matter of marking out a special class of events. For then our claim to self-determination can be founded in a conception of human agents as the kind of beings who consciously act under the influence of a wide variety of considerations, including so-called normative reasons. And an account of agents and their motivation can then make allusion to quite disparate factors, including, for instance, traits of character and emotional reactions.[25] Provided that human beings themselves are acknowledged to be part of the subject matter in action-explanation, a story about what someone does on occasion need not be focused upon actions and their history among other events, states and processes; it can be focused upon the agent and the difference that she made.

4

The idea that human beings make a difference – that they cause things, or bring them about – is surely a very ordinary and familiar one. Bratman tells us that 'it is difficult to know what it means to say that the agent, as distinct from relevant psychological events, processes and states, plays … a basic role in the aetiology and explanation of action.'[26] But I think that Bratman's difficulty must be a consequence of his espousal of an events-based account of agency. When one reflects upon what is present in that account, it can seem as if the only alternative to thinking of actions as 'embedded in an event causal order' were to treat agents as 'fundamentally separate and distinct elements in the metaphysics'[27] – as if any agent would have to encroach upon the causal chains that lead up to actions.

There is another view, however; and I think that it is a part of common sense. If we want to know what it means to say that an agent (as distinct from events and so on) brings things about, then we need only to think about what is ordinarily meant when this is said. That is what I explore next (4.1). We shall discover that events-based accounts are ruled out when it is accepted that agents bring about the things that they actually do (4.2). When the actual causal role of agents is grasped, it becomes evident why the standard story is not a story of human agency (4.3).

4.1 An event of someone's doing something is usually an event of their bringing something about. A driver slams on the brakes and she brings it about that the car comes to a sudden stop; the event that is her slamming on the brakes brings it about that the car comes to a sudden stop. A tea drinker puts her cup on the table; the result of the event of her putting it there is that the cup is on the table. The thought here – that a person's doing something is typically that person's bringing something about – relies on the fact that typical action verbs are causatives of one or another sort. The causative character of action language reflects agents' abilities to affect things. When agents do things by moving their bodies, they draw on causal knowledge, some of which is knowledge of relations of event causation, including knowledge of what their bodies' movements cause. (A foot pressed against the appropriate pedal applies the brakes; braking causes stopping; and so on.) In taking up the language of events, then, one is able to recapitulate in an explicit way a kind of knowledge that agents exploit in affecting things beyond themselves.

The idea that actions are events that can be redescribed in terms of their effects or results was part of the background of events-based accounts. We see now that this idea fits in with a general way of spelling out the causative character of action language: something the driver did was to bring the car to a sudden stop, and the car's arriving at a sudden stop was an effect of the driver's action; something the tea drinker did was

to put the cup on the table, and the cup's being on the table was a result of her putting it there. Although an event ontology is made explicit here, there is no call to import the two assumptions of an events-based account of agency. In the first place, to claim that there are events which merit the title 'actions' is not to adopt a conception of agency which confines examples of agency to the occurrence of events. For the upshot of agents' drawing on their causal knowledge can perfectly well be that they *don't* move their bodies. (So it was in the case of A, B and C, who, knowing that their moving would not have conduced to what they wanted, did things intentionally without there being any *action*.) Secondly, the claim that actions are events that are usually described in terms of their effects and results says nothing about the aetiology of actions. Taking a view about the language of action and its causative character can hardly settle the question of what kind of story to tell about the causation and explanation of action. Accepting that actions are events is one thing, endorsing an events-based account of agency quite another.

4.2 Advocates of events-based accounts are not alone in thinking that once events are on the scene, any causal question relating to human agency concerns the causation of the events that are actions. There are also the Agent Causationists who say that *agents* are causes of actions.[28] It is when this is said that it looks as though agents were intruders among events states and processes, encroaching there as 'fundamentally separate and distinct elements in the metaphysics'.

But in order to defend the causal role of agents, there is no need to say that they cause actions. Indeed there is every reason to say that agents do *not* cause actions. Consider again the examples of the driver and the tea drinker. What did they cause, or bring about? The driver caused (among other things) the car's coming to a halt; the tea drinker brought it about that (among other things) her cup was on the table. These things, which they caused or brought about, are the effects or results of their actions. What agents cause, then, are not the events that are their actions, but the effects or results in terms of which their actions may be described.[29] And when we think of agents causing things, we don't think of them imposing themselves in causal chains that lead up to their actions.[30]

Those who speak as if an action were an event one candidate for whose cause is an agent make it seem as if an action might be identified independently of any agent. But an event that merits the title 'action' is *a person's* intentionally doing something. And such events do not belong in a causal order from which people themselves might be missing. Their effects and results are caused by people situated in the causal world in which they intervene, and knowledge of which they rely on for their doings to lead to outcomes they want. Evidently this world, which we know and inhabit, although it is not a world from which events are absent, is not 'the event causal order' of which Bratman spoke. But nor is it a world into which people intrude.

Bratman and Smith, when they raised questions about what it is for an agent of a certain sort to be at work, turned these into questions about what sort of psychological cause is in operation. Like others who tell the standard story, they suppose that citing states and events that cause a bodily movement carries the explanatory force that might have been carried by mentioning the agent. But unless there is an agent, who causes whatever it is that her action does, questions about action-explanation do not even arise. An agent's place in the story is apparent even before anyone enquires into the history of the occasion.

To see this, consider that when one has an action-explanation, one knows why someone did something, and that that is to know why they played a particular causal role – why *a* brought it about that *p*, say. The explanation does not tell one *what* causal role *a* played: one already knows this when one knows what *a* did. If one finds out *why a* did whatever it was, then one comes to know things about *a* which make it understandable that she should have brought it about that *p*. But it then becomes more fully intelligible why it came about that *p* only insofar as this had already been understood by reference to *a*'s part in bringing it about. It might be that the agent actively intervened – so that there was a "positive performance" on her part –, or it might be that the agent intentionally let matters take their course. Either way, one must have taken a view of what the agent did – what role she played –, before one can speak to the question of why she did it. In cases where the agent can be said to have intervened, there will be an event that was her action.

But that could not mean that one needs to switch one's attention to an event causal order in order to uncover the agent's motives and reasons in such cases.

The fact that our attention is never directed towards an event causal order when it comes to action-explanation makes it clear why the same sort of explanation should subsume cases where there is no event which is an action as well as cases where there is (§1.1). And it helps to show why (SS) of §1.2 ought never to command our assent, although (*) perfectly well can.

4.3 Before concluding, I should say something about *bodily movements*. (I indicated that I would postpone expression of my own disbelief in the standard story's accounting of these back at the start of §1.) What it will be important now to realize is that the agent's role – as cause of what her actions cause – still has application in connection with moving the body. Recognizing this will help to pin-point where the standard story goes wrong. And it will also enable us to understand better why Hume should have been led to say that we can only produce effects totally different from any that we intend.

We move our bodies in order to effect changes beyond them. The driver, for instance, produced a movement of her foot for a purpose. Thanks to her causal knowledge, her moving her foot on the brake pedal belonged in a causal sequence that culminated in the car's coming to a halt. Her action then is describable as her moving her foot, as her slamming on the brakes, and as her bringing the car to a halt. But there is no possible reason to say that it is a foot's movement. Would anyone be inclined to think of someone's moving her foot as a foot's movement unless they imagined that a person's activity could be dissolved into the goings-on of states and events? The movement of a foot is not an action: it is not an agent's doing anything.

It is not a mere quibble to insist that someone's moving a bit of their body is their doing something, and that the movement they produce is not. For when the label 'action' is attached to bodily movements – to events which aren't actions – the events which *are* actions (to which 'action' had always been supposed to apply) are left out of account. Proponents of the standard story identify actions with bodily movements.

And the identification gives their game away. Given that agents cause what their actions cause, an agent's place in any causal story must be the place of her actions. But then agents and the events that really are actions are obliterated with a single stroke when bodily movements are identified with actions. In the standard story no-one ever does anything.

When actions are removed from the scene, not only are agents removed, but also their capacities cannot be recorded. We saw that when one considers the teachings of anatomy as Hume relates these, human agents, with their usual powers of movement and abilities intentionally to do things, are not in sight. Hume denied us our normal capacities of movement. But if it is allowed, against Hume, that we can move our bodies, and can produce such effects as we know would be produced by moving them, then our actions will be thought of as exercises of our capacities. (When the driver, who is capable of moving her right foot [and knows how to put the brakes on etc.] exercises a capacity of movement, there is an event/action of her slamming on the brakes.) Agents then are seen as bodily beings who have a place in causal sequences which lead from influences upon them to the comprehensible effects that they have beyond them. It is only to be expected now that the facts about what we do are not recorded by speaking of items which operate 'in such a manner as is wholly beyond our comprehension'.

5

I hope to have elicited the force of my claim that human agents are ineliminable from any proper story of their agency. Nagel was right to think that the very idea of agency is threatened when we try to picture action from an objective or external standpoint. For in any picture of action, agents will be seen causing things. And since agents are not visible from the external standpoint, we must refuse the suggestion that we might account for agency from it. Some philosophers are inured to the external standpoint; others impose it as their own – for instance whey they are led from the idea that actions are events to events-based accounts of agency. But we have established now that this was never the standpoint of anyone who had anything to say about people and what they do;

and that treating actions as events incurs no commitment to any events-based account.

It may yet be thought that I exaggerate when I say that the standard story is not a story of human agency at all. Many people suppose that it is only a kind of shorthand that leads philosophers to favour a slogan like the summary version of the standard causal story – 'beliefs and desires cause actions'. What this means, so these people say, is that 'a person's believing something and a person's desiring something causes that person's doing something'. According to this line, agents' mental states and their actions are really mentioned, even if agents themselves are not highlighted, in the language of the shorthand and of the standard story. Well, I think that what is represented now as shorthand is actually a way of talking that changes the subject. And I want to say something about why the change of subject should so frequently go unobserved.

Notice that even when what is alleged to be shorthand is given in its unabbreviated version, still the agent's role in action could not be conveyed. For when an account of the causal transaction in a case of agency is given in the claim that a person's believing something and a person's desiring something causes that person's doing something, it is assumed that the whole of the causal story is told in an action-explanation. The fact that the person exercises a capacity to bring something about is then suppressed. It is forgotten that the agent's causal part is taken for granted as soon as she is said to have done something. The species of causality that belongs with the relevant idea of a person's exercising her capacities is concealed.

There are many reasons why this should remain concealed, and why so many philosophers should have settled for a picture of agency like the one presented in the standard story's events-based account. There is the ease with which it is forgotten that 'action' is used in a semi-technical, philosophers' sense when the causal underpinnings of agency are in question (see §1.1). There is the readiness with which the very different uses of the word 'state' are confused (see §1.2). And perhaps there is a tendency simply (unreflectively) to equate a person's moving her body with the movement that she makes. But none of these slides and confusions is as powerful as the outlook which encourages them and which they encourage. From this outlook, the only possible reality is one in which any causal fact fits into an account in which everything that does any causal work is an event or state. Thus the correct and ordinary idea that to explain what human beings do is to give a kind of causal explanation is thought to be amenable to reconstruction as the idea that some events have causes belonging in a category of psychological occurrences.

Many philosophers with this outlook nod in the direction of the standard story, and offer it a sort of shallow endorsement. They assume that what they have to say about human agency is compatible with the story, without troubling to investigate it. I examined Bratman's account of full-blown agency in order to see where the standard story leads when it is explicitly told and taken seriously. I hoped to show that, whatever our metaphysical outlook might be, we can appreciate that we need to be released from the straitjacket of the standard story to give a realistic account of human agency. (Bratman's second-order reflexive policies should strike us, I think, as states at best of superhumans – states introduced in order to compensate for a deficiency in what can be uncovered among what is 'embedded in the event causal order'.)

Bratman's work is instructive because he follows where the story leads. Those whose endorsement of the story is more shallow than Bratman's might be less willing than he is to accept what I take to be its consequences. But given the prevailing 'naturalistic' outlook, it is not surprising that so many philosophers should sometimes pay the standard story lip service. And the widespread acceptance of the story among philosophers of mind may make it seem as if the outlook itself had some support. Thus even those whose accounts of agency actually exclude the standard story may blithely suppose that they might always be recast to conform to it. After all, the standard story isn't *obviously* wrong. It is obvious only that its vocabulary is inadequate. This obvious thought leads to the idea that the story needs to be supplemented; the question whether the causal notions that belong in an account of human agency are contained in the story is then overlooked.

I suggest that a 'naturalistic' outlook engenders the story, and that the story sustains that outlook; we have an orthodoxy whose presuppositions aren't examined by most of those who perpetuate it. Peter Strawson once said that it takes a really great philosopher to make a really great mistake.[31] I can't help thinking that, these days, it takes a really great number of philosophers to contrive in the persistence of a really great mistake.

Notes

Editors' note: some footnotes have been abbreviated, with the author's permission.

1. Michael Smith, 'The Structure of Orthonomy', in *Agency and Action*, ed. J. Hyman and H. Steward (Cambridge University Press, 2004), 165–93.
2. This use of 'rationalize' is taken from Donald Davidson's 'Actions, Reasons, and Causes', reprinted as Chapter 19 in this volume, in which the seeds of the standard story were sown.
3. In 'The Possibility of Philosophy of Action', in *Human Action, Deliberation and Causation*, ed. Jan Bransen and Stefaan Cuypers (Dordrecht: Kluwer Academic Publishers, 1998), 17–41, Michael Smith defends the standard story, which he there calls the basic Humean story, to the hilt. He aims to show just how widely the story has application (however much one might need to embellish it in order to deal with all of the various cases). My present concern, one might say, is not with any of the particular claims in that paper, but with the general picture of agency that lies behind it.
4. For a defence of the idea that actions are described in terms of effects they have and the thesis about the individuation that underlies this claim, see Davidson's 'Agency', reprinted as Chapter 2 in this volume.
5. Cited in previous note. That paper begins with the question 'What events in the life of a person reveal agency?'. The question puts in place the assumption that the phenomenon of human agency will be delimited when it is said which events are actions.
6. The doubt about assimilating actions to bodily movements mentioned a few paragraphs back is different. The question there was this: Assuming that an agent moved her body on some occasion when there was an action, then is it her bodily *movement* with which the action is to be identified? Here the question is

this: Should the class of actions be so circumscribed that it is required that an agent move her body for there to be an event which is an action?

7. There are no such things as negative particulars: cp. D. H. Mellor, *The Facts of Causation* (London: Routledge, 1995), 131–4. Notice that the presence of the word 'not' in a verb-phrase that applies to some agent need not correspond to there being no action: it could correspond to the occurrence of an action that is negatively described. Equally a positive description can sometimes be given of cases where there is no action (in the standard story's sense): she spoiled the show by not turning up.

8. The simplification assumes that *w* is a cause of that of which *d* and *b* are a cause. It is actually unclear how the 'and' of '*d* and *b* caused *m*' (a desire and a belief caused a movement) is supposed to work: cp. nn.13 and 15 *infra*. But I take it that those who tell the standard story will assent to 'Desires cause actions', just as they assent to 'Desires and beliefs cause actions'.

9. I cannot defend the idea that action-explanation is causal in the present paper. About it, I would say what I say, in n.5 *supra* about the idea that actions are events.

10. I don't think that I need to take issue with Davidson's claims in 'The Logical Form of Action Sentences', reprinted in his *Essays on Actions and Events* (Oxford University Press, 1980): one can accept that some of the sentences that give the explanantia of some action-explanations implicitly contain an existential quantifier whose domain is events, without thinking that any of the explanations is focused on the occurrence of an event. The objection that may be raised here will be that someone who allows any sort of equivalence between 'a Φ-d' and 'there was an event of a's Φ-ing' is compelled to think that action-explanation is the explanation of events' occurrences. But I think the objection relies on a failure to appreciate the hypersensitivity of 'explains why …' contexts. Consider that there may be circumstances in which we are interested to know why *Mary* stole the bicycle, and other circumstances in which we are interested to know why Mary *stole* the bicycle; and different answers to the questions will satisfy our interests in the different circumstances. (See Jonathan Bennett, §14 of *Events and Their Names* (Oxford University Press, 1988), 32–3 for a spelling out of this example.) My claim is that when someone seeks an action-explanation, typically what she is interested to know is why someone did something.

11. Helen Steward's challenge, in Part II of *The Ontology of Mind: Events, Processes and States* (Oxford University Press, 1997), is devastating. There is no ontological category into which can be lumped both the things which those who tell the standard story call 'states' and the things which they call 'events'.

12. 'Cause' is sometimes used in such a way that any 'because'-statement (or, perhaps, any 'because'-statement which is genuinely causal) licenses a statement of the form 'C causes E'. I needn't quarrel with this usage, insofar as 'Q because P' might be equivalent to 'C causes E' *where 'C' and 'E' abbreviate 'the fact that P' and 'the fact that Q'*. My quarrel here is with the move from 'Q because P' to '*c* caused *e*', where '*c*' and '*e*' are taken to name something in the category of particulars.

13. A different way to undermine this habit is to show that there are no intelligible causal statements which mix together things in a category of events with things in a category of conditions (where so-called 'token' states would need to be reckoned in the category of conditions). This is the conclusion of an argument of Davidson's 'Causal Relations' (reprinted in his *Essays on Actions and Events*, cit. n.10, 149–62). For a spelling out and endorsement of the relevant argument, see Helen Steward, 'On the notion of cause "philosophically speaking"', *Proceedings of the Aristotelian Society*, XCVII (1997), 125–40. From the perspective of Steward's article, it must seem an irony that Davidson's writings about action should so much have influenced those who tell the standard story.

14. I hope that it will be evident now that the view about the operation of causality that I put into question need not be founded in the standard story's conception of events. At the outset of §1, I noted that some philosophers draw on a different conception: an example would be Jaegwon Kim. The criticisms of the standard story in §1 have relied upon a specific conception of events (upon the only conception, I should say, which allows that they are genuinely particulars). But I believe that my claims against "events"–based accounts have application also when "events" is understood in different (but all of them philosophically familiar) ways.

15. *An Enquiry Concerning Human Understanding* (1748), §7.I.

16. Hume's denial of causal powers is well-known of course. But I think that its consequences for an account of human agency are insufficiently appreciated. (I take these consequences to be revealed in the particular passage, though no doubt there could be more argument about this. I don't suggest that Hume really thought that no one can move their limbs. His compatibilist arguments always take it quite for granted that human beings can take their place in the causal nexus.)

17. See *The View from Nowhere* (Oxford University Press, 1986), 110–11.

18. In Ch.VII of op. cit. n.17, Nagel discusses a question which 'applies even to the activity of spiders' before he introduces two different problems relating specifically to human agency. I have not been careful to distinguish here between Nagel's various problems, thinking as I do that they should all be solved together. I have said more about the problem that Nagel calls the problem of autonomy in 'Agency and Causal Explanation', in *Mental Causation*, ed. J. Heil and A. Mele (Oxford University Press, 1993), 129–53 (reprinted in *Philosophy of Action*, ed. A. Mele, Oxford University Press, 1997).

19. David Velleman introduces his problem about agency by reference to Nagel's puzzle in 'What Happens When Someone Acts?', *Mind* 101 (1992), 461–81 (reprinted at 123–43 in his *The Possibility of Practical Reason*, Oxford University Press, 2000); but he settles for the view that the standard story is adequate if someone's agency falls short of what is needed for a case of 'agency *par excellence*'. I think then that Velleman fails to address what Nagel had supposed to be a *quite general* puzzle. I discuss Velleman's treatment in this and subsequent of his papers in my 'Agency and Alienation', in *Naturalism in Question*, ed. Mario De Caro and David Macarthur (Harvard University Press, 2004).

20. The paper by Bratman on which I mainly focus in the present section is 'Two Problems About Human Agency,' *Proceedings of the Aristotelian Society* (2000–2001), 309–26. (I have just quoted from p. 311.) I also draw on his 'Reflection, Planning, and Temporally Extended Agency', *The Philosophical Review* 109 (2000), 35–61: the phrase 'embedded in the event causal order' occurs there. In this, Bratman not only endorses 'naturalistic psychology', but also maintains that an agent's identity over time should be treated as consisting 'primarily in overlapping strands of various kinds of psychological ties' between 'states and attitudes'. It is a good question whether such a reductionist conception of personal identity is enforced by 'naturalistic psychology', but certainly no accident that someone should subscribe to both.

21. See his *Intention, Plans and Practical Reason* (Harvard University Press, 1987).

22. 'Two Problems …', op. cit. n.20, p.312.

23. Ibid. p.310.

24. Ibid. pp.321–4.

25. I say this in order to point towards a different direction from Bratman's in which to go in order to answer questions like Bratman's. I don't mean to deny that there are plenty of good questions in the region of Bratman's own.

26. See 'Reflection, Planning', op. cit. n.20, p.39.

27. Ibid.

28. I introduce the initial capitals in 'Agent Causation' in order to suggest a distinctive doctrine – that of e.g. Richard Taylor (see further, next n.). Robert Kane, in *The Oxford Handbook of Free Will* (2002), 23, talks about the common practice of introducing a hyphen in 'agent causation' in order to indicate that a special kind of relation is intended. Well, many philosophers have had particular theoretical intentions when they have defined notions of agent causation; save for that, I don't think that we'd be inclined to think that there's anything special about it.

Others who are called agent causationists include Timothy O'Connor and John Bishop. There is much agreement between the view I put forward here and theirs. But O'Connor and Bishop both define actions as *relations* (and perhaps, then, they do introduce a notion which is 'special' in the sense meant by Kane). Thus they abandon the idea in the background of events-based accounts, which, as it seems to me, can be perfectly acceptable.

29. And that is why it is not an ordinary notion of agent causation which is used when Agents are said to Cause actions (see preceding n.). Bringing in an agent to do some of the causal work of the states and events of an events-based theory can be a consequence of confusing actions with their effects or results. One sees this confusion in the following passage from Richard Taylor's *Action and Purpose* (Englewood Cliffs, N.J.: Prentice-Hall, 1966). The quotation is at p. 111 of the 1973 edition reprinted by Humanities Press, New York; I have added the numbering):

> (1) In acting, I make something happen, I cause it.… (2) It seem[s] odd that philosophers should construe this as really meaning, not that I, but rather some event process or state not identical with myself should be the cause of that which is represented as my act. (3) It is plain that … I am not identical with any such event process or state as is usually proposed as the 'real cause' of my act. (4) Hence, if … I sometimes cause something to happen, … it is false that an event process or state not identical with my self should be the real cause of it.

The philosophers, the oddness of whose construal Taylor points out at (2), claim that an event, state or process causes his action. But in order to arrive at their claim, one has to confuse 'acting' with the 'something' that he makes happen, or causes, in acting. In putting the cup on the table (say) that which he makes happen, or causes, is that the cup is on the table. His action, however, is his putting the cup on the table. Thus to represent that some event process or state caused the cup to be on the table is not to represent that some event state or process caused his putting it there. Nothing is said about the cause of his putting it there. Thus Taylor's assertion at (4) can be rejected. An event not identical with the agent (sc. an action) is a cause of that which an agent causes to happen. This does not conflict with Taylor's claims at (1) and (3), which are obviously true.

30. In Ch.VII of *Actions* (Routledge, 1980), I suggested that the question of the irreducibility of agent causation comes down to the question whether 'is an action of' can be analysed in terms of event-causal notions. It now seems to me that the principal thesis of that book – namely that actions are events that we always describe in terms of their effects – leads rather directly to the answer *No*. We don't know which events are *a*'s actions unless we know what *a* – the agent – caused. And we couldn't know what it is for something to be *a*'s action without knowing that things like *a* can cause things.

31. 'Self, Mind and Body', in *Freedom and Resentment and Other Essays* (London: Methuen & Co. Ltd., 1974).

Part II

Willing and Trying

Introduction to Part II

1.

Wittgenstein asked, perhaps rhetorically, what is left when we subtract my arm's going up from my raising it (Chapter 1). One answer is: my trying to raise it. Other answers include: my attempting, undertaking, striving, heeding, setting out, exerting an effort, willing, wishing, deciding, or intending to raise it (though we shall for the most part deal with intention in another part). The precise relation between these arguably distinct phenomena – and, for many of them, their very existence – is a matter of great controversy. In this part we concentrate on the notions of willing and trying.

Ryle (Chapter 8) famously argued that the concepts of 'volition' and 'act of will' have no utility and should consequently be discarded alongside other illegitimate concepts such as that of phlogiston. This was not to deny that people may try to do things, or exhibit great strength (or weakness) of will; Ryle only denies that such an effort requires the prior occurrence of a volition, something that takes place in the mind and stands behind (or before) the ordinary action (or attempt to act). Many thinkers disagree with Ryle, thinking that we cannot avoid postulating the occurrence of volitions (even if we cannot discern their occurrence introspectively), which they identify variously with 'inner' (mental or neurological) acts or processes or events such as desiring. As we saw in Part I, if there are such mental events as volitions, we need to answer further questions about the relation of such things to (ordinary, physical) action. Some think that volitions are not actions themselves, but precede or cause physical actions. Others think they are purely mental actions that precede physical actions, and yet others think these mental actions are identical to the relevant physical actions, so that some actions are both mental and physical. No philosophy of action could be complete without giving some answers to these questions. Let us now look at some of the most popular accounts more closely.

Wittgenstein followed his question with another rhetorical question: "are the kinesthetic sensations my willing?" If there is to be such a thing as a willing, it had better not be a feeling or sensation that accompanies a bodily movement. Indeed, such sensations need not even be present when I act. William James famously mentions a patient of Landry's who had no bodily sensations at all, though he could still move around (James 1891: 490; Landry 1855). When the patient was asked to close his eyes and move his arm to the top of his head, Landry held the arm down (though the patient could not feel this). Upon opening his eyes the patient was surprised to see that no movement had taken place. In her early work (Chapter 9) Hornsby appealed to this experiment to support the claim that the patient *tried* to move his arm (James himself does not use this word but talks instead of exerting an effort). Indeed, Hornsby concluded that all actions are tryings of this kind,

Philosophy of Action: An Anthology, First Edition. Edited by Jonathan Dancy and Constantine Sandis.
© 2015 John Wiley & Sons, Inc. Published 2015 by John Wiley & Sons, Inc.

regardless of whether or not they are followed by the relevant (mere) bodily movements. (In recent years Hornsby (e.g. 2010) has moved away from this view in favor of an account according to which the ubiquity of trying suggests that our activities extend beyond our own minds and bodies.)

This view of action (or 'voluntary action') as volition may also be found in the writings of Descartes (1970), Berkeley (1998), Prichard (2004), and O'Shaughnessy (1980). In Chapter 7 Prichard writes that "[W]here we think of ourselves or of another as having done a certain action, the kind of activity of which we are thinking is that of willing ... when I move my hand, the movement of my hand, though an effect of my action, is not itself an action ... or even part of an action." In Prichard's time, it was mainly moral philosophers who were interested in the nature of action, and their concern was largely about the nature and scope of our moral obligations. What can be required of us? Can we be required to help others? Prichard's earlier view had been that we cannot be obligated actually to bring about certain changes, e.g. to ensure that others are helped, since we can never know (and cannot ensure) that our actions will have those changes as effects. He concluded that our obligation must be to set ourselves to bring about those changes. On this account, an act is not the bringing about of a change but, rather, that which brings it about; hence this identification of action with willing.

James himself held the rather different view that though there are volitions, they are not actions. The actions are the bodily movements that the volitions cause: "I will to write, and the act follows. I will to sneeze and it does not. I will that the distant table slide over the floor towards me; it also does not." Variants of this account may also be found in Locke (1975) and Hume (1974).

A third approach claims that actions come in two distinct forms, internal acts of mind and external acts of the body. Bentham gives the example of striking as a 'corporeal act' and that of intending to strike as a 'mental act'. Other proponents of this sort of view include Hobbes (1968) and Reid (1969).

A fourth volitionist account sees action as a complex made up of two parts, a volition (which is not itself an action) followed (causally or otherwise) by a bodily movement. Mill (1843), for example, writes that an action is "not one thing, but a series of two things: the state of mind called a volition followed by an effect." A variant of this view may be found in Lowe (Chapter 10).

2.

Criticisms of volitionism also come in various forms. Perhaps the most striking are those of Wittgenstein and Ryle, already mentioned. Wittgenstein's worry was with those views which saw the will as an 'instrument' through which bodily movements were brought about (Chapter 1, §§614–616, in this volume; see also the discussion of basic actions in our introduction to Part I). Consider Reid's claim that "the cause of the volition is the man that willed it." If agents can cause events in this sort of way, why should they not be capable of causing a bodily act directly and be restricted to causing acts of will? The view that we can only perform a bodily act *via* a mental one, Wittgenstein maintains, turns all action into a form of telekinesis: we will with our minds that our arm should move and then wait for the movement to follow. Yet nobody tries to move their arm, or wills it to move in the way in which the would-be telekinesist wills that the matchbox moves. Indeed, as with intending, we do not will or try *that* something happens but *to* do something, to move the matchbox.

Ryle's worry with volitions was of a rather different sort. If what makes an action voluntary is its relation to some act of willing, we are left with the puzzle of what makes the latter acts voluntary. If the answer appeals to some other volition (willing to will), we are faced with an infinite regress. The notion of volition, then, fails to do the work it is supposed to. This leads Ryle to characterize it as a useless postulate. If, on, the other hand, we can say what it is for a volition to be voluntary without appealing to further volitions we may wonder why we felt the need to bring in volitions to explain the voluntariness of (other) actions. Ryle maintains accordingly that what makes an action voluntary has nothing to do with volitions but with a lack of coercion, duress, and so on. But not all volitionists appeal to the will in order to elucidate *voluntariness*. Some think willing or volition is the mark of *intentional* action instead.

Whatever we make of the above accounts, the fact that we can try (attempt, decide, strive) to do things that we fail eventually to do may be thought to show that the trying is one thing, one action and the action being attempted (which may or may not materialize) another. Thinking this, one is not far from supposing that there are two actions involved in every case of successful trying, and to contrast the inner (mental) act with the outer (physical) one. This contrast remains even if we understand the mental act as a neural event in the brain; it is still inner as opposed to outer. It does not really help, either, to insist that it is the person herself who is doing these acts (rather than her sub-parts, her mind or her body); it remains tempting to think that we do the trying with our minds and the other action with our bodies, so that we are still dealing with two actions. But it would be a mistake (common to all arguments from error or illusion) to infer, from the fact that there can be trying without the physical action ensuing, that no trying is itself a physical act (Wittgenstein, Chapter 1, §615, p. 1, this volume). A successful trying can just be a physical action (either the very act that one is trying to do or some other action which either precedes or encompasses it); and the same might go for a successful willing. Moreover, while we may succeed in doing things without even trying this just means no more than that we do such things with minimal effort.

In opposition to the sorts of view which allow us to at least sometimes separate the willing from the action willed is O'Shaughnessy's dual aspect theory according to which willing is an action with both psychological and physical aspects. Under its psychological aspect it is an object of direct awareness, akin to a sensation. Under its physical aspect, by contrast, willing is to be identified with a kind of exertion of effort (which empirical psychologists typically distinguish from trying) which sets the muscles in motion.

One doesn't need to accept O'Shaughnessy's view to hold that one's attempting to do one thing is frequently identical to one's succeeding in doing something else. My failing to hit the tennis ball, for example, may be identical to my swinging my racket in an awkward manner. If, following Anscombe (1957: §§23–27) and Davidson (Chapter 2), we allow that one and the same action can have such multiple descriptions, then it appears plausible that all actions are successful under some description, unless we allow for 'slips' in which even our most basic intentions misfire.

Might there be basic (or 'naked') acts of trying or willing, viz. ones that cannot be redescribed as acts of succeeding in doing something else? The Landry patient would seem to be the best example for this sort of case, but there are two readings of this case: the first is that he tried to raise his arm and failed, the second simply that he mistakenly thought he had raised it. How then are we to tell which of these readings is correct? We cannot simply rely on the patient's verbal report of what he thought he did or tried to do, or of what he expected to see when he opened his eyes. A more helpful approach might be to ask in virtue of what he might have thought he had tried to move his arm. It cannot be a kinesthetic sensation in his arm since he couldn't feel anything in it. Might he have had a mental sensation of trying, then? We have already seen that it is suspect to claim that trying is a mental act, so that one does it with one's mind, as opposed to with one's hands, feet, or whichever part of one's body one is attempting to move. And if trying were a mental act, would it be one that one could try but fail to do? Some people undergoing brain surgery and asked to try to move their hand report that they can no longer even try to do that.

References

Anscombe, G. E. M. (1957), *Intention* (Oxford: Blackwell).

Berkeley, G. (1998), *A Treatise Concerning the Principles of Human Knowledge and Three Dialogues Between Hylas and Philonous*, ed. J. Dancy (Oxford: Clarendon Press).

Descartes, R. (1970), *Philosophical Letters*, trans. and ed. A. Kenny (Oxford: Clarendon Press).

Hobbes, T. (1968), *Leviathan*, ed. C. B. Macpherson (London: Penguin).

Hornsby, J. (2010), "Trying to Act", in T. O'Connor and C. Sandis (eds.), *A Companion to the Philosophy of Action* (Oxford: Wiley-Blackwell), 18–25.

Hume, D. (1974), *An Enquiry Concerning Human Understanding*, 3rd edn., ed. L. A. Selby-Bigge and P. H. Nidditch (Oxford: Oxford University Press).

James, W. (1891), *The Principles of Psychology*, vol. 2 (London: Macmillan).

Landry, O. (1855), *Mémoire sur la paralysie du sentiment d'activité musculaire* (Paris: Plon).

Locke, J. (1975), *An Essay Concerning Human Understanding*, ed. P. H. Nidditch (Oxford: Clarendon Press).

Mill, J. S. (1843), *A System of Logic* (London).

O'Shaughnessy, B. (1980), *The Will: A Dual Aspect Theory* (Cambridge: Cambridge University Press).

Prichard, H. A. (2004), *Moral Writings*, ed. J. MacAdam (Oxford: Clarendon Press).

Reid, T. (1969), *Essays on the Active Powers of the Human Mind*, ed. B. A. Brody (Cambridge, Mass.: MIT Press).

Further Reading

Amaya, S. (2013), "Slips," *Noûs* 47 (3), 559–576.

Dancy, J. (2009), "H. A. Prichard," rev. 2014, *Stanford Encyclopedia of Philosophy*: http://plato.stanford.edu/entries/prichard/.

McCann, H. (1974), "Volition and Basic Action," *Philosophical Review* 83 (4), 451–473.

Ruben, D.-H. (2013), "Trying in Some Way," *Australasian Journal of Philosophy* 91 (4), 719–733.

7

Acting, Willing, Desiring

H. A. Prichard

The question 'What is acting or doing something?' seems at first unreal, i.e. a question to which we already know the answer. For it looks as though everyone knows what doing something is and would be ready to offer instances. No one, for instance, would hesitate to say to another 'You ought to go to bed', on the ground that neither he nor the other knows the kind of thing meant by 'going to bed'. Yet, when we consider instances that would be offered, we do not find it easy to state the common character which we think they had which led us to call them actions.

If, as a preliminary, we look for help to the psychologists, from whom we naturally expect to get it, we find we fail. We find plenty of talk about reflex actions, ideo-motor actions, instinctive actions, and so on, but no discussion of what actions are. Instead, they seem to take for granted that our actions are physical processes taking place within our body, which they certainly are not.

We should at first say that to do something is to originate or to bring into existence, i.e., really, to cause, some not yet existing state either of ourselves or of someone else, or, again, of some body. But, for clearness' sake, we should go on to distinguish those actions in doing which we originated some new state

Prichard, H. A. (1945), "Acting, Willing, Desiring," in *Moral Obligation* (Oxford: Oxford University Press, 1949), 272–281. Reprinted with permission of Oxford University Press.

directly from those in which we did this only indirectly, i.e. by originating directly some other state, by originating which we indirectly originated the final state. As instances of the former we might give moving or turning our head, and as instances of the latter, curing our toothache by swallowing aspirin, and killing another by pressing a switch which exploded a charge underneath him. If challenged, however, we should have to allow that even in instances of the former kind we did not originate directly what the instances suggest that we did, since what we did originate directly must have been some new state or states of our nerve-cells, of the nature of which we are ignorant. We should, however, insist that in doing any action we must have originated *something* directly, since otherwise we could not originate anything indirectly.

The view that to act is to originate something was maintained by Cook Wilson in a paper on *Means and End*. In the course of this paper he also maintained (1) that an action required the desire to do it, and (2) that it is important to avoid the mistake of thinking that the origination of something X is the willing of X, apparently on the ground that if it were, X would exist as soon as we willed it, and yet it usually does not. He also appeared to hold that the origination of X, though not identical with willing the origination, required it, so that when I originated a movement of my hand, this required as an antecedent my willing this origination, and this

Philosophy of Action: An Anthology, First Edition. Edited by Jonathan Dancy and Constantine Sandis.
© 2015 John Wiley & Sons, Inc. Published 2015 by John Wiley & Sons, Inc.

willing in turn required the desiring to originate the movement.

According to Cook Wilson, then, in considering an action we have to distinguish three things: first, the action itself, the originating something; second, the required willing to originate this; and third, the required desire to originate this. And according to him what we will and what we desire are the same, viz. the action.

Professor Macmurray, in a Symposium[1] on 'What is action?', takes substantially the same view of what an action is. He says: 'An action is not the concomitance of an intention in the mind and an occurrence in the physical world: it is the *producing* of the occurrence by the Self, the *making* of a change in the external world, the *doing* of a deed. No process which terminates in the mind, such as forming an intention, deciding to act, or willing, is either an action or a component of action.' But he goes on to add: 'In certain circumstances such a mental event or process may be followed *necessarily* by action.'

Now, so far as I can see, this account of what an action is, though plausible and having as a truth underlying it that usually in acting we do cause something, is not tenable.

Unquestionably the thing meant by 'an action' is an activity. This is so whether we speak of a man's action in moving his hand, or of a body's action such as that of the heart in pumping the blood, or that of one electron in repelling another. But though we think that some man in moving his hand, or that the sun in attracting the earth, causes a certain movement, we do not think that the man's or the sun's activity *is* or *consists in* causing the movement. And if we ask ourselves: 'Is there such an activity as originating or causing a change in something else?', we have to answer that there is not. To say this, of course, is not to say that there is no such thing as causing something, but only to say that though the causing a change may require an activity, it is not itself an activity. If we then ask: 'What is the kind of activity required when one body causes another to move?', we have to answer that we do not know, and that when we speak of a force of attraction or of repulsion we are only expressing our knowledge that there is some activity at work, while being ignorant of what the kind of activity is. In the case, however, of a man, i.e., really, of a man's mind,

the matter is different. When, e.g., we think of ourselves as having moved our hand, we are thinking of ourselves as having performed an activity of a certain kind, and, it almost goes without saying, a *mental* activity of a certain kind, an activity of whose nature we were dimly aware in doing the action and of which we can become more clearly aware by reflecting on it. And that we are aware of its special nature is shown by our unhesitatingly distinguishing it from other special mental activities such as thinking, wondering, and imagining. If we ask 'What is the word used for this special kind of activity?' the answer, it seems, has to be 'willing'. (I now think I was mistaken in suggesting that the phrase in use for it is 'setting oneself to cause'.) We also have to admit that while we know the general character of that to which we refer when we use the word 'willing', this character is *sui generis* and so incapable of being defined, i.e. of having its nature expressed in terms of the nature of other things. Even Hume virtually admits this when he says: 'By the *will*, I mean nothing but *the internal impression we feel and are conscious of, when we knowingly give rise to any new motion of our body or new perception of our mind*',[2] and then goes on to add that the impression is impossible to define. Though, however, the activity of willing is indefinable, we can distinguish it from a number of things which it is not. Thus obviously, as Locke insisted, willing is different from desiring, and again, willing is not, as some psychologists would have it, a species of something called conation of which desiring is another species. There is no such genus. Again, it is not, as Green in one passage[3] implies, a species of desiring which is desiring in another sense than that ordinary sense in which we are said to desire while hesitating to act.

In addition, plainly, willing is not resolving, nor attending to a difficult object, as James holds, nor for that matter attending to anything, nor, again, consenting to the reality of what is attended to, as James also maintains, nor, indeed, consenting to anything, nor, once more, identifying ourself with some object of desire, as Green asserts in another passage.[4]

Consequently, there seems to be no resisting the conclusion that where we think of ourselves or of another as having done a certain action, the kind of activity of which we are thinking is that of willing (though we should have to add that we are thinking of our particular act of willing as having been the doing of the action in question, only because we think it caused a certain change), and that when we refer to some instance of this activity, such as our having moved our finger or given some friend a headache, we refer to it thus not because we think it was, or consisted in, the causing our finger to move or our friend's head to ache, but because we think it had a certain change of state as an effect.

If, as it seems we must, we accept this conclusion, that to act is really to will something, we then become faced by the question: 'What sort of thing is it that we will?'

Those who, like Cook Wilson, distinguish between acting and willing, answer that what we will is an action, which according to him is the originating some change. Thus Green says: 'To will an event' (i.e. presumably some change) 'as distinguished from an act is a contradiction.' And by this he seems to mean that, for instance, in the case which he takes of our paying a debt, what we will is the paying of our debt and not our creditor's coming into possession of what we owe him. Again, James and Stout, though they do not consider the question, show by their instances that they take for granted that what we will is an action. Thus James says: 'I will to write, and the act follows. I will to sneeze and it does not.'[5] And Stout illustrates a volition by a man's willing to produce an explosion by applying a lighted match to gunpowder.[6] But, unfortunately, James speaks of what he has referred to as, the act of writing which I will, as certain physiological movements, and similarly Stout speaks of, the production of an explosion which I will, as certain bodily movements. And, of course, the bodily movements to which they are referring are not actions, though they may be the effects of actions. Plainly, then, both are only doing lip-service to the idea that what we will is an action. And James, at least, drops doing even this. For immediately after making the statement just quoted, viz. 'I will to write, and the act follows. I will to sneeze and it does not', he adds: 'I will that the distant table slide over the floor towards me; it also does not.' Yet no one would say that the sliding of the table, as distinct from my sliding it, was an action.

In this connexion it is well for clearness' sake to bear two things in mind. The first is that some transitive verbs used for particular actions are also used intransitively. Thus one not only speaks of turning one's head but also says that one's head turned. And the second is that, while the phrase 'turning one's head' stands for an action and so for an activity of one's mind, yet when I say 'my head turned' I am speaking simply of a movement of my head which is a change of place and not an action. The difference is made clear by considering what is plainly a mistake made by Professor Macmurray. He says that the term 'action' is ambiguous. He says: 'It may refer either to what is done or to the doing of it. It may mean either "doing" or "deed". When we talk of "an action" we are normally referring to what is done. … To act is to effect a change in the external world. The deed is the change so effected.' And he emphasizes what he considers the ambiguity in order to indicate that it is doings and not deeds that he is considering. Obviously, however, there is no ambiguity whatever. When I move my hand, the movement of my hand, though an effect of my action, is not itself an action, and no one who considered the matter would say it was, any more than he would say that the death of Caesar, as distinct from his murder, was an action or even part of an action.

This difference between, e.g., my moving my hand and a movement of my hand, is one which James and Stout seem to ignore, as becomes obvious when James speaks of the sliding of a table as, like writing, an action. We find the same thing, too, in Locke. For though, e.g., he says that 'we find by experience, that, barely by willing it, we can move the parts of our bodies',[7] yet in contrasting a human with a physical action he implies that what we will is a movement of our body. Probably, if pressed, he would have said that, strictly speaking, what we will is a movement and so not an action. In addition, James and Stout seem to treat the distinction between an act of willing, or, as they prefer to call it, a volition, and what is willed, as if it were the same as the distinction between an act of willing and its effect, although they are totally different.

It should be clear from what I have just said that those who hold that what we will is an action must, to be successful, mean by an action something which really is an action. They may, of course, maintain that what we will is a physical process, such as a movement of my hand, but if they do they are really denying that what we will is an action.

It should also now be clear that if we face the question 'What sort of thing do we will?', we have only two answers to consider: (1) that it is some change of state of some thing or person; and (2) that it is an action. If, however, we are forced to conclude, as we have been, that doing something is an act of willing, we seem forced to exclude the second answer, simply on the ground that if it were true, then whenever we think of ourselves as having done some action, we must be thinking of ourselves as having willed some action, i.e. as having willed the willing of some change X; and to think this seems impossible. By the very nature of willing, it seems, what we will must be something other than willing, so that to will the willing of a change X must be an impossibility. And if we even try to deny this, we find ourselves forced to admit that the willing of X, which (we are contending) is what we will, must in turn really be the willing the willing of something else, and so on, and thus become involved in an infinite regress. It is true that Cook Wilson, in a long unpublished discussion, tried to vindicate the analogous idea that in certain limiting cases, viz. those in which the desire moving us is not the desire of some change but the desire to cause it ourselves, as happens in playing golf or patience, what we originate is identical with our origination of something. But he never seems to me to succeed in meeting the objection that this identity must be impossible. Similarly, it seems to me, it is impossible for there to be a case in which the willing the willing of X is identical with willing X.

We are thus left with the conclusion that where we think we have done some action, e.g. have raised our arm or written a word, what we willed was some change, e.g. some movement of our arm or some movement of ink to a certain place on a piece of paper in front of us. But we have to bear in mind that the change which we willed may not have been the same as the change we think we effected. Thus, where I willed some movement of my second finger, I may at least afterwards think that the change I effected was a movement of my first finger, and, only too often, where I willed the existence of a certain word on a piece of paper, I afterwards find that what I caused was a different word. Again, in two cases of the act we call trying to thread a needle, what I willed may have been the same, though the changes I afterwards think

I effected were very different, being in the one case the thread's going through the needle and in the other its passing well outside it.

Suppose now that it be allowed that so far I have been right. Then the following admissions must be made:

1. An action, i.e. a human action, instead of being the originating or causing of some change, is an activity of willing some change, this usually causing some change, and in some cases a physical change, its doing or not doing this depending on the physical conditions of which the agent is largely ignorant.

2. Sometimes, however, we have performed such an activity without, at any rate so far as we know, having caused any physical change. This has happened when, e.g., we willed a movement of our hand, at a time when it was either paralysed or numb with cold, whether we knew this or not. No doubt in such cases our activity would not ordinarily be called an action, but it is of the same sort as what we ordinarily call and think of as an action.

3. There is no reason to limit the change which it is possible to will to a movement of some part of our body, since, as James says in effect, we can just as much will the sliding of a table towards us as a movement of our hand towards our head. Indeed, we may, in fact, will this in order to convince ourselves or someone else that by doing so we shall not cause the table to slide. And it looks as though we sometimes will such things in ordinary life, as when in watching a football match we want some player's speed to increase, and will it to increase.

4. Where we have willed some movement of our body and think we have caused it, we cannot have directly caused it. For what we directly caused, if anything, must have been some change in our brain.

5. Where we think that by willing some change we effected some change in the physical world, we are implying the idea that in doing so, we are butting into, or interfering with, the physical system, just as we think of an approaching comet as effecting a breach in the order of the solar system, so long as we do not regard the comet as

part of the system. This idea is, of course, inconsistent with our belief in the uniformity of nature unless we include in nature minds as well as bodies; and in any case it is inconsistent with our belief in the conservation of energy. But so long as we think, as we do, that at any rate on some occasions we really effect something in the physical world, we must admit this. And if we knew that such effecting was impossible, we should give up acting.

We have now to face another question, viz. 'Does acting require a desire, and if it does, the desire of what?'

It is at least very difficult to avoid Aristotle's conclusion that acting requires a desire, if only for the reason he gives, viz. that διάνοια αὐτὴ οὐθὲν κινεῖ. [Thought itself moves nothing.] It seems that, as Locke maintained, if we never desired something we should never do anything. But what is the desire required?

Here only one or other of two answers seems possible, viz. (1) that it is a desire of the change X which we will, and (2) that it is a desire of the willing of X. And when we try, we do not find it easy to decide between them. For on the one hand, the desire required seems to have to be the desire of X, on the ground that, if we are to will X, we must desire X. And on the other hand, it seems that it must be the desire to will X, since unless we *desired* to will X we could not will X. Indeed, just for this reason Plato seems to have gone too far in the *Gorgias* when he maintained that in acting we never desire to do what we do, but only that for the sake of which we do it. For, if acting is willing, it seems that the desire required must be a desire of the willing, even though the desire be a dependent desire, i.e. a desire depending on the desire of something else for its own sake, viz. that for the sake of which we do the action. And Plato's mistake seems to have been that of restricting desiring to desiring something for its own sake.

The two answers are, of course, radically different. For if the desire required is the desire of X, the thing desired and the thing willed will be the same, as indeed Green implies that they are when he maintains that willing is desiring in a special sense of 'desiring'. But if so, while the willing of X will require what for

want of a better term we seem to have to call the thought of X, as being something involved in the desire of X, it will not require either the desire of the willing of X or, for that reason, even the thought of willing X. On the other hand, if the desire required is the desire to will X, the thing desired and the thing willed will necessarily be different, and while the willing of X will require the desire of willing X and so also the thought of willing X, it will not require the desire of X, though it will require the thought of X, as being something involved in the thought of willing X. It should, however, be noted that in the case of the latter alternative, the desire of X may in some cases be required indirectly as a condition of our desiring the willing of X.

To repeat here for clearness' sake what is central – if the desire required is the desire of X, the willing of X will not require either the desire of the willing of X or even the thought of willing X, while, if the desire required is the desire of willing X, the willing of X will not require the desire of X, though it will require the thought of X.

On consideration, however, we have to reject the idea that the desire required is the desire of X, on three grounds. First, if it were true, we should always will any change which we desired to happen, such as the sliding of the table, whether or not we thought that if we were to will it to happen we should thereby cause it to happen; and obviously we do not. Second, we occasionally will a change to happen without any desire for it to happen. This must occur, e.g., if a man ever does an act moved solely by the desire for revenge, willing, say, the movement of a switch which he is confident will result in the death of another, not from any desire for his death but solely from the desire to cause it by willing the movement. And even if there are no acts animated solely by the desire for revenge, there are certainly actions approximating to this. At all events, in the case of playing a game the desire at work must be not the desire of some change but the desire to cause it. A putter at golf, e.g., has no desire for the ball to fall into the hole; he only desires to cause it to fall in. This contention is, I think, not met by maintaining, as Cook Wilson in fact does, that the player desires the falling into the hole as caused by his action, and so desires the falling as part of, or an element in, his action. Its falling is neither a part of, nor an element in, his action; at best it is only an effect of it. And the player could only be said to desire the falling if, as he does not, he desired it to happen irrespectively of what would cause it to happen. And in this connexion it may be added that if the desire required were the desire of X, it would be impossible to do any act as one which we think would or might fulfil some obligation, since *ex hypothesi* the desire required will be a desire for a change X and not a desire to *will* a change X. Then, third, there is a consideration which comes to light if we consider more closely what it is that we will in certain cases, and more especially in those in which we describe an action as one of trying to do so and so. Suppose, e.g., I have done what we describe as having tried to jump a ditch, and so imply that beforehand I was doubtful of success. Obviously I did not will a movement of my body which I was sure would land me, say, two clear yards on the other side, since if I had thought of willing this I should have realized that willing this would not result in my getting across. I willed that movement the willing of which, if I were to will it, I thought the most likely of all the willings of movements in my power to result in my landing on the farther bank. And in this connexion it seems worth nothing that what we call trying to do something is as much doing something as what we ordinarily call doing something, although the word 'trying' suggests that it is not. It is the willing a change described in the way in which I have just described what I willed in trying to jump a ditch.

It therefore seems that the desire required must be the desire of the willing of a certain change X. Yet this conclusion is exposed to two objections. The first is that if it were true, it would be impossible to will something X for the first time. For in this context we mean by a desire to will X a desire we can only have in consequence of thinking that if we were to will X, our doing so would be likely to cause something else, and ultimately something which we desire for its own sake. But we cannot desire to will something X, unless we at least have a conjecture that if we were to will X, our willing X might cause some change which we desire for its own sake. And this conjecture requires the thought that on some previous occasion we have willed X and thence concluded from what we think followed this willing of X that it may have caused something else Y. Yet *ex hypothesi* we cannot have willed X on this

previous occasion from the desire to will X, since then we had no idea of what willing X might cause. James expresses what is really this objection, though in a misleading way, when he says: 'If, in voluntary action properly so-called' (i.e. in what is really an action), 'the act must be foreseen, it follows that no creature not endowed with divinatory power can perform an act voluntarily for the first time.'[8] The statement as it stands is, of course, absurd, because no one before acting *knows* what his act will be, or even that he will act. But it can be taken as an inaccurate way of expressing the thought that an act of will requires an idea of something which we may cause if we perform the act.

To this objection I have to confess that I cannot see an answer. Yet I think that there must be an answer, since, however it has come about, for us as we are now an act of will does seem to require the desire of it, and so some idea of something which it might effect. I need hardly add that it is no answer to maintain that the desire immediately required by willing something X is in some cases the desire of X, and in others the desire of willing X.

The second objection is one which seems to me, though insidious, an objection which can be met. It can be stated thus: 'It is all very well to say that the desire immediately presupposed by willing X is the desire to will X. But to say this is not enough. For we often desire to will X, and yet do not, as when we hesitate to get out of bed or out of a warm bath, and when this is so, obviously something else is required, and this something can only be the willing to will X, so that after all there must be such a thing as willing to will.' But to this the reply seems clear. Though it is possible to desire to desire, as when I desire to desire the welfare of my country more than I do, it is impossible to will to will, for the reason already given. And where we hesitate to will X, what is required is not the willing to will X but either a certain increase in our desire to will X or a decrease in our aversion to doing so. Certainly, too, we often act on this idea, hoping, e.g., that by making ourselves think of the coldness of our breakfast if we stay in bed we shall reach a state of desire in which we shall will certain movements of our body. And sometimes we succeed, and when we do, we sometimes, as James puts it, suddenly find that we have got up, the explanation of our surprise apparently being that we, having been absorbed in the process of trying to stimulate our desire to get up, have not reflected on our state of desire and so have not noticed its increase.

There is also to be noticed in this connexion a mistake into which we are apt to fall which leads us to think that there must be such a thing as willing to will. We of course frequently want certain changes to happen and also want to will certain changes. But we are apt not to notice that the objects of these desires differ in respect of the conditions of their realization, and in consequence to carry the account of the process of deliberation described by Aristotle one step too far – as Aristotle did not. According to him, when we want the happening of something Z which is not an action of ours and which we think we cannot cause directly, we often look for something else Y from the happening of which the happening of Z would result, and then if necessary for something else X from the happening of which Y would result, until we come to think of something A from the happening of which

X, Y, and Z would in turn result, and which we also think it in our power to cause by a certain act α. And when we have found A the process stops. We, however, are apt to carry the process one step farther, and apply to the act α, i.e. the willing of something β, the willing of which we think likely to cause A, the same process that we applied to Z, Y, X, and A, thus treating the willing of β as if it were not the willing of something (which it is), but a change which some act of willing might cause. As a result of doing this we ask 'From what act of willing would the willing of β result?', and the answer has to be 'The willing the willing of β'. But the very question is mistaken, because the willing of β is not a change like Z, Y, X, and A. The only proper question at this stage must be not 'From what *willing* would the willing of β result?' but 'From what *something* would the willing of β result?' And the proper answer must be: 'From a certain increase in our desire to will β.'

Notes

1. *Proceedings of the Aristotelian Society*, Supplementary Volume XVII (1938).
2. D. Hume, *A Treatise of Human Nature*, ed. L. A. Selby-Bigge (Clarendon Press, 1896), p. 399.
3. T. H. Green, *Prolegomena to Ethics*, ed. A. C. Bradley (Clarendon Press, 1884), §§140–2.
4. Ibid., §146.
5. W. James, *Principles of Psychology* (Harvard University Press, 1890), ii, p. 560.
6. G. F. Stout, *A Manual of Psychology* (London: W. B. Clive, 1898–9), iv, p. 641.
7. J. Locke, *An Essay Concerning Human Understanding*, ii, 21, §4.
8. James, *Psychology*, ii, p. 487.

8

The Will

Gilbert Ryle

1. Foreword

MOST of the mental-conduct concepts whose logical behaviour we examine in this book, are familiar and everyday concepts. We all know how to apply them and we understand other people when they apply them. What is in dispute is not how to apply them, but how to classify them, or in what categories to put them.

The concept of volition is in a different case. We do not know in daily life how to use it, for we do not use it in daily life and do not, consequently, learn by practice how to apply it, and how not to misapply it. It is an artificial concept. We have to study certain specialist theories in order to find out how it is to be manipulated. It does not, of course, follow from its being a technical concept that it is an illegitimate or useless concept. 'Ionisation' and 'off-side' are technical concepts, but both are legitimate and useful. 'Phlogiston' and 'animal spirits' were technical concepts, though they have now no utility.

I hope to show that the concept of volition belongs to the latter tribe.

Ryle, G. (1949), "The Will," in *The Concept of Mind*, 60th anniversary edn. (Abingdon: Routledge, 2009), 62–74. Reprinted with permission of Taylor & Francis Books.

2. The Myth of Volitions

It has for a long time been taken for an indisputable axiom that the Mind is in some important sense tripartite, that is, that there are just three ultimate classes of mental processes. The Mind or Soul, we are often told, has three parts, namely, Thought, Feeling and Will; or, more solemnly, the Mind or Soul functions in three irreducibly different modes, the Cognitive mode, the Emotional mode and the Conative mode. This traditional dogma is not only not self-evident, it is such a welter of confusions and false inferences that it is best to give up any attempt to re-fashion it. It should be treated as one of the curios of theory.

The main object of this chapter is not, however, to discuss the whole trinitarian theory of mind but to discuss, and discuss destructively, one of its ingredients. I hope to refute the doctrine that there exists a Faculty, immaterial Organ, or Ministry, corresponding to the theory's description of the 'Will' and, accordingly, that there occur processes, or operations, corresponding to what it describes as 'volitions'. I must however make it clear from the start that this refutation will not invalidate the distinctions which we all quite properly draw between voluntary and involuntary actions and between strong-willed and weak-willed persons. It will, on the contrary, make clearer what is meant by 'voluntary' and 'involuntary', by 'strong-willed' and 'weak-willed', by emancipating these ideas from bondage to an absurd hypothesis.

Philosophy of Action: An Anthology, First Edition. Edited by Jonathan Dancy and Constantine Sandis.
© 2015 John Wiley & Sons, Inc. Published 2015 by John Wiley & Sons, Inc.

Volitions have been postulated as special acts, or operations, 'in the mind', by means of which a mind gets its ideas translated into facts. I think of some state of affairs which I wish to come into existence in the physical world, but, as my thinking and wishing are unexecutive, they require the mediation of a further executive mental process. So I perform a volition which somehow puts my muscles into action. Only when a bodily movement has issued from such a volition can I merit praise or blame for what my hand or tongue has done.

It will be clear why I reject this story. It is just an inevitable extension of the myth of the ghost in the machine. It assumes that there are mental states and processes enjoying one sort of existence, and bodily states and processes enjoying another. An occurrence on the one stage is never numerically identical with an occurrence on the other. So, to say that a person pulled the trigger intentionally is to express at least a conjunctive proposition, asserting the occurrence of one act on the physical stage and another on the mental stage; and, according to most versions of the myth, it is to express a causal proposition, asserting that the bodily act of pulling the trigger was the effect of a mental act of willing to pull the trigger.

According to the theory, the workings of the body are motions of matter in space. The causes of these motions must then be *either* other motions of matter in space *or*, in the privileged case of human beings, thrusts of another kind. In some way which must forever remain a mystery, mental thrusts, which are not movements of matter in space, can cause muscles to contract. To describe a man as intentionally pulling the trigger is to state that such a mental thrust did cause the contraction of the muscles of his finger. So the language of 'volitions' is the language of the para-mechanical theory of the mind. If a theorist speaks without qualms of 'volitions', or 'acts of will', no further evidence is needed to show that he swallows whole the dogma that a mind is a secondary field of special causes. It can be predicted that he will correspondingly speak of bodily actions as 'expressions' of mental processes. He is likely also to speak glibly of 'experiences', a plural noun commonly used to denote the postulated non-physical episodes which constitute the shadow-drama on the ghostly boards of the mental stage.

The first objection to the doctrine that overt actions, to which we ascribe intelligence-predicates, are results of counterpart hidden operations of willing is this. Despite the fact that theorists have, since the Stoics and Saint Augustine, recommended us to describe our conduct in this way, no one, save to endorse the theory, ever describes his own conduct, or that of his acquaintances, in the recommended idioms. No one ever says such things as that at 10 a.m. he was occupied in willing this or that, or that he performed five quick and easy volitions and two slow and difficult volitions between midday and lunch-time. An accused person may admit or deny that he did something, or that he did it on purpose, but he never admits or denies having willed. Nor do the judge and jury require to be satisfied by evidence, which in the nature of the case could never be adduced, that a volition preceded the pulling of the trigger. Novelists describe the actions, remarks, gestures and grimaces, the daydreams, deliberations, qualms and embarrassments of their characters; but they never mention their volitions. They would not know what to say about them.

By what sorts of predicates should they be described? Can they be sudden or gradual, strong or weak, difficult or easy, enjoyable or disagreeable? Can they be accelerated, decelerated, interrupted, or suspended? Can people be efficient or inefficient at them? Can we take lessons in executing them? Are they fatiguing or distracting? Can I do two or seven of them synchronously? Can I remember executing them? Can I execute them, while thinking of other things, or while dreaming? Can they become habitual? Can I forget how to do them? Can I mistakenly believe that I have executed one, when I have not, or that I have not executed one, when I have? At which moment was the boy going through a volition to take the high dive? When he set foot on the ladder? When he took his first deep breath? When he counted off 'One, two, three—Go', but did not go? Very, very shortly before he sprang? What would his own answer be to those questions?

Champions of the doctrine maintain, of course, that the enactment of volitions is asserted by implication, whenever an overt act is described as intentional, voluntary, culpable or meritorious; they assert too that any person is not merely able but bound to know that he is willing when he is doing so, since volitions are defined as a species of conscious process. So if ordinary men and women fail to mention their volitions in their descriptions of their own behaviour, this must be due to their being untrained in the dictions appropriate to the description of their inner, as distinct from their overt, behaviour. However, when a champion of the doctrine is himself asked how long ago he executed his last volition, or how many acts of will he executes in, say, reciting 'Little Miss Muffet' backwards, he is apt to confess to finding difficulties in giving the answer, though these difficulties should not, according to his own theory, exist.

If ordinary men never report the occurrence of these acts, for all that, according to the theory, they should be encountered vastly more frequently than headaches, or feelings of boredom; if ordinary vocabulary has no non-academic names for them; if we do not know how to settle simple questions about their frequency, duration or strength, then it is fair to conclude that their existence is not asserted on empirical grounds. The fact that Plato and Aristotle never mentioned them in their frequent and elaborate discussions of the nature of the soul and the springs of conduct is due not to any perverse neglect by them of notorious ingredients of daily life but to the historical circumstance that they were not acquainted with a special hypothesis the acceptance of which rests not on the discovery, but on the postulation, of these ghostly thrusts.

The second objection is this. It is admitted that one person can never witness the volitions of another; he can only infer from an observed overt action to the volition from which it resulted, and then only if he has any good reason to believe that the overt action was a voluntary action, and not a reflex or habitual action, or one resulting from some external cause. It follows that no judge, schoolmaster, or parent ever knows that the actions which he judges merit praise or blame; for he cannot do better than guess that the action was willed. Even a confession by the agent, if such confessions were ever made, that he had executed a volition before his hand did the deed would not settle the question. The pronouncement of the confession is only another overt muscular action. The curious conclusion results that though volitions were called in to explain our appraisals of actions, this explanation is just what they fail to provide. If we had no other antecedent grounds for applying appraisal-concepts to the actions of others, we should have no reasons at all for inferring from those actions to the volitions alleged to give rise to them.

Nor could it be maintained that the agent himself can know that any overt action of his own is the effect of a given volition. Supposing, what is not the case, that he could know for certain, either from the alleged direct deliverances of consciousness, or from the alleged direct findings of introspection, that he had executed an act of will to pull the trigger just before he pulled it, this would not prove that the pulling was the effect of that willing. The connection between volitions and movements is allowed to be mysterious, so, for all he knows, his volition may have had some other movement as its effect and the pulling of the trigger may have had some other event for its cause.

Thirdly, it would be improper to burke the point that the connection between volition and movement is admitted to be a mystery. It is a mystery not of the unsolved but soluble type, like the problem of the cause of cancer, but of quite another type. The episodes supposed to constitute the careers of minds are assumed to have one sort of existence, while those constituting the careers of bodies have another sort; and no bridge-status is allowed. Transactions between minds and bodies involve links where no links can be. That there should be any causal transactions between minds and matter conflicts with one part, that there should be none conflicts with another part of the theory. Minds, as the whole legend describes them, are what must exist if there is to be a causal explanation of the intelligent behaviour of human bodies; and minds, as the legend describes them, live on a floor of existence defined as being outside the causal system to which bodies belong.

Fourthly, although the prime function of volitions, the task for the performance of which they were postulated, is to originate bodily movements, the argument, such as it is, for their existence entails that some mental happenings also must result from acts of will. Volitions were postulated to be that which makes actions voluntary, resolute, meritorious and wicked. But predicates of these sorts are ascribed not only to bodily movements but also to operations which, according to the theory, are mental and not physical operations. A thinker may ratiocinate resolutely, or imagine wickedly; he may try to compose a limerick and he may meritoriously concentrate on his algebra. Some mental processes then can, according to the theory, issue from volitions. So what of volitions themselves? Are they voluntary or involuntary acts of mind? Clearly either answer leads to absurdities. If I cannot help willing to pull the trigger, it would be absurd to describe my pulling it as 'voluntary'. But if my volition to pull the trigger is voluntary, in the sense assumed by the theory, then it must issue from a prior volition and that from another *ad infinitum*. It has been suggested, to avoid this difficulty, that volitions cannot be described as either voluntary or involuntary. 'Volition' is a term of the wrong type to accept either predicate. If so, it would seem to follow that it is also of the wrong type to accept such predicates as 'virtuous' and 'wicked', 'good' and 'bad', a conclusion which might embarrass those moralists who use volitions as the sheet-anchor of their systems.

In short, then, the doctrine of volitions is a causal hypothesis, adopted because it was wrongly supposed that the question, 'What makes a bodily movement voluntary?' was a causal question. This supposition is, in fact, only a special twist of the general supposition that the question, 'How are mental-conduct concepts applicable to human behaviour?' is a question about the causation of that behaviour.

Champions of the doctrine should have noticed the simple fact that they and all other sensible persons knew how to decide questions about the voluntariness and involuntariness of actions and about the resoluteness and irresoluteness of agents before they had ever heard of the hypothesis of the occult inner thrusts of actions. They might then have realised that they were not elucidating the criteria already in efficient use, but, tacitly assuming their validity, were trying to correlate them with hypothetical occurrences of a para-mechanical pattern. Yet this correlation could, on the one hand, never be scientifically established, since the thrusts postulated were screened from scientific observation; and, on the other hand, it would be of no practical or theoretical use, since it would not assist our appraisals of actions, depending as it would on the presupposed validity of those appraisals. Nor would it elucidate the logic of those appraisal-concepts, the intelligent employment of which antedated the invention of this causal hypothesis.

Before we bid farewell to the doctrine of volitions, it is expedient to consider certain quite familiar and authentic processes with which volitions are sometimes wrongly identified.

People are frequently in doubt what to do; having considered alternative courses of action, they then, sometimes, select or choose one of these courses. This process of opting for one of a set of alternative courses of action is sometimes said to be what is signified by 'volition'. But this identification will not do, for most voluntary actions do not issue out of conditions of indecision and are not therefore results of settlements of indecisions. Moreover it is notorious that a person may choose to do something but fail, from weakness of will, to do it; or he may fail to do it because some circumstance arises after the choice is made, preventing the execution of the act chosen. But the theory could not allow that volitions ever fail to result in action, else further executive operations would have to be postulated to account for the fact that sometimes voluntary actions are performed. And finally the process of deliberating between alternatives and opting for one of them is itself subject to appraisal-predicates. But if, for example, an act of choosing is describable as voluntary, then, on this suggested showing, it would have in its turn to be the result of a prior choice to choose, and that from a choice to choose to choose....

The same objections forbid the identification with volitions of such other familiar processes as that of resolving or making up our minds to do something and that of nerving or bracing ourselves to do something. I may resolve to get out of bed or go to the dentist, and I may, clenching my fists and gritting my teeth, brace myself to do so, but I may still backslide. If the action is not done, then, according to the doctrine, the volition to do it is also unexecuted. Again, the operations of resolving and nerving ourselves are themselves members of the class of creditable or discreditable actions, so they cannot constitute the peculiar ingredient which, according to the doctrine, is the common condition of any performance being creditable or discreditable.

3. The Distinction between Voluntary and Involuntary

It should be noticed that while ordinary folk, magistrates, parents and teachers, generally apply the words 'voluntary' and 'involuntary' to actions in one way, philosophers often apply them in quite another way.

In their most ordinary employment 'voluntary' and 'involuntary' are used, with a few minor elasticities, as adjectives applying to actions which ought not to be done. We discuss whether someone's action was voluntary or not only when the action seems to have been his fault. He is accused of making a noise, and the guilt is his, if the action was voluntary, like laughing; he has successfully excused himself, if he satisfies us that it was involuntary, like a sneeze. In the same way in ordinary life we raise questions of responsibility only when someone is charged, justly or unjustly, with an offence. It makes sense, in this use, to ask whether a boy was responsible for breaking a window, but not whether he was responsible for finishing his homework in good time. We do not ask whether it was his fault that he got a long-division sum right, for to get a sum right is not a fault. If he gets it wrong, he may satisfy us that his failure was not his fault, perhaps because he had not yet been shown how to do such calculations.

In this ordinary use, then, it is absurd to discuss whether satisfactory, correct or admirable performances are voluntary or involuntary. Neither inculpation nor exculpation is in point. We neither confess to authorship nor adduce extenuating circumstances; neither plead 'guilty' nor plead 'not guilty'; for we are not accused.

But philosophers, in discussing what constitutes acts voluntary or involuntary, tend to describe as voluntary not only reprehensible but also meritorious actions, not only things that are someone's fault but also things that are to his credit. The motives underlying their unwitting extension of the ordinary sense of 'voluntary', 'involuntary' and 'responsible' will be considered later. For the moment it is worth while to consider certain consequences which follow from it. In the ordinary use, to say that a sneeze was involuntary is to say that the agent could not help doing it, and to say that a laugh was voluntary is to say that the agent could have helped doing it. (This is not to say that the laugh was intentional. We do not laugh on purpose.) The boy could have got the sum right which he actually got wrong; he knew how to behave, but he misbehaved; he was competent to tie a reef-knot, though what he unintentionally produced was a granny-knot. His failure or lapse was his fault. But when the word 'voluntary' is given its philosophically stretched use, so that correct as well as incorrect, admirable as well as contemptible acts are described as voluntary, it seems to follow by analogy with the ordinary use, that a boy who gets his sum right can also be described as having been 'able to help it'. It would then be proper to ask: Could you have helped solving the riddle? Could you have helped drawing the proper conclusion? Could you have helped tying a proper reef-knot? Could you have helped seeing the point of that joke? Could you have helped being kind to that child? In fact, however, no one could answer these questions, though it is not at first obvious why, if it is correct to say that someone could have avoided getting a sum wrong, it is incorrect to say that he could have avoided getting it right.

The solution is simple. When we say that someone could have avoided committing a lapse or error, or that it was his fault that he committed it, we mean that he knew how to do the right thing, or was competent to do so, but did not exercise his knowledge or competence. He was not trying, or not trying hard enough. But when a person has done the right thing, we cannot then say that he knew how to do the wrong thing, or that he was competent to make mistakes. For making mistakes is not an exercise of competence, nor is the commission of slips an exercise of knowledge *how*; it is a failure to exercise knowledge *how*. It is true in one sense of 'could' that a person who had done a sum correctly could have got it wrong; in the sense, namely, that he is not exempt from the liability to be careless. But in another sense of 'could', to ask, 'Could you have got it wrong?' means 'Were you sufficiently intelligent and well-trained and were you concentrating hard enough to make a miscalculation?', and this is as silly a question as to ask whether someone's teeth are strong enough to be broken by cracking nuts.

The tangle of largely spurious problems, known as the problem of the Freedom of the Will, partly derives from this unconsciously stretched use of 'voluntary' and these consequential misapplications of different senses of 'could' and 'could have helped'.

The first task is to elucidate what is meant in their ordinary, undistorted use by 'voluntary', 'involuntary', 'responsible', 'could not have helped' and 'his fault', as these expressions are used in deciding concrete questions of guilt and innocence.

If a boy has tied a granny-knot instead of a reef-knot, we satisfy ourselves that it was his fault by first establishing that he knew how to tie a reef-knot, and then by establishing that his hand was not forced by external coercion and that there were no other agencies at work preventing him from tying the correct knot. We establish that he could tie reef-knots by finding out that he had been taught, had had practice, usually got them right, or by finding that he could detect and correct knots tied by others, or by finding that he was ashamed of what he had done and, without help from others, put it right himself. That he was not acting under duress or in panic or high fever or with numb fingers, is discovered in the way in which we ordinarily discover that highly exceptional incidents have not taken place; for such incidents would have been too remarkable to have gone unremarked, at least by the boy himself.

The first question which we had to decide had nothing to do with the occurrence or non-occurrence of any occult episode in the boy's stream of consciousness; it was the question whether or not he had the required higher-level competence, that of knowing how to tie reef-knots. We were not, at this stage, inquiring whether he committed, or omitted, an extra public or private operation, but only whether he possessed or lacked a certain intelligent capacity. What satisfied us was not the (unattainable) knowledge of the truth or falsity of a particular covert cause-overt effect proposition, but the (attainable) knowledge of the truth or falsity of a complex and partially general hypothetical proposition—not, in short, that he did tie a shadowy reef- or granny-knot behind the scenes, but that he could have tied a real one with this rope and would have done so on this occasion, if he had paid more heed to what he was doing. The lapse was his fault because, knowing how to tie the knot, he still did not tie it correctly.

Consider next the case of an act which everyone would decide was not the agent's fault. A boy arrives late for school and on inquiry it turns out that he left home at the usual time, did not dally on his way to the omnibus halt and caught the usual omnibus. But the vehicle broke down and could not complete the journey. The boy ran as fast as he could the rest of the way, but was still late. Clearly all the steps taken by the boy were either the same as those which normally bring him to school in time, or were the only steps open to him for remedying the effects of the breakdown. There was nothing else that he could have done and his teacher properly recommends him to follow the same routine on future occasions. His late arrival was not the result of a failure to do what he was capable of doing. He was prevented by a circumstance which was not in his power to modify. Here again the teacher is judging an action with reference to the capacities and opportunities of the agent; his excuse is accepted that he could not have done better than he did. The whole question of the involuntariness of his late arrival is decided without the boy being asked to report any deliverances of consciousness or introspection about the execution or non-execution of any volitions.

It makes no difference if the actions with which an agent is charged either are or embody operations of silent soliloquy or other operations with verbal or non-verbal images. A slip in mental arithmetic is the pupil's fault on the same grounds as a slip made in written arithmetic; and an error committed in matching colours in the mind's eye may merit the reproach of carelessness in the same way as an error committed in matching colours on the draper's counter. If the agent could have done better than he did, then he could have helped doing it as badly as he did.

Besides considering the ordinary senses of 'voluntary', 'involuntary', 'responsible', 'my fault' and 'could' or 'could not help', we should notice as well the ordinary uses of such expressions as 'effort of will', 'strength of will' and 'irresolute'. A person is described as behaving resolutely when in the execution of difficult, protracted or disagreeable tasks he tends not to relax his efforts, not to let his attention be diverted, not to grumble and not to think much or often about his fatigue or fears. He does not shirk or drop things to which he has set his hand. A weak-willed person is one who is easily distracted or disheartened, apt to convince himself that another time will be more suitable or that the reasons for undertaking the task were not after all very strong. Note that it is no part of the definition of resoluteness or of irresoluteness that a resolution should actually have been formed. A resolute man may firmly resist temptations to abandon or postpone his task, though he never went through a prefatory ritual-process of making up his mind to complete it. But naturally such a man will also be disposed to perform any vows which he has made to others or to himself. Correspondingly the irresolute man will be likely to fail to carry out his often numerous good resolutions, but his lack of tenacity of purpose will be exhibited also in surrenders and slacknesses in courses of action which were unprefaced by any private or public undertakings to accomplish them.

Strength of will is a propensity the exercises of which consist in sticking to tasks; that is, in not being deterred or diverted. Weakness of will is having too little of this propensity. The performances in which strength of will is exerted may be performances of almost any sort, intellectual or manual, imaginative or administrative. It is not a single-track disposition or, for that and other reasons, a disposition to execute occult operations of one special kind.

By 'an effort of will' is meant a particular exercise of tenacity of purpose, occurring when the obstacles are notably great, or the counter-temptations notably strong. Such efforts may, but need not, be accompanied by special processes, often of a ritual character, of nerving or adjuring oneself to do what is required; but these processes are not so much ways in which resoluteness is shown as ways in which fear of irresoluteness manifests itself.

Before we leave the concept or concepts of voluntariness, two further points need to be made. (1) Very often we oppose things done voluntarily to things suffered under compulsion. Some soldiers are volunteers, others are conscripts; some yachtsmen go out to sea voluntarily, others are carried out to sea by the wind and tide. Here questions of inculpation and exculpation need not arise. In asking whether the soldier volunteered or was conscripted, we are asking whether he joined up because he wanted to do so, or whether he joined up because he had to do so, where 'had to' entails 'no matter what he wanted'. In asking whether the yachtsman went out to sea of his own accord or whether he was carried out, we are asking whether he went out on purpose, or whether he would still have gone out as he did, even if he had

meant not to do so. Would bad news from home, or a warning from the coastguard, have stopped him?

What is involuntary, in this use, is not describable as an act. Being carried out to sea, or being called up, is something that happens to a person, not something which he does. In this respect, this antithesis between voluntary and involuntary differs from the antithesis we have in mind when we ask whether someone's tying of a granny-knot, or his knitting of his brows, is voluntary or involuntary. A person who frowns involuntarily is not forced to frown, as a yachtsman may be forced out to sea; nor is the careless boy forced to tie a granny-knot, as the conscript is forced to join the army. Even frowning is something that a person does. It is not done to him. So sometimes the question 'Voluntary or involuntary?' means 'Did the person do it, or was it done to him?'; sometimes it presupposes that he did it, but means 'Did he do it with or without heeding what he was doing?' or 'Did he do it on purpose or inadvertently, mechanically, or instinctively, etc.?'

(2) When a person does something voluntarily, in the sense that he does it on purpose or is trying to do it, his action certainly reflects some quality or qualities of mind, since (it is more than a verbal point to say) he is in some degree and in one fashion or another minding what he is doing. It follows also that, if linguistically equipped, he can then tell, without research or conjecture, what he has been trying to accomplish. But these implications of voluntariness do not carry with them the double-life corollaries often assumed. To frown intentionally is not to do one thing on one's forehead and another thing in a second metaphorical place; nor is it to do one thing with one's brow-muscles and another thing with some non-bodily organ. In particular, it is not to bring about a frown on one's forehead by first bringing about a frown-causing exertion of some occult non-muscle. 'He frowned intentionally' does not report the occurrence of two episodes. It reports the occurrence of one episode, but one of a very different character from that reported by 'he frowned involuntarily', though the frowns might be photographically as similar as you please.

9

Acting and Trying to Act

Jennifer Hornsby

1

We began with descriptions of actions that have been taken (for certain purposes) to be the basic ones – *bodily movements*$_T$ –, and saw grounds for locating actions further back in time than the overt movements$_I$ of the body.★ Then we turned to descriptions of actions in (causally speaking) even more basic terms – *contractions*$_T$ *of muscles* –, and found that we cannot make space for these, unless actions are 'right inside the body'. The trail from bodily movements back to muscle contractions may be followed further. We can ask whether there are descriptions of actions so basic that they are free of any specific commitment to consequences like the body's movings$_I$ or the muscles' contractings$_I$. Is there any type of event instances of which can be shown to occur before the muscles contract, and instances of which can be shown to be actions?

I shall answer these questions 'Yes' in this chapter. Every action is an event of *trying* or attempting to act,

Editors' note: Hornsby here uses the subscripts $_T$ and $_I$ to mark the difference between the transitive sense of "bodily movement," in which the verb takes an object (my moving my body – moving$_T$), and the intransitive sense in which it doesn't (my body's moving – moving$_I$). She further characterizes the latter as a mere bodily movement (see Hornsby, *Actions* [London: Routledge, 1980], pp. 2–3).

Hornsby, J. (1980), "Acting and Trying to Act," in *Actions* (London: Routledge and Kegan Paul), 33–45. Reprinted with permission of Taylor & Francis Books.

and every attempt that is an action precedes and causes a contraction$_I$ of muscles and a movement$_I$ of the body.

The chief thing that the sceptical will require me to establish is that the province of *trying* can be as large as this implies. My view is that occasions on which a man tries to do something are not only some of the occasions on which in trying to do something he succeeds in doing something else. For first, we try to act in a certain way whenever we intentionally act in that way (§2.1 and §2.2); and second, we may try to act though there is no action at all (§3.2). The first point suggests that every action is accompanied by a trying. The second will help to demonstrate that at least some tryings do not reach to the surface of the body. But if that can be shown to be true of all tryings (§3.3), then, if actions may be identified with the tryings that accompany them (§2.3), we shall reach the general conclusion that actions themselves lie within the body (§4).

2

2.1 It seems that it is only appropriate for a speaker to say that an agent tried to ϕ, if, for some reason or other, the agent did not – or it was thought that he did not – straightforwardly and easily ϕ. Perhaps the agent needed to exert himself specially in order to ϕ, or perhaps, through bad luck or bad judgment, he failed to ϕ; in such cases it may well be said that he tried to ϕ. In Grice's idiom, there is a disjunctive set of doubt or denial ('D-or-D') conditions – here of doubt whether or denial that the agent succeeded –, and a speaker who says 'He tried to ϕ' will normally be taken to hold that one of the conditions in the set is fulfilled (Grice, 1961). But 'the fulfilment of the relevant D-or-D condition is not a condition of either the truth or the falsity of a statement [to the effect that someone tried. It is only that] if this condition is not fulfilled, the utterance of a statement [that says that he tried] may well be extremely misleading in its implication.' (I adapt here one of Grice's claims about perception, p. 139, to make my claim about action.)

If this is right, then the province of trying can extend much wider than would be supposed by someone who was content with asking when we should normally have cause to say that someone tried. It can be argued that it spreads very wide indeed. So far from failure or its possibility providing a necessary condition of trying, success gives a sufficient condition: we try to do everything which we intentionally do. (For the substance of the argument, I am indebted to Brian O'Shaughnessy (1973). I endeavour to formulate a quite general version.)

One can imagine an onlooker who has excellent grounds for thinking that a certain agent has every incentive to do a certain thing, but who also has excellent grounds for thinking that the agent will not succeed. The onlooker knows moreover that the reasons he has for thinking that the agent will not succeed have never been brought to the agent's attention. In the particular case, his belief that the agent will fail to do what he wants, though justified, is false. In fact the agent straightforwardly does what he had an incentive to do. Then, on the basis of his knowing of the agent's reasons, and of his knowing that the agent thought there was no obstacle, the onlooker is surely right if he says that he knew the agent would *try* to do it. So the agent did try.

The onlooker might, for example, know that a friend of his thinks there is treasure hidden under a boulder in the garden. The onlooker does not suppose that his friend will succeed in shifting the boulder, because he has been told that the boulder is much too heavy for his friend to move. But he has been misinformed. In the event, the friend simply and effortlessly rolls the boulder to one side. The onlooker admits that he was

mistaken. But he says 'I was right about one thing at least. I knew that my friend would try to move it.'

What such examples bring to light is this: the kind of doubt or denial that in the ordinary way makes it appropriate to speak of trying need not impinge upon the agent himself, and thus need not affect whether it is true that he tried. It was only the onlooker who had any doubts that his friend would move the boulder, and the friend did not exert himself specially. But then, recognizing that we can tell a story which leaves everything where it was for the agent, and yet which shows that it is obviously true to say that the agent tried to act, we may come to see that agents do try to ϕ in every case where they set out to ϕ and succeed in ϕ-ing.

The critical step in the argument is the step from 'None of those things that went on outside the agent and that prompted the spectator to say that the agent tried impinged upon the agent' to 'Therefore even if these things had not gone on, the agent would still have tried'. Can we be sure that the spectator's doubts, or the grounds for them, really make no difference to whether the agent tried? After all, it can make all the difference to whether you know that p whether it is true that p; and whether or not you count as knowing that p can also be affected simply by whether others have found reason to doubt that p. (cp. Harman, 1973, p. 146). Might not the question whether an agent *tried* also depend upon how things were outside himself, or upon how they were thought to be?

Now there is one perfectly good sense in which what a man tries to do does depend upon how he and the world are related. Whether someone is now trying to learn a Shakesperian sonnet, for instance, may depend upon whether it is a Shakesperian sonnet that he is now trying to learn by heart – a question he may be misinformed or have no particular views about. But this creates no general problem, because there is no need to assume that the agent's states of mind are given exhaustively in the premises of the argument. We can insist that the question how the agent's action is to be characterized should always be settled at the start of any particular use of the argument; and, provided that it contains a true description of the agent's action which can properly be used in stating both what the agent knows he has reason to do and also the onlooker's belief about the agent's reasons, the argument will proceed.

There would be a genuine threat to the argument if someone could show that, in circumstances where both A and B know that A intends to ϕ, an uncommunicated doubt on the part of B as to whether A will actually ϕ in itself affects the question whether A will try to ϕ. But however plausible something analogous to this may be in the case of knowledge, there is nothing to support it in the case of trying. And if that is right, the critical step is unobjectionable.

2.2 There may be doubts about the scope of the argument. If it is to be seen to establish anything general about action, then evidently we must say which pieces of human behaviour count as actions. We observed that there are fewer actions than there are events that can be mentioned in answering the question 'What did he do?' (Chapter One, §3.1); but we need now to state explicitly what the extra condition is of something's being an action beyond its being someone's doing something.

I take over Davidson's claim that all and only actions have descriptions under which they are intentional (1971) (with a caveat to be entered below, n. 3 at §3.3). This characterization explains our view of the cases in Chapter One. We do not say that a person who snores *acts*, because there is no description of the event of his making the sounds he makes that can be used to tell us of anything he intentionally does. We readily allow that the trooper who stood at attention and the man who did sums in his head both behaved as *agents*, because we do not have far to go to find values of ϕ such that 'He ϕ-d intentionally' is true of them: very likely the trooper stood at attention intentionally, and the man did his sums intentionally. So we have support for the idea, which Davidson defends much more amply, that if we go through a list of things that were done when there was someone's action – a catalogue of the different kinds that subsume this action of his –, then we shall find at least one thing in the list such that we can truly say 'He did that intentionally'.[1]

Granted this, the argument about trying can be applied (potentially at least) to every action, provided it need only be assumed that the agent intentionally did what he had incentive to do. And nothing more than that is needed. It doesn't have to be taken for granted that the agent *forms* an intention to act, or that he has the thought of his action at the front of his mind. Consider Brown who has a daily routine of waking up, getting dressed ..., which he carries out habitually, without reflection or ado. One day someone is provided with a reason to think that Brown ate something on the previous night that causes specific motor disturbances, and to think that as a result Brown will not be able to knot his tie this morning. Brown none the less is unaffected, and carries out his routine absolutely as normal, knotting his tie in his usual unthinking way. The person who knew what he had eaten is surprised to learn that Brown had done this. But he always knew that he would *try* to knot his tie.

Of course we cannot always invent examples that show it would be natural to say that people have tried to act. But anyone who thought that that was an objection to the argument would be missing its point. It is not claimed that whenever anyone does anything intentionally, we could imagine someone else on the scene who could say with all propriety 'He tries to do that thing'. It is rather that, by way of seeing that we can often envisage a person in that position, we should be persuaded (defeasibly perhaps) that 'He tried to ϕ' is not merely compatible with a man's success in ϕ-ing, but integral to his having ϕ-d intentionally. The examples help us to recognize (the analogue of what Grice recognized for perception) that what makes it true of someone that he tries to ϕ has nothing to do with whether ϕ-ing is difficult for him, or with whether he thinks that it may be difficult for him. What makes it true that he tries to ϕ has little to do with his attitudes – except in so far as his having those attitudes actually brings it about that he does something, which, if there is no difficulty, is to ϕ.

2.3 What is it though to try to act in some way?

Sometimes it is to act in some other way. Jane tries to return a service at tennis, and hits the ball into the net. One thing she did was try to hit the ball, and another thing she did was hit it into the net. But it is not that one has to do first the one thing and then the other in such cases, that having tried to hit the ball over the net (having had a shot at it), one then has to mitigate one's failure to get it over the net by now hitting it into the net. Having attempted ineptly to hit the ball over the net, one has already done all that one needs to do to have hit it into the net. One's trying to return it *is* one's hitting it into the net.

It seems that matters cannot be otherwise if one succeeds in doing exactly what was attempted. If someone's trying to hit the ball somewhere can be the same as his hitting it elsewhere, then his actually hitting it where he meant to could scarcely be different from his trying to hit it there. One thing that is done then is try to ϕ, and another thing that is done is ϕ. But having made a movement that is an attempt at ϕ-ing, no further doing is called for from the agent if he is to have ϕ-d. His attempt is then a success.

This recalls Chapter One (§ 2.4). And indeed we have to believe in identities between tryings and actions – to accept that attempts may be successes – because among the verbs from which more complex verbs can be made in construction with 'by' are verbs that result from embedding in the context 'try –'. 'He knocked the picture off the wall by trying to straighten it.' 'He tried to turn on the light by flicking the switch.'

Suppose that John does try to turn on the light by flicking the switch, but that the bulb has gone. A spectator who knew that the bulb had gone and who disbelieved that John would succeed in turning on the light may have known that John, in his ignorance, would at least try to turn it on. He could take his flicking the switch as proof that he tried to turn it on. And it seems that he has his proof because John's switch flicking was his trying to turn on the light. But if (by § 2.1) flicking the switch was something else that John tried to do, and yet John did not make two attempts at getting the light on, then there was only one (variously describable) trying on his part. Thus his switch flicking must equally be his trying to flick the switch. His succeeding in ϕ-ing is his trying to ϕ.

2.4 If ever we ϕ intentionally, then we try to ϕ (§ 2.1); if ever we try to ϕ and succeed in ϕ-ing, then our trying is our succeeding (§ 2.3). Thus, provided that every action of anyone is his intentionally doing something (§ 2.2), it is the same as some trying. At this point all that is needed for the conclusion that no action includes an overt bodily movement, is that no trying includes an overt bodily movement.

3

3.1 Some philosophers have thought that we cannot speak of trying where merely moving the body is in question, that 'He tried to –' does not make its ordinary sense unless '–' is filled by a description of an action that is non-basic (Davidson, 1971, p. 18 in this volume; Danto, 1966, p. 58). But one of these philosophers has an argument that a man may both try to ϕ and succeed in ϕ-ing which suits me very well.

> I dial Jones's number … If I fail to reach Jones, I say I will try again, meaning that I will again dial that number, and if I reach Jones, I will have succeeded, even though *I* did nothing differently on that occasion than on the one before (Danto, 1966, p. 57).

Thus we can say that at the second attempt, when I try again to reach Jones, my attempt is my reaching him. But similarly we could argue that someone's second attempt to move his body might be his moving his body. If a man has a disorder in virtue of which he suffers intermittently from partial paralysis, he may try to move his arm and fail, and say that he will try to move it later. Then when he tries, he may succeed.

The Gricean argument also can be applied to the case of bodily movement. Indeed since that argument provides us with a quite general strategy for showing that one who intentionally ϕ-s may also try to ϕ, it makes it difficult to deny that move the body is something one can try to do. But still, any purported proof of that will have at least to acknowledge the possibility that a person should try to move his body and fail to move it. And probably it is this possibility that has seemed so hard to credit.

3.2 Hume did not think that it needed arguing that we can fail in attempts to move our bodies. In discussing knowledge of causation, he used this example:

> A man, suddenly struck with a palsy in the leg or arm, or who had newly lost those members, frequently endeavours, at first, to move them, and employ them in their usual offices (*Enquiry*, Sect. 7, pt 1).

Another useful example is Landry's patient, mentioned by William James. He had lost all sensation in one arm, and when he was asked to put the affected arm on top of his head with his eyes closed, he could do so if he wasn't prevented. But when he was prevented, when, unknown to him, his arm was held down, he was surprised to find upon opening his eyes that no movement had taken place. Again it seems that he tried in vain to move a part of his body (James, at p. 490 of vol. II of [1950] edn). (Silber (1963) reports that the phenomenon is found also in non-diseased subjects whose fingers have been anaesthetized.)

These natural statements of what goes on in the two examples have met with much resistance, however.

About the first, it has been said that we tend to think that a man with the palsy tries to move his leg only because we conceive of him learning of his paralysis through this little piece of reasoning: 'I try to move my leg, it doesn't move; therefore, I cannot move it' (cp. R. Taylor, 1966, pp. 77–85). But we surely do better to suppose that the man's knowledge that he cannot move his leg is direct and non-inferential: what he learns is that he cannot move it, and that he is not in a position even to try to move it now. Some people hold that this latter description gives a complete account of the man who discovers he is paralysed, because (they say) we do not really have any conception of what a pure trying without outward and visible signs would be. A man who claims he is trying to wiggle his ears simply will not be believed unless there is some external manifestation of his efforts.

All of the power of this objection may be derived from our reluctance to suppose that one will try to do what one *knows* to be impossible. We interpret a man's action by seeing it as his doing something that he had some motive to do. We know that he wants to ϕ, that his movements can be construed as his ϕ-ing, and then sometimes we know why he is doing what he is doing. But this style of interpretation will make sense of a person only if we are prepared to add that he does not think that ϕ-ing is something he cannot do. For, even if we know that a man wants to ϕ, if we also think that he thinks that there is no way that he will ϕ, then we can expect his desire to be to that extent inert. Where he lacks the relevant belief, then, we shall usually have no reason to think that he will try to ϕ, and (unless we know that he has a motive for trying

to ϕ that is additional to any motive he might have for ϕ-ing[2]) we shall have a reason to think that he will not try to ϕ. That will explain why we are apt to disbelieve those who would claim that they are trying to wiggle their ears: most of us know whether we are able to do this or not. It would explain, too, why we soon cease to think that a man whose leg has become paralysed can go on trying to move it: at some point he will surely have learnt that it is impossible. But the man who concerns us is someone who discovers that a part of him is unexpectedly paralysed. *Ex hypothesi*, he has no knowledge of the impossibility at the time.

Landry's patient certainly did not realize that it had been made impossible for him to move his arm. He was surprised on occasion to find that he had failed to move it. And here it has to be explained not only that he believes (if he does believe it) that he has tried, but also that he believes that he has succeeded. The patient did not suppose that he had moved his arm except on those occasions where he has been asked to move it. On those occasions where he was asked to move it, and also, unknown to him, was prevented from moving it, no movement would explain his belief, and the supposition that he tried to move his arm seems to be inescapable if we want to make any sense of the episode. There is no question that he learns of his failure by inference from his having tried. It is rather that unless *we* say of him that he tried, we cannot see why he should think he succeeded. We cannot understand why he should be curious to know exactly what went on when he finds out that his arm has not moved.

But there is a line of objection directed specifically against the case of the patient. It will be said that his reaction is best explained by supposing not that he tried but that he *acted*. He is an authority on what he does; and so, since he believes that he has done whatever he does when he actually moves his arm, he must have done whatever he does when he moves his arm. It has even been suggested that we should say 'So far as he, or the mental side of him, but not necessarily his arm, is concerned, he moved his arm' (Vesey, 1961, pp. 363, 364. Davis also thinks that there is an action; 1979, p. 41, n. 16).

One of the remarks made in objection to the first case can be turned to advantage here. If an agent really were authoritative about when he had acted, and could know that he had moved his arm so far as the mental side of him was concerned, then why are we not always inclined to think that, whenever people claim pokerfaced to be trying to wiggle their ears, they must be doing something – to wit, wiggling their ears as far as the mental side of them is concerned? But they are not. And it seems equally obvious that the man who discovered that his leg was paralysed cannot be said to have done anything. He discovered precisely that he could not do what he wanted.

But there is one difference between the two cases which might seem to affect the question whether the patient who had lost sensation in his arm acted. Didn't he, unlike the man with the recently paralysed leg, show some signs of trying? Wasn't some force needed to prevent his arm from rising? Or perhaps there were contractions of muscles that could have been detected with suitable equipment. And if there was nothing of this sort, then working with normal assumptions about what it takes to move an arm, we shall suspect that the patient really did not try. (We do not feel this about the newly paralysed man, because we take paralysis to act high up in the nervous system.) This is all true. But it must be remembered that the patient intended to do no more than move his arm. He did not set out to tense it, or to contract his muscles. Of course if the muscles do contract, that will be excellent evidence that he has tried to move his arm. But unless his arm also moves$_I$, there is no evidence that he moved$_T$ it. Even if all actions are tryings, not all tryings are actions.

3.3 It is significant that it would alter things to change the last example slightly, by supposing that the patient was someone who had learnt that he could contract certain muscles by moving his arm, and that his intention was to contract those muscles. Then, provided only that they contracted$_I$, we would, I think, say that there was an action. He did what he set out to do.[3]

And now it seems that there could be an event that was actually not an action, but that might have been an action. If the patient whose muscles contracted when he was prevented from moving his arm had set out to contract those muscles, then nothing that went on inside him beyond a certain point would need to have been different in any way. Certainly he wouldn't have done anything differently, because he would have known that all he needed to do in order to

contract his muscles was to move his arm. So if only the unintended consequences of his trying to move his arm had been intended, the event of his trying would have been his doing something intentionally, an action of contracting the muscles.

Further thoughts of this kind will explain what temptation there is to say that the patient who did not move his arm nevertheless acted. We feel that if the patient was surprised that his arm had not moved, then there must have occurred something exactly like what would have occurred if his arm had moved. But if we allow that there is an event of the patient's trying, then certainly there is an event of the same kind whether his arm moves or not. Not only that: we may also think that the very event that occurred when his arm did not move might have been a moving$_I$ of his arm. If only his arm had not been prevented from moving$_I$, it would have moved$_I$, and then his trying to move it would have been an action of moving$_I$ the arm.

We can also understand why one should be inclined to think that an agent is authoritative about whether he acts. There are types of events – trying to act in certain ways – with respect to the occurrence of which the agent may have a certain authority, and instances of such types may be actions. This is to say that there are events that the agent is particularly well placed to know about, and that some of them are actions. But it is not to say that an agent always knows, or knows better than anyone else does, whether he has acted. For in order to be actions such events must result in bodily movements$_I$ (or in contractions of muscles, if they are all that the agent tries to produce); and the agent need not have any special authority whether bodily movements$_I$ have occurred, as the sensationless patient shows. (Of course kinaesthetic sensations, which are missing for Landry's patient, will in more ordinary circumstances put the agent in a peculiar epistemic position with respect to the results of his attempts to move his body.)

Some of this is speculation. But even if it is wrong to hold to the strong claim that particular tryings that are not actions could, except for the impediments, have been tryings that are actions, the weaker claim I need, which the speculation does something to support, is that attempts to move the body that are not successes have very much the same status as attempts to move the body that succeed. This is certainly true of people's attempts to turn on lights: these may be flickings of switches, movings of fingers, tryings to flick switches … whether or are not they are successful. Why should matters be different in the case of attempts to move the body, which, if they fail, have no overt effects? What leads some people to think that even unsuccessful attempts to move the body are actions should rather make one think that, as with all other attempts, the principal difference between the successful and unsuccessful sort is that the unsuccessful ones do not have the intended effects. ▼

4

4.1 If there is an action that is someone's intentionally moving his body, then that someone tries to move his body (§ 2.1 and § 3.1). Moreover his trying to move it is his moving it (§ 2.3). Trying to move the body if it is not an action is an internal event, possibly with external signs (§ 3.2). But it need make little difference to trying events *per se* whether or not they are actions (§ 3.3). So the tryings that are actions are also internal events.

Stated in this general way, the argument applies only to actions that are intentional-described-as-bodily-movements; and it is not obvious that all actions have this property. Nevertheless, if the argument can be carried through for particular instances of a wide range of action kinds (and it can), then at least it will show that some actions from a wide range of kinds are internal events. It would be strange, though, if some but not all actions of any kind were internal events. And again it would be strange if

actions of very many kinds were internal events and yet not all actions were.

It may help to appreciate the cogency of a general claim to review the underlying strategy of the argument. Take an action describable in various ways – as a ϕ-ing, as a ψ-ing, as a χ-ing …. Under some of these descriptions under which it is intentional it will be redescribable again as a trying to act in that way – a trying to ϕ, a trying to ψ …. (There may also be further descriptions of it as a trying – if the agent was unsuccessful on some score.) Next, we can often construct examples to make it clear that for some one description in the series of action descriptions, and for some one description in the series of descriptions of tryings, the action is to be identified with the trying. (Trying to turn on a light was flicking a switch.) But then, in any particular case, however the action is described as an action and however the action is described as a trying, we can affirm an identity. It remains only to show that it is clear for tryings as they are described in some way that they are always internal events. This is made clear for trying to move the body.

4.2 The first two chapters of the book from which this chapter is taken purported to show that actions are causes of bodily movements$_1$, this chapter (*inter alia*) that actions are tryings to move$_T$ the body or bring about bodily movements$_1$. Together the claims entail that, where successful, trying to move the body is causing it to move. If that has any independent merit, then the argument from causing reinforces the argument from trying, and vice versa. But the argument from trying gives us an independent route to the conclusion that actions are internal events.

Notes

Editors' note: Hornsby no longer accepts the views presented in this chapter; for her more recent views on trying to act, see her "Trying to Act," in *A Companion to the Philosophy of Action*, ed. T. O'Connor and C. Sandis (Wiley-Blackwell, 2010), pp. 18–25.

1. Someone might retort that the most interesting question about any doing is whether it can show anything at all about a person's psychological states; and then he might say that a serious concept of action should include in its domain *senseless* actions such as tapping the feet or the fingers, or rattling the keys in one's pocket for no apparent reason. We take such activities to reflect a person's states of mind, though they are not carried out intentionally (O'Shaughnessy, 1973; Locke, 1974). To this the reply can only be that it is doubtful whether we can straightforwardly effect any cut-off between movements which do and movements which do not have a psychological history (cp. Williams,

1978, p. 284), and that we have to draw boundaries where we can find significant boundaries to draw. If we take an interest in regarding ourselves as rational creatures much of whose behaviour receives a satisfying explanation when it is seen to issue from our beliefs, and desires, interests and concerns, then the restriction of actions to events that can be characterized in such a way that we can see that something was intentionally done when they occurred will enable us to deal with a vast area that we take to matter.

2. All the examples I have met of someone's trying to do what he knows to be impossible are examples of a person who has a reason to try to ϕ that persists even if any reason he has for ϕ-ing is eliminated. (Sometimes we lose face if we aren't seen to make an effort, for example.) See e.g. Williams, 1978, p. 172, and Thalberg, 1962 (though Thalberg's examples are cited as examples of *intending* the known impossible which may be more problematic).

3. This contrast, between the case where he meant his muscles to contract and the case where he did not, provides nice support for Davidson's idea that something

intentionally done is required for action. But we must modify Davidson's criterion of action now that we have seen that, in special cases, someone may try to do something without also doing any of the things that he tried to do. The problem is that it seems possible that in at least some such cases the patient *intentionally tries to move his arm*. But if that is so, then we have an answer to the question 'What did he do?' which cites something that he did intentionally, although we do not have an action. Call *simplex* any description of a doing which does not contain any other description of a doing embedded in the context 'try to —'. Then actions are all and only the events that have simplex descriptions under which they are intentional.

(Perhaps there is a sense of 'do something' (DO something) in which trying to do something is never DOING anything. If that were right, then we could stick to Davidson's formulation, taking over this sense of 'do'. Note, however, that treating *his trying to* — as a species of *his doing something* (§2.3 above) relies only upon a fact about ordinary usage, that '*He* tried to ϕ' sometimes does give an appropriate answer to 'What did he do?')

References

Danto, A. (1966), 'Freedom and forbearance', in *Freedom and Determinism* (ed.) K. Lehrer (New York: Random House).

Davidson, D. (1971), 'Agency', in *Agent, Action, and Reason* (ed.) R. Binkley, R. Bronaugh, and A. Marras (Toronto: University of Toronto Press). Reprinted here as Chapter 2.

Davis, L. H. (1979), *Theory of Action* (Englewood Cliffs, N.J.: Prentice-Hall).

Grice, H. P. (1961), 'The causal theory of perception, part I', *Proceedings of the Aristotelian Society* supp. vol. 35, 121–152.

Harman, G. (1973), *Thought* (Princeton, N.J.: Princeton University Press).

Hume, D. (1748), *Enquiry Concerning Human Understanding* (ed.) L. A. Selby-Bigge (Oxford: Oxford University Press, 1975).

James, W. (1890), *Principles of Psychology*, authorized edition in two unabridged volumes (New York: Dover, 1950).

Locke, D. (1974), 'Action, movement, and neurophysiology', *Inquiry* 17 (1-4), 23–42.

O'Shaughnessy, B. (1973), 'Trying (as the mental "pineal gland")', *Journal of Philosophy* 70 (13), 365–386.

Silber, J. R. (1963), 'Human action and the language of volitions', *Proceedings of the Aristotelian Society* 64, 199–220.

Taylor, R. (1966), *Action and Purpose* (Englewood Cliffs, N.J.: Prentice-Hall).

Thalberg, I. (1962), 'Intending the impossible', *Australian Journal of Philosophy* 40, 49–56.

Vesey, G. (1961), 'Volition', *Philosophy* 36, 325–365.

Williams, B. (1978), *Descartes: The Project of Pure Inquiry* (Harmondsworth: Penguin).

10

Action and Volition

E. J. Lowe

Persons or selves do not merely *perceive* their world – they also *act* upon it intentionally. Indeed, the self's capacities for perception and action are inseparably intertwined, even if these capacities may be exercised independently on some occasions. For example, a person incapable of voluntary self-movement cannot spontaneously generate the kind of motion parallax which, as we saw in the previous chapter, is vital to extracting information about the spatial structure of his environment from the light energies encountered by his eyes. And a person incapable of self-perception is deprived of the information feedback necessary for executing fine-grained movements of her limbs. In this chapter I shall be arguing that there must exist a class of mental acts corresponding to the traditional notion of a *volition* or *act of will*, and that any human action properly described as *voluntary* must involve the occurrence of at least one such mental act. Volitions, I maintain, play an indispensable causal role in the genesis of voluntary bodily movement, a role for which mental states like belief and desire are constitutionally unsuited, even though states of the latter sort are indeed normally to be included amongst the causal antecedents of volitions. Volitions are different from states like belief and desire not only in respect of their distinctive causal

role, but also in respect of their distinctive intentional content, which, as we shall see, always has an ineliminably self-referential character.

1. Agents and Actions

Let me begin by introducing some basic terminology and explaining the theoretical framework I mean to deploy. In what follows I shall, at least to start with, be using the terms *agent* and *action* in very broad senses. An agent, in this sense, may be any sort of enduring object (or 'continuant') capable of entering into causal relationships with other such objects. It need not, thus, be a person or an animal, though persons and animals *are* agents in my broad sense, and most of what I have to say will concern them. By an *action sentence* I mean a sentence of the form '*a* is Fing' (in the present tense case), where '*a*' names an agent and '*F*' is a verb or verb-phrase describing some sort of *activity*, in the broadest sense of that term, whereby it betokens a change (or indeed a non-change) either in the agent itself or in some object causally affected by it. For instance, '*a* is falling', '*a* is breathing' and '*a* is opening the window' are all action sentences, in my terminology. An *action* (or *act*), correspondingly, is something whose occurrence is necessary for the truth of an action sentence, and may be referred to by a noun-phrase of the form '*a*'s Fing'. So, for example, *a*'s falling, *a*'s breathing and *a*'s opening the window are all actions.

Philosophy of Action: An Anthology, First Edition. Edited by Jonathan Dancy and Constantine Sandis.
© 2015 John Wiley & Sons, Inc. Published 2015 by John Wiley & Sons, Inc.

Very often action sentences submit to a *causal* analysis. That is to say, an action sentence of the form '*a* F*ed*' (to use the past tense case) may very often be analysed as entailing a sentence of the form '*a* caused *x* to *G*', where '*x*' names an object and '*G*' again describes an activity. For instance, 'Smith opened the window' may be analysed as entailing 'Smith caused the window to open' and 'Smith killed Jones' may be analysed as entailing 'Smith caused Jones to die'. (Observe that I do not claim that 'Smith killed Jones' is *logically equivalent to* 'Smith caused Jones to die' – a claim which has been much disputed of late.[1] However, this is not because I am convinced that there is no such equivalence, but only because the weaker claim made above is all that I need for my current purposes.)

Consider now a sentence of the form '*a* caused *x* to *F*'. We can, it seems, always ask *how a* caused *x* to *F*, and be entitled to expect that an answer will at least in principle be forthcoming. And the answer will be of the form 'by *Ging*' or, more fully, '*a* caused *x* to *F* by *Ging*'. The 'how' and the 'by' invoked here we may call the 'how' and the 'by' of *causal means* (to distinguish them from certain other 'hows' and 'bys' which need not presently concern us). Now, where we have such an answer to the how-question, two possibilities arise concerning the further action sentence '*a* G*ed*' (the sentence which reports an action *by* doing which *a* caused *x* to *F*). Either '*a* G*ed*' will submit to a causal analysis, or it will not. Suppose it *will not*. Then I contend that '*a* caused *x* to *F* by *Ging*' entails '*a*'s *Ging* caused *x*'s *Fing*'. Suppose, alternatively, that '*a* G*ed*' *will* submit to a causal analysis, as entailing, say, '*a* caused *y* to *H*'. Then I contend that '*a* caused *x* to *F* by *Ging*' entails '*a* caused *y* to *H* and *y*'s *Hing* caused *x*'s *Fing*'.

Some examples will help to make these contentions clearer and more persuasive. Consider first, then, the action sentence 'Smith caused Jones to fall'. Suppose we ask *how* Smith caused Jones to fall and the answer returned is 'Smith caused Jones to fall by colliding with him'. Now, 'Smith collided with Jones', it seems clear, is *not* causally analysable. And accordingly I propose that 'Smith caused Jones to fall by colliding with him' entails 'Smith's colliding with Jones caused Jones's falling'. Next consider the action sentence 'Smith caused the light to go on' and suppose we again ask *how*, receiving this time the answer 'Smith caused the light to go on by turning the switch'. This time,

'Smith turned the switch', unlike 'Smith collided with Jones', *is* causally analysable, entailing as it does 'Smith caused the switch to turn'. So what I want to say here is that 'Smith caused the light to go on by turning the switch' entails 'Smith caused the switch to turn and the switch's turning caused the light's going on'.

Suppose I am right in what I have said so far (and I have, to be fair, glossed over some subtleties which are not pertinent to the general thrust of my argument). Then the following important result may be deduced. All causal action sentences in which the name of an *agent* appears as the grammatical subject of the verb 'to cause' depend for their truth upon the truth of causal sentences in which noun-phrases solely referring to *actions* appear as grammatical subjects of this verb. Sentences of the first type are ones of the form '*a* caused *x* to *F* (by *Ging*)' and sentences of the second type are ones of the form '*a*'s *Ging* caused *x*'s *Fing*' (or are conjunctions of such sentences). Let us call the two types of causal sentence *agent-causal* and *action-causal* sentences respectively. Then our interesting result is that all agent-causal sentences depend for their truth upon the truth of action-causal sentences. (Whether this means that agent-causal sentences are in principle altogether eliminable in favour of action-causal sentences is another question, though I am inclined to think that they are.)

The proof of this result is simple enough, given my earlier contentions. For suppose we have an agent-causal sentence of the form '*a* caused *x* to *F*' and that in answer to the how-question this is expanded as '*a* caused *x* to *F* by *Ging*'. Then if '*a* G*ed*' is *not* causally analysable we immediately have the consequence that our original agent-causal sentence depends for its truth upon the truth of the action-causal sentence '*a*'s *Ging* caused *x*'s *Fing*'. If on the other hand '*a* G*ed*' *is* causally analysable, say as '*a* caused *y* to *H*', then we have the consequence that our original agent-causal sentence depends for its truth upon the truth of the causal sentence '*a* caused *y* to *H* and *y*'s *Hing* caused *x*'s *Fing*', which is partly agent-causal and partly action-causal. But now the same considerations may be applied to the agent-causal part, '*a* caused *y* to *H*', which has exactly the same form as our original agent-causal sentence, '*a* caused *x* to *F*'. Hence, on pain of an infinite regress which would certainly appear to be vicious, that original agent-causal sentence must ultimately depend for its truth upon the truth of some *purely* action-causal sentence (one which will be conjunctive in form). Moreover, the grammatical subject of the first conjunct of that sentence will necessarily be a noun-phrase referring to an action of *a*'s which is *not causally analysable*. I shall call this action the *original* action of the causal chain of actions terminating in *x*'s F*ing* (though there is no presumption here that the 'original' action is itself *uncaused*, nor even that it in any sense 'initiates' the subsequent chain of actions). Thus, if the agent-causal sentence '*a* caused *x* to *F*' is ultimately dependent for its truth upon the truth of the action-causal sentence '*a*'s G*ing* caused *y*'s H*ing* and *y*'s H*ing* caused *x*'s F*ing*', then *a*'s G*ing* is what I would call the 'original' action of the causal chain of actions terminating in *x*'s F*ing*. And *a*'s G*ing* will be an action of *a*'s that is not causally analysable.

2. Bodily Movements and Bodily Motions

So far I have not, officially, been concerned exclusively with human agents and actions, but from now on I shall concentrate on these. Assuming – as seems reasonable unless we are given good grounds to think otherwise – that human actions provide no exception to the general conclusions reached so far, it is clear that at least *some* human actions must fail to be causally analysable – in particular, those that are 'original' in causal chains of human action. Evidently, then, these original actions cannot be *bodily movements* of any sort, if by bodily movements we are talking of human agents' *movings of their bodies*: for all such actions *are* causally analysable. For instance, 'Smith raised his arm' is analysable as entailing 'Smith caused his arm to rise'. Of course, there is *another* sense of 'bodily movement' in which it denotes not a moving by an agent of his body, but simply a movement of his body – and to avoid ambiguity and confusion I shall call this a *bodily motion*, reserving the term 'bodily movement' exclusively for agents' movings of their bodies. A bodily motion in this sense is an action which is *not* causally analysable. For instance, the action sentence 'Smith trembled', as it is normally used, reports a bodily motion. Only in exceptional circumstances would this sentence be used to report a

bodily movement, when it would be causally analysable as entailing 'Smith caused himself to tremble'.

Now, the peculiarity of human agents (and of some animal agents, I assume) is that they can perform *voluntary* actions. And in the case of voluntary actions it is sufficiently clear that the 'original' actions of the causal chains involved must be *mental* acts of some sort (and *not*, say, items such as mere bodily motions). The reason why I say this is simply that the possession of a mind is so obviously the distinguishing feature of the sort of agent that is capable of engaging in voluntary action, while some actual *exercise* of that mind's capacities must equally evidently be what makes the difference, in any particular case, between a voluntary action and an action that might just as well have been attributable to an agent altogether devoid of a mind. These distinctive mental acts we shall shortly identify as *volitions*. But before we reach that point, I need to comment briefly on the view of some philosophers that certain bodily movements are 'basic' in the sense that in the case of such movements there is *no* answer to the question of *how*, or by doing what, they are done.[2] For if this view were correct, it would totally undermine the volitional theory that I wish to defend.

Consider again the action sentence 'Smith raised his arm', which is causally analysable as entailing 'Smith caused his arm to rise'. And suppose we ask *how* Smith did this. I expect an answer of the form 'Smith caused his arm to rise by F*ing*', entailing in turn the action sentence 'Smith F*ed*'. But the philosophers of whom I speak seem to think that very often there is *no* such answer to a question such as this, and that then the arm-raising is what they call a 'basic' action. At other times they *would* allow an answer, such as 'by tugging on a rope attached to his arm via a pulley'. But in all *normal* cases of arm-raising, they would say, there is simply *no* answer to a question such as 'By doing *what* did Smith raise his arm?' However, this creates a considerable difficulty, for it then appears that there must be agent-causal sentences which do not depend for their truth upon the truth of action-causal sentences – although only, it seems, where human and perhaps animal agents and voluntary actions are concerned. This makes for unnecessary mystery, suggesting as it does the operation, in certain cases of human and animal action, of a *kind* of causation not to be found in the realm of inanimate things.

A naturalistic view of animate beings certainly cannot tolerate such a suggestion. (I should perhaps add, however, that I do not dispute that there *is* something special about 'normal' cases of voluntary bodily movement, which justifiably motivates the description of such actions as 'basic' – I merely dispute the view of 'basicness' adverted to above. An alternative view will be proposed later.)

3. Voluntary Actions and Volitions

I asserted a little while ago that in the case of voluntary human actions, it is clear that the actions which are 'original' in causal chains of human action must be *mental* acts of some sort. That is to say, if *a*'s causing *x* to *F* was a *voluntary* action of *a*'s, then it appears that the causal chain of action terminating in *x*'s *F*ing must have had as its original action a certain sort of mental act of *a*'s. Such a mental act will, of course, not be causally analysable. Plainly, though, we cannot assume that just *any* sort of causally unanalysable mental act which is original in a causal chain of human action would suffice to render that chain of action voluntary. The sort of mental act which *would* suffice I shall call – by definition, in effect – a *volition*, or *willing*, or *act of will*. I am contending, thus, that what distinguishes voluntary from involuntary human actions is the *kind* of mental origin they involve, and I am further assuming that there is some *single* kind of original mental acts which are characteristically involved in all chains of voluntary human action. (This is a view of voluntary action which, while held in some disrepute in recent decades, has a venerable history.[3]) And the assumption that I am making seems a reasonable hypothesis, in the absence of countervailing argument. (Later I shall offer a positive defence of it.) But if it is correct, then there is no question but that *there are* volitions or acts of will, since undoubtedly human agents do sometimes voluntarily cause things to happen. All that remains, then, is to try to characterize volitions more closely.

Suppose, then, that *a* caused *x* to *F*, and did so voluntarily. Then by my account this means that the sentence '*a* caused *x* to *F*' depends for its truth upon the truth of some sentence of the form '*a*'s *G*ing caused … *x*'s *F*ing', where the gap may or may not (but almost always will) be capable of containing further noun-phrases referring to intermediate steps in a causal chain of actions, and where '*a*'s *G*ing' denotes what we have decided to call a *volition*. Thus in such a case the ultimate answer to the question of *how a* caused *x* to *F* is 'by willing'. But by willing *what*? It is clear that the mental activity of willing, if it is to play the causal role we have assigned it in voluntary human action, must always have an intentional object: willing must always be willing *something*. But *what* is it that the agent wills, when by so willing he voluntarily causes something to happen? Two principal possibilities suggest themselves.[4] One is that the agent wills *something to do something* – for instance, wills *x* to *F*. The other is that the agent wills *to cause something to do something* – for instance, wills to cause *x* to *F*. (Some would prefer to say that willing is a propositional attitude, that is, a matter of willing *that such-and-such be the case*.[5] But for a number of reasons, which need not be gone into just now, I find this proposal unacceptable. I shall return to the issue later.) Which of these two possible accounts should we prefer?

In order to settle this question, let us consider a relatively simple case of an agent *a*'s voluntarily causing a motion of his own body, for example, causing his arm to rise. And suppose, for the sake of simplicity, that he does this 'in the normal way', rather than as in the rope and pulley example (so that his action is what many philosophers would call a 'basic' action). On my view, the ultimate answer in such a case to the question of *how a* caused his arm to rise is that he did it *by willing*. And now our further question is by willing *what*? In such a case, the two rival hypotheses supply the following two answers respectively: (1) by willing *his arm to rise*, and (2) by willing *to cause his arm to rise*.[6] My own opinion is that the former answer is quite untenable. One simply cannot, I believe, 'will' one's arm to rise any more than one can 'will' a table across the room to move. Indeed, I think it is this erroneous view of the intentional objects of acts of will that has, as much as anything, brought into such ill repute the belief that such acts exist at all. For if willing *were* like this it would apparently be purely a matter of *a posteriori* discovery that some acts of will happened to be causally efficacious and others not, and this seems incomprehensible. Can it really be supposed that I just *discover* (by trial and error?) that if I will my arm to move, it does move, but that if I will the table to move, it does not?[7] Surely not: this would make willing too much like mere wishing. (Whether or not our wishes come true is not in general up to us.) I believe, on the contrary, that the very concept of an act of will must be of a kind of mental activity that is (normally) efficacious with respect to its own intentional content (see section 6 below) – and that this feature of willing is much easier to accommodate within the alternative account mentioned earlier, precisely because that account incorporates an intention to *cause* a specific effect into the very content of an act of will and thereby secures a constitutive connection between what it *is* to will and the expectation that an act of will should be causally efficacious in the relevant way. (This is *not* to say that I think that an act of will realizes its own intentional content by virtue of a logical or conceptual necessity – a view which some opponents of volitionism have attempted to foist upon it – for this would be incompatible with the *causal* role of such acts, as well as being utterly mysterious.)

Having rejected what I like to call the 'magical' account of willing, my view is, then, that when *a* voluntarily causes his arm to rise 'in the normal way', he causes his arm to rise *by willing to cause it to rise*, so that, in this sort of case, we may say that *a*'s willing to cause his arm to rise causes his arm to rise. But if this is so, then it turns out that we haven't, after all, yet fully specified the intentional content of *a*'s act of will. For if what *a* wills is *to cause his arm to rise*, then earlier considerations of ours require that *a* must, at least implicitly, will *to cause his arm to rise by Fing* (for some appropriate *F*), and that, in fact, *F*ing in such a ('basic') case must be none other than *willing*. That is to say, a fuller specification of the (perhaps only implicit) content of *a*'s act of will must have it that *a* wills *to cause his arm to rise by willing* – the point being that, as was explained earlier, we are always entitled to expect an answer to the question of *how* an act of causing is (to be) done, and in this case 'by willing' seems to be the only answer that is ultimately acceptable. After all, it is barely comprehensible that *a* should, in such a case, will to cause his arm to rise by doing anything *other* than willing. (Even in the rope and pulley case, where *a* wills to cause his arm to rise by tugging on the rope, there is *something* that he wills to cause by willing: thus here he wills to cause his *other* hand to move *by willing*.

Of course, I don't mean to suggest that ordinary, philosophically untutored human agents necessarily *think* of themselves as 'willing to cause things by willing' – that is, think of the contents of their volitions under this sort of description.)

Now, however, another difficulty looms. I have just argued that when *a* voluntarily causes his arm to rise 'in the normal way', he must cause it to rise by willing *to cause it to rise by willing*. But then the question again arises, with respect to the willing mentioned in the specification of the content of *a*'s act of will, as to what *its* content is – for all willing, we have agreed, is willing *something*. An infinite regress seemingly threatens: we appear to be in danger of having to say that *a* causes his arm to rise by willing to cause his arm to rise by willing to cause his arm to rise by willing … and so on *ad infinitum*. But in fact I don't believe that there is a serious difficulty here. The lesson to be drawn from the threatened regress is that *a*'s act of will must be, in respect of its content, *self-referential*.[8] What we must say is that when *a* voluntarily causes his arm to rise 'in the normal way', he causes it to rise by willing *to cause it to rise by performing THAT act of will*, where 'THAT' refers to the very act of will whose content is being specified. (Henceforth, I shall reserve the capitalized form, 'THAT', exclusively for this sort of self-referential use.) In this way, we respect both the demand that the content of *a*'s act of will should be *fully* specifiable and the demand that its content should specify *willing* as the means by which the arm is to be caused to rise.

One phenomenon that this self-referential characterization of willing seems to illuminate is our feeling that when, after a period of deliberation and hesitation, we suddenly go ahead and *do* something, we reached a 'point of no return' in our deliberations, at which action immediately and irrevocably followed: we sometimes call such points 'moments of decision', and use metaphors such as tipping a balance or releasing a spring to describe them. This is quite understandable on the account of willing advanced above: for once I *do* perform the mental act of willing to cause something to happen by performing THAT very act of will, there is no holding back. Provided my neural mechanisms are functioning normally, the willed action is already underway, that is, the causing is already in process of occurring – for if it were not, the willing would *already* have failed to realize its intentional content, which would imply some defect of neural functioning (since willing is by its very nature normally causally efficacious). I often can, it is true, subsequently will to reverse matters, and thus *undo* voluntarily something that I have voluntarily begun to do: but undoing what has begun to be done is quite different from withholding from doing, and moreover *feels* quite different. The alternative account of willing rejected earlier cannot, it seems, properly accommodate these facts.[9] For if, say when I raise my arm voluntarily, all that I will is *my arm to rise a short time hence*, it is not at all obvious why this act of will may not be immediately countermanded and the arm-raising withheld. Performing an act of will should *commit* the agent to realizing (or at least to *beginning* to realize) the content of his willing, or else it is not even clear how willing can be causally sufficient (in the circumstances) for its intended effect. For willing cannot be sufficient if the absence of a countermanding act of will is necessary.

4. Basic and Non-basic Voluntary Actions

I should make it clear that the foregoing account of volitional content strictly applies only in the case of voluntary actions which would standardly be called 'basic', such as raising one's arm 'in the normal way'. But this now provides us with the material for an account of *basicness* (or, more precisely, of *basic voluntary causing*) which has considerable advantages over the account rejected earlier. According to that earlier account, *a* caused *x* to *F* – for example, caused his arm to rise – as a basic (voluntary) action only if *a* caused *x* to *F* but *not* by doing anything else (where the 'by' is the 'by' of causal means). I reject this because – for one thing – I want to say that even where *a* voluntarily caused his arm to rise 'in the normal way', he did it *by* doing such things as causing the muscles in his shoulder and back to contract (even if *a* may not have been *aware* that this was how he did it). But, more fundamentally, of course, I reject it because I also want to say that in such a case *a* caused his arm to rise not least *by willing*. (There is, incidentally, no inconsistency in saying *both* of these things – that he did it *both* by causing his muscles to contract *and* by willing. For he *also* caused

his muscles to contract *by willing* – though not by willing *to cause them to contract*, but only by willing *to cause his arm to rise*. And the 'by' of causal means is transitive.)

However, what *is* special about voluntarily raising one's arm 'in the normal way' is that in such a case the bodily movement in question is made *the direct object of one's volition*: in such a case, as we have seen, one causes one's arm to rise precisely by willing *to cause one's arm to rise* (by performing THAT act of will). And *this* is why the action is properly described as 'basic'. By contrast, consider a non-basic voluntary action such as causing a ball to move. One cannot (I think) cause a ball to move precisely by willing *to cause it to move* (by performing THAT act of will). Rather, one's volition must be directed upon a bodily movement of one's own body, albeit in the knowledge or belief that the bodily motion so brought about will cause motion in the ball. So, typically, one might cause a ball to move by willing *to cause one's foot to move into contact with the ball* (by performing THAT act of will).

Thus we may offer the following as a definition of basic voluntary causing:

> *a* voluntarily caused *x* to *F* basically (or as a basic action) if and only if *a* caused *x* to *F* by willing to cause *x* to *F* by performing THAT act of will.

Instances of *non*-basic voluntary causing will fall into two categories. First, there are familiar cases such as the one just discussed of causing a ball to move, in which *a* causes *x* to *F* voluntarily by voluntarily causing something *y* to *G* as a basic action – for example, he voluntarily causes a ball to move by voluntarily causing his foot to move into contact with the ball as a basic action. Here *a*'s willing causes *y*'s *G*ing which causes *x*'s *F*ing. Secondly, there are more esoteric cases like the one mentioned earlier concerning the causation of muscle contractions, in which *a* causes *x* to *F* voluntarily by willing to cause something *y* to *G* and where, typically, *x*'s *F*ing will be an intermediate cause of *y*'s *G*ing – for example, he voluntarily causes his shoulder and back muscles to contract by willing to cause his arm to rise, and the contraction of his shoulder and back muscles causes the rising of his arm. For in such a case I see no reason to deny that *a* causes his shoulder and back muscles to contract *voluntarily*, even though he may be unaware that he is doing so.

(A voluntary action need not be *intentional*, even though an intentional action must be voluntary.[10]) These, then, are cases in which, typically, *a*'s willing causes *x*'s F*ing* which causes *y*'s G*ing*.

I repeat, then, that what is peculiar to basic voluntary actions is that they are made the direct object of the agent's will – and for the most part such actions are limited in practice to the agent's movement of various parts of his own body 'in the normal way'. We may appropriately say of such actions that they are done 'at will'. One may raise one's arm or kick one's foot 'at will' (unless one is disabled or impeded), but cannot in general do such things as contract one's shoulder muscles or move a ball 'at will'. I say 'in general' because it must be recognized that an agent can with practice *extend* his repertoire of basic actions (thus infants have to learn to walk and talk 'at will'), and so it would be dangerous to attempt to lay down *a priori* limits to the range of basic actions. Some people can indeed learn to do such things as control their heart-beat 'at will', and one might equally wish to ascribe to a competent typist an ability to type the word THE 'at will'. But although there may not be specific *a priori* limits, limits there certainly must be, for we are not God and do not, *pace* Descartes, have an infinite or boundless will.

We can understand now, while still rejecting, the alternative account of basicness discussed earlier. The reason why one may be tempted to *say* that where *a* voluntarily caused *x* to *F* as a basic action he did not do it *by* doing anything else is simply that no other action will in such a case *enter into the content of a's volition* as constituting a causal means to the end of bringing about *x*'s F*ing* (apart, of course, from that very act of volition itself). But this is just to say that *a* need not *will* to do something else by doing which he may cause *x* to *F*: it is not to imply that he need not in fact *do* any such further thing.

5. In Defence of Volitions

It is now time to answer some familiar objections to the kind of account of voluntary action that I have just offered. One particularly well-known objection, due to Gilbert Ryle, is that such an account is driven into an infinite regress of willings (a different sort of regress, however, from the one which we earlier

evaded by recognizing the self-referential character of volitional content).[11] The argument is that if only those actions are voluntary that originate in an act of will, then we need to ask whether acts of will themselves are voluntary or not, which presents the following dilemma. If they are not, then it is hard to see how they can serve to make the actions which originate in them *voluntary* (because we normally regard the consequences of involuntary actions as being themselves involuntary). On the other hand, if it is said that acts of will *are* voluntary, then by the volitional theorist's own lights this will apparently have to mean that acts of will themselves originate in *other* acts of will, these in yet others, and so on *ad infinitum*.

My own response to this objection – in which I differ from some other volitionists[12] – is to accept quite happily that acts of will are *not* themselves voluntary and to deny that the first horn of the alleged dilemma presents a genuine difficulty. Here it should be recalled that I effectively *define* 'willing' as that kind of mental activity which is characteristically 'original' in those causal chains of human action which we would ordinarily describe as voluntary. (This does indeed presuppose – though as far as I can see quite unproblematically – that we can very often recognize actions as being voluntary other than by means of identifying their causal origins.) So there is no mystery as to why 'willed' causings should be voluntary, particularly since our further characterization of the causal and intentional features of volitions has, I hope, gone some way towards explaining their suitability for the theoretical role that has been assigned to them. The fact that *other* sorts of involuntary human activities, such as twitches and blinks, do *not* render voluntary the causal chains of action which issue from them is quite irrelevant. (Here I should perhaps emphasize that I am not concerned to try to define or explicate *what we ordinarily mean* in describing an action as 'voluntary'. What I am interested in is the question of what *in fact* makes a voluntary action voluntary, and this in my view unquestionably has to do with the special nature of its causal provenance.)

One reason why I am quite happy to deny that acts of will are voluntary is that by my account, it will be recalled, such acts are necessarily not causally analysable, and I am only prepared to regard as voluntary those actions that *are* causally analysable. (Willing is not *itself* a matter of causing something to happen – in the way that killing is a matter of causing death – even though *by* willing one may, and typically does, cause something to happen.) But I should add that while I have denied that willing can be voluntary, I do not mean to rule out *a priori* the possibility that an agent might *voluntarily cause himself* to perform a certain act of will. In the simplest case, this would occur if the agent were to cause himself to will to do something by willing to cause himself so to will by performing THAT act of will. In such a case, the voluntary causing of volition would of course be 'basic' – though in fact I very much doubt whether it is possible even in principle for an agent to cause himself to *will* 'at will', any more than it appears that he can cause himself to *believe* 'at will'.[13] If one can voluntarily cause volitions in oneself, one can I think only do this in a roundabout way – for instance, by voluntarily conjuring up thoughts of certain attractive or desirable prospects (as a weight-watcher may invoke the image of a desirably slender future self in order to prompt a volition to resist eating a cream cake). Thus we see that a volitional theory of the sort that I am advancing need not represent agents as being the perfect slaves of their wills, since it may allow that they can have a measure of voluntary control over some of the operations of the will itself.

Another time-worn objection to volitions is that we are, supposedly, quite ignorant of their existence – and this is put down to their being the mere inventions of the overspeculative philosophical imagination.[14] To this I have a twofold reply. First, we are *not* in fact universally oblivious of our volitions (though most of us, of course, will not recognize them by that name). Second, there are very good reasons why too conscious an awareness of our volitions would impede us in the performance of voluntary actions. On the first point, I should say that we *are* sometimes made aware of our volitions, especially in circumstances in which, contrary to our expectations, we fail in the attempt to perform some voluntary action. Thus there is the famous example of the patient cited by William James who, lacking kinaesthetic sensations in his arm, was surprised to be told that he had failed to raise it when instructed to do so, the arm being (unbeknownst to him) kept under restraint.[15] The patient was evidently conscious of having done *something* but not, obviously,

of having raised his arm – since he failed to do this. What I would say, of course, is that he was conscious of *willing* to raise his arm – what else? Furthermore, the fact that when we *are* made aware of our volitions our perception of them is often only confused and indistinct (as this patient's evidently was) should be unsurprising to anyone who has abandoned the Cartesian view of the mind as peculiarly transparent to itself. Here I might add that although nothing quite equivalent to my use of the term 'volition' seems to exist in ordinary language, the vocabulary of *trying* comes close to capturing its sense – a point to which I shall return.

As for the second point made above – that too conscious an awareness of our volitions would impede us in the performance of voluntary actions – this is just a corollary of a more general observation, that too conscious an awareness of *any* of the actions *by* doing which we do some further thing intentionally (of which willing is of course one) tends to impede us in the performance of that further intended action. For instance, a competent typist who attends to the movements of his fingers tends to make more errors than one who does not.

One last objection that I shall mention concerns the *number* of willings or volitions we execute in the course of performing some train of voluntary action. Thus Ryle asks, with heavy sarcasm, how many acts of will one executes in, say, reciting 'Little Miss Muffet' backwards.[16] Now, the first thing to say about this objection is that volitions are not in any way peculiar amongst actions in raising problems of enumeration and, by implication, of individuation. One might equally well ask, with as little expectation of receiving an obvious and uncontentious reply, how many *utterances* one executes in reciting 'Little Miss Muffet' backwards – but this does not, or should not, engender scepticism about the existence of utterances.

At another level, however, the enumeration question does raise some important, though in no way embarrassing, issues about volitions and voluntary action. In particular, it raises the question of whether complete action-routines or only the components of such routines can constitute the intentional objects of volitions. For instance, when a competent typist types the sentence 'The cat sat on the mat', should we suppose that he simply has a volition to type that sentence, or should we suppose rather that he first has a volition to type 'The', then a volition to type 'cat', and so forth? (I stipulate that the typist is a 'competent' one because it seems clear that in the case of a novice the typing even of each letter will be a non-basic voluntary action: recall our earlier discussion.) I do not consider that this is a question that can be settled conclusively without recourse to empirical psychological evidence: either hypothesis seems tenable, *a priori*. What is clear, however, is that not *every* component action of *every* action-routine can individually be the intentional object of some volition of the agent. (After all, even so 'simple' an action as raising one's arm 'in the normal way' involves many component actions.) What also seems clear is that as competence in performing an action-routine improves with practice, fewer of its components or sub-routines need individually to be made the intentional

objects of volitions of the agent. If this implies that someone well-rehearsed in reciting 'Little Miss Muffet' backwards executes *fewer volitions* in reciting it than someone not so well-rehearsed – as it may well do – then I do not regard this as a consequence which a volitionist need feel embarrassed about accepting. The only reason, I suspect, why the enumeration question may *appear* at first to present an embarrassing difficulty for the volitionist is that it is tacitly being supposed that the volitionist is committed to regarding introspective awareness of one's own volitions as a transparent and infallible source of all that one ever needs to know about them – in short, it is being supposed that the volitionist must adhere to the Cartesian conception of the mind. For since introspection provides no conclusive answer to the enumeration question, it is then inferred that acts of will as the volitionist supposedly conceives of them cannot really exist.[17]

Notes

1. See, e.g., Judith Jarvis Thomson, *Acts and Other Events* (Ithaca: Cornell University Press, 1977), p. 128.
2. See, e.g., Arthur C. Danto, 'Basic Actions', *American Philosophical Quarterly* 2 (1965), pp. 141–8.
3. See, in particular, John Locke, *An Essay Concerning Human Understanding*, bk. II, ch. XXI, sect. 5. I discuss Locke's theory in my 'Necessity and the Will in Locke's Theory of Action', *History of Philosophy Quarterly* 3 (1986), pp. 149–63 and in my *Locke on Human Understanding* (London: Routledge, 1995), ch. 6. Volitionism is now enjoying a revival amongst a minority of action-theorists: see further Lawrence E. Davis, *Theory of Action* (Englewood Cliffs, NJ: Prentice-Hall, 1979), ch. 1 and Carl Ginet, *On Action* (Cambridge: Cambridge University Press, 1990), ch. 2. Ginet arrives at his position through a train of reasoning somewhat similar to mine in sections 1 and 2 above: see his *On Action*, pp. 4 ff.
4. Cf. H. A. Prichard, 'Acting, Willing, Desiring', Chapter 7 in this volume. I disagree with Prichard's answer to the question, however.
5. See, e.g., Hugh McCann, 'Volition and Basic Action', *Philosophical Review* 83 (1974), pp. 451–73, especially p. 468 and Ginet, *On Action*, pp. 31-2.
6. I would be happy to treat (2) as equivalent to 'by willing *to raise his arm*' – but, as I mentioned in section 1, this

sort of putative equivalence has been disputed by some philosophers of action, so I shall not insist on it here.
7. To suppose that this sort of thing could be discovered by *trial* and error is manifestly absurd, at least if generalized to embrace all acts of will – for 'trial' itself implies the performance of voluntary action. Yet what other method of discovery could there be, if what is to be discovered is merely an empirical truth?
8. Other recent authors have similarly contended that *intentions* are self-referential: see, e.g., John R. Searle, *Intentionality* (Cambridge: Cambridge University Press, 1983), ch. 3. See also Ginet, *On Action*, pp. 35–6, where the claim is made for both volitions and intentions.
9. Similarly, it is at most this other account which succumbs to the objection raised by G. E. M. Anscombe in her 'Will and Emotion', in R. M. Chisholm & R. Haller (eds.), *Die Philosophie Franz Brentanos* (Amsterdam: Rodopi, 1978), pp. 145 f. Anscombe remarks: 'That an act is voluntary doesn't mean that it is preceded by an act of will ... In proof of this, consider how, whatever inner event precedes an act, one can still ask *if it* [i.e., the act] *was voluntary when it occurred*.' But if the 'inner event' is willing as I have characterized it, and *does* cause the intended effect as specified in the content of that willing, then this question is *not* genuinely still open.

10. For more on the distinction between voluntariness and intentionality, see my 'An Analysis of Intentionality', *Philosophical Quarterly* 30 (1980), pp. 294–304.

11. See Gilbert Ryle, 'The Will', Chapter 8 in this volume.

12. See, e.g., McCann, 'Volition and Basic Action', p. 472.

13. Cf. Bernard Williams, 'Deciding to Believe', in his *Problems of the Self* (Cambridge: Cambridge University Press, 1973).

14. See, e.g., Ryle, op. cit.

15. See William James, *Principles of Psychology* (New York: Henry Holt & Co., 1890), vol. 2, p. 490. This is the famous case of Landry's patient.

16. See Ryle, op. cit.

17. [A section on belief, desire, and will has been omitted here.]

Part III

Intention and Intentional Action

Introduction to Part III

1.

Why are philosophers of action interested in intention? One reason is that philosophers of action are not interested in *all* actions. They are not interested in the actions of the wind and the tides. And some human actions don't interest them either, such as breathing and giving birth. What distinguishes the actions that interest them, supposedly, is that they are intentional.

Another reason is that philosophers are interested in what it is to act for a reason, and they tend to think that all intentional actions are done for a reason, and all actions done for a reason are intentional. (Hursthouse challenges the first part of this in Chapter 22; see also Knobe in Chapter 16; Knobe and Kelly 2009.)

But even if not all the actions that interest us are intentional, and not all intentional actions are done for a reason, there are other things that might interest us in the idea of an intentional action. There is the apparently simple phenomenon of forming an intention to do something and then doing it (and doing it intentionally) when the time comes. It would not be so surprising if there were a relation between these two things – the intention and the eventual intentional action; but what is that relation? One thought is that for an action to be intentional it needs to be accompanied by a mental state called an intending (or an intention), so that walking across the road intentionally is a kind of combination of walking across the road and intending to do just that – but the

intending could have started long before the action got going. (See here Bratman, Chapter 14.) Pursuing this line, we are likely to want to know what is meant by 'accompanied'; surely more is required than just co-presence, so perhaps we should say 'accompanied and caused by'. A very different suggestion is that the intentionality, the intendedness, of an action is not an extra, mental accompaniment to (and cause of) the physical process of moving one's limbs in such a way that one ends up on the other side of the road, but somehow more closely connected to that process. (The basic idea here is associated with Anscombe, Chapter 11.) But if it is, we can ask whether the sort of intending that is at issue when one does something intentionally is the same *sort* of intending as goes on when one is now intending to act later. Are these to be thought of as two utterly different things that have somehow got very similar names? This is not a very plausible hypothesis; but it is very hard to do better. (See McDowell, Chapter 15.)

We can also ask how it is that we know what we intend, and whether our ability to know what we are doing is the same ability as the ability to know what we intend (or, come to that, as the ability to know what we mean, or how we are feeling). Is it that the special way in which I seem to know what I am doing (which appears not to require observation) is really the same special way in which we know what we intend? If so, what is that way? Is it a sort of introspection? (See here Donnellan, Chapter 12.)

Philosophy of Action: An Anthology, First Edition. Edited by Jonathan Dancy and Constantine Sandis.
© 2015 John Wiley & Sons, Inc. Published 2015 by John Wiley & Sons, Inc.

We can also ask whether intending is itself something that can be done for a reason. If we suppose that it can, and that two people can act for the same reason, are we then to think that people can share an intention (an intending)? If so, does it makes sense to think of an intending as a mental state that two people can both be in at once? Or should we say that my intending is mine and yours is yours, and that a joint intention is not the same as a shared intention? (See here Stoutland, Chapter 18.)

2.

We suggested that there are two ways in which we speak of intentions. There are the so-called *prior intentions*, which are formed when the time for action has not yet arrived, and which once formed lie low, somehow, waiting for that time to come. One can set oneself up now to act later, in such a way that when the time comes there is no need, or call, for further deliberation, and one just starts off doing what one had earlier decided to do; as we might say, the decision was made long ago and there is no need to revisit it. Then there is the sense in which the action as we are doing it is intentional, which is not the same as being what we had a prior intention to do, since many intentional actions are not decided on in advance. Clearly, then, we need an account of the relation between what are called prior intentions and what are called *intentions in action*. Anscombe however starts her *Intention* (Chapter 11 here) by suggesting that there are *three* ways in which we speak of intention. When someone says "I am going to do such-and-such," this is an expression of a prior intention; we can also speak of an action as intentional, meaning by this to refer to an intention in action; and we can ask with what intention the thing was done, where this refers perhaps to something that lies in the future, to a purpose, or *further intention* with which it was done. Anscombe says that we want our account of intention to fit all these three, but that this does not mean that we need to treat them all at once. And she proceeds to start from the first, the prior intention, only to abandon that after several sections as fruitless, and to proceed to tackle the second.

As if these complexities were not enough, Davidson starts his paper "Intending" (Chapter 13 here) by saying that he is going to treat what he calls 'pure intention': intention without conscious deliberation or any overt consequence such as action. He supposes that, whatever this is, it must be present whenever anyone intends as a result of deliberation, or acts with an intention. His conclusion is that to purely intend to act in a certain way is to make an all-out unconditional judgment that acting in that way is desirable. What is interesting here is Davidson's determination to find some form of desire or belief that he can identify with a pure intending. It is as if intendings have got to be analyzable in terms of something more familiar, or at least already on the table. (See also Davidson 1970.)

Bratman (Chapter 14) takes the view that intending is neither a form of desiring nor a form of believing, nor a combination of the two. To intend to act in a certain way is to have a plan of action. That plan need not be formulated in advance, but it can be. There are significant advantages to having the ability to form plans; without this ability, we would be far less able to cope with the problems that life can throw up. Still, though one can act on a plan without having formed that plan in advance, the primary case for Bratman is the preconceived plan. When asked what it is to have a preconceived plan, his answer is that it is to be in a 'planning state'. So in a way his account of intending is similar to Davidson's; they agree that intentions are mental states of the agent, and only disagree about what sort of state they are. For Davidson, it is a specific form of belief-state, an all-out unconditional judgment; for Bratman, it is a state distinct from such other mental states as belief and desire.

This debate is conducted as if the primary case of intending is the prior intention. Whatever a prior intention is, an intention in action has got to be either just that state, or something completely different. Since that state can exist before the action starts, it is distinct from the action itself, and must therefore be something that, if it continues during the action, is, as it were, a distinct accompaniment to the action. Alternatively, the prior intention may cease when the action begins, so that an intention in action (as when one is doing what one intends to do, rather than just what one previously intended to do) somehow supplants the prior intention at the moment when the action starts. Both of these pictures of the relation between prior intention and intention in action are awkward. Perhaps we should be approaching the matter the other way round, trying to make sense of the intention in action first, and then somehow understand a prior intention in that light. This is the strategy of McDowell's chapter. McDowell (Chapter 15) does not think of the intention in action as a distinct mental accompaniment to the physical process that is the acting – an accompaniment that could in principle exist separately – and did so, before the action got started. For him, the action is at once mental and physical; it has two aspects, intentionality and physicality. (There is a history to this view; it can be found in Hegel – see chapters in Laitinen and Sandis 2010.)

This, of course, raises the difficulty in reverse: how could something that is a mere aspect of an action somehow have existed for a while before the action started? So McDowell's reversal of the Bratman/Davidson approach has its own awkwardness, as he would be the first to admit.

A different sort of difficulty derives from the fact that intending is something that we can do. Is intending to act itself an action, then? Perhaps not, but surely forming an intention is, or at least can be, an action. As Bratman would put it, sometimes one needs a plan, and one can settle down and make one. If so, is it something we can do for a reason? If it is, it seems to follow that the reasons to form the intention to act in a certain way can be different from the reasons to act in that way. Normally, of course, they won't be. Our reasons for writing this introduction today are the same reasons as the reasons we had yesterday to form the intention to write it today. But if forming an intention is an action, and the reasons for forming that intention can be different from the reasons to act in the way intended, various awkward questions arise. First, there is Kavka's now famous toxin puzzle (Chapter 17): why can't I form the intention to act tomorrow, and simultaneously form the intention to change that intention before the time for action comes? Second, is forming an intention itself something we can do either intentionally or unintentionally?

More plausible, perhaps, is the idea that forming a prior intention is something we can do, and do for a reason, but the reasons for which we form the intention will be such things as that we won't have time to work out a proper plan of action when the time comes – which is quite different from the reasons in favor of this plan rather than that one. So there will be the reasons for making some plan or other at all, and the reasons for making this plan rather than that one. The latter may be identical with the reasons for doing this action rather than that.

The Kavka problem cannot be escaped so easily.

3.

Another issue debated here is the question whether, and in what sense, there can be shared intentions. If prior intention, at least, is to be understood in terms of planning, can there be plans that are made by two people, in addition to those that are made only by one?

We tend to think of an intention in terms of cases where an individual, call her Mary, intends to go to the dentist. Going to the dentist is something that she does; it is an action done by an individual. But some actions seem to be done by two or more people acting together. When the team wins the game, it is not as if each member of the team wins. They together win the game. When David and John lift a piano, we cannot carve their action up into what David does and what John does. It is not as if David lifts half the piano and John lifts the other half. So it seems that, though there are many things that David does and John does not do and vice versa, while they are both lifting the piano, the only agent to whom the action of lifting the piano can be ascribed is a joint agent consisting somehow of David and John. Of course not all collective action is like this. Our editing of this volume was done in little bits, with Constantine making his contributions and Jonathan making his, going backwards and forwards. But again, this is quite unlike a relay race. There are cases and cases.

Having got this far, we can then ask about the intention to lift the piano, which David and John formed yesterday. Between then and now, they continuously intended to lift the piano today. Is this to be understood as a sort of combination of individual intentions (that is, of intentions one of which belongs to David and the other to John), or as an indivisible joint intention which they somehow share? Some thinkers feel a *reductive urge* when thinking about joint intention that they do not feel when thinking about joint action, leading them to try to find ways of dividing the joint intention up into separate bits each of which belongs either to David or to John, but not to both. Others fight this partial (and as they would say unmotivated) reductive tendency, trying to make as much sense of a joint intention as of a joint action. In between these two views would be one that supposed the two agents to be in distinct intending-states that have a common content, expressed with a 'we'; each of us intends that we shall together lift the piano.

This debate is in danger of assuming that if David and John do the action, David does it and so does John. And this pattern may not always be applicable. A committee may intend to act in a certain way even though none of its members intends to act in that way; there might even be actions that can *only* be done by the committee, so that the individual members *cannot* intend to do it.

4.

Finally, a reminder: we should be wary of simply asking of some action whether it was an intentional action or not. Every action has many true descriptions, and it may be intentional under some and not under others of those descriptions. So I say the words "I go from a corruptible to an incorruptible crown, where no disturbance can be." In saying these words, I say the last words of King Charles I before his death on the scaffold. But what if I know nothing of that? If we think of these as two descriptions of the same action, it seems that my action is intentional under one of them and not under the other. So no action is intentional (or unintentional) as such. This of course leaves it possible for there to be an action that is not intentional under any description whatever.

References

Davidson, D. (1970), "How is Weakness of the Will Possible?," in J. Feinberg (ed.), *Moral Concepts* (Oxford: Oxford University Press), 93–113; reprinted in Davidson's *Essays on Action and Events* (Oxford: Oxford University Press, 1980), 21–42.

Knobe, J., and Kelly, S. D. (2009), "Can One Act for a Reason without Acting Intentionally?," in Sandis (ed.), 169–183.

Laitinen, A., and Sandis, C. (eds.) (2010), *Hegel on Action* (Basingstoke: Palgrave Macmillan).

Further Reading

Anscombe, G. E. M. (1979), "Under a Description," *Noûs* 13 (2), 219–233; reprinted in her *Metaphysics and the Philosophy of Mind: Collected Papers Volume II* (Oxford: Blackwell, 1981), 208–219.

Austin, J. L. (1957), "A Plea for Excuses," *Proceedings of the Aristotelian Society* 57, 1–30.

Bratman, M. (2014), *Shared Agency: A Planning Theory of Acting Together* (Oxford: Oxford University Press).

Holton, R. (1999), "Intention and Weakness of Will," *Journal of Philosophy* 96 (5), 241–262.

Holton, R. (2008), "Partial Belief, Partial Intention," *Mind* 117 (465), 27–58.

Moran, R., and Stone, M. (2009), "Anscombe on Expression of Intention," in Sandis (ed.), 132–168.

Sandis, C. (ed.) (2009), *New Essays in the Explanation of Action* (Basingstoke: Palgrave Macmillan).

11

Intention §§1–9

G. E. M. Anscombe

1. Very often, when a man says 'I am going to do such-and-such', we should say that this was an expression of intention. We also sometimes speak of an action as intentional, and we may also ask with what intention the thing was done. In each case we employ a concept of 'intention'; now if we set out to describe this concept, and took only one of these three kinds of statement as containing our whole topic, we might very likely say things about what 'intention' means which it would be false to say in one of the other cases. For example, we might say 'Intention always concerns the future'. But an action can be intentional without being concerned with the future in any way. Realising this might lead us to say that there are various senses of 'intention', and perhaps that it is thoroughly misleading that the word 'intentional' should be connected with the word 'intention', for an action can be intentional without having any intention in it. Or alternatively we may be tempted to think that only actions done with certain further intentions ought to be called intentional. And we may be inclined to say that 'intention' has a different sense when we speak of a man's intentions *simpliciter* – i.e. what he intends to do – and of his intention *in* doing or proposing something – what he aims at in it. But in fact it is implausible to say that the word is equivocal as it occurs in these different cases.

Anscombe, G. E. M. (1957), *Intention §§1–9* (omitting 2 and parts of 8) (Cambridge, Mass.: Harvard University Press), 1–16. Copyright © 1957, 1963 by G. E. M. Anscombe. Reprinted by permission of the publisher.

Where we are tempted to speak of 'different senses' of a word which is clearly not equivocal, we may infer that we are in fact pretty much in the dark about the character of the concept which it represents. There is, however, nothing wrong with taking a topic piecemeal. I shall therefore begin my enquiry by considering expressions of intention.

[…]

3. We need a more fruitful line of enquiry than that of considering the verbal expression of intention, or of trying to consider what it is an expression of. For if we consider just the verbal expression of intention, we arrive only at its being a – queer – species of prediction; and if we try to look for what it is an expression of, we are likely to find ourselves in one or other of several dead ends, e.g.: psychological jargon about 'drives' and 'sets'; reduction of intention to a species of desire, i.e. a kind of emotion; or irreducible intuition of the meaning of 'I intend'.

Looking at the verbal expression of intention is indeed of use for avoiding these particular dead-ends. They are all reached in consequence of leaving the distinction between estimation of the future and expression of intention as something that just is intuitively obvious. A man says 'I am going for a walk' and we say 'that is an expression of intention, not a prediction'. But how do we know? If we asked him, no doubt he would tell us; but what does he know, and how? Wittgenstein has shown the impossibility of

Philosophy of Action: An Anthology, First Edition. Edited by Jonathan Dancy and Constantine Sandis.
© 2015 John Wiley & Sons, Inc. Published 2015 by John Wiley & Sons, Inc.

answering this question by saying 'He recognizes himself as having, or as having had, an intention of going for a walk, or as having meant the words as an expression of intention'. If this were correct, there would have to be room for the possibility that he misrecognizes. Further, when we remember having meant to do something, what memory reveals as having gone on in our consciousness is a few scanty items at most, which by no means add up to such an intention; or it simply prompts us to use the words 'I meant to …', without even a mental picture of which we judge the words to be an appropriate description. The distinction, then, cannot be left to be intuitively obvious, except where it is used to answer the question in what sense a man meant the form of words 'I am going to …' on a particular occasion.

We might attempt to make the distinction out by saying: an expression of intention is a description of something future in which the speaker is some sort of agent, which description he justifies (if he does justify it) by reasons for acting, sc. reasons why it would be useful or attractive if the description came true, not by evidence that it is true. But having got so far, I can see nowhere else to go along this line, and the topic remains rather mystifying. I once saw some notes on a lecture of Wittgenstein in which he imagined some leaves blown about by the wind and saying 'Now I'll go this way … now I'll go that way' as the wind blew them. The analogy is unsatisfactory in apparently assigning no role to these predictions other than that of an unnecessary accompaniment to the movements of the leaves. But it might be replied: what do you mean by an 'unnecessary' accompaniment? If you mean one in the absence of which the movements of the leaves would have been just the same, the analogy is certainly bad. But how do you know what the movements of the leaves would have been if they had not been accompanied by those thoughts? If you mean that you could calculate their movements just by knowing the speed and direction of the winds and the weight and other properties of the leaves, are you insisting that such calculations could not include calculations of their thoughts? – Wittgenstein was discussing free will when he produced this analogy; now the objection to it is not that it assigns a false role to our intentions, but only that it does not describe their role at all; this, however, was not its purpose. That

purpose was clearly *some* denial of free will, whether we take the wind as a symbol for the physical forces that affect us, or for God or fate. Now it may be that a correct description of the role of intention in our actions will not be relevant to the question of free will; in any case I suspect that this was Wittgenstein's view; therefore in giving this anti-freewill picture he was at liberty simply to leave the role of intention quite obscure.

Now our account of expressions of intention, whereby they are distinguished from estimates of the future, leaves one in very much the same position as does the picture of the wind blowing the leaves. People do in fact give accounts of future events in which they are some sort of agents; they do not justify these accounts by producing reasons why they should be believed but, if at all, by a different sort of reason; and these accounts are very often correct. This sort of account is called an expression of intention. It just does occur in human language. If the concept of 'intention' is one's quarry, this enquiry has produced results which are indeed not false but rather mystifying. What is meant by 'reason' here is obviously a fruitful line of enquiry; but I prefer to consider this first in connexion with the notion of intentional action.

4. I therefore turn to a new line of enquiry: how do we tell someone's intentions? or: what kind of true statements about people's intentions can we certainly make, and how do we know that they are true? That is to say, is it possible to find types of statement of the form 'A intends X' which we can say have a great deal of certainty? Well, if you want to say at least some true things about a man's intentions, you will have a strong chance of success if you mention what he actually did or is doing. For whatever else he may intend, or whatever may be his intentions in doing what he does, the greater number of the things which you would say straight off a man did or was doing, will be things he intends.

I am referring to the sort of things you would say in a law court if you were a witness and were asked what a man was doing when you saw him. That is to say, in a very large number of cases, your selection from the immense variety of true statements about him which you might make would coincide with what he could say he was doing, perhaps even without reflection, certainly without adverting to observation. I am sitting in a chair writing, and anyone grown to the age of reason in the same world would know this as soon as he saw me, and in general it would be his first account of what I was doing; if this were something he arrived at with difficulty, and what he knew straight off were precisely how I was affecting the acoustic properties of the room (to me a very recondite piece of information), then communication between us would be rather severely impaired.

In this way, with a view to shewing roughly the range of things to be discovered here, I can take a short cut here, and discuss neither how I am to select from the large number of true statements I could make about a person, nor what is involved in the existence of such a straight-off description as 'She is sitting in a chair and writing'. (Not that this does not raise very interesting questions. See *Philosophical Investigations*, p. 59, (*b*): 'I see a picture: it shows a man leaning on a stick and going up a steep path. How come? Couldn't it look like that if he were sliding downhill in that position? Perhaps a Martian would give that description.' *Et passim.*) All I am here concerned to do is note the fact: we can simply say 'Look at a man and say what he is doing' – i.e. say what would immediately come to your mind as a report to give someone who could not see him and who wanted to know what was to be seen in that place. In most cases what you will say is that the man himself knows; and again in most, though indeed in fewer, cases you will be reporting not merely what he is doing, but *an* intention of his – namely, to do that thing. What is more, if it is not an intention of his, this will for the most part be clear without asking him.

Now it can easily seem that in general the question what a man's intentions are is only authoritatively settled by him. One reason for this is that in general we are interested, not just in a man's intention *of* doing what he does, but in his intention *in* doing it, and this can very often not be seen from seeing what he does. Another is that in general the question whether he intends to do what he does just does not arise (because the answer is obvious); while if it does arise, it is rather often settled by asking him. And, finally, a man can form an intention which he then does nothing to carry out, either because he is prevented or because he changes his mind: but the intention itself can be complete, although it remains a purely interior thing. All this conspires to make us think that if we want to know a man's intentions it is into the contents of his mind, and only into these, that we must enquire; and hence, that if we wish to understand what intention is, we must be investigating something whose existence is purely in the sphere of the mind; and that although intention issues in actions, and the way this happens also presents interesting questions, still what physically takes place, i.e. what a man actually does, is the very last thing we need consider in our enquiry. Whereas I wish to say that it is the first. With this preamble to go on to the second head of the division that I made in §1: intentional action.

5. What distinguishes actions which are intentional from those which are not? The answer that I shall suggest is that they are the actions to which a certain sense of the question 'Why?' is given application; the sense is of course that in which the answer, if positive, gives a reason for acting. But this is not a sufficient statement, because the question "What is the relevant sense of the question 'Why?'" and "What is meant by 'reason for acting'?" are one and the same.

To see the difficulties here, consider the question, 'Why did you knock the cup off the table?' answered by 'I thought I saw a face at the window and it made me jump'. Now, so far I have only characterised reason for acting by opposing it to evidence for supposing the thing will take place – but the 'reason' here was not evidence that I was going to knock the cup off the table. Nor can we say that since it mentions something previous to the action, this will be a cause rather than a reason; for if you ask 'Why did you kill him?' the answer 'He killed my father' is surely a reason rather than a cause, but what it mentions is previous to the action. It is true that we don't ordinarily think of a case like giving a sudden start when we speak of a reason for acting. "Giving a sudden start", someone might say, "is not *acting* in the sense suggested by the expression 'reason for acting'. Hence, though indeed we readily say e.g. 'What was the reason for your starting so violently?' this is totally unlike 'What is your reason for excluding so-and-so from your will?' or 'What is your reason for sending for a taxi?'" But what *is* the difference? In neither case is the answer a piece of evidence. Why is giving a start or gasp not an 'action', while sending for a taxi, or crossing the road, is one? The answer cannot be "Because the answer to the question 'why?' may give a *reason* in the latter cases", for the answer may 'give a reason' in the former cases too; and we cannot say "Ah, but not a reason for *acting*"; we should be going round in circles. We need to find the difference between the two kinds of 'reason' without talking about 'acting'; and if we do, perhaps we shall discover what is meant by 'acting' when it is said with this special emphasis.

It will hardly be enlightening to say: in the case of the sudden start the 'reason' is a *cause*; the topic of causality is in a state of too great confusion; all we know is that this is one of the places where we do use the word 'cause'. But we also know that this is a rather strange case of causality; the subject is able to give the cause of a thought or feeling or bodily movement in the same kind of way as he is able to state the place of his pain or the position of his limbs.

Nor can we say: "– Well, the 'reason' for a movement is a cause, and not a reason in the sense of 'reason for acting', when the movement is involuntary; it is a reason, as opposed to a cause, when the movement is voluntary and intentional.' This is partly because in any case the object of the whole enquiry is really to delineate such concepts as the voluntary and the intentional, and partly because one can also give a 'reason' which is only a 'cause' for what is voluntary and intentional. E.g. "Why are you walking up and down like that?" – "It's that military band; it excites me". Or "What made you sign the document at last?" – "The thought: 'It is my duty' kept hammering away in my mind until I said to myself 'I can do no other', and so signed."

It is very usual to hear that such-and-such are what we *call* 'reasons for acting' and that it is 'rational' or 'what we *call* rational' to act for reasons; but these remarks are usually more than half moralistic in meaning (and moralism, as Bradley remarked, is bad for thinking); and for the rest they leave our conceptual problems untouched, while pretending to give a quick account. In any case, this pretence is not even plausible, since such remarks contain no hint of what it is to act for reasons.

6. To clarify the proposed account, "Intentional actions are ones to which a certain sense of the question

'why?' has application", I will both explain this sense and describe cases shewing the question *not* to have application. I will do the second job in two stages because what I say in the first stage of it will be of use in helping to explain the relevant sense of the question 'why?'.

This question is refused application by the answer: 'I was not aware I was doing that'. Such an answer is, not indeed a proof (since it may be a lie), but a claim, that the question 'Why did you do it (are you doing it)?', in the required sense, has no application. It cannot be plausibly given in every case; for example, if you saw a man sawing a plank and asked 'Why are you sawing that plank?', and he replied 'I didn't know I was sawing a plank', you would have to cast about for what he might mean. Possibly he did not know the word 'plank' before, and chooses this way of expressing that. But this question as to what he might mean need not arise at all – e.g. if you ask someone why he is standing on a hose-pipe and he says 'I didn't know I was'.

Since a single action can have many different descriptions, e.g. 'sawing a plank', 'sawing oak', 'sawing one of Smith's planks', 'making a squeaky noise with the saw', 'making a great deal of sawdust' and so on and so on, it is important to notice that a man may know that he is doing a thing under one description, and not under another. Not every case of this is a case of his knowing that he is doing one part of what he is doing and not another (e.g. he knows he is sawing but not that he is making a squeaky noise with the saw). He may know that he is sawing a plank, but not that he is sawing an oak plank or Smith's plank; but sawing an oak plank or Smith's plank is not something else that he is doing besides just sawing the plank that he is sawing. For this reason, the statement that a man knows he is doing X does not imply the statement that, concerning anything which is also his doing X, he knows that he is doing that thing. So to say that a man knows he is doing X is to give a description of what he is doing *under which* he knows it. Thus, when a man says 'I was not aware that I was doing X', and so claims that the question 'Why?' has no application, he cannot always be confuted by the fact that he was attentive to those of his own proceedings in which doing X consisted.

7. It is also clear that one is refusing application to the question 'Why?' (in the relevant sense) if one says:

'It was involuntary', even though the action was something of which one was aware. But I cannot use this as it stands, since the notion of the involuntary pretty obviously covers notions of exactly the type that a philosophical enquiry into intention ought to be elucidating.

Here, digressing for a moment, I should like to reject a fashionable view of the terms 'voluntary' and 'involuntary', which says they are appropriately used only when a person has done something untoward. If anyone is tempted by this view, he should consider that physiologists are interested in voluntary action, and that they are not giving a special technical sense to the word. If you ask them what their criterion is, they say that if they are dealing with a grown human they ask him, and if with an animal, they take movements in which the animal is e.g. trying to get at something, say food. That is, the movement by which a dog cocked its ear at a sudden sound would not be used as an example.

This does not mean that every description of action in which its voluntariness can be considered is of interest to physiologists. Of course they are only interested in bodily movements.

We can also easily get confused by the fact that 'involuntary' neither means simply non-voluntary, nor has an unproblematic sense of its own. In fact this pair of concepts is altogether very confusing. Consider the four following examples of the involuntary:

(a)   The peristaltic movement of the gut.
(b)   The odd sort of jerk or jump that one's whole body sometimes gives when one is falling asleep.
(c)   'He withdrew his hand in a movement of involuntary recoil.'
(d)   'The involuntary benefit I did him by a stroke I meant to harm him.'

Faced with examples like (c) and (d), how can I introduce 'It was involuntary' as a form for rejecting the question 'Why?' in the special sense which I want to elucidate – when the whole purpose of the elucidation is to give an account of the concept 'intentional'? Obviously I cannot. There is however a class of the things that fall under the concept 'involuntary', which it is possible to introduce without begging any questions or assuming that we understand notions of the very type I am professing to investigate. Example (b)

belongs to this class, which is a class of bodily movements in a purely physical description. Other examples are tics, reflex kicks from the knee, the lift of the arm from one's side after one has leaned heavily with it up against a wall.

8. What is required is to describe this class without using any notions like 'intended' or 'willed' or 'voluntary' and 'involuntary'. This can be done as follows: we first point out a particular class of things which are true of a man: namely the class of things which he *knows without observation*. E.g. a man usually knows the position of his limbs without observation. It is without observation, because nothing *shews* him the position of his limbs; it is not as if he were going by a tingle in his knee, which is the sign that it is bent and not straight. Where we can speak of separately describable sensations, having which is in some sense our criterion for saying something, then we can speak of observing that thing; but that is not generally so when we know the position of our limbs. Yet, without prompting, we *can say* it. I say however that we *know* it and not merely *can say* it, because there is a possibility of being right or wrong: there is point in speaking of knowledge only where a contrast exists between 'he *knows*' and 'he (merely) *thinks* he knows'. Thus, although there is a similarity between giving the position of one's limbs and giving the place of one's pain, I should wish to say that one ordinarily *knows* the position of one's limbs, without observation, but not that being able to say where one feels pain is a case of something known. This is not because the place of pain (the feeling, not the damage) has to be accepted by someone I tell it to; for we can imagine circumstances in which it is not accepted. As e.g. if you say that your foot, not your hand, is very sore, but it is your hand you nurse, and you have no fear of or objection to an inconsiderate handling of your foot, and yet you point to your foot as the sore part: and so on. But here we should say that it was difficult to guess what you could mean. Whereas if someone says that his leg is bent when it is straight, this may be surprising but is not particularly obscure. He is wrong in what he says, but not unintelligible. So I call this sort of being able to say 'knowledge' and not *merely* 'being able to say'.

Now the class of things known without observation is of general interest to our enquiry because the class of intentional actions is a sub-class of it. I have already said that 'I was not aware I was doing that' is a rejection of the question 'Why?' whose sense we are trying to get at; here I can further say 'I knew I was doing that, but only because I observed it' would also be a rejection of it. E.g. if one noticed that one operated the traffic lights in crossing a road.

[…]

9. I first, in considering expressions of intention, said that they were predictions justified, if at all, by a reason for acting, as opposed to a reason for thinking them true. So I here already distinguished a sense of 'Why?', in which the answer mentions evidence. 'There will be an eclipse tomorrow'. – 'Why?' 'Because …' – and an answer is the reason for thinking so. Or 'There was an ancient British camp here'. 'Why?' – and an answer is the reason for thinking so. But as we have already noted, an answer to the question 'Why?' which does not give reason for thinking the thing true does not *therefore* give a reason for acting. It may mention a cause, and this is far from what we want. However we noticed that there are contexts in which there is some difficulty in describing the distinction between a cause and a reason. As e.g. when we give a ready answer to the question 'Why did you knock the cup off the table?' – 'I saw such-and-such and *it made me jump.*'

Now we can see that the cases where this difficulty arises are just those where the cause itself *qua* cause (or perhaps one should rather say: the causation itself) is in the class of things known without observation.

12

Knowing What I Am Doing

Keith S. Donnellan

I

OTHER people come to know what I am doing by observing me, by asking me, or by more round-about means. In the case of my own intentional actions, such means of finding out are reserved for other people; it is absurd to suppose that I come to know what I am doing in these ways. This seems to be a logical or conceptual absurdity, as much so as the absurdity of supposing that I find out I am in pain by listening for my groans and seeing myself wince.

Of course there are occasions on which one might ask himself what he is doing. An absent-minded person may "forget what he is doing" and "find out" by observation. Seeing the telephone directory open to his friend's number, he infers that he was in the process of calling him up. But the conceptual point is preserved by noticing that the normal question to oneself is in the past tense, "Now what *was* I doing?" What one learns or remembers is how he had been occupied before the siege of absent-mindedness, not what he is now doing.

A sleepwalker or a person in a daze may awaken to his surroundings and discover what he is doing. He may be appalled to find himself strolling the streets in his nightclothes. But though this is something he is doing, it is not, of course, something he is doing intentionally.

Finally, because of the well-known fact that what I am doing may be intentional under one description, but not under another, it is possible for me to discover, in the same way others do, that some further description correctly applies. I may discover that I am not only drawing the bath water, but making the well run dry. The latter, however, would not then describe an intentional action.

II

Recently, several writers have said that one's own intentional actions are known to one without a basis in evidence or observation.[1] Now one very persuasive reason that could be given for this view is the conceptual point just mentioned, the absurdity of supposing that one can come to know what he is (intentionally) doing by watching himself in action. And the fact that people have often talked as if our knowledge of our own intentional actions were *necessarily* without observation suggests that they do have this conceptual point in mind. One point I would like to establish is that, if this is so, then the explanations that have been given of the expression 'knowledge without observation' are not wholly appropriate to the case of intentional actions.

The expressions 'knowledge without observation' and 'knowledge not based on evidence' can lead us to think of at least two quite distinct sorts of cases.

Donnellan, K. S. (1963), "Knowing What I Am Doing," *Journal of Philosophy* 60 (14), 401–409. Reprinted with permission of The Journal of Philosophy.

Philosophy of Action: An Anthology, First Edition. Edited by Jonathan Dancy and Constantine Sandis.

And it is important to see to which pattern intentional actions are being assimilated. In the first place, there are those first-person, present-tense, psychological statements which most philosophers accept as made without the sort of grounds that their third-person equivalents require. Reports of one's present headache, anger, beliefs, etc. are the usual examples. Should one's statements about what he is (intentionally) doing be assimilated to these?[2] In the second place, there are such examples as the kind Wittgenstein[3] and Anscombe (§8) supply: knowledge of the position of one's limbs and the ability most of us have to estimate roughly what time it is without the benefit of clocks. Is my knowledge of my own intentional actions rather like these cases? I should like to show that neither of these models is appropriate.

III

The difficulty of placing statements about one's intentional actions in the same category with reports of one's present headache or anger is that we many times must revise the former in a way in which we do not revise the latter. "What are you doing?" "I'm turning on the radio." "That's not the radio, that's the record player." "I *thought* I was turning on the radio." Or, to take a different possibility: "What are you doing?" "I am turning on the nine o'clock news." "You can't, the radio doesn't work." (To someone else) "I was trying to turn on the news, but the radio doesn't work." In these cases we would not continue to say that I *was* turning on the radio or the news; we move instead to a weaker statement. There does not seem to be the same possibility of revision concerning statements made by me about my present headache.

Many philosophers, in fact, would decline to say that I can *know* I have a headache precisely because my assertion that I do is immune to revision in the light of further discoveries. Where there is no contrast between states of knowledge and states of mere opinion, they would say that one cannot correctly speak of knowledge. But in the case of my own intentional actions, I can say sincerely that I am doing such and such although it is not true that I am doing it. Error is

possible; hence there have not been qualms about saying that, when I make no error, I *know*.[4]

IV

If we abandon the model of statements about one's headaches, anger, etc. as showing what we mean by the expressions 'knowledge without observation' and 'knowledge not based on evidence', the second sort of model fails for another reason.

Blind men sometimes have the ability to say when they are approaching obstacles, though, of course, they cannot see them. They can sometimes do this though they have nothing which acts as *evidence* for them. People sometimes have the ability to estimate with some accuracy the passage of time, though they do not consult their watches or count their heartbeats. Wittgenstein's example (§151 ff.) of knowing when one can continue a series before he has thought of the next member of it may also fall in this group.

In such circumstances we often have no hesitation about attributing knowledge to the people concerned. Yet it would seem correct to say of them that they do not know from observation or from evidence.

We may, of course, have an explanation of "how they do it." And without one we are perplexed, for example, about the ability of the blind man. But the explanations do not refer to items of evidence or to observations made. It might be discovered, for example, that minute changes in the sound of the blind man's tapping cane are produced in the proximity of obstacles in his path. It may further be found that without his cane he loses the ability to tell when he is approaching something. We then have the ingredients of an explanation. But though we explain his ability in this way, the blind man may not know how he does it. He may not know that the tip-tap of his cane is connected with the presence or absence of objects. He does not utilize the minute changes in sound as evidence from which to draw a conclusion. Nor is there anything here comparable to ordinary observation. The blind man does not listen for the changes in sound, nor would he justify his claim that he is approaching an object by reference to what he hears. We are dealing here with what are often called "cues," but "cues" in this sense are quite different from "clues." And they are also quite different from the cue that an actor listens for in order to know when to go on stage. For a cue, in this sense, may be operative without the individual realizing it or even suspecting it.

There is, very possibly, point to characterizing such cases as "knowledge without observation" and "knowledge not based on evidence." This will mean that the particular content of what is known is not the result of observation or consideration of evidence. The blind man does not say that there is an object in front of him or that his path is clear because he has observed this or because he has evidence that it is so.

But this should not lead us to suppose that evidence and observations are totally irrelevant. For even though the *content* of what is known on particular occasions does not result from them, *confidence* in what is known may well be based on evidence or observation. If asked how he knows, the blind man or the time-teller can only answer, "I just know." But if asked why he should be so confident that he is correct, he can very possibly refer to his record of past successes. He can show, by reference to evidence, that he has the power to say what is the case in these circumstances.

Anscombe's paradigm case of knowledge without observation seems to me to fall in with the examples just discussed. And, hence, she seems to me to assimilate knowledge of our own intentional actions to these cases. She points to the knowledge we can have of the position and movement of our limbs as showing what she means by "knowledge without observation" (§8). I know, without looking at them, as others usually must, that my legs are crossed or that my elbow is crooked. Anscombe must, of course, face the natural reply that *I feel* my legs to be crossed, that kinesthetic sensations inform me of this fact. After all when my arm is numb, when I have no such sensations, I cannot say without looking how it is disposed. But though she admits that having feeling in one's arm is perhaps a necessary condition of such knowledge, sensations are not data, she argues, from which we *infer* the position of our arm. I cannot back up my claim to know by any description of these sensations nor specify what sensations indicate what position.

Kinesthetic sensations may not be evidence of the position of our limbs. But this does not mean that they play no role. The sounds from the tapping of the blind man's cane are not evidence for him of the presence or absence of objects, but they figure in the explanation of "how he does it." So, too, kinesthetic sensations may figure in the explanation of how we know the position of our limbs.

Anscombe admits, of course, that we can be mistaken. (In fact she accepts that as a necessary condition for knowledge.) So too can the blind man and the time-teller be mistaken. But it does not follow from the fact that observation can show one mistaken that observation must be the basis for claiming to know. Knowledge can be claimed, as Wittgenstein points out (§324), on the basis of success.

V

There is, however, a significant difference between the sorts of cases just discussed and knowledge of one's own intentional actions. The fact from which we began was the logical absurdity of supposing that one learns of his own intentional actions by observing himself. But in the cases brought up in the last section no such *logical* absurdity is present. The blind man may lose his ability to detect objects in his special way. But he then merely reverts to feeling his way about, discovering by touch when he is confronted with an obstacle. The time-span detector *can* use a watch. One can lose the ability to tell without looking the movement and disposition of one's limbs temporarily under local anesthesia or when one's arm or leg has "gone to sleep." The very same thing, the position of a part of the body, may be known to one in either of two ways – through observation or without it.

In contrast, the argument for holding that the special knowledge we have of our own intentional actions is knowledge without observation rests on the *logical* absurdity of supposing that it is ever acquired in one's own case by looking at oneself. As paradigms to compare intentional actions to, the blind man, the time-span detector, and the example of the position and disposition of the body do not seem adequate. In the sense in which these are cases of knowledge without evidence or observation, the range of things that *could* be known without observation is vast. It is possible that someone have the ability to pick winners at the track without relying on form, past performance, etc. A long enough string of successes, I should imagine, would give us reason to say that he knew the winner and knew it, in this sense, without observation or evidence.

The group of cases we have been considering would, if taken as illustrating the status of our knowledge of our own intentional actions, lead us to think that knowing what we are doing intentionally without observation is a knack we might lose, just as the blind man may lose his special ability. But it rather seems otherwise: that being able to say what one is doing intentionally without observation is an essential, a logically necessary, condition on intentional action.

I think, in fact, that those writers who have stressed this aspect of intentional actions have all taken the thesis that we have knowledge without observation of our own intentional actions as a necessary truth. Anscombe, for example, makes it a defining condition in her analysis of intentional action: "Intentional actions are a sub-class of the events in a man's history which are known to him *not* just because he observes them" (op. cit., p. 24). Without adding some such qualifier as 'usually,' one would not, for example, say the same thing about the position of one's limbs, since under an anesthetic a person may have to revert to looking to know where his arm is.

VI

We are led by different considerations to reject the two sets of paradigms for knowledge without observation as applicable to the case of intentional actions. We reject the ones represented by first-person present-tense reports of pain and anger because of the fact that we often are forced to revise our statements about our intentional actions. We reject the ones represented by the ability of the blind man and our knowledge of the position of our limbs because we were in the first place led to use the term 'knowledge without observation' in reference to intentional actions through noting a logical absurdity in supposing that we could come by our knowledge of our own intentional actions through observation.

Yet at the same time we are pulled back toward our two sets of paradigm cases because each of them seems to exhibit one of the features of intentional actions. The absurdity of discovering by observation what one is doing intentionally appears to be like the absurdity of discovering that one is in pain by noting one's groans. The possibility of error and revision is seen in the blind man's ability to say without observation when he is confronted by an obstacle.

What this suggests is that knowledge of our own intentional actions is complex, that it divides up, so to speak, into an element of "direct awareness," to be assimilated to the examples of pain and anger, and other elements to which observation is relevant. Different aspects of our knowledge would account for the two characteristics we have all along noted. The absurdity of supposing that we come to have knowledge by observing ourselves stems from the fact that one element of an intentional action is the *intention* and this is not known to us through observation, just as our pains are not so known to us. The possibility of mistake and the need for revision arise from a quite different source. If I say that I am turning on the news, the radio may be, unknown to me, in a state of disrepair. But this is something I might have checked up upon by looking and probing.

An analogy for this possibility might be this: suppose that the affliction known as "sciatica" essentially involves both a characteristic pain and characteristic physiological aberrations. A person cannot then come to know that he has sciatica entirely through observation, for the pain will be something he cannot become aware of by such means. But he nevertheless can make a mistake, because he can err about the physiological conditions.

Consider this example of Anscombe's: "I shut my eyes and write something. I can say what I am writing. And what I am writing will almost always in fact appear on the paper. Now here it is clear that my capacity to say what is written is not derived from any observation" (op. cit., p. 53). I may make a mistake here: what I say I am writing on the paper may not appear on the paper. This is, also, as her example shows, something about which I often or usually have knowledge without observation. Even with my eyes open, my ability to say what is on the paper may not be the result of looking at what appears there. But there is not yet enough to make it *essentially* or *necessarily* a case of knowledge without observation, any more than knowing when obstacles are in front of him is *essentially* or *necessarily* knowledge without observation for the blind man. For he may have been told or struck his foot on them. And while I normally do not rely upon observation to know what appears on the paper when I write on it intentionally, I may have to. One is inclined to suppose that if one writes on a piece of paper with his eyes closed for the first time, he would usually then look to see what did appear on the paper. It may also be true that when I do know without observation in such cases, the explanation of "how I do it" involves the fact that it is an intentional action. But that does not make intentional actions *a species of* things known to a man without observation.

The fact that in such a case I *may* know without observation what has been written by me is a point about intentional actions quite distinct from the fact that it is absurd to suppose that I might come to know what I am doing intentionally by watching myself in action. The former is possibly the usual thing; the latter is necessarily always the case.

When I declare that I am turning on the news, there seem to be two things I am telling you: what I *mean* to be doing, my intention, which will exist whatever I am in fact doing; and what is getting done by me. What I *cannot* discover by observation is the former, and that is a conceptual impossibility; it is not merely that I have the ability to say without looking. What I may know without observation, in the sense in which the blind man knows something to be in front of him and we usually know the position of our limbs, is the latter.

If this account correct, then we have pulled apart the features of knowledge of intentional actions. We seem to support the traditional account, which, in Anscombe's words, holds that "what one knows as intentional action is only the intention ... and the rest is known by observation to be the *result*" (op. cit., p. 51).[5] Though we should modify the last clause to read, "... *may* be known by observation...."

VII

I want to question, however, the correctness of assimilating one aspect of knowledge of our intentional actions to the model of pain and anger. Is my relationship to my intention, to what I *mean* to be doing, that which I have to my pain? The absence of the possibility of a mistake suggests it. But there is a significant difference. In the case of a pain, what others see and go on in deciding that I am in pain are *expressions* of pain, the groans, winces, etc. But, those aspects of my behavior which others go on in ascertaining what I mean to be doing are not *expressions* of my intention. I cannot hold them in, the way I can suppress a groan or control my face when I am angry. Looking at my watch, turning some knobs on the machine, etc. may tell others that I mean to turn on the news (though the radio, without my knowing it, is broken). But these are not expressions of my intention as a groan is an expression of pain.

Secondly, reports of pain and anger are not reports of dispositions to exhibit the expressions of pain and anger. But if one says he is turning on the radio, we have been informed of what he means to be doing even if, e.g., the radio is broken or his arm paralyzed. And has he not told us of a disposition: if the radio is not broken and his arm not paralyzed, etc., the radio will be turned on by him?

If the thesis that "what one knows as intentional action is only the intention ... and the rest is known by observation to be the result" means that one aspect of our knowledge is to be assimilated to such paradigms as knowledge of one's own pain or anger and the other aspects to knowledge of external events, then it now seems to me wrong. If my intention, what I mean to do, were a mental event or state, then what others go on in ascribing it to me would have the status of an "outward expression." It could be controlled or repressed. And a dispositional analysis of my report of it would seem out of place.

If we call my ability to say what I mean to be doing, to report my intention, "knowledge without observation," it does not seem to fit in with either of the two sorts of paradigms we tried out for that expression. It seems rather to be a special case in its own right. And there, I think, lies the mystery. If intending is not an "inner state" such as pain or anger, how can it be *conceptually* absurd to suppose that we learn of our intentions by observation?

Notes

1. G. E. M. Anscombe, *Intention* (Ithaca, N.Y.: Cornell University Press, 1957); Stuart Hampshire and H. L. A. Hart, "Decision, Intention and Certainty," *Mind*, 67: 1–12; A. I. Melden, *Free Action* (London: Routledge and Kegan Paul, 1961), ch. IV; P. F. Strawson, *Individuals* (London: Methuen and Co., 1959), pp. 111–112.

2. Possibly Strawson comes closest to doing this when he says that such predicates as 'going for a walk', 'coiling a rope', 'playing ball', 'writing a letter', "… have the interesting characteristic of many P-predicates, that one does not, in general, ascribe them to oneself on the strength of observation, whereas one does ascribe them to others on the strength of observation" (111). P-predicates also include, e.g., 'is in pain'.

3. *Philosophical Investigations*, translated by G. E. M. Anscombe (New York: The Macmillan Co., 1953), §607 and sec. viii. Hereafter all references to Wittgenstein are to *Investigations*.

4. See, for example, Anscombe, *loc. cit.*

5. We have not, however, said anything to support the causal analysis of the traditional account.

13

Intending

Donald Davidson

Someone may intend to build a squirrel house without having decided to do it, deliberated about it, formed an intention to do it, or reasoned about it. And despite his intention, he may never build a squirrel house, try to build one, or do anything whatever with the intention of getting a squirrel house built. Pure intending of this kind, intending that may occur without practical reasoning, action, or consequence, poses a problem if we want to give an account of the concept of intention that does not invoke unanalysed episodes or attitudes like willing, mysterious acts of the will, or kinds of causation foreign to science.

When action is added to intention, for example when someone nails two boards together with the intention of building a squirrel house, then it may at first seem that the same problem does not necessarily arise. We are able to explain what goes on in such a case without assuming or postulating any odd or special events, episodes, attitudes or acts. Here is how we may explain it. Someone who acts with a certain intention acts for a reason; he has something in mind that he wants to promote or accomplish. A man who nails boards together with the intention of building a squirrel house must want to build a squirrel house, or think that he ought to (no doubt for further reasons),

and he must believe that by nailing the boards together he will advance his project. Reference to other attitudes besides wanting, or thinking he ought, may help specify the agent's reasons, but it seems that some positive, or pro-, attitude must be involved. When we talk of reasons in this way, we do not require that the reasons be good ones. We learn something about a man's reasons for starting a war when we learn that he did it with the intention of ending all wars, even if we know that his belief that starting a war would end all wars was false. Similarly, a desire to humiliate an acquaintance may be someone's reason for cutting him at a party though an observer might, in a more normative vein, think that that was no reason. The falsity of a belief, or the patent wrongness of a value or desire, does not disqualify the belief or desire from providing an explanatory reason. On the other hand, beliefs and desires tell us an agent's reasons for acting only if those attitudes are appropriately related to the action as viewed by the actor. To serve as reasons for an action, beliefs and desires need not be reasonable, but a normative element nevertheless enters, since the action must be reasonable in the light of the beliefs and desires (naturally it may not be reasonable in the light of further considerations).

What does it mean to say that an action, as viewed by the agent, is reasonable in the light of his beliefs and desires? Suppose that a man boards an airplane marked "London" with the intention of boarding an

Davidson, D. (1978), "Intending," in Y. Yovel and D. Reidel (eds.), *Philosophy of History and Action* (Jerusalem: The Magnes Press, The Hebrew University), 41–60. First published by D. Reidel. Reprinted with permission of Springer.

airplane headed for London, England. His reasons for boarding the plane marked "London" are given by his desire to board a plane headed for London, England, and his belief that the plane marked "London" is headed for London, England. His reasons explain why he intentionally boarded the plane marked "London." As it happens, the plane marked "London" was headed for London, Ontario, not London, England, and so his reasons cannot explain why he boarded a plane headed for London, England. They can explain why he boarded a plane headed for London, Ontario, but only when the reasons are conjoined to the fact that the plane marked "London" was headed for London, Ontario; and of course his reasons cannot explain why he intentionally boarded a plane headed for London, Ontario, since he had no such intention.[1]

The relation between reasons and intentions may be appreciated by comparing these statements:

1. His reason for boarding the plane marked "London" was that he wanted to board a plane headed for London, England, and he believed the plane marked "London" was headed for London, England.
2. His intention in boarding the plane marked "London" was to board a plane headed for London, England.

The first of these sentences entails the second, but not conversely. The failure of the converse is due to two differences between (1) and (2). First, from (2) it is not possible to reconstruct the specific pro-attitude mentioned in (1). Given (2), there must be some appropriate pro-attitude, but it does not have to be wanting. And second, the description of the action ("boarding the plane marked 'London' ") occupies an opaque context in (1), but a transparent context in (2). Thus "boarding the plane headed for London, Ontario" describes the same action as "boarding the plane marked 'London,' " since the plane marked "London" *was* the plane headed for London, Ontario. But substitution of "boarding the plane headed for London, Ontario" for "boarding the plane marked 'London' " will turn (1) false, while leaving (2) true. Of course the description of the intention in (2), like the description of the contents of the belief and pro-attitude in (1), occupies an opaque context.

Finally, there is this relation between statements with the forms of (1) and (2): although (2) does not entail (1), if (2) is true, *some* statement with the form of (1) is true (with perhaps another description of the action, and with an appropriate pro-attitude and belief filled in). Statement (1), unlike (2), must describe the agent's action in a way that makes clear a sense in which the action was reasonable in the light of the agent's reasons. So we can say, if an agent does A with the intention of doing B, there is some description of A which reveals the action as reasonable in the light of reasons the agent had in performing it.

When is an action (described in a particular way) reasonable in the light of specific beliefs and pro-attitudes? One way to approach the matter is through a rather abstract account of practical reasoning. We cannot suppose that whenever an agent acts intentionally he goes through a process of deliberation or reasoning, marshalls evidence and principles, and draws conclusions. Nevertheless, if someone acts with an intention, he must have attitudes and beliefs from which, had he been aware of them and had the time, he *could* have reasoned that his action was desirable (or had some other positive attribute). If we can characterize the reasoning that would serve, we will in effect have described the logical relations between descriptions of beliefs and desires, and the description of an action when the former give the reasons with which the latter was performed. We are to imagine, then, that the agent's beliefs and desires provide him with the premises of an argument. In the case of belief, it is clear at once what the premise is. Take an example: someone adds sage to the stew with the intention of improving the taste. We may describe his belief: He believes that adding sage to the stew will improve its taste. So his corresponding premise is: Adding sage to the stew will improve its taste.

The agent's pro-attitude is perhaps a desire or want; let us suppose he wants to improve the taste of the stew. But what is the corresponding premise? If we were to look for the proposition toward which his desire is directed, the proposition he wants true, it would be something like: He does something that improves the taste of the stew (more briefly: He improves the taste of the stew). This cannot be his premise, however, for nothing interesting follows from the two premises: Adding sage to the stew will improve its taste, and the agent improves the taste of the stew. The trouble is that the attitude of *approval* which the agent has toward the second proposition has been left out. It cannot be put back in by making the premise "The agent wants to improve the taste of the stew": we do not want a *description* of his desire, but an *expression* of it in a form in which he might use it to arrive at an action. The natural expression of his desire is, it seems to me, evaluative in form; for example, "It is desirable to improve the taste of the stew," or "I ought to improve the taste of the stew." We may suppose different pro-attitudes are expressed with other evaluative words in place of "desirable."

There is no short proof that evaluative sentences express desires and other pro-attitudes in the same way that the sentence "Snow is white" expresses the belief that snow is white. But the following consideration will perhaps help show what is involved. If someone who knows English says honestly "Snow is white," then he believes snow is white. If my thesis is correct, someone who says honestly "It is desirable that I stop smoking" has some pro-attitude towards his stopping smoking. He feels some inclination to do it; in fact he will do it if nothing stands in the way, he knows how, and he has no contrary values or desires. Given this assumption, it is reasonable to generalize: if explicit value judgments represent pro-attitudes, all pro-attitudes may be expressed by value judgments that are at least implicit.

This last stipulation allows us to give a uniform account of acting with an intention. If someone performs an action of type A with the intention of performing an action of type B, then he must have a pro-attitude toward actions of type B (which may be expressed in the form: an action of type B is good (or has some other positive attribute)) and a belief that in performing an action of type A he will be (or probably will be) performing an action of type B (the belief may be expressed in the obvious way). The expressions of the belief and desire entail that actions of type A are, or probably will be, good (or desirable, just, dutiful, etc.). The description of the action provided by the phrase substituted for "A" gives the description under which the desire and the belief rationalize the action. So to bring things back to our example, the desire to improve the taste of the stew and the belief that adding sage to the stew will improve its taste serve to rationalize an action described as "adding sage to the stew". (This more or less standard account of practical reasoning will be radically modified presently.)

There must be such rationalizing beliefs and desires if an action is done for a reason, but of course the presence of such beliefs and desires when the action is done does not suffice to insure that what is done is done with the appropriate intention, or even with any intention at all. Someone might want tasty stew and believe sage would do the trick and put in sage thinking it was parsley; or put in sage because his hand was joggled. So we must add that the agent put in the sage because of his reasons. This "because" is a source of trouble; it implies, so I believe, and have argued at length, the notion of cause. But not any causal relation will do, since an agent might have attitudes and beliefs that would rationalize an action, and they might cause him to perform it, and yet because of some anomaly in the causal chain, the action would not be intentional in the expected sense, or perhaps in any sense.[2]

We end up, then, with this incomplete and unsatisfactory account of acting with an intention: an action is performed with a certain intention if it is caused in the right way by attitudes and beliefs that rationalize it.[3]

If this account is correct, then acting with an intention does not require that there be any mysterious act of the will or special attitude or episode of willing. For the account needs only desires (or other pro-attitudes), beliefs and the actions themselves. There is indeed the relation between these, causal or otherwise, to be analysed, but that is not an embarrassing entity that has to be added to the world's furniture. We would not, it is true, have shown how to *define* the concept of acting with an intention; the reduction is not definitional but ontological. But the ontological reduction, if it succeeds, is enough to answer many puzzles about the relation between the mind and the body, and to explain the possibility of autonomous action in a world of causality.

This brings me back to the problem I mentioned at the start, for the strategy that appears to work for acting with an intention has no obvious application to pure intending, that is, intending that is not necessarily accompanied by action. If someone digs a pit with the intention of trapping a tiger, it is perhaps plausible that no entity at all, act, event or disposition, corresponds to the noun phrase "the intention of trapping a tiger" – this is what our survey has led us to hope. But it is not likely that if a man has the intention of trapping a tiger, his intention is not a state, disposition or attitude of some sort. Yet if this is so, it is quite incredible that this state or attitude (and the connected event or act of *forming an intention*) should play no role in acting with an intention. Our inability to give a satisfactory account of pure intending on the basis of our account of intentional action thus reflects back on the account of intentional action itself. And I believe the account I have outlined will be seen to be incomplete when we have an adequate analysis of pure intending.

Of course, we perform many intentional actions without forming an intention to perform them, and often intentional action is not preceded by an intention. So it would not be surprising if something were present in pure intending that is not always present in intentional action. But it would be astonishing if that extra element were foreign to our understanding of intentional action. For consider some simple action, like writing the word "action." Some temporal segments of this action are themselves actions: for example, first I write the letter "a." This I do with the intention of initiating an action that will not be complete until I have written the rest of the word. It is hard to see how the attitude towards the complete act which I have as I write the letter "a" differs from the pure intention I may have had a moment before. To be sure, my intention has now begun to be realized, but why should that necessarily change my attitude? It seems that in any intentional action that takes much time, or involves preparatory steps, something like pure intending must be present.

We began with pure intending – intending without conscious deliberation or overt consequence – because it left no room for doubt that intending is a state or event separate from the intended action or the reasons that prompted the action. Once the existence of pure intending is recognized, there is no reason not to allow that intention of exactly the same kind is also present when the intended action eventuates. So though I may, in what follows, seem sometimes to concentrate on the rather special case of unfulfilled intentions, the subject in fact is all intending –

intending abstracted from a context which may include any degree of deliberation, and any degree of success in execution. Pure intending merely shows that there is something there to be abstracted.

What success we had in coping with the concept of intentional action came from treating talk of the intention with which an action is done as talk of beliefs, desires, and actions. This suggests that we try treating pure intentions – intendings abstracted from normal outcomes – as actions, beliefs or pro-attitudes of some sort. The rest of this paper is concerned with these possibilities.

Is pure intending an action? It may be objected that intending to do something is not a change or event of any kind, and so cannot be something the agent does. But this objection is met by an adjustment in the thesis; we should say that the action is forming an intention, while pure intending is the state of an agent who has formed an intention (and has not changed his mind). Thus all the weight is put on the idea of forming an intention. It will be said that most intentions are not formed, at least if forming an intention requires conscious deliberation or decision. What we need then is the broader and more neutral concept of coming to have an intention – a change that may take place so slowly or unnoticed that the agent cannot say when it happens. Still, it is an event, and we could decide to call it an action, or at least something the agent does.

I see no reason to reject this proposal; the worst that can be said of it is that it provides so little illumination. The state of intention just is what results from coming to have an intention – but what sort of a state is it? The coming to have an intention we might try connecting with desires and beliefs as we did other intentional actions (again with a causal chain that works "in the right way"). But the story does not have the substantial quality of the account of intentional action because the purported action is not familiar or observable, even to the agent himself.

Another approach focuses on overt speech acts. *Saying* that one intends to do something, or that one will do it, is undeniably an action, and it has some of the characteristics of forming an intention. Saying, under appropriate circumstances, that one intends to do something, or that one will do it, can commit one to doing it; if the deed does not follow, it is appropriate to ask for an explanation. Actually to identify saying one intends to do something with forming an intention would be to endorse a sort of performative theory of intention; just as saying one promises to do something may be promising to do it, so saying one intends to do it may be intending (or forming the intention) to do it. Of course one may form an intention without saying anything aloud, but this gap may be filled with the notion of speaking to oneself, "saying in one's heart."[4] A variant theory would make forming an intention like (or identical with) addressing a command to oneself.

I think it is easy to see that forming an intention is quite different from saying something, even to oneself, and that intending to do something is quite different from having said something. For one thing, the performative character of commands and promises which makes certain speech acts surprisingly momentous depends on highly specific conventions, and there are no such conventions governing the formation of intentions. Promising involves assuming an obligation, but even if there are obligations to oneself, intending does not normally create one. If an agent does not do what he intended to do, he does not normally owe himself an explanation or apology, especially if he simply changed his mind; yet this is just the case that calls for explanation or apology when a promise has been made to another and broken. A command may be disobeyed, but only while it is in force. But if an agent does not do what he intended because he has changed his mind, the original intention is no longer in force. Perhaps it is enough to discredit these theories to point out that promising and commanding, as we usually understand them, are necessarily public performances, while forming an intention is not. Forming an intention may be an action, but it is not a performance, and having an intention is not generally the aftermath of one.

None of this is to deny that saying "I intend to do it" or "I will do it" is much like, or on occasion identical with, promising to do it. If I say any of these things in the right context, I entitle a hearer to believe I will do it, and since I know I entitle him to believe it, I entitle him to believe I believe I will do it. Perhaps a simpler way to put it is this: if I say "I intend to do it" or "I will do it" or "I promise to do it" under certain conditions, then I *represent myself* as believing that I

will. I may not believe I will, I may not intend that my hearer believe I will, but I have given him ground for complaint if I do not. These facts suggest that if I not only say "I intend" or "I will" in such a way as to represent myself as believing I will, but I am sincere as well, then my sincerity guarantees both that I intend to do it and that I believe I will. Some such line of argument has led many philosophers to hold that intending to do something entails believing one will, and has led a few philosophers to the more extreme view that to intend to do something is identical with a sort of belief that one will.

Is intending to act a belief that one will? The argument just sketched does not even show that intending implies belief. The argument proves that a man who sincerely says "I intend to do it" or "I will do it" under certain conditions must believe he will do it. But it may be the saying, not the intention, that implies the belief. And I think we can see this is the case. The trouble is that we have asked the notion of sincerity to do two different pieces of work. We began by considering cases where, by saying "I intend to" or "I will," I entitle a hearer to believe I will. And here it is obvious that if I am sincere, if things are as I represent them, then I must believe I will. But it is an assumption unsupported by the argument that any time I sincerely say I intend to do something I must believe I will do it, for sincerity in this case merely requires that I know I intend to do it. We are agreed that there are cases where sincerity in the utterer of "I intend to" requires him to believe he will, but the argument requires that these cases include all those in which the speaker knows or believes he intends to do it.

Once we have distinguished the question how belief is involved in avowals of intention from the question how belief is involved in intention, we ought to be struck with how dubious the latter connection is.

It is a mistake to suppose that if an agent is doing something intentionally, he must know that he is doing it. For suppose a man is writing his will with the intention of providing for the welfare of his children. He may be in doubt about his success, and remain so to his death; yet in writing his will he may in fact be providing for the welfare of his children, and if so, he is certainly doing it intentionally. Some sceptics may think this example fails because they refuse to allow that a man may *now* be providing for the welfare of his children if that welfare includes events yet to happen. So here is another example: in writing heavily on this page I may be intending to produce ten legible carbon copies. I do not know, or believe with any confidence, that I am succeeding. But if I am producing ten legible carbon copies, I am certainly doing it intentionally. These examples do not prove that pure intending may not imply belief, for the examples involve acting with an intention. Nevertheless, it is hard to imagine that the point does not carry over to pure intending. As he writes his will, the man not only is acting with the intention of securing the welfare of his children, he also intends to secure the welfare of his children. If he can be in doubt whether he is now doing what he intends, surely he can be in doubt whether he will do what he intends.

The thesis that intending implies believing is sometimes defended by claiming that expressions of intention are generally incomplete or elliptical. Thus the man writing his will should be described as intending to try to secure the welfare of his children, not as intending to secure it, and the man with the carbon paper is merely intending to try to produce his copies. The phrases sound wrong: we should be much more apt to say he *is* trying, and intends to do it. But where the action is entirely in the future, we do sometimes allow that we intend to try, and we see this as more accurate than the bald statement of intention when the outcome is sufficiently in doubt. Nevertheless, I do not think the claim of ellipsis can be used to defend the general thesis.

Without doubt many intentions are conditional in form – one intends to do something only if certain conditions are satisfied – and without doubt we often suppress mention of the conditions for one reason or another. So elliptical statements of intention are common. Grice gives us this exchange:

X. I intend to go to that concert on Tuesday.
Y. You will enjoy that.
X. I may not be there.
Y. I am afraid I don't understand.
X. The police are going to ask me some awkward questions on Tuesday afternoon, and I may be in prison by Tuesday evening.
Y. Then you should have said to begin with, "I intend to go to the concert if I am not in prison," or, if you wished to be more reticent, something like, "I should

probably be going," or "I hope to go," or, "I aim to go," or, "I intend to go if I can."[5]

Grice does not speak of ellipsis here, but he does think that this example, and others like it, make a strong case for the view that "X intends to do A" is true, when "intends" is used in the *strict* sense, only if X is sure that he will do A. The man in the example must intend *something*, and so if we knew what it was, we could say that his remark "I intend to go to the concert" was elliptical for what he would have said if he had used "intend" in the strict sense. What would he have said? "I hope to go" is not more accurate about the intention, since it declares no intention at all; similarly for "I aim to go" and "I should probably be going." "I intend to go if I can" is vague and general given the particularity of X's doubts, but there seems something worse wrong with it. For if an agent cannot intend what he believes to be impossible, then he asserts neither more nor less by saying "I intend to do it if I can" than he would by saying "I intend to do it." How about "I intend to go to the concert if I am not in prison"? Intuitively, this comes closest to conveying the truth about the situation as X sees it. But is it *literally* more accurate? It is hard to see how. On the view Grice is arguing for, if X said in the strict sense, and honestly, "I intend to be at the concert," he would imply that he believed he would be there. If X said in the strict sense, and honestly, "I intend to be at the concert if I am not in jail," he would imply that he believed he would be at the concert if he were not in jail. Now obviously the first belief implies the second, but is not implied by it, and so an expression of the second belief makes a lesser claim, and may be thought to be more accurate. Of course, the stronger claim cannot, by its contents, lead Y into error about what X will do, for whether X says he will be at the concert, or only that he will be there if he is not in jail, both X and Y know X will not be at the concert if he is in jail. Where Y might be misled is with respect to what X believes he will do, and hence intends, if the thesis we are examining is true. For on the thesis, "I intend to be at the concert if I am not in jail" implies a weaker belief than "I intend to be at the concert." If this is right, then greater accuracy still would result from further provisos, since X also does not believe he will be at the concert if he changes his mind, or if something besides imprisonment prevents him. We are thus led further and further toward the nearly empty "I intend to do it if nothing prevents me, if I don't change my mind, if nothing untoward happens." This tells us almost nothing about what the agent believes about the future, or what he will in fact do.

I think X spoke correctly and accurately, but misleadingly, when he said "I intend to go to the concert." He could have corrected the impression while still being accurate by saying "I now intend to go to the concert, but since I may be put in jail, I may not be there." A man who says "I intend to be there, but I may not be" does not contradict himself, he is at worst inscrutable until he says more. We should realize there is something wrong with the idea that most statements of intention are elliptical until tempered by our doubts about what we shall in fact do when it is noticed that there is no satisfactory *general* method for supplying the more accurate statement for which the original statement went proxy. And the reason is clear: there can be no finite list of things we think might prevent us from doing what we intend, or of circumstances that might cause us to stay our hand. If we are reasonably sure something will prevent us from acting, this does, perhaps, baffle intention, but if we are simply uncertain, as is often the case, intention is not necessarily dulled. We can be clear what it is we intend to do while being in the dark as to the details, and therefore the pitfalls. If this is so, being more accurate about what we intend cannot be a matter of being more accurate about what we believe we will bring off.

There are genuine conditional intentions, but I do not think they come in the form "I intend to do it if I can" or "if I don't change my mind." Genuine conditional intentions are appropriate when we explicitly consider what to do in various contingencies; for example, someone may intend to go home early from a party if the music is too loud. If we ask for the difference between conditions that really do make the statement of an intention more accurate, and bogus conditions like "if I can" or "if nothing comes up" or "if I don't change my mind," it seems to me clear that the difference is this: bona fide conditions are ones that are reasons for acting that are contemporary with the intention. Someone may not like loud music now, and that may be why he now intends to go home early from the party if the music is too loud. His not

being able to go home early is not a reason for or against his going home early, and so it is not a relevant condition for an intention, though if he believes he cannot do it, that may prevent his having the intention. Changing his mind is a tricky case, but in general someone is not apt to view a possible future change of intention as a reason to modify his present intention unless he thinks the future change will itself be brought about by something he would now consider a reason.

The contrast that has emerged between the circumstances we do sometimes allow to condition our intentions and the circumstances we would allow if intentions implied the belief that we will do what we intend seems to me to indicate pretty conclusively that we do not necessarily believe we will do what we intend to do, and that we do not state our intentions more accurately by making them conditional on all the circumstances in whose presence we think we would act.

These last considerations point to the strongest argument against identifying pure intending with the belief one will do what one intends. This is that reasons for intending to do something are in general quite different from reasons for believing one will do it. Here is why I intend to reef the main: I see a squall coming, I want to prevent the boat from capsizing, and I believe that reefing the main will prevent the boat from capsizing. I would put my reasons for intending to reef the main this way: a squall is coming, it would be a shame to capsize the boat, and reefing the main will prevent the boat from capsizing. But these reasons for intending to reef the main in themselves give me no reason to believe I will reef the main. Given a lot more assumptions, that a squall is coming may be a reason to believe I believe a squall is coming, and given some even more fancy assumptions, that it would be a shame to capsize the boat may be a reason to believe I want to prevent the boat from capsizing. And given that I have these beliefs and desires, it may be reasonable to suppose I intend to reef the main, and will in fact do so. So there may be a loose connection between reasons of the two kinds, but they are not at all identical (individual reasons may be the same, but a smallest natural set of reasons that supports the intention to act cannot be a set that supports the belief that the act will take place).

It is often maintained that an intention is a belief not arrived at by reasoning from evidence, or that an intention is a belief about one's future action that differs in some other way in its origin from an ordinary prediction. But such claims do not help the thesis. How someone arrived at a belief, what reasons he would give in support of it, what sustains his faith, these are matters that are simply irrelevant to the question what constitute reasons for the belief; the former events are accidents that befall a belief, and cannot change its logical status without making it a new belief.

Is intending to do something the same as wanting to do it? Clearly reasons for intending to do something are very much like reasons for action, indeed one might hold that they are exactly the same except for time. As John Donne says, "To will implies delay," but we may reduce the delay to a moment. I am writing the letter "a" of "action," and I intend to write the letter "c" as soon as I finish the "a." The reason I intend to write the letter "c" as soon as I finish the "a" is that I want to write the word "action," and I know that to do this I must, after writing the letter "a," write the letter "c." Now I have finished the "a" and have begun "c"! What is my reason for writing the "c"? It is that I want to write the word "action," and I know that to do this I must ... So far the reasons sound identical, but if we look closer a tiny difference will emerge. When I am writing the "a" I intend to write the "c" in just a moment, and part of my reason is that I believe this moment looms in the immediate future; when I am writing the "c," my reasons include the belief that *now* is the time to write the "c" if I am to write "action," as I wish to. Aristotle sometimes neglects this difference and as a result says things that sound fatuous. He is apt to give as an example of practical reasoning something of this sort: I want to be warm, I believe a house will keep me warm, straightway I build a house. It is an important doctrine that the conclusion of a piece of practical reasoning may be an action; it is also important that the conclusion may be the formation of an intention to do something in the future.

Now I would like to draw attention to an aspect of this picture of what it is like to form an intention that seems to make for a difficulty. Consider again a case of intentional action. I want to eat something sweet, that is, I hold that my eating something sweet is desirable. I believe this candy is sweet, and so my eating this candy will be a case of my eating something sweet, and I conclude that my eating this candy is desirable. Since nothing stands in the way, I eat the candy – the conclusion is the action. But this also means I could express the conclusion by using a demonstrative reference to the action: "This action of mine, this eating by me of this candy now, is desirable." What seems so important about the possibility of a demonstrative reference to the action is that it is a case where it makes sense to couple a value judgment directly to action. My evaluative reason for acting was, "My eating something sweet is desirable." But of course this cannot mean that any action of mine whatsoever that is an eating of something sweet is something it makes sense to do – my judgment merely deals with actions in so far as they are sweet-consuming. Some such actions, even all of them, may have plenty else wrong with them. It is only when I come to an actual action that it makes sense to judge it as a whole as desirable or not; up until that moment there was no object with which I was acquainted to judge. Of course I can still say of the completed action that it is desirable in so far as it is this or that, but in choosing to perform it I went beyond this; my choice represented, or perhaps was, a judgment that the action itself was desirable.

And now the trouble about pure intending is that there is no action to judge simply good or desirable. All we can judge at the stage of pure intending is the desirability of actions of a sort, and actions of a sort are generally judged on the basis of the aspect that defines the sort. Such judgments, however, do not always lead to reasonable action, or we would be eating everything sweet we could lay our hands on (as Anscombe pointed out in *Intention*).[6]

The major step in clearing up these matters is to make a firm distinction between the kind of judgment that corresponds to a desire like wanting to eat something sweet and the kind of judgment that can be the conclusion of a piece of practical reasoning – that can correspond to an intentional action.[7] The first sort of judgment is often thought to have the form of a law: any action that is an eating of something sweet is desirable. If practical reasoning is deductive, this is what we should expect (and it seems to be how Aristotle and Hume, for example, thought of practical reasoning). But there is a fundamental objection to this idea, as can be seen when we consider an action that has both a desirable and an undesirable aspect. For suppose the propositional expression of a desire to eat something sweet were a universally quantified conditional. While holding it desirable to eat something sweet, we may also hold that it is undesirable to eat something poisonous. But one and the same object may be sweet and poisonous, and so one and the same action may be the eating of something sweet and something poisonous. Our evaluative principles, which seem consistent, can then lead us to conclude that the same action is both desirable and undesirable. If undesirable actions are not desirable, we have derived a contradiction from premises all of which are plausible. The cure is to recognize that we have assigned the wrong form to evaluative principles. If they are judgments to the effect that *in so far as* an action has a certain characteristic it is good (or desirable, etc.), then they must not be construed in such a way that detachment works, or we will find ourselves concluding directly that the action is simply desirable when all that is warranted is the conclusion that it is desirable in a certain respect. Let us call judgments that actions are desirable in so far as they have a certain attribute *prima facie* judgments.

Prima facie judgments cannot be directly associated with actions, for it is not reasonable to perform an action merely because it has a desirable characteristic. It is a reason for acting that the action is believed to have some desirable characteristic, but the fact that the action is performed represents a further judgment that the desirable characteristic was enough to act on – that other considerations did not outweigh it. The judgment that corresponds to, or perhaps is identical with, the action cannot, therefore, be a *prima facie* judgment; it must be an all-out or unconditional judgment which, if we were to express it in words, would have a form like "This action is desirable."

It can now be seen that our earlier account of acting with an intention was misleading or at least incomplete in an important respect. The reasons that determine the description under which an action is intended do not allow us to *deduce* that the action is simply worth performing; all we can deduce is that the action has a feature that argues in its favour. This is enough, however, to allow us to give the intention with which the action was performed. What is misleading is that the reasons that enter this account

do not generally constitute all the reasons the agent considered in acting, and so knowing the intention with which someone acted does not allow us to reconstruct his actual reasoning. For we may not know how the agent got from his desires and other attitudes – his *prima facie* reasons – to the conclusion that a certain action was desirable.[8]

In the case of intentional action, at least when the action is of brief duration, nothing seems to stand in the way of an Aristotelian identification of the action with a judgment of a certain kind – an all-out, unconditional judgment that the action is desirable (or has some other positive characteristic). The identification of the action with the conclusion of a piece of practical reasoning is not essential to the view I am endorsing, but the fact that it can be made explains why, in our original account of intentional action, what was needed to relate it to pure intending remained hidden.

In the case of pure intending, I now suggest that the intention simply is an all-out judgment. Forming an intention, deciding, choosing and deliberating are various modes of arriving at the judgment, but it is possible to come to have such a judgment or attitude without any of these modes applying.

Let me elaborate on this suggestion and try to defend it against some objections. A few pages ago I remarked that an all-out judgment makes sense only when there is an action present (or past) that is known by acquaintance. Otherwise (I argued) the judgment must be general, that is, cover all actions of a certain sort, and among these there are bound to be actions some of which are desirable and some not. Yet an intention cannot single out a particular action in an intelligible sense, since it is directed to the future. The puzzle arises, I think, because we have overlooked an important distinction. It would be mad to hold that any action of mine in the immediate future that is the eating of something sweet would be desirable. But there is nothing absurd in my judging that any action of mine in the immediate future that is the eating of something sweet would be desirable *given the rest of what I believe about the immediate future*. I do not believe I will eat a poisonous candy, and so that is not one of the actions of eating something sweet that my all-out judgment includes. It would be a mistake to try to improve the statement of my intention by saying

"I intend to eat something sweet, provided it isn't poisonous." As we saw, this is a mistake because if this is the road I must travel, I will never get my intentions right. There are *endless* circumstances under which I would not eat something sweet, and I cannot begin to foresee them all. The point is, I do not believe anything will come up to make my eating undesirable or impossible. That belief is not part of what I intend, but an assumption without which I would not have the intention. The intention is not conditional in form; rather, the existence of the intention is conditioned by my beliefs.

I intend to eat a hearty breakfast tomorrow. You know, and I know, that I will not eat a hearty breakfast tomorrow if I am not hungry. And I am not certain I will be hungry, I just think I will be. Under these conditions it is not only not more accurate to say "I intend to eat a hearty breakfast if I'm hungry," it is *less* accurate. I have the second intention as well as the first, but the first implies the second, and not vice versa, and so the first is a more complete account of my intentions. If you knew only that I intended to eat a hearty breakfast if I was hungry, you would not know that I believe I will be hungry, which is actually the case. But you might figure this out if you knew I intend to eat a hearty breakfast tomorrow.

I think this view of the matter explains the trouble we had about the relation between intending to do something and believing one will – why, on the one hand, it is so strange to say "I intend to do it but perhaps I won't," and yet is so impossible to increase the accuracy of statements of intention by making the content of the intention conditional on how things turn out. The explanation is that the intention assumes, but does not contain a reference to, a certain view of the future. A present intention with respect to the future is in itself like an interim report: given what I now know and believe, here is my judgment of what kind of action is desirable. Since the intention is based on one's best estimate of the situation, it merely distorts matters to say the agent intends to act in the way he does only if his estimate turns out to be right. A present intention does not need to be anything like a resolve or a commitment (though *saying* one intends to do something may sometimes have this character). My intention is based on my present view of the situation; there is

no reason in general why I should act as I now intend if my present view turns out to be wrong.

We can now see why adding "if I can" never makes the statement of an intention more accurate, although it may serve to cancel an unwanted natural suggestion of the act of saying one intends to do something. To intend to perform an action is, on my account, to hold that it is desirable to perform an action of a certain sort in the light of what one believes is and will be the case. But if one believes no such action is possible, then there can be no judgment that such an action consistent with one's beliefs is desirable. There can be no such intention.

If an intention is just a judgment that an action of a certain sort is desirable, what is there to distinguish an intention from a mere wish? We may put aside wishes for things that are not consistent with what one believes, for these are ruled out by our conception of an intention. And we may put aside wishes that do not correspond to all-out judgments. ("I wish I could go to London next week": my going to London next week may be consistent with all I believe, but not with all I want. This wish is idle because it is based on some only of my *prima facie* reasons.) But once we put these cases aside, there is no need to distinguish intentions from wishes. For a judgment that something I think I can do – that I think I see my way clear to doing – a judgment that such an action is desirable not only for one or another reason, but in the light of all my reasons, a judgment like this is not a mere wish. It *is* an intention. (This is not to deny that there are borderline cases.)

How well have we coped with the problem with which we began? That problem was, in effect, to give an account of intending (and of forming an intention) that would mesh in a satisfactory way with our account of acting with an intention, and would not sacrifice the merits of that account. With respect to the first point, finding an account of intending that would mesh with our account of intentional action, we devised a satisfactory way of relating the two concepts, but only by introducing a new element, an all-out judgment, into the analysis of intentional action. Given this sort of judgment and the idea of such a judgment made in the light of what is believed about the future course of affairs, we were able, I think, to arrive at a plausible view of intending.

There remains the question whether the sort of judgment to which I have appealed, an all-out judgment, can be understood without appeal to the notions of intention or will. I asked at the beginning of this last section of my paper whether intending to do something is wanting to do it; if it were, we might consider that our aim had been achieved. What we intend to do we want, in some very broad sense of want, to do. But this does not mean that intending is a form of wanting. For consider the actions that I want to perform and that are consistent with what I believe. Among them are the actions I intend to perform, and many more. I want to go to London next week, but I do not intend to, not because I think I cannot, but because it would interfere with other things I want more. This suggests strongly that wanting and desiring are best viewed as corresponding to, or constituting, *prima facie* judgments.

If this is correct, we cannot claim that we have made out a case for viewing intentions as something familiar, a kind of wanting, where we can distinguish the kind without having to use the concept of intention or will. What we can say, however, is that intending and wanting belong to the same genus of pro-attitudes expressed by value judgments. Wants, desires, principles, prejudices, felt duties and obligations provide reasons for actions and intentions, and are expressed by *prima facie* judgments; intentions and the judgments that go with intentional actions are distinguished by their all-out or unconditional form. Pure intendings constitute a subclass of the all-out judgments, those directed to future actions of the agent, and made in the light of his beliefs.

Notes

1. I take the "intentionally" to govern the entire phrase "boarded a plane headed for London, Ontario." On an alternative reading, only the boarding would be intentional. Similarly, in (1) below his reason extends to the marking on the plane.
2. See my "Freedom to Act," in *Essays on Freedom of Action*, ed. T. Honderich, London, 1973.
3. This is where my "Actions, Reasons, and Causes," Chapter 19 in this volume, left things. At that time I believed it would be possible to characterize "the right way" in non-circular terms.
4. See P.T. Geach, *Mental Acts*, London, 1957.
5. H.P. Grice, "Intention and Uncertainty," British Academy Lecture, Oxford, 1971, pp. 4, 5.
6. G.E.M. Anscombe, *Intention*, Oxford, 1957, p. 59.
7. No weight should be given the word "judgment." I am considering here the *form* of propositions that express desires and other attitudes. I do not suppose that someone who wants to eat something sweet necessarily *judges* that it would be good to eat something sweet; perhaps we can just say he *holds* that his eating something sweet has some positive characteristic. By distinguishing among the propositional expressions of attitudes I hope to mark differences among the attitudes.
8. I have said more about the form of *prima facie* evaluative judgments, and the importance of distinguishing them from unconditional judgments, in "How is Weakness of the Will Possible?" in *Moral Concepts*, ed. J. Feinberg, Oxford, 1969.

14

Two Faces of Intention

Michael Bratman

We do things intentionally, and we intend to do things. Our commonsense psychology uses the notion of intention to characterize both our actions and our mental states: I might intentionally start my car, and I might intend to start it. My intention to start it clearly does not guarantee that I do. But beyond that it is not obvious how these two phenomena are related. A central problem for a theory of intention is to provide a plausible account of this relation.

One thing seems clear: it is part of our common-sense psychological framework that these phenomena are not completely unrelated. In classifying both our actions and our states of mind in terms of some root notion of intention, commonsense psychology clearly assumes that there is some important commonality. Our problem is to say what this commonality is, by spelling out the relation between intentional action and intending (or, having an intention) to act.

There are two common approaches to this problem. The first – the *desire-belief* model – sees intentional action as action that stands in appropriate relations to the agent's desires and beliefs.[1] This is a reductive model: it sees intentions to act as reducible to certain desires and beliefs.[2] On this approach, the problem of the relation between acting intentionally and having an intention to

act becomes the problem of the relation of the complex of desires and beliefs constitutive of the latter to those desires and beliefs necessary for the former.

I think this approach is mistaken. We are planning creatures. We frequently settle in advance on plans for the future. On occasion, this even involves settling on one of several conflicting options each of which is, in light of our desires and beliefs, equally attractive. These plans help guide our later conduct and coordinate our activities over time, in ways in which our ordinary desires and beliefs do not. Intentions are typically elements in such coordinating plans. Once we recognize this central role intentions play in our lives the natural view to take, I think, is that intentions are distinctive states of mind, not to be reduced to clusters of desires and beliefs.

So I have argued in several recent papers.[3] Here my argument against the desire-belief model will be only indirect. I will try to show what a part of a theory of intention would look like once we reject that model. Insofar as the account sketched is plausible, it will constitute an indirect argument against that model.

This brings us back to our problem of the relation between intending to act and acting intentionally. Once we see intentions as distinctive phenomena, how should we understand this relation? Here is where the second common approach comes in. I may intend to start my car later today: this is a future-directed intention. But I may also intend to start my car now: this is a present-directed intention. Such a

Bratman, M. (1984), "Two Faces of Intention," *Philosophical Review* 93 (3), 375–405. Copyright © 1984 Cornell University. All rights reserved. Republished by permission of the copyright holder and current publisher Duke University Press, www.dukeupress.edu.

Philosophy of Action: An Anthology, First Edition. Edited by Jonathan Dancy and Constantine Sandis.
© 2015 John Wiley & Sons, Inc. Published 2015 by John Wiley & Sons, Inc.

present-directed intention does not guarantee that I actually start my car. But if I do start my car intentionally then, it seems plausible to suppose, I have such a present-directed intention to start it. After all, while starting the car I surely intend to do something. Given that what I do intentionally is start it, it seems that what I intend will include starting it.

This suggests a general solution to our problem: for me intentionally to A I must intend to A; my mental states at the time of action must be such that A is among those things I intend. I will call this the *Simple View*.[4]

The Simple View is a special case of a more general conception, the *Single Phenomenon View*. On this more general view, intentional action and the state of intention both involve a certain common state, and it is the relation of an action to this state that makes that action intentional. The Simple View adds to this more general conception the requirement that this state is just an intention so to act.

The Simple View has its virtues. It recognizes the distinctiveness of intentions, and provides a straightforward and initially plausible account of the relation between such intentions and intentional action. It is a view towards which commonsense initially leans, as well as a view implicit in many discussions of intention in moral philosophy.[5] Nevertheless, while I will be accepting a version of the more general, Single Phenomenon View, I find the Simple View unacceptable. Our conception of the state of intention is that of a single state tied to two very different sorts of phenomena. Intention is Janus-faced, tied both to coordinating plans and intentional action. The Simple View does not allow sufficient theoretical room for both these faces of intention.

In Sections 1 and 2 of this paper I explain why. In Section 3 I show how one might naturally be led to the Simple View by an unacceptable reduction of another kind: a reduction of present-directed intention to volition. Finally, in Sections 4 through 6 I sketch a route between the desire-belief model and the Simple View, a route that remains within the framework of the more general Single Phenomenon View. My proposal sees intentions as distinctive, and sees the intentionality of an action as dependent on its relation to such intentions. But it rejects the account of this relation provided by the Simple View. It holds, instead, that while to A intentionally I must intend to do something, I need not intend to do A. This leads to a distinction between what I intend and the motivational potential of my intention. I conclude by arguing that this distinction has a further virtue: it allows our concern with the ascription of responsibility to shape our classification of actions as intentional without thereby distorting our classifications of mental states in ways which undermine critical regularities.

1. Consistency of Intention and the Simple View

My argument against the Simple View is rooted in my conception of intentions as elements in coordinating plans. So I need to say more about that conception.

We have been speaking of present-directed intentions. But there is a tension in saying that I intend to do what I am now doing: talk of what I intend to do seems normally reserved for my attitude towards my future conduct. When I am actually starting my car it may seem natural to say that I no longer intend to start it, I am starting it. I think we should take this strain as a philosophical hint: not that there are no present-directed intentions, but that to understand what intentions are we should begin by concentrating on the future-directed case.[6] This is the *methodological priority of future-directed intention*.[7]

Future-directed intentions are typically elements in larger plans.[8] Such plans help me to coordinate my activities over time, and my activities with yours. The ability to settle in advance on such plans enables us to achieve complex goals we would not otherwise be able to achieve. This ability to settle on coordinating plans is a kind of universal means: it is of significant use in the pursuit of goals of very different sorts.

Intentions aid coordination as elements in larger plans. The concern with coordination exerts pressure towards unification of our various intentions. So if our intentions are to be well-suited to aid coordination, we should be able to put them together into a larger plan which can serve this coordinating role well. But to coordinate my activities over time a plan should be, other things equal, internally consistent. Roughly, it should be possible for my entire plan to be realized.[9] Further, a good coordinating plan is a plan for the world I find myself in. So, assuming my beliefs are consistent, such a plan should be consistent with my beliefs, other things equal. Roughly, it should be possible for my entire plan to be realized while my beliefs are true.[10]

Let us say that my intentions are weakly consistent if they could all be put together into an overall plan that is internally consistent. My intentions are strongly consistent, relative to my beliefs if all my intentions could be put together into an overall plan that is consistent with those beliefs. To be well-suited to aid coordination, my intentions will need to be, other things equal, strongly consistent relative to my beliefs. Since it is largely to aid such coordination that we bother with future-directed intentions in the first place, we have a pragmatic rationale for a rational demand that future-directed intentions be strongly consistent, relative to the agent's beliefs. This is a demand that should be respected in our further practical reasoning and planning.

This demand for strong consistency distinguishes intentions from ordinary desires. I might, without irrationality, both desire to play basketball today and desire to finish this paper today, all the time knowing I cannot do both. In contrast, intentions to play and to finish would, given my beliefs, convict me of a criticizable form of irrationality.

The demand for strong consistency provides the basis of my argument against the Simple View. But first I need to make one more point about that view. Suppose I intentionally start my car. On the Simple View it follows that

(1) I intend to start my car.

The point to note is that I can have the intention reported in (1) whether or not I actually do start my car. As we might say, the form of (1) is not

(2) aRb

where b is replaced by a singular term denoting an actual, particular action of starting my car.[11] This clarification in mind, let us turn to a series of three examples.[12] In the first case I am playing a video game in which I am to guide a "missile" into a certain target. I am quite skilled at such things, but it is a difficult game and I am doubtful of success. Still, I aim at the target and try to hit it. As it happens, I succeed in just the way I was trying. My success was not merely a matter of luck; it depended heavily on my considerable skills at such games. Further, hitting the target was what I wanted to do; I was not just aiming at the target as a way of ensuring that the "missile" would go several inches to the right. Do I hit the target intentionally? It seems that I do. I want to hit it and so am trying to hit it. My attempt is guided by my perception of the target. I hit the target in the way I was trying, and in a way that depends on my relevant skills. And it is my perception that I have hit it that terminates my attempt. So even though I am doubtful of success while I am trying, if I do succeed in hitting the target I hit it intentionally. On the Simple View, then, I must intend to hit the target. And this is, for all we have said, an acceptable result.[13] Even though I am doubtful that I will hit the target, the intention to hit it need not violate the demand for strong consistency.

Suppose now that a second game is added, a game which also involves guiding a "missile" into a certain target. Since I am ambidextrous and can play one game with each hand, I decide to play both games simultaneously. As before, the games are difficult and I am doubtful of success at either of them. As it happens, I miss target 2 but I do succeed in hitting target 1 in the way I was trying and in a way that depended on my relevant skills. Here again, it seems to me, I hit target 1 intentionally. The mere fact that I was also trying unsuccessfully to hit target 2 does not prevent me from intentionally hitting target 1.

The Simple View must say, then, that I intend to hit target 1. And this seems plausible. But what about my intentions concerning target 2? I was trying equally hard, and with equal skill, as well as with equally weak confidence of success, to hit target 2. It seems clear from the symmetry of the case that if I intend to hit target 1 I also intend to hit target 2. Of course, in the example I do not hit target 2, whereas I do hit target 1. But, as we noted above, this difference does not prevent me from intending to hit target 2.

So the defender of the Simple View must suppose that in this case I intend to hit each target. This sets the stage for my argument against this view, an argument which requires one more addition to our example.

Let us now suppose that the two games are known to me to be so linked that it is impossible to hit both targets. If both targets are about to be hit simultaneously the machines just shut down. Both targets remain visible to me, so I can see which target I hit if I hit either target. And there is a reward for hitting either target. But I know that while I can hit each target, I cannot hit both targets. Still, I know it is difficult to hit either target, so I again decide to play both games simultaneously; I see the risk of shutting down the machines as outweighed by the increase in my chances of hitting a target. I proceed to try to hit target 1 and also to try to hit target 2. I give each game a try.

Suppose I do hit target 1 in just the way I was trying to hit it, and in a way which depends heavily on my considerable skills at such games. It seems, again, that I hit target 1 intentionally. So, on the Simple View, I must intend to hit target 1. Given the symmetry of the case I must also intend to hit target 2. But given my knowledge that I cannot hit both targets, these two intentions fail to be strongly consistent. Having them would involve me in a criticizable form of irrationality. But it seems clear I need be guilty of no such irrationality: the strategy of giving each game a try seems perfectly reasonable. If I am guilty of no such irrationality I do not have both of these intentions. Since my relevant intentions in favor of hitting target 1 are the same as those in favor of hitting target 2, I have neither intention. So the Simple View is false. If it were true I would be guilty of a form of criticizable irrationality; but I need be guilty of no such irrationality. The Simple View imposes too strong a link between intention and intentional action, a link that is insensitive to differences in the demands of practical reason.

This argument against the Simple View appeals to constraints on intention that do not apply in the same way to intentional action. In this respect it is similar to an alternative argument that has been sketched in the literature. It will be useful to discuss this argument briefly.

Suppose I intend now to go to the concert tonight. What must I believe about my future concert-going? Some philosophers[14] accept the strong thesis that I must now believe I will go. Their reasons for this strong thesis tend to be of two sorts. There is, first, the need to explain the apparent oddness of remarks like:

"I intend to go to the concert, but I may not go."[15] Second, there is the idea that by seeing intention in this way we can best explain the role of intentions in various kinds of practical thinking.[16] I will not examine such arguments for this strong belief condition here. It suffices for my purposes to note that once we are given this strong belief requirement on future-directed intention it will be natural to suppose that present-directed intentions are subject to a similar belief condition; and this leads directly to an argument against the Simple View.[17]

This argument has two premises. The first is just this strong belief requirement. The second is the observation that a person can do something intentionally even though, at the time of action, he is in doubt whether he is so acting. We have already seen an example of this: I might intentionally hit the target even while being doubtful of success. Donald Davidson offers another example.[18] A person might try hard to make ten carbon copies on a typewriter, while being skeptical of success. Still, if this is what he wants to do, and if he does, in fact, make ten copies in the way he was trying and in a way that depends on his relevant skills, then it seems that he intentionally makes ten copies. Again, we have intentional action despite lack of belief.

So we have two premises: a strong belief requirement on intending to act, and the observation that one may A intentionally even while doubting that one is A-ing. These two premises entail that the Simple View is false. Given the strong belief requirement, when I act intentionally in a way in which I do not believe I am acting I will not intend so to act.

Like my initial argument, the present argument tries to cite a constraint on intention that does not similarly apply to intentional action. But whereas I cited the constraint that rational intentions are to be strongly consistent, given the agent's beliefs, the present argument cites a strong belief condition on intention. Now it seems to me that this strong belief condition is problematic in ways in which the demand for strong consistency is not. It seems plausible to suppose that sometimes intentions just do not satisfy such a strong belief condition. For example, I might intend now to stop at the bookstore on the way home while knowing of my tendency towards absent-mindedness – especially once I get on my bike and go into "automatic pilot." If I were to reflect on the matter I would be skeptical about my stopping there, for I know I may well forget. It is not that I believe I will not stop; I just do not believe I will. Still, my plan is to stop.

Examples like this seem at least to show that the strong belief requirement is no more obvious than the Simple View itself. So a philosopher committed to the Simple View could plausibly resist the present argument by turning it on its end and seeing it as an objection to the strong belief requirement. One person's *modus ponens* is another's *modus tollens*.[19]

In contrast, the demand for strong consistency of intentions is more difficult to avoid. First, instead of requiring an actual belief that I will A for me to intend to A, it demands only that (other things equal, and if my intentions are to be rational) I not have beliefs inconsistent with the belief that I will A.

Second, this constraint is even compatible with the possibility of my intending to stop at the bookstore and believing I will not. It just requires us to say that, other things equal, I would then be guilty of a form of critizable irrationality. Finally, it will be more difficult to turn the tables on my argument, rejecting the requirement of strong consistency in order to hold onto the Simple View. This is because this consistency constraint seems to be firmly grounded in a basic feature of intentions: their role in coordinating plans.

Nevertheless, objections to my argument remain. I turn now to consider some of these.

2. Objections and Replies

My argument depends on two claims about the final video games case in which the games are known to be linked and I succeed in hitting target 1:

i.   If in this case I had present-directed intentions which failed to be strongly consistent, I would be criticizably irrational.

and

ii. I hit target 1 intentionally.

Let us consider some ways in which a defender of the Simple View might try to challenge these claims. Begin with (i).

It might be urged that, for all that I have said, only future-directed intentions are subject to the strong

consistency requirement. So I can intend to hit target 1 now, and similarly concerning target 2, without being criticizably irrational, contrary to (i).

This objection is inadequate for two reasons. First, the argument for the demand for strong consistency depended on the observation that intentions typically play a coordinating role. Now, while this is clearest in the case of future-directed intentions, this is also an important role of some present-directed intentions. Suppose my intentions concerning the video games are embedded in a larger plan for the day. I begin the day with what are then future-directed intentions concerning these games. When the time comes these become present-directed intentions. But they continue to be part of my coordinating plan. So they continue to be subject to the demand for strong consistency.

Second, the very idea that some present-directed intentions escape the consistency demands to which most other intentions are subject seems to me not very plausible. After all, they are all equally intentions. Notice that we do not think belief works this way. That is, we do not see certain beliefs about the present as subject to weaker demands of consistency than beliefs about the future.

A second objection to (i) grants that there is a general presumption against such inconsistency, but urges that this presumption can sometimes be overridden and, indeed, is overridden in the present case. I have strong pragmatic reasons for intending to hit each target, since that is how I best pursue the reward. Given these pragmatic reasons to have both intentions, the fact that they fail to be (given my beliefs) strongly consistent need not convict me of criticizable irrationality, contrary to (i).

My response is to reject the contention that I must intend to hit each target in order best to pursue the reward. What I need to do is to try to hit each target. But this does not mean that I must intend to hit each target. Perhaps I must intend something – to try to hit each target, for example. But it seems that I can best pursue the reward without intending flat out to hit each target, and so without a failure of strong consistency.[20] Given a presumption against such a failure, that is what I should do. If I nevertheless do intend to hit each target I am criticizably irrational. So (i) remains plausible. What about (ii), the claim that what I do intentionally is hit target 1? Here the defender of the

Simple View might urge that what I do intentionally is only to hit one of the two targets. So all that the Simple View requires is that I intend to hit one of the two targets. And that intention is not threatened by the demand for strong consistency.

In assessing this objection we must be careful to distinguish my case from other, superficially similar cases. For example, suppose there is a single target in front of you and you know it is either target 1 or target 2. But since the targets are labelled on the back you do not know which target it is. Still, you do know that you get a reward for hitting target 1 or for hitting target 2. So you shoot at, and hit the target in front of you, which turns out to be target 1.

Now, on one natural reading of 'trying', you were not trying specifically to hit target 1. You were only trying to hit whichever target it was that was in front of you. Further, on a natural reading of 'knowingly', you did not hit target 1 knowingly; for you did not know that it was target 1, rather than target 2, that you were hitting. Such observations make it plausible to say that while in hitting target 1 you intentionally hit one of the two targets, you did not intentionally hit target 1.

Again, suppose there are two targets close together, and one gun. You only have enough skill to aim in the vicinity of the pair of targets, trying to hit one or the other. And that is what you do. Suppose you hit target 1. Then it is plausible to say that in hitting target 1 you have intentionally hit one of the two targets without intentionally hitting target 1.

In both these cases, then, it might plausibly be insisted that you do not intentionally hit target 1. It is important to note, however, that my case is different from these. I am trying to hit each of two targets (though I am not trying to hit both). I am not just trying to hit a single target which, for all I know, is one or the other of two different targets. Nor am I just aiming the same shot at both targets in the attempt to hit one or the other. Rather, each of the two targets separately guides my attempt to hit it. Further, I know that if I successfully hit target 1 my endeavor to hit it will be terminated by my knowledge that I have hit that very target. So my case differs from yet a third variation in which I know, rather, that the machine will only tell me if one of the targets is hit, without telling me which one. In this third variation it may be

plausible to insist that all I do intentionally is hit one of the targets. But, again, my case is importantly different.

These contrasts with variant cases highlight features of my case which argue for the claim that I intentionally hit target 1. First, I want to hit target 1 and so am trying to do so. Second, my attempt to hit target 1 is guided specifically by my perception of that target, and not by my perception of other targets. Relevant adjustments in my behavior are dependent specifically on my perception of that target. Third, I actually hit target 1 in the way I was trying, and in a way that depends on my relevant skills. Fourth, it is my perception that I have hit target 1, and not merely my perception that I have hit a target, that terminates my attempt to hit it. Granted, if I had instead hit target 2 that also would have terminated my endeavor to hit target 1, given my knowledge of how the games are linked.

Nevertheless, what actually does terminate my attempt to hit target 1 is my perception that I have hit that target. When all this is true it seems to me too weak just to say that I have intentionally hit one of the targets. Rather, I have intentionally hit target 1.

Both crucial claims in my argument against the Simple View are, then, quite plausible. But this is not the end of the matter. We need also to know the larger theoretical advantages and disadvantages of giving up the Simple View. The remainder of this paper pursues some of these larger issues. Insofar as the alternative framework it sketches is independently plausible, it provides further support for the rejection of the Simple View.

3. Intention and Volition

I have followed the Simple View in eschewing the reduction of intention to desire and belief. But I have also rejected the Simple View's detailed conception of the relation between intentional action and the state of intention. I now want to examine one natural way of arriving at the Simple View, a way that depends on a different sort of reduction – this time, of intention to volition. I want to do this for two reasons. First, such a reduction is a natural way of arriving at the Simple View, and so deserves some comment here.

Second, this will allow me to show how one can be led to an alternative conception of what is common to both intention and intentional action. This alternative conception accepts the Single Phenomenon View, but supposes that the element common to both intentional action and the state of intention is volition, rather than intention itself. Since I will be defending a version of the Single Phenomenon View which sees intention as the common element (though, of course, not the version expressed in the Simple View), it is important for me to say why I reject this alternative.

When I A intentionally – and not merely by accident, by mistake, unwittingly, inadvertently and so on – it may seem plausible to say that I am in a sense "committed" to A-ing. There may seem here to be a kind of "practical commitment" to A-ing that goes beyond mere desire. This suggests that all cases of intentionally A-ing share a special pro-attitude in favor of A-ing, a pro-attitude distinct from an ordinary desire to A. The presence of this pro-attitude in favor of A guarantees the kind of commitment to A-ing characteristic of intentionally A-ing. We may call this special attitude willing or, alternatively, volition, and this suggestion the Volitional Thesis. On the Volitional Thesis, then, in intentionally A-ing I will to A (or, perhaps, that I A): I have a volition to A (that I A).

If one accepts the Volitional Thesis one needs to say more about willing. In particular, one needs to say what the relation is between willing to A and intending to A. Here we are faced with an important theoretical decision. On one conception willing and intending are completely distinct mental elements: my volition to A is itself neither an intention to A nor a necessary part of such an intention. When we see willing this way the Volitional Thesis, while compatible with the Simple View, provides no direct support for that view and could be accepted by one who rejected the Simple View. In this paper I leave open the question of the acceptability of the Volitional Thesis when willings are understood, in this way, as completely distinct from intentions.

More germane to present concerns is a second conception which supposes there to be a much tighter connection between intention and volition. One version of this second conception sees the volition to A, required by the Volitional Thesis for intentionally A-ing, as at least a necessary component of a

present-directed intention to A. This is the Necessity Thesis Finally, on an even stronger version of this conception a volition to A, in the sense of the Volitional Thesis, just is a present-directed intention to A. This is the *Identification Thesis*. And with the Identification Thesis we have arrived at the Simple View.

The Identification Thesis amounts to a reduction of present-directed intention to volition. Such a reduction seems fairly natural.[21] Yet, taken together with the Volitional Thesis it leads to the Simple View. Having rejected the Simple View we must block this reasoning at some point. Where? Return to the last video games example. This example does not threaten the Volitional Thesis taken by itself. It remains open, for all that that thesis says, that I both will to hit target 1 and will to hit target 2. This is because by itself the Volitional Thesis offers no reason for supposing that willings are subject to the same demands of strong consistency to which intentions are subject. Nor does the example directly challenge the idea that willings, of the sort required by the Volitional Thesis, are necessary components of corresponding intentions. What the example precludes is that willings of the sort required by the Volitional Thesis be identified with corresponding intentions. If my willings to hit each target were just present-directed intentions to hit them, I would be criticizably irrational; but I am not. To avoid the Simple View we must reject the reduction of present-directed intentions to volitions of the sort required by the Volitional Thesis.

In light of our discussion, we can see what goes wrong with such a reduction. The Volitional Thesis introduces the notion of volition to capture the special commitment it supposes to be characteristic of intentional action. In contrast, the idea of an intention to act is partly tied to future-directed intentions and plans, and to their characteristic commitment to future action. When we identify present-directed intentions with such volitions we implicitly assume that these two roles do not bring with them conflicting demands. But what we learn from the video games example is that they do. So we should reject this reduction.

Having rejected the Identification Thesis, could we still retain the Necessity Thesis, the view that a volition to A is a necessary part of a present-directed intention to A? This would be to see a volition to A, rather than a full-blown intention to A, as the element common to both intentionally A-ing and having a present-directed intention to A. This would lead naturally to an alternative version of the Single Phenomenon View. On this alternative version the basic, single phenomenon is volition; it is a volition to A that is common to both my intentionally A-ing and the intention to A. While I may intend to A in intentionally A-ing, I need not: I need only will to A. An intention to A is a volition to A *together with something else.*

What else? In his important British Academy lecture[22] H. P. Grice in effect pursues a version of this strategy. Grice first introduces a general notion of willing which has the feature that I will that I A whenever I either intentionally A or intend now to A later. Gricean willings, while embodying (in the present-directed case) the special commitment characteristic of intentional action, are not confined to the present. Grice then goes on to claim that my intention to A is my willing that I A together with my belief that I will, as a result, A. There is a single phenomenon involved in both intentional action and the state of intention, but it is not intention itself. It is, rather, volition – understood as a proper part of intention.

This view has several virtues. It avoids the identification of present-directed intention and volition that we have seen to founder on the demand for strong consistency of intention. At the same time it provides an explanation of why intentions are subject to such consistency demands, namely: because beliefs are, and an intention to A includes the belief that one will. In this way it provides for a more complex connection between the commitment characteristic of intentional action, and that characteristic of future-directed intentions and plans, than is allowed by the Simple View.

The problem is that this view requires a return to the strong belief requirement on intention. And we have seen reason to be doubtful of that requirement. Further, there is no obvious way to weaken this belief requirement without creating other difficulties. For example, suppose we try saying that an intention to A is a volition that one A together with a belief that, as a result, one is more likely than not to A. The problem now will be that we have undermined the general capacity of rational intentions to be unified into larger,

rational plans. This is because we have now blocked the inference from

a. I rationally intend to A and rationally intend to B

to

b. It would not be irrational for me to intend to A and B.

It is not generally true that if I rationally believe of *each* of A and B that I am more likely than not so to act, I can rationally believe the same of my performing both actions. So the inference from (a) to (b) will not go through. But, as we have seen, intentions are at least potentially elements in larger coordinating plans. To be rational my intentions should at least be capable of combining into a larger plan that is not irrational. So we will want to retain the inference from (a) to (b).

In light of these difficulties perhaps we should put aside such belief requirements on intention and appeal directly to the constraint of strong consistency. One way to do this might be to say that my intention to A is my volition to A together with my disposition to impose this constraint on that volition. The problem now is that we make the step from volition to intention appear arbitrary. Recall that it is not generally appropriate to impose the demand for strong consistency on one's volitions: this is the lesson of the video games example. So, on the suggested view, to intend to A I must be disposed to treat my volition to A in a special way, a way not generally appropriate for volitions. But, having given up the belief condition on intention, the suggested view leaves us with no explanation of why this special treatment is appropriate in this case. We have no explanation of why I should impose the demand for strong consistency on this volition but not on others.

The strategy of constructing intentions out of volitions and other things, we now see, faces a dilemma in providing for the consistency constraints characteristic of intention. If it tries to account for these constraints by adding to volition a further belief condition, this condition will be too strong. If it tries just to tack onto volition a disposition to impose the relevant consistency constraints, it makes the step from volition to intention seem arbitrary. Faced with this dilemma, I propose taking a different tack.

4. Intention and Motivational Potential

Both the Simple View and the Volitional Thesis agree in supposing that – pace the desire-belief model – intentional action involves a special pro-attitude, distinct from the agent's desires and beliefs. The problem has been to say more precisely what that special attitude is. On the Simple View it is an intention to act in the way one acts intentionally; and we have seen this idea to be at odds with the requirement that intentions be strongly consistent. On the Volitional Thesis all intentional action involves a distinctive volition so to act. I have not criticized this view directly. I have instead focused my critical attention on attempts to weld such a view to either a reduction of present-directed intention to volition (which just returns us to the Simple View) or the Gricean view of volitions as proper parts of intentions.

Both the Simple View and the Volitional Thesis share a common assumption. They both assume that if there is a distinctive pro-attitude involved in intentionally A-ing, it will be a pro-attitude specifically in favor of A-that there must be a tight fit between what is done intentionally and what is intended (willed). This is the assumption of tight fit. Together with our video games example, this assumption leads us to reject the idea that intentional action generally involves an intention, that intention is the element common to both the state of intention and intentional action.

I propose to give up the assumption of tight fit and to distinguish between what is intended, and the sorts of intentional activity in which an intention may issue. Making this distinction, we can say that when I A intentionally I intend something, but I may not specifically intend to A. Our notion of intentional action embodies a complex scheme for the classification of actions (or, perhaps, actions "under a description"). To understand the relation between intention and intentional action we must recognize that the factors that determine what is intended do not completely coincide with the factors that, on this scheme, determine what is done intentionally.

Recognizing this, we can accept a version of the Single Phenomenon View which sees intention as the common element in both intentional action and the state of intention. To find a common element we need not retreat to some proper part of intention, volition. Actions are intentional in part because of their relations to intentions. But the admissible relations are more complex than those envisaged by the Simple View.

In the theory of action one can be led into two different mistakes (among others!). The first, built into the desire-belief model, is to suppose that intentional action involves no distinctive state of intention at all. The second, made by the Simple View, is to suppose that intentional action always involves an intention so to act – a supposition that does not do justice to the role of intentions in coordinating plans. I am proposing a way between. In acting intentionally there is something I intend to do; but this need not be what I do intentionally.

Supposing, then, that there are cases in which I intentionally A and yet do not intend to A but only intend to B, for some appropriate B, a full account of our scheme for classifying actions as intentional will need to sort out just when this can be so. Whatever its details, such an account will implicitly specify a four-place relation between intentions, desires, beliefs and types of actions. It will say what types of actions may be performed intentionally in the course of executing a certain intention, given a certain background of desires and beliefs. This allows us to define a useful notion, that of the motivational potential of an intention. A is in the motivational potential of my intention to B, given my desires and beliefs, just in case it is possible for me intentionally to A in the course of executing my intention to B. If I actually intend to A then A will be in the motivational potential of my intention. But we need not suppose that if A is in the motivational potential of an intention of mine then I intend to A. Consider the last video games example. My intention includes my hitting target 1 in its motivational potential: it is possible, given my desires and beliefs, for me to hit target 1 intentionally in the course of executing my intention. Nevertheless, I do not intend flat-out to hit target 1. While hitting target 1 is in the motivational potential of my intention, it is not what I intend.

What then do I intend? There are several possibilities. I might intend to try to hit target 1, and also to try to hit target 2. I might intend to hit target 1 if I can, and similarly concerning target 2. I might even just intend to hit one of the two targets; though we must be careful to distinguish this case from the cases discussed in Section 2 in which, though I intend to hit one of the two targets, my intention does not include hitting target 1 in its motivational potential. The important point is just that my intention may include hitting target 1 in its motivational potential without including it in what is intended.

That my intention includes hitting target 1 in its motivational potential, even though it is not an intention to hit target 1, does not by itself explain why it is true that I hit target 1 intentionally. This is clear from the definition of motivational potential. The notion of motivational potential is intended to mark the fact that my intention to B may issue in my intentionally A-ing, not to explain it. It is a theoretical placeholder: it allows us to retain theoretical room for a more complex account of the relation between intention and intentional action while leaving unsettled the details of such an account. Such an account would not itself use the notion of motivational potential but would, rather, replace it with detailed specifications of various sufficient conditions for intentional conduct.

Let me put the point this way. On the theory just sketched, if I A intentionally then I A in the course of executing some intention to B and, given my desires and beliefs, this intention contains A in its motivational potential. This means that there will be some true statements) along the lines of:

If S intends to B and S A's in the course of executing his intention to B and — then S A's intentionally.

A full-blown theory of intentional action will tell us how such blanks should be filled in. For example, our discussion of the video games example suggests that one such specification of sufficient conditions would be roughly along the lines of the following:
S intentionally A's if

1. S wants to A and for that reason intends to try to A, and
2. S A's in the course of executing his intention to try to A, and
3. S A's in the way he was trying to A, and
4. (2) and (3) depend, in an appropriate way, on S's relevant skills.

Without working out the details, we can see that such a specification would use conditions like (3) and (4) to fill in the theoretical space opened up by our distinction between what is intended and what is in the motivational potential of an intention.

This new theoretical space allows us to formulate a more satisfactory alternative to the desire-belief model than those so far considered. In contrast with the desire-belief model, we can grant that intentional action at least typically involves a distinctive pro-attitude that is not reducible to the agent's desires and beliefs. In particular, intention is a distinctive pro-attitude involved in intentionally A-ing, though it need not be an intention to A. By allowing this flexibility in what is intended we do better than the Simple View in providing for the consistency demands on intentions. We can allow, for example, that when I intentionally hit target 1 what I intend need not involve me in inconsistency.

This flexibility also takes away a main source of motivation for accepting the Necessity Thesis and treating an intention to A as consisting of a volition to A plus something else. Having given up the assumption of tight fit, we no longer must choose between an intention to A and a volition to A – understood as a proper part of such an intention – in order to locate a distinctive pro-attitude generally involved both in an intention to A and in intentionally A-ing. Further, since all intentions are subject to a demand for strong consistency, we avoid an analogue of the puzzle, faced by the defender of the Necessity Thesis, about why we should impose such constraints on only some proper sub-set of our volitions.

In response one might still worry that the distinction, between what is intended and what is in the motivational potential of an intention, is illusory. As Anscombe famously remarks, "the primitive sign of wanting is *trying to get*."[23] But what is true about wanting seems even more clearly true about intention: the "primitive sign" of an intention to A is trying to A. In the face of this I have tried to drive a wedge between an intention whose execution may involve both trying to A and intentionally A-ing, and an intention to A. I have claimed that one might have the former intention and yet still not intend to A. But how is that possible? Differences in what I intend should reveal themselves in differences in the roles played by my intentions. But the basic role present-directed intentions play is in motivating and guiding present conduct. So it may seem unclear that there is a real difference between intending to A and having an intention whose role includes the motivation of intentionally A-ing.

The response to this worry is that intentions play other important roles. Differences in these roles can discriminate between two intentions, both of which include A in their motivational potential but only one of which is an intention to A. That there are these other important roles is clear from the methodological priority of future-directed intention; for a basic role played by future-directed intentions is as elements in coordinating plans. There are differences in the role played in such plans by an intention to A and that played by other intentions which include A in their motivational potential. Included among these will be differences in the constraints imposed on yet other intentions, given the demand for strong consistency. What I intend, when I have a future-directed intention, will be in part reflected in the ways in which my intention constrains my other intentions by way of this consistency demand. Thus, if my future-directed intentions concerning targets 1 and 2 do not convict me of criticizable inconsistency then, given my beliefs, they are not intentions to hit target 1 and to hit target 2. This is so even though my intention concerning target 1 includes hitting it in its motivational potential, and similarly with my intention concerning target 2.

A similar point applies to present-directed intentions. What I intend when I have a present-directed intention will not be simply a matter of the sorts of intentional conduct in which my intention might issue. I can have a present-directed intention which includes hitting target 1 in its motivational potential even though I do not intend flat-out to hit target 1. For my intention to be an intention to hit target 1 it must constrain my other intentions accordingly, by way of the demand for strong consistency. And, as we have seen, my intentions concerning targets 1 and 2 may have hitting each target in their motivational potential without constraining each other in the ways characteristic of intentions to hit these targets.

5. Motivational Potential Extended

Let us sum up so far. Desires, beliefs and intentions are basic elements in the commonsense psychology underlying intentional action. Intentions are typically elements in plans. Intentional action generally involves an intention to act. The state of intention is itself the common element in both the states and the actions included within our conception of intention: the Single Phenomenon View is correct. The intention involved in intentional action need not, however, be an intention so to act. My intention may include A in its motivational potential even though I do not, strictly speaking, intend to A. The coherence of this latter idea is ensured by the role intentions play in coordinating plans. All this is neutral on the question of whether intentional action involves a special volitional element that is completely distinct from intention. But it does eliminate the need to introduce volitions as special psychological elements related to intentions as part to whole, and serving as the common element in intentional action and intending to act.

This approach depends on driving a wedge between what I intend and the motivational potential of my intention. Now, the wedge I have so far argued for has been rather thin: it has directly concerned only certain special cases in which the demand for strong consistency created problems for the Simple View. But once we have this wedge we can widen it in ways that promise to be useful. Let me briefly sketch two such ways.

Suppose I intend to run the marathon and believe that I will thereby wear down my sneakers. Now it seems to me that it does not follow that I intend to wear down my sneakers, and in a normal case I will not so intend. One sign of the absence of such an intention will be the fact that I am not at all disposed to engage in further reasoning aimed at settling on some means to wearing down my sneakers. In contrast, if I intended to get to the track by 9 a.m., as a means to running the race, I would be disposed to engage in reasoning aimed at figuring out how to do that.[24] My attitude towards wearing down my sneakers does not play the role in further means-end reasoning that an intention to wear them down would normally play.

Even so, if I proceed to run the marathon and actually do wear down my sneakers then I might well do so intentionally. Perhaps this is clearest in a case with two further features.[25] First, I not only believe I will wear them down; I consciously note this while I am running. Second, wearing them down has some independent significance to me; perhaps they are a family heirloom. In a case with these two further features I think we would classify my action as intentional. Yet it does not seem that these further features must change what I intend in running the race. Given my relevant beliefs and desires, in executing my intention to run the race I may intentionally wear down my sneakers; and this even though I do not intend to wear them down. So while what I intend does not include wearing down my sneakers, the motivational potential of my intention does.

Generalizing, we can expect a full theory of intentional action to generate true statements along the lines of

> If S intentionally B's in the course of executing his intention to B, and S believes that his B-ing will result in X, and his B-ing does result in X and —, then S intentionally brings about X.

For present purposes we can leave aside the subtle issue of just how the blank should be filled in (e.g., must it add that S is aware that he is bringing about X and is not indifferent as to whether or not he does bring it about?). The important point is that these sufficient conditions will not include the requirement that S actually intends to bring about X. This means that motivational potential can be extended by our beliefs about the upshots of what we intend, even when what we intend is not thereby extended.

Consider a second sort of case. I intend to shoot a jump shot. I know that my jump shot will have to contain certain sub-components, for example: stopping on my left foot. But as a skilled jump-shooter I need not intend all this, for my intentions and plans are typically at a level of abstraction appropriate to my skills. I may just intend to shoot the jump shot, perhaps as part of a larger plan to score and then to try to steal the in-bounds pass.

We may say that my stopping on my left foot is a *necessary constitutive means* of my shooting the jump

shot. What this case suggests is that I may, while guilty of no criticizable irrationality, intend to B, know that A is a necessary constitutive means of B-ing, and yet not intend to A. Rational intention need not be transmitted along the lines of known, necessary constitutive means.

Nevertheless, it seems that the motivational potential of my intention may be transmitted along such lines even when what I intend is not. If I successfully execute my intention and shoot the jump shot, and if in so doing I stop on my left foot, then I may well have stopped on that foot intentionally. So the motivational potential of my intention to shoot the jump shot may include stopping on my left foot. Here again this may be clearest for cases which have two further features. First, I not only know I must stop on my left foot; I consciously note this as I am shooting. Second, stopping on my left foot has some independent importance to me; perhaps I have recently injured it and it behooves me to go easy on it. In a case with these two further features I think we would classify my stopping on my left foot as intentional. Yet it does not seem that these further features force a change in what I intend. What I intend may remain just to shoot the jump shot. But given my background of beliefs and desires my intention includes stopping on my left foot in its motivational potential: it is possible for me to stop on my left foot intentionally in the course of executing my intention.

Generalizing again, we can expect a theory of intentional action to issue in true statements along the lines of

> If S intentionally B's in the course of executing his intention to B, and S believes that his A-ing is a necessary constitutive means of his B-ing and S A's in the course of executing his intention to B and …, then S intentionally A's.

Here again the important point is not the details concerning how to fill in the blank, but just that an intention to A is not required. This means that motivational potential can be extended by means-end beliefs, even when what is intended is not thereby extended.

These cases illustrate some of the complexities of our scheme for the classification of actions as intentional. The Simple View forces us to read these complexities back into the agent's intentions: it includes in what is intended everything done intentionally. Our view loosens the connection between what is intended and what is done intentionally: it sees what is intended as a fact about the agent's mind which need not reflect all the complexities of our scheme for classifying actions as intentional. It does this by using the notion of motivational potential to provide a buffer between the considerations that influence the intentionality of action and those that influence what a person intends.

6. Motivational Potential and the Distinctiveness of Intention

I now want to argue that this buffer helps support the central claim that intentions are distinctive states of mind. It does this by protecting regularities important to the defense of this claim.

The classificatory schemes involved in our commonsense framework play certain roles in our lives, and we can expect the details of such schemes to be shaped by those roles. An important role played by our scheme for classifying actions as intentional is that of identifying ways of acting for which an agent may be held responsible: our concern is not limited to the description and explanation of actions, but extends to the assessment of agents. This is why it seems natural to classify as intentional my wearing down my sneakers. After all, as Sidgwick notes in defending his proposal to "include under the term 'intention' all the consequences of an act that are foreseen as certain or probable": "we cannot evade responsibility for any foreseen bad consequences of our acts by the plea that we felt no desire for them."[26]

Now, the case for seeing intentions as distinctive states of mind depends on locating them in an explanatory system connecting environment and behavior, and on identifying their distinctive role in this system. To do this there need to be underlying regularities connecting intentions with each other and with other states and processes. Further, these regularities must be significantly dependent on what is intended; a regular connection between, say, intentions formed during winter quarter and nervousness is not the sort of

regularity we need. To the extent to which our scheme for determining what is intended is shaped by our concern, not only with explanation of action, but with the assignment of responsibility, it will be harder to find such regularities. This is because such a concern would tend to lead to the ascription of intentions which do not play their normal roles in motivation and practical reasoning.

To see this, consider again my intention to get to the track by 9 a.m., as a means to running the race. This intention plays a pair of roles important to attempts at explanation. First, it triggers further means-end reasoning concerning how to get to the track by then. Second, when the time comes it motivates activity guided by my beliefs (many of them perceptual) about where the track is.[27] In these respects it contrasts with my mere expectation that I will wear down my sneakers as a result of running. I am neither disposed to engage in reasoning aimed at settling on a means to wearing them down, nor do I guide my running of the race by keeping track of the state of my sneakers.[28]

There are, then, distinctive regularities connecting what is intended with further practical reasoning and with what beliefs guide our activity. The Simple View undermines such regularities. By reading back from the intentionality of my wearing down my sneakers to an intention to wear them down, it ascribes to me an intention which is outside the web of these regularities; for my attitude toward wearing down my sneakers does not play the roles characteristic of an intention to do so. To support such regularities we need to allow our concern with responsibility to shape what is done intentionally without similarly shaping what is intended. We need to allow our concern with responsibility to lead us to classify my wearing down my sneakers as intentional, without forcing us to say that I intend to wear them down. This is what the notion of motivational potential allows our theory to do. Returning to our video games example, we can make a similar point. Here the relevant regularity is a general tendency towards equilibrium. Generally, when an agent notices that his intentions fail to be strongly consistent there will be an attempt at revision, aimed at achieving consistency. But this regularity is undermined if we suppose that in cases such as our video games example there are strongly inconsistent intentions and yet no tendency towards appropriate revision. The notion of motivational potential allows us to protect this regularity and yet still grant that I hit target 1 intentionally.

7. Two Faces of Intention

Intention is Janus-faced, tied both to intentional action and coordinating plans. I have tried to sketch a version of the Single Phenomenon View that provides room for both of these faces of intention, and for an appropriate link between them. In doing this I have tried to avoid the oversimplifications of the Simple View and the Identification Thesis, as well as the difficulties that arise when we try to construct intentions out of volitions and other things. I have also tried to leave room for the different effects which our concern with the ascription of responsibility has on the different classificatory schemes included within our conception of intention. And, finally, I have tried to do this in a way that recognizes, exploits and supports the distinctiveness of an agent's intentions and plans.

Notes

Editors' note: some notes have been abbreviated or omitted, with the author's permission.

1. This is one of the guiding themes in Davidson's classic paper, "Actions, Reasons, and Causes," Chapter 19 in this volume. See also A. Goldman, *A Theory of Human Action* (Englewood Cliffs, N.J.: Prentice-Hall, 1970).

2. Philosophers who explicitly defend a reduction of the state of intention to certain desires and beliefs include R. Audi, "Intending," *Journal of Philosophy* 70 (1973), pp. 387–403; M. Beardsley, "Intending," in A. Goldman and J. Kim, eds., *Values and Morals* (Dordrecht: Reidel, 1978); and P. Churchland, "The Logical Character of Action-Explanations," *The Philosophical Review* 79 (1970), pp. 214–236.

3. "Intention and Means-end Reasoning," *The Philosophical Review* 90 (1981), pp. 252–265; "Taking Plans Seriously," *Social Theory and Practice* 9 (1983), pp. 271–287; "Davidson's Theory of Intention," in M. Hintikka and B. Vermazen, eds., *Essays on Davidson: Actions and Events* (Oxford: Clarendon Press, 1985), pp. 13–26.

4. Note that the Simple View does not say that there must be a separate event of intending to A for each intentional A-ing. The Simple View only imposes a requirement on one's mental states. Philosophers who accept something tantamount to the Simple View include B. Aune in *Reason and Action* (Dordrecht: Reidel, 1977), Chapter II, esp. pp. 89–102, and J. Searle in *Intentionality* (Cambridge: Cambridge University Press, 1983), Chapter 3. Searle says that the rejection of what I have called the Simple View is "a mistake that derives from a failure to see the difference between prior intentions [what I have called future-directed intentions] and intentions in action [what I have called present-directed intentions]" (p. 94n). But, as will be seen, my objection to the Simple View does not depend on such a failure.

5. See, for example, Charles Fried, *Right and Wrong* (Cambridge, Mass.: Harvard University Press, 1978), esp. pp. 20–24.

6. Note that even my present-directed intention to start my car is an intention to perform an action that continues somewhat into the future. Indeed, I doubt whether it is possible to have a present-directed intention to perform an instantaneous action, for reasons outlined by Brian O'Shaughnessy in *The Will* (Cambridge: Cambridge University Press, 1980), vol. 2, pp. 312–313.

7. Here I diverge from a long-standing tradition in the philosophy of action. This tradition begins with Anscombe's decision in her ground-breaking monograph to treat intentional action, rather than intending to act, as the basic case in terms of which to understand intention. See *Intention* (Ithaca, N.Y.: Cornell University Press, 1963), esp. §4.

8. There is a certain ambiguity in talk about plans. Sometimes we are talking about states of the agent - states of having certain plans. Other times we are talking about an appropriate abstract structure – some sort of partial function from circumstances to actions, perhaps – that may be used to describe the planning-states of different people. A more careful usage might reserve 'plan' for the latter and 'having a plan' for the former; but this is frequently stylistically awkward. In this essay I use 'plan' to mean 'having a plan' – that is, a state of mind. Thus plans are in the same category as (though different from) desires and beliefs.

It is worth noting that the importance of plans, and the associated phenomenon of planning, to our understanding of intention is sometimes blocked from view simply by the terminology we employ. For example, in his paper, "Intention and Punishment," in *Punishment and Responsibility* (Oxford: Oxford University Press, 1968), H. L. A. Hart writes "Intention is to be divided into three related parts....The first I shall call 'intentionally doing something'; the second 'doing something with a further intention', and the third 'bare intention' because it is the case of intending to do something in the future without doing anything to execute this intention now" (p. 117). This scheme forces us to see most future-directed intentions merely as "bare intentions," and this tends to block from view the roles of such intentions in plans, and the resulting constraints on these intentions.

9. I assume a broad notion of realization such that a conditional intention to A if p is realized if not-p.

10. I do not think that these brief explanations of the relevant notions of consistency are without their difficulties. There are deep problems here analogous to problems that arise when we try to say, for example, in what sense our beliefs about the morning star (that is, the evening star), or Cicero (that is, Tully) should be consistent. But I think this gloss on consistency will suffice for my purposes here.

11. This explains why I did not include Donald Davidson among those who accept the Simple View, even though he comes close to endorsing the view that if I intentionally start my car then I must intend my particular act of starting it. See his essays, "How Is Weakness of the Will Possible?," in *Essays on Actions and Events*, op. cit., and "Intending," Chapter 13 in this volume.

12. These examples take off from an example sketched by Robert Audi, op. cit., esp. p. 401.

13. One might even here object to the Simple View if one thought that to intend to hit the target I must believe I will. Below I discuss this line of argument against the Simple View, and why I do not take it.

14. For example, H. P. Grice, "Intention and Uncertainty," *Proceedings of the British Academy* 57 (1971), pp. 263–279; and G. Harman, "Practical Reasoning," *Review of Metaphysics* 29 (1976), pp. 431–463.

15. Grice, op. cit., pp. 264–266.

16. For example, one of Harman's arguments in favor of this strong thesis is that it allows for a natural account of the role of intentions in means-end reasoning. Op. cit., p. 435.

17. As Harman explicitly notes. Ibid., p. 433.

18. In "Intending," op. cit.

19. Of course, if we reject the strong belief requirement, we will need alternative explanations of the linguistic data and the data about practical reasoning originally summoned in its support. I sketch an alternative explanation of the latter in my "Intention and Means-End Reasoning," op. cit. I think an alternative explanation of the former can also be constructed, though I will not try here.

20. Perhaps there are other cases of trying to achieve each of two goals known to be incompatible in which, due to peculiarities of one's character, one really must intend to achieve each goal in order best to pursue each goal. But we need not suppose that my case is like this.

21. Aune accepts the Identification Thesis in *Reason and Action*, op. cit., Chapter II, Section 4. Searle also seems to be guided by some such reduction in *Intentionality*, op. cit.

22. Op. cit.

23. Op. cit., p. 68.

24. I introduce this further intention to make it clear that I am not just denying that I intend to wear down my sneakers "as an end." I do not intend to get to the track by 9 a.m. as an end; but I still do intend to do so. In contrast, I may not intend at all to wear down my sneakers. For probing discussions of related matters see Jonathan Bennett, *Morality and Consequences: The Tanner Lectures on Human Values*, ed. S. M. McMurrin (Cambridge: Cambridge University Press, 1980), lecture III; and Gilbert Harman, "Rational Action and the Extent of Intentions," *Social Theory and Practice* 9 (1983), pp. 123–141.

25. As Allan Gibbard helped me see. Note that I do not say that I run the race with the intention of wearing down my sneakers. I do not discuss acting with a further intention in this paper.

26. Henry Sidgwick, *The Methods of Ethics* (7th edn.) (New York: Dover, 1966), p. 202.

27. Of course, to play this motivational role my intention need not be an intention to get to the track by 9 a.m. It might just be an intention to try, or to get there by then if my old car holds up. Still, if I do intend to get there by 9 a.m. (and do not merely expect that I will) my intention will normally play the cited role.

28. I *might* guide my running of the race by keeping track of the state of my sneakers – for example, if I use them as a pedometer. Since even then I would not intend to wear them down, the presence of such guidance does not ensure intention. My point here is only that its absence indicates an absence of intention.

15

Acting As One Intends

John McDowell

1. In *Mind and World* I recommended that we understand the perceptual experience of rational creatures as an actualization in their sensory consciousness of conceptual capacities, capacities that belong to their rationality. The thought was that conceptual capacities inform sensory consciousness itself, rather than being confined to intellectual activity in which we put a construction on something that sensory consciousness affords to us anyway, independently of our power of judgment.

I want to urge an analogous conception of the bodily movements we make when we act. I want to urge that we conceive our intentional bodily movements as themselves instances of conceptual capacities in operation. The parallel thought in this case is that conceptual capacities inform our active bodily movements themselves, rather than being confined to conceptual states or goings-on to which the movements might be seen as responses. In both cases the main interest of the proposal, from my point of view, is the way it flies in the face of a dualistic separation of the rationality of rational animals from their animal nature.

There are two reasons why a conception of bodily action on these lines is attractive. First, it definitely avoids the idea that conceptual goings-on belong as such in a more or less mysterious inner realm, hidden from others. And, second, it definitely avoids the idea that the true self, the seat of reason, needs to be distanced from the embodied animal nature of the rational animal.

A good way to begin on elaborating such a conception of bodily action would be to think about the concept of intention in action. That is what I am going to start doing here.

2. Philosophers sometimes treat the expression 'intention in action' as a technical term. Robert Brandom hyphenates it into a single word, which signals that he is not conceiving it as a bit of ordinary language.[1] John Searle also hyphenates it, in his second treatment of the topic in *Rationality in Action*.[2] (In *Intentionality*,[3] with the same doctrine apart from some details, he left it as three words.)

But I want to resist the tendency to locate the idea of intention in action in some technical region of philosophy. I think common sense can easily accommodate the idea. And I want to be guided by how the phrase might be used to help express a conception of agency and action that we acquire in doing no more than learning relevant regions of our ordinary language.

3. Ultimately I want to suggest an interpretation of the phrase 'intention in action' according to which the intentions so characterizable are not distinct from the actions in which they are said to be. But I am

McDowell, J. (2009), "Acting As One Intends." This chapter was prepared by Jonathan Dancy from McDowell's Hägerström Lectures, given at Uppsala University in 2005. © John McDowell. It appears here by kind permission of the author.

going to work up to the non-distinctness of intentions from actions by degrees, starting with some
things that can be said without yet implying anything
in that area.

The most obvious way to begin isolating an idea of
intention in action is to distinguish it from the idea of
intention for the future. An intention in action would
need to be contemporaneous with the action it is in.
Intentions in action stand in contrast with prior
intentions, intentions to do such-and-such at some
future time. A prior intention predates the action that
is its execution, if indeed there is any such action, as
there will not be if the agent is prevented or changes
her mind or forgets.

Searle introduces intention in action by exploiting
this contrast. He describes two kinds of case in which
there is an intention in action without there having
been any relevant prior intention. In the first kind of
case, there was no prior intention in the vicinity at all;
one simply sets to and starts doing something. Searle's
example is a case in which, without premeditation,
while reflecting on a philosophical problem, he stands
up and starts pacing about. In the second kind of case,
there was a prior intention, but its content did not
embrace some detail of what one is now intentionally
doing in the course of executing it. Searle's example is
a case in which, in the course of executing an intention he formed in advance to drive to his office, he
changes gear as he accelerates out of a turn.

4.   Of course Searle does not restrict intentions in
action to cases in which there was no relevant prior
intention. His point in starting with such cases is that
they compel us to recognize intentions in action, as a
kind of item that cannot be identified with intentions
formed in advance of acting. But if a concept of intention in action has application at all, there must be
intention in action whenever someone is intentionally
doing something, including cases in which she formed
an intention ahead of acting. So we should consider
cases in which acting intentionally is executing what
was a prior intention. How does the prior intention
relate to the intention in action that we implicitly
acknowledge when we say the acting is intentional?

Searle's answer is that intentions in action are new
items, which a prior intention starts to generate when
the time to execute it comes. In Searle's picture prior

intentions and intentions in action are different
kinds of thing even apart from the difference in their
temporal relation to stretches of activity. A prior
intention has as its object an action, doing such-and-
such at some future time. But an intention in action,
generated by the prior intention at its due time, has as
its object not the action the agent is embarking on,
but something else, which Searle conceives as a component of that action.

Consider, for instance, an intention harboured by
someone standing on a kerb: the intention to cross the
street when the light turns green. On Searle's account,
when the person sees the light turn green, her prior
intention to cross the street starts to generate intentions in action. The object of the prior intention was
crossing the street, but the objects of the intentions in
action that it starts to generate when the agent starts
acting are the limb movements that need to happen if
the person is to do that. As those limb movements
begin, the person begins crossing the street. If all goes
well, she gets to the other side, thereby completing an
action of crossing the street. As Searle sees things, the
action is a causally structured complex: its components are, first, the intentions in action that the prior
intention began to generate when the agent saw the
light turn green, and, second, the limb movements on
which the intentions in action are targeted, which the
intentions in action will have caused.

I want to exploit Searle's theory as a helpful foil, to
bring into relief a different answer to the question
how intentions in action are related to intentions for
the future. On this different account, when one sees
the light turn green and starts crossing the street, it is
not that an intention for the future starts to generate
new items, intentions in action as Searle conceives
them. Rather, what was an intention for the future
becomes an intention in action. When one starts to do
something one had a prior intention to do, say crossing the street, one's intention, now in action, still has
that as its object. One does not start having new
intentions directed at limb movements that might be
seen, with Searle, as components in crossing the street.
One goes on having the same intention – directed at
crossing the street – that used to be a prior intention.
It is no longer a prior intention, but that is simply
because the time for acting that figures in its content is
no longer in the future. When its time comes, something

that was an intention for the future takes a new shape as an intention in action. At any rate that happens if the agent knows the time has come, does not forget what she intended to do, does not change her mind when the moment for acting arrives, and is not prevented from acting accordingly.

On this picture, what were prior intentions become intentions in action through the operation of an ability to retain thoughts – the same thoughts – while keeping track of the passage of time. My street-crossing case involves a very simple instance of that ability. A future time for acting is determined, in the thought that the agent's intention is, as the time at which a recognizable thing is going to happen: the time at which the light is going to turn green. When that recognizable thing happens, the agent recognizes that the time has come, and the intention becomes an intention in action – which is just to say that the agent starts executing her intention.

Of course the ability to keep track of time has more sophisticated forms also, involving the use of clocks and so forth. And of course the relevance of this ability to a subject's psychological history is not restricted to the persistence through time of intentions. The ability to keep track of time is called on whenever one keeps hold of time-specific thoughts as time passes. For instance, one can retain for a while a bit of knowledge one might have expressed, at the time at which one acquired it, by saying 'The light is turning green'. One needs to express it differently later, perhaps by saying 'The light turned green a while ago' – or, with a more sophisticated form of the ability to keep track of time, something like 'The light turned green thirty seconds ago'. But it is the *same* bit of knowledge, persisting through the passage of time, that needs to be expressed in these different ways.[4] Just so, it is the *same* intention, persisting through the passage of time, that alters from being an intention for the future to being an intention in action when its time comes, provided that it does not lapse through change of mind or forgetfulness, and provided that the agent knows its time has come and is not prevented from acting.

5. Searle's picture in its original form implies that intentions for the future lapse when the relevant acting starts, giving way to the intentions in action that they cause. Brian O'Shaughnessy, objecting to Searle,

points out that at any moment in a period in which one is intentionally crossing a street – to stay with the same example – one has an intention directed at the future. At any time during the crossing, one intends to go on crossing from the point one has reached to the other side.[5] O'Shaughnessy works with an example involving swimming from Dover to Calais. But the structure is the same, and I shall stay with my example.

The intention to finish crossing is not an intention in action in Searle's sense. This intention has as its object a prospective action: going from the point one has reached to the other side of the street. But the intentions in action, in Searle's sense, that are supposed to be operative in going on crossing would have as their objects the limb movements that need to happen if one is to do that, items that are not themselves actions but that figure in Searle's picture as components of actions.

In response to O'Shaughnessy, Searle makes a partial concession. He acknowledges that after one has embarked on executing a prior intention, an intention that is still for the future persists into the time of acting. Searle envisages this as an ever-shrinking residue of the original prior intention, present throughout the time of acting as an intention whose object is still in the future. In my example, this is an intention that at any time in the crossing is the intention to go on from the point one has reached to the other side. (Searle writes of 'the remains of the prior intention'.[6]) But Searle insists that acknowledging this shrinking residue of the prior intention does not obviate the need to recognize the intentions in action that, as he sees things, bring about the limb movements required for acting as one intended to act. As before, when one realizes that the time determined for acting by the original prior intention has come (when one sees the light turn green, in my example), the prior intention starts to generate, directly, suitable intentions in action, and thereby indirectly to generate suitable limb movements, directly caused by the intentions in action. Thereafter, persisting in its increasingly residual form, it goes on indirectly generating limb movements, by directly generating intentions in action, as one goes on crossing.[7]

And this picture presumably applies also where there was no prior intention. Suppose one intentionally crosses a street without having had a prior intention to cross it; one simply started crossing on the spur of the moment. Even so, throughout the crossing, given that it is intentional, there must be an intention of the sort that, where there was a prior intention, Searle conceives as a shrinking residue of that: an intention directed, at each moment, towards a future action, going on from the point one has reached to the other side. Searle's picture must be that whether or not there was a prior intention, intentionally crossing a street involves a shrinking intention for the future that progressively discharges itself, by generating intentions in action that in turn generate suitable limb movements.

Now contrast the alternative picture I described. On this picture, when acting is executing a prior intention, an intention in action is what the prior intention *becomes* when the time it determines for action arrives. When its time comes and the agent knows its time has come, the intention takes on the new guise of an intention that is expressing itself in action, provided it is not thwarted and does not lapse through change of mind. And now the phenomenon O'Shaughnessy points to, the directedness towards a diminishingly future stretch of action, falls straightforwardly into place. It is just what one would expect of a persisting intention that has become an intention in action because its time has come, and that continues to be operative throughout the acting in which it expresses itself. Similarly with an intention that begins its career as an intention in action – one starts acting on the spur of the moment – rather than becoming an intention in action after a phase in which it is an intention for the future.

In the background of this phenomenon, we need more than the ability to keep track of time, which was enough for making sense of the alteration from a prior intention to an intention in action. Now we need also the ability to know how one's action is progressing. Unless one knows how far one has come, one cannot intelligibly intend to go on from there to the other side of the street. But this is clearly not a gratuitous new requirement. The ability to be aware of the progress of one's action is a condition for being able to do things like intentionally crossing streets at all.

O'Shaughnessy multiplies intentions beyond what I am envisaging here. In his picture, there is an overarching intention of crossing the street, which may or may not have previously been an intention for the

future, but which, in either case, persists after one has begun crossing the street, though more and more of the street-crossing it is directed at recedes into the past as one goes on crossing. And there is in addition a continuum of distinct intentions for the future, one for any instant during the period in which one is crossing the street, directed at progressively less extensive completions of the crossing. O'Shaughnessy conceives these future-directed intentions as caused by the overarching persisting intention of crossing the street, and so as distinct from it.[8]

This continuum of differently future-directed intentions is O'Shaughnessy's way of dealing with the phenomenon Searle aims to accommodate by envisaging a single shrinking intention, in some cases a residue of what used to be a prior intention, intelligibly shifting in its future-directed content as one makes progress in one's action. But O'Shaughnessy's conception of the overarching and persisting intention of crossing the street seems enough to accommodate that phenomenon. What Searle conceives as shrinkage in an intention directed exclusively to the future is just as well conceived as shrinkage in what one still needs to do in order to execute the persisting intention, that is, to cross the street. And as far as I can see, this picture of the persisting intention to cross the street leaves unmotivated O'Shaughnessy's idea that there is *also* a continuum of future-directed intentions, each directed at a different remainder of the street-crossing, caused by the overarching intention and hence distinct from it. The shifting future-directedness is just what is to be expected of the overarching intention itself, as it progressively finds expression in crossing the street. The multiple intentions O'Shaughnessy invokes, over and above the persisting intention of crossing the street, with their orientation towards smaller and smaller continuations into the future of what one is doing, are better conceived, not as distinct effects of the persisting intention in action, but as successive shapes taken by it.

The general form of this shifting future-directedness in the content of intention in action is this: at any point, one intends to do whatever it takes to finish doing what one is doing. In the street-crossing example this idea functions in a particularly simple way. At any time in the course of crossing the street, what one still needs to do is to go on from the point one has reached to the other side of the street. But the same structure fits projects with more complex shapes, for instance baking a cake or building a house. In these cases, when we spell out what is required if one is to finish doing what one is doing, at a moment at which one is some way into doing it, we need to introduce things to do with more complex relations to what one has already done. Having beaten the eggs, one needs to fold in the flour, and so on until the cake is baked. But the idea of going on until one has finished doing what one is doing still fits, for the content of the diminishingly future-directed intention that, on the picture I am recommending, an intention in action is.

6. O'Shaughnessy countenances, besides the overarching intention of crossing the street (to stay with my example), a continuum of distinct exclusively future-directed intentions, one for each moment in crossing. I suggested a unification: instead of those distinct and multiple future-directed intentions, focus on the diminishingly future-directed aspect of the persisting overarching intention itself.

Now O'Shaughnessy also envisages another set of intentions, contemporaneous with their expression in action, that would be operative when someone is crossing a street: intentions directed at moving one's limbs as the project requires.[9] Intentions of this sort reflect motor skills – not just the ability to make the movements needed for the routine exercise of a skill such as walking, but sometimes a more finely tuned responsiveness to circumstances, as when one puts a foot down carefully to compensate for an unevenness in the surface.

Here we are closer to Searle's intentions in action than anything so far has brought us. But as O'Shaughnessy insists, these intentions are still distinct from intentions in action in Searle's sense. An intention in action in Searle's sense would have as its object a limb's moving thus and so, whereas an intention of this kind has as its object one's moving the limb thus and so.

Here too I see no need to multiply intentions as O'Shaughnessy does. O'Shaughnessy conceives these detailed motor intentions as generated by the overarching intention, and so distinct from it. But we need not follow him in this. We can exploit again the idea of different shapes taken by the overarching intention as it expresses itself. In the picture as we already have

it, persisting intentions change their shape from being intentions purely for the future to being intentions in action, as a subject keeps track of time. And once they have taken on the guise of intentions in action, they change to having less in prospect and more behind them of what they are intentions to do, as an agent makes progress in a project. In the same spirit, we can say that these same intentions, intentions to do things like crossing streets, change from one determinate short-term motor shape to another as they express themselves in acting.

Motor skills are anyway presupposed by the very idea of intentions to do things like crossing streets. But in making their role explicit, I have added a third item to the background against which the shifting career of a persisting intention is intelligible. I was already appealing to the ability to hold on to thoughts, including intentions, through the passage of time, and the ability to keep track of the progress of actions. The third item is motor competence, the ability to gear one's movings of one's limbs to the circumstances in which one engages in bodily action. These are all things on which the changes of shape undergone by an intention to do something like crossing a street depend.

7. I hope I have made plausible a conception with the following features. (All I have aimed to do is to reformulate some obvious common sense in terms of the idea of intention in action.) An intention in action is a kind of item that can be in place in advance of the action in which it is, in the guise of an intention for the future. In a different kind of case, however, an intention in action begins to be in place only when one begins acting. That is how it is with unpremeditated intentional action. Once an intention is in action, it shifts its shape at a coarse-grained level of description, as more of what it is an intention to do gets to have been done and less remains to do. It also shifts its shape at a more fine-grained level of description, as it expresses itself in the detailed exercises of motor skills that are called for in executing one's project. An intention in action is in action throughout the action in which it is, not just at the start.

In laying out this conception, I exploited Brian O'Shaughnessy's objections against John Searle. But the picture I want to recommend is not O'Shaughnessy's own.

There are two divergences. The first is the one I elaborated in §§5 and 6. This is that O'Shaughnessy multiplies intentions in a way in which the picture I have just summarized does not. But the picture I want to recommend diverges in a second way from O'Shaughnessy's picture, and that is what I want to consider now. O'Shaughnessy does not allow the title 'intention in action' to any of the intentions he countenances. In fact he thinks there is something wrong with the very idea of an intention in action. I have been working with the thought that we might reject what Searle wants to conceive as intentions in action, supposed intentions whose objects are that one's limbs should move in certain ways, but that we might recognize different candidates for being intentions in action: in particular, the persisting overarching intentions that O'Shaughnessy himself acknowledges. But O'Shaughnessy would have no sympathy with that.

This takes me to my main purpose. The ultimate point of talking about intentions in action was to be that it would enable me to fill out a proposal I put on the table at the beginning of this chapter. The proposal is that the bodily goings-on involved in, for instance, intentionally crossing a street are themselves exercises of conceptual capacities, somewhat as, according to me, the sensory goings-on involved in the perceptual experience of rational animals are themselves actualizations of conceptual capacities.

I began this inquiry into how to think about intention in action by remarking that the force of 'in', in that phrase, is at least partly temporal. An intention in action would need to be contemporaneous with the action it is in. But if the idea of intention in action is to fit the thought that bodily goings-on can themselves be exercises of conceptual capacities, 'in' needs to have a force that is not exhausted by the idea of an intention that is contemporaneous with its action.

So far as it goes, the merely temporal interpretation of 'in' is uncontroversial. That is not what arouses O'Shaughnessy's scepticism about the very idea of an intention in action. His doubts impinge directly on my proposal. I can express my proposal by saying that the intention operative in doing such-and-such is not distinct from the bodily movements one makes when one does such-and-such. And that is just what O'Shaughnessy finds unintelligible.

8. O'Shaughnessy's scepticism is in the first instance directed at Searle, but its spirit applies more widely.

Searle's intentions in action are not just contemporaneous with the actions they are said to be in. They are supposed to be components of them. Against this, O'Shaughnessy finds it unintelligible that anything deserving to be conceived as an intention might, as he puts it, 'actually enter the precincts of the action itself'.[10]

This thought threatens other ideas besides Searle's idea that an intention might be in an action by being part of it. Consider the implications of O'Shaughnessy's prohibition on intentions entering the precincts of action. It would follow that the intention of crossing a street – to fix on the single item to which I have suggested we can reduce the multiplicity of contemporaneous intentions he countenances – relates to someone's crossing the street only from outside. A model for this might be the way in which an intention that a tree should fall might relate to the tree's falling, say if the intention is realized in one's sawing through the tree's trunk, with the result that it falls. I do not want to defend Searle's idea that intention might be in an action by being part of it. But I want to resist any suggestion that the relation between intention and bodily movement might be appropriately modelled on the relation between an intention operative in sawing through a tree's trunk and the falling of the tree, where the falling is the result of the intention, so that – to echo O'Shaughnessy – the intention does not enter the precincts of the falling itself. I think an intention of crossing the street, conceived in the protean shape-shifting way I have recommended, should not be conceived as related to one's bodily movements in crossing the street only from outside.

To elaborate this, I shall exploit another region of O'Shaughnessy's own thinking.

In his ground-breaking work on the will (a phenomenology of acting spirit), O'Shaughnessy presents a dual aspect conception of physical, or bodily, action.[11] Acting physically is exercising motor capacities. And exercising a motor capacity is as such a bodily phenomenon. But according to the dual aspect conception, it is also psychological, and not just in an isolable component but through and through. A psychological concept, expressible by 'willing' in a sense O'Shaughnessy attaches to that verb, applies not to some supposed psychic initiating occurrence, but to the relevant bodily goings-on, those describable as a subject's exercising a motor capacity, in their entirety. Willing is not something that causally initiates bodily acting and perhaps supervises it from outside. Willing is in the acting, not in the Searle-like sense that willing is part of an action, but in the sense that 'willing' is a characterization of the acting itself, apt for capturing its psychological aspect.

Why, now, does O'Shaughnessy find it unintelligible that intending might enter the precincts of action? Well, he is impressed – surely correctly, so far as this goes – by the thought that willing, conceived as he conceives it, belongs to animal life as such, whereas intending does not. Intending is not universal in animals. O'Shaughnessy marks the restriction by saying that intention can be attributed only to animals whose behaviour is future-directed in a certain distinctive way. Consider a cat slinking along, belly to ground and with whiskers twitching, in a way that can be explained by saying it is stalking a bird. That explanation implicitly invokes a projected future in which the bird has been caught.[12] 'It's stalking a bird' answers a version of the question 'Why?' in terms of which G. E. M. Anscombe famously isolates intentional action. In fact this example of the attribution of intention to animals other than human beings is Anscombe's own.[13]

So the concept of intention does not have as broad a scope as O'Shaughnessy's concept of willing, even before we consider the special form in which the concept of intention applies to rational animals. And O'Shaughnessy accommodates this by holding that intending is *additional* to the willing that, according to his dual aspect conception, is just acting under a description that brings out its psychological aspect. He locates intending in a higher region of the psychological, which he marks out with a technical use of the word 'mental'. Intending, he holds, is not merely psychological, as willing is, but mental. It causally initiates willing – that is, acting – and supervises it from outside its precincts.

It is clear that the idea of intending is different from the idea of willing plain and simple, willing as it is found in animals that do not have intention. But do we have to agree with O'Shaughnessy that intending is *additional* to willing? Why not conceive intending as a special form taken by willing, in animals that are at

least, as we might put it, proto-rational? That would allow us to go further than O'Shaughnessy does with the dual aspect conception of bodily action, as both physical through and through and psychological through and through. If we conceive intending as a species of willing, we can hold that, like the willing plain and simple to which O'Shaughnessy restricts the concept of willing, intending can be in action, not in the Searle-like sense that it is a component in actions, but in an O'Shaughnessy-like sense, that it just is acting, characterized in a way that captures a now more sophisticated psychological aspect that this kind of acting has.

It may seem a problem for this proposal that willing in O'Shaughnessy's sense just is acting. In contrast, intending figures not only as intention in action, but also – in rational animals – as intention purely for the future. Intention purely for the future cannot be just what willing is: that is, acting, characterized in a way that brings out its psychological aspect. But surely intention in the course of being acted on should be just what intention purely for the future is except that its time is present.

But everything depends on the direction in which we take that equation. We might think it requires us to start with intention purely for the future and conceive intention in action as just what that is except for the time difference. That would threaten the possibility of supposing that intention in action just is acting described in such a way as to highlight its psychological aspect. But we should take the equation in the other direction; we should start with intention in action and conceive intention purely for the future as just what that is apart from the time difference.

Once intentions purely for the future are on the scene, we are concerned with the special form that intending takes in rational animals. The cat whose intention is captured by saying it is stalking a bird can drop out of the picture, and we can say an intention is the kind of thing that can be arrived at by practical reasoning (though intentions need not be acquired by reasoning). Of course practical reasoning, reasoning directed at the question what to do, can be for the future. I can reason about which bus to take tomorrow, and conclude by forming an intention to take the one that leaves at 8.28. But that should not dislodge us from holding that when practical reasoning is about what to do here and now, drawing the conclusion is acting, as Aristotle says.

The conclusion of practical reasoning about what to do here and now is, if you like, a kind of thought. It is practical thought, in the strong sense that assenting to such a thought just is beginning to act in a certain way, for instance beginning to cross a street; and continuing to assent − not revoking one's assent − is continuing to act, for instance continuing to cross the street. An intention for the future is, by all means, a thought of the same kind, apart from the time difference. But the way to accommodate that is not to distance intention for the here and now from acting, on the ground that intending purely for the future is not acting, but to conceive an intention for the future as a prospective action biding its time. When its time comes, provided the agent knows its time has come and is not prevented, and provided she does not change her mind, it will become an instance of willing − that is, acting. On these lines we can sustain an O'Shaughnessy-like dual aspect conception for intending, not just for willing in general. We can say intention in action is the form taken, in intending animals, by willing, conceived as O'Shaughnessy conceives it. Intention in action just is acting, under a characterization that brings out its psychological aspect, a psychological aspect that is more sophisticated than the one captured by talk of willing plain and simple.

The picture of intention for the future as prospective action biding its time is no more than an application of the idea I urged in §4: that intentions for the future become intentions in action when their time comes, provided the agent knows the time has come, and is not prevented, and does not change her mind. To talk of intention in action is just to talk of acting intentionally. Since there can be intentions for the future, acting intentionally can be, though it need not be, the mature form of something that was already present before acting was under way. An intention for the future stands to the acting one engages in when one starts to execute it, or, equivalently, to the intention in action that it becomes at that point, as a caterpillar stands to the butterfly it becomes in metamorphosis.

9. My talk of shape-shifting intentions may have seemed metaphysically extravagant. But from the vantage point I have reached now, it should be clear that there was less to that talk than there may have seemed. One kind of shape-shifting, the shift from intention purely for the future to intention in action, is what I am now in a position to redescribe as the transition from action in waiting to action in progress. Action in waiting is something whose nature is that in due course, failing prevention or change of mind or failure to keep track of time, it matures into action in progress. For the rest, talk of a persisting intention that changes its shape as time passes now emerges as no more than a way of talking, surely harmlessly, of the unfolding of an action intentionally undertaken.

Not that that is a completely straightforward topic. I am going to spend the rest of this chapter on it, and I shall be only scratching the surface.

10. Earlier in this chapter, I suggested that the exercises of motor skills involved in the execution of a project such as walking across a street should be seen as shapes assumed by the persisting intention of crossing the street as one progresses with the project. Now even if all the motor activity is routine, an advance intention of crossing a street will not be at all points determinate in respect of precisely what motor performance is to come at each juncture of the crossing: whether to step off the kerb with the left foot or the right, and so on throughout. So even if the crossing is routine, there is an *improvisational* character to the way the intention that is in action in it acquires determinacy as it expresses itself in acting. This comes out more vividly when we consider cases in which routine motor activity is not enough to get things done, as when a competent walker copes on the fly with uneven terrain. For a more extreme case, suppose that, as one is making one's way across the street, an earthquake begins to open up fissures in the surface, and getting to the other side starts to require a special deftness in how one places one's feet.

These cases provide analogues, for projects as low grade as merely achieving a change in one's physical location, to examples of action in connection with which it might come more easily to speak of creativity. Consider, for instance, how an intention of making a wood sculpture would need to acquire determinacy as one proceeds, dealing as one goes along with unforeseeable knots and irregularities of grain. Of course mere motor skills matter here too; a clumsy woodworker will botch attempts to work around a knot. But now there is room for a different sort of evaluation of intentions in action. Artistic talent is not exhausted by dexterity. Perhaps we might judge a street-crossing that gracefully overcomes obstacles in something like the spirit in which we might judge a bit of ballet.

The detailed intentions with which one responds to circumstances, in the course of executing an overarching intention that is initially only partly determinate, can be formed as a result of practical reasoning engaged in as problems arise. The wood sculptor thinks: 'I can't make a straight cut there, because the wood will split at the knot. So what shall I do?' And the result of her reflection determines the shape her intention takes during the phase of her activity in which she is overcoming that obstacle. So there can be practical reasoning in the background of this kind of coping with problems that arise in the course of a project. But there need not be. As with intentions in general, the right thing to say about short-term executive intentions of this sort is that they are instances of a kind of thing that *can* be formed as a result of practical reasoning, not that all instances of the kind *are* formed in that way. This kind of creative dealing with circumstances as they arise can be unreflective.

11. The bodily goings-on involved in walking across a street have an internal organization in which one thing is causally related to another. For instance, forward motion on the part of a human being who stays upright and balanced is a causal outcome of the familiar, though quite hard to describe, things she does with her legs, pushing back with one foot and swinging the other forward in a smooth sequence of movements. Now it seems infelicitous to insist here on separating the result, the upright and balanced forward motion, from doings on the part of the agent specified in terms of how she moves her legs, doings that we would perhaps, on this kind of view, see as designed to achieve that result. This causal organization is internal to the agent's doing, rather than being a matter of connections between the doing under a minimal specification and something external to the doing so specified.

Similarly with simple manipulation of objects. Picking up a book, say, is causally organized, in that the book's change of position is a causal outcome of the agent's motions of grasping and lifting. And here too it seems infelicitous to separate the book's change of place from doings on the part of the agent specified in terms of how she moves her hands and arms, perhaps seen as designed to achieve that result. Here too it seems better to regard the causal relation as internal to the agent's doing, rather than as connecting the agent's doing under a minimal specification with an outcome external to the doing so specified. A picture on those lines falsifies the structure of the case, even if we insist that a further description *of the agent's doing* – a further specification of what she is doing or has done – is available by virtue of the occurrence of the outcome.

What I am suggesting here may become clearer if we contrast a different kind of case, where it is natural to say that an external outcome allows for a new specification of what an agent is doing or has done. Suppose one has a project of rolling a boulder down a slope. The boulder is balanced at the top of the slope. One applies enough force to push it past the tipping point. Now gravity takes over; the boulder falls outward, and rolls down the slope, as one intended that it should. When the boulder reaches the bottom of the slope, it becomes true that one has rolled it down the slope. But there is no need to go on exerting effort, which is the shape willing takes here,[14] after one has moved the boulder's centre of gravity enough to cause it to topple. If the boulder gets to the bottom of the slope, one has rolled it down the slope; but one's active, willing part in the proceedings is finished at the moment at which gravity takes over.

In cases of this sort, there is a familiar tendency to behave as if one could exert one's will magically, so as to go on having an impact on how things happen. If a threat arises that the boulder will stop rolling on a less steep stretch of the slope, it may be natural, as one watches from a distance, to do things with one's body as if to urge it on. Baseball hitters sometimes contort their bodies after the ball has left the bat, in a way that makes what sense it does only as an attempt to cause the ball to stay fair by magically influencing its trajectory. But one smiles at this tendency, and that brings out vividly the real structure of this sort of case. Here we do have a separable outcome of a doing, by virtue of which a further specification of what one has done becomes available. This kind of structure is central to Donald Davidson's discussion of agency.[15]

In this kind of case an outcome – the boulder rolling down the slope, the ball landing fair – is temporally separate from a bit of willing, or equivalently acting, on the part of the agent. By virtue of its having that outcome, the bit of acting becomes describable in a way that alludes to the outcome – rolling the boulder down the slope, hitting a fair ball. This temporal separateness makes it particularly obvious how natural it is to apply the Davidsonian structure in these cases.

But a temporal separation of the outcome is not necessary for the Davidsonian structure to be a comfortable fit. Suppose that as one is crossing a street one is leaving a trace on the recording medium of a surveillance camera. Perhaps this is intentional; imagine that one's plan is to provide oneself with an alibi in respect of a crime one's associates are committing. Here it is natural to see the appearance of the trace on the recording medium as an outcome, distinct from one's doing conceived under the specification 'crossing the street'. By virtue of the fact that it leads to this outcome, the doing can be redescribed as leaving a trace on the recording medium. And here the emergence of the outcome is not something that begins to happen only as the willing that is one's acting comes to an end.

So how does this case differ from achieving balanced and upright forward motion when one walks, or bringing about a change in the position of a book that one picks up, where I suggested it is infelicitous to apply the Davidsonian structure?

I think the point is this. One's movings of one's limbs, in walking, or in grasping and lifting something, are indeed intentional, but not, so to speak, autonomously so. If we acknowledge that one acts intentionally under specifications framed in terms of the way one moves one's limbs in this kind of case, the intentions in action that we thereby implicitly acknowledge have no place in the picture except as shapes taken by the overarching intention to cross the street or to pick up the book. The overarching intention takes such shapes through the operation of motor skills, without any need for even implicit practical reasoning. There is no application here for the idea of adopting means to ends. Crossing the street, say, is something one immediately sets to and does, not something one does by doing something else.

Contrast the case in which one intentionally leaves a trace on the recording medium of a surveillance camera as one crosses a street. The intention of crossing the street is autonomous, as the intention of doing whatever one does with one's legs when one does some routine walking is not, because crossing the street is a means to the end of leaving a trace on the recording medium. We can find a sort of confirmation of this suggestion by considering cases in which, for special reasons, the unreflective operation of motor skills does not suffice to yield motor intentions apt for forward motion or manipulation of objects, and one has to think about how to work one's legs or arms. Such cases comfortably fit the Davidsonian structure. In such cases the intentions to do suitable things with one's limbs are autonomous, and now there is nothing counter-intuitive about the idea that a doing describable in those terms gets to be redescribable in terms of locomotion or manipulation of objects by virtue of leading to outcomes external to itself.

12.   In my boulder-rolling example the agent's intention was to roll the boulder down the slope. But we can consider a different version. Suppose the agent's intention is only to see if she can topple the boulder from its balanced position. She does not think ahead to what is likely to happen next if it topples. Perhaps she is horrified when, rather than simply coming to rest away from its original position, it starts to roll, gaining momentum and perhaps threatening a party of picnickers in its path. If the boulder reaches the bottom of the slope, then, no less than the person for whom its getting to the bottom of the slope was the plan, she will be describable as having rolled it down the slope. That she has done that may, for instance, be the basis for accusing her of recklessly endangering the picnickers. This kind of specification of what someone has done, alluding to an outcome that has resulted from her doing something, is neutral as to whether the doing specified in a way that alludes to the outcome – as 'rolling the boulder down the slope' alludes to the outcome consisting in the boulder's rolling down the slope – is intentional under that specification or not. Similarly, if a surveillance camera is recording one's crossing of a street, one is leaving a trace on its recording medium as one crosses, whether or not one is even aware of the camera, let alone intending that one's crossing should have that effect.

To embark on a bit of physical or bodily acting is to intervene in objective reality. Things start to change in the world, in a way that simply is one's intention expressing itself. For instance a certain human body – one's own – starts to move across a street. Intentions express themselves in happenings in objective reality. Just for that reason, the idea of intention in action is well captured by the image of dropping a stone in a pool, causing ripples that spread out in all directions. One's intentions in action, *qua* happenings in objective reality, have effects that radiate out in time and space from the initial intervention. There seems to be no principled way of drawing a limit to the possible extent of the causal reverberations of a bit of acting. They are bound to outrun the agent's capacity for foresight, let alone her capacity to include them in what she intends, as the first boulder-roller includes the boulder's rolling down the slope in what she intends. And any outcome of one's doing, however unforeseen or unintended, generates a truth about what one has done, as the unforeseen and unintended rolling of the boulder down the slope in the second boulder-rolling example generates the possibility of saying truly that the agent has rolled the boulder down the slope. So there is a perfectly intelligible conception according to which what one is doing or has done is determined by what alterations in the objective world can be traced to one's intentional interventions in it, independently of whether the alterations were intended or even foreseen. What one is doing or has done, on this interpretation of the phrase, can be a topic of discovery for one, for instance as one watches in horror while the boulder that one thoughtlessly toppled over ploughs through a group of picnickers. The discovery may not even be feasible for the agent herself; it may be only after someone's death that she can be known to have started the train of events that led to a revolution.

What one is doing or has done, on this interpretation, can escape one's control. One has no special authority in saying what one is doing or has done. Others may be more knowledgeable than one is about the consequences of one's interventions. As if throwing a stone into a pool, one throws out one's intentional doing into objective reality, where it takes on a life of its own as the objective happening it is, collecting new characterizations as its effects unfold.

But what one is doing, or has done, *intentionally* cannot escape one's control like that. It is true that in cases with the Davidsonian structure investigation may be required to confirm that one has done something one intended to do. One needs to watch what happens in order to know whether one has succeeded in rolling a boulder down a slope, and one needs to check that a camera has functioned properly in order to know whether one has succeeded in leaving a trace on its recording medium. But that would be confirming that things have happened as one intended that they should. We would lose a distinction that we ought not to be willing to lose if we supposed that, in the second boulder-rolling example, it turns out, as the boulder rolls down the slope, that rolling it down the slope is after all the content of an intention the agent has.

When I say that what one is doing intentionally cannot escape one's control, I am not implying that there is no room for surprise at a form that one's intention takes. In the simple case of crossing the street there is, according to the picture I have been recommending, an initially indeterminate intention, to get across the street, that takes on determinate motor shapes as one responds to the shifting circumstances under which at any moment the next move needs to be made. Now consider the version of the street-crossing example in which finishing the crossing starts to require a special nimbleness as one dodges clefts opening in the roadway because of an earthquake. If one succeeds in crossing in these circumstances, one might look back at the detailed motor shapes that one's overarching intention took, under the pressure of the unusual circumstances, with a thought like 'I didn't know I had it in me to be so nimble'. In a case like this, one discovers something about one's capacities as agent by intentionally doing something that one did not know in advance one was capable of doing.

As I said, the structure here is analogous to the structure of cases where a concept of creativity finds more obvious application, as an initially indeterminate intention takes determinate shapes in response to obstacles that arise in the course of, say, making a sculpture. Anyone who writes, even if it is only utilitarian prose, will recognize the experience of surprise at the determinate shape that an initially indeterminate intention of expressing a certain thought, at first only vaguely conceived, takes as one starts to string words together.

One can be surprised, then, at a determinate shape one's intention takes. But it is not that one finds out, with surprise, what the intention that takes that determinate shape already was. If that were the appropriate picture here, it might be appropriate, in the second boulder-rolling example, to take the line I have resisted, and claim that an intention that the agent is initially aware of only in an indeterminate guise turns out to have been an intention to roll the boulder down the slope. But in that case the agent's doing comes to be characterizable as rolling the boulder down the slope by virtue of a result's merely happening, without further involvement on her part. In contrast, when an initially indeterminate intention becomes more determinate as one walks across a street or makes a sculpture, that is not something that merely happens, without intervention on one's part, as one thing causally leads to another. In these cases, an intention's taking a determinate shape is the agent's *giving* her intention a further determination. In neither case do we have an intention turning out to have already had some determinacy that comes to light only as events unfold.

It may seem problematic to say that an intention's acquiring determinacy as someone goes on crossing a street is her giving it more determinacy. Did I not say that at least in routine cases an intention to walk, for instance, acquires short-term determinacy, in respect of what limb movements to make, through the unreflective operation of motor skills? But that would threaten my saying that the agent further determines her intention only if one could not further determine an intention except by taking thought about what to do. Of course there is no need for that when an agent, say, steps off a kerb with her right foot, thereby further determining, for the moment, an intention to cross the street. To emphasize that she does not take thought about what to do, it can be right to say she finds herself stepping off with her right foot. But she does find herself *doing* that. She does that intentionally. And in intentionally doing that, she determines her intention in action to take that shape at that moment. (That is simply to say that that is what she does at that moment.)

One gives determinacy to an initially indeterminate intention by progressively giving it expression in objective reality. When one gets to the other side of the street, one will have accomplished a complete street-crossing by intentionally making just the movements one has made — at least those of the movements one has made that were relevant to the execution of the project (of course there may have been others, for instance waving to a friend).

One may not succeed in one's project. An attempt to cross a street may be cut off in mid-crossing. More interestingly, suppose I finish my sculpture, and it is not the elegant construction I vaguely had in mind, but a clumsy mess. Everything I did in making it I did intentionally. So should we say the clumsy mess is what, as it turns out, I intended to make? That making *this* — or perhaps making something with just *these* features — is the determinacy I gave my intention as I proceeded? That would be like saying endangering the picnickers is what the second boulder-roller, as it turns out, intended to do. And we should not say such a thing.

Making the clumsy mess is indeed what I have achieved by my intentional sculpting activities. That is like saying endangering the picnickers is what I have achieved by my intentional boulder-toppling activities. My doing under these sorts of specification is not under my control: in one case because the determinate object I threw out into objective reality has, as it were of its own accord, acquired a new description in terms of an effect it had as the objective event it was; in the other because the specification reflects the failure of the object I threw out into objective reality (I mean my making the sculpture, though the wording would fit the sculpture too) to conform to a specification I intended for it. In the sculpting case, I learn something about myself when I see that the clumsy mess is the best I can produce in pursuit of elegance. But what I learn is something about my powers, not something about what my intention after all was. I have failed to execute — to effect a determinate objective realization of — an indeterminate intention. I have not succeeded in giving an intention of mine a determinacy with which I am then disappointed. Perhaps we should say I learn that what I thought was an intention was really only a wish or a hope. I do not have it in me to intend what I thought I intended, when I told myself I intended to make an elegant construction, any more than I have it in me to intend to do a high jump with the bar set at two metres.

I am insisting on preserving a special place, among differences an agent makes to how things happen in the objective world, for differences she makes intentionally. As objectively real deflections of the course of events, the differences one makes are all public matters, those intentionally made no less than the others. When one acts intentionally one puts into the public domain an item that collects further determinations, by having further effects, outside one's control. So one runs the risk of turning out, in the public view, which is the only view that counts for these purposes, to have done something one would not have dreamed of doing. It is also true that what one has objectively done — what others can authoritatively say one has done — can diverge from what one intended because of sheer failure on one's part. It is essential to agency that one retains the right to make just that sort of separation: 'I did that, but not intentionally.' All the differences one makes are one's doing, but only some of them are one's intentional doing. Over the question which of the differences are her intentional doing, public though they are, the agent must have a special authority. If we denied ourselves this distinction, we would not be able to distinguish the special sort of difference-maker an agent is from the sort of difference-maker that, for instance, a meteorite can be, when it crashes into the earth and causes a mass extinction of animal species.

Of course if we concede this special authority to agents, we open up a possibility for abusing it. It can be tempting to disavow an intention one really has in order to cut a better figure. But here as elsewhere, the possibility of abuse is not a ground for rejecting a claim of authority altogether.

Notes

This chapter was prepared by Jonathan Dancy from my Hägerström Lectures, given at Uppsala University in 2005. It partly coincides with my Amherst Lecture in Philosophy for 2011, 'Some Remarks on Intention in Action,' published at www.amherstlecture.org.

1. Robert B. Brandom, *Making It Explicit: Reasoning, Representing, and Discursive Commitment* (Cambridge, Mass.: Harvard University Press, 1994).
2. John Searle, *Rationality in Action* (Cambridge, Mass.: MIT Press, 2001).
3. John Searle, *Intentionality* (Cambridge: Cambridge University Press, 1983).
4. On keeping track of time, see Gareth Evans, *The Varieties of Reference* (Oxford: Clarendon Press, 1982), especially 192–6.
5. See Brian O'Shaughnessy, 'Searle's Theory of Action', in Ernest Lepore and Robert Van Gulick, eds., *John Searle and His Critics* (Oxford: Blackwell, 1991), 271–88.
6. See Searle's 'Response: The Background of Intentionality and Action', in *John Searle and His Critics*, 289–99.
7. Ibid., 298; see also *Rationality in Action*, 50–1.
8. See 'Searle's Theory of Action', 274–5.
9. Ibid., 278.
10. Ibid., 282.
11. See Brian O'Shaughnessy, *The Will: A Dual Aspect Theory* (Cambridge: Cambridge University Press, 1980, two volumes). There is a helpful brief statement of the dual aspect conception in the opening pages of O'Shaughnessy's paper 'The Epistemology of Physical Action', in Johannes Roessler and Naomi Eilan, eds., *Agency and Self-Awareness* (Oxford: Clarendon Press, 2003), 345–57.
12. On the future-directedness of intention, see *The Will*, vol. 2, 303–30.
13. See G. E. M. Anscombe, *Intention* (Oxford: Blackwell, 1957), 86–7.
14. I put this in because willing (in O'Shaughnessy's sense) is not necessarily effortful.
15. See Donald Davidson, 'Agency', Chapter 2 in this volume.

16

Intentional Action and Side Effects in Ordinary Language

Joshua Knobe

The chairman of the board of a company has decided to implement a new program. He believes

1. that the program will make a lot of money for his company

and

2. that the program will also produce some other effect x.

But the chairman doesn't care at all about effect x. His sole reason for implementing the new program is that he believes it will make a lot of money for the company. In the end, everything proceeds as anticipated: the program makes a lot of money for the company and also produces effect x.

Here it appears that, although the chairman foresaw that x would result from his behaviour, he did not care either way whether x actually occurred. Let us say, then, that x was a 'side effect' of his behaviour. The question I want to address here is: Shall we say that the chairman brought about this side effect *intentionally*?

This question goes to the heart of a major controversy regarding the proper analysis of the concept of intentional action. So, for example, on Alfred Mele's

(2001) analysis, it is always wrong to say that a side effect was brought about intentionally.[1] By contrast, on Michael Bratman's (1984; 1987) analysis, there are circumstances under which side effects can truly be said to have been brought about intentionally. Numerous other authors have come down on one side or the other of this issue.

Now, when we encounter a controversy like this one, it can sometimes be helpful to ask ourselves what people would ordinarily say about the situation under discussion. Would people ordinarily say that the side effects of a behaviour were brought about intentionally? Clearly, ordinary language does not here constitute a court of final appeal. (Even if it turns out that people ordinarily call side effects 'intentional', we might conclude that they are truly unintentional.) Still, it does seem plausible that the examination of ordinary language might provide us with some useful guidance about difficult cases like this one.

In an earlier publication, the experimental psychologist Bertram Malle and I provided empirical support for the conclusion that people only consider an effect to have been brought about 'intentionally' when the agent was specifically trying to bring about that effect (Malle & Knobe 1997). I now think that this conclusion was too hasty. The truth is that a person's intuitions as to whether or not a given side effect was produced intentionally can be influenced by that person's attitude toward the specific side effect in question (Harman 1976). Thus, it would be a mistake to ask for a general

Knobe, J. (2003), "Intentional Action and Side Effects in Ordinary Language," *Analysis* 63 (3), 190–194. Reprinted with permission of Oxford University Press.

answer to the question as to whether people will think that an agent intentionally brought about 'some side effect *x*'. People's judgements depend in a crucial way on what *x* happens to be. In particular, it makes a great deal of difference whether they think that *x* is something good or something bad.

1. First Experiment

To test this hypothesis, I conducted a simple experiment. Subjects were 78 people spending time in a Manhattan public park. Each subject was randomly assigned to either the 'harm condition' or the 'help condition'. Subjects in the harm condition read the following vignette:

> The vice-president of a company went to the chairman of the board and said, 'We are thinking of starting a new program. It will help us increase profits, but it will also harm the environment.'
>
> The chairman of the board answered, 'I don't care at all about harming the environment. I just want to make as much profit as I can. Let's start the new program.'
>
> They started the new program. Sure enough, the environment was harmed.

These subjects were then asked to determine how much blame the chairman deserved for what he did (on a scale from 0 to 6) and to say whether they thought the chairman *intentionally* harmed the environment.

Subjects in the help condition received a vignette that was almost exactly the same, except that the word 'harm' was replaced by 'help':

> The vice-president of a company went to the chairman of the board and said, 'We are thinking of starting a new program. It will help us increase profits, and it will also help the environment.'
>
> The chairman of the board answered, 'I don't care at all about helping the environment. I just want to make as much profit as I can. Let's start the new program.'
>
> They started the new program. Sure enough, the environment was helped.

These subjects were then asked to determine how much praise the chairman deserved (on a scale from 0 to 6) and whether they thought the chairman *intentionally* helped the environment.

As predicted, the two conditions elicited two radically different patterns of responses. In the harm condition, most subjects (82%) said that the agent brought about the side effect intentionally, whereas in the help condition, most subjects (77%) said that the agent did not bring about the side effect intentionally. This difference was highly statistically significant, $\chi^2(1, N = 78) = 27.2, p < .001$.

2. Second Experiment

Of course, we should be reluctant to reach any general conclusions on the basis of just one experiment. Perhaps the results obtained in experiment can be explained in terms of some highly specific fact about the way people think about corporations and environmental damage. To test the generality of the effect, I therefore ran a second experiment. The vignettes used in this second experiment had the same basic structure as those used in experiment 1, but the story was transposed from a corporate setting (with a chairman affecting the environment) to a military setting (with a lieutenant affecting a squad of soldiers).

Subjects were 42 people spending time in a Manhattan public park. Once again, subjects were randomly assigned to either a 'harm condition' or a 'help condition.' Subjects in the harm condition were asked to read the following vignette:

> A lieutenant was talking with a sergeant. The lieutenant gave the order: 'Send your squad to the top of Thompson Hill.'
>
> The sergeant said: 'But if I send my squad to the top of Thompson Hill, we'll be moving the men directly into the enemy's line of fire. Some of them will surely be killed!'
>
> The lieutenant answered: 'Look, I know that they'll be in the line of fire, and I know that some of them will be killed. But I don't care at all about what happens to our soldiers. All I care about is taking control of Thompson Hill.'
>
> The squad was sent to the top of Thompson Hill. As expected, the soldiers were moved into the enemy's line of fire, and some of them were killed.

These subjects were then asked to determine how much blame the lieutenant deserved for what he did and whether or not he intentionally put the soldiers in the line of fire.

Subjects in the help condition received a quite similar vignette:

> A lieutenant was talking with a sergeant. The lieutenant gave the order: 'Send your squad to the top of Thompson Hill.'
>
> The sergeant said: 'If I send my squad to the top of Thompson Hill, we'll be taking the men out of the enemy's line of fire. They'll be rescued!'
>
> The lieutenant answered: 'Look, I know that we'll be taking them out of the line of fire, and I know that some of them would have been killed otherwise. But I don't care at all about what happens to our soldiers. All I care about is taking control of Thompson Hill.'
>
> The squad was sent to the top of Thompson Hill. As expected, the soldiers were taken out of the enemy's line of fire, and they thereby escaped getting killed.

These subjects were then asked to determine how much praise the lieutenant deserved for what he did and whether or not he intentionally took the soldiers out of the line of fire.

Once again, the two conditions elicited two radically different patterns of responses. In the harm condition, most (77%) subjects said that the agent brought about the side effect intentionally, whereas in the help condition most (70%) subjects said that the agent did not bring about the side effect inten-

tionally. This difference was statistically significant, $\chi^2(1, N = 42) = 9.5, p < .01$.

3. Explaining the Results

Why do people respond so differently to vignettes that seem, at least in certain respects, to be so similar? Here subjects' ratings of praise and blame may provide an important clue. I therefore combined the praise and blame ratings from the two experiments and ran a new series of tests.

Overall, subjects said that the agent deserved a lot of blame in the harm condition ($M = 4.8$) but very little praise in the help condition ($M = 1.4$), $t(120) = 8.4$, $p < .001$, and the total amount of praise or blame that subjects offered was correlated with their judgements about whether or not the side effect was brought about intentionally, $r(120) = .53, p < .001$.

In other words, there seems to be an asymmetry whereby people are considerably more willing to blame the agent for bad side effects than to praise the agent for good side effects. And this asymmetry in people's assignment of praise and blame may be at the root of the corresponding asymmetry in people's application of the concept *intentional*: namely, that they seem considerably more willing to say that a side effect was brought about intentionally when they regard that side effect as bad than when they regard it as good.

Note

1. Mele (2003) now retracts this view in response to an earlier version of the present paper.

References

Bratman, M. 1984. Two faces of intention. Chapter 14 in this volume.

Bratman, M. 1987. *Intention, Plans, and Practical Reason.* Cambridge, MA: Harvard University Press.

Harman, G. 1976. Practical reasoning. *Review of Metaphysics* 29: 431–63.

Malle, B. F. and J. Knobe. 1997. The folk concept of intentionality. *Journal of Experimental Social Psychology* 33: 101–21.

Mele, A. 2001. Acting intentionally: probing folk notions. In *Intentions and Intentionality: Foundations of Social Cognition*, ed. B. F. Malle, L. J. Moses & D. Baldwin, 27–43. Cambridge, MA: M.I.T. Press.

Mele, A. 2003. Intentional action: controversies, data, and core hypotheses. *Philosophical Psychology* 16 (2): 325–340.

17

The Toxin Puzzle

Gregory S. Kavka

You are feeling extremely lucky. You have just been approached by an eccentric billionaire who has offered you the following deal. He places before you a vial of toxin that, if you drink it, will make you painfully ill for a day, but will not threaten your life or have any lasting effects. (Your spouse, a crack biochemist, confirms the properties of the toxin.) The billionaire will pay you one million dollars tomorrow morning if, at midnight tonight, you *intend* to drink the toxin tomorrow afternoon. He emphasizes that you need not drink the toxin to receive the money; in fact, the money will already be in your bank account hours before the time for drinking it arrives, if you succeed. (This is confirmed by your daughter, a lawyer, after she examines the legal and financial documents that the billionaire has signed.) All you have to do is sign the agreement and then intend at midnight tonight to drink the stuff tomorrow afternoon. You are perfectly free to change your mind after receiving the money and not drink the toxin. (The presence or absence of the intention is to be determined by the latest 'mind-reading' brain scanner and computing device designed by the great Doctor X. As a cognitive scientist, materialist, and faithful former student of

Doctor X, you have no doubt that the machine will correctly detect the presence or absence of the relevant intention.)

Confronted with this offer, you gleefully sign the contract, thinking 'what an easy way to become a millionaire'. Not long afterwards, however, you begin to worry. You had been thinking that you could avoid drinking the toxin and just pocket the million. But you realize that if you are thinking in those terms when midnight rolls around, you will not be intending to drink the toxin tomorrow. So maybe you will actually have to drink the stuff to collect the money. It will not be pleasant, but it is sure worth a day of suffering to become a millionaire.

However, as occurs to you immediately, it cannot really be necessary to drink the toxin to pocket the money. That money will either be or not be in your bank account by 10 a.m. tomorrow, you will know then whether it is there or not, and your drinking or not drinking the toxin hours later cannot affect the completed financial transaction. So instead of planning to drink the toxin, you decide to intend today to drink it and then change your mind after midnight. But if that is your plan, then it is obvious that you do not intend to drink the toxin. (At most you intend to intend to drink it.) For having such an intention is incompatible with planning to change your mind tomorrow morning.

At this point, your son, a strategist for the Pentagon, makes a useful suggestion. Why not bind yourself to

Kavka, G. S. (1983), "The Toxin Puzzle," *Analysis* 43 (1), 33–36. Published by Oxford Journals, Oxford University Press, Oxford. Reprinted with permission of Oxford University Press.

drink the stuff tomorrow, by today making irreversible arrangements that will give you sufficient independent incentive to drink it? You might promise someone who would not later release you from the promise that you will drink the toxin tomorrow afternoon. Or you could sign a legal agreement obligating you to donate all your financial assets (including the million if you win it) to your least favourite political party, if you do not drink it. You might even hire a hitman to kill you if you do not swallow the toxin. This would assure you of a day of misery, but also of becoming rich.

Unfortunately, your daughter the lawyer, who has read the contract carefully, points out that arrangement of such external incentives is ruled out, as are such alternative gimmicks as hiring a hypnotist to implant the intention, forgetting the main relevant facts of the situation, and so forth. (Promising *yourself* that you will drink the toxin could help if you were one of those strange people who take pride in never releasing oneself from a promise to oneself, no matter what the circumstances. Alas, you are not.)

Thrown back on your own resources, you desperately try to convince yourself that, despite the temporal sequence, drinking the toxin tomorrow afternoon is a necessary condition of pocketing the million that morning. Remembering Newcomb's Problem, you seek inductive evidence that this is so, hoping that previous recipients of the billionaire's offer won the million when and only when they drank the toxin. But, alas, your nephew, a private investigator, discovers that you are the first one to receive the offer (or that past winners drank less often than past losers). By now midnight is fast approaching and in a panic you try to summon up an act of will, gritting your teeth and muttering 'I will drink that toxin' over and over again.

We need not complete this tale of high hopes disappointed (or fulfilled) to make the point that there is a puzzle lurking here. You are asked to form a simple intention to perform an act that is well within your power. This is the kind of thing we all do many times every day. You are provided with an overwhelming incentive for doing so. Yet you cannot do so (or have extreme difficulty doing so) without resorting to exotic tricks involving hypnosis, hired killers, etc. Nor are your difficulties traceable to an uncontrollable fear of the negative consequences of the act in question – you would be perfectly willing to undergo the after-effects of the toxin to earn the million.

Two points underlie our puzzle. The first concerns the nature of intentions. If intentions were inner performances or self-directed commands, you would have no trouble earning your million. You would only need to keep your eye on the clock, and then perform or command to yourself at midnight. Similarly, if intentions were simply decisions, and decisions were volitions fully under the agent's control, there would be no problem. But intentions are better viewed as dispositions to act which are based on *reasons to act* – features of the act itself or its (possible) consequences that are valued by the agent. (Specifying the exact nature of the relationship between intentions and the reasons that they are based on is a difficult and worthy task, but one that need not detain us. For an account that is generally congenial to the views presented here, see Davidson's 'Intending', Chapter 13 in this volume.) Thus, we can explain your difficulty in earning a fortune: you cannot intend to act as you have no reason to act, at least when you have substantial reasons not to act. And you have (or will have when the time comes) no reason to drink the toxin, and a very good reason not to, for it will make you quite sick for a day.

This brings us to our second point. While you have no reasons to drink the toxin, you have every reason (or at least a million reasons) to *intend* to drink it. Now when reasons for intending and reasons for acting diverge, as they do here, confusion often reigns. For we are inclined to evaluate the rationality of the intention both in terms of its consequences and in terms of the rationality of the intended action. As a result, when we have good reasons to intend but not to act, conflicting standards of evaluation come into play and something has to give way: either rational action, rational intention, or aspects of the agent's own rationality (e.g., his correct belief that drinking the toxin is not necessary for winning the million).

I made some similar points in an earlier article ('Some Paradoxes of Deterrence', *Journal of Philosophy*, June 1978), but there I was discussing an example involving conditional intentions. The toxin puzzle broadens the application of that discussion, by showing that its conclusions may apply to cases involving unconditional intentions as well. It also reveals that intentions are only partly volitional. One cannot intend whatever one wants to intend any more than one can believe whatever one wants to believe. As our beliefs are constrained by our evidence, so our intentions are constrained by our reasons for action.[1]

Note

1. The puzzle discussed here emerged from a conversation, some years ago, with Tyler Burge about 'Some Paradoxes of Deterrence'.

18

The Ontology of Social Agency

Frederick Stoutland

0. Introduction

Philosophers of action have not paid much attention to social agency, that is, to actions performed not by individual persons but by social groups of various kinds. Discussion has centered on what individuals, do, believe, or desire, and on the reasons each has for acting, the standard story being that actions consist of bodily movements that are rationalized and caused by the agent's beliefs and desires. Although we often describe an agent's actions in terms of their results rather than in terms of the bodily movements involved, the claim is that *what* we are describing are the agent's bodily movements. Since each of us has a distinct body and moving it is something we do on our own, this view apparently rules out genuinely social agency, that is, agency that is not reducible to the agency of individuals.

Recently, however, there has been increased interest in social agency, which has received careful discussion from a number of philosophers.[1] But most of these discussions, while taking social action seriously, display an individualist, anti-social bias about agents. Many of them focus, for example, on cases like painting a house together or moving a piano, which involve actions people do together but which they could have done separately. Given pianos and our

limited strength, most of us could not move a piano alone but it is not incoherent to think of so doing. It is, therefore, not difficult to think of the actions of social groups like these in terms of the actions of each of its members that are coordinated in various ways.

That is not the case for actions like playing a Mozart symphony, passing a law, appointing a president of a university, declaring a stock dividend, or winning the World Series. Those are not actions individuals can perform on their own. Only an orchestra can play a Mozart symphony, only a parliament pass a law, only a university name its president, only a corporation declare a stock dividend, and only a baseball team win the World Series. Only social agents can do or intend to do these things, and while the actions of individual agents are essential to their doing them, it is the groups that act intentionally in these ways.

Philosophers who are biased toward individualism respond to this in different ways. Some take the eliminativist view that there really are no social agents; we may speak in social terms but what we say applies only to the actions, intentions, beliefs, and reasons of individual agents. Others respond, not by denying that social agents have intentions or beliefs and act for reasons, but by arguing that these are reducible to – definable in terms of – the intentions, beliefs, actions, and reasons of members of the group. Still others reject reductionism, claiming in particular that social intentions and beliefs cannot be defined in terms of individual intentions and beliefs since their content

Stoutland, F. (2008), "The Ontology of Social Agency," *Analyse & Kritik* 30, 533–551.

must be mutually referring in distinctive ways. But the anti-social bias remains because the intentions and beliefs themselves are not ascribed to social groups but to their members.

My aim in what follows is to undermine the individualist bias in accounts of the ontological status of social agency by showing, in particular, that social groups – not all of them but many – are not ontologically secondary but have a reality of their own. This involves showing that it is legitimate to ascribe actions, reasons, intentions and beliefs to social groups as such, not only to their individual members. In short, there are, I shall argue, social agents in addition to individual agents.

This is a relatively narrow topic and a uniquely philosophical one, which is only indirectly relevant to claims about the social explanation of behavior, about how individuals are dependent on society, or other claims made by social scientists. The social groups that I am concerned with are not a primary source of the social constraints Durkheim articulated (cf. Aron 1967, 72f.). Orchestras, parliaments, corporations, or baseball teams constrain their members in various ways but that is secondary to their role in making possible a range of actions and attitudes that would not be possible outside the groups. My focus, however, is not on that – on what social groups constitute – but on what constitute groups as social agents and what it is to ascribe to them actions, attitudes, and reasons.

1. Social Agents

In our discourse together we constantly speak of the agency not only of individuals but also of social groups. We speak in terms of social agents, of their actions and their reasons for acting, and of their intentions, beliefs and other attitudes. I shall say something about each of these in the course of this paper.

Let us distinguish two kinds of *social agents*. One is *plural* agents, where the agent is referred to as 'they' and agency expressed by 'we': thus they played a Mozart quartet, they played chess, we nailed up that long board, we moved the piano, we took turns, we had a quarrel. The other is *collective* agents, where the agent is not plural but singular, referred to by a name or definite description or as 'it', not as 'they', though

typically *expressed* as 'we'. Thus the Senate debated a new tax law but *it* hasn't passed it yet, the Company laid off a lot of employees but *it* will lay off more, and – as an expression of agency – we intend to appoint a new president of the university, and so on.

What I have just said reflects American rather than British English. In the former it is said that the government *is* planning to do such and such, whereas in the latter that the government *are* planning to so such and such. This shows that the line between these two kinds of agents is not sharp. There are, nevertheless, significant differences. Plural agents come into being just by people coming together and doing things jointly – nailing up a board, playing a string quartet having a dinner party. Collective agents cannot come to be in that way: they require a history of practice. Even if they are established by fiat – 'we formed a new company yesterday' – the fiat is effective only against the background of social groups of that kind that were not established by fiat. The group cannot therefore be transitory or ephemeral: collective agents have a permanence plural agents do not. The senate, the company, or the family outlive particular members or the actions they perform. Plural agents in general do not: the we who nailed up that board does not exist as a we beyond that act.[2]

Another difference is that collective agents typically involve structures that institutionalize authority relations.[3] These enable the decisions of certain members to be decisions of the social group and permit persons to speak on behalf of the group, so that statements they make are statements of the group. When the president of the university speaks, for instance, the university, as a matter of institutional structure, speaks. This is in general not the case for plural agents, which do not institutionalize authority. Individuals may have special authority but it is informal and fluid, based on others letting them have it rather than on their office or status.

Collective agents and plural agents are alike, however, in that neither kind is identical with individual agents. The senate does things individual senators cannot do, such as pass laws or issue a resolution. The university appoints a new president, which no member of the university can do. The quintet plays Schubert's 'Trout', which is something no individual musician can do.[4] This point may be obscured in the case of types of actions that either an individual or a social agent could perform. An example is our holding up a board so we can get it nailed in place, a type of action either of us could (with great difficulty) do alone. This particular act is, nevertheless, the act of a social agent because it is not divisible between the two of us. That entails, I contend, not only that each of us performs the same *type* of action – namely, lifting a board – but that we perform a single act *token*. Lifting a board is something *we* do as a social agent. It is true that in lifting the board, each of us also acts as an individual agent, exercising his own strength and moving in a distinctive way, which makes the social action possible, but these individual acts are not identical with the act performed by the social agent. It was neither you nor I who did so but *we*, that is, the group of which we are members.

2. Social Actions

Social agents perform social actions, which are similar to the actions of individual agents in a number of ways. First, there is no acting where there is no *intentional* acting. What distinguishes mere behavior – where things happen but there is no agency – from acting, is that the latter is intentional under at least one description. Acting, that is to say, is *essentially* intentional, and insofar as it falls short of being intentional, it is a diminished form of acting. Second, whenever an agent acts, his so acting is not intentional under other descriptions. Acting always has unintended results, which are diminished forms of acting: in acting intentionally, agents also do things in ignorance, by mistake, accidentally, and so on.

Third, an agent who acts does so, in general, for a reason that yields a description under which her acting is intentional. An agent may act for no reason – whistle idly, for instance – but that is necessarily exceptional and, moreover, an act that could have been done for a reason.[5] It is exceptional because the capacity to act for reasons is essential to agency and hence for the capacity to act intentionally (and hence to act). If one acts for a reason, one acts intentionally (under a description): one cannot have a reason for acting inadvertently or in ignorance because if one did so act for a reason, it would not be acting inadvertently or in ignorance. And if one acts intentionally, one knows what one is doing

under a description, which means one knows at least the immediate reason for what one is doing.

These claims, assumed in most conceptions of individual action, apply straightforwardly to social action. The Senate acts only when it acts intentionally under a description, but in so acting it does not act intentionally in all respects. For example, it intentionally passes a budget law, but in so doing, it inadvertently increases unemployment in certain sectors and angers some citizens. Its passing a budget law was intentional because it did so for a reason, namely, because the law was required to bring down the deficit. Its reason for action did not include increasing unemployment or angering citizens, so it was not intentional in those respects. A quartet intentionally plays Beethoven's last quartet because a patron requested it, but unintentionally wakes up a baby or inspires a bad review (which were not requested by a patron). The same analysis, so familiar for the actions of individuals, applies straightforwardly to social action generally.

Many philosophers, however, even among those sympathetic to social action, will reject this account. They may admit that there are social actions in the guise of 'joint actions', which are social in that they are not divisible among the individual agents who make up the group. But they will deny that this indivisibility entails that there is one *token* action the group itself performs.

Take four persons playing a string quartet. If this is a genuine social action, there is, I maintain, one token action that the quartet performs, namely, playing a quartet, which involves a complex pattern of blended sounds. The four players also perform actions of their own, each playing from a score that marks out the notes she will play. But the quartet played consists of the joint sounds that result from the players playing together, which must be heard together to hear the quartet. The harmony, dissonance, tempo, or what have you, that marks a quartet, is played not by individuals but by the quartet: there is numerically one act that it alone performs, namely, producing those sounds that jointly constitute the quartet.

The reaction to this is sometimes reductionism: there is nothing to a quartet other than four individual players coming together, and the so-called social action of playing a quartet is reducible to the individual actions of four persons performed at the same time, meeting certain conditions of harmony and coopera-tiveness. Philosophers sympathetic to social action usually reject reductionism, however, on the ground that it fails to admit that there is anything unique about social actions, in particular for failing to take account of their indivisibility. Four persons do not *each* play a quartet, and while it is true that each player plays a distinct part, the joint sounds – the harmonies and dis-sonances and patterns – are not divisible among them.

But philosophers with an individualist bias deny that there is one *token* action performed by the quar-tet, claiming rather that the only token actions are those performed by each individual player. What marks out these actions as social is that the action of each individual player is a *type* of action it would not be were it performed in isolation. Reductionism misses this point in claiming that the type of actions players perform when playing on their own is no dif-ferent from the type of actions they perform when playing a quartet. On the contrary, when playing a quartet, each player must not only play his own part; he must also contribute to the quartet, pay attention to his colleagues, aim at harmony, and the like, all of which involve characteristics his action would not have were he not a member of a group. Social actions are not reducible to individual actions because the former are types of action the latter are not. They can, in other words, be described in ways the actions of isolated individual agents cannot.

On this view, however, social actions still consist of numerically different act tokens performed by distinct individuals: a social action is performed by a social group, not because there is a token action the group itself performs, but because individual persons act in ways they would not act were they not in the group. This individualist bias is more subtle than individualist reductionism in that it recognizes a difference between social and individual actions. But the difference is not between social and individual *agents* – the agents are individuals, each performing a distinct action – but between the kinds of descriptions of the actions performed by individuals.

This individualist view rests on a number of claims, of which I will consider three. First, the attitudes nec-essarily involved in agency – intentions and beliefs in particular – can be ascribed only to individuals not to social groups, and hence there are no genuinely social

agents. Second, action is intentional only if the agent is capable of what Weber called 'subjectively under-standable action', but social agents do not have such self-understanding. Third, actions not only always involve bodily movements (if they are not merely mental acts), but actions *consist* of an agent's moving his body in various ways, and since only individual agents have bodies and can directly move only their own, there cannot be genuine social agents. I shall discuss each of these objections in the rest of this paper.

3. Social Attitudes

The first objection is the most common, and a great deal of energy and ingenuity has been expended showing how to avoid ascribing intentions, beliefs, and other intentional attitudes to social groups. In my view, this is a mistake: since social actions are not divisible among individual agents, the social attitudes involved are also not divisible among individual agents but are the attitudes of groups as social agents. By social atti-tudes, then, I do not merely mean intentional attitudes with social *content*. Nor do I mean attitudes directed toward some social rather than individual good, or which involve social rather than individual interests.[6] I mean attitudes whose *subjects* are social agents.

There are numerous examples of such attitudes. A corporation has beliefs and intentions, and while its employees may share the content of some of those attitudes, they are the corporation's attitudes. More typi-cally, its employees will not share its attitudes, and, indeed, there may be attitudes ascribable to the corpora-tion which are not ascribable to any of its members. The corporation may, for example, have set a certain level of sales as its aim for the next fiscal year, even if no member of the corporation shares that aim (perhaps the figure is a compromise, different from the aims of any of the managers or board members[7]). But even if the cor-porate attitudes are shared by some members, they are *corporate* attitudes, not attitudes of individual agents.

The examples may be extended. Intentions, beliefs, and desires are ascribed to universities, churches, parlia-ments, charitable organizations, and orchestras, which their members may or may not share, but that in any case are the intentions, beliefs, and desires of the social group. No doubt social agents would not have attitudes if their members did not, and in many cases their attitudes reflect the attitudes of their members. But the converse is also true; individual agents not only reflect the attitudes of the groups to which they belong, but there are attitudes they would not have did the group not have them. Expecting to vote in the next election presupposes that the government intends to hold one. Believing that the parliament will raise taxes assumes that it wants to do so. Wanting to cash a check presupposes banks that intend to cash them.

Many philosophers find this objectionable. Reductionists argue that so-called social attitudes are no different from the attitudes of individual agents: they have no distinctive contents that the attitudes of solitary individuals do not have. The beliefs or desires of a church, for example, are just the attitudes of its members, and their contents do not presuppose any social group. To speak of what a church believes is to speak of what is believed by most of its members, beliefs they could in principle have all by themselves.

Individualists who take social action more seriously reject reductionism by maintaining there are attitudes with distinctively social contents that solitary individuals do not have. Consider a social belief, for example, one expressed by a congregation saying, 'We believe in God'. If that is a genuine social belief, it is, on this view, not simply a case of each member believing in God, for there is nothing social about that. It involves in addition each member believing of the other members that they believe in God, and believing that the other members believe that, and so on, with perhaps other attitudes as well. Attitudes with such mutually referring contents are, it is claimed, distinctive of social beliefs, marking out a type of *contents* individual beliefs do not have. But attitudes with such contents are still not genuinely social if only individuals and not social groups have them,[8] and, indeed, the point of this kind of proposal is precisely to avoid ascribing attitudes to agents other than individuals.

This is, in my view, a mistake: social agency requires not only that attitudes have social content but that they be ascribed to social agents. This is most evident in the case of intentions. The proposal that intentions are social if they have mutually referring contents maintains that to ascribe an intention to a social group is just to ascribe to each member of the group an intention

with the *same* mutually referring content. Social intentions, on this view, are individual intentions with distinctive *common* contents. But there are, I conclude, no such intentions: different agents cannot have intentions whose content is common in the relevant sense.

The reason for this is that intentions necessarily include reference to the agent who has them. An agent can intend only to do something *herself*: she cannot intend anyone else to act, but at best only intend to do something herself that might induce someone else to act. I cannot intend *you* to buy *me* a dinner, but only intend to do something that might have that result. But if the content of an intention always includes an implicit reference to the agent who intends, the intentions of different agents do not have a common content. Art can intend to go to a film and Mary can intend to do the same; but their intentions do not have a common content since Art's intention is *his* going to the film and Mary's is *her* going to the film. This means that the notion of 'we intend' cannot be analyzed in terms of the notion of 'I intend' since they involve the intentions of different agents. We must either construe social actions in terms of intentions with individual contents or recognize that intentions are social attitudes to be ascribed straightforwardly to social agents.[9]

The first alternative is unacceptable. If an agent can intend only to do something herself, then the only intentions an agent can *fulfill* by her actions are her own. It follows that if a social action fulfills an intention, the intention must be the intention of the agent who performed that action, namely, a social agent. Otherwise the action would be fulfilling the intention of someone other than the agent of the act (an individual agent), which is not coherent since agents can fulfill only their own intentions.

A number of proposals have been made to avoid this objection by arguing that it is, after all, possible to construct a notion of intentions that have *common*, hence social, contents *shared* by members of a group. Here is Michael Bratman's analysis (1993, 104):

We intend to J if and only if:

1. (a) I intend that we J and (b) you intend that we J
2. I intend that we J because of 1a and 1b; you intend that we J because of 1a and 1b
3. 1 and 2 are common knowledge between us.

Bratman takes this analysis to yield intentions with common contents that individual agents share, thus avoiding the objection that actions performed by individual agents cannot fulfill intentions that are social in the sense of being shared. Since the contents of 'we-intend's' are distinct from the contents of 'I-intend's', in that the former are ascribable to individuals only as members of a group, it is not a reductivist analysis. But while it allows actions to fulfill intentions that are social in that agents can have them only as members of a group, it does not allow social *agents* to have intentions. A shared intention, Bratman notes, is

"a state of affairs that consists in attitudes […] of the *participants* and interrelations between those attitudes […]. It consists primarily of a web of attitudes of the individual participants [and involves] two main elements: (1) a general treatment of the intentions of *individuals* and (2) an account of the special contents of the intentions of the *individual* participants in a shared intention." (107 f.; my emphasis)

Bratman explicitly recognizes the problem I have posed:

"What I intend to do is to perform actions of my own; I cannot intend to perform the joint action J. So how will the conception of the joint action get into the intentions of the individuals?" (101)

To resolve that, Bratman introduces the technical notion of *intention that*, which does not require that what the agent intends be an act of that same agent. I can intend *that* you buy me dinner, and one person can, in general, intend *that* another person do something. If that is so, then an individual can intend *that* a group do something. Since it is just this notion that plays the key role in Bratman's analysis of 'we intend […]' – it is given in clause 1 – it is not surprising that we get a notion of shared intention with common content.[10]

There are two objections to this proposal. The first is that Bratman's analysis simply *postulates* a technical notion of intention whose point is just to permit common content, and that begs the question, namely, *whether* the intentions of different agents can have common content. The other is that intentions do not take propositional objects: we may intend to do something or we may act with an intention, but in either case the object of our intending is an activity, not a fact or state of affairs. An agent intends to drive *to* Minneapolis, or is driving *to* Minneapolis with the intention to buy a piano, or intends *to* buy a piano because he intends *to* learn how to play. If these intentions are construed as having propositional objects, they cease to have the distinctive features of intentions and become attitudes of a different kind.[11]

Bratman contends that his notion of *intention that* is not "some new and distinctive attitude [but one] […] already needed in an account of individual intelligent agency. But we are allowing this attitude to include in its content joint activity." (ibid., 102) While intentions are indispensable to individual agency, *intention that* is not, because an individual can only intend to do something herself. *Allowing* the attitude to include in its content joint activity is not to *establish* that an agent can intend a joint activity but to construct a new attitude that is essentially different from the intentions we ascribe to individual agents.

An analogous point applies to beliefs. Unlike intentions, beliefs take propositional objects, and their contents may be common to different agents. But the beliefs that play an essential role in explaining an agent's actions as intentional must be beliefs of the agent himself. One may, for instance, act in a certain way because it is necessary for some end, but the necessity of the action will explain one's acting only if one *believes* it is necessary, and that must be the agent's own belief. He may, of course, see that the act is necessary because someone else believes it is and tells him so, but that the act is necessary explains his acting only if he himself comes to believe it is necessary. For a belief to play a role in explaining a social group's action, therefore, it must be a belief of the group itself, not of its members. Its members' beliefs may underlie the beliefs of the group but they play a role in the reasons for which the group acts only by way of beliefs of the group as such.

4. Ascribing Attitudes to Social Agents

Not every intentional attitude is ascribable to social agents, any more than every type of action can be performed by a social agent; indeed, those claims are necessarily related. Social agents cannot walk or jump or engage in other bodily actions, and so they cannot intend to do them or believe they are doing them. Since social agents cannot weep or laugh, the range and kind of emotions ascribable to them are also restricted (though perhaps there are metaphorical senses in which social groups weep or laugh). Although more could be said about the kinds of attitudes and emotions that *cannot* be ascribed to social agents, my concern here is to articulate a view that shows why many intentional attitudes *can* be so ascribed.

I want first to consider a primary reason many philosophers refuse to ascribe attitudes of any kind to social agents, namely, a mistaken but entrenched view about the nature and role of the attitudes in explaining action. On this view, the attitudes are causally efficacious events or states internal to an agent's mind/brain, which cause events in his nervous system that in turn cause his bodily movements. They have rational content that are an agent's reason for acting, and if they cause the agent's bodily movements in accord with that content (not accidentally or deviantly), they are intentional under a description and hence are actions of the agent. An agent's action *consists*, then, in his moving his body, and although we describe that in terms of many things, in particular in terms of what the bodily movements cause in the world beyond his body, *what* we are describing are his bodily movements.[12]

This is the so-called 'standard story' of action, which comes in a number of versions that develop in sophisticated ways the simple points set out above. My concern here is with aspects of the story that bear directly on the individualist bias in philosophy of action and thereby rule out an adequate account of social agency. One is its claim that actions consist in bodily movements (which I will discuss in section 6), while the others concern the attitudes: that they are events or states internal to an agent's mind/brain, their fundamental explanatory role being the causal production of bodily movements in accordance with their content.

If these claims are accepted, attitudes like intentions, beliefs, and desires cannot be ascribed to social agents because doing so would require that social agents have brains and nervous systems that causally produce their actions. Or it would require that they have super-personal, collective minds, which might

have some metaphorical point but would not fulfill the causal function attitudes have on this view, namely, to be causally productive of an agent's actions. The absurdity of these alternatives is sufficient to account for the individualist refusal to ascribe attitudes to social agents.

But if those claims about the attitudes are rejected, then it is not absurd to ascribe the attitudes to social agents. I think they should be rejected on the ground that they yield an inadequate account even of individual agency. The attitudes are not entities, they are not located in an agent's mind/brain, and their explanatory role is not the causal production of bodily movements (or anything else). Although I cannot adequately defend these counter claims in this paper, I will articulate the conception of the attitudes they presume and show how they apply to social agency.[13]

I have written indifferently of events and states (which is common among defenders of the standard story), but they should be clearly distinguished. Events are particulars in having numerous intrinsic properties (or descriptions), many of which may be undiscovered, and they are causally efficacious in that they are causally related to other events (or things) that they produce. Claims about such causal relations are extensional in that they are true under every description of the events; they are not true *in virtue of* some property of the events (and hence false *in virtue of* some other property).

If attitudes were events, they would be causally efficacious, but they are states and not events. Events happen at a time but attitudes do not happen: states, hence attitudes, obtain through time. Nor are attitudes particulars that are located at some time or place or that have undiscovered intrinsic properties. They are property-like and not referred to (as events are) but *predicated* of a subject.[14] It is agents that intend, believe, or desire, and in characterizing an agent as intending to write, believing that it will rain, desiring to own a house, we do not refer to entities in his mind/brain but we characterize *him* as intending to write, and so on. Those are properties of an agent that are individuated by their content – to write, that it will rain, to own a house. We may predicate the very same attitude of different agents, who may have the same belief, the same desire, even (with the important qualifications discussed above) the same intention: each of us may have the intention to write or see a film, although it will be directed in each case to the one who has the intention.

As states, attitudes are not causally efficacious: they are not causally related to – do not produce – bodily movements or other events or things. But they play a role in the explanation of actions (or other attitudes) by being *causally relevant* to actions, other events, states, and so on. A property is causally relevant to an outcome just in case the outcome would have been different had the property been different (or absent). 'Being rotten', for instance, is a causally relevant (but not causally efficacious) property: that the tree was rotten did not cause the tree to fall down; but it was causally relevant because, had the tree not been rotten, it would not have fallen over in the wind. So it is with the attitudes; an agent's beliefs do not causally produce his action, but had he not believed what he did, he would not have (or probably would not have) acted intentionally as he did. There may, of course, be an explanation of why an attitude – intending to build a garage, desiring to own a house – is causally relevant to an action, but causal relevance does not depend on our knowing that explanation, or even on there being one. Many explanations refer to causally relevant states, and their explanatory power does not depend on our knowing why they are causally relevant.[15]

This view of the nature and explanatory role of the attitudes is essentially Davidson's, and I would appeal to his status in the philosophy of action in defense of the view. In any case, it allows the ascription of attitudes, not only to individual agents, but also to social groups of various kinds. We can ascribe to a quartet an intention to play a piece by Mozart, a belief that it should keep a fast tempo, a desire to satisfy its patron's request. It is irrelevant that the quartet has no brain or nervous system or that attitudes directed toward its own actions as a quartet are not causally productive of its actions. The attitudes that we ascribe to the quartet, no more than those we ascribe to individual agents, are not located in a mind/brain; they are properties predicated of the quartet that are causally relevant to its actions as a social agent. Had the quartet not intended to play a piece by Mozart, not believed it should keep a fast tempo, not wanted to please its patron, its actions would have been very different. A complicated story might be constructed about why those attitudes are causally relevant, but we do not know that story, and the explanation does not depend on it.

A similar account can be given of the attitudes of numerous social agents – universities, parliaments, corporations, banks, churches, social agencies, etc. We speak often of their beliefs, intentions, what they want, even what they fear or hope for, and there is no reason to feel uneasy in so doing or to take solace from the philosophical analysis of those committed to individualism. It is true that there would be no social agents without manifold complex relations between individuals more or less like those that philosophers spell out so carefully. But those relations will vary a great deal depending on the social group: they may be cooperative, but they may not; they may not involve mutual knowledge; they may or may not be institutional; there might not be significant intentions shared by members of the group. But what those diverse relations make possible is something new – a social agent to which attitudes are ascribed that are not ascribed to individuals who are members of the group. This is something that need not be resisted given an adequate understanding of the nature and explanatory role of the attitudes.

5. Social Agents' Knowledge of What They are Doing

I want now to consider briefly the claim that action is intentional only if it is what Max Weber called "subjectively understandable", which in his view is not true of social actions.

Weber defended 'methodological individualism', which he defined as the view that "in sociological work collectivities must be treated as solely the resultants and modes of organization of the particular acts of individual persons". He argued that only individuals "can be treated as agents in a course of subjectively understandable action" (Weber 1968, 13) on the ground that social inquiry is different from that of natural science in that it aims at an interpretive understanding [*verstehen*] of social phenomena. That entails, he held, that intentional action must be the focus of investigation because (as Joseph Heath puts Weber's claim) "actions can be understood in a way that other phenomena cannot, precisely because they are motivated by intentional states". Methodological individualism comes into the picture because Weber also held (in Heath's words) that "only individuals possess intentional states, and so the methodological privileging of actions entails the methodological privileging of individuals".[16]

The connection of all this with 'subjectively understandable action' is that investigators aiming at an interpretive understanding of social phenomena must grasp the intentional states that motivate the agent, which means they must grasp the agent's *own (subjective) understanding* of her action: what she intends to be doing, what she believes is necessary to fulfill her intention, how she perceives situations in the world as reasons for her to act, and so on. The agent herself may not have a perfect understanding of such things, but as an agent who acts, she must know what she is doing intentionally, which means she must have a grasp of what she is intending, what she takes to be necessary to achieve her ends, her own reason for initiating action, etc. While investigators must *interpret* an agent to know these things, the agent knows them about herself directly, without interpretation.

Weber is, in my view, right about much of this – about the role of interpretation, about the centrality of intentional action, about the latter being 'subjectively understandable'. But he is wrong in maintaining that these claims apply only to individual agents and not to social groups. His claim that only individuals 'can be treated as agents in a course of subjectively understandable action' presumes (if Heath understands him correctly) that only individuals possess intentional states. But this premise, I have argued, is false: we can ascribe attitudes like beliefs and intentions to social agents.

Even if is granted that social agents can have intentional attitudes, it may be argued that it does not follow that social action is 'subjectively understandable', which I take to mean that social agents do not know what they are doing intentionally and what their intentions, beliefs, or other attitudes are. I think that the relevant sense of 'know' here is, as Anscombe has argued, 'know without observation'. If we know what we are doing only by observing our action, then we are not the agents of the action but only observers of it. Similarly, if we need evidence to discover what we intend to do, or what we believe necessary, or what is our own reason for initiating action, then those

attitudes are at best remotely connected with our acting intentionally. The issue is whether social agents have such knowledge, at least with respect to more primitive descriptions of their action and their more short term reasons for acting.

In my view, social agents do have such knowledge. If it were a matter of introspection, if it required that an agent have introspective access to the content of her mind, then such knowledge by a social agent would be unintelligible. But since, in my view, an *individual* agent's knowledge of what she is doing intentionally is not based on introspection, and the attitudes are not items in her mind/brain, there is no reason to think of *social* agents in that way. The knowledge required, I suggest, is what Anscombe called *practical* as opposed to theoretical: agents know what they are doing intentionally not by matching their judgment to their actions but by matching their actions to their intentions. If they are mistaken, the mistake is not in their judgment but in their performance: they fail to do what they intend.

A corporation, for instance, decides to do something, and then its employees are instructed to carry out the decision: if things do not go as decided, the problem is not that the corporation is wrong about how things went but that the decision was not properly executed, that external conditions changed, or that things went wrong in some other way. The mistake with regard to how things went is not in the judgment (the reports) but in the performance. When it is discovered by investigation that things did not go as intended, there is *theoretical* knowledge of the action. But if things did go as decided, the corporation knows what it is doing simply because its decision was carried out as intended: it has *practical* knowledge of its action – knowledge of what is happening by doing it.[17]

6. Bodily Movements and Action

A third objection to the notion of social agents that I shall discuss is that actions *consist* of bodily movements, and since each of us has a distinct body that we move directly only on our own, individuals are the real agents of action. To counter this objection, we should consider carefully how bodily movements actually figure in the actions of individual agents.

Individual agents are, of course, necessary if there are to be social agents. A corporation could not refocus its efforts, declare a dividend, or build a new plant if there were not individual agents at work doing what is relevant to such corporate actions. A quartet could not play Beethoven if each of its members did not play an instrument according to the score. Moreover, the actions of individual agents are, in a sense, sufficient for the actions of a social agent. Once the employees of a corporation have completed their assigned tasks, there is not a *further* action done by the corporation, and once the members of the quartet have played the parts assigned to them, there is no *further* playing on the part of the quartet. The reason these individual actions are 'in a sense' sufficient is that conditions must be right for them so to be. The employees of a corporation must complete their tasks successfully, there must be suitable coordination, their actions must not be countermanded, and so on. Similar things apply to the quartet because what individuals play is not always sufficient for the playing of a quartet.

It is crucial to recognize that analogous points apply to the relation between an individual's bodily movements and his action. An agent acts in the world (and not merely mentally) only if he moves his body, and having moved his body in very complex ways, there is nothing *further* to do in order to act in various ways – provided conditions are right and things work out as he intended. If the world cooperates, then his moving his body is his moving his pen, which is his writing a sentence, which is his writing a letter, which is his pleasing his friend, etc. In moving his body, he may do many things; that is, his acting may have many descriptions that do not mention his moving his body, under some of which his acting is intentional, under many of which it is not.

The standard story of action takes this point to mean that an agent's action *consists* of his moving his body; that is what an action is, the rest being descriptions (or properties) of the bodily movements. The descriptions are true of the agent's moving his body because of what those movements result in, but his acting just *is* his moving his body. In Quine's terms, that is the ontology of action and everything else is ideology. Since only individuals move their bodies directly, it follows immediately that the agents of action must be individuals.

In my view, the standard story is mistaken: even if an agent's moving her body is both necessary and, given the right conditions, sufficient for her acting it does not follow that her acting *consists* of her moving her body. It does not follow, that is, that when we describe the many things an agent is doing, *what* we are describing is her moving her body – that the many descriptions of her acting are only *true of* her moving her body. As Anscombe wrote: "The proper answer to 'What is the action, which has all these descriptions?' is to give one of the descriptions. Any one, it does not matter which; or perhaps it would be best to offer a choice, saying, 'Take which ever you prefer'." (Anscombe 1981, 209) This is the right answer, although it does not rule out contexts in which one description is more basic than others and hence can, in that sense, be taken as specifying *what* we are describing when we describe an action.

Bodily movement descriptions are rarely basic in that sense because to specify *what* action we are describing, we specify *an* action, that is, something that has a unity as action, and this is rarely a matter of the bodily movements involved. I am, for instance, now writing a paper, which has been my primary task over many days. The ways in which I have moved my body in acting are complex and extremely diverse, and as such they have no unity but are merely a miscellany. My writing a paper, however, is *an* action, one that has a unity so that *it* can be described in many ways. Whatever unity there is to my bodily movements as action derives from my writing a paper and not vice versa, and it is, indeed, more plausible to say that what the bodily movement descriptions are true of is my writing a paper, than to say that what the paper-writing descriptions are true of is my moving my body. Moreover, an explanation of what I am doing that cites my reason for doing it explains my writing a paper, and it is the latter that explains my moving my body as I do.

Given this, it is evident that the actions of individual agents can be both necessary and (given the right conditions) sufficient for the actions of social agents without the latter *consisting* of the actions of individuals or without descriptions of social agents being *true of* individual agents. The members of any social group perform numerous and diverse actions as members of the group. White collar employees of a corporation write letters, hold meetings, offend colleagues, waste time, make decisions, etc., actions that are intentional under a description, but that viewed simply as the actions of individuals are a miscellany with no unity. If we understand, however, that the corporation intends to down-size and focus on one central mission, then we can grasp the unity in those individual actions as directed toward that goal. There is *an* action performed (or intended) by the corporation, an action individual agents cannot perform, and although the individuals' actions are (given the right conditions) sufficient for the corporation's actions, descriptions of the corporation's actions are not true of the individual actions. Moreover, it is not the actions of its employees that explain the corporation's action; on the contrary, the corporation's action explains the actions of its employees. It is because the corporation is down-sizing that its employees have reasons to be active in those diverse ways.

The point is, then, that although bodily movements are necessary and (in a sense) sufficient for individual actions, and although individual actions are necessary and (in a sense) sufficient for social actions, individual actions do not *consist* of bodily movements nor do social actions *consist* of individual actions. Ascribing actions to social agents presumes that we can ascribe attitudes to them that are explanatorily relevant to the actions of the individuals involved, hence causally relevant to the bodily movements of individuals. But it does not presume that social agents have bodies that they are able to move directly.

7. Individuating Agents

The underlying issue in this paper can be formulated as how to *individuate* agents and actions. When several descriptions are descriptions of the same thing, then that same thing has been individuated – that is, distinguished from other things – so that different descriptions can be asserted of it. The standard story assumes that there is one right way of individuating agents and actions, namely, in terms of an individual agent's own bodily movements. Philosophers who defend that story disagree on the so-called problem of the individuation of action – whether action should be individuated in a fine-grained or coarse-grained

fashion. But these differences are built on agreement that actions consist of an agent's bodily movements, the differences being how finely we should individuate *them*.

There is in current philosophy of action an admirable pluralism about admissible descriptions of intentional action. Most philosophers agree that there are numerous correct ways of describing our action, that most such descriptions are not in terms of bodily movements, that there is no such thing as *the* right way of *describing* what we do. But there is no corresponding pluralism as far as *individuation* is concerned. An action *consists* in an agent's bodily movements, which is *what* we describe in describing action, the reigning view being that no matter how diversely we describe action, we must individuate ultimately in physical terms. Only the latter identify an action about which we can ask whether *it* is intentional under some description or what an agent's reasons for doing it might be.

What I am urging is that we also be pluralistic about individuation. Just as we do not think it necessary to designate one way of *describing* an agent acting as *the* right way, so we should not think it necessary to designate one way of *individuating* an agent acting as *the* (ultimately) right way. Individualists think there is one right way to individuate, a view assumed by proponents of the standard story who maintain that action consists in the bodily movements of individual agents. The contrary mistake is made by collectivists: they think that *social* individuation is *the* (ultimately) right way to individuate, and that collective agents are therefore more ultimate – more well-founded, more explanatorily or conceptually basic – than individual agents. Pluralism about individuation means the rejection of both: social agency is neither more nor less ultimate, well-founded or basic than non-social agency.[18]

The ontology of action, therefore, is much broader than is allowed by individualists of various kinds. There are in the world social agents that we describe in various ways and to which we ascribe intentional attitudes. That we describe agents and actions in social ways is taken for granted; we ought in the same way to set aside our individualist, anti-social bias and take it for granted that what we are thus describing are genuine social realities.

Notes

1. Bratman 1992; 1993; 1999; Gilbert 1989; 1990; 2000; Pettit 2007; Searle 1995; Tuomela 1984; 1991; 2007. For further references see Baier 1997.

2. Plural agents can become collective agents. Four musicians who play a quartet together may establish themselves as the Toledo Quartet, which institutionalizes itself and may outlast all the players who began it.

3. This is not always the case, for example, with families, which are natural rather than instituted social agents. There usually are authority relations in a family, and they may be fairly strict, but they stem neither from the institutional structures typical of collective agents nor from the informal power relations of plural agents. They show another sense in which there is no sharp distinction between the two kinds of social agents.

4. Numerous real life instances of social agents are discussed in writings about corporate responsibility and similar topics. A good example is French 1984. He discusses the case of the Ford Motor Company being sued for murder in the Pinto case, involving a car it produced with a faulty fuel tank. The suit was against the company, not against its officers or employees; the company itself, it was contended, was morally responsible for knowingly killing innocent people. A more recent case is the Minneapolis School Board appointing a company to be superintendent of its schools. The president of the company was interviewed but it was made clear that not he but his company would manage the schools. (This arrangement did not last very long.)

5. 'No reason' is a relevant answer to the question why you were whistling, whereas it would not be a relevant answer to the question of why you tripped on the rug.

6. This distinction does not line up with the ones I am making here. A social agent, for example, need not act for the social or common good but for its own good or for the good of some individual, just as an individual person may act not for his own good but for the common (or social) good.

7. If the aim was set by the board, this does not mean a social action has been reduced to individual actions, for the board is itself a social agent.

8. The same is true of Tyler Burge's anti-individualist arguments, which aim to show that the content of attitudes is socially determined, for example, by one's language. Burge assumes that however social the content of attitudes may be, they will be ascribed to individual persons. See, for example, Burge 1979.

9. This does not mean that I consider Mary and Art's going to the film to be the action of a social agent. The point of the example is simply to illustrate the point that the only intentions agents, either individual or social, can fulfill are their own.

10. Wilfrid Sellars introduced a notion of 'intend that' that is like Bratman's, but he noted that it presupposes the concept of 'intend to' and emphasized "the conceptual priority of intentions to do even in the case of intentions that someone do". To intend that such and such be the case, he said, means, roughly that I intend to do that which is necessary to make it the case that such and such. Insofar as there is a non-technical notion of intending that such and such, Sellars' view is surely the correct one. Cf. Sellars 1968, 184.

11. For an excellent discussion of intention that is directly relevant to this point, cf. Moran/Stone 2008.

12. In this paper, I use 'bodily movements' both transitively, to mean 'moving one's body', and intransitively, to mean 'one's body moves', because the distinction is not relevant for my discussion.

13. The best defense of these claims is Steward 1997. They are claims Davidson has made. See, for example, Davidson 2003, 499 and 654; and Davidson 1993.

14. On this point see Steward 1997, chap. 4. She argues convincingly that the notion of a *token* state (which is to turn a state into a particular) is incoherent.

15. This way of formulating the distinction is from Steward 1997. I developed the distinction, though formulated differently, in Stoutland 2008.

16. Cf. Heath 2005. This is an excellent article though I am not certain that Heath gets Weber exactly right.

17. This is a view articulated by Anscombe 1957, 33, 34, 45, 46. Since she did not discuss social agency, I do not know if she would agree with my applying her view as I do. She gives an example that does, however, suggest she might agree. It concerns a man "directing a project, like the erection of a building which he cannot see and does not get reports on, purely by giving orders [...]. He is not like a man merely considering speculatively how a thing might be done [...]. *His* knowledge of what is done is practical knowledge."

18. Here is another way to put the point. If there is one right way of individuating the world, then the world must consist of a single ultimate domain of individuals, and hence whatever there is must consist ultimately of the same individuals. It may be reasonable to think that those ultimate individuals are physical, which sets the Chinese box analysis going: social action consists

of (complex) individual actions, which consist of bodily motions ..., etc., down to physical micro-states which are the ultimate individuals. My claim is that there is no such thing as a single, ultimate domain of individuals. Just as there are alternative ways of describing the world, none of which is ultimate or privilege in a general sense, so there are alternative ways of individuating the world, none of which is ultimate or privilege in a general sense. Social discourse individuates in various ways, depending on the discourse, but we should refuse to admit that this way of individuating lines up with the way of individuating when our concern is with non-social agents or with the explanations of the physical sciences.

References

Anscombe, G. E. M. (1957), *Intention*, Oxford

Anscombe, G. E. M. (1981), *Metaphysics and the Philosophy of Mind*, Minneapolis

Aron, R. (1967), *Main Currents in Sociological Thought 2*, New York

Baier, A. (1997), Doing Things with Others: The Mental Commons, in: L. Alanen/S. Heinämaa/T. Wallgren (eds.), *Commonality and Particularity in Ethics*, New York, 15–44

Bratman, M. (1992), Shared Cooperative Activity, in: *Philosophical Review* 101(2), 321–341

Bratman, M. (1993), Shared Intentions, in: *Ethics* 104(1), 97–113

Bratman, M. (1999), *Faces of Intention*, Cambridge

Burge, T. (1979), Individualism and the Mental, in: *Midwest Studies in Philosophy* 4, 73–121

Davidson, D. (1993), Reply to Ralf Stoecker, in: R. Stoecker (ed.), *Reflecting Davidson*, Berlin, 287–290

Davidson, D. (2003), Replies, in: L. E. Hahn (ed.), *The Philosophy of Donald Davidson*, Illinois

French, P. (1984), *Collective and Corporate Responsibility*, New York

Gilbert, M. (1989), *On Social Facts*, Princeton

Gilbert, M. (1990), Walking Together: A Paradigmatic Social Phenomenon, in: *Midwest Studies* 15, 1–14

Gilbert, M. (2000), *Sociality and Responsibility: New Essays in Plural Subject Theory*, Lanham

Heath, J. (2005), Methodological Skepticism, in: *Stanford Encyclopedia of Philosophy* http://www.science.uva.nl/~seop/entries/methodological-individualism/

Moran, R./M. Stone (2008), Anscombe on Expression of Intention, in: C. Sandis (ed.), *New Essays on the Explanation of Action*, Basingstoke

Pettit, P. (2007), Responsibility Incorporated, in: *Ethics* 117, 171–201

Sandis, C. (2008) (ed.), *New Essays on the Explanation of Action*, Basingstoke

Searle, J. (1995), *The Construction of Social Reality*, New York

Sellars, W. (1968), *Science and Metaphysics*, London

Steward, H. (1997), *The Ontology of Mind: Events, Processes, and States*, Oxford

Stoutland, F. (2008), Indeterminism, Intentional Action, and Bodily Movements, in: C. Sandis (ed.), *New Essays on the Explanation of Action*, Basingstoke

Tuomela, R. (1984), *A Theory of Social Action*, Dordrecht-Boston

Tuomela, R. (1991), Intentional Single and Joint Action, in: *Philosophical Studies* 62, 235–262

Tuomela, R. (2007), *The Philosophy of Sociality: The Shared Point of View*, Oxford

Weber, M. (1968), *Economy and Society*, ed. by C. Roth and C. Wittig, Davis

Part IV

Acting for a Reason

Introduction to Part IV

1.

If the last part was (partly) about what it is to act intentionally, Part IV is about what it is to act for a reason. A strategy here is to treat the two questions separately and then see how the answers to them line up.

When one acts for a reason, one is motivated in a certain way to do what one does. What is that way? There is a classic theory that one needs to understand in order to locate oneself in the debate. This theory, known as Humeanism because of some similarity to views propounded by Hume, maintains that what it is for an action to be done for a reason is for it to be caused in a certain way by a certain combination of mental states in the agent. These mental states need to be of the right sorts and to be related to one another, to be linked, in the right sort of way. As Davidson expresses it in his classic "Actions, Reasons, and Causes" (Chapter 19), what it is for an action to be done for a reason is for it to be caused by the agent's having both a pro-attitude to actions of a certain kind and a belief that the action will be of that kind. Here we have two mental states, pro-attitude and belief, and a link given by the common focus on the kind of action at issue.

Sometimes this Humean theory is expressed as a *theory of motivation*: the sort of motivation that is at issue when people do things for reasons occurs when their so acting is caused by the right sort of combination of beliefs and pro-attitudes. Sometimes the theory is offered as an answer to the question what form the *explanation of action* is to take. (This topic, action-explanation, is addressed more directly in Part V of this volume.) So Davidson's account of acting for a reason can also be seen as a theory of what is required to explain action; his Humean theory of action-explanation is that we explain such an action by citing the combination of beliefs and pro-attitudes that caused it. It emerges that Humeanism is at once a theory of acting for a reason, of action-explanation, and of motivation.

Of course this 'triple' theory is concerned only with the sort of action that is action done for a reason, and with the sort of motivation appropriate to that. Other actions, instinctive ones, perhaps, and those done under strong emotion or hypnosis, may be motivated in other ways. So the theory is not a theory of motivation in general, but of motivation by reasons, as one might say, and this is sometimes called *rational motivation*. Instinctive and emotional actions may be sensible, but they will not in this sense be 'rational'.

It is important to notice here that the notion of an action is being taken for granted. We already know what actions are, supposedly, and we are asking, of those things, what it is for one of those to be done for a reason. But Humeanism can also offer an account of what an action is, which we have seen in Part I: actions are bodily movements, of which the rationally motivated ones are those caused by suitable combinations of beliefs and pro-attitudes. On this account, sneezing

Philosophy of Action: An Anthology, First Edition. Edited by Jonathan Dancy and Constantine Sandis.
© 2015 John Wiley & Sons, Inc. Published 2015 by John Wiley & Sons, Inc.

and breathing are actions, but not rationally motivated ones (normally, anyway) – which might be right.

One final comment: Davidson speaks of suitable combinations of beliefs and pro-attitudes. But he is fairly broad-minded (at least in the article reprinted here) about what is to count as a pro-attitude; he includes among pro-attitudes such things as 'moral views', which would be ordinarily taken to be some form of belief. This means that moral motivation may occur when an action is caused by the combination of two beliefs: a belief that acting in a certain way is here obligatory and a belief that to do some proposed action would be to act in that way. More normally, however, Humeanism is expressed as the view that actions are caused by suitable combinations of beliefs and *desires*, and the argument for the theory depends crucially on there being some significant difference between beliefs and desires, which explains why one needs one of each if one is to get rational motivation. Now the notion of a desire being used here is pretty vague, or perhaps one should say flexible; it needs to be vague if it is to cover all cases of actions, since it certainly happens that people do things that they would not say they desire to do at all, such as sacrifice themselves for the sake of others. They are more likely to say that they have to do this than that they want to do it. To insist that they did it because they wanted to would be to cheapen the sacrifice.

So what is the crucial difference between belief and desire? The standard answer to this question appeals to what is called a difference in 'direction of fit'. An example in Anscombe's *Intention* (§32) is used to make the point, which concerns two sorts of mistake. A man goes to the supermarket with a list of things to buy. But his wife is suspicious of him and sets a detective to record his actions. The detective makes a list of what the man buys in the store. The two lists should coincide. If they don't, where is the mistake? There are two possible answers: either the man did not buy all and only what was on the list, or he did, but the detective's list does not record all and only what the man bought. The latter case is analogous to the relation between belief and fact. If there is a mismatch between a belief and the facts, the mistake lies in the belief. We would hardly say that we should work to change the facts so as to make the belief true. The former case is analogous to the relation between desire and thing desired. If there is a mismatch here, the mistake does not lie in the desire. We would think that the way to rectify things is to change the world so that things are as desired.

The point of this long analogy is that we can see here that rational motivation requires one state of each sort in the agent. Beliefs alone could not motivate, because when one acts for a reason there must be something one is trying to achieve, something that is not yet the case, and one is trying to change the world so as to achieve it. Desires alone could not motivate, because without belief one would not know whether one needs to change anything in order for things to be as one desires.

This is the argument that drives the Humean account of rational motivation.

2.

But of course Humeanism, as we have expressed it so far, simply assumes that rational motivation occurs when action is the effect of mental states of some kind or other in the agent. The assumption here is that the reasons for which we act are our own mental states, causing us to do the things we have reason to do. There are two ways in which this assumption can be fleshed out. The first is to suppose that one's reasons *are* one's relevant beliefs and desires; the second is to suppose that one's reasons are always of the form 'that I believe this'; or 'I want that'. The excerpts from Dancy's book (Chapter 20) argue against each of these in turn.

On the first view, Dancy points out that the reasons for us to do one thing rather than another are normally such things as that it is a fine day, and that she needs our help. These things are not mental states of the agent at all, but they do seem to be able to be reasons for doing one thing rather than another – going out for a walk, in the first case, and offering support in the second. The theory that maintains that any reason for which we act must be a mental state of the agent announces, with little argument, that it is impossible to act for these reasons, even though they are admittedly good reasons. So most of the reasons we have are ones that cannot motivate us; the only things that can motivate us are states of ourselves.

The second view, which Dancy calls 'the new theory', does not claim that the reasons for which we act are always states of ourselves, but holds instead that they are always correctly specified as 'that I believe this' or 'that I want that'. So his reason for running is that he believes that the train is leaving (rather than just that the train is leaving), or that he wants to help her (rather than just that doing this will help her). Dancy argues from example that this second view distorts our reasons. There is a difference between the motivations of the person who calls the pest control officer for the reason that there are pink rats in his boots, and that of the person who calls the psychiatrist for the reason that he believes that there are pink rats in his boots. And Humeanism of this second form cannot really recognize that difference. It turns all our rational motivation into a form of self-absorption.

Of course it is one thing to decide on the nature of the reasons for which we act and another to work out what must be the case for us to act for those reasons. No doubt it is impossible to act for a reason unless one has certain beliefs and desires, or purposes; but this does nothing to show that those beliefs and desires are themselves the reasons for which one is acting. When we act for such a reason as her need for help, we do want to help; but our wanting to help is not our reason for doing what we do.

Hursthouse (Chapter 22) argues that there are many 'arational' but still intentional actions that the Humean belief-desire story does not fit. These actions are not preceded by desires to do an action of a certain sort and a belief that the action is of that sort. The true explanation of why I intentionally defaced her photo was that I was furious with her, and it is impossible to convert this explanation into a belief-desire explanation without distortion. More generally, there is a tendency to suppose that intentional actions are actions done for a reason, and the explanation of such actions is given by specifying the good that the agent saw in so acting. Of course there are lots of actions like this. But there are others, too. When I vent my anger by defacing the photo, it is not that I see some good in venting my anger (the pro-attitude), and believe this to be an easy way to do it, ready to hand. But my action is intentional nonetheless.

Hursthouse's arguments can however be turned against non-Humean accounts of acting for a reason.

If the true explanation of my defacing her photo is that I was furious with her, my fury will not have been my reason for doing what I did. The non-Humeans maintain that our reasons consist in real or supposed features of the situation. But not any old feature of the situation will do. Why is it impossible to run a marathon for the reason that Tuesday comes after Monday? It is because the ordering of days of the week is (normally) irrelevant to one's choice of whether to run or not. Which features are relevant in the sense here intended? The obvious answer is: those features that cast running in a favorable light or unfavorable, or which affect the eligibility or ineligibility of the running option. A reason *for* action, then, is a consideration that casts such action in a favorable light. Raz (Chapter 23) calls this view the 'classical view', and he defends it against various objections, including those derived from Hursthouse's 'expressive' actions.

Korsgaard (Chapter 21) starts in a familiar place by asking whether the reasons for which we act are states of ourselves or the facts on which those states are based. Her answer is that both of these suggestions are wrong. The best form of the second answer holds that the agent's reasons are the features that make the action seem eligible to the agent. But to Korsgaard this seems insufficiently normative. She suggests that rational action is action motivated by (consciousness of) the appropriateness of its own motivation. To make sense of this, she argues that Aristotle and Kant agree that an action done for a reason is not one thing, the action, done in the light of another, the reason; the action includes its own reason. The action is to be understood as a 'this-for-the-sake-of-that'. The 'that' here is the agent's purpose, or reason. This is the way Korsgaard tries to make sense of the idea that an action is motivated by consciousness of its own appropriateness; the appropriateness is the fit between the 'this' and the 'that'. We might wonder whether the 'this' here is not just the action, motivated by the 'that for the sake of which'. But Korsgaard suggests here a distinction between act and action. (A similar distinction between act and action is to be found in Ross 1930: ch. 1.) The act is the thing done for the sake of that; the action is the doing of it for that reason. An action is an 'act-for-the-sake-of-an-end'. We explain the act by explicating (laying out) the purpose for which it was done, and our explication succeeds as an explanation if the act–purpose combination (i.e. the action) is indeed appropriate. An agent who acts in the light of the appropriateness of act to purpose is one who is motivated by consciousness of the appropriateness of his own motivation.

The standard case of rational motivation is a case where the agent does what she takes herself to have most reason to do, and does it exactly for that reason. But there are occasions where agents do something else instead. They have perfectly good views about reasons, but do not act accordingly. How are we to understand such actions? This is the old problem of the weakness of the will. We have two ways of failing to do the action that we judge best: weakness and compulsion (where what compels one is the strength of one's desires). How are we to distinguish between these? In both cases the agent is unable to do what he judges best; his preferences lead him one way and his desires another. Watson (Chapter 24) suggests that the agent is weak when the desires on which he acts are ones that an agent with ordinary powers of self-control would have no difficulty in ignoring, or mastering. The agent is under compulsion when the desires are so strong that ordinary powers of self-control would not enable the agent to master them. Weaker desires than those may be ones that our agent cannot resist, without our needing to think of him as under compulsion in this sense.

Reference

Ross, W. D. (1930), *The Right and the Good* (Oxford: Clarendon Press).

Further Reading

Anscombe, G. E. M. (1957), *Intention* (Oxford: Blackwell).

Davidson, D. (1970), "How is Weakness of the Will Possible?," in J. Feinberg (ed.), *Moral Concepts* (Oxford: Oxford University Press), 93–113; reprinted in Davidson's *Essays on Action and Events* (Oxford: Oxford University Press, 1980), 21–42.

Davidson, D. (1987), "Problems in the Explanation of Action," in P. Pettit, R. Sylvan, and J. Norman (eds.), *Metaphysics and Morality: Essays in Honour of J. J. C. Smart* (Oxford: Blackwell), 35–49; reprinted in Davidson's *Problems of Rationality* (Oxford: Oxford University Press, 2004), 101–116.

Hieronymi, P. (2011), "Reasons for Action," *Proceedings of the Aristotelian Society* 111, 407–427.

Setiya, K. (2007), *Reasons without Rationalism* (Princeton, N.J.: Princeton University Press).

Smith, M. (1987), "The Humean Theory of Motivation," *Mind* 96 (381), 36–61.

19

Actions, Reasons, and Causes

Donald Davidson

WHAT is the relation between a reason and an action when the reason explains the action by giving the agent's reason for doing what he did? We may call such explanations *rationalizations*, and say that the reason *rationalizes* the action.

In this paper I want to defend the ancient – and common-sense – position that rationalization is a species of ordinary causal explanation. The defense no doubt requires some redeployment, but not more or less complete abandonment of the position, as urged by many recent writers.[1]

I

A reason rationalizes an action only if it leads us to see something the agent saw, or thought he saw, in his action – some feature, consequence, or aspect of the action the agent wanted, desired, prized, held dear, thought dutiful, beneficial, obligatory, or agreeable. We cannot explain why someone did what he did simply by saying the particular action appealed to him; we must indicate what it was about the action that appealed. Whenever someone does something for a reason, therefore, he can be characterized as (a) having

some sort of pro attitude toward actions of a certain kind, and (b) believing (or knowing, perceiving, noticing, remembering) that his action is of that kind. Under (a) are to be included desires, wantings, urges, promptings, and a great variety of moral views, aesthetic principles, economic prejudices, social conventions, and public and private goals and values in so far as these can be interpreted as attitudes of an agent directed toward actions of a certain kind. The word 'attitude' does yeoman service here, for it must cover not only permanent character traits that show themselves in a lifetime of behavior, like love of children or a taste for loud company, but also the most passing fancy that prompts a unique action, like a sudden desire to touch a woman's elbow. In general, pro attitudes must not be taken for convictions, however temporary, that every action of a certain kind ought to be performed, is worth performing, or is, all things considered, desirable. On the contrary, a man may all his life have a yen, say, to drink a can of paint, without ever, even at the moment he yields, believing it would be worth doing.

Giving the reason why an agent did something is often a matter of naming the pro attitude (a) or the related belief (b) or both; let me call this pair the *primary reason* why the agent performed the action. Now it is possible to reformulate the claim that rationalizations are causal explanations, and give structure to the argument as well, by stating two theses about primary reasons:

Davidson, D. (1963), "Actions, Reasons, and Causes," *Journal of Philosophy* 60 (23), 685–700. Reprinted with permission of The Journal of Philosophy.

Philosophy of Action: An Anthology, First Edition. Edited by Jonathan Dancy and Constantine Sandis.
© 2015 John Wiley & Sons, Inc. Published 2015 by John Wiley & Sons, Inc.

1. For us to understand how a reason of any kind rationalizes an action it is necessary and sufficient that we see, at least in essential outline, how to construct a primary reason.
2. The primary reason for an action is its cause.

I shall argue for these points in turn.

II

I flip the switch, turn on the light, and illuminate the room. Unbeknownst to me I also alert a prowler to the fact that I am home. Here I do not do four things, but only one, of which four descriptions have been given.[2] I flipped the switch because I wanted to turn on the light, and by saying I wanted to turn on the light I explain (give my reason for, rationalize) the flipping. But I do not, by giving this reason, rationalize my alerting of the prowler nor my illuminating of the room. Since reasons may rationalize what someone does when it is described in one way and not when it is described in another, we cannot treat what was done simply as a term in sentences like 'My reason for flipping the switch was that I wanted to turn on the light'; otherwise we would be forced to conclude, from the fact that flipping the switch was identical with alerting the prowler, that my reason for alerting the prowler was that I wanted to turn on the light. Let us mark this quasi-intensional[3] character of action descriptions in rationalizations by stating a bit more precisely a necessary condition for primary reasons:

> C1. *R* is a primary reason why an agent performed the action *A* under the description *d* only if *R* consists of a pro attitude of the agent toward actions with a certain property, and a belief of the agent that *A*, under the description *d*, has that property.

How can my wanting to turn on the light be (part of) a primary reason, since it appears to lack the required element of generality? We may be taken in by the verbal parallel between 'I turned on the light' and 'I wanted to turn on the light'. The first clearly refers to a particular event, so we conclude that the second has this same event as its object. Of course it is obvious that the event of my turning on the light can't be referred to in the same way by both sentences, since the existence of the event is required by the truth of 'I turned on the light' but not by the truth of 'I wanted to turn on the light'. If the reference were the same in both cases, the second sentence would entail the first; but in fact the sentences are logically independent. What is less obvious, at least until we attend to it, is that the event whose occurrence makes 'I turned on the light' true cannot be called the object, however intensional, of 'I wanted to turn on the light'. If I turned on the light, then I must have done it at a precise moment, in a particular way – every detail is fixed. But it makes no sense to demand that my want be directed at an action performed at any one moment or done in some unique manner. Any one of an indefinitely large number of actions would satisfy the want, and can be considered equally eligible as its object. Wants and desires often are trained on physical objects. However, 'I want that gold watch in the window' is not a primary reason, and explains why I went into the store only because it suggests a primary reason – for example, that I wanted to buy the watch.

Because 'I wanted to turn on the light' and 'I turned on the light' are logically independent, the first can be used to give a reason why the second is true. Such a reason gives minimal information: it implies that the action was intentional, and wanting tends to exclude some other pro attitudes, such as a sense of duty or obligation. But the exclusion depends very much on the action and the context of explanation. Wanting seems pallid beside lusting, but it would be odd to deny that someone who lusted after a woman or a cup of coffee wanted her or it. It is not unnatural, in fact, to treat wanting as a genus including all pro attitudes as species. When we do this and when we know some action is intentional, it is empty to add that the agent wanted to do it. In such cases, it is easy to answer the question 'Why did you do it?' with 'For no reason', meaning not that there is no reason but that there is no *further* reason, no reason that cannot be inferred from the fact that the action was done intentionally; no reason, in other words, besides wanting to do it. This last point is not essential to the present argument, but it is of interest because it defends the possibility of defining an intentional action as one done for a reason.

A primary reason consists of a belief and an attitude, but it is generally otiose to mention both. If you tell me you are easing the jib because you think that will stop the main from backing, I don't need to be told that you want to stop the main from backing; and if you say you are biting your thumb at me because you want to insult me, there is no point in adding that you think that by biting your thumb at me you will insult me. Similarly, many explanations of actions in terms of reasons that are not primary do not require mention of the primary reason to complete the story. If I say I am pulling weeds because I want a beautiful lawn, it would be fatuous to eke out the account with 'And so I see something desirable in any action that does, or has a good chance of, making the lawn beautiful'. Why insist that there is any *step*, logical or psychological, in the transfer of desire from an end that is not an action to the actions one conceives as means? It serves the argument as well that the desired end explains the action only if what are believed by the agent to be means are desired.

Fortunately, it is not necessary to classify and analyze the many varieties of emotions, sentiments, moods, motives, passions, and hungers whose mention may answer the question 'Why did you do it?' in order to see how, when such mention rationalizes the action, a primary reason is involved. Claustrophobia gives a man's reason for leaving a cocktail party because we know people want to avoid, escape from, be safe from, put distance between themselves and, what they fear. Jealousy is the motive in a poisoning because, among other things, the poisoner believes his action will harm his rival, remove the cause of his agony, or redress an injustice, and these are the sorts of things a jealous man wants to do. When we learn a man cheated his son out of greed, we do not necessarily know what the primary reason was, but we know there was one, and its general nature. Ryle analyzes 'he boasted from vanity' into "he boasted on meeting the stranger and his doing so satisfies the lawlike proposition that whenever he finds a chance of securing the admiration and envy of others, he does whatever he thinks will produce this admiration and envy" (*The Concept of Mind*, 1949, 89). This analy-

sis is often, and perhaps justly, criticized on the ground that a man may boast from vanity just once. But if Ryle's boaster did what he did from vanity, then something entailed by Ryle's analysis is true: the boaster wanted to secure the admiration and envy of others, and he believed that his action would produce this admiration and envy; true or false, Ryle's analysis does not dispense with primary reasons, but depends upon them.

To know a primary reason why someone acted as he did is to know an intention with which the action was done. If I turn left at the fork because I want to get to Katmandu, my intention in turning left is to get to Katmandu. But to know the intention is not necessarily to know the primary reason in full detail. If James goes to church with the intention of pleasing his mother, then he must have some pro attitude toward pleasing his mother, but it needs more information to tell whether his reason is that he enjoys pleasing his mother, or thinks it right, his duty, or an obligation. The expression 'the intention with which James went to church' has the outward form of a description, but in fact it is syncategorematic and cannot be taken to refer to an entity, state, disposition, or event. Its function in context is to generate new descriptions of actions in terms of their reasons; thus 'James went to church with the intention of pleasing his mother' yields a new, and fuller, description of the action described in 'James went to church'. Essentially the same process goes on when I answer the question 'Why are you bobbing around that way?' with 'I'm knitting, weaving, exercising, sculling, cuddling, training fleas'.

Straight description of an intended result often explains an action better than stating that the result was intended or desired. 'It will soothe your nerves' explains why I pour you a shot as efficiently as 'I want to do something to soothe your nerves', since the first in the context of explanation implies the second; but the first does better, because, if it is true, the facts will justify my choice of action. Because justifying and explaining an action so often go hand in hand, we frequently indicate the primary reason for an action by making a claim which, if true, would also verify, vindicate, or support the relevant belief or attitude of the agent. 'I knew I ought to return it', 'The paper said it was going to snow', 'You stepped on *my* toes', all, in appropriate reason-giving contexts, perform this familiar dual function.

The justifying role of a reason, given this interpretation, depends upon the explanatory role, but the converse does not hold. Your stepping on my toes neither explains nor justifies my stepping on your toes unless I believe you stepped on my toes, but the belief alone, true or false, explains my action.

III

In the light of a primary reason, an action is revealed as coherent with certain traits, long- or short-termed, characteristic or not, of the agent, and the agent is shown in his role of Rational Animal. Corresponding to the belief and attitude of a primary reason for an action, we can always construct (with a little ingenuity) the premises of a syllogism from which it follows that the action has some (as Miss Anscombe calls it) "desirability characteristic."[4] Thus there is a certain irreducible – though somewhat anemic – sense in which every rationalization justifies: from the agent's point of view there was, when he acted, something to be said for the action.

Noting that nonteleological causal explanations do not display the element of justification provided by reasons, some philosophers have concluded that the concept of cause that applies elsewhere cannot apply to the relation between reasons and actions, and that the pattern of justification provides, in the case of reasons, the required explanation. But suppose we grant that reasons alone justify in explaining actions; it does not follow that the explanation is not also – and necessarily – causal. Indeed our first condition for primary reasons (C1) is designed to help set rationalizations apart from other sorts of explanation. If rationalization is, as I want to argue, a species of causal explanation, then justification, in the sense given by C1, is at least one differentiating property. How about the other claim: that justifying is a kind of explaining, so that the ordinary notion of cause need not be brought in? Here it is necessary to decide what is being included under justification. Perhaps it means only what is given by C1: that the agent has certain beliefs and attitudes in the light of which the action is reasonable. But then something essential has certainly been left out, for a person can have a reason for an action, and perform the action, and yet this reason not be the reason why he did it. Central to the relation between a reason and an action it explains is the idea that the agent performed the action *because* he had the reason. Of course, we can include this idea too in justification; but then the notion of justification becomes as dark as the notion of reason until we can account for the force of that 'because'.

When we ask why someone acted as he did, we want to be provided with an interpretation. His behavior seems strange, alien, outré, pointless, out of character, disconnected; or perhaps we cannot even recognize an action in it. When we learn his reason, we have an interpretation, a new description of what he did which fits it into a familiar picture. The picture certainly includes some of the agent's beliefs and attitudes; perhaps also goals, ends, principles, general character traits, virtues or vices. Beyond this, the redescription of an action afforded by a reason may place the action in a wider social, economic, linguistic, or evaluative context. To learn, through learning the reason, that the agent conceived his action as a lie, a repayment of a debt, an insult, the fulfillment of an avuncular obligation, or a knight's gambit is to grasp the point of the action in its setting of rules, practices, conventions, and expectations.

Remarks like these, inspired by the later Wittgenstein, have been elaborated with subtlety and insight by a number of philosophers. And there is no denying that this is true: when we explain an action, by giving the reason, we do redescribe the action; redescribing the action gives the action a place in a pattern, and in this way the action is explained. Here it is tempting to draw two conclusions that do not follow. First, we can't infer, from the fact that giving reasons merely redescribes the action and that causes are separate from effects, that therefore reasons are not causes. Reasons, being beliefs and attitudes, are certainly not identical with actions; but, more important, events are often redescribed in terms of their causes. (Suppose someone was burned. We could redescribe this event "in terms of a cause" by saying he was burned.) Second, it is an error to think that, because placing the action in a larger pattern explains it, therefore we now understand the sort of explanation involved. Talk of patterns and contexts does not answer the question of how reasons explain actions, since the relevant pattern or context contains both reason and action. One way we can explain an event is by placing it in the context of its cause; cause and effect form the sort of pattern that explains the effect, in a sense of 'explain' that we understand as well as any. If reason and action illustrate a different pattern of explanation, that pattern must be identified.

Let me urge the point in connection with an example of Melden's. A man driving an automobile raises his arm in order to signal. His intention, to signal, explains his action, raising his arm, by redescribing it as signaling. What is the pattern that explains the action? Is it the familiar pattern of an action done for a reason? Then it does indeed explain the action, but only because it assumes the relation of reason and action that we want to analyze. Or is the pattern rather this: the man is driving, he is approaching a turn; he knows he ought to signal; he knows how to signal, by raising his arm. And now, in this context, he raises his arm. Perhaps, as Melden suggests, if all this happens, he does signal. And the explanation would then be this: if, under these conditions, a man raises his arm, then he signals. The difficulty is, of course, that this explanation does not touch the question of why he raised his arm. He had a reason to raise his arm, but this has not been shown to be the reason why he did it. If the description 'signaling' explains his action by giving his reason, then the signaling must be intentional; but, on the account just given, it may not be.

If, as Melden claims, causal explanations are "wholly irrelevant to the understanding we seek" of human actions (184) then we are without an analysis of the 'because' in 'He did it because ...', where we go on to name a reason. Hampshire remarks, of the relation between reasons and action, "In philosophy one ought surely to find this ... connection altogether mysterious" (166). Hampshire rejects Aristotle's attempt to solve the mystery by introducing the concept of wanting as a causal factor, on the grounds that the resulting theory is too clear and definite to fit all cases and that "There is still no compelling ground for insisting that the word 'want' *must* enter into every full statement of reasons for acting" (168). I agree that the concept of wanting is too narrow, but I have argued that, at least in a vast number of typical cases, some pro attitude must be assumed to be present if a statement

of an agent's reasons in acting is to be intelligible. Hampshire does not see how Aristotle's scheme can be appraised as true or false, "for it is not clear what could be the basis of assessment, or what kind of evidence could be decisive" (167). Failing a satisfactory alternative, the best argument for a scheme like Aristotle's is that it alone promises to give an account of the "mysterious connection" between reasons and actions.

IV

In order to turn the first 'and' to 'because' in 'He exercised *and* he wanted to reduce and thought exercise would do it', we must, as the basic move,[5] augment condition C1 with:

C2. A primary reason for an action is its cause.

The considerations in favor of C2 are by now, I hope, obvious; in the remainder of this paper I wish to defend C2 against various lines of attack and, in the process, to clarify the notion of causal explanation involved.

A. The first line of attack is this. Primary reasons consist of attitudes and beliefs, which are states or dispositions, not events; therefore they cannot be causes.

It is easy to reply that states, dispositions, and conditions are frequently named as the causes of events: the bridge collapsed because of a structural defect; the plane crashed on takeoff because the air temperature was abnormally high; the plate broke because it had a crack. This reply does not, however, meet a closely related point. Mention of a causal condition for an event gives a cause only on the assumption that there was also a preceding event. But what is the preceding event that causes an action?

In many cases it is not difficult at all to find events very closely associated with the primary reason. States and dispositions are not events, but the onslaught of a state or disposition is. A desire to hurt your feelings may spring up at the moment you anger me; I may start wanting to eat a melon just when I see one; and beliefs may begin at the moment we notice, perceive, learn, or remember something. Those who have argued that there are no mental events to qualify as causes of actions have often missed the obvious because they have insisted that a mental event be observed or noticed (rather than an observing or a noticing) or that it be like a stab, a qualm, a prick or a quiver, a mysterious prod of conscience or act of the will. Melden, in discussing the driver who signals a turn by raising his arm, challenges those who want to explain actions causally to identify "an event which is common and peculiar to all such cases" (87), perhaps a motive or an intention, anyway "some particular feeling or experience" (95). But of course there is a mental event; at some moment the driver noticed (or thought he noticed) his turn coming up, and that is the moment he signaled. During any continuing activity, like driving, or elaborate performance, like swimming the Hellespont, there are more or less fixed purposes, standards, desires, and habits that give direction and form to the entire enterprise, and there is the continuing input of information about what we are doing, about changes in the environment, in terms of which we regulate and adjust our actions. To dignify a driver's awareness that his turn has come by calling it an experience, much less a feeling, is no doubt exaggerated, but whether it deserves a name or not, it had better be the reason why he raises his arm. In this case, and typically, there may not be anything we would call a motive, but if we mention such a general purpose as wanting to get to one's destination safely, it is clear that the motive is not an event. The intention with which the driver raises his arm is also not an event, for it is no thing at all, neither event, attitude, disposition, nor object. Finally, Melden asks the causal theorist to find an event that is common and peculiar to all cases where a man intentionally raises his arm, and this, it must be admitted, cannot be produced. But then neither can a common and unique cause of bridge failures, plane crashes, or plate breakings be produced.

The signaling driver can answer the question 'Why did you raise your arm when you did?', and from the answer we learn the event that caused the action. But can an actor always answer such a question? Sometimes the answer will mention a mental event that does not give a reason: 'Finally I made up my mind'. However, there also seem to be cases of intentional action where we cannot explain at all why we acted when we did. In such cases, explanation in terms of primary reasons parallels the explanation of the collapse of the bridge from a structural defect: we are ignorant of the event or sequence of events that led up to (caused) the collapse, but we are sure there was such an event or sequence of events.

B. According to Melden, a cause must be "logically distinct from the alleged effect" (52); but a reason for an action is not logically distinct from the action; therefore, reasons are not causes of actions.[6]

One possible form of this argument has already been suggested. Since a reason makes an action intelligible by redescribing it, we do not have two events, but only one under different descriptions. Causal relations, however, demand distinct events.

Someone might be tempted into the mistake of thinking that my flipping of the switch caused my turning on of the light (in fact it caused the light to go on). But it does not follow that it is a mistake to take 'My reason for flipping the switch was that I wanted to turn on the light' as entailing, in part, 'I flipped the switch, and this action is further describable as having been caused by my wanting to turn on the light'. To describe an event in terms of its cause is not to identify the event with its cause, nor does explanation by redescription exclude causal explanation.

The example serves also to refute the claim that we cannot describe the action without using words that link it to the alleged cause. Here the action is to be explained under the description: 'my flipping the switch', and the alleged cause is 'my wanting to turn on the light'. What possible logical relation is supposed to hold between these phrases? It seems more plausible to urge a logical link between 'my turning on the light' and 'my wanting to turn on the light', but even here the link turned out, on inspection, to be grammatical rather than logical.

In any case there is something very odd in the idea that causal relations are empirical rather than logical. What can this mean? Surely not that every true causal statement is empirical. For suppose 'A caused B' is true. Then the cause of $B = A$; so, substituting, we have 'The cause of B caused B', which is analytic. The truth of a causal statement depends on *what* events are described; its status as analytic or synthetic depends on *how* the events are described. Still, it may be maintained that a reason rationalizes an action only when the descriptions are appropriately fixed, and the appropriate descriptions are not logically independent.

Suppose that to say a man wanted to turn on the light *meant* that he would perform any action he believed would accomplish his end. Then the statement of his primary reason for flipping the switch would entail that he flipped the switch – "straightway he acts," as Aristotle says. In this case there would certainly be a logical connection between reason and action, the same sort of connection as that between 'It's water-soluble and was placed in water' and 'It dissolved'. Since the implication runs from description of cause to description of effect but not conversely, naming the cause still gives information. And, though the point is often overlooked, 'Placing it in water caused it to dissolve' does not entail 'It's water-soluble'; so the latter has additional explanatory force. Nevertheless, the explanation would be far more interesting if, in place of solubility, with its obvious definitional connection with the event to be explained, we could refer to some property, say a particular crystalline structure, whose connection with dissolution in water was known only through experiment. Now it is clear why primary reasons like desires and wants do not explain actions in the relatively trivial way solubility explains dissolvings. Solubility, we are assuming, is a pure disposition property: it is defined in terms of a single test. But desires cannot be defined in terms of the actions they may rationalize, even though the relation between desire and action is not simply empirical; there are other, equally essential criteria for desires – their expression in feelings and in actions that they do not rationalize, for example. The person who has a desire (or want or belief) does not normally need criteria at all – he generally knows, even in the absence of any clues available to others, what he wants, desires, and believes. These logical features of primary reasons show that it is not just lack of ingenuity that keeps us from defining them as dispositions to act for these reasons.

C. According to Hume, "we may define a cause to be an object, followed by another, and where all the objects similar to the first are followed by objects similar to the second." But, Hart and Honoré claim, "The statement that one person did something because, for example, another threatened him, carries no implication or covert assertion that if the circumstances were repeated the same action would follow" (52). Hart and Honoré allow that Hume is right in saying that ordinary singular causal statements imply generalizations, but wrong for this very reason in supposing that motives and desires are ordinary causes of actions. In brief, laws are involved essentially in ordinary causal explanations, but not in rationalizations.

It is common to try to meet this argument by suggesting that we do have rough laws connecting reasons and actions, and these can, in theory, be improved. True, threatened people do not always respond in the same way; but we may distinguish between threats and also between agents, in terms of their beliefs and attitudes.

The suggestion is delusive, however, because generalizations connecting reasons and actions are not – and cannot be sharpened into – the kind of law on the basis of which accurate predictions can reliably be made. If we reflect on the way in which reasons determine choice, decision, and behavior, it is easy to see why this is so. What emerges, in the *ex post facto* atmosphere of explanation and justification, as *the* reason frequently was, to the agent at the time of action, one consideration among many, *a* reason. Any serious theory for predicting action on the basis of reasons must find a way of evaluating the relative force of various desires and beliefs in the matrix of decision; it cannot take as its starting point the refinement of what is to be expected from a single desire. The practical syllogism exhausts its role in displaying an action as falling under one reason; so it cannot be subtilized into a reconstruction of practical reasoning, which involves the weighing of competing reasons. The practical syllogism provides a model neither for a predictive science of action nor for a normative account of evaluative reasoning.

Ignorance of competent predictive laws does not inhibit valid causal explanation, or few causal explanations could be made. I am certain the window broke because it was struck by a rock – I saw it all happen; but I am not (is anyone?) in command of laws on the basis of which I can predict what blows will break which windows. A generalization like 'Windows are fragile, and fragile things tend to break when struck hard enough, other conditions being right' is not a predictive law in the rough – the predictive law, if we had it, would be quantitative and would use very different concepts. The generalization, like our generalizations about behavior, serves a different function: it provides evidence for the existence of a causal law covering the case at hand.

We are usually far more certain of a singular causal connection than we are of any causal law governing the case; does this show that Hume was wrong in claiming that singular causal statements entail laws? Not necessarily, for Hume's claim, as quoted above, is ambiguous. It may mean that 'A caused B' entails some particular law involving the predicates used in the descriptions 'A' and 'B', or it may mean that 'A caused B' entails that there exists a causal law instantiated by some true descriptions of A and B.[7] Obviously, both versions of Hume's doctrine give a sense to the claim that singular causal statements entail laws, and both sustain the view that causal explanations "involve laws." But the second version is far weaker, in that no particular law is entailed by a singular causal claim, and a singular causal claim can be defended, if it needs defense, without defending any law. Only the second version of Hume's doctrine can be made to fit with most causal explanations; it suits rationalizations equally well.

The most primitive explanation of an event gives its cause; more elaborate explanations may tell more of the story, or defend the singular causal claim by producing a relevant law or by giving reasons for believing such exists. But it is an error to think no explanation has been given until a law has been produced. Linked with these errors is the idea that singular causal statements necessarily indicate, by the concepts they employ, the concepts that will occur in the entailed law. Suppose a hurricane, which is reported on page 5 of Tuesday's *Times*, causes a catastrophe, which is reported on page 13 of Wednesday's *Tribune*. Then the event reported on page 5 of Tuesday's *Times* caused the event reported on page 13 of Wednesday's *Tribune*. Should we look for a law relating events of these *kinds?* It is only slightly less ridiculous to look for a law relating hurricanes and catastrophes. The laws needed to predict the catastrophe with precision would, of course, have no use for concepts like hurricane and catastrophe. The trouble with predicting the weather is that the descriptions under which events interest us – 'a cool, cloudy day with rain in the afternoon' – have only remote connections with the concepts employed by the more precise known laws.

The laws whose existence is required if reasons are causes of actions do not, we may be sure, deal in the concepts in which rationalizations must deal. If the causes of a class of events (actions) fall in a certain class (reasons) and there is a law to back each singular causal statement, it does not follow that there is any law connecting events classified as reasons with events classified as actions – the classifications may even be neurological, chemical, or physical.

D. It is said that the kind of knowledge one has of one's own reasons in acting is not compatible with the existence of a causal relation between reasons and actions: a person knows his own intentions in acting infallibly, without induction or observation, and no ordinary causal relation can be known in this way. No doubt our knowledge of our own intentions in acting will show many of the oddities peculiar to first-person knowledge of one's own pains, beliefs, desires, and so on; the only question is whether these oddities prove that reasons do not cause, in any ordinary sense at least, the actions that they rationalize.

You may easily be wrong about the truth of a statement of the form 'I am poisoning Charles because I want to save him pain', because you may be wrong about whether you are poisoning Charles – you may yourself be drinking the poisoned cup by mistake. But it also seems that you may err about your reasons, particularly when you have two reasons for an action, one of which pleases you and one which does not. For example, you do want to save Charles pain; you also want him out of the way. You may be wrong about which motive made you do it.

The fact that you may be wrong does not show that in general it makes sense to ask you how you know what your reasons were or to ask for your evidence. Though you may, on rare occasions, accept public or private evidence as showing you are wrong about your reasons, you usually have no evidence and make no observations. Then your knowledge of your own reasons for your actions is not generally inductive, for where there is induction, there is evidence. Does this show the knowledge is not causal? I cannot see that it does.

Causal laws differ from true but nonlawlike generalizations in that their instances confirm them; induction is, therefore, certainly a good way to learn the truth of a law. It does not follow that it is the only way to learn the truth of a law. In any case, in order to know that a singular causal statement is true, it is not necessary to know the truth of a law; it is necessary only to know that some law covering the events at hand exists. And it is far from evident that induction, and induction alone, yields the knowledge that a causal law satisfying certain conditions exists. Or, to put it differently, one case is often enough, as Hume admitted, to persuade us that a law exists, and this amounts to saying that we are persuaded, without direct inductive evidence, that a causal relation exists.

E. Finally I should like to say something about a certain uneasiness some philosophers feel in speaking of causes of actions at all. Melden, for example, says that actions are often identical with bodily movements, and that bodily movements have causes; yet he denies that the causes are causes of the actions. This is, I think, a contradiction. He is led to it by the following sort of consideration: "It is futile to attempt to explain conduct through the causal efficacy of desire – all *that*

can explain is further happenings, not actions performed by agents. The agent confronting the causal nexus in which such happenings occur is a helpless victim of all that occurs in and to him" (128, 129). Unless I am mistaken, this argument, if it were valid, would show that actions cannot have causes at all. I shall not point out the obvious difficulties in removing actions from the realm of causality entirely. But perhaps it is worth trying to uncover the source of the trouble. Why on earth should a cause turn an action into a mere happening and a person into a helpless victim? Is it because we tend to assume, at least in the arena of action, that a cause demands a causer, agency an agent? So we press the question; if my action is caused, what caused it? If I did, then there is the absurdity of infinite regress; if I did not, I am a victim. But of course the alternatives are not exhaustive. Some causes have no agents. Primary among these are those states and changes of state in persons which, because they are reasons as well as causes, make persons voluntary agents.

Notes

1. Some examples: G. E. M. Anscombe, *Intention*, Oxford, 1959; Stuart Hampshire, *Thought and Action*, London, 1959; H. L. A. Hart and A. M. Honoré, *Causation in the Law*, Oxford, 1959; William Dray, *Laws and Explanation in History*, Oxford, 1957; and most of the books in the series edited by R. F. Holland, *Studies in Philosophical Psychology*, including Anthony Kenny, *Action, Emotion and Will*, London, 1963, and A. I. Melden, *Free Action*, London, 1961. Page references in parentheses will all be to these works.

2. We would not call my unintentional alerting of the prowler an action, but it should not be inferred from this that alerting the prowler is therefore something different from flipping the switch, say just its consequence. Actions, performances, and events not involving intention are alike in that they are often referred to or defined partly in terms of some terminal stage, outcome, or consequence.

    The word 'action' does not very often occur in ordinary speech, and when it does it is usually reserved for fairly portentous occasions. I follow a useful philosophical practice in calling anything an agent does intentionally an action, including intentional omissions. What is really needed is some suitably generic term to

bridge the following gap: suppose '*A*' is a description of an action, '*B*' is a description of something done voluntarily, though not intentionally, and '*C*' is a description of something done involuntarily and unintentionally; finally, suppose *A = B = C*. Then *A*, *B*, and *C* are the same – what? 'Action', 'event', 'thing done', each have, at least in some contexts, a strange ring when coupled with the wrong sort of description. Only the question "Why did you (he) do *A?*" has the true generality required. Obviously, the problem is greatly aggravated if we assume, as Melden does (*Free Action*, 85), that an action ("raising one's arm") can be identical with a bodily movement ("one's arm going up").

3. "Quasi-intentional" because, besides its intensional aspect, the description of the action must also refer in rationalizations; otherwise it could be true that an action was done for a certain reason and yet the action not have been performed. Compare 'the author of *Waverley*' in 'George IV knew the author of *Waverley* wrote *Waverley*'.

4. Miss Anscombe denies that the practical syllogism is deductive. This she does partly because she thinks of the practical syllogism, as Aristotle does, as corresponding to a piece of practical reasoning (whereas for me it is only

part of the analysis of the concept of a reason with which someone acted), and therefore she is bound, again following Aristotle, to think of the conclusion of a practical syllogism as corresponding to a judgment, not merely that the action has a desirable characteristic, but that the action is desirable (reasonable, worth doing, etc.).

5. I say "as the basic move" to cancel the suggestion that C1 and C2 are jointly *sufficient* to define the relation of reasons to the actions they explain. I believe C2 can be strengthened to make C1 and C2 sufficient as well as necessary conditions, but here I am concerned only with the claim that both are, as they stand, necessary.

6. This argument can be found, in one or more versions, in Kenny, Hampshire, and Melden, as well as in P. Winch, *The Idea of a Social Science*, London, 1958, and R. S. Peters, *The Concept of Motivation*, London, 1958. In one of its forms, the argument was of course inspired by Ryle's treatment of motives in *The Concept of Mind*.

7. We could roughly characterize the analysis of singular causal statements hinted at here as follows: '*A* caused *B*' is true if and only if there are descriptions of *A* and *B* such that the sentence obtained by putting these descriptions for '*A*' and '*B*' in '*A* caused *B*' follows from a true causal law. This analysis is saved from triviality by the fact that not all true generalizations are causal laws; causal laws are distinguished (though of course this is no analysis) by the fact that they are inductively confirmed by their instances and by the fact that they support counterfactual and subjunctive singular causal statements.

20

How to Act for a Good Reason

Jonathan Dancy

1. Psychologism: The Three-Part Story and the Normative Story

Psychologism is a view about motivation; it is the claim that the reasons for which we act are psychological states of ourselves. I will be assuming here that the form of psychologism to be attacked is the best form, namely the view that the psychological states that constitute the reasons for which we act consist entirely of beliefs, which I call pure cognitivism. (The previous chapter of the book from which this paper is taken argues this point.) This has the great advantage that we do not have to introduce complicating considerations about desires. The only psychological states relevant are beliefs, and we can discuss the matter entirely in terms of the relation between the belief (the believing, that is) and the thing believed.

In what follows, I will operate with a distinction about which I have some doubts. This is the distinction between motivating reasons and normative reasons. This distinction seems to suggest that there are two *sorts* of reasons: the motivating sort and the normative or good sort. I don't accept this suggestion, but I will still work with the distinction here, because

the positions that I am here working to reject are best formulated in its terms. Those positions do hold that though we speak of motivating *reasons* and normative or good *reasons*, we are genuinely dealing with two distinct *sorts* of reason, in a way that raises the question whether the word 'reason' is not awkwardly ambiguous. I am going to allow this way of speaking in the course of an attempt to argue that it is incoherent.

So – are any motivating reasons psychological states of the agent? The reasons we actually give, in explaining either our own actions and those of others, seem to be expressed sometimes in terms of a psychological state of the agent, and sometimes not. I might say that we are sending our child to this school because we believe it will suit her better; and I might say that I am taking my car down to the garage because it is time for it to be serviced. Admittedly, in the second sort of case, I must believe that it is time for a service if I am to act in the light of that fact. But still it seems to be not so much my believing this as what I believe that is being offered as my reason for doing what I propose to do. So, we may say, some reason-giving offers a belief of the agent as a reason, and others offer what is believed by the agent instead; and there is a world of difference between these. If our motivating reasons are all 'what is believed', no reasons are psychological states of the agent. If those reasons are all psychological states of the agent, none are properly, fully specifiable in the form 'A acted because *p*'. The proper, philosophically revealing form will be 'A acted because

Dancy, J. (2000), "How to Act for a Good Reason," excerpts from *Practical Reality* (Oxford: Oxford University Press), chs. 5 and 6. Reprinted with permission of Oxford University Press.

A believed that *p*'; and we will understand this sort of explanation as specifying a psychological state of the agent as explanans.

Psychologism has a large and enthusiastic following. But any complete theory of practical reasons has to deal not only with motivating reasons but also with normative reasons. With that in mind, three possibilities are available for us. We can understand both normative and motivating reasons as psychological states of the agent. We can understand all reasons as what the agents believe, rather than as their believings of those things. Or, finally, we can hold that motivating reasons are psychological states of the agent, while normative reasons are what agents (we hope) believe.

Of these three possibilities, I think that the first is clearly implausible. It is implausible because it is so extreme. It is not the view that all normative reasons are *grounded* in psychological states of the agent. The view that all practical reasons derive their normative status from a relation to some desire of the agent is of that sort; and it is worth arguing against. But the view we are currently considering is that all normative reasons *are* psychological states of the agent. This would rule out any such reasons as that she asked me to do it, that this is an opportunity I have long been waiting for, and that I will be too busy to have time to do it next week. There would have to be an amazingly strong argument to persuade us that considerations like these are altogether of the wrong sort to count as reasons in favour of an action. The only argument that I can see in the offing is that all motivating reasons are psychological states of the agent, and that normative reasons must be a subset of motivating reasons. Whatever the merits of such an argument (and I confess that it would seem to me to vindicate Nagel's view that psychologism should cause us to abandon the very idea of acting for a reason) it returns us to the question whether motivating reasons are or are not psychological states.

What I want to examine, then, is the respective merits of the second and the third possibilities. I am interested in promoting the second alternative, under which no reasons at all, either motivating or normative, are psychological states of the agent. But this requires me to argue against a position that appears well entrenched. It is worth taking a moment to build up an initial version of this third theory, as follows.

When we speak of reasons for action, the little word 'for' cloaks an ambiguity, or at least a distinction. There are reasons in favour of acting, and reasons why we acted. Favouring is one thing; it is a normative relation, and the reasons that favour actions can include such things as normative states of the world, for certainly they are unlikely to be psychological states of the agent. The reasons why we act, however, are not themselves things that favour actions; they are things that explain them. These are all psychological states of the agent – believings, if pure cognitivism is the truth; pairs of believings and desirings, if it is not. Now there is a constraint on any theory about the relation between normative and motivating reasons. This is that the theory show that and how any normative reason is capable of contributing to the explanation of an action that is done for that reason. Call this the 'explanatory constraint'. There is a way in which it is easy to meet that constraint. The believings that explain the action can themselves be explained, of course, and on occasions at least we do so by appeal to their truth. He believed that there was a rhinoceros before him because there was one there; she believed that he needed her help because he did. So the reasons that favour an action can explain the reasons that explain the action. So though normative reasons do not explain actions directly, they explain them indirectly. The explanatory constraint is met by appeal to the transitivity of explanation. We emerge with a three-part story in which everything has its place, and nothing is missed out. The story is: normative reason → motivating reason → action. The arrows in this story indicate relations of explanation, though of course there is more to the matter than those explanatory relations alone.

Opposed to this three-part story is one which denies the existence of motivating states as reasons of any sort, and tries to make do with normative reasons. These normative reasons are also able to play the role of motivating reasons; that is, in ordinary English, the reason why we should act is to be (at least able to be) the reason why we do act. What is believed is what motivates as well as what makes it the case that what we did was the right thing to have done. The believing, which of course occurs (though even this will be disputed), does not play the role of motivating reason; some other role must be found for it. Motivating reasons are what is believed; and some of the things believed are normative reasons as well.

Let us call this alternative story the 'normative story', because it takes its start from normative reasons. It is obviously going to be hard to develop, let alone sustain. In order to gain it some credibility, as it were, I am now going to run through a list of potential objections to the three-part story. For if the three-part story collapses under attack, the prospects for the normative story are obviously much better.

2. Against the Three-Part Story

I start by considering a standard argument for the claim that motivating reasons are psychological states of the agent, specifically believings, which runs as follows:

The statement

    1. *A*'s reason for F-ing was that *p*

can only be true if

    2. *A* believed that *p*.

Therefore

    3. *A*'s reason for F-ing was that *A* believed that *p*.

This argument is of course rather peculiar and not obviously valid. But I want to say two further things about it. The first is that it is not an argument for psychologism. Its conclusion is not that X's reason for doing A was his believing that *p*, but that his reason was that he believed that *p*. That is to say, the motivating reason it 'discovers' is not itself a psychological state of the agent but the 'fact' that the agent was in such a state. That X believed that *p* is not itself a psychological state of X's. If it were, X could be in it; but the sense in which X is in the fact that X believed that *p* is surely not the sense in which X is in a psychological state.

We could of course rewrite the argument with, as its conclusion, not (3) but the genuinely psychologistic

    3*. *A*'s reason for F-ing was *A*'s believing that *p*.

The point I am trying to make, however, is directed at those who have become psychologists, in my sense, by arguing for (3) and then misunderstanding their own conclusion as the psychologistic (3*) – a train of thought which I take to be fairly common.

Second, the argument as I have given it above says nothing about how it is to be interpreted. In particular, it does not say whether its 'conclusion' is to be understood as replacing its first premise, or as related to that premise in some other way. I don't want to suggest that there would be any incoherence in an argument whose conclusion is inconsistent with one of its premises. We are all used to such things. The point is rather that, for all the argument tells us, it may be that the conclusion is intended as a sort of philosophical explication of, rather than a replacement for, the premise. In general, as will emerge, I have no quarrel with the idea that (1) and (3) are somehow more or less equivalent, i.e. that (3) is a restatement of (1). It is true that we move without strain from the simple form of action-explanation (1) to the psychologised form (3) and back again. We should accept this and cater for it in our overall account of the explanation of action. Problems only arise when it is supposed that (1) is an incomplete specification of a reason that is only fully characterised by (3) – something on which the argument given above is officially silent. In my view, if there is a difference between (1) and (3), it speaks entirely in favour of (1) as the normal form in which to give a reason. The argument for this view comes below.

It is one thing, however, to undermine supposed arguments for a position, and another to show the position itself to be false. So I now make three direct objections to the three-part story. The first is one that I have already offered in print (Dancy 1995). This objection amounts to the introduction of a further constraint, which we can call the normative constraint, in addition to the explanatory constraint that we have already seen. This requires that a motivating reason, that in the light of which one acts, must be the sort of thing that is capable of being among the reasons in favour of so acting; it must, in this sense, be possible to act for a good reason. The explanatory constraint held that all normative reasons should be the right sorts of things to contribute to motivation, since that is what they must be if they are to be capable of contributing to the explanation of action in the right sort of way. The normative constraint goes in the other direction, claiming that motivating reasons should be the right sort of thing to be normative reasons.

The three-part story fails the normative constraint in a very blatant way, for it renders us more or less incapable of doing an action for any of the reasons that make it right. It makes it impossible, that is, for the reasons why we act to be among the reasons in favour of acting. If I am trying to decide what to do, I decide which action is right, noticing (we hope) the reasons that make it right; and then I act in the light of those reasons. They are the reasons why I do what I do (my motivating reasons). According to the three-part story, this is impossible. For the three-part story announces that motivating reasons are psychological states and that normative reasons are quite different, including even such things as normative facts about the world. The three-part story has set itself up in such a way that it is bound to breach the normative constraint; which is to say that it has introduced far too great a gap between the explanatory and the normative. And this makes the three-part story paradoxical at its core.

It is not just that, by thinking of motivating reasons as psychological states of the agent, the three-part story breaches the normative constraint. I want to agree with psychologism that we should not be looking among psychological states of the agent for the normative reasons that favour the action. The psychologists are right about this. For no – or only very few – psychological states of the agent are normative reasons; it is not normally psychological states of the agent that make her action the right one to do. In a way I expect this point to be obvious. What makes my action wrong is that she badly needed help and I just walked away from her. What makes overtaking on the wrong side of a bend not a very sensible thing to do is that there may well be something coming the other way. Once one has started in this vein one can go on for ever. Psychologism must be right to think of normative reasons as facts, as states of affairs, or as features of the situation, and must be wrong, therefore, to think of motivating reasons as psychological states of the agent.

What confuses the issue is that it is possible to think that the agent's mental states do make a difference to the question whether he acted rightly. And so they do,

in a way; for that he believed she would welcome his advances surely makes him (or his action) less reprehensible than he (or it) would have been if he had believed the opposite, especially if his belief was reasonable. But, first, that belief, even if reasonable, need not make the action right. His believing this can serve as some defence or excuse for his doing what he did, without making that action right. The normative relevance of the belief lies primarily at the evaluative level, rather than at the deontic level where reasons lie. And, second, there remains the awkward difference between the suggestion that it is his belief, conceived as a mental state that he is in, that is the reason and the suggestion that it is that he so believes that is the reason. For that he so believes is not a mental state that he is in, but a state of affairs; just as his nervousness is a mental state that he is in, but that he is nervous is a state of affairs rather than a mental state. At the moment we are only discussing the less plausible view that the normative reason is a mental state of the agent.

In my now fairly wide experience, the normal response of those attracted to the three-part story is to say, when accused of paradox in this sort of way, that the matter is wildly exaggerated. The normative reason, they say, can perfectly well be thought of as a motivating reason in any case where its being the case that p makes right an action that is done because of the belief that p. For if A explains B and B explains C, A is part of the explanation of C; and motivating reasons include anything that contributes to the explanation of the action. But this seems to me not so much to defend the story as to abandon it. The core of the three-part story is the claim that normative reasons cannot be motivating ones, a claim that rests on psychologism about motivating reasons and a (correct) sense that normative reasons are in general nothing like psychological states of the agent. The sorts of things that are normative reasons are things like the pain the other is suffering, the wrong I will be doing her if I persist, and other features of the world that call for certain responses from us. These normatively significant states of affairs are metaphysically different beasts from psychological states of the agent. Having insisted on this difference, the three-part story cannot then go on to ignore it, and to say in spite of it that we can perfectly well speak of those normative states of affairs as motivating reasons, even though their official view (indeed, the core of their position) is that only psychological states of the agent can play that role. This would be far too much like trying to have one's cake and eat it.

Finally, I want to stress one feature of this argument. This is the constant stress on the phrase 'right sort of thing'. A motivating reason must, I claimed, be the right sort of thing to be a normative reason. This is really a metaphysical point. Some motivating reasons cannot be good reasons. Perhaps the downfall of others cannot be a good reason for satisfaction. Perhaps, as some hold, the rightness of an action cannot be among the reasons for doing it. But these features are, still, metaphysically speaking, the right sort of thing to be a good reason. They are ruled out, if they are indeed ruled out, not by being the wrong sort of thing, but by being wrong ones of the right sort.

[Several sections are omitted here.]

So far I have argued against psychologism, the claim that all motivating reasons are psychological states of the agent. My general line has been that motivating reasons are not so far removed from the normative as psychologism leads us to suppose. Of course my attack on psychologism has done nothing directly to refute the rather different theory that insists that agent's reasons, motivating reasons, are more properly formulated as 'because he believes that *p*' than as simply 'that *p*'. This theory needs separate treatment, which it will receive next.

3. Because He Believes That *p*

If the reasons that motivate us are not psychological states of ourselves, our believings or belief-states, we might still feel that the things we believe cannot be those reasons either. The main reason for saying so is a worry about the case where things are not as the agent conceives them to be. Surely, in such a case, we cannot say that his reason for acting as he did was that *p*. We have to say that his reason for acting was that he believed that *p*. Accepting this for the case where the relevant belief is false, then, we might still hope that 'that *p*' can indeed be the explanation of the action in cases where it is the case that *p*, but that where it is not the case that *p* the explanation can only be 'that he believed that *p*'. But, as Bernard Williams puts it

(1980, p. 102), the true/false distinction should not be allowed to affect the form of the relevant explanation. Supposing, therefore, that our explanation should take the same form whether it is or is not the case that *p*, and having already accepted that the correct explanation in cases where it is not the case that *p* is 'that he believed that *p*' we are driven to say the same of cases where the relevant belief is true rather than false. We may of course allow that the simpler explanation 'that *p*' is not actually false or wrong as an explanation. But we suppose that, properly understood, it should be seen as enthymematic, i.e. as an acceptable shorthand version of the full explanation.

This new theory has one great advantage over psychologism. This is that it provides as reasons things that can be believed, things properly expressible using that-clauses. That I believe that *p* is something that can itself be believed and that is capable both of being the case and of not being the case. It therefore meets the constraint sometimes put by demanding that all motivating reasons be propositional in form (Bond 1983, p. 22; Darwall 1983, p. 33). Now in my view we do not want to end up supposing that good reasons are true propositions, or indeed propositions of any sort. But by 'propositional in form' we need only take ourselves to mean that a motivating reason must be capable of being believed, asserted, doubted, supported and so on, in the sorts of ways that many philosophers have supposed that only propositions can be.

Though it has this advantage over psychologism, the new theory is very close to it. Indeed, some find it hard to distinguish between the theory that holds that motivating reasons are psychological states of the agent, conceived as believings, and the theory that holds that they are such things as that the agent believes that *p*. The two theories unite in opposition to the view that motivating reasons are things that the agent believes, which is the position I am trying to defend. Because they are so close, we need to be sure that they are genuinely distinct.

One important potential difference between them is that the states which psychologism offers as motivating reasons are thought of as static events, and so as capable of being causes of actions (also conceived of as events). A psychological state understood in this way can play this role of cause of action – cause of bodily movement, probably – without strain. Construed as a static event, it is fitted to play its part in the relation commonly called 'event-causation' – an extensional relation between particulars. That the agent believes that *p*, by contrast, can only be conceived as a cause of his subsequent action if we allow that that-clauses can specify causes. If they do, and if the sort of cause that they specify is not reducible to event-causation in some way, we are dealing with the sort of causation sometimes called 'fact-causation', though whether the thing specified by the that-clause is a fact or a state of affairs seems to be a matter of debate. However that may be, it remains the case that if there is a difference between fact-causation and event-causation, there is the same difference between our two theories.

There are of course other differences. The mental state can be interrupted; that I believe that *p* cannot. The mental state, understood as a static event, occurs; that I believe that *p* obtains, or is the case. The mental state has some sort of location; that I believe that *p* does not. The mental state is at least potentially identifiable with a neural state, and may be conceived as a functional state. That I believe that *p* cannot be conceived functionally, nor can it possibly be identified with a neural state of any sort. It is quite the wrong sort of thing for that.

Consider the difference between my nervousness, which is a mental state, and that I am nervous, which is not. My nervousness may explain my jumping whenever there is a loud noise; that I am nervous explains why I take beta-blockers when I have to sing in public, since my reason for doing so is that I am nervous, while my nervousness is not my reason for jumping at loud noises. (In fact I don't do this for a reason at all.) So explanations that appeal to mental states as *explanantia* are not equivalent to explanations that appeal to such things as 'that the agent is in such-and-such a mental state'.

It seems then that the new theory, as a theory of motivating reasons, is genuinely distinct from psychologism. We should also note that various arguments, often offered as arguments in favour of psychologism, are really only arguments in favour of the new theory. We saw one of these in section 2:

1. *A*'s reason for F-ing was that *p*

can only be true if

2. *A* believed that *p*.

Therefore

3. *A*'s reason for F-ing was (*really*) that *A* believed that *p*.

There is also the argument mentioned above, that if it is not the case that *p*, we are forced to understand the reason why the agent acted as 'that he believed that *p*' *rather than* as the simpler 'that *p*'. We then infer that we must say the same sort of thing of all cases, including those where the agent is not wrong about whether it is the case that *p*.

These two arguments raise questions that need to be answered. The first asks what role we are to attribute to the fact that the agent believed that *p* in cases where we nonetheless want to explain the action by appeal to the simpler 'that *p*'. I will address this question in the next section. The second asks about the relation between cases where it is, and where it is not, the case that *p*. Can the simpler explanation 'that *p*' be run in cases where it is not the case that *p*? I address this in section 5 below.

So these arguments do need to be addressed, and I will address them. But still their conclusion is false, and can be shown to be false. The crucial point is this. There are indeed cases in which (1) gets the agent's reason wrong and (3) gets it right, but that these are rather unusual, and the way in which they are unusual reveals the falsehood of the new theory as a general view about reasons and motivation. Consider a case where my reason for acting is genuinely that I believe that *p*. For instance, that I believe that the cliff is crumbling is my reason for avoiding climbing it, because having that belief I am more likely to fall off (I will get nervous). This is a case where that I believe what I do is genuinely my reason for action, in a way that is independent of whether the belief is actually true. As I might say, whether the cliff actually is crumbling or not doesn't matter. I believe that it is crumbling, and this alone is sufficient to motivate me to stay away from it. I recognise that if the cliff were not crumbling, I would still have just the same reason not to climb it as if it were, so long as I continue to believe it to be crumbling. But this is a quite unusual situation, not at all the normal case.[1] Normally, I suppose that if things are not as I believe them to be, I do not in fact have the reason that I take myself to have. It would be quite peculiar to suppose that no practical reasons are like this, and that all are of the special sort that we found in the case of the crumbly cliff.

The suggestion here is that we determine what our reason is by considering what it varies with. If the reason remains when the supposed ground for it vanishes, that supposed ground was not the actual ground. Normally we take our reasons to be grounded in objective features of the situation, and to disappear if those features disappear. If my reason for not climbing had been that the cliff was crumbly, that is how I would have been thinking of things; I would have supposed my reason to persist until the cliff ceases to be crumbly. But in the case of the example as I have given it, I know that my reason for not climbing persists *as long as I continue to believe* that the cliff is crumbly. This is how I conceive of my own reason. So this is genuinely a case where it is 'that I believe that *p*' that is my reason for action.

There are other such cases once one begins to look for them. Someone who believes that there are pink rats living in his shoes may take that he believes this as a reason to go to the doctor or perhaps a psycho-analyst. This is quite different from the person who takes (his belief) that there are pink rats living in his shoes as a reason to call in the pest control officer. Such contrasts show that we will distort what we have been calling the light in which the agent acted, or the agent's reasons, if we insist that they are properly specified as 'that he believed that *p*'. If there is a significant difference between the explanation 'that he believed that *p*' and the simpler 'that *p*', the advantage is normally all on the side of the simpler version. 'That I believe that *p*' is almost never the right way to specify the light in which I act, my reasons for doing what I do, if it is taken as significantly different from the simpler 'that *p*'.

The form of argument that I have been using here is unusual, but surely none the worse for that. It involves showing, of some supposedly general thesis, that the situations of which it is most obviously true are very uncommon ones (and in the present case necessarily so), so that the general thesis must be false as a general thesis just because of the peculiar nature of the cases which it correctly characterises.

So the 'new theory' is false, and false for different reasons from those that toppled psychologism. But we cannot just dismiss the arguments offered in support of the new theory. As I have already said, those arguments raise questions that need to be addressed. I now turn to consider the first of those arguments. How should we explain the fact that, where the agent's reason for acting is that *p*, the agent must believe that *p*, if not by saying that the agent's reason for acting is 'really' that he believes that *p*?

4. The Role of Belief in the Psychologising Restatement of a Reason

Whenever the agent acts in the light of the fact that *p*, the agent must take it that *p* (and I understand this sort of 'taking it that' as a weak form of belief). And ordinarily, we have claimed, the psychologised explanation of the action is to be understood as the same explanation as the non-psychologised one. Sometimes the psychologised explanation is inappropriate, even misleading. The opportunities for use of the explanation 'I am doing this because I think I am married' are rare, one might say; to use this form of words definitely gives one to understand that there is something odd about the situation (as if one might not be quite sure whether the divorce had come through). Nonetheless, if I act in the light of the fact that I am married, I must believe that I am. So what role does 'that I believe I am married' play in the explanation? It seems as if the belief must be there but is not allowed to make much of a contribution, and this is very odd. So what role can the normative story assign to the belief?

Collins' view is that I insert an 'I believe that' into the explanation of my action (actual or intended) when I am in some doubt as to whether I am right; the phrase signals that uncertainty (Collins, 1997). Equally, in the third person case we move to the psychologised explanation when we take it that the matter is dubious or that the agent is mistaken. In the first person case, the transaction as a whole is to be understood in terms of a Gricean conversational implicature.

The implication of uncertainty can be cancelled, as when one says, perhaps, 'The reason why I am going to do it is that I believe that p, though I have to say that I am not in any doubt about the matter.' There is clearly much truth in this, but it seems to me not to be an answer to our question. The question is not one about when we do and when we don't adopt the psychologised form of explanation. It is about the role of the belief in the story as a whole if it is not playing the focal role normally attributed to it.

What other account of the role of belief is available to the normative story? I can think of two. The first involves a structural distinction in the theory of explanation. There is a difference between a consideration that is a proper part of an explanation, and a consideration that is required for the explanation to go through, but which is not itself a part of that explanation. I call the latter 'enabling conditions'. For instance, that England is not sinking beneath the waves today is a consideration in the absence of which what explains my actions would be incapable of doing so. But that does nothing to show that England's not submerging today is part of the explanation of why I do what I do (or more generally of my doing what I do). It is therefore an enabling condition in this case, though of course it is a proper part of the explanation of some other things, for instance of why the ports are not disappearing under water. The suggestion therefore is that the believing, conceived traditionally as a psychological state, is an enabling condition for an explanation which explains the action in terms of the reasons for (i.e. in favour of – the good reasons for) doing it. This condition is required for that explanation to go through. That is, in the absence of the believing what in fact explains the action would not then explain it, either because the action would not then have been done at all, or because, if it had, it would have been done for another reason and so been explained in another way. But the believing does not contribute directly to the explanation.

The difficulty that I see with this move is not so much that the notion of an enabling condition requires theoretical support that I have not provided here. It is rather that there is no clear account of where the line that it draws is to come, case by case. It is not clear what one is to say to someone who insists that the believing is a proper part of the explanation. And so we can have no confidence that there won't be plenty of occasions in which the believing will end up within the explanation rather than outside it, returning us to our starting point.

I have something of a reply to this point, which is that the appeal to enabling conditions is made after we have established that motivating reasons must be able to be normative ones, to be good reasons, and shown therefore that motivating reasons do not standardly include psychological states of the agent. It is also made after we have established that explanations of the form 'that I believe that p' are not normally the correct way of specifying the light in which I act, if they are conceived of as distinct in style from the simpler explanation they are intended to replace. Having got this far, however, we have a principled reason for insisting that the believing, or that the agent so believed, is not to be taken as a proper part of the relevant explanation. We were looking for a way of recognising the fact that it is never wrong to admit a reference to the agent's belief in the story; we can do this, consistently with the results we have already accepted, only by allowing that the believing, or that the agent believes, counts as an enabling condition rather than as a part of the motivating reason. We could not, for instance, say that the believing is part of the motivating reason, the rest being constituted by the normative reason. For this would return us to the point that the (now complex) motivating reason is incapable of being the normative reason. Nor could we say that 'that the agent believes that p' is really the agent's reason, or among the agent's reasons; for to insist on this would be to distort our account of the light in which the agent acted. So there is a principled explanation of the fact that the believing must be seen as an enabling condition rather than as a proper part of the explanation on each occasion.

However, I do not feel confident enough in this reply to rely on it entirely. This motivates me to look for another account of the reference to belief in 'he is doing it because he believes that p'. The one that appeals to me is what I call the appositional account. This hears 'he is doing it because he believes that p' as 'he is doing it because p, as he believes'. The 'as he believes' functions paratactically here, attaching itself to the '*p*'. Again, it is not part of the specification of his reason, but is a comment on that reason, one that is required by the nature of the explanation that we are giving. That explanation specifies the features *in the light of which* the agent acted. It is required for this sort of explanation that those features be present to the agent's consciousness – indeed, that they be somehow conceived as favouring the action; so there must always be a way of making room for this fact, in some relation to the explanation that runs from features as reasons to action as response. It is not required, however, that the nature of the agent's consciousness itself constitute the *explanans*. The appositional account tells us how to hold all these things together in a coherent whole.

More needs to be said about this paratactic comment. How, for instance, are we to understand statements like 'If I had not believed that *p*, I would not have done it'? Is there any possibility of running some paraphrase such as 'If it had not been the case, as I believed, that *p*, I would not have done it'? This seems strained to me, at best; on its most natural hearing, it sounds equivalent to 'If it had not been the case that *p*, I would not have done it', which is not at all what we want. But we are not here in the business of contributing to the famous Davidsonian research programme. There is perhaps a harder question whether we can, understanding the phrase 'I believe that *p*' appositionally, retain the validity of *modus ponens* and other inference schemata. In general, however, I offer the appositional account as a philosophical explication of the sense of 'I believe that *p*', rather than as a contribution to formal philosophy of language. It is only if it is taken in the latter way that these hard-edged questions get a bite.

There are interesting questions here about the relation between the appositional account and the enabling conditions account. One view is that they are distinct. For the enabling conditions account may seem to be committed to the existence of the belief as a psychological state, while the appositional account is consistent with the more radical suggestion that belief is more a stance or commitment than a state. The appositional account, that is, leaves it open what sort of a philosophical story we should tell about belief, in a way that the enabling condition account does not.

So the appositional account enjoys a considerable strategical advantage, and we should adopt it in preference to the enabling conditions account.

Still, we can never deny that the agent believes that *p*, if we once explain his action by saying that he did it for the reason that *p*, as he supposes. Indeed, as I see it the two sentences at issue:

his reason for doing it was that *p*, as he supposed

his reason for doing it was that he supposed that *p*

entail each other.[2] What is more, the second of them is to be understood as entailing that the agent supposed/believed that *p*. So on either account, appositional or enabling condtions, we have to allow that, had the agent not believed that *p*, he could not have acted for the reason that *p*. And this is really all that it amounts to to say that his belief that *p* is an enabling condition for his acting for the reason that *p*. What is more, if there is sufficient reason to deny that belief is a psychological state, that reason must be compatible with some positive account of what is going on in ordinary belief-attributions. It is not as if we are forced to allow that the reference to belief in the appositional clause is a reference to a psychological state, just because the appositional clause entails the straightforward claim that the agent believed that *p*. So perhaps the correct view is that there are two versions of the enabling condition account, one that takes the belief as a psychological state and the other that does not. The appositional version of things is not committed to either version as such.

Why not just say that what explains the action is that *p* and that the agent believed that *p*? Because this just opens the door for those who want to argue that the 'that *p*' is redundant – for in cases where what the agent believes is not the case, we just drop the first conjunct without our explanation being at all damaged or diminished thereby. And we have already seen that this is wrong. Psychologised explanations give the wrong explanation of action, if we conceive of them as somehow preferable to the simpler non-psychologised ones. That the agent believed that *p* is not the sole correct explanation of the action, even in a case where the belief was false.

5. Factive and Non-Factive Explanations

The previous section concerned the difficulties thought to arise because of the universal insertability of the 'I believe that', and the admission that if the agent does not believe that p, his reason for acting cannot be that p. This new section concerns the relevance of the claim that, if it is not the case that p, the reason why the agent acted cannot be that p and must be that he believed that p. The case of the false belief, as we might put it, drives a wedge between the psychologised and the non-psychologised explanation, in favour of the former. And once this point has been made about cases where the relevant belief is false, we will have to say the same thing about cases where it is true. For we are allowing that the true/false distinction should not affect the form of the relevant explanation.

There is a distinction between the reasons why we do what we do and the good reasons for acting in that way. Explanation of action in terms of the reasons that motivated the agent is only one way of explaining why the agent did what he did. All explanations can be given in terms of reasons, after all, even those that are not explanations of action. We can ask for the reason why the sun goes down the sky towards evening, even though we know perfectly well that the sun does not do this for a reason of its own, as it were. We are not, impossibly, supposing that the trajectory of the sun is something intentionally chosen by the sun in the light of these and those considerations. Even when we restrict ourselves to the explanation of intentional action, which will still be offered in terms of reasons, we need not always suppose that the reasons we offer in explanation of why the agent did what he did are among what we have been calling 'the agent's reasons', or that the agent acted in the light of those reasons. We may, for instance, explain an action by saying that the agent is shy, or ignorant of certain relevant facts. So explaining in terms of the reasons that motivated the agent is a special case of explaining (giving the reason) why he acted as he did.

Now one form of pressure in favour of the psychologised explanation of intentional action derives from the simple thought that all explanation is factive. What this means is that from an explanation of the form 'the reason why it is the case that p is that q' we can infer both that p and that q. This is no different from the relation between 'he knows that p' and 'p', or between 'he has forgotten that p' and 'p'. For him to know that p or to have forgotten that p or indeed to have remembered that p, it must be the case that p. In this sense, we say that knowledge and remembering are factive; and so is forgetting. Equally, various locutions in which we characteristically give explanations are factive. As I said above, 'the reason why it is the case that p is that q' is doubly factive, entailing both that p and that q. So is 'the explanation of its being the case that p is that q'. The question then arises whether all explanations are factive in this sense. Suppose that my question 'what were his reasons for doing that?' is a request for explanation, and that the explanation can be given by laying out the considerations in the light of which he determined to do what he did. Suppose also that, in those considerations, the agent was mistaken. Things were not as he supposed them to be in relevant respects. Does this mean that we cannot base our explanation on those considerations? Is explanation in terms of motivating reasons always factive, like other explanation, or is it non-factive? If it is non-factive, it is different from other sorts of explanation. But we should not beg the question by assuming that such a thing is impossible, though no doubt it will affect our general conception of explanation should things so turn out. The question, then, is whether there is a way of explaining an action by laying out the considerations in the light of which the agent acted without committing ourselves to things being as the agent there conceived them to be.

I take it that the answer to this question is yes. I suggest that locutions such as

> His reason for doing it was that it would increase his pension

> The ground on which he acted was that she had lied to him

are not factive. To test this, we only need to consider whether it is possible without contradiction to continue by denying that things were as the agent took them to be. Consider the following sentences:

> His reason for doing it was that it would increase his pension, but in fact he was quite wrong about that.

The ground on which he acted was that she had lied to him, though in fact she had done nothing of the sort.

Neither of these sentences sounds self-contradictory to me. Not everyone's ears agree with me about this, I know. But there seems to be no reason why there should not be a way of revealing the light in which the agent saw things as a way of explaining why he did what he did, but without asserting that he was right to see things that way. I think that the two locutions above are ways of doing that. They are not, of course, the only ways of doing it. We can achieve the same thing by saying:

He did it because he took it that it would increase his pension.

What explains his doing it was that he thought it would increase his pension.

The reason why he did it was that he fondly imagined that it would increase his pension.

He did it for the reason that, as he imagined, it would increase his pension.

He did this because, as he supposed, she had lied to him.

In the first two of these five cases, we have apparently recognised the factive nature of the locution we are using, in offering after the 'because' and 'explains' a sentence that is true. The same is true of the third. In the last two cases, matters are a little more delicate. Suppose that she did not lie to him, but that he thought that she had lied. Is it true that, as he supposed, she had lied to him? No. It is not quite clear what truth value this sentence now has, but it does seem clear that it does not have the truth value true. So the insertion of the apposition 'as he believed' does not take us from a falsehood to a truth in the way that the insertion of 'he believed that. . .' does, or at least can do. What it does is to remove the speaker's commitment to things being as the agent supposed. So the appositional use is a sort of halfway house. The relevant context is not factive, since any commitment to the truth of the contained clause can be removed without incoherence, but it has something of the style of a factive explanation, for if you take the apposition out, there is a strong *suggestio veri*.

It may be that there are some forms of action explanation that are factive and some that are not. I see no need to decide this issue. Of the ones that are not, there is no real need to include the apposition in order to avoid commitment to things being as the agent supposed. If the explanation is not factive, it is not factive. Any commitment there may be will be more in the style of a conversational implicature than an entailment. So we might want to include the apposition in order to guard ourselves against the implicature otherwise carried by some forms of explanation, that the agent was right about the matter. Some hear 'He did this because she had lied to him' as factive, and so as the wrong explanation of his action if she had not lied to him. Others hear it as carrying a *suggestio veri*, but a cancellable one, so that where the agent is mistaken we can still explain his action by saying 'He did this because, as he supposed, she had lied to him'. And this pattern of choices repeats with the other styles that our action-explanation can take, e.g. 'his reason for doing this was that *p*'.

What conclusions can we draw from all this? The most general conclusion is now familiar, that there are explanations of action that do not succeed simply by laying out the agent's reasons for action in the terms that the agent would have done if asked. Restricting ourselves now to attempts to specify the agent's reasons, in the sense that we have given to that phrase, we have decided that though some such attempts may involve a factive context, others do not. The ones that do not are ones that involve a contained intensional context, such that the whole can be true as an explanation though the contained part, the thing doing the explaining, is not. There are, then, both factive and non-factive ways of laying out the considerations in the light of which the agent acted.

If this is so, it seems to me that the difference between the factive and the non-factive cannot be of any real significance when it comes to the explanation of action. We can phrase our explanation as we like, and that is the end of the matter. So it cannot be that the very notion of explanation drives us to the use of the phrase 'because he believed that . . .'

in order to live up to the factive demands associated with the explanation of events. In this sense, a thing believed that is not the case can still explain an action.

It follows from this that if we do decide to use the factive turn of phrase in giving our explanation of his action, this cannot be because we are driven by the need to find a factive explanation. We do not need to do this, and there are available plenty of effectively equivalent turns of phrase that would have enabled us to have done things differently. If the agent's conception of the situation is mistaken, there are some ways of explaining his action that are now ruled out. But this does not show that only factive ones are left in, forcing us toward the phrasing 'he did it because he believed that p'. If we do use the factive ones, this will be a comparatively arbitrary choice.

The picture that is emerging here reminds us that for the agent the psychologised and the non-psychologised explanations are effectively equivalent. We tend to suppose that, once we move to the third-person perspective, things are very different in this respect, on the grounds that the purposes of explanation force us to move to a different explanation of the action – one whose general structure consists in a relation between the action and the psychology of the agent rather than in a relation between the action and the light in which the agent saw it. But this is a distortion of what is going on when we move from one form of explanation to the other. The distinction between first and third person does not allow us to suppose that in the third person case, there is a radical distinction between the psychologised and the non-psychologised forms of explanation, when there is no such radical difference in the first person case. There is only one sort of explanation, though the form in which we may choose to give that explanation may vary according to the circumstances. What is more, the most revealing form, perhaps I should say, the form least likely to mislead philosophers, is the simple form which contains no visible reference to belief at all.

I close with a summary of the position I have reached. The fact that the agent would not have performed the action had he not believed that p should not persuade us that the proper way of specifying the reason in the light of which he acted was as 'that he believed that p'. This sort of counterfactual test takes us in the wrong direction, since it invites us to ignore the differences between two relations: first, the special relation that holds between the reason for which the action was done and the action done for that reason, and second the more general relation that holds between the action and any other condition in the absence of which it would not have been done for the reason that it was. And anyway, there are examples that show the need to distinguish between those special cases of reasons that involve the agent's belief and those that don't. The counterfactual test invites us to blur that distinction. One may feel some unease about saying 'his reason was that p' when we don't ourselves believe that p. But this too should not drive us to saying 'his reason was that he believed that p', supposing that by this device we are respecting the factive nature of explanation; we can avoid any apparent commitment on our part to things being as the agent supposed by use of one of a number of special constructions such as 'as he supposed'.

It seems, then, that the explanation of action, at least that of intentional action, can always be achieved by laying out the considerations in the light of which the agent saw the action as desirable, sensible, or required. If things were as the agent supposed, there is no bar against the agent's reasons being among the reasons in favour of doing what he actually did. That is to say, the reasons that motivated the agent can be among or even identical with the good reasons in the case, those that favour acting as he did. Equally, the good reasons can motivate him, since they can be the considerations in the light of which he acted, and citing them can explain the action directly rather than only being able to do so indirectly as part of the content of a suitable psychological state. Good reasons explain action in any case where the agent chose to do that action in the light of those reasons. The psychological state that the agent is in is not, of course, simply irrelevant to the explanation. But neither is it the focus of that explanation. Equally, that the agent has the relevant beliefs is not irrelevant, but is not the focus of the explanation either.

Notes

1. I have borrowed this form of argument from Joseph Raz (1986, pp. 142–3). A different and maybe better example would be where the reason for me not to climb the cliff is that I believe that I can't climb it.

2. Except in the special sorts of case discussed in section 3 above.

References

Bond, E. J. (1983) *Reason and Value* (Cambridge: Cambridge University Press).

Collins, A. W. (1997) 'The Psychological Reality of Reasons', *Ratio* 10, pp. 108–23.

Dancy, J. (1995) 'Why There is Really No Such Thing as the Theory of Motivation', *Proceedings of the Aristotelian Society* 95, pp. 1–18.

Darwall, S. (1983) *Impartial Reason* (Ithaca, NY: Cornell University Press).

Raz, J. (1986) *The Morality of Freedom* (Oxford: Clarendon Press).

Williams, B. (1980), 'Internal and External Reasons', in his *Moral Luck* (Cambridge: Cambridge University Press, 1981), pp. 101–13.

21

Acting for a Reason

Christine Korsgaard

---

1. Introduction: Reason and Reasons

The question I am going to discuss in this essay is what a practical reason is: that is, what we are referring to when we talk about "the reason for an action," and what happens when someone acts for a reason. The answer I am going to present is one that I believe is common to Aristotle and Kant, and that distinguishes them from nearly everyone else. I am also going to suggest that their answer is correct, for an important reason. As I will try to explain, the view I believe we find in Aristotle and Kant enables us to connect their account of what *reasons* are with an important feature of their account of what *Reason* is: namely, that Reason is in a particular way the *active* aspect or dimension of the mind.

More generally, when we talk about reason, we seem to have three different things in mind. In the philosophical tradition, reason refers to the active rather than the passive or receptive aspect of the mind. Reason in this sense is opposed to perception, sensation, and perhaps emotion, which are forms of, or at least involve, undergoing. The contrast is not unproblematic, for it seems clear that receptivity itself cannot be understood as wholly passive. The perceived world does not merely enter the mind, as through an open door. In sensing and responding to the world our minds interact with it, and the activity of our senses themselves makes a contribution to the character of the perceived world. Though at some level innate and automatic, this contribution may be shaped and extended by learning, changed by habituation and experience, and perhaps even consciously directed. But the mental activity that we associate with reason goes beyond that involved in even the most sophisticated receptivity. Reasoning is self-conscious, self-directing activity through which we deliberately give shape to the inputs of receptivity. This happens both in the case of theoretical reasoning, when we are constructing a scientific account of the world, and in the case of practical reasoning, where its characteristic manifestation is choice.

Reason has also traditionally been identified with either the employment of, or simply conformity to, certain principles, such as the principles of logical inference, the principles that Kant identified as principles of the understanding, mathematical principles, and the principles of practical reason. A person is called reasonable or rational when his beliefs and actions conform to the dictates of those principles, or when he is deliberately guided by them. And then finally, there are the particular considerations, counting in favor of belief or action, that we call "reasons."

The use of the English word "reason" in all of these contexts, and the way we translate equivalent terms from other languages, suggests a connection, but what exactly is it? Aristotle and Kant's conception of what

Korsgaard, C. (2008), "Acting for a Reason," in *The Constitution of Agency* (Oxford: Oxford University Press), 207–229. © C. Korsgaard 2008. Reprinted with permission of Oxford University Press.

practical reasons are, I believe, can help us to answer this question, by bringing out what is distinctive, and distinctively active, about acting for a reason. That, at least, is what I am going to argue.

2. Three Questions about Reasons

There are actually three, or at least three, questions about the ontology of reasons for action. The first question is what sorts of items count as reasons for action – in particular, whether reasons are provided by our mental states and attitudes, or by the facts upon which those states and attitudes are based. (I'll explain this contrast in greater detail below.) The second question is what kinds of facts about actions are relevant to reasons, and in particular whether reasons always spring from the goals achieved through action or sometimes spring from other properties of the actions, say that the action is just or kind. This question is most familiar to us from the debate between consequentialists and deontologists. The third question is how reasons for action are related to actions themselves, and in particular whether this relation is to be understood causally or in some other way.[1] Put in more familiar terms, this is the question what we mean when we say that someone is "motivated."

How do we answer these questions? Most philosophers would agree that practical reasons have at least some of the following properties. (1) They are normative, that is, they make valid claims on those who have them. (2) They are motivating, that is, other things equal, the agents who have them will be inspired to act in accordance with them.[2] And (3) they are motivating in virtue of their normativity, that is, people are inspired to do things by the normativity of the reasons they have for doing them, by their awareness that some consideration makes a claim on them. I will call this property being "normatively motivating," and, although it is not uncontroversial, I am inclined to assume that this is what a practical reason should essentially be: a normatively motivating consideration. We answer questions about the ontology of reasons by asking whether our candidate items could possibly have the properties in question, and by keeping our eye on the connection between Reason and reasons.

The first question – whether reasons are provided by mental states or by the facts upon which those states are based – leads to a problem, which I will call the problem of the reflexive structure of reasons, and which I will describe in the next section. I will then show how Aristotle and Kant's view solves that problem, by the way that it answers the second question, about whether the value of actions rests in their consequences or elsewhere. Finally, in the last section, I will say a little about the question how reasons and actions are related, the question of motivation.

3. Mental States and Good-making Properties

Bernard Williams once wrote: "Desiring to do something is of course a reason for doing it."[3] Joseph Raz disagrees. "Wants … are not reasons for action," he writes. "The fact that [actions] have a certain value – that performing them is a good thing to do because of the intrinsic merit of the action or of its consequences – is the paradigmatic reason for action."[4] The debate about whether reasons are provided by mental states or by facts about the value of the actions arises in part because our ordinary practice of offering reasons seems to go both ways. Suppose I ask: "Why did Jack go to Chicago?" Sometimes we offer as the answer some mental state of Jack's. We might say "he wanted to visit his mother," for instance. The mental state might be a desire, as in the example I have just quoted, or it might be a belief. "He believed his mother needed his help." Many philosophers, of course, think that the reason is given by a belief/desire pair. For instance, he wanted to visit his mother, and believed that she was to be found in Chicago; or, he wanted to help his mother, and believed that he could help her by going to Chicago. On that showing, the answers I gave earlier are partial, offered on the assumption that the questioner can easily work out the rest for herself. When I reply "he wanted to visit his mother," for instance, I leave the questioner to conclude that he believed his mother was to be found in Chicago.

But philosophers like Raz insist that, despite the fact that we answer questions in this way, the reason is not given by Jack's mental states, but rather by certain facts that those mental states are a response to: facts about what I will call the good-making properties of the actions. An important caveat here: I do not mean by using the phrase "good-making properties" to pre-judge the question whether agents always act for the sake of what they regard as good in any moral or sub-stantial sense.[5] I am using the term "good" here to refer to whatever it is about the action that makes it seem eligible to the agent. If St Augustine is right, then the badness of an action may be one of its good-making properties in the formal sense in which I am using the term.[6] We can still ask whether what gave the young Augustine a reason to steal those famous pears is the fact that the action is bad or his desire to do something bad. The defenders of the view that good-making properties are reasons will say that it is the *fact* that the action is bad, not his desire to do the bad. After all, these philosophers urge, reasons are things that agents act *on*. The agent is confronted by the reason, and the reason makes a kind of claim on him, it calls out to him that a certain action is to be done, or at least is eligible to be done. So we should identify as reasons the kinds of items that first-person deliberators take to be reasons, the kind of items that play a role in deliberation. And – leaving Augustine and returning to the more benign Jack – unless Jack is really a very self-absorbed character, what he takes to make a claim on him are not his own mental states, but what's good about the action he proposes to do. After all, if you ask Jack why he is going to Chicago, it would seem a bit odd for him to say "because I want to." He might of course say "Because I want to help my mother," but according to the defenders of good-making properties, we should not take this formula-tion to express the idea that his desire is his reason, for he could equally say, with exactly the same force, "Because my mother needs my help." Certainly it seems likely that when he talks to *himself* about the situation, and decides what to do, he talks to himself about his mother and her troubles, not about his own mental states. So if he does say "I am going because I want to help my mother," instead of taking that to mean that his desire is his reason, we should take it as a kind of announcement that he thinks he both has, *and is responding to*, a reason. Here he describes his response to the reason as a want, a desire. But he could equally well, or perhaps even better, say "I *need* to help my mother," or "I *have to* help my mother" where

"need" or "have to" refers not merely to a psychologi-cal state (or not to a *merely psychological* state), but to a normative response – something along the lines of "I feel that I am under an obligation to help my mother."

But the view that the reasons are given by the good-making properties of the proposed actions also runs into certain objections. For there seem to be problems about saying that the (supposedly) good-making properties of action, all by themselves, can be normative or motivating. For one thing, there are the standard objections to normative realism. Objectors to realism insist that facts and natural prop-erties by themselves (such as the fact that an action would help one's mother) are normatively inert. And for another, there are problems about explaining motivation and the sense of obligation by appeal to the good-making properties of actions alone. After all, people who are aware of the good-making properties of action sometimes fail to be motivated by them or to acknowledge that they present any sort of norma-tive claim. For the good-making properties of actions to have normative and motivational effects, to exert a claim on the agent in light of which he acts, there must be a certain uptake: the agent must *take* them to be good-making properties and be moved accordingly. And the defender of mental states will argue that when someone fails to respond to the good-making proper-ties in question, we can identify what we would need to *add* in order to provoke the response. To the person who is not motivated by his mother's need for help, we might add a desire to help her. To the person who finds no normative claim associated with helping his mother, we might add the belief that one ought to help one's family. And in this way we seem to come back around to the view that reason-giving force arises at least in part from the agent's mental states after all.

But the defender of good-making properties will deny this. The problem I just described, he will say, only arises from a shift in standpoint. When we talk third-personally about the fact that an agent did or did not respond to the reasons before him, we talk about his mental states, since those constitute the responses in question. But that doesn't mean that the mental states are part of the reason, or that they play any role in the agent's own deliberations. The good-making properties of the action provide the reason, and to say that the agent desires to help or feels himself obliged to help is only to say that he is responding appropriately to the good-making properties of helping. After all, if the good-making properties have no motivating or normative force on their own – if we have to *add* the mental states, in order to get the motivating or normative force – then someone who lacks the mental states in question will quite properly be unmoved by the supposedly good-making properties. But surely we *do* want to say that there is something amiss with someone who, say, finds no normatively motivating consideration in the fact that his mother needs help. The mental states are not *added*, in order to *explain* or *provide* the normative and motivational force of the reason; rather, they are simply identified third-personally as the *appropriate response* to the normative and motivational force of the reason.

A minor problem with this argument is that there appear to be two kinds of cases, running roughly along the lines of the permissible and the obligatory. There are cases in which the reason does seem to depend for its existence on a mental state, in particular a desire, and cases in which it does not. Suppose Jack's mother is not in need of help, and his only possible reason for going to Chicago would be that he would enjoy a visit with her. In that case, whether the fact that a trip to Chicago would procure his mother's company is a good-making property of going on the trip *does* depend on whether Jack desires to see his mother. And this may seem to suggest that some reasons do after all depend on mental attitudes and states. But this little difficulty may easily be finessed. The defender of the view that reasons are good-making properties may agree that one of the possible good-making properties of an action is that it satisfies the agent's desire – or perhaps more simply that it satisfies someone's desire.

But there is a deeper problem with the view that the mental states we sometimes mention when we are asked for our reasons are really just the appropriate responses to reasons that exist independently of them. For what does it mean to say that motivation or a sense of obligation is the *appropriate* response? That claim itself appears to be normative – we are not saying merely that it is the usual or natural response. So the idea seems to be that the mental states in question – desire or a sense of obligation or a belief in

obligation or whatever it might be – are responses that there is reason to have. So now we seem to have reasons to be motivated and obligated by our reasons. The first layer of reasons are certain facts about the good-making properties of actions, and the second layer of reasons are facts about how it is appropriate to respond to those good-making properties. Do we then need a further layer of reasons about how it is appropriate to respond to the reasons in the second layer, and so on forever?

But the defender of good-making properties will again deny this. If someone fails to respond appropriately to the good-making properties of an action, one may argue, then he just is irrational, and that is all there is to it. That's what the normativity of the good-making properties of the action amounts to – that you are irrational if you don't respond to them in a certain way. In other words, rationality may simply be *defined* in terms of the appropriateness of certain responses. A practically rational being is *by definition* one who is motivated to perform actions by the perception or awareness of their good-making properties.[7]

But now we need to be more specific about what this means, for there are two possibilities here. One may perceive or be aware of X, but not under the description X. Does a rational agent find his reason in the good-making properties of the action themselves, or in the *fact* that those properties make the action good? Suppose it is good for a mother to protect her children from harm. Is a lioness who protects her cubs from a marauding male lion then acting for a reason, or rationally? Perhaps we do not know exactly how to think about the lioness's mental representations, but she is an agent, not a mechanism, and it seems clear that there is some sense in which she does what she does *in order to protect her cubs*.[8] That aim guides her movements, and in that sense motivates them; and given the risks to herself that she is prepared to run for the sake of her cubs, one may even be tempted to say that she acts under the influence of a normative claim. If this is all there is to rational agency, then of course it does not involve the exercise of any specifically human power which we might identify with the faculty of Reason: it is just a way we describe certain actions from outside, namely, the ones that conform to rational principles or to the particular considerations we call "reasons."

On the other hand, we may insist that there *is* something different in the human case, something that does involve the faculty of Reason. The human being is aware of the reason *as a* reason; she identifies the good-making properties of the action under the description "good" or "reason" or "right," or some such normative description. She does not act merely in accordance with a normative consideration but *on* one. So rational action is not just a matter of being motivated by certain facts about the good-making properties of actions – say, that the action will help one's mother, or that it would satisfy one's desire. Rather, it is a matter of being motivated by the awareness or belief that these facts *constitute* good-making properties of the action. To act rationally is to act from the belief that what you are doing is in some way good. But doesn't that show that the normative force belongs to a mental state after all?

To understand the answer, we must first ask what it means to believe that the facts constitute good-making properties. Recall that we are using "good" here in a minimal and formal sense. To say that the facts constitute good-making properties in this sense is just to say that they provide the agent with what the agent regards as appropriate grounds for motivation. That's all goodness in this context is – appropriate grounds for motivation. So to say that you are motivated by the awareness that the good-making properties of the action make it good is just to say that you are motivated by the awareness that you have appropriate grounds for motivation. You are motivated by the idea that your motives are good. So rational motivation in a sense takes *itself* for its object. It has an essentially reflexive structure.[9] Kant at one point actually says something like this: he says we should act on maxims that can have as their objects *themselves* as universal laws of nature (G 4:437; my emphasis). It sounds very mysterious, and as if we had run into a problem, but I don't think that we have. I think this is just a way of saying that rational action is action that is *self-consciously* motivated, action whose motivation is essentially dependent on consciousness of its own appropriateness. It is this property – *consciousness of its own appropriateness* – that the lioness's motivation lacks.[10]

So to have a reason is to be motivated by the consciousness of the appropriateness of your own motivation. How is it possible to be in such a state? I will call this the problem of the reflexive structure of reasons. The problem is that you might think we have to choose between the two elements involved in the motivation. Either Jack is motivated by his mother's need for help, in which case one may complain that he is no more exercising reason than the lioness is; or Jack is motivated by the thought of his action's goodness, in which case one may complain that he is a self-absorbed jerk who really ought to be thinking about his mother instead of about how good his own actions are.

Aristotle and Kant, I am about to argue, show us the way around this: how the two elements of motivation, its content and the judgment of its goodness, may be combined. And this is no surprise, for to say that a rational agent is motivated by the appropriateness of being motivated in exactly that way is to articulate the deep root of Kant's dictum that a morally good agent acts not merely in accordance with duty but *from* it. In fact what I've just argued is that the problems usually associated with Kant's idea of acting from duty – the appearance that it somehow excludes acting from more attractive motives like a direct concern for others – is a problem that arises from the very nature of a reason for action. That is, once we understand that acting for a reason requires that one be conscious that one has a reason, we can also see that asking "Did he do it in order to help his friend, or because he thought it was his duty?" makes just as little sense as it would to ask, "Did he do it in order to help his mother, or because he thought he had a reason?" In order to explain how Aristotle and Kant solve the problem of the reflexive structure of reasons, I now turn to the second of the three questions I raised: whether the reason for an action always rests in the goal that is achieved by it, or in other facts about the action.

4. The Goodness of Action

According to a number of familiar theories of goodness, the standards of goodness for a thing are given by the nature of the thing itself, especially by its functional nature. A thing is good when it has the properties that make it good at being what it is, or doing what it does. If these theories are correct, then to determine what makes an action good, we ought first to ask what an action is – what its functional nature is – and then we will know what makes it good, to what standards it is subject.

Now John Stuart Mill thought he knew the answer to both of these questions. In the opening remarks of *Utilitarianism*, he says:

> All action is for the sake of some end, and rules of action, it seems natural to suppose, must take their whole character and color from the end to which they are subservient.[11]

According to Mill, action is essentially production, and therefore its function is to bring something about, to achieve some end. Whether an action is good, Mill concludes, depends on whether *what* it brings about is good, or as good as it can be.[12]

But it has not always seemed obvious to philosophers that action is essentially production. In Book 6 of the *Nicomachean Ethics*, Aristotle says:

> Among the things that can be otherwise are included both things made and things done; making and acting are different ... so that the reasoned state of capacity to act is different from the reasoned state of capacity to make. Nor are they included one in the other, for neither is acting making nor is making acting. (NE 6.4 1140a1–15)

According to Aristotle, action and production are two different things. And in the following section Aristotle remarks on one of the most important differences between them, namely that:

> while making has an end other than itself, action cannot; for good action itself is its end. (NE 6.5 1140b5–10)

Actions, or at least good actions, Aristotle says, are chosen for their own sakes, not for the sake of something they produce.

Actually, this is one of three different things Aristotle tells us about why good actions are done by virtuous agents. First of all, in at least some cases an act is done for some specific purpose or end. For instance, Aristotle tells us that the courageous person who dies in battle lays down his life for the sake of his country

or his friends (NE 9.8 1169a17–30). In the same way, it seems natural to say that the liberal person who makes a donation wants to help somebody out; the magnificent person who puts on a play wants to give the city a treat, the ready-witted man wants to amuse his audience, and so on. At the same time, as I've just mentioned, Aristotle says that virtuous actions are done for their own sakes. And finally, Aristotle also tells us that virtuous actions are done for the sake of the noble – *to kalon* (e.g. NE 3.7 1115b12; 3.8 116b3; 3.9 1117b9; 3.9 1117b17; 3.11 1119b15; 4.1 1120a23; 4.2 1122b6).

If we suppose that the reason for an action rests in its purpose, as Mill does, these will look like three inconsistent or competing accounts of the purpose or aim of virtuous action. But when we consider Aristotle's own conception of an action we can see why there is no inconsistency here. What corresponds in Aristotle's theory to the description of an action is what he calls a *logos* – as I will render it, a principle. A good action is one that embodies the *orthos logos* or right principle: it is done at the right time, in the right way, to the right object, and – importantly for my purposes – with the right aim. To cite one of many such passages, Aristotle says:

> anyone can get angry – that is easy – or give or spend money; but to do this at the right time, with the right aim, and in the right way, that is not for everyone, nor is it easy; that is why goodness is both rare and laudable and noble. (NE 2.9 1109a25–30)

The key to understanding Aristotle's view is that the *aim* is included in the description of the action, and that it is the action as a whole, *including the aim*, which the agent chooses. Let us say that our agent is a citizen-soldier, who chooses to sacrifice his life for the sake of a victory for his polis or city. The Greeks seem to think that is usually a good aim. Let's assume that our soldier also sacrifices himself at the right time – not before it is necessary, perhaps, or when something especially good may be achieved by it – say cutting off the enemy's access to reinforcements. And he does it in the right way, efficiently and unflinchingly, perhaps even with style, and so on. Then he has done something courageous, a good action. Why has he done it? His *purpose* or *aim* is to secure a victory for his city.

But the object of his choice is the whole action – sacrificing his life in a certain way at a certain time in order to secure a victory for the city. He chooses this whole package, that is, to-do-this-act-for-the-sake-of-this-end – he chooses *that*, the whole package, as a thing worth doing for its own sake, and without any further end. "Noble" describes the kind of value that the whole package has, the value that he sees in it when he chooses it.

Now this means that Aristotle's view of the nature of action is the same as Kant's. Kant thinks that an action is described by a maxim, and the maxim of an action is also of the "to-do-this-act-for-the-sake-of-this-end" structure. Kant is not always careful in the way he formulates maxims, and that fact can obscure the present point, but on the best reading of the categorical imperative test, the maxim which it tests includes both the act done and the end for the sake of which that act is done. It *has* to include both, because the question raised by the categorical imperative test is whether there could be a universal policy of pursuing *this sort of* end by *these sorts of* means. For instance, in Kant's own *Groundwork* examples the maxims tested are something like "I will commit suicide in order to avoid the personal troubles that I see ahead" and "I will make a false promise in order to get some ready cash." What the rejection of these maxims identifies as wrong is the whole package – committing suicide in order to avoid the personal troubles that you see ahead, and making a false promise in order to get some ready cash. The question of the rightness or wrongness of, say, committing suicide in order to save someone else's life, is left open, as a separate case to be tested separately. Indeed, Kant makes this clear himself, for in the *Metaphysics of Morals* he raises the question whether a man who has been bitten by a rabid dog and commits suicide in order to avoid harming others when he goes mad from the rabies has done something wrong or not (MM 6:423–424). Committing suicide in order to avoid seriously harming others is a different action from committing suicide in order to avoid the personal troubles that you see ahead, and requires a separate test.

And "moral worth" or being done "from duty" functions in Kant's theory in the same way that nobility does in Aristotle's. It is not an alternative purpose we have in our actions, but a characterization of a specific kind of value that a certain act performed for the sake of a certain end may have. When an agent finds that she *must* will a certain maxim as a universal law, she supposes that the action it describes has this kind of value. Many of the standard criticisms of the Kantian idea of acting from duty are based on confusion about this point. The idea that acting from duty is something cold, impersonal, or even egoistic is based on the thought that the agent's *purpose* or *aim* is "in order to do my duty" *rather than* "in order to help my friend" or "in order to save my country" or whatever it might be. But that is just wrong. Sacrificing your life in order to save your country might be your duty in a certain case, but the duty will be to do that act *for that purpose*, and the whole action, both act and purpose, will be chosen as one's duty.

Let me introduce some terminology in order to express these ideas more clearly. Let's say that the basic form of a Kantian maxim is "I will do act-A in order to promote end-E." Call that entire formulation the description of an action. An action, then, involves both an act and an end, an act done for the sake of an end. In the examples we've been looking at, making a false promise and committing suicide are what I am calling "acts," or, as I will sometimes say, "act-types." Making a false promise in order to get some ready cash, committing suicide in order to avoid the personal troubles that you see ahead, and committing suicide in order to avoid harming others are what I am calling "actions."

Now a slight complication arises from the fact that *acts* in my sense are also sometimes done for their own sakes, for no *further* end, from some non-instrumental motive like anger or sympathy or the sheer pleasure of the thing.[13] In this case, doing the *act* is itself the end. To describe the whole *action*, in this kind of case, we have to put that fact into the maxim, and say that we are doing it for its own sake, for its inherent desirability, or however it might be. So for instance, if you choose to dance for the sheer joy of dancing, then *dancing* is the *act*, and *dancing for the sheer joy of dancing* is the *action*. We might contrast it to the different action of someone who dances in order to make money, or to dodge the bullets being shot at his feet. As I said before, it is the action that is strictly speaking the object of choice. And according to both Aristotle and Kant, it is the *action* that strictly speaking is, as

Kant would have it, morally good, permissible, or bad; or as Aristotle would have it, noble, or at least not ignoble, or base.

The view that actions, acts-for-the-sake-of-ends, are both the objects of choice and the bearers of moral value sets Aristotle and Kant apart from many contemporary moral philosophers, less because of overt disagreement than because of unclarity about the issue. Here again, our ordinary practices of offering reasons give us unclear guidance. Earlier I noticed that when we ask for the reason for an action, we sometimes cite a fact, and sometimes a mental state. But another way we often answer such questions, cutting across that debate, is to announce the agent's purpose. "Why did Jack go to Chicago?" "In order to visit his mother" is the reply. Jack's purpose is offered in answer to the question about his reason. This makes it appear as if his purpose is the reason for his choice, and as if what he chooses, in response to having that purpose, is only the act. But this appearance, I believe, is misleading.

To explicate this point I will first take a detour. One way to accommodate talk of reasons to the distinction I've just made between acts and actions would be to distinguish the reasons for acts from the reasons for actions. We could say that the act is performed for the sake of the purpose it serves, while the whole action is performed for its own sake – say, because of its nobility or lawfulness or rightness. Then we might think that confusion arises from thinking there is always "a reason" for what someone does, when in fact the phrase "the reason for what he does" is ambiguous between the reason for the act and the reason for the action.

This proposal, although tempting, is not satisfactory. One problem with it springs from the fact that reasons are supposed to be normative. If a reason for an act is its purpose, and reasons are supposed to be normative, then it follows that the purpose itself is normative for the agent. This is certainly not what either Aristotle or Kant thinks. Kant does think that there are some purposes we ought to have – our own perfection and the happiness of others, which are identified as obligatory by his contradiction in the will test. These we must stand ready to promote if an opportunity comes in our way. But he does not think that our purposes are *in general* normative for us in this

way. In Kant's theory, normativity arises from autonomy – we give laws to ourselves. But we do not first choose a purpose, enact it into law, and then scramble around for some way to fulfill it, now being under a requirement to do so.[14] If it worked that way, we *would* be in violation of a self-legislated requirement every time we gave up a purpose because we were unable to find a decent and reasonable way to achieve it. But this isn't what happens. If you can't get to Paris without stealing the ticket money, stowing away on a boat or risking your life trying to cross the Atlantic in a canoe, then you may drop the project, and you have not thereby violated any norm.[15] What we will as laws are maxims, which describe actions, and we normally adopt a purpose as a *part* of an action.

Another problem with the proposal is that it suggests that in asking for "the reason" for what someone does, ordinary language is misleading, because there are always, so to speak, two reasons, one for the act and one for the action. But that in turn suggests a different way of looking at the situation, which does not require us to say that the idea of a reason is ambiguous, but only that we tend to misinterpret what we are doing when we offer a reason. If Aristotle and Kant are right about actions being done for their own sakes, then it seems as if every action is done for the same reason, namely because the agent thinks it's worth doing for its own sake. This obviously isn't what we are asking for when we ask for the reason why someone did something, because the answer is always the same: he thought it was worth doing. What may be worth asking for is an *explication* of the action, a complete description of it, which will show us *why* he thought it was worth doing. Now normally we already know what the act was, so the missing piece of the description of the action is the purpose or end. "Going to Chicago in order to visit one's mother" is intelligible as a worthwhile thing to do, so once we have that missing piece in place, we understand what Jack did. That the purpose by itself couldn't really be the source of the reason shows up clearly in this fact: if the purpose supplied is one that fails to make the whole action seem worthwhile, even though the purpose is indeed successfully served by the act, we will not accept the answer. Suppose Jack lives in Indianapolis, 165 miles away from Chicago. Then if I tell you that Jack went to Chicago to buy a box of paperclips, you will not accept the answer, even though one can certainly buy a box of paperclips in Chicago. You will say "that can't be the reason," not because the purpose isn't served by the action, but because going from Indianapolis to Chicago just to buy a box of paperclips is so obviously not worthwhile. Thus when we ask for the reason we are not just asking what purpose was served by the act – we are asking for a purpose that makes sense of the whole action. And as Aristotle saw, there will be cases where supplying the purpose will not be sufficient to make the action intelligible even where it is, so to speak, weighty enough to support the act. "Why did Jack go to Paris?" we ask. "He has always wanted to see the Eiffel Tower" is the reply. "No, but why just now?" urges the questioner, for Jack has taken off quite suddenly in the middle of the semester. And as Aristotle says, in order to be worthwhile the action must also be done at the right time and in the right way. So the practice of answering the motivational question "why?" by citing the agent's purpose does not really suggest that what we choose are acts, and our reasons are provided by our purposes. It is just that the purpose is often, though not always, the missing piece of the agent's maxim, the piece we need to have in place before we can see why the agent thought that this action as a whole was a thing worth doing.[16]

The way Kant presents the hypothetical and categorical imperatives in the *Groundwork* suggests that he himself may have fallen into the kind of confusion that I've been describing, at least about bad actions. He presents them as two different kinds of imperatives, on a footing with each other, and occasionally makes remarks suggesting that we are acting on either one *or* the other.[17] For instance, at one point, after distinguishing the two imperatives, Kant contrasts someone who avoids making a false promise because it is "in itself evil" (G 4:419) with someone who avoids making a false promise because it will damage his reputation if it comes to light.

As I have already said, what Kant's view actually implies is "in itself evil" is making a false promise in order to get some money. But the slip is understandable, although this will take a moment to explain. As I mentioned before, on the best reading of the categorical imperative test, the question whether we can universalize the maxim is a question about whether

we can will the universal practice of pursuing *that* end by *that* means. Or, to put the point more carefully, you ask whether you could will to be part of an order of things in which this was the universal practice, and at the same time rationally will the maxim in question yourself. For instance, you ask whether you could will to be part of an order of things in which everyone who needed money attempted to get it by means of a false promise, and at the same time will the maxim of getting money by means of a false promise yourself. According to Kant, in such an order of things people would just laugh at promises to repay money as vain pretenses, rather than lending money on the strength of them (G 4:422). Since making a false promise would then not *be* a means of getting the money you need, you could not rationally will to get money by that means. And so the maxim fails the test.

This is not the place to discuss in detail how well this test works as a guide to moral judgment.[18] What I want to point out now is that there is one sort of case in which it works almost too well. Some act-types are purely natural, in the sense that they depend only on the laws of nature for their possibility. Walking and running, slugging and stabbing, tying up and killing – these are acts-types that are made possible by the laws of nature, and accordingly, one can do them in any society. Elsewhere I have noticed the difficulty of using the universal law test to rule out maxims involving these kinds of acts.[19] But other act-types depend for their possibility not just on natural laws, but also on the existence of certain social practices or conventions. Writing a check, taking a course, running for office are act-types of this kind: you can do them only in societies with the sorts of institutions and practices that make them possible. Now where an action involves an act-type that must be sustained by practices and conventions, and at the same time violates the rules of those very practices or conventions, it is relatively easy to find the kind of contradiction that Kant looks for in the universalization test. This is because practices and conventions are unlikely to survive their universal abuse. Thus it hardly seems to matter *what* the purpose is for which you perform such an act; nearly every action involving such an act will fail the categorical imperative test. Charitably interpreted, Kant is recording this fact when he says that false promising is "in itself evil." Yet the remark is misleading at best. Even if Kant were right in thinking that any action involving the act-type "false promise" will fail the test, that would not show that the act-type is inherently evil. It would only show that members of the class of actions involving that act-type are inherently evil.

No doubt remarks like the one about false promising being "in itself evil" are part of what has led to the widespread misconception that Kant's ethical system is supposed to generate rules against act-types. But this is not just a confusion about Kant's theory. It is a familiar confusion about ethics itself. And another thing that supports this confusion is the existence of words in the language that seem to name wrong act-types, but actually name wrong actions, though somewhat schematically described. Aristotle himself trips over this one when he says:

> But not every action nor every passion admits of a mean; for some have names that already imply badness…in the case of actions, adultery, theft, murder…nor does goodness or badness with regard to such things depend on committing adultery with the right woman, at the right time, and in the right way, but simply to do any of them is to go wrong. (NE 2.6 1107a 9–15)

In fact, Aristotle is running together slightly different kinds of cases, but none of them shows that there are act-types that are inherently wrong. The example that best fits the point I want to make is murder. To say that murder is wrong is not to say that there is an act-type, murder, that is wrong no matter what end you have in view when you do it. Rather, "murder" is the name of a class of *actions*. A murder is a homicide committed for *some end or other* that is inadequate to justify the homicide. We don't call execution or killing in battle or killing in self-defense "murder" unless we believe that those actions are not justifiable, that punishment or war or self-defense are not ends that justify killing.

"Theft," another of Aristotle's examples, is not quite like that, or rather, it depends on how we are using the word. If by "theft" we mean "taking property that is not legally your own," we do have an act-type, but one that doesn't already imply wrongness, although it certainly gestures at a very likely reason for wrongness. It is like false promising – a violation of social practices that is *almost* sure to turn out wrong no

matter what your end is. So here Aristotle may have been derailed by the same thing that derailed Kant. But of course there is a sort of colorful use of terms like "theft" in which we do use them to indicate wrongness, precisely because the case *isn't* legally one of theft. Thus if a shop charges too much for an article people desperately need, we say "that's highway robbery!" to express our disapproval. In that usage, robbery or theft, like murder, already implies wrongness, but in that usage, theft is not an act-type. It is a class of actions, roughly those that take people's property away for ends that can't justify doing that.

As for adultery, it also depends on the usage. If it means "having sexual relations with someone other than the person to whom you are married, or with a person who is married to someone else" it is like theft. It is an act-type, but again Aristotle is wrong. It is intelligible to ask whether perhaps at this time and in this place and with this particular person it is all right to commit adultery, just as it's intelligible to ask whether it is all right to violate society's property arrangements for some extraordinary purpose. Perhaps if your love is true and mutual and faithful, your spouse has been in a coma for the last fifteen years, the doctors say he is brain-dead but the law forbids removing life support, and divorce in these circumstances isn't legal, then adultery in this strictly legal sense isn't wrong – at least it makes sense to ask. But the word "adultery" may be used, like the word "murder," only to indicate *unjustifiable* violations of the marriage conventions. If one may say, without any misuse of language, "it isn't really adultery, for my husband and I have a very special understanding…" then "adultery" is like "murder", a term only used when we think the whole action is wrong.[20]

5. Motivation: The Relation between Reasons and Actions

According to Aristotle and Kant, then, the object of choice is an action, in the technical sense I have explained – an act for the sake of an end. The reason for the action is expressed in the agent's *logos* or principle. Roughly speaking, what happens when an agent chooses an action is something like this: the agent is attracted on some occasion to promoting some end or other. The end may be suggested by the occasion, or it may be one he standardly promotes when he can. He reasons about how he might achieve this end, or what he might do in its service, and he arrives at a possible maxim or *logos*. He considers promoting a certain end by means of a certain act done in a certain way at a certain time and place. That is to say, he considers an action, and he asks himself whether it is a thing worth doing. And he determines the action to be noble or at least not base, morally worthy or at least permissible. Kant thinks he makes this determination by subjecting the maxim to a test, the categorical imperative test, and Aristotle does not, but for present purposes that is not important. Determining the action to be good, a thing worth doing for its own sake, he does the action. He is therefore motivated by the goodness of being motivated in the way he is motivated: or, to put it more intelligibly, he is motivated by his awareness that his end is one that justifies his act in his circumstances, that the parts of his maxim are related in the right way.[21] Aristotle and Kant's view, therefore, correctly identifies the kind of item that can serve as a reason for action: the maxim or *logos* of an action, which expresses the agent's endorsement of the appropriateness of doing a certain act for the sake of a certain end.

At the same time, their view brings out one of the ways in which having a reason is an exercise of an agent's activity. On their view, the agent chooses not only the act, but also the purpose or end – he chooses the act for the sake of the end, but in doing so he chooses to promote or realize the end. Although his attraction to the end may be thrust upon him by nature, the decision to pursue the end is not. So choice on this view is a more fully active state than on the view that what we choose are mere acts, motivated by ends that are given to us. The agent does not just choose an act as a reaction to an end that is given him by his desire or even by his recognition of some external value. Since both the end and the means are chosen, the choice of an action is an exercise of the agent's own free activity.

But there is one last problem. Suppose someone objects that Aristotle and Kant's view does not actually solve the problem posed by the reflective structure of reasons. The Aristotelian or Kantian agent, the objec-

tor will say, is motivated by the nobility or moral worth of the whole action *rather than* by its content, by the end that it serves. I have still not shown that you can be motivated, as it were, in both ways at once. Nor (therefore) have I successfully shown that the agent is active in the way I've just claimed. On my theory of motivation, the agent's choice of the action is just a reaction to the goodness of the whole action, in the same way that, on the alternative theory, the choice of an act is just a reaction to the goodness of the end. So goes the objection.[22,23]

This objection, I believe, is based on a fundamental misunderstanding of what it means to be motivated – a misunderstanding of the way in which reasons and actions are related. The objection assumes that a motivating reason is related to an action in the same way that a purpose is related to an act. The purpose is something separate from or outside of the act, for the sake of which one does the act. But the reason for an action is not related to an action in that way. So this brings us to the third question: how reasons and actions are related, or what it means to be motivated.

An essential feature of the view I have attributed to Aristotle and Kant is that the reason for an action is not something outside of, or behind, or separate from, the action. Giving a description or explication of the action, and giving a description or explication of the reason, are the same thing. The *logos* or maxim that expresses the reason is a kind of description of the action, and could be cited in response to the question: *what is he doing?* just as easily as it can in response to the question *why is he doing that?* Indeed – to make one last appeal to our ordinary practices – their view explains why in ordinary language these questions are pretty much equivalent. For the demand for justification can as easily take the form: *what are you doing?* or more aggressively and skeptically *what do you think you are doing?* as it can *why are you doing that?*[24] The reason for an action is not something that stands behind it and makes you want to do it: it is the action itself, described in a way that makes it intelligible.

I can best convey what I have in mind here by drawing your attention briefly to the middle player in the trio of items that we associate with the idea of reason – principles. The agent's *logos* or maxim is, as Kant puts it, his subjective principle. What exactly is a principle, metaphysically speaking, and what does it mean to say that an agent has one or acts on one? Some recent moral philosophers have been critical of principles, thinking of them as something like rules that function as deliberative premises. "I believe in the principle of treating people equally, and therefore I will show these particular people no favoritism, though they happen to be my relatives." And then it may seem as if there is an option to acting on principle, such as being moved by love or compassion or loyalty instead.

But I don't believe that, at least for a rational agent, there is any option to acting on principle.[25] To believe in a principle is just to believe that it is appropriate or inappropriate to treat certain considerations as counting in favor of certain acts. Because that's what a principle is: a principle is a description of the mental act of *taking* certain considerations to count in favor of certain acts.[26] Suppose that Jack is tempted to take a trip to Chicago by the fact that it will help his mother, and he decides to act accordingly. The belief that the trip will help his mother does not cause him to act. Rather, he takes it to provide him with a reason for the action. We may represent this fact – his taking the fact that it would help his mother to count in favor of making the trip – by saying that it is his *principle*, his *logos* or maxim, to take a trip to Chicago in order to help his mother. So to say that he acts on principle is just to *record the*

fact that he is active and not merely causally receptive with respect to his perception of the good-making properties of the action.[27] Jack's actively, self-consciously, taking the fact that it will help his mother to count in favor of making the trip *amounts to* his judging that the whole action is good. And his taking the fact that it would help his mother as a reason for making the trip, and in so doing judging that the whole action is good, is coincident with his *doing it*.[28] I don't mean that he doesn't think, he just acts: as I said earlier, reasoned action is above all self-conscious. What I mean is that the judgment that the action is good is not a mental state that precedes the action and causes it. Rather, his judgment, his practical thinking, is embodied in the action itself. That's what it means to say that the action is motivated and not merely caused. For a motive is not merely a mental cause. And an action is not merely a set of physical movements that happens to have a mental cause, any more than an utterance is a set of noises that happen to have a mental cause. An action is an essentially intelligible object that *embodies* its reason, the way an utterance is an essentially intelligible object that embodies a thought. So being motivated by a reason is not a reaction to the judgment that a certain way of acting is good. It is more like an announcement that a certain way of acting is good. The person who acts for a reason, like God in the act of creation, *declares* that what he does is good.

Notes

1. The answers admit of a rough, though only a rough, grouping. Empiricists tend to think that reasons are provided by our mental states, especially our desires; that the relevant facts concern the desirability of the goals to be achieved through action; and that the relation between reasons and actions is causal. Rationalists tend to think that reasons are provided by the facts in virtue of which the action is good, that these facts need not be limited to the desirability of the goals that are achieved through action, but may concern intrinsic properties of the action itself; and that the action is caused not by the reason, but rather by the agent's response to the reason. To some extent, this essay follows the familiar Kantian strategy of making a case by showing how the debate between rationalists and empiricists leads to an impasse.

2. These remarks are of course tautological; this is because the properties in question are essentially indefinable. These two properties I've just gestured at are sometimes referred to as normative and motivational internalism, respectively, but I prefer to avoid these terms.

3. Bernard Williams, *Ethics and the Limits of Philosophy*, p. 19.

4. Joseph Raz, *Engaging Reason*, p. 63. Raz actually says "options" not actions, but he means the actions among which we are choosing, so I've changed the quotation for clarity in this context.

5. In other words, I am looking for what it means to act for a reason in the descriptive sense of reason. An important feature of the terms "reason," "rational" and

so forth is that they admit of either a descriptive or a normative use. In the descriptive sense, one can act "rationally" while acting for either a good reason or a bad one; rational action is opposed to non-rational action or perhaps mere movement or expression. In the normative sense, one counts as acting rationally only when the reason is good. Hence we can say either "that's a terrible reason" (descriptive sense) or "that's no reason at all" (normative sense) and mean the same thing. The point of focusing on the descriptive sense is that once we have identified which action or activity we have in mind when we talk about "acting for a reason," we may then be able to locate the normative sense by asking what counts as being *good at* this activity. As I will observe below, I think that the account of acting for a reason that I give in this essay supports the claim that acting in accordance with the categorical imperative is a way of being good at acting for a reason. See note 26.

6.   St Augustine, *Confessions*, Book 2, section 4, p. 47.

7.   Elsewhere I have argued that this strategy cannot work, because it effectively blocks the attempt to give a descriptive account of what rationality is. See my "The Normativity of Instrumental Reason," Essay 1 in CA, pp. 55–6. The argument of this essay is making good on that claim, even though in this essay I do not directly attack the idea of defining reason in terms of reasons.

8.   For an argument that non-human animals count as agents, see my *Self-Constitution: Agency, Identity, and Integrity*.

9.   I can think of two other things that philosophers have claimed to have an essentially reflexive structure, or to take themselves for their objects. One is God, as conceived by Aristotle in *Metaphysics* 12.9, where God is identified with the divine activity of thinking on thinking – for Aristotle, the most perfect and purely active activity there can be. The other is personal identity. Some philosophers have claimed, rightly as I believe, that persons are not incidentally but essentially conscious of themselves. It's not as if you have a personal identity which might or might not be conscious of; rather; if you are not conscious of your personal identity, then you don't have it. So the state of being a person takes itself for its object (see, for example, Robert Nozick, *Philosophical Explanations*, chapter 1, part 2, pp. 71–114). I am claiming reasons are like that, and in my view this is no accident, since, as I argue in *Self-Constitution: Agency, Identity, and Integrity*, being a person is essentially an activity, and a person is in a sense constituted by her reasons.

10.   Now at this point the defender of good-making properties may wish to argue as follows. The tangled formulation at which I have just arrived is the result of the extremely broad definition of good-making property that I adopted at the outset. You will recall that I said that by good-making property I did not mean "good" in any substantial sense, but only whatever it is about the action that makes it seem eligible to the agent. If "eligible" means "appropriately motivating" then of course it follows that to be aware of the good-making properties is just to be aware of appropriate grounds for motivation. But the philosopher who proposes to define a rational agent as one who is moved by good-making properties does not mean good in this minimal or formal sense. Rather, the proposal here is that we define a rational agent as one moved by those properties that are genuinely good, in a substantial sense.

But this will not do. For we still have the problem of the lioness, and again she leaves us with two options. If protection of her cubs is genuinely good, in whatever substantial sense we have in mind, and to be rational is to be moved by the genuinely good, then on this showing she is a rational agent. Or if to avoid that, this philosopher accepts the claim that she must know that her action is genuinely good, then all that this maneuver does is add an additional clause to my definition of a rational agent. A rational agent is one who is motivated by the consciousness that her grounds for action are appropriate grounds for normative motivation *and gets it right*. This is not really a way of avoiding the issue. What I have just said amounts to an argument to the effect that we must identify a descriptive sense of reason. See also notes 5 and 7.

11.   John Stuart Mill, *Utilitarianism*, p. 2.

12.   Actually, Mill is wrong about this. The theories of goodness I mention in the text seek to identify what are sometimes called "internal" or "constitutive" standards of goodness. These are standards that hold of an object in virtue of what it is. On Mill's own theory of action, the only constitutive standard of actions is effectiveness. The achievement of a good end, as opposed to whatever end is aimed at, is only an external standard for actions. Technically speaking, aiming at the good is a side constraint on action. For more on internal or constitutive standards, see "The Normativity of Instrumental Reason," Essay 1 in CA, pp. 61–2; "Self-Constitution in the Ethics of Plato and Kant," Essay 3 in CA, pp. 110–13; and the Introduction to CA, pp. 7–10.

13. Kant's notorious example, from the first section of the *Groundwork*, of the sympathetic person who lacks moral worth, is like this: Kant specifies that he "has no further motive of vanity or self-interest" and does the action for its own sake (G 4:398). The agent who acts from duty also does the action for its own sake. Discussions of the argument of the first section of the *Groundwork* frequently overlook this, and suppose instead that Kant is contrasting two different purposes one may have in one's actions, one's own pleasure and duty. For further discussion, see my "From Duty and for the Sake of the Noble: Kant and Aristotle on Morally Good Action," Essay 6 in CA especially pp. 176–87. Kant does describe another of his *Groundwork* exemplars, the prudent merchant, as performing an action for an instrumental reason (G 4:397). If the argument of this essay is correct, Kant should not have done that: the prudent merchant in fact chooses something like "to charge my customers a fair price in order to profit from the good reputation of my business" as an action worth doing for its own sake.

14. In the past I have sometimes suggested that Kant could be interpreted as allowing for maxims of having purposes – for instance, in "Morality as Freedom," I imagine a maxim like this: "I will make it my end to have the things that I desire" (CKE, p. 164). I now think that is wrong, and that purposes are adopted only as parts of whole actions, for reasons given in the text. The maxims associated with the contradiction in the will test should be understood not as maxims of having purposes, but as schematic maxims of action: roughly "I will do whatever I (decently and reasonably) can to promote the happiness of others and my own perfection."

15. I now think that what I say about this in "The Normativity of Instrumental Reason," Essay 1 in CA, on pp. 57–8, where I portray an agent as enacting ends into law prior to enacting means into law, is misleading. At the time I wrote that essay, I believed that its argument showed that hypothetical imperatives depended on categorical ones; as I say in the Afterword to that essay, I now believe it shows that, strictly speaking, there are no separate hypothetical imperatives. See note 17.

16. Gisela Striker reminds me that a word often translated from Greek as "reason" in the sense of "a reason" is *aition*, the why or the cause. The purpose of an action is its final cause, which appears as a part of the *logos*. Translations of this kind thus pick up the tendency to identify the reason with the purpose.

17. I have in mind remarks that suggest that bad or heteronomous action is done on hypothetical imperatives, while good or autonomous action involves categorical imperatives. See, for instance, G 4:441, where Kant associates heteronomous accounts of morality with hypothetical imperatives. In fact, if actions are chosen for their own sakes, then every action is chosen in accordance with a law that has elements of both imperatives. The action must be chosen as something good in itself, which means it is governed by the categorical imperative. And every action must involve an act that is a means to an end, in a very broad sense of "means" – it may cause the end, constitute it, realize it or whatever it might be. The right way to think of the law governing action, I now believe, is as a practical categorical imperative, where the instrumental element enters with the thought that the law must be practical.

18. For more extensive discussion, see my "Kant's Formula of Universal Law," CKE essay 3.

19. "Kant's Formula of Universal Law," CKE essay 3, pp. 84–5 and 97–101.

20. It is a different question whether there are categories of actions that are always regrettable because they violate the (in this case, Kantian) ideal of human relationships – that there should be no coercion or deception. In "The Right to Lie: Kant on Dealing with Evil" (CKE essay 5), I argue for a "double-level" interpretation of Kant's theory, with the Formula of Universal Law representing an absolute but minimal standard of justification, and the Formula of Humanity representing an ideal of human relations. When dealing with evil agents or certain kinds of tragic circumstances, we may have to violate our ideal standards, but we are never justified in violating the Universal Law formula. The argument of this essay takes place in the terms of the Formula of Universal Law, and so is about what can be justified given the circumstances, not about the ideal. I thank Marian Brady for pressing this question, and Tamar Schapiro for discussion of the issue.

21. Elsewhere I have argued that Kant's notion of the form of a maxim can be understood in terms of Aristotle's sense of "form." A thing's form in Aristotle's sense is the arrangement of its parts that enables it to perform its function. In a good maxim, the act and the end are related to each other in such a way that it can serve as a universal law (SN 3.3.5, pp. 107–8). I have also suggested that we might understand Aristotle's notion of the *orthos logos* in the same way – the parts are all related in a way that gives the action its nobility.

See "From Duty and for the Sake of the Noble: Kant and Aristotle on Morally Good Action," Essay 6 in CA, pp. 193–4.

22. Notice that if this objection were correct, merely permissible action would not be possible, or at least there would be a difficulty about it, since in that case the action is judged to be "not bad" or "not ignoble" and that hardly sounds like a reason for doing it. The content of the maxim must play a role in motivation if permissible action is possible. The account I am about to give shows how permissible action is compatible with autonomy.

23. Another way to put the objection, or at least a similar objection, is to wonder why "doing my duty" should not be regarded as a further end, to which the action as a whole serves as a kind of means. In this case the answer is to start the argument over, and to ask whether it is the fact that the action is a means to doing one's duty, or the agent's belief that the action is a means to doing his duty, that serves as the reason for doing it. We can only solve the problem by supposing that reasons have a reflexive structure, and to explain how that is possible, we have to come around once more to a view like Aristotle and Kant's – understood as I have presented it in the text.

24. Despite the apparent complexity of their view, the idea behind Aristotle and Kant's conception of what it means to have a reason is in one way simpler than that of their contemporary competitors. To have a reason is to be motivated by certain considerations, taking them to be appropriate grounds for motivation.

To have a reason, in other words, is to *know what you are doing.*

25. Actually, I believe that there is also a sense in which non-human animals act on principle: their instincts serve as their principles. See my "Motivation, Metaphysics, and the Value of the Self: A Reply to Ginsborg, Guyer, and Schneewind," especially pp. 49–51, and *Self-Constitution: Agency, Identity, and Integrity.*

26. The categorical imperative, in its universal law formulation, is in a way both descriptive of and normative for this act. It is descriptive insofar as the agent who takes end-E to count in favor of doing Act-A in effect makes "doing Act-A for the sake of End-E" her law, the law that governs her own action. It is normative insofar as it indicates what counts as performing this act well – namely, reflecting on whether that maxim is really fit to serve as a law. See note 5.

27. For further discussion of the kind of activity involved in rational action, see "From Duty and for the Sake of the Noble: Kant and Aristotle on Morally Good Action," Essay 6 in CA, especially p. 187.

28. It is frequently argued that intentions must exist separately from actions because we often decide what we will do (and why) in advance of the time of action. I believe, however, that we begin implementing or enacting our decisions immediately, for once a decision is made, our movements must be planned so that it is possible to enact it, and that planning is itself part of the enacting of our decision. I thank Luca Ferrero for illuminating discussions of this issue.

References

Aristotle. *Nicomachean Ethics* (NE), from *The Complete Works of Aristotle: The Revised Oxford Translation.* Edited by Jonathan Barnes. Princeton: Princeton University Press, 1984. NOTE: *In quoting from this edition I have deviated from the translation in two ways: I have always translated "ergon" as "function" rather than "work," and I have always translated "arete" as "virtue" rather than "excellence."*

Augustine, Saint. *Confessions.* Translated by R.S. Pine-Coffin. Harmondsworth: Penguin Books, 1961.

Kant, I. *Groundwork of the Metaphysics of Morals* (G), Cambridge Texts in the History of Philosophy. Translated and edited by Mary Gregor with an Introduction by Christine M. Korsgaard. Cambridge: Cambridge University Press, 1998.

Kant, I. *The Metaphysics of Morals* (MM), Cambridge Texts in the History of Philosophy. Translated and edited by Mary Gregor with an Introduction by Roger J. Sullivan. Cambridge: Cambridge University Press, 1996.

Korsgaard, C. *The Constitution of Agency* (CA). Cambridge: Cambridge University Press, 2008.

Korsgaard, C. *Creating the Kingdom of Ends* (CKE). Cambridge: Cambridge University Press, 1996.

Korsgaard, C. "Motivation, Metaphysics, and the Value of the Self: A Reply to Ginsberg, Guyer, and Schneewind," *Ethics* 109 (1998), 49–66.

Korsgaard, C. *Self-Constitution: Agency, Identity, and Integrity.* Cambridge: Cambridge University Press, 2009.

Korsgaard, C. *Sources of Normativity* (SN). Cambridge: Cambridge University Press, 1996.

Mill, J. S. *Utilitarianism*. Edited by George Sher. Indianapolis: Hackett Publishing Company, 1979.

Nozick, R. *Philosophical Explanations*. Cambridge, MA: The Belknap Press, 1981.

Raz, J. *Engaging Reason*. Oxford: Oxford University Press, 1999.

Williams, B. *Ethics and the Limits of Philosophy*. Cambridge, MA: Harvard University Press, 1985.

22

Arational Actions

Rosalind Hursthouse

It is often said that there is some special irrationality involved in wreaking damage or violence on inanimate objects that have angered one, and, correspondingly, something rational about striking people or animals in anger. The explanation of this seems obvious, for the first surely manifests the irrational belief that inanimate things are animate and can be punished, whereas the second has no such flaw. But behind this seemingly innocuous observation lies, as I shall argue, a false account of action explanation and a false semantic theory. According to the standard account of actions and their explanations, intentional actions are actions done because the agent has a certain desire/belief pair that explains the action by rationalizing it. Any explanation of intentional action in terms of an appetite or occurrent emotion (which might appear to be an explanation solely in terms of desire) is hence assumed to be elliptical, implicitly appealing to some appropriate belief.[1] In this paper, I challenge this assumption with respect to the "arational" actions of my title – a significant subset of the set of intentional actions explained by occurrent emotion. These actions threaten the standard account, not only by forming a recalcitrant set of counterexamples to it, but also, as we shall see, by undercutting the false semantic theory that holds that account in place.

Hursthouse, R. (1981), "Arational Actions," *Journal of Philosophy* 88 (2), 57–68. Reprinted with permission of Rosalind Hursthouse and The Journal of Philosophy.

I define these actions ostensively by means of a list of examples, and then define them explicitly, thereby making it obvious why I call them "arational" actions (rather than "irrational," on the model of the distinction between "amoral" and "immoral"). I cluster the examples around the emotion (or emotions) that would, usually, explain the actions; the explanation would, usually, be of the form "I ϕ-ed because I was so frightened (or happy, excited, ashamed . . . so overwhelmed by hatred or affection or …) that I just wanted to, or felt I had to." Arational actions:

a. explained by a wave of love, affection, or tenderness – kissing or lightly touching in passing, seizing and tossing up in the air, rumpling the hair of, or generally messing up the person or animal one loves; talking to her photograph as one passes, kissing it;

b. explained by anger, hatred, and sometimes jealousy – violently destroying or damaging anything remotely connected with the person (or animal, or institution) one's emotion is directed toward, e.g., her picture, letters or presents from her, awards from her, books or poems about her; the chair she was wont to sit in, locks of her hair, recordings or "our" song, etc.;

c. explained by anger with inanimate objects – doing things that might make sense if the things were animate, e.g., shouting at them, throwing an "uncooperative" tin opener on the ground or out

Philosophy of Action: An Anthology, First Edition. Edited by Jonathan Dancy and Constantine Sandis.
© 2015 John Wiley & Sons, Inc. Published 2015 by John Wiley & Sons, Inc.

of the window, kicking doors that refuse to shut and cars that refuse to start, tying towels that keep falling off a slippery towel rail on to it *very* tightly and then consolidating the knots with water; muttering vindictively 'I'll show *you*', or 'You *would* would you';

d. explained by excitement – jumping up and down, running, shouting, pounding the table or one's knees, hugging oneself or other people, throwing things;

e. explained by joy – running, jumping, leaping up reaching for leaves on trees, whistling or humming tunelessly, clapping one's hands;

f. explained by grief – tearing one's hair or clothes, caressing, clutching, even rolling in, anything suitable associated with the person or thing that is the object of grief, e.g., pictures, clothes, presents from her (cf. anger above). (The example of rolling in comes from a novel in which a man takes his dead wife's clothes out of the wardrobe, puts them on the bed and rolls in them, burying his face in them and rubbing them against his cheeks);

g. explained by shame – covering one's face *in the dark*, or when one is alone; washing with violent attention to scrubbing and scouring;

h. explained by horror – covering one's eyes when they are already shut;

i. explained by fear – hiding one's face, burrowing under the bed clothes;

j. explained by feeling proud, or self-satisfied, or pleased with oneself – talking to or posturing to oneself in the mirror.

I maintain, with respect to these examples, that on very many (though *not* necessarily all) occasions on which such actions were performed, it would be true to say the following of them: (i) that the action was intentional; (ii) that the agent did not do it for a reason in the sense that there is a true description of action of the form "*X* did it (in order) to . . ." or "*X* was trying to . . ." which will "reveal the favorable light in which the agent saw what he did,"[2] and hence involve, or imply, the ascription of a suitable *belief*; and (iii) that the agent would not have done the action if she had not been in the grip of whatever emotion it was, and the mere fact that she was in its grip explains the action as much as anything else does.

I shall say that when and only when these three conditions hold of an action it is, by definition, an *arational action*, and appropriate to the emotion or emotions that explain it. The examples are of action types, most of whose tokens would be arational actions, but, as noted above, I am not insisting that they always would be. Many of them, for instance, might be done on occasion without the agent's being aware of what she was doing, thus violating condition (i), and many might be done, on occasion, in order to . . ., thus violating condition (ii). On such occasions, the actions are not, as performed, arational actions; whether or not an agent has performed an arational action on some occasion is determined by whether the three conditions obtain.

I have encountered great resistance, both explicitly in discussion and implicitly in philosophy-of-action literature, to the very idea of arational actions as defined. What people want to do is deny that when condition (i) obtains, condition (ii) *can* obtain. "If an action is intentional," they say, "it *must* be done for a reason, i.e., because of an appropriate desire and belief" – for this is, indeed, the standard account. Now I do not want to quarrel about senses of 'done for a reason'; the central point at issue is certain belief ascriptions to agents performing intentional actions of the sort described above. I am just using 'not done for a reason' here to capture my claim that these actions are explained solely by reference to desire – "I was so angry/delighted, etc., I just wanted to" – not to an appropriate belief.

To get quite clear about what is at issue, let us consider as an example, Jane, who, in a wave of hatred for Joan, tears at Joan's photo with her nails, and gouges holes in the eyes. I can agree that Jane does this because, hating Joan, she wants to scratch her face, and gouge out her eyes; I can agree that she would not have torn at the photo if she had not believed that it was a photo of Joan; and if someone wants to say, "So those are the reasons for the action," I do not want to quarrel, for these "reasons" do *not* form the appropriate desire-belief pair assumed by the standard account. On the standard account, if the explanatory desire in this case is the desire to scratch Joan's face, then the appropriate belief has to be something absurd, such as the belief that the photo of Joan *is* Joan, or that scratching the photo will be causally efficacious in defacing its original. And my disagreement is with adherents of the standard account, who must think that some *non*absurd candidates for appropriate beliefs to ascribe to agents performing arational actions are available.

An exhaustively detailed rebuttal of the various candidates that may be offered cannot be given, of course, but I now review the most plausible.

When one attempts to think of appropriate beliefs, it becomes clear quite rapidly that there is no point in trying to find them piecemeal, token by token – beliefs such as the belief that by harming a photo one harms the original. Viewed abstractly, the desires to perform arational actions when in the grip of an emotion provide, apparently, a rich fund of those cases which Gary Watson[3] neatly characterized as those in which "one in no way values what one desires" (*ibid.*, p. 201), and what is needed to show this is mere appearance, is a belief, ascribable to the agent in every case, about the value of what she is doing. My claim was that these actions are not done in order to ϕ; the counterclaim, coming from the standard account, should be that they *are* done in order to ϕ, where the agent always wants to ϕ and where the appropriate belief, showing in what way the agent values the action, would be of the form "and the agent believes that doing this (gouging out the eyes on the photo or whatever it is) is ϕ-ing."

We seem to find the promise of a candidate in the thought that tokens of the types in question are done *in order to express the emotion*, to relieve it, or vent it, or make it known. This, it is said, reveals the standard desire-belief reason for which arational actions are done: the agent desires to express her emotion, and believes that whatever she is doing *is* expressing it.

But quite generally, what is wrong with this suggestion once again is that it involves ascribing a belief to the agent which should not be ascribed. If I ϕ in order to express or relieve my emotion, I do so in the belief that my ϕ-ing will indeed have (or is likely to have) this upshot. And in such cases, there is the possibility that I am not setting about fulfilling my intention in the right way; that I am open to correction. But arational actions would not usually admit of any possibility of mistake in this way; they are not the sort of action an agent would usually do in the (possibly erroneous) belief that they would achieve this effect.

Nor should we accept it as obvious that in every case the agent has the desire *to express this emotion*, a desire whose content is distinct from that of the desire to, say, throw the tin opener violently on the floor. The ascription of this extra desire requires an extra justification.

Of course, I grant that, on some particular occasion, such a justification may be available; as before, I am not insisting that *no* token of an arational action type is ever done in order to express an emotion. I might indeed, on occasion, break up the furniture in the belief that this is expressing my rage and wanting to express it, because my psychotherapist has convinced me that I have hitherto suppressed my emotions too much, that it is better to express them than to bottle them up. Here, my decision to follow the therapist's advice provides the justification for ascribing to me the extra desire *to express this emotion* – and, significantly, it also introduces the possibility of my being open to correction. "You're not really expressing your rage," knowledgeable onlookers may say. "Why don't you really *scream!*"

Similarly, I might tousle someone's hair in the belief that this will make it known to them that I am feeling a wave of affection for them, and that they would like to know this. Or I might deliberately try to get my corrosive hatred for Joan out of my system and tear at her photo in the belief that doing so will bring me this relief. In such cases, the information that my belief is false, that I am not going to succeed in making known or relieving my emotion, or that my expressing it in this way on this occasion is not a good idea would be seen by me as a reason for stopping what I am doing. Granted, this can happen on occasion. But on most occasions, this is not how things are; usually the agent will not be *trying* (successfully or unsuccessfully) to express her emotion, in the belief that this is a good idea, at all.

Notwithstanding this, there seems to be something right about the idea that arational actions are done "to express the emotion" that has not yet been brought out. Let us consider the claim, not that the agent does the action *in order to* express the emotion, but rather qua expression of emotion.

What does this mean? If it is saying that arational actions *are* "expressions of emotion" or "expressive of emotion," this is, I think, obviously true, but it adds nothing to the claim that arational actions are as defined – i.e., intentional actions appropriate to certain emotions, whose only explanation is that, in the grip of the relevant emotion, the agent just felt like doing them. Indeed, it is less explicit than the definition, for both unintentional actions (such as unknowingly gnashing one's teeth) and intentional actions done for further reasons (such as tearing at someone's eyes in order to hurt them) also count as expressions of emotions. But if the 'done qua expression' turn of phrase is intended to capture something more explicit, what could this be?

Given the obvious fact that in some sense the agent does arational actions "(just) because she wants to," or "for their own sake," prompted by the occurrent desire, it is natural to compare arational actions with actions prompted by appetite, and to look to Stephen Schiffer's[4] account of actions prompted by "reason-providing desires," such as eating a piece of chocolate because I am seized by a desire for chocolate. These, according to Schiffer, are done "for pleasure" – not in quite the same sense in which one goes to the ballet "for pleasure," where I desire to go to the ballet because I believe I shall enjoy it, but still in the sense that they are done *in the belief* that satisfying the desire will yield pleasure. This being so, the obvious cases of actions prompted by Schifferian reason-providing desires can be given a standard belief-desire reason explanation; the agent desires physical pleasure, and believes that acting in accordance with the currently aroused appetite will yield this, and so acts. And similarly, it might be said, in the case of arational actions; the agent desires pleasure, and the appropriate belief, ascribable in every case, is that acting in accordance with the occurrent desire to do whatever it is – tear up the photo, cover one's eyes, throw the tin opener out of the window – will yield this.

But the difficulty with extending Schiffer's account in this way is that the ascription of the relevant belief is plausible only with respect to the standard bodily appetites. It is indeed "almost always" true, as he says, that the bodily appetites, once aroused, are pleasurable to satisfy, which is why we talk of the pleasures of food and drink and sex, why we have the concept of *physical* pleasure, and why actions prompted by appetite can so often be described as done "for pleasure." The belief that we shall get physical pleasure from actions done

to satisfy such appetites may plausibly be ascribed to any one of us. But the ascription is either implausible or vacuous in other cases.

Suppose I am seized by a sudden desire to lick something furry, and do so because of that desire. Do I do so *in the belief* that doing so will yield me pleasure? A philosopher could indeed, parodying Thomas Nagel,[5] introduce the notion of a motivated belief; the description of an agent as doing something "because she wants to do it" simply entails that the agent believed that doing whatever it is would "give her pleasure." This "motivated belief" could then be ascribed to the person who licks something furry "because she wants to"; but in such a case the ascription is clearly vacuous. There are no grounds on which she could believe it will give her *physical* pleasure – quite the contrary, in fact. She does not necessarily believe she will enjoy it – indeed, if one were seized by such an odd desire, one might well act on it because one was curious to find out whether doing so was enjoyable or not. The only "pleasure" the agent believes in is "the 'pleasure' of desire-satisfaction," and this is an entirely formal and empty concept of pleasure.

Now, the desires to perform arational actions (unlike the aroused bodily appetites but like the desire to lick something furry) are not generally known as being pleasurable to satisfy; on the contrary, we know of some of the cases that acting in accordance with the desires makes one feel terrible, and of others that acting in accordance with them is neither pleasant nor unpleasant. To ascribe to the agent of an arational action, in every case, the belief that satisfying this desire now will yield pleasure is hence, implausibly, to ascribe an absurd belief – one for which the agent has no grounds, and which she knows is probably false. Or it is the vacuous ascription of a "motivated" belief.

Actions prompted by odd physical cravings are, I claim, genuine examples of cases in which "one in no way values what one desires" and are thereby counter-examples to the standard account of intentional action, albeit so odd and rare that they might be dismissed as fringe cases. Arational actions, however, are not, in the same way, odd or rare; if they do indeed resist appropriate belief ascription, as I have maintained, then the standard account is shown to be fundamentally flawed.[6]

For not only do arational actions provide a large set of counterexamples, but they also, once their resistance to belief ascription is acknowledged, justify our looking with a skeptical eye at actions done in the grip of an emotion to which the full rational panoply of belief, desire, and "intention with which" is usually ascribed. It is generally said, for example, that, if someone flees in terror from a lion, she is doing so in order to get to safety and preserve herself from danger or death; she desires self-preservation and believes that flight is the best way in the circumstances to get it. And, it is said, if someone strikes a person with whom she is angry, or says cruel things to him, she does so in order to hurt, or even to punish him; once again, an appropriate desire-belief pair is ascribed.

Anyone who confidently holds the view that these ascriptions of reasons or "intention with which" must apply in such cases is committed to seeing a great disanalogy between them and cases such as feeling frightened of burglars, ghosts, or thunder and burrowing under the bed clothes (to safety?), feeling angry and kicking furniture (to hurt it?), and muttering imprecations under one's breath (for whose ears?), or to making them analogous by ascribing quite lunatic beliefs to the agent.

If there really is a great disanalogy, the account of the "rational" cases provides us with no clue about the account to be given of the arational ones, which must then seem utterly mysterious. Nor is the problem they present solved – not at least for anyone interested in giving a systematic account of action – by denying that arational actions are intentional. For they are clearly not unintentional, and to say they form a significant class of actions that are neither intentional nor unintentional is to admit that, within the standard account, they present a formidable problem.

If, on the other hand, they are accepted as analogous and the lunatic beliefs are ascribed, these will show up nowhere else in behavior, be sincerely and vigorously repudiated by the agent, and that agent's momentary acquisition of them will, in turn, be utterly mysterious.

A deep problem is found here by anyone who holds that whether or not an action is intentional or was done for a reason (because of a desire and a belief), whether or not an emotion was motivated by emotion e, and whether or not an agent believes that p

must be all-or-nothing matters. And this view is held by people in the grip of the false semantic theory according to which predicates such as 'intentional', 'for a reason', 'motivated by emotion e', and 'believes that p' have clearly determinate, necessary and sufficient satisfaction conditions. On this theory, an action must be intentional or not, done for a reason or not, motivated by an occurrent emotion or not; an agent must believe that p or not. And then we find these mysteries.

The new "solution" to this problem is to say that, if the world proves thus recalcitrant to our attempts to carve it up with our predicates, this shows that there is something wrong with the predicates and the concepts they express; that, under the pressure of the facts about human behavior, they "fragment" or "come apart." So "intentional" and "belief" (for example) must be abandoned, and replaced by more accurate concepts derived from neurophysiology.[7]

But suppose we abandoned this false semantic theory, and instead said the following. Actions done because one is in the grip of an emotion do not form discrete groups, but a range. In the grip of an emotion, we do some things quite involuntarily, such as sweating, trembling, and coloring up. These are things over which, as things are, I have no direct control at all. There are other doings over which I can exercise direct control but can also do involuntarily, without realizing that I am doing them. I can clench or unclench my fists at will, smile or frown, but these are also things I can easily do unawares. I may begin to do some things, e.g., scream or cry or run without realizing that I am doing so, and once started, find it easier to go on than to stop; here perhaps I may be said to refrain intentionally from stopping. Other actions I do intentionally because, in the grip of the emotion, I just want to do them, though I do not do them in the belief that there is anything good about them at all (arational actions). Then there are actions that I do, momentarily believing that there is something good about them, though, looking back, I may not be able to understand how I could have (some cases of *akrasia*); and finally there are actions I do for a reason, in order to do or achieve something I believe to be good or desirable. Although there are clear cases in each of these groups, some of the actions that are clearly done "because the agent is in the grip of an emotion" will have features in common with some two adjacent groups, and there will be nothing that does or could settle to which group it "really" belongs.

Fleeing in terror might well be a case in point. It may be, on occasion, that one has a reason for fleeing – that it will get one out of danger – and flees, but it still may be that one did not flee, on that occasion, in order to get out of danger. Perhaps, after all, it is simply the case that one of the desires we are seized by when seized by fear is the desire to run or hide – such a desire would have good survival value – and that sometimes we act on it as impulsively, and with as little thought, as we act on the desire to scream or jump for joy.

Now, if this is indeed how things are with us, what are the consequences for the roles of reason and emotion in action? Well, let us go back to the thought with which I started – the contrast between the supposed irrationality of striking inanimate objects in anger and the supposed rationality of striking animate ones. If what I have argued is correct, then both sides of this contrast may be false. It may be that neither is irrational nor rational, but rather that both are arational, in the sense of being done without reason.

Moreover, insofar as one can see the potential for rationality or irrationality in either, the ascription goes the other way. I have deliberately stayed away from the murky waters of the topic of *akrasia* or weakness of will, but it is, I take it, perfectly obvious, and consistent with all I have said, that on some occasions an arational action may be irrational in the standard akratic way, i.e., contrary to some practical judgment about the good or necessity of refraining from it. If I throw the only tin opener out of the window, I certainly shall not be able to open the tin and may have to go hungry to bed; if I wreak violence on someone else's valuable antique furniture, I violate her rights. So, assaulting inanimate objects in anger may be irrational in the sense of being akratic. But it is surely the case that assaulting animate ones is much more likely to be so. Reason may well have nothing to say against assaulting the inanimate, but the fact that the animate can be hurt and harmed always stands as a potential reason against assaulting them.

In highlighting this point, I do not mean to ally myself with those who see emotion as opposed, in some important sense, to reason (or Reason) or who think that the practical rationality manifested in moral action must be somehow independent of the desiderative faculty. On the contrary, I stand firmly on the Aristotelian side of the Aristotelian-Kantian debate. But those of us who follow Aristotle should not, I think, push our luck too far, and I want to conclude by showing how the existence of arational actions creates something in the way of a problem even for us.

·An important fact about human beings, stressed in neo-Aristotelian virtue-based ethics, is that we are creatures such that our appetites and passions may prompt us where reason would also have lead. In this fact lies the sense in which we are "constituted by nature to receive the virtues,"[8] the possibility of harmony between our desiderative and rational faculties, of the virtuous person's grasp of "truth in agreement with right desire" (*ibid.*, 1139 a31). Aristotle maintains, (and Dennis Stampe[9] has recently reiterated) that desire is for the seeming (or apparent) good (or pleasant); when what seems good in the faculty of desire is truly good, then the desire is right, and the true judgment of reason about what is good will be in agreement with it.

Now, the apparent pleasures to which the bodily appetites prompt us may indeed be judged truly good and pleasant by reason. In relation to the bodily appetites, Watson rightly emphasizes the fact that we may "judge that to cease to have such appetites is to lose something of worth" (*op. cit.*, p. 213) and thereby both desire *and* value (some of) the actions to which the appetites prompt us. A human being *can* be seen "in his role as Rational Animal"[10] while eating, drinking, and making love (if it is in the right way, on the right occasions, and so on), odd as that may initially seem, not because he is, necessarily, acting "for a reason" of the standard sort, but because these are activities that can properly form part of a flourishing human life; reason may correctly judge that such actions are good and endorse them.

The same is true of most of the emotions. Reason may judge truly that to cease to have many of the emotions to which we are subject would be to lose something of worth, thereby conferring value on many of the actions to which they prompt us which it would endorse. Once again, a human being can be seen in her role as a rational animal when she flees the dangerous, honors the dead, repels aggressors, punishes wrongdoers, makes recompense for her own wrongdoing, cherishes her children, celebrates joyful occasions, and so on. Reason may correctly judge that such actions are good.

The only sense in which Reason and emotion are opposed, according to Aristotelian ethics, is that (except, perhaps, in people who have "natural virtue") the untrained passions tend to represent things as good and pleasant (or bad and unpleasant) which are not truly so. We have to be trained to fear dishonor more than death, to desire sexual intercourse as an expression of love within a lifelong partnership rather than as simply fun or the exercise of power, to be angered by injustice rather than deserved criticism. Unless they are properly trained, the passions will prompt us to action contrary to reason, or, even worse, corrupt our reason so that we judge things to be good and pleasant falsely. But, properly trained, most of them – it has been said, all[11] – will be in agreement with rational judgment.

But can the same be said about the arational actions to which our emotions prompt us? It seems to me that, by and large, it cannot, though we might make out a plausible case for some of the actions appropriate to a wave of affection or tenderness. Reason can find good in touching and caressing the people and animals one loves (in the right way on the right occasions, etc.); it forms and endorses loving bonds, is found innocently pleasurable, reassuring, or endearing by the recipients, may speak louder than words, especially to the pre- or nonlinguistic, and so on. Although we usually do not rumple our children's hair for these excellent reasons, we could. But I do not see how one could even begin to make out a case for finding any good in any of the others; they are arational not merely in the sense that one is prompted to them only by desire and not by reason (which is equally true of actions prompted solely by appetite) but further, in the sense that they cannot be *made* rational; reason cannot endorse them.

We might still think, however, that our lives would not, quite generally, be better if emotion never prompted us to act in these ways, or if we always resisted the prompting. We might well find something rather touching or endearing about people's performing many of the arational actions;[12] even the disturbingly violent ones seem to evoke some sort of bond of sympathy. When I have read this paper to discussion groups, I have found that the list of the examples at the beginning always provokes instant delighted recognition; everyone knows what it is like to act in some of these ways, and is somehow pleased to hear it acknowledged and described. Now, someone might maintain that this is just a case of the weak and fallible taking (improper) pleasure in having company. But to me it suggests that we value ourselves and each other as emotional creatures – not as *rational*-emotional in the way pinpointed by Aristotle, but as just plain emotional – and do not believe that the perfect human being would never act arationally.

The importance of this fact, if it is a fact, should not be overemphasized. It leaves general claims about the connections between human perfection, moral agency, and practical *rationality* intact, *if* it is remembered that we make these claims in the area where things are, as Aristotle says, not true of necessity but "for the most part."

Notes

1. So, for instance, Donald Davidson has said in lectures that 'She fled out of fear' (or 'because she was frightened') and 'She killed him out of hatred' are to be construed in terms of the actions' being caused by appropriate beliefs and desires.
2. "Explanations of action in terms of reasons work by revealing the favourable light in which the agent saw what he did (or at least what he attempted)" – John McDowell, "Reason and Action," *Philosophical Investigations*, V, 4 (October 1982): 301–5.
3. Gary Watson, "Free Agency," *Journal of Philosophy*, LXXII, 8 (April 24, 1975): 205–220.
4. Stephen Schiffer, "A Paradox of Desire," *American Philosophical Quarterly*, XIII, 3 (1976): 195–203.
5. Thomas Nagel, *The Possibility of Altruism* (Oxford: Clarendon Press, 1970), pp. 29–30.
6. I am not, of course, unaware of further variations on the appropriate belief which might be tried, but only space prevents me from showing that they fail, too. The belief that in performing the arational action one will

eliminate discomfort or agitation (rather than achieve actual pleasure) does not turn the trick; nor does the fascinatingly symbolic nature of many of the examples of arational actions yield anything helpful, as many people are initially tempted to suppose.

7. Cf. Patricia and Paul Churchland's and Stephen Stich's writings, *passim;* e.g., Patricia Churchland, *Neurophilosophy: Toward a Unified Science of the Mind/Brain* (Cambridge, MA: MIT, 1986), p. 382.

8. *Nicomachean Ethics*, 1103 a24–6.

9. Dennis Stampe, "The Authority of Desire," *Philosophical Review*, XCVI, 3 (1987): 335–81.

10. Davidson, "Actions, Reasons, and Causes," Chapter 19 in this volume.

11. In "Aristotle's Doctrine of the Mean," *American Philosophical Quarterly*, X (1973): 223–30, J. O. Urmson maintained that, according to Aristotle, there is no emotion that one should never exhibit. In "Plato on the Emotions," *Proceedings of the Aristotelian Society*, Supplement, LVII, 1 (1984): 81–96, I argue, following Aquinas (*Sum. Theo.* 1a2ae Q24 a.4.), that, on the contrary, some passions may be bad in themselves, insofar as they involve an attachment to the truly bad or an aversion to the truly good, for example, envy and *accidie*. But the intrinsically bad emotions are few.

12. I owe this point to Gary Watson in discussion.

23

Agency, Reason, and the Good

Joseph Raz

One approach to the explanation of agency, with origins in the writings of Plato and Aristotle,[1] takes acting for a reason[2] to be the distinctive and central case of human[3] agency. Other forms of action are either irrelevant (e.g. 'as I fell I hit the vase and shattered it', 'my breathing got heavier') or to be explained by reference to the central case (e.g. 'I opened the door by mistake', 'I hurt him inadvertently'). Reason is then explained in part by invoking value: valuable aspects of the world constitute reasons.[4] This approach, the classical approach, it may be called, can be characterized as holding that the central type of human action is intentional action; that intentional action is action for a reason; and that reasons are facts in virtue of which those actions are good in some respect and to some degree.[5]

This way of understanding the connection between action, reason, and value has been challenged by various writers.[6] Suppose for example that in a fit of rage at my unfaithful husband I gouge out his eyes in his photograph (which I find while going through his wallet) and then tear it up. I did that because I was mad at him, but I do not claim that the action was good or wise, or even permissible. I agree that I should never have touched his property, and that the whole thing was foolish if not worse. Nor do I claim that I had a reason for doing what I did. I did it because

I was mad at him, but not in order to accomplish anything (not even to hurt him – I did not for a moment believe that it would), nor in the belief that the action was a worthwhile or good action. Actions like this are not particularly rare and, it is claimed, they show the inadequacy of the classical approach. They are intentional, but neither done for a reason, nor seen by the agent as good.

I will examine this challenge in two stages. First, I will consider the possibility that reasons need not be connected to value in the way the classical approach alleges.[7] Then I will consider the case for denying the identification of intentional action with action for a reason.

1. Reason and the Good

(a) The Objection

Let me start with what I will take to be a common assumption. Generally speaking, humans have the capacity to act in light of an appreciation of their situation in the world. That capacity is primarily manifested in intentional actions: they are actions under the control of the agents who take them. They are undertaken because of what the agents believe about themselves, and the world around them, and that means that they are intelligible to their agents. So, typical intentional actions are actions about which their agents have a story to tell[8] (i.e. actions manifesting an internal

Raz, J. (2001), "Agency, Reason, and the Good," in *Engaging Reason* (Oxford: Oxford University Press), 22–45. Reprinted with permission of Oxford University Press.

viewpoint about what one is doing, or is about to do), a story which explains why one acted as one did. Moreover, and this point is crucial, the explanation makes intelligible not only why the action happened; it makes it intelligible as an action chosen, or otherwise undertaken, by the agent. It is a story which shows what about the situation or the action made it, the action, an intelligible object of choice for the agent, given who he is and how he saw things at the time.

I have put the point in as vague a way as I can for the task of explaining human agency is precisely the task of making sense of this common assumption. The classical approach is one route one can follow in attempting such an explanation. According to it the 'story' is of what the agents took to be facts which show the act to be good, and which therefore constitute a reason for its performance, making it eligible.

At this point the objector comes in. The classical approach, he contends, confuses the features which make an action an intelligible object of choice with what might make it a good action. True, what makes it good also makes its choice intelligible. But good-making features are just one kind of feature capable of explaining the eligibility of actions, that is their possible attraction for an agent. That an action will cure someone's illness makes it eligible because it makes it good. But that an action hurts another makes it an intelligible object of choice too, says the objector. Those who understand people understand that a desire to hurt, and to watch the other being hurt, exercises great appeal for many people. That an action is hurtful does not make it good, but it makes it intelligible by making its appeal to some agents intelligible. Another example: that one has a duty to perform an action is a reason to perform it, which also shows it to be good, at least in some respect. But that an action will violate one's duty, or that it will break all the norms, also makes it an intelligible object of choice. Again, we know that often people do what they do precisely because it is the wrong thing to do, because it is the anomic choice.

Once we draw a clear distinction between features which show an act to be an intelligible object of choice and ones which show it to be good or of value we will see, the objection continues, that reasons belong with the first, and not with the second. People will acknowledge, or brag, that they did something because it would hurt X, or because it was against all the rules. These are often their openly avowed reasons. And that is how it should be, for reasons are those considerations which make the act eligible from the point of view of the agent, and not necessarily those which make it good.

(b) Some Background

To deal with the objection, using the examples I have given, we need some initial simplifications and clarifications. First, the kind of case we are dealing with is often complicated by the presence of multiple reasons and motives, ambiguities in their interpretations, and by occurrences of self-deception and rationalization. We will just assume that our examples are not infected by any of these.

Second, sometimes people act to hurt others, etc. because they mistakenly believe in what they take to be values, for example, they may believe that women whose husbands betrayed them should kill their children and commit suicide. Such women are acting for what they regard as good reasons, reasons, that is, which make their actions the best or the right actions in the circumstances.[9] While many such actions are bad and wrong, and some even monstrously bad, they are not counter-examples to the classical approach, for in the eyes of their agents they are good. The objection relies on cases where agents intentionally do what they take to be bad because, as they see it, it is bad.

Third, reference to mistaken beliefs in reasons serves to remind us that while, according to the classical approach, reasons are facts which endow an action with some good-making properties, when we explain actions by the reasons for which they were undertaken the focus is on the agents' beliefs that they had such and such reasons, beliefs which may be false. In explanatory contexts we sometimes refer to such beliefs themselves as reasons, and we always do so when we take those beliefs to be false, that is, when we think that (in the primary sense of the term) the agents had no reason for their actions. Even then their actions are susceptible of explanation by reasons, which here means by their beliefs in reasons. I will leave it to the context to clarify whether reference to reasons is really to reasons or to belief in them.

Finally, it may be objected that the alleged counter-examples above fail because they are incomplete. That

an action will hurt another is no reason for performing it for if it were then everyone would have such a
reason, and those who did not act for them would be
irrational. That is absurd, and therefore the examples
fail to embarrass the classical approach. How is this
response to be squared with the fact that some people
will openly admit that they did what they did solely
because they knew that it would hurt someone? The
argument is that this states only part of their reason.
They also believed that their victims deserved to be
hurt, or that they had a duty to hurt them. Once the
missing component of their reason is added the case is
seen to be clearly consistent with the classical
approach.

There is no doubt that this analysis is true of some
cases, but it need not be true of all. The objection to
the classical approach is based on the possibility of
cases in which agents would deny any thought that
what they did was right. They acted to hurt others and
never thought that what they were doing was other
than bad or wrong. This, one may reply, still leaves
their reasons incomplete and therefore incomprehensible. Surely, if asked 'Why did you do what you did?'
they will say 'Because we wanted to hurt'. Their
desires are their reasons, and that an act will satisfy
one's desire makes it *pro tanto* good. This reply is, however, not available for defenders of the classical
approach, for they deny that agents' desires are (some
special cases apart) reasons for their actions at all, let
alone that they are good-making reasons.[10] Moreover,
the classical approach allows that in any given situation people may well be confronted with quite a
number of incommensurate options, so that there is
no reason to expect every rational agent in a similar
situation to choose the same. This is as true when the
options are entirely benevolent (going to the theatre,
collecting for a charity, working out, etc.) as when
they are hurting others, acting immorally, etc.

(c) Refuting the Objection

With these clarifications let us turn to an examination
of the objection. It is aimed at the classical approach,
while accepting the common assumption, that is, the
assumption that reasons make actions eligible by
making their choice intelligible from the point of view
of their agents. The objection is, therefore, committed

to the availability of an explanation of how it is that
non-good-making qualities make an action eligible. I
find it difficult to imagine such an explanation. For
example, suppose one were to say that the intelligibility
of certain reasons lies simply in the fact that we know
(or believe) that human beings are often motivated by
them. We know that people are often motivated to
hurt, whereas they are not commonly motivated to
swallow pieces of paper. Therefore, we find it intelligible that people act to hurt, and strange if they swallow
pieces of paper (for no further reason).

But this explanation misses the point of the common assumption. Naturally, when we know that a
certain pattern of conduct is common we are not
surprised when it happens. That does not make it
intelligible, except in that we assume that, if it is
intentional, then it is intelligible to the agents. They
have reasons, we assume, even though we do not
know what they are, nor are we interested in finding
out. Contrariwise, if the conduct is rare it may be
more difficult for us to imagine what reasons the
agents had for their conduct, but the rarity of the conduct is no proof that it is unintelligible, irrational –
not even proof that the agents' action is based on false
beliefs in reasons.

It is not surprising that applying the distinction
between different kinds of explanations, those giving
the agents' reasons and those which are from 'outside',
from an 'external point of view', is not always easy in
practice. Our interest in explanations is of many kinds,
and when we provide an explanation we often try to
cater for a demand whose nature is not always
perspicuous, or one which may be ambiguous in
nature. This is true even when it is our own interest or
curiosity that the explanation is meant to satisfy.
Consequently explanations themselves are often
ambiguous, and multipurpose. Besides, sometimes the
very divide between reason-based and other explanations is rather thin. Pleasure provides the clearest
example. We know that many people prefer sweet
food, and if we plan marketing, investing, etc. that is all
we need to know. But we understand why a person
prefers sweet food from that person's point of view
only if we discover, for example, that sweet food gives
them pleasure, that they enjoy such food. That taste is,
as I said, common. Suppose however that someone
claims to have pleasure in chewing paper. We will be

surprised, but once we are convinced that the claim is truthful we will accept it. There is no accounting for taste, we will say.[11] Here, as with pure pleasures of the senses generally, there is not much rational depth to the reason. We cannot ask for further and further rational explanations (as we can when someone does something because it is only just to do so, for example). It is merely a matter of one's physical constitution. But that should not disguise the difference between 'many people prefer sweet food' and 'many people enjoy eating sweet food'.

The difficulty in explaining the eligibility of actions in ways other than by reference to good-making qualities may make one doubt the objection. But is it just failure of imagination which makes the classical approach seem the only coherent account to have? I do not think so. The problem is of finding conceptual room for an alternative. Suppose we concede the objection and allow that one has reason to hurt others. It would seem to follow that those who do not hurt others, or who deny that the fact that an action would hurt others is in and of itself a reason to perform it, are irrational, or at least imperfectly rational, for they fail to acknowledge such reasons. If cogent this argument constitutes a refutation of the objection, its *reductio ad absurdum*. The refutation cannot be avoided by claiming that bad-making properties are permissive reasons. They are not, and it is wrong to follow them. The objector may try to avoid the *reductio* by pointing out that it presupposes what he denies, that is it presupposes that reasons not only render actions eligible for choice by the agent, but that they also *pro tanto* justify them. According to the objector everyone may find hurting people attractive just as everyone may find bananas tasty. It does not follow that doing what is attractive is justified.

But does this way of explaining reasons independently of value preserve the normativity of reasons? Does it account for the fact that defying reasons is irrational, that one may disregard a reason only to follow a more stringent one? The problem is not in the reality of the example the objector produces in support. The problem is in providing a coherent account of reasons, which allows for agents (*a*) believing that possession of properties other than good-making properties can provide reasons for actions, and (*b*) allows for the normative force of reasons, i.e. for the fact that failure to conform to them is a fault.

The classical approach allows that a gap may open between what is good and what attracts agents. But it accounts for the gap by the fact that agents can make mistakes. Certain actions appear to them attractive because they appear to them to possess good-making properties, but in fact they do not possess them. The gap acquires a stronger, more troubling profile when the mistake is due to motivated irrationality, such as self-deception, or wishful thinking. The objection, on the other hand, fails to provide an account of the attractiveness of the reason-constituting properties which preserves their normativity.

(d) Are There Reasons which are Neutral in Value?

Yet the force of the counter-examples is still troubling, though they may well be suspected of overkill. Why, we may wonder, need one go for reasons which involve badness? If the argument is that reasons need not be related to the good the natural counter-examples would be cases where reasons are simply neutral regarding the good, cases where reasons are neither good nor bad. Yet such examples are much harder to come by. What could be such an example? That a person when at home closes the door to the room he is in because he feels queasy and uncomfortable being in an open rather than a closed room, or the other way round, that one opens the door because … Or suppose that, walking in the street, I hear people singing round the corner, and curiosity makes me deviate from my route to see what is going on. Entirely intelligible, but does it show that the action is good in any respect?

It seems fairly clear that such reasons do not make the action morally good, nor do they manifest any moral virtue in their agents. Nor do they realize any other important impersonal value (beauty?), nor manifest any non-moral virtue or skills of their agents. Does it mean that these reasons are not constituted by good-making properties? Some may say that there is just one other way in which they can be good: they can be good because they contribute to the well-being of their agents, that is to the overall success (or quality, or what not) of their lives. But then, conformity with the reasons in my examples does not contribute to the agents' well-being either.

I do not want to get hung up on the examples I used. If you disagree choose your own. Imagine, however, that the person who, when at home, closes the doors to the rooms he is in, would, were he not to do so, soon become absorbed in whatever he is doing and forget that the door remained open. His closing the door does not affect his well-being for it does not affect his life. Or think again of the person who makes a momentary detour to see who is singing round the corner. His life is not affected one way or another by his action, which he will completely forget a few minutes later, and which has no other consequences. Some people would insist that such actions do favourably affect the person's well-being. They merely do so to a minuscule degree, so that the difference they make escapes our notice. Well-being, however, is in part about how people feel about their life, and in part about the values of their actions. Factors which make no difference to either do not affect their well-being. I will accept therefore that there are cases of people acting for reasons which are morally neutral, contribute to no value, not even to the well-being of their agents, manifest no virtue, moral or other, and display no skill or accomplishment of any note.

Does not that disprove the classical approach? I do not think so. I do not believe that for an action to be of value, or to be good, it must possess a good-making property connecting it to big values, like justice or beauty, or well-being or any other value for which we have an abstract name. Small goods are small but good none the less, nor need they be trivial instances of big values. This is a conceptual point, about the nature of concepts of value, and of what is valuable. It is not, of course, to be tested entirely by its conformity to the meaning of the words 'value' or 'good', though they are relevant to the issue. The notion of value used here, and in many philosophical discussions of axiological issues, does duty for a whole range of English words and expressions: 'value', 'good', 'best', etc., are just some of them. Others include many (but not all) uses of 'important', 'worthy', 'significant', 'meaningful', 'useful', 'meritorious', 'attractive', 'estimable', 'a good thing to do', and others. The notion is meant to generalize over the concepts of the pleasurable, enjoyable, of beauty, etc. We learn its scope by example, and we fix its contours by understanding its function within an explanatory account.[12] Theories falling within the classical approach do so, and they are not to be faulted by the counter-examples, for those presuppose that small values must be instances of big values, a supposition the classical approach is of course committed to denying. It should be admitted that talk of value in the context of what I call 'small values' is an extension of the normal use of the term, and may mislead. But the cases involved are cases where we may well say that the person's action was a good one, or use some other related expression.

(e) The Objection to 'Small' Values

A possible objection to this 'small values' view runs as follows. The small values view loses the concept of value altogether. It collapses into the concept of a reason, and is no longer an independent concept which provides part of the explanation of the concept of a reason for action. So long as the notion of value is tied to what I loosely call big values we have a grasp of its meaning which is partly independent of the role of value in providing reasons for action. We know roughly how to argue about beauty, justice, freedom, well-being, and other values. The moment the essential link to big values is severed – the objection proceeds – we no longer have any way of understanding value except through the maxim that whatever constitutes a reason is of value. Value now is entirely dependent on reason and plays no independent explanatory role.

The objection is, however, unjustified. As it recognizes, all the concepts involved – intention, reason, rationality, intelligibility, and value – are interdependent. We cannot but explain one in terms of the others. This interdependence, far from being vicious, is the reason for our ability to explain each of them by means of the others. This ability is lost if one concept entirely depends on just one other. This is, according to the objection, what happens to the notion of 'being of value', if it is not to be understood as tied to what I called big values as well as to reasons. But the objection overlooks other contexts to which value is central, such as the contexts of justification and of evaluation, and thus it also overlooks the connection between value and rationality. To put the point briefly: values not only show how certain actions are intelligible but also how they are justified. It is central to the classical approach that the same concept is crucial both for intelligibility and to justification (and therefore also to evaluation). Of course, intelligibility and justification can come apart. Intelligibility depends, according to the common assumption, on how things looked to the agents at the time. Justification and evaluation depend on how things really were at the time, though they allow for different types or dimensions of evaluation which take greater or lesser account of the agents' subjective perspective.

According to the classical approach, the role of values in justification and evaluation allows us to check on any claim that some consideration is a reason because it makes an act an intelligible object of choice: if this is so then the same consideration must also show that the act is justified or at least that there is something to be said in its justification, something that in the absence of contrary considerations makes it justified. Justifications (at least some kinds of justifications) do not depend on the agents' perspective, and do not depend on the reasons for which agents actually acted. We have a (relatively) independent grasp of the notions of evaluation and justification, and therefore the objection fails.

(f) Anomic Tendencies

The argument so far has disposed of the objection to the classical approach in so far as it relies on the claim that features which make an action an intelligible object of choice need be neither good nor bad. This may seem to offer little comfort to the supporters of the classical approach for it fails to dispose of cases relying on the intelligibility of actions for reasons which the agents acknowledge not to justify the actions (special circumstances always excluded). Hence, the challenge to the classical approach is not yet answered. When people take what they believe to be bad-making features to be their reasons I will say that they act for anomic reasons.

Some may be tempted to deny the possibility and intelligibility of action for anomic reasons. We can understand people saying 'I am doing this because it is bad', if what they mean is 'because it is conventionally taken to be bad', or if another reinterpretation is available. Otherwise we must judge them to be conceptually confused. Literally speaking, they say nothing in

uttering the sentence 'I am doing this because it is bad', that is, they are totally incoherent. I do not, however, believe that such reinterpretations are always adequate to the phenomena. That is, I think that there are cases of action for a reason where the best description or explanation of what the agents did is that they took those actions because they believed them to be wrong or evil. True, the classical approach judges these ways of describing or explaining the agents' action to involve a degree of conceptual confusion and incoherence. But not all confusions render the thought totally empty, nor beyond all comprehension. Many people's beliefs include contradictions, and while the notion of believing in a contradiction is to a degree incoherent, it is nevertheless not devoid of all content. It provides the best description of many people's state of belief.

The objector to the classical approach does not, of course, regard anomic reasons as incoherent. Rather, he regards them as disproving the classical approach. But there is no reason to agree with him. The objector faces two difficulties. First, he has to explain why, if the classical approach is mistaken, if the possession of good-making characteristics is not the only thing which can constitute reasons, we do not have reasons which are neither good nor bad. It seems to follow that only what has value or disvalue can constitute a reason. Secondly, he has to provide an alternative explanation of what makes an action an intelligible object of choice. I am facing the proverbial saucer of mud, and proceed to eat it, moving my hands and mouth as I would normally do when eating. Something has gone wrong with me. In the absence of any good-making characteristic which I believe eating the mud possesses I will not be able to understand what I am doing. I will be more horrified at myself behaving in this way than other people will be. For to me this will signify that I have lost control over myself, that I am possessed by something which makes me act in ways I do not understand, ways which I disavow, protesting that it is not really me. The objector agrees with this description of the saucer-of-mud case. His task is to explain how it differs from cases in which agents have reasons which make their actions intelligible to themselves, but which are not conceived by them as good-making. This is where he fails. He has no explanation as to how reasons not conceived as good-making differ from the mud-eating example. He can neither identify what would count as such reasons (why not the fact that what is in the saucer is mud?), nor explain how they function as reasons, as factors rendering actions intelligible objects of choice.

These two difficulties are inter-related. Had the objector been able to answer the question about the intelligibility of actions he would have been able to produce examples of reasons where the factors which render actions intelligible are neither good nor bad. His failure to do so makes it possible to deal with anomic reasons as an anomalous, degenerate case.

What the objector promises, or at any rate what he must deliver to succeed, is a new account of normativity of reasons, independent of their relations to value. The objector should be able to specify what we have a non-value-dependent reason to do in a way which is free from any reference to values. All he delivers are anomic reasons, which are clearly not independent. They are generated from real reasons by inversion. There is no way of understanding them except as an inversion of values. That establishes that they are a degenerate case, an exception which proves the rule, rather than an objection to it. They are non-reasons (that is, facts which are of the wrong kind to be reasons) which through some corruption of a psychological process are taken for reasons. As an anomaly we can understand anomic reasons and their allure, to the extent that any incoherent thought can be understood. We know what they are, how to identify them: by inversion of true reasons. And we know how to explain their allure, by the appeal of contrariness.

The appeal of contrariness is an established psychological phenomenon.[13] Not being psychologists it does not fall to us to explain it. Its existence is well attested in a wide range of otherwise very different types of cases. Nor is it either good or bad in itself. Much creativity arises out of contrariness. Knowing of its existence we should have predicted the existence of anomic reasons even before we came across them. The only doubt might have been whether conceptual constraint set a limit to the possibility of contrariness. But we know from other cases that it does not. Contrariness quite often leads to nonsense. Had nonsense been totally beyond comprehension, anomic reasons would have been impossible, there would have been no content to them; but it is not. As

I have just remarked, sometimes the best description and explanation of people's beliefs and actions involve conceptual confusions. That is what makes anomic reasons possible, and what enables us to understand them up to a point. Anomic reasons are possible, and we can understand them, only because they are a degenerate case of the normal. They vindicate rather than challenge the classical approach.

But does contrariness explain in the right way how the bad can be appealing, that is, how it renders actions an intelligible object of choice for certain agents? If it does not, if it merely provides an explanation from 'outside', it fails to explain anomic reasons. The answer is yes and no. The classical approach denies that anomic reasons are really reasons. They are a perversion of reasons. They are non-reasons masquerading as reasons. Therefore, there is no call to extend the notion of the normative, and explain how possession of non-good-making characteristics can be a reason. What is needed is an explanation of how they can masquerade as reasons, that is, an explanation of what attraction they can hold for agents who take them to be bad. Contrariness delivers that explanation, or rather a full phenomenological description of it would. It can do that because it works by inversion. It takes some elements of the norm and ascribes them to the opposite of the norm. Of course, when it transgresses conceptual constraints our ability to understand the process is limited. In those cases it descends into incoherence. What we expect is that the phenomena will reveal the same impenetrability, the same resistance to complete understanding. Anomic reasons, the claim is, do just that. We can understand them only so far, but not completely.

The fact that contrariness is a general and structural psychological tendency, working by inversion, means that it is capable of generating forms of behaviour providing apparent counter-examples to any norm. Had the classical approach been misguided, had the true explanation been different, contrariness would have generated not anomic reasons, but some other reasons being apparent counter-examples to the true approach. In other words, whatever the nature of reasons, we would expect contrariness to produce degenerate cases of non-reasons masquerading as reasons. Reasons generated by contrariness are not counter-examples for accounts which are psychologically acute and sensitive. These accounts allow that, given that human beings are capable of self-understanding, their conduct can be influenced by knowledge of explanations of human conduct, influences leading to a whole range of deviations, of which action for anomic reasons is just an example. This means that explanations consist of explaining the standard case and some of the possible ways in which deviations can be generated.

(g) A Moderate Objection: On Degrees of Intelligibility

At this point a moderate objector may break rank with the others to deny that my argument against the objection affects him. He does not wish to extend the normative beyond its dependence on good-making qualities. He agrees that actions for anomic reasons are irrational. But they are actions for real reasons. My suggestion that these are non-reasons masquerading as reasons is not credible. Nor are actions for anomic reasons that exceptional. They are just one type of irrational action, similar in many respects to akratic actions. That is why I am wrong in thinking that the classical approach can absorb their existence unmodified, taking them to be a degenerate case of the norm.

On one point the moderate objector and I agree, namely that actions for anomic reasons are irrational, and therefore exceptional. They are, however, a good deal more exceptional than typical akratic actions. I say, 'typical akratic actions' for what kinds of psychologically deviant actions should count as akratic, or as displaying weakness of the will, is of course a controversial matter. Typical akratic actions are actions for ordinary reasons: smoking because one enjoys it or to avoid the unpleasant sensations and feelings induced by nicotine deprivation, being disloyal to a friend because doing so advances one's career or job prospects, etc. What makes them akratic is that the agents judge them to be wrong or unwise. They act against their better judgement. Moreover, given that they are irrational they are not entirely open to explanation by reason. We can understand why the action was done for it was done for a reason which we can understand. But we also cannot understand why it was done, cannot understand it from the inside. For the agents themselves say that they knew

they should not have done it, and there was nothing to prevent them from following their judgement. So why did they do it after all? Akratic agents are themselves in the same situation. They understand their akratic actions in the sense that they know what attracted them, and they felt the force of the attraction. But on the other hand, they do not understand why they acted as they did, in spite of the fact that they thought that they should not. They do not understand why it is so difficult for them to resist the temptations, or the fears, or whatever it is that makes them act against their better judgement.[14]

Akratic actions fit the classical approach. The reasons for them are ordinary reasons, and their irrationality, being an irrationality, should not be eliminated by an alternative account which makes it more intelligible and rational than it is. Action for anomic reasons is not akratic, for the agents may not display the internal conflict typical of akrasia. They may be entirely happy acting as they do. It is also more anomalous than akrasia for it is intentional action for a pseudo reason, rather than for a real reason (that is, for a fact which renders the action, in the eye of the agent, bad – at least to a degree – rather than good). But, given that both akratic actions and actions for anomic reasons can be accommodated by the classical approach, the moderate objector's claim that they require a modification to it remains unproven.

2. Expressive Action

(a) Reason and Expression in Action

Was the example with which I introduced this chapter, in which I find a photograph of my husband and in a rage gouge out his eyes, a case of action for anomic reasons? It is not detailed enough to tell. It might have been, or it may be a case of akratic action. It is clear, however, that not all its features which seem at odds with the classical approach have yet been explained. It requires an examination of the second challenge to the classical approach: allowing that reasons are facts which show the act to be good in some respect and to some degree, that is allowing that reasons are essentially related to the good in this way, the second challenge denies that all intentional actions are actions for reasons.

Various reasons prompt people to doubt the thesis that to act intentionally is to act for a reason. Some actions are too spontaneous or their effects too negligible to count as actions for a reason. For example, what is my reason when I instinctively move my arm across my face when becoming aware of a fly hovering above my nose, or turn my head to the left when becoming aware of something moving on my left? Some actions are part of a whole sequence of actions where there may be a reason for undertaking the sequence but not for a particular step in it. What is my reason when I put one foot in front of the other in the course of getting out of the room?

I will not discuss these objections here.[15] They seem to be based on a misguided notion of what it is to act for a reason (parallel to the denial of small values we discussed above), leading to the conclusion that one acts for a reason only when one's action is preceded by deliberation about what to do. They also misunderstand the role of routines (such as moving one's leg to walk, or following a familiar route across town when returning home from work). While routines require the finessing of reason-based explanations, they also require, for the same reasons, finessing our understanding of intentional action. The case I wish to examine is of expressive action, that is action which is intentional at least in part because – it would seem – it is expressive, not because it is undertaken for a reason. The most persuasive example of this kind of action may well be the simplest: in the course of a conversation I suddenly get annoyed by something said, or by a recollection, and I bang the table in exasperation, for example. But before I examine such cases a few general observations about reason and expression in action.

We can start by picking up where the previous section left off, for a word of explanation arising out of that discussion may connect the two parts of my argument. I emphasized that in as much as intentional actions are actions for reasons they are intelligible, that is, they can be understood from within, their agents and others can understand what, in the eyes of the agents, made the actions eligible. Naturally not all aspects of people's actions are intelligible in that way. When I drive a car I do not have a reason to corrode

its tyres, nor do I have a reason for the precise posture in which I sit in the car. The wearing out of my tyres and my body posture are both side-effects of my driving. Why does the fact that many aspects of our actions are not susceptible to reason-based explanations, that they are not intelligible in the way aspects of actions which are reason-based are, why does that not undermine the relevance and importance of reasons for the understanding of agency? Furthermore, many actions are not intentional, and thus they too cannot be explained by reasons (at least not by reasons alone). I do things by mistake, or accidentally, or inadvertently, and so on. Does that not show that the emphasis on the internal perspective, on the intelligibility of the action as an object of choice, is misguided? And if reasons are as central as the classical approach suggests, why do we not consider these actions as irrational as we do akratic actions, actions for anomic reasons, and others?

These matters require much more detailed analysis than they can receive here. In principle, however, the answers are not far to seek. In many of these cases we do not mean to control certain aspects of our actions, we just let the body, or the environment, take care of itself. This 'not meaning' may be reasoned ('I cannot significantly affect the rate of erosion of my tyres', 'I will be even less comfortable if I try to sit in a posture of my choice, than if I let my body determine my posture') or not. Cases of action other than intentional ones are mostly either the bringing about of further consequences by intentional actions (in which case they are further aspects of the intentional action we did not mean to control) or they are cases of failure in an intentional action (or both). But these failures (as in action by mistake, inadvertent action, etc.) are not failures of rationality, but of execution. Being unintended failures[16] they cannot be explained from the inside, even though an external explanation is often easy to find.

These observations leave one important class of case: intentional action undertaken in the belief that the reasons against the action (or for some incompatible alternative to it) are not worse than the reasons for it.[17] In these cases one understands (or thinks one does) what renders the action eligible. But one also understands (or believes one understands) that incompatible alternatives are also eligible, and not inferior to this action. It follows that one cannot understand from the inside one's preference for this particular action. So far as reasons can enlighten one, one might just as well have chosen one of the other options. These cases, however, are not irrational for one is not defying reason. Reason, so to speak, has exhausted itself. One cannot explain one's choice from the inside for there is no inside story to tell on that point. (I can explain why I chose to drink spirits rather than wine, but not why the Macallan rather than the Balvenie – though sometimes I can do that too. Sometimes I may well have reason to choose one rather than the other.) Some people find this puzzling and in need of explanation. But it is just a fact of life. We can explain how it is possible that reason will not determine all aspects of one's choices (it would have been very surprising if it could), and explain which aspects it fails to determine in a particular situation and why. Beyond that it is just a fact that when there is no internal story to have we have none.

The fact that so many aspects of actions are not explained by the agents' reasons makes it possible for them to express people's character, their personality traits, and tastes.[18] This statement suggests a greater bifurcation between reason and expression than is the case. In acting rationally we express our rational nature. Much more, however, is expressed by the manner of our actions (willing or grudging, eager or hesitant), by involuntary aspects of conduct (posture expressing confidence, for example), or by choices among options where reason does not indicate that any of them is better than all the others (which may show taste for adventure, sense of fun, physical exuberance, and much more).

(b) Purely Expressive Intentional Actions: The Relevance of Control

When we have an interest in our own actions or those of others, it may be both in the reasons for which the actions were done, and in the way they express the agents' personality. In many cases one or the other interest dominates. But in all cases, according to the classical approach, it is people's responsiveness to reason which accounts for their ability to act intentionally. Moreover, to identify people's intentions one needs to identify their reasons. They fix the intentions.

What the action expresses may dominate our interest in it, but it does not determine the intention with which it is done.

This is doubted by the second objection to the classical approach. According to it actions can be intentional in virtue (in part at least) of being expressive, and not merely because they are undertaken for reasons. The clearest evidence to start the argument will be cases of actions which are intentional even though they are not undertaken for reasons, cases of purely expressive intentional actions. My kicking or banging the table in frustration is an example of such cases. The actions in question typically express emotions, feelings, and moods. If they express character or personality they do so through expressing emotions, etc.

I call such actions purely expressive to distinguish them from actions undertaken in order to express something. Some expressive actions are communicative actions: since it is the anniversary of the revolution I fly a flag on top of my house. Or, I turn my back on a person, to express my disapproval of his conduct. I fly the flag, and turn my back, to communicate to others that I mean to express whatever it is I mean to express. But expressive action may be undertaken for reasons not involving a communicative intention. Seeing me teeming with anger you may say to me (they do so in films) 'Why do you not smash some crockery?' and in order to relieve my tension I do just that. My examples are different. They are cases in which people just act, or if you like, they just act out their frustration, or anger, or joy, and so on. They do not do what they do in order to express their emotions. They just act and their actions express their emotions.

This distinction is real enough, and it is the basis of the claim that purely expressive actions are not done for reasons. Yet they are intentional actions. Their intentionality can be established by the fact that they are under the control of their agents, control that is manifested in two crucial respects. First, the initiation of the action is up to the agent, and second, the execution of the action is also under the agent's control. Let me take the second point first. A mother hits her child in exasperated rage. Her arms hit the child: their movements could be as well directed and controlled in strength as they would be were she acting for an ordinary reason, for example, giving a demonstration.

Expressive actions need not be marked by any lessening in control over the manner of their execution. They can display as much skill and dexterity as any action.

Similarly, turning to the first point, their initiation and continuation is under the agents' control. People who smash an object in anger usually choose one which is not very expensive. If they choose one which is very expensive this is deliberate, it is understood to show the strength of their feeling. Strong reasons to desist coming to mind at the last minute will typically cause one to desist, and so on. I describe control over the initiation partly as ability to stop it or to avoid it. But that does not equate such acts with semi-voluntary acts like breathing, which count as our acts at all only in a marginal sense, and only because of a limited ability to suppress them, or control their manner (fast breathing, etc.). The body's autonomous system initiates breathing. All we can do is exercise a limited degree of control. There is nothing comparable with purely expressive acts. If they happen they do because we choose them. But we are reluctant to describe it like that because that makes them more like actions for reasons than they are. They are more spontaneous. They explode within us, we feel. That is why it is easier to concede that we can suppress them than that we initiated them, chose them. But we did, or else they would not be intentional.

But while control is necessary to intentional action it is not sufficient. To show that an act is intentional it is not enough to show that its initiation and conduct are under the agents' control. They also must have a story to tell about it, a story which makes its performance intelligible. It explains why they exercised their control to perform it, rather than to avoid it. That is where the expressive aspect of the action comes in and provides the missing element which in other actions is filled by the reason for which the action was performed.

This, then, is the challenge to the classical approach's claim that intentional actions are actions for reasons. Pure expressive actions express emotions, feelings, or moods but are not done in order to express them, nor for any other reason. In spite of this they are intentional for they are under the control of their agents. This challenge is stronger than the challenge based on anomic reasons, for it contains the germ of an alternative account of intentionality based on control and expressiveness. Still, even this challenge is not without weaknesses. We expose them when examining the connection between control and reason. To be convinced of the strength of the challenge we need to be convinced that acting for a reason and being in control of the action, while clearly different concepts, are not inter-related in application. The reason why this is a potential weak point is that while we feel that there is some awkwardness in describing purely expressive actions as actions for reasons, we also suspect that they involve some loss of control.

I conceded that there is no respect with regard to which purely expressive actions necessarily involve loss of control. Yet they typically involve some loss of control. We expect people expressing emotions by throwing the crockery at the door or at a person, or a picture, to be less successful in finding their target than the same people would normally be. We expect people kicking the table to miss the table's leg more often than they normally would. We also expect such people to be less good in judging the prudent degree of force to apply, and are not surprised when often they hurt themselves (physically) more than they expected the action to hurt them, or cause more damage than they expected to cause. Could it be that while there is no necessary loss of control in any specific respect, a purely expressive action must involve some loss of control somewhere?

First, note that many aspects of purely expressive actions are not merely subject to their agents' control, but are also governed by reason. Even if the mother hitting the child does not do so for a reason, the action merely giving vent to her frustration, and even if people throwing crockery at others with whom they quarrel do so just in anger, and not for any reason, they aim at the child or at the people with whom they quarrel *because* they are the appropriate target for their expressive action. What counts as expressive action is in part a matter of cultural convention. In some cultures you can express contempt for a person by spitting in their direction. In other cultures this would not express anything. Is it surprising that only where it is recognized culturally as expressive do people express themselves through such actions? Purely expressive actions are not merely under our control, they are also under our guidance and we guide them to be what they are, that is, to be purely expressive, and to do no more, not to cause too much hurt to ourselves or to others, not to make us look ridiculous, etc. Even if we do not undertake them for a reason, we are guided by reasons when we engage in them. Given that in so many respects purely expressive actions are guided by reasons, why do we feel that there is something odd in taking them to be actions for a reason?

Possibly the answer, and with it the key to the explanation of purely expressive actions, is that they involve a small loss of control, and that is why they are not typical examples of actions for a reason. This brings me back to the question left hanging in the paragraph before last: do purely expressive actions necessarily involve loss of control? The answer, I am afraid, is yet again both yes and no. First the yes: I think that it is not just that some diminished control over the execution of purely expressive action is typical. I suspect that it is necessary. Purely expressive actions are non-identical twins of actions for a purely expressive reason, that is actions one undertakes when the emotion swells within, and one says to oneself, 'Why should I not let rip? It will do me good', or 'I am entitled to', or something like that. That is, when the action is just a tiny bit more calculated it is an ordinary action for a reason, albeit a purely expressive one. The hesitation in saying that purely expressive actions are identical with their twins is that they explode from within without this element of calculation. But that explosion is a matter of diminished control over the initiation of the action.

The diminished control I identified is not located where I looked for it above. There the question was whether there is some diminution in agents' control over the manner and skill involved in purely expressive acts. My tentative answer is that in principle no such diminution is required, but that in practice it will be difficult to convince anyone, including the agents themselves, that an action which is perfectly controlled in manner and execution is not under perfect control at the point of initiation, and is therefore purely expressive. Since conceptual boundaries in such matters cannot be sharp, it may be too sharp, too definitive, to say that purely expressive actions need involve diminished control only over their initiation, but not over their manner and skill in

execution. But they certainly involve the first kind of diminished control.

(c) Do Purely Intentional Actions Refute the Classical Approach?

Why then did I answer no as well as yes? For one thing, I had to. If purely expressive actions are actions over the initiation of which we have no control they are not intentional actions.[19] They will be more like breathing, that is, semi-voluntary actions, in virtue of our limited control over their execution. I need not deny that there are expressive actions which fit the bill. There are times when we lose control over ourselves altogether. We are subject to irresistible impulses which we cannot control, or something like that. There is no need to consider such cases here. They are the sort of exceptional cases which do not require a revision in the classical approach, nor in any other approach, but exist as (one hopes) exceptional breakdowns of human agency, rather than as examples of it. The challenge that purely expressive actions pose to the classical approach is that they are supposed to be ordinary intentional actions, and yet not actions for reasons. If they are ordinary intentional actions they are actions the initiation of which is controlled by their agents. The examples of purely expressive actions used throughout this chapter are not cases of total loss of control over the initiation of the action (I will not throw the vase in rage if I realize at the last minute that it is a very expensive one, etc.), and are meant to be ordinary intentional actions.

There is another way of seeing why the thought that agents do not control the initiation of purely expressive actions of the kind our examples illustrate is incorrect. In all these examples the agents do not disapprove of their actions. Of course, one can regret having kicked the table, as one can regret any other action one may have performed. But at the time of action the agents are not conflicted. Their actions are not akratic for they do not believe that they should not perform them. No doubt there can be purely expressive actions which are akratic as well, but that is not part of their nature. So let us confine our attention to those which are not akratic, to normal purely expressive actions. People who perform them are as happy with the fact that they performed them as with any other normal intentional actions.[20]

This last point seems to me to provide a clue to an explanation of purely expressive actions. It suggests that people who perform normal, purely expressive actions have, in the terms of the common assumption with which we started, a story to tell about their performance. They know why they did what they did. They are, at the time of action, content to have done as they did. Moreover, their explanations as to why they acted as they did are based on the same direct, non-evidential knowledge as we have of our reasons, intentions, decisions, and their like. Finally, their explanations invoke considerations which are in fact reasons for actions, and which could have been their reasons. For example, they may say that they acted out of rage, adding, or more commonly implying, that the action was an appropriate expression of rage. Typically such explanations invoke motives rather than reasons, but they state facts (that I was enraged and the action was an appropriate expression of my rage) which are also reasons for the actions thus explained.

In all, purely expressive actions are almost like actions for reasons. They differ in that while they do not involve loss of control over their initiation they involve diminution of that control (that is the Yes side of the answer, which was explained above). This makes it somewhat awkward to say that they are actions for reasons. It makes them differ slightly from their non-identical twins, in which the factors invoked by agents to explain their actions actually serve as reasons for those actions. The difference between the twins is in a slight loss of control in the purely expressive twin. But their similarity is so great that in spite of the difference the purely expressive actions are actions with a story from the point of view of the agent, a story which can serve as a reason – it merely did not function as a reason. Can we describe how it did function in a way which will bring out both the similarity and the difference between the twins? My suggestion is that we can think of people who perform normal purely expressive actions as people who let themselves express their emotions, feelings, or moods in action. They permit themselves to do so. They allow their emotions, feelings, or moods to express themselves in action, rather than taking an action in order to express their emotions. It is as if their will is less active (less in

control) than in ordinary actions for reasons. Normally, we will the actions because of, what we take to be, the reasons for them. When we act for an expressive reason we take the fact of our emotion to be (part of) a reason for an action appropriate for its expression in the circumstances. In the case of purely expressive actions we merely allow the emotion to express itself, the will acting as a non-interfering gate-keeper.

These metaphors show, I hope, how subtle and thin is the difference between the twins. Does it justify regarding purely expressive action as an objection to the classical approach? I do not think so. In part the difference between such actions and normal actions for reasons is just too slight to make this case any more than a small modulation of the classical approach. But even this is to allow purely expressive actions the wrong role in the argument. The crucial point is that the very loss of control which makes them cases of letting oneself act for a reason rather than cases of acting for a reason also makes them somewhat less than typically intentional. This is where their use as an objection to the classical approach goes wrong. Control over the initiation of the action is an element in intentional action. When this control is absent the action is not intentional. When it is slightly impaired, and it is no more than that in our case, it is no longer a paradigmatic intentional action. Hence, the intentionality of actions and their character as actions for reasons go hand in hand, even if their alignment is not entirely tight.[21] This is what the classical approach maintains.

3. How Strong are These Arguments?

The argument of this chapter, and much of the argument of the book, aims at establishing essential features of some of the concepts which play a key role in our thought. If successful they achieve a dual goal: in as much as they provide an account of these concepts they contribute to an explanation of some central features of people's lives as rational agents. In as much as the concepts they explain are those we commonly use when thinking about ourselves and others as rational agents, they explain some central features of our self-understanding. They can succeed in one goal only if they succeed in both. Given that the understanding of people as rational agents which we seek is an understanding gained through the use of concepts which are pivotal to our thinking about ourselves, their analysis cannot contribute to the explanation of human beings as rational agents unless it contributes to the explanation of our self-understanding, and vice versa.

No claim is made here, however, that it is impossible to understand humans in any other way, through the use of other sets of interlocking concepts. Arguably a complete understanding of rational agents requires success in the dual task. That is, no explanation which is alien to people's self-understanding can adequately account for their character as rational agents. But it is also possible that in some cultures past or future, or in the past or future of our own culture, people's self-understanding may depend on the use of different sets of concepts. If so then the conclusions expounded here are not undermined. The truths which different sets of concepts enable us to grasp are consistent, or they would not be truths. But the explanations they provide are, on that assumption, incomplete. They have to be complemented by an account of those alternative ways of understanding people's rational nature. Cultural histories serve to remind us of this need. But so long as new ways of conceptualising ourselves may emerge in the future the task of explanation is inherently incomplete, incomplete not in having left undone something which can and needs to be done, but because changes in the ways persons conceive of themselves will require new explanations to enable us to understand them. Even if we succeed in stating the preconditions of any way of conceptualizing rational thought these preconditions will not be sufficient in themselves to explain all the puzzles to which their specific instantiations give rise. Claims of philosophical success are not to be seen as claims of philosophical finality. The ever open possibility of conceptual change is but one reason for the conclusion that the thought that the task of philosophical explanation can be discharged once and for all is illusory.[22]

Notes

Editors' note: some notes have been abbreviated or amended, with the author's permission.

1. So far as I know much of the interest in it in recent philosophical writings is due to Anscombe's *Intention* (Oxford: Blackwell, 1957).
2. Whenever I refer to reasons I will have reasons for action in mind. In fact the conclusions here advanced apply equally to all practical reasons (reasons for attitudes, emotions, etc.), that is to all reasons other than reasons for belief.
3. Where this way of identifying the kind of agency involved is not meant to imply that only human beings are capable of such actions (nor that all human beings are), but only to pick out the class of action as one which is typical of humans.
4. 'Reason', like 'father', is both a one-place and a two-place predicate: 'People's vulnerability', one may say, 'is a basic moral reason.' But if that is so it is because some relational application of the predicate is true (e.g. 'that people are vulnerable is a reason for us all to protect them from harm'). This example presents reasons as a relation between two facts: the fact that people are vulnerable is a reason for (the fact of) people protecting others from harm (to obtain). Alternatively, and more naturally in many contexts, we conceive of reasons as a relation between a fact which is the reason (when used as a one-place predicate), a (class of) person(s), and an action(-type). It is also possible to claim that all reasons are properties of the action for which they are reasons, i.e. properties which make it *pro tanto* good. Here 'reasons' is given a slightly different, though closely connected, sense. I doubt that much illumination can be derived from a careful study of the grammatical or logical form of reason-sentences.

   Note that in regarding facts as reasons (as explained here) one indicates that reasons are aspects of the world only in the sense that it is not a fact that so and so unless the world is such and such (e.g. unless a certain action was performed, or an event occurred, or unless some object has some property, etc.). In this way identifying reasons as facts is neutral regarding the ultimate 'ontological' character of reasons. I believe that events, acts, states, and more can be reasons, and that nothing much turns on that. [...]
5. The agents' belief that there is a reason for their action, or a specific belief of theirs in something which they take to be a reason can also be said to be a reason, in a slightly different sense which I will call an 'explanatory

reason'. An explanatory reason may exist even when there is no reason for the agents to do what they did (i.e. when they mistakenly believe that there is a reason for their action). Nor can a reason explain agents' behaviour unless they were aware of it (though not necessarily of the fact that it is a reason).

6. e.g. Rosalind Hursthouse, 'Arational Actions' Chapter 22 in this volume.

7. The challenge to be examined relates to the type of examples mentioned. I will not consider objections arising out of belief in the conceptual or other independence of deontic considerations, which can constitute reasons while not being related to the good, etc.

8. Or they are parts of sequences of action – getting up, walking to the left, stopping at the door, turning the handle, etc. – about which one has a story to tell.

9. In this chapter I do not deal with another objection to the classical approach, namely that right action (or that some categories of right action) has to be understood independently of the good, that deontic considerations are independent of considerations of value. I assume that whatever one must (or must not) do for deontic reasons is at least also good (or bad).

10. For my arguments to that effect see my *Engaging Reason* (Oxford, 2000), ch. 3. See also W. Quinn, 'Putting Rationality in its Place', in his *Morality and Action* (Cambridge: Cambridge University Press, 1993).

11. I am not suggesting that such claims cannot be empirically tested, nor that people cannot be wrong about what gives them pleasure. But that is another story.

12. In other words, the concept is not hostage to the linguistic accident of the existence or absence of an abstract noun naming one value or another.

13. Notice that I am not claiming that people who act for anomic reasons act in order to be contrary, if that means that the contrariness of their action is their reason for it. This too may sometimes happen, but it misses the point of actions for anomic reasons. It

represents them as undertaken for what are perceived to be good-making features (even though the perception is mistaken). Anomic agents perceive themselves as acting in pursuit of the bad, not the good. I invoke contrariness not as a reason, but as a psychological explanation of their action.

14. Complications and qualifications abound. Here are two. (1) Both the akratic agents, and others observing them, may have a different kind of understanding of the situation, an understanding consisting of familiarity: they may know what it feels like. They may even predict how they or others will react to the temptation. (2) Sometimes the irrationality of weak-willed actions is hidden from their agents by self-deception, or faulty reasoning. For example, people may say: 'Overall we should not have this cigarette, but it would be so good to have it, and there is nothing wrong in not doing what one should do overall once in a while.'

15. They are partially discussed in *Engaging Reason*, ch. 10.

16. Cases of unconscious intentions excluded.

17. Though not better either. Where they are believed to be better the action is akratic.

18. Needless to say, not all aspects of our actions which are not controlled by reason do that. Normally I express nothing when, in driving my car, I wear out its tyres.

19. Admittedly they can be borderline cases: even if their agents cannot control their initiation, to the extent that they control and guide their manner and execution, and especially if they can and do not terminate them, they possess characteristics of intentional actions and can be said to be more or less intentional.

20. Nor are they in fact irrational, at least not necessarily so, for there may be good reasons for the agents to act expressively, even if they did not act for these reasons.

21. This remark is meant to acknowledge that we feel more clearly that they are not typical actions for reasons than that they are not typical intentional actions.

22. [Raz further explores some aspects of this topic in his *From Normativity to Responsibility* (Oxford, 2012).]

24

Skepticism About Weakness of Will

Gary Watson

Two Kinds of Skepticism

Although it occurs with deplorable frequency, weakness of will has seemed to many philosophers hard to understand. The motivation of weak behavior[1] is generally familiar and intelligible enough: the desire to remain in bed, or the desire for another drink are ordinary examples. Nevertheless, our common ways of describing and explaining this phenomenon have been thought to involve serious difficulties. These descriptions and explanations can, upon reflection, seem incoherent.

Accordingly, weakness of will has given rise to various forms of skepticism. The most notorious form is socratism, which denies the possibility of such behavior. Another form of skepticism admits its possibility but casts doubt upon a complex of distinctions and moral attitudes involved in the common view. Briefly, it argues that no one who acts contrary to his or her better judgment does so freely, that weakness of will cannot be significantly distinguished from psychological compulsion,[2] and that therefore certain moral distinctions implicit in the common view cannot be justified.

My concern in this paper will be to explore and develop a version of nonsocratic skepticism. In my view, socratism is incorrect, but like Socrates, I think

that the common understanding of weakness of will raises serious problems. Contrary to socratism, it is possible for a person knowingly to act contrary to his or her better judgment. But this description does not exhaust the common view of weakness. Also implicit in this view is the belief that actions which are contrary to one's better judgment are free in the sense that the agent could have done otherwise. The grounds for skepticism about this belief will be my theme.[3]

To clear the way and to introduce some important distinctions, it will be helpful to begin with a discussion of socratic skepticism. Then I will set out what I take to be the crucial elements in the common account of weakness, and consider the apparent emptiness of that account as an explanatory model; it is said that one takes the drink *because* one's will is weak, for example, and this explanation is supposed to contrast with the compulsive case in which one takes the drink because one's desire is too strong. Finally, I will discuss and compare the merits of an alternative way of drawing the distinction between weakness and compulsion.

Socrates and Davidson

A brief look at Donald Davidson's essay, "How is Weakness of Will Possible?",[4] will help us to isolate the errors of socratism. His paper is worth considering because, among other reasons, it contains an excellent

Watson, G. (1977), "Skepticism about Weakness of Will," *Philosophical Review* 86 (3), 316–339. Copyright © 1977 Cornell University. All rights reserved. Republished by permission of the copyright holder and the present publisher, Duke University Press, www.dukeupress.edu.

Philosophy of Action: An Anthology, First Edition. Edited by Jonathan Dancy and Constantine Sandis.
© 2015 John Wiley & Sons, Inc. Published 2015 by John Wiley & Sons, Inc.

formulation of some principles which have caused much of the traditional philosophical trouble. Although I believe his own solution to have difficulties of its own, I wish rather to examine the way in which he generates the problem.

Davidson sees the problem of "incontinence" as arising from the apparent incompatibility between two principles which connect judgment, motivation, and action, and the belief that incontinence (possibly) exists. He characterizes incontinence in this way:

> In doing *x* an agent acts incontinently if and only if: (*a*) the agent does *x* intentionally; (*b*) the agent believes there is an alternate action *y* open to him; and (*c*) the agent judges that, all things considered, it would be better to do *y* than to do *x* (p. 94).

The principles with which the belief in the existence of incontinence is at odds are these:

P1. If an agent wants to do *x* more than he wants to do *y* and he believes himself free to do either *x* or *y*, then he will intentionally do *x* if he does either *x* or *y* intentionally.

P2. If an agent judges that it would be better to do *x* than to do *y*, then he wants to do *x* more than he wants to do *y* (p. 95).

As Davidson says, P1 connects "wanting" with "acting intentionally," whereas P2 connects "judging better" with "wanting." He insists that the tension cannot be alleviated by modifying these principles to make them both true and consistent with the belief in incontinence – not that P1 and P2 are crystal clear and unambiguous as they stand: but "the problem will survive new wording, refinement, and elimination of ambiguity" (p. 96).

Since Davidson accepts these principles and believes incontinence exists, he must deny that these principles logically conflict with this belief. The main burden of his paper is to show how we may accept them and still maintain weakness to be possible. The first point to notice, then, is that with the appropriate addition of the phrase "all things considered" to P2, the principles and the belief in incontinence clearly are contradictory. The incontinent are supposed to act against their all-things-considered judgments; but P2 is stated in terms of judgment *simpliciter*. It is this

apparent difference that Davidson exploits. What he thinks happens in incontinence (so defined) is that one acts contrary to one's all-things-considered judgment; but in so acting one acts in accordance with one's "unconditional" or "unqualified" judgment, or with one's judgment *simpliciter* (pp. 110–113).

Several questions arise about Davidson's position. First, is the distinction between a judgment all-things-considered and an unqualified or unconditional judgment sound? It might well be supposed that an all-things-considered judgment is precisely an unqualified judgment made on the basis of all considerations thought relevant by the agent. Second, even if this distinction were made out, is there not equally good reason to think that people act contrary to their unqualified or unconditional judgments, as there is to think that people act contrary to their all-things-considered judgments? Davidson's theses entail that this is impossible. Third, are P1 and P2 true?

Davidson's remarks on practical reasoning are certainly novel and interesting; but it is this last question that will concern me here, for the problem lies with these socratic principles. Aside from the fact that P1 and P2 lead to a denial of what intuitively seems to exist, there are strong general reasons for rejecting them. To see this, recall the reasoning in Plato's *Protagoras* which led Socrates (or the early Plato) to deny the possibility of *akrasia*. In this work Socrates denied the common account, according to which agents may knowingly fail to do what they believe best in the situation, because they yield to temptation, or short-term pleasure, or are overcome by appetite. Socrates denied this account because he believed that human beings always most desire, and hence pursue, what is (thought to be) best (compare P1 and P2). On this supposition, in acting weakly they would have to be pursuing what they believe to be best, believing it not to be best.

Instead, Socrates insisted that what is called weakness of will (*akrasia*) is really a species of ignorance. The weak agent suffers from a kind of evaluation illusion, very like an optical illusion – the nearer, more immediate good looks the greater. The so-called weak agent lacks the art of measurement, the art of correctly weighing nearer and farther goods, and to have this art is to have knowledge of good and evil. (Hence the thesis that virtue is a kind of knowledge, to which I shall return.)

Despite the ingenuity of this appeal to evaluational illusions (which I think in fact occur), the later Plato came to see this matter differently. He came to realize that we are generally susceptible to motivation which is independent, in strength and origin, of our judgments concerning how it is best to act. Plato's distinction between the rational and nonrational parts of the soul may be taken as a distinction between sources of motivation. The rational part of the soul is the source of evaluations – judgments as to the value or worth of a particular course of action or state of affairs. The nonrational part of the soul is the source of such desires as arise from the appetites and emotions. These desires are blind in the sense that they do not depend fundamentally upon the agent's view of the good. Since these sources of motivation differ, they may conflict, and in certain cases, the desires of the nonrational soul may motivate the agent contrary to his or her "desires" for the good. In some such way, Plato tried to account for motivational conflict and for the possibility of both self-mastery and its opposite.[5]

On the basis of this distinction, then, Plato rejected Socrates' (or his own earlier) view that a person's desires are always desires for the "good" and that what a person most desires is what is (thought) best. Elementary as these points are, they suffice to show the possibility of weakness of will. The desires of hunger and sex, the desires of anger and fear, do not depend upon one's assessment of the value of doing what one is thereby inclined to do. But if such desires exist, as they surely do, then it is possible that they are strong enough to motivate one contrary to one's judgment of what is best; it is possible that one's evaluations and desires diverge in certain cases in such a way that one is led to do things which one does not think worth doing, or as much worth doing as some available option. Hence socratism is false. There are no good theoretical grounds for denying *akrasia*.

To bring these points to bear on Davidson's principles: let us distinguish two senses of "wants more" or "wants most," an evaluational sense and motivational sense.[6] In the first sense, if one wants to do x more than one wants to do y, one *prefers* x to y or ranks x higher than y on some scale of values or "desirability matrix." In the second sense, if one wants to do x more than y, one is more strongly motivated to do x than to do y. Thus, $P2$ may be true if understood in

the language of evaluation, but false if understood in the language of motivation; whereas $P1$ is true if understood in the language of motivation, but false if understood in the language of evaluation. If a person judges x to be better than y, then he or she values x more than y. But as we have seen, it does not follow that the agent's desire or want for x, rather than for y, will motivate the agent to act (if either does). But this must follow if $P1$ and $P2$ are jointly to have the consequences that Davidson accepts. There is no univocal interpretation of the key phrases of $P1$ and $P2$ on which these principles turn out to be true, or even very plausible.

Thus, even though Davidson wishes to allow the existence of "incontinence," in these principles we encounter the socratic viewpoint once again. It is important to note in addition that the above principles also rule out the possibility of being compulsively motivated to act contrary to one's practical judgment. Once we are disabused of the idea that the strength of one's desire is necessarily proportional to the degree to which one values its object, there is conceptual room for compulsion as well as weakness.[7] The real problem, as we shall see, is not to admit but to distinguish them. But first it will be instructive to look at some related distortions implicit in the socratic theory of virtue.

Self-Control and the Socratic Theory of Virtue

Consider the virtue of courage, and how this virtue is misconceived by the socratic view. Courage is a virtue which it is in the interest of everyone to have, and is in this respect like continence. Now for Socrates, courage is, as it should be, the virtue which applies to situations of danger. But for him it applies in the following eccentric way: courage is the knowledge of what is really dangerous or not. Since Socrates thought that the only danger is evil, or doing evil, all that it takes to possess the virtue of courage, and to act courageously in appropriate circumstances, is the knowledge of what is good and evil. (This is the keystone of his doctrine of the unity of the virtues: each virtue is a special case of wisdom (knowledge of good and evil) applied to particular contexts: courage is wisdom about danger, temperance is wisdom about what is really pleasant, justice is wisdom applied to social relationships and statecraft, and so on. If you have wisdom in general, then you will have the other virtues, and if you lack one of these, you will lack wisdom). Hence the coward is one who has a false view of what is really dangerous. The courageous person is one who is able to distinguish apparent from real dangers.

But surely courage is not like this. Courage is the capacity to deal with one's fear in contexts where one is thereby spontaneously inclined to actions which are contrary to one's view of what should be done. The virtue of courage has a role only because we are not as Socrates says we are; it is needed because of the irrational part of the soul, because our inclinations do not always harmonize with our judgments of the good. Socrates thinks that the courageous person's virtue is that he or she sees there is nothing really to fear, whereas the coward is benighted about this. But the truth appears to be that courage is needed precisely where there *is* something to fear, but where this emotion would lead one to act contrary to one's better judgment.

Courage is thus a special type of self-control; it is self-control in situations of personal danger. Consequently, self-control has a broader application than to pleasure and temptation. If human psychology were as Socrates assumes, such a virtue would have no use. Self-control is a virtue only for beings who are susceptible to motivation which is in potential conflict with their judgments of what is good to pursue; only to beings like ourselves who have appetites and emotions which may incline them contrary to their better judgments.[8]

In passing, it is worth noting that possessing the capacity to make one's practical judgments effective in action is generally in the interest of every being with some sort of view of how to live, and does not presuppose a particularly austere or "rationalistic" ethic. Even those who favor spontaneity and propose to follow their inclinations should want the virtue of self-control. To use an example of Thomas Nagel,[9] even those who favor a spontaneous life will want to be able to resist the sudden urge to join the Marine Corps – or more generally, to resist those inclinations the satisfaction of which would render them unable to act impulsively in the future.

As I see it, then, the virtue of self-control is the capacity to counteract recalcitrant motivation, that is, motivation which is contrary to one's better judgment. It is this virtue that the weak agent lacks, or at least fails to exercise; and for this virtue, knowledge in the ordinary sense is clearly insufficient. Now both compulsion and weakness of will involve a failure of self-control. In the next section, I want to consider some common ways of distinguishing these types of failure.

Weakness and Compulsion

Suppose that a particular woman intentionally takes a drink. To provide an evaluative context, suppose also that we think she ought not to have another because she will then be unfit to fulfill some of her obligations. Preanalytically, most of us would insist on the possibility and significance of the following three descriptions of the case. (1) the reckless or self-indulgent case; (2) the weak case; and (3) the compulsive case. In (1), the woman knows what she is doing but accepts the consequences. Her choice is to get drunk or risk getting drunk. She acts in accordance with her judgment. In (2) the woman knowingly takes the drink contrary to her (conscious) better judgment; the explanation for this lack of self-control is that she is weak-willed. In (3), she knowingly takes the drink contrary to her better judgment, but she is a victim of a compulsive (irresistible) desire to drink.

These variations reveal the leading features of the common conception of weakness. On this model, the weak drinker is like the compulsive drinker in that she acts contrary to her better judgment,[10] but she is like the reckless drinker in that she is able to resist the drink. Accordingly, she is placed morally somewhere "in between" the others. Since she acted contrary to her judgment, she is not, like the reckless drinker, just morally "bad" – her values and judgment are not in question. But unlike the compulsive, she is not a victim of irresistible desires. She shares with the reckless the ability to resist, and for this reason we hold her responsible.

The common account, then, insists that the weak person has, but fails to exercise, the capacity of self-control. It is this requirement that nonsocratic skepticism challenges. Before posing the challenge, I will illustrate and clarify the concept of motivational compulsion, and then raise some preliminary difficulties in distinguishing it from weakness. Subsequently, I will argue that this common way of making the distinction is untenable, and will propose an alternative way that does not rest upon this requirement.

The notion of psychological or motivational compulsion is probably an extension of the ordinary notion of interpersonal compulsion, in which one person is forced by another to act "against his will." Although psychological compulsion may not be widely recognized in ordinary life, I think that the concepts of mania, phobia, and addiction imply its possibility.[11] I shall assume that when an action is literally compelled motivationally, the agent is motivated by a desire (or "impulse" or "inclination") that he or she is unable to resist. In illustration, a man might have a dread fear of spiders or rats so overwhelmingly strong that, even when it is urgently important for him to do so, he is literally unable to handle one. Or a starving woman may be driven by her hunger to do such acts as she would rather die than perform. Or a drug addict, because of his or her unconquerable craving for the drug, may be unable (at least over a span of time) to refuse the opportunity to obtain and consume some heroin.

It is not true that manic and phobic actions are necessarily compulsive; the motivations may raise the cost of alternative actions prohibitively, and thus "coerce" rather than compel. If I give in to my fear of flying, recognizing all the while that this fear is baseless, it does not follow that I was compelled to remain grounded. It may rather be that the difficulties and anxieties involved in my overcoming my admittedly irrational fear make doing so too costly. (Nor would this be a case of weakness of will; here I act on my judgment that flying is not worth the suffering.) However, there may be circumstances in which I am unable to overcome my phobia, even when it is practically urgent for me to fly. Nevertheless, even though manic or phobic desires do not necessarily compel, they are potentially compulsive in that their strength is to a large degree independent of the person's will.

In what follows, I wish to exclude from consideration cases of unconscious or "semi-conscious" or self-deceptive actions. Where one deceives oneself about what is best, or about one's situation of action, one does not act contrary to one's better judgment, but rather in accordance with one's self-deceptive judgment. Or perhaps in such cases, it is radically unclear what the real judgment *is*. Self-deception is itself philosophically troublesome, and as a matter of fact many actions we call weak may involve self-deception of some sort. But no philosophical reasons drive us to redescribe the phenomenon in this way, and certainly the common view insists on the possibility of "clear-headed" action contrary to better judgment. Furthermore, the problems raised by weakness of will differ distinctively from the problems raised by self-deception. The former problem is how a judgment can fail to lead to appropriate action. The latter problem concerns the way in which beliefs and judgments can be influenced by desires. Consequently, I will restrict my attention to actions involving failures of the former kind.[12]

Preliminary Difficulties

It is important to emphasize that "weakness of will," in ordinary usage, purports to be an explanatory concept; weakness of will is not just any sort of action contrary to the agent's judgment. To identify behavior in this way is to offer a minimal kind of explanation: one acts contrary to one's better judgment *because* one is weak; one *yields* to temptation, *allows* oneself to give in to appetite, and so forth.

Now the force of this explanation is quite unclear, especially if it is supposed to contrast with an explanation in terms of compulsion. For the present, the problem of distinguishing weakness from compulsion may be expressed in the following way. In those examples given earlier, what is most striking, and leads naturally to the invocation of the notion of compulsion, is that the agents' actual motivation is independent of any conception that they have of the worth of their actions. Their motivation is in this way "alien" to them. In some significant sense, they seem motivated contrary to their own wills. Clearly, the "will" here cannot be the *strongest* motive; for compulsives do not act contrary to their strongest motive. They act contrary to their judgments of the worth of their actions. It is plausible, then, to identify the "will" with practical judgment. This suggests that the mark of a compulsive desire is its capacity to motivate the agent contrary to practical judgment. But it follows that the weak agent acts contrary to his or her judgment in exactly the same sense, and therefore acts under compulsion.

This consequence is admittedly counterintuitive. Surely if it is plausible in some circumstances to say that a starving person is unable to resist taking the bread, that in general compulsives are driven ineluctably to acts beyond their control, it is quite implausible to say this of the well-nourished who capitulate to their fondness for bagels.

Similarly, we are inclined to contrast weakness and compulsion like so: in the case of compulsive acts, it is not so much that the will is too weak as that the contrary motivation is too strong; whereas, in weakness of will properly so-called, it is not that the contrary motivation is too strong, but that the will is too weak.

There is, I think, something correct in this contrast; but the following difficulty remains. This talk of strength of desires is obscure enough, but insofar as it has meaning, there does not appear to be any way of judging the strength of desires except as they result in action. For why is it said that the compulsive's desires are too strong? Isn't it just because these agents are motivated contrary to their wills? Isn't the only relatively clear measure of strength of desires the tendency of those desires to express themselves independently of the agent's will? If this is so, the desires which motivate the weak contrary to their judgments are "too strong" as well, and explanations of weakness and compulsion come to the same thing. We are left again with the conclusion that weakness is a case of compulsion.[13]

We have seen why socratism is to be rejected, but a real problem remains. If a sufficient condition of compulsive motivation is that the motivation be contrary to the agent's practical judgment, then weakness of will is a species of compulsion. And if compulsive behavior is involuntary and unfree, weak behavior is involuntary and unfree. In any case, weakness and compulsion are on a par. The intuition that the agent's will is too weak, whereas in the other case, the contrary motivation is too strong, appears to rest on an illusion.

One way to avoid this conclusion – that all weak actions are compulsive – would be to argue that no actions are compulsive, since no desires are irresistible.

One philosopher who is skeptical about the idea of an irresistible desire is Joel Feinberg. "There is much obscurity in the notion of the strength of a desire," Feinberg writes, but he thinks several points are clear:

> The first is that strictly speaking no impulse is irresistible; for every case of giving in to a desire, I would argue, it will be true that, if the person had tried harder he would have resisted it successfully. ... Nevertheless, it does make sense to say that some desires are stronger than others and that some have an intensity and power that are felt as overwhelming.[14]

Feinberg's confidence on these points puzzles me. One may well be dubious in practice about particular pleas of irresistibility. And, if one is in the dark about the notion of strength, one may well have blanket doubts about such claims. But if it is granted that desires may be *hard* to resist, on what grounds can it be denied that sometimes desires may be *too* hard to resist? Why must the feeling that some desires are overwhelmingly "intense and powerful" be mistaken? What puzzles me is how the possibility of irresistible desires can be rejected a priori unless the notion of strength here is altogether empty.

Not only do many psychologists assume this possibility, the common view of weakness seems committed to it as well. For it insists that the weak person has but does not exercise the capacity to resist. This insistence presupposes the intelligibility of lacking this capacity. In any case, even if it is true, as Feinberg believes, that in all cases, "if the person had tried harder, he would have resisted," this does not show that no desires are irresistible. For a person may be unable to try harder and for this reason be unable to resist.

Therefore, it seems unjustified to hold that no desires are too strong for an agent to resist. In fact, we very frequently compare the strengths of desires, both when they are those of a particular individual at a given time, and when the desires belong to different persons or the same person at different times. (*P*'s desire to lounge in bed is stronger than his desire to keep appointments; *Q* has stronger sexual desires than most, or than she herself had when she was fifteen.) It is not clear what criteria we invoke in such comparisons, but two obvious criteria are clearly unhelpful. Motivational efficacy will not do because on this measure any desire which motivates would thereby be the strongest.[15] And this measure would not allow for significant interpersonal comparisons. Nor, once again, will independence of the agent's will or better judgment do, for then the desires of the weak and the compulsive will be equally strong.

Strength and Resistibility

It might help at this point to return to my earlier description of self-control as the capacity to resist recalcitrant desires; such desires are strong to the extent to which they *need* to be resisted. For again, not all actual desires which one does not in the end act upon are therefore resisted. To resist cannot simply be to refrain from acting upon some desire one has. As Aristotle observed (*Nicomachean Ethics*, 1152a1 ff.), there is a difference between the "continent" and the "temperate" person which rests upon the notion of strength. For both types, "choice" regulates action – both act upon their evaluations – but while the temperate person has moderate appetites, the continent person acts rightly *despite* strong contrary inclinations. A person's desires are moderate to the degree to which they do not require resistance.

The important point is that practical conflict may assume both a decision-theoretic and a psychological form. When the conflict takes the first form, it arises from the question of what to do. But motivational conflicts may persist after this question is settled. Here the strength of desires is revealed and the need for resistance emerges. The temperate are less susceptible than others to this motivational conflict. Their souls are harmonious. The continent are so susceptible, but manage to resist. The weak fail.

Why then do the continent manage successfully to resist, whereas the weak do not? The answer cannot be that the weak are subject to stronger desires than the continent, for this would not explain why they are weaker; nor would it enable us to distinguish weakness from compulsion. The proposal I now wish to entertain is the following. The weak and the strong may be subject to desires of exactly the same strength. What makes the former weak is that they give in to desires which the possession of the normal degree of self-control would enable them to resist. In contrast, compulsive desires are such that the normal capacities of resistance are or would be insufficient to enable the agent to resist. This fact about compulsive desires is what gives substance to the claim that they are too strong. The fact that weak agents' desires would be controlled by the exercise of the normal capacities of resistance gives point to the claim that these agents are weak.

Something like this distinction is suggested by a passage of Aristotle. He remarks that the difference between weakness and what we have called compulsion might depend on the fact that the desires which defeat the weak person are such that most people could have resisted:

> ... if a man is defeated by violent and excessive pleasures or pains, there is nothing wonderful in that; indeed we are ready to pardon him if he has resisted [is overcome while offering resistance – Ostwald] ... But it is surprising if a man is defeated by and cannot resist pleasures and pains which most men can hold out against, when this is not due to heredity and disease ... (*Nicomachean Ethics*, 1150b7 ff., Ross trans.).

This way of expressing the point is unfortunate; for it may suggest that desires are like barbells which most people can or cannot lift. Whatever the ontological status of desires, it does not seem intelligible to say of an inclination that a particular person has on a particular occasion, that most others would be able to hold out against that very inclination. It makes better sense to ask not whether other people could have resisted that particular motivation – but whether the individual would have been able to hold out had he or she possessed and exercised the kinds of capacity of self-control normally possessed by others, or whether persons of normal self-control would resist similar desires of the same strength. Such a counterfactual is no doubt formidable to establish, but at least it is intelligible. I suggest that when we believe it, or something like it, to be true of people who do not resist, we think them weak (the fault is with them, not with the opposing desires); when we believe that they could not have resisted even so, then we think of them as victims of compulsion (the fault is not with them, but rather their desires are too strong). (Perhaps this way of looking at the matter also presupposes that we believe weak persons both could and should possess and exercise those skills – otherwise it would not be their *fault*.) In this manner, we can distinguish among "temperance" and "continence" (in Aristotle's sense), weakness and compulsion. And we can avoid saying either that no desires are irresistible or that weakness is a case of compulsion.

In summary, then, there are capacities and skills of resistance which are generally acquired in the normal course of socialization and practice, and which we hold one another responsible for acquiring and maintaining. Weak agents fall short of standards of "reasonable and normal" self-control (for which we hold them responsible), whereas compulsive agents are motivated by desires which they could not resist even if they met those standards. That is why we focus on the weakness of the agent in the one case (it is the agent's fault), but on the power of the contrary motivation in the compulsive case. And this view allows explanations in terms of weakness of will to be significantly different from explanations in terms of compulsion. In the case of weakness, one acts contrary to one's better judgment *because one has failed* to meet standards of reasonable or normal self-control; whereas, this explanation does not hold of compulsive behavior.

Let us now note some of the implications of this proposal. One obvious point is that, on this account, a desire is compulsive (irresistible) or not only relative to certain norms of self-control; only relative to the capacities of the normal person, and this probably means the typical adult in our society. It may be true, for example, that having undergone from childhood an intensive program of discipline, such as yoga, would have enabled a person to resist certain desires now. But this fact would not incline us at all to withdraw the claim that the individual was suffering from compulsive desires. Hence the fact that one would be a weak person in a community of yogis does not mean that one would not be compulsive among us. (It does not follow from this account, however, that weak agents are those with less self-control than most others in their society *in fact* have. Weakness is relative to expectations and norms, and it is conceivable that a whole community could fall short of these.)

The relativity of this viewpoint may conflict with our ordinary view of weakness; perhaps prior to reflection we think that a desire is either resistible or it isn't. Even so, it seems to me that this relativity is a desirable feature of the present account. We could define an absolute concept of compulsion in something like the following manner: an agent is motivated by a compulsive desire if *no* degree of training and discipline would have enabled him or her to resist. But it is an open question whether *any* desires are compulsive on this definition, and it does not seem to apply in the right way to the cases we think of as compulsive. Relativity is in any case a feature of the concept of weakness in general – for example, the concept of physical weakness. The possible existence of races of creatures who could lift 500-pound weights, or of training programs which would enable most of us to do so, would not mean that those of us who cannot lift this weight were physically weak.[16]

This doctrine accords fairly closely with typical moral attitudes toward weakness as well. In contrast to "bad characters," we do not criticize weak agents for their principles or values but for their failure to develop or maintain the capacities necessary to make those values effective in action. The appropriate blaming attitudes toward the weak, by themselves and others, are shame and (if one goes in for this sort of thing) contempt, not guilt and indignation. For the fault is not injustice, but lack of control. And since they have (or may have) the right values, they are as much an object of pity as reproach – from any point of view, *especially their own*,[17] they are in a bad way. Since shame characteristically involves falling short of shared standards of excellence in conduct, shame will often be appropriate in the case of weakness in a way in which it will not be for compulsion.[18]

The Proposed Account versus the Common Account

The proposed account entails that the desires of weak agents are resistible in the sense that had they developed and maintained certain normal capacities of self-control, they would have resisted them. And to the degree to which we judge such agents blame-worthy and responsible for their weak behavior, we believe they could and should have developed and maintained these capacities. So the weak must be constitutionally capable of meeting these standards. But these implications are consistent with their being unable at the time of action to resist. Hence, this account differs significantly from the common one. On the latter the ability to resist at the time of action is a distinguishing feature of weakness.

Morally, the proposed account likens weakness to negligence in its emphasis on the point that blameworthiness does not require that one be able to resist or that weak behavior be fully under voluntary control. For negligence is a paradigm case of blameworthy but nonvoluntary behavior. Engrossed in an interesting conversation, a man forgets to look both ways at the intersection and therefore collides with another vehicle. He does not do so voluntarily, or even intentionally, and yet we may judge him blameworthy for failing to meet standards (or the "duty") of reasonable care. (To be sure, the man is engaged in numerous voluntary actions at the time of the collision, but colliding, for which he is blamed, is not among them.) Could he have remembered? It is not at all clear that he could have. Remembering is not in this case even an action. What we believe is that he should have remembered to look and because of this, that he falls short of standards of reasonable care. The accident is explained by his fault (just as weak behavior is explained by the agent's fault).[19]

Perhaps to think him blameworthy we must also believe that he could have been or become the kind of person who exercises reasonable care. But these beliefs do not entail that he was able, at the time of action, to avoid the accident. On the proposed account, the case of weak behavior is quite parallel. The weak person may be seen as negligent for failing to acquire the relevant capacities. And like the standard of normal self-control, the standard of reasonable care (and thus what counts as negligence) is relative to social norms and particular contexts. Moreover, like the weak person in the above example, the negligent person is not criticized for his values and judgments (he is not bad or unjust) but for failing to ensure that his behavior is informed by, and conforms to, those values and judgments. (However, unlike the negligent person, but like the compulsive, the weak person does of course act intentionally.)[20]

Therefore, the fact that on the proposed account weak agents may be no more able at the time of action to conform their behavior to their judgments than compulsives does not rob the distinction between weakness and compulsion of its moral significance.

That distinction can be significantly drawn without requiring ability. I shall now argue that, furthermore, there are strong reasons for doubting that this requirement can be satisfied, and thus for rejecting this central feature of the common account. By the common account, the culpability of the drinker in our earlier example is located not in her failure to develop or maintain the normal capacity of resistance, but in her failure to exercise the capacity she possesses. The challenge to this account is to find a pertinent explanation of this failure.

Generally, people fail to perform some action for a combination of the following kinds of reason: (*a*) they are unaware of the action as an option; (*b*) they do not want or choose to do it; or (*c*) they are unable to do it. Given awareness, nonperformance indicates lack of "power" or lack of "will" or both.[21] This is why inquiries into capacities and knowledge are relevant in contexts of moral appraisal. For instance, if you know that the curtains are burning, and you are able to extinguish the fire, I infer from your nonperformance that you did not want or choose to put the fire out. I thereby learn something important about your values and priorities. On the other hand, of course, if you did not choose to let the curtains burn, or did not even do it knowingly, you would not necessarily be exculpated, for your action or omission may be explained by your culpable ignorance or carelessness. Generally, then, culpable failures or omissions are explained either by lack of choice, or by culpable lack of care, knowledge, or ability.

The proposed account fits weakness into a scheme of this kind. Weak agents fail or neglect to meet certain standards of self-control, and their culpability does not require choice or ability at the time of action. The explanation of the weak agent's failure to act upon practical judgment involves attributing this failure to another culpable failure to develop or maintain the relevant capacities.

The challenge to the common account is to provide a similarly pertinent explanation of the weak person's failure. This failure is due neither to lack of knowledge nor, putatively, to lack of ability or negligence. To return to the case of the weak drinker, the woman judges that she should resist and therefore, by her own lights, has sufficient reason for exercising her alleged capacity. What might explain her not doing so?

There seem to me only two possible explanations. (1) She *chooses* not to. (2) Her *effort* to resist is culpably insufficient. Both of these explanations will be found inadequate.

(1) First, the notion of choice (and also decision) seems to me to involve the notion of applying one's values to the perceived practical options. (Aristotle is close when he speaks of choice as desire in accordance with deliberation.) In this sense, it is of course generally true that one may choose not to exercise some capacity that one has. But the capacity of self-control is special in this respect. For the capacity of self-control involves the capacity to counteract and resist the strength of desires which are contrary to what one has chosen or judged best to do. The weak drinker's failure to resist her desire to drink is a failure to implement her choice not to drink. To choose not to implement this choice would be to change her original judgment, and the case would no longer be a case of failure to implement judgment. Therefore, the weak agent's failure to resist the drink cannot intelligibly be explained by her choice.

Equally important, even if it made sense to explain her failure in this way, doing so would result in the moral assimilation of the weak case to the reckless case. The common account rightly wishes to distinguish these, but the difference would collapse if both involved choice.

(2) Second, it might be supposed that the drinker's failure is to be explained by her culpably insufficient *effort*. Sometimes we attribute a person's failure, not to absence of ability or choice, but to lack of sufficient effort. I may try and fail to throw a coin across the Schuylkill River even when I wanted very much to do so and was able to do so. The explanation may be that I misjudged either the amount of effort required or the distance across. Or in a basketball game, my failure to make a jump-shot from the free-throw line might be explained by insufficient concentration rather than lack of capability or will. Using "effort" to include both physical exertion and psychological factors such as concentration and "keeping one's head," in both cases, we may suppose, I not only would have succeeded with greater effort, but could have made the requisite effort.

Perhaps weakness of will is commonly viewed as involving insufficient effort. In order to help here, an explanation of this kind must be conjoined with the assumption that the weak person is able to make the requisite effort to resist. For obviously, if effort of a certain kind and degree is necessary to successful resistance, it will be true that the drinker is able to resist only if she has the capacity to make an effort of that kind and degree to resist. Our focus is thus shifted to her failure of effort, and everything now turns on why she does not make *it*. But it is far from clear what explanation is forthcoming.

The explanation cannot be that making the effort is not thought to be worth it. For once again, implicit in the judgment that it is best not to drink is the judgment that it is best to resist contrary desires. If the drinker really judges that it is not worth that much effort, she either changes her mind or originally only made a conditional judgment of the form: it is best not to drink unless not doing so requires too much effort.

The explanation cannot be that she misjudged the amount of effort required. I may have underestimated how much exertion would be required to throw the coin across the Schuylkill, or how much concentration was necessary to make the basket. But it is not clear what the analogue to this in the case of resisting a drink would be. And even if misjudgment were involved, that would be a different fault from weakness of will.

So we do not seem to have a pertinent explanation of why the weak drinker fails to exert adequate effort. No doubt her failure has something to do with the relative strengths of her desires to resist and to drink. But *this* is not enough for the common account, since it is consistent with her being unable to make the effort. Inasmuch as she has the same good reasons for making the effort to resist as for not drinking, we need an explanation which makes it clear that she is able to resist. For even if some (further) effort would enable her to resist, the desire to drink may generate desires not to make this effort (in the way that desires frequently cause other desires for the means to their fulfillment) and these may be irresistibly strong.

Given her strong motive for making an effort (namely, her considered practical judgment), and in the absence of a special explanation for her not making it (such as "I didn't think it was worth it", or "I didn't think it was necessary"), we are entitled to be skeptical about the common view, and to conclude that the person was unable to resist.

Conclusion

Socrates found the common conception of weakness of will to be confused. However, his reasons for rejecting that account are unsound. They deny the morally and psychologically important complexity of human motivation, and in particular the potential divergence between certain kinds of desire and judgments of the good. This divergence is what makes room for the virtue of self-control and, obversely, the vice of weakness of will.

Just the same, I have offered doubts of a nonsocratic sort about the common account of weakness. To take seriously the possibility of acting contrary to one's better judgment is at the same time to raise problems about the distinction between weakness and compulsion. I have argued that the common view, according to which the differentiating feature is that the weak are able to conform their behavior to their practical judgments, is unjustified. Instead, I have proposed that weakness of will involves the failure to develop certain normal capacities of self-control, whereas compulsion involves desires which even the possession of such capacities would not enable one to resist.

Notes

1. Weakness of will occurs only if one knowingly does something contrary to one's better judgment. We will see that this condition does not distinguish between weakness and compulsion.
2. I shall assume throughout that if someone is psychologically compelled to do something, he or she is unable to refrain from doing it (though not necessarily conversely). The compulsive's motivation is literally irresistible. This concept is discussed further on page 248.
3. In the socratic dialogues of Plato, the view that Socrates denies is often formulated as the view that people often, *freely and voluntarily*, act contrary to their better judgments. This position will be rejected by both forms of skepticism. But the focus of Socrates' arguments is the weaker proposition that one can knowingly act contrary to one's better judgment. Hence I call "socratic" only this version of skepticism.
4. In *Moral Concepts*, edited by Joel Feinberg, Oxford University Press, 1970.
5. I develop this distinction, and apply it to the concept of free action, in "Free Agency", *Journal of Philosophy*, April 24, 1975.

   An interpretative point: Plato appears to have held that the distinction between knowledge and belief is relevant in some way I fail to appreciate. Hence he may still have denied the possibility of acting contrary to one's *knowledge*.
6. The distinction between the language of motivation and the language of evaluation is clearly drawn by G. Santas, in "Plato's *Protagoras*, and Explanations of Weakness", *The Philosophical Review*, 1966. His discussion of weakness is one of the best that I know of. In insisting upon this distinction, I do not wish to assert a semantical ambiguity of "want." The point is rather that there are different, and noncoincident criteria for whether someone wants to do one thing *more than* another.
7. The existence of weakness of will, or generally the divergence between evaluation and motivation, reveals one kind of limitation on decision theory, conceived as an explanatory theory of behavior. Decision theory will be correct only on the assumption (often unjustified) of "continence." Explaining weak action will require a different branch of psychology.
8. The appetites and emotions are not the only sources of such motivation. Perhaps appetites (like hunger, thirst, sex) may be distinguished from emotions (like anger, fear, resentment) in that the latter essentially involve beliefs (that something is dangerous, that one has been wronged, that another is obstructing one), whereas appetites do not. But the following examples do not seem to fit clearly into either category – the inclinations arising from pain, the inclination to excrete, the inclination to sleep (arising from sleepiness) – and these surely belong to the "nonrational" part of the soul. Why isn't sleepiness, like hunger, an appetite?

   Let me hasten to add that, as Ruth Mattern has pointed out to me, self-control should not be conceived as a unified capacity, such that if one has it in one area, one will have it in all areas. A person may be "soft" with respect to pain, but never yield to temptation, or one may be perfectly courageous, but continually give in to the desire to drink.
9. In *The Possibility of Altruism*, Oxford, The Clarendon Press, 1970.
10. Acting contrary to one's better judgment is not, however, a necessary condition of compulsion; one's desire might be compulsive and happen to accord with one's judgment.

11. See the leading psychological study, *Fears and Phobias*, by Marks. In his discussion of "obsessive-compulsive" neuroses, Freud also speaks of being unable to resist certain "impulses".

12. On a larger view, this distinction may prove to be superficial. If, as I suggest, self-control or strength of will is the capacity to ensure that one's practical judgment is effective in action, then presumably it would be part of this capacity to maintain clarity of judgment in the face of temptation. In a significant sense, one's practical judgment is ineffective in self-deceptive action, and one can yield to bad reasoning as well as directly to temptation. But I shall adhere in the text to this characterization of weakness as action contrary to one's conscious and immediate practical judgment, both for simplicity and because this case is conceptually most problematic for my concerns.

13. A few remarks on internalism may be in order here. I am supposing, as I think we ordinarily do, that when one acts weakly, one wants to some degree to do what one judges best. Weakness of will is marked by conflict and regret. However, this supposition does not entail a commitment to a general internalist view that a person necessarily wants what he or she judges best. (Note that even this general view is a weaker internalism than Davidson's *P2*.) For even if it is possible not at all to want what one judges best, it would be a distortion to describe such a case as weakness of will. For such an externalist agent would have a strong and undivided will – and what he or she lacked certainly would not be self-control. I think one trouble with Davidson's discussion (op. cit.) is that it leaves untouched the way in which weakness of will is supposed to involve weakness; "incontinence" turns out to be a "surd" noncompliance with the "principle of continence," and hence is construed as merely practical irrationality. (Compare Nietzsche's remark: "When the mind is made up, the ear is deaf to even the best arguments. This is the sign of a strong character. In other words, an occasional will to stupidity." [*Beyond Good and Evil*, sec. 107] Consider also a cartoon I recently saw. On his way to the local bar, the character encounters his priest, who asks him, "Have you no self-control?" He replies, "Yes, Father, I have, but I will not be a slave to it.")

14. "What is So Special about Mental Illness?", in *Doing and Deserving*, Princeton University Press, 1970, pp. 282–283.

15. This needs some qualification. The motivational efficacy of desire could be understood counterfactually. For example, it may be that a woman is motivated by her thirst rather than her hunger, even though the latter is stronger than the former in this sense: if she had thought she could satisfy her hunger, that desire rather than her thirst would have motivated her. But

the statement in the text seems to hold for *competing* desires, where two desires are competing if the agent believes it is now possible to satisfy either but not both. I owe this notion of a competing desire to Robert Audi.

16. Note, however, that on this account I could easily be mistaken about whether my action was weak or compulsive, because I could be mistaken about what the relevant standards were. Indeed, in the absence of shared expectations and norms the distinction might come to lose its force altogether.

17. For one's "point of view" includes preeminently the values which determine one's better judgment.

18. To say that there is generally a moral contrast between weak and compulsive behavior is neither to deny that a compulsive may sometimes be blameworthy, nor to imply that a weak person always is. Just as compulsive agents may sometimes be responsible and blameworthy for having allowed themselves to become or remain compulsive, so the failure of the weak agent might be excusable, as Aristotle intimates, if it were due to "disease." Perhaps we would not or should not classify such a person as weak of will; we would not call a person negligent who was subnormally careless due to disease. If so, weakness of will differs in this respect from physical weakness, which carries no implication of responsibility.

19. I do not suppose that the phenomenon of negligence is well understood; it poses some hard questions for the theory of responsibility. I would claim, however, that weakness resembles negligence in this respect, that both are nonvoluntary behavior thought to be open to blame. The important point is that the responsibility of weak agents is no more (or less) problematic than the responsibility of negligent agents.

20. Some may wish to deny that compulsive behavior is, or can be, intentional if it is not free. This denial seems to me unjustified. For one thing, on leading views of intentionality, both compulsive and weak action will count as intentional. Both the compulsive and the weak person act on a "primary reason" (in Davidson's sense: "Actions, Reasons, and Causes", Chapter 19 in this volume). Their behavior is consciously motivated; hence both may have "practical knowledge" and be able to answer a certain kind of question "Why?" (See E. Anscombe, *Intention*.) More decisively, compulsive and weak behavior both involve at least a minimal form of practical reasoning: the person with a dread fear of spiders may reason about how best to escape, a weak person about how best to obtain some cigarettes. To deny intentionality here is unjustifiably to conflate intentional with free action.

21. This theme is pursued in Chapter 2 of Stuart Hampshire's *Freedom of the Individual*.

Part V

The Explanation of Action

Introduction to Part V

1.

What form of explanation is appropriate for intentional actions? Answers to this question come under two broad headings: causal and non-causal. Surely, we might say, either they are causal – that is, we explain an action by specifying its causes – or they are not – that is, we explain actions in some other way. But this disjunction depends for its bite on our having a clear account of what it is to specify a cause, and no such account is at present available. Without one, we will have to struggle on as best we can.

We saw in Part IV that there is broad agreement that the question "why did he do that?" is standardly answered by saying "because he believed this and wanted, or intended, that." Let us call explanations of this sort 'standard explanations'. Our use of the word 'because' in them, though it does signal that we are involved in explanation, does not show that the explanation we give is causal. There are uses of 'because' in mathematics and in ethics that are not causal (that was wrong because you promised not to do it). More to the point, however, the fact that we allude to belief, desire, and intention in these explanations does not yet tell us how such explanations function. The question what is going on in these standard explanations is wide open.

We now consider five distinct interpretations of standard explanations. The first interpretation would claim to take standard explanations quite literally.

They appeal to psychological states of the agent, and appeal to them as causes of the action. But these explanations are still incomplete as they stand. Explanations in science work by subsuming the event to be explained under a law, and our explanation specified no law. Still, for the explanation to succeed there must be a law which will be generally of the form "Whenever someone believes this and wants/intends that, they will act in such a way." This is a psychological law for creatures like us. Explanations of intentional action will then be similar in form to explanations of natural events; the only real difference between them is that the laws that ground them are psychological rather than physical, or perhaps best psycho-physical (insofar as we might think of them as relating the mental to the bodily, something disputed by the next interpretation).

The second interpretation focuses on the neuro-physiological bases for belief and desire. It looks through the psychological to the neural level that underpins it. It understands our standard explanation as implicitly appealing to neurophysiological laws of the form "whenever such and such neural changes occur, such and such bodily changes will occur." There is, according to this view, nothing wrong with the psychological reading of the explanation, any more than there is on the first interpretation; but the reference to belief and desire in them is really a reference to the neural states that make it the case that the agent believes this and wants that.

Philosophy of Action: An Anthology, First Edition. Edited by Jonathan Dancy and Constantine Sandis.
© 2015 John Wiley & Sons, Inc. Published 2015 by John Wiley & Sons, Inc.

So we have two competing causal interpretations of our original explanation. Of the chapters in this section, two are related to this matter. Malcolm (Chapter 29) argues that the appeal to the psychological cannot be to psychological states as causes, because the supposed psychological laws are conceptual truths rather than empirical regularities. His main reason for saying this is that if someone fails to act when he sees an opportunity to get something he wants and there is no countervailing consideration, we take this to show that he did not really want it. If the relevant laws are not contingent, an explanation that appeals to them cannot be causal, because cause and effect must be logically distinct entities, and any laws linking them must therefore be contingent.

Dretske (Chapter 31) is not concerned with the nature of any relevant laws. (As we will see shortly, it is anyway contentious to suppose that causal explanation necessarily involves an appeal to laws.) He asks rather how the neural and the psychological could be combined in a complete causal explanation of action. Rejecting the idea that psychological changes are the effects of neural changes, so as to give us a sort of passage (a causal chain?) from the neural to the psychological and thence to action, he suggests that psychological events are 'structural' causes of action while neural events are 'triggering' causes. A triggering cause of the light going on is the operation of the switch; a structuring cause is what established the causal pathway from the triggering cause to this effect, for instance the way the electrical system in the house is set up. It is true that the light went on because the system is set up that way, but it is not the same sort of causal truth as, and is not in competition with, the claim that it went on because of pressure on the switch. It is worth considering carefully whether Dretske's distinction, even if sound, really captures the relation between the causal roles of the neural and the psychological. He seems to say that the person's desire for more light plays the same sort of causal role as does the way the system is set up; they are both structural causes of the light's going on when the switch is pressed.

The first two interpretations have taken our standard explanation of action and asserted that it is incomplete. Both assert that some reference to a law is implicit in the explanation offered, differing only on what sort of law is involved. A third interpretation, while still causal, drops this requirement and allows that though there must be a law if such explanations are successful, the explanations themselves are silent on the nature of such laws (beyond the claim that such a law exists). This interpretation is associated with Davidson; it requires that the terms in which, in giving our explanation, we specify the required causal relation between particulars (whether they be events, as Davidson here takes them to be, or some other objects) need not be at all revealing of the nature of the law that must hold if the explanation is to be successful. So when I say "he did it because he believed this and wanted that," I am committed to there being a law of the form 'whenever p, then q', which connects the cause and effect under some descriptions, but not committed to anything about the terms in which p and q are to be characterized (neural, psychological, chemical, whatever). In addition to this, Davidson denies that there are any (strict) psycho-physical laws; so the claim "she did this because she wanted that and believed that doing this would be a good way to get it" certainly does not reveal the nature of the law that sustains it.

One might ask, of these causal explanations, how it is that they serve to explain, if they don't give us any sense of a regularity under which the relevant events are to be subsumed. They say (or at least are committed to saying) that there is one, certainly, but they don't say anything about what it might be. What sort of explanation is that? The most prominent answer is that the explanatory power of our standard explanation is not derived from any relation to a supposed regularity. What makes our explanation genuinely explanatory is that it reveals what point the agent saw in doing what he did. It shows us how he came to be attracted to acting in that way, indeed how he came to be sufficiently attracted by this course of action to prefer it to all others available. And it reveals this by imputing to the agent an appropriate set of beliefs and desires, which, it says, caused him so to act.

A fourth interpretation of our standard explanation of action agrees on all that, except for the last remark about causation. It is true, according to this interpretation, that our explanation works by revealing the favorable light in which the agent viewed his action. It shows us what the supposed good was in acting in that way. But we need not go on to say that the explanation represents the action as the effect of the agent's believings and desirings, understood as causes. The action is now conceived as a response, not to the agent's believing this and wanting that, but to what he believed and wanted. The appeal here is to the world – and to the prospects – as he conceives them, rather than to his so conceiving. And since what is appealed to may not be the case, it cannot generally be being appealed to as a cause.

On this fourth account, the standard explanation is not wrong in the way it appeals to the agent's beliefs and desires; it is the philosophical account that is mistaken, since it is misled by the surface of our explanation to suppose that 'because he believed that *p*' means 'caused by his believing that *p*' rather than 'for the reason that *p*, as he supposed'. It focuses our attention on his psychological state rather than on what really drives the explanation, namely the supposed good in so acting. This account is closely connected to the non-Humean (anti-psychologistic) accounts of acting for a reason discussed in the introduction to Part IV.

A fifth interpretation of our standard explanation is teleological. It says that what the explanation does is to reveal the purposes of the agent. A more revealing form in which our explanation could have been given is 'he did it in order to V', where V-ing is some goal or aim of the agent's. So we can say "he did it in order to stay on course," or we can say "he did it because he wanted to stay on course and he thought that this would be a way of achieving that." Understood in the first, explicitly teleological way (the Greek 'telos' means 'aim', 'end' or 'purpose') our explanation apparently appeals to something quite incapable of being a cause, namely 'to stay on course' (see Schueler 2003). The question then is whether we would be justified in insisting that despite this difference, the teleological explanation is really a causal one in disguise. In the paper reprinted here, Collins argues (Chapter 30) that it is not (at least not in the contemporary sense; one of Aristotle's four causes was the 'teleological cause'). He allows that whenever a teleological explanation is appropriate, there is also a causal explanation available (since there must be a way in which it all works). But he maintains that this does nothing to show that the two explanations are equivalent.

We now return to the difference between the third and the fourth interpretations. One might suppose that there is a simple contrast between these two: the first is causal and the second is evaluative. But this contrast is too stark. The first interpretation is causal, true, but it is also evaluative, because the explanation works by revealing something of value that the agent is pursuing. Of course the agent may be mistaken in supposing it to be of value. But if he is mistaken, it has to be a comprehensible mistake, for if it is not, the action has not really been explained at all; we are still left more or less in the dark. A version of an example of Anscombe's makes the point. Suppose we ask "why are you putting all those books on your roof?" and the answer we get is "because they are green." So far, one might think, we are none the wiser; but if the explanation were merely causal, we should have been satisfied, because understood causally the answer means 'my doing so is the effect of my believing that they are green' – and this could be true. Of course we would still not see any point in what the agent was doing – but that notion of 'seeing the point' means 'see anything worthwhile in it' – and this was not what the explanation, understood causally, was offering. But there is a way of adapting the causal explanation so that it does offer the sort of evaluative perspective that we are looking for here. Smith (Chapter 28) takes a hint from Hempel (a hint that seems entirely absent in the paper by Hempel here reprinted as Chapters 25 and 27). Let us suppose that for the explanation of intentional action, we need to specify the psychological states that together caused the bodily movement that is the action. Still, it is also required that the agent, as the host of these various changes, can be thereby displayed as acting rationally. If that can be shown, it will be by revealing the sort of point in the action that makes it an instance of practical rationality – that is, that it shows how the action makes sense. For what we learn is not only the point in so acting, but also we come to understand the agent's motivation as the sort of motivation characteristic of rational creatures.

2.

We have divided Hempel's "Explanation in Science and in History" into two parts, and inserted a chapter from Dray's *Laws and Explanation in History* between them (Chapter 26). The reason why we have done things in this seemingly peculiar way is that the first part of Hempel's paper gives a very clear account of what he there calls 'deductive-nomological' explanation. Explanations of natural events, especially scientific explanations, are supposed to have this structure, and the question then is whether other explanations, say explanations of intentional action, may not have that structure, too. Of course the explanations we actually give do not look much like deductive-nomological explanations as Hempel understands them; but that does not decide the issue, because it is easy to think that the explanations we standardly give are a sort of shorthand version of the real thing.

So we have a model of explanation in science, and we may suppose that explanation in general must be of that same sort: whatever we explain, we explain by subsumption under some relevant law. Dray argues (Chapter 26), against Hempel, that this model is completely inapplicable to explanation in history, and more generally to the explanation of action; the remainder of Hempel's paper, which follows (Chapter 27), is an attempt to show that he can assimilate Dray's main points without damage. His argument hinges on the thought that to show that action was rational or appropriate to a situation is not to explain why it was done, for it may have in fact been performed for some unrelated reason. Smith's

chapter starts with an interesting distinction between constitutive and non-constitutive explanations of action. A constitutive explanation is one whose availability makes the thing explained an action. (This should remind us of Anscombe's view that an intentional action is something to which the relevant question 'Why?' is appropriate.) So a Humean explanation of action as a bodily movement caused by certain beliefs and desires of the agent's is constitutive if we suppose that being caused in this way is what makes a bodily movement an action in the first place: actions are those bodily movements that are so caused. A non-constitutive explanation of action takes it as established independently that what is being explained is an action, and goes beyond that; Smith's examples are of actions that are especially good in one way or another. So one way in which we might give a non-constitutive explanation of an action would be to show that it was done in the service of a *rational* desire – to get something which the agent rationally wanted. This is very close to saying 'to get something that the agent was right to want', and this would take us to the idea that we explain the action by showing how sensible it was, or by showing the good the agent rightly saw in doing it. Such an explanation would be both causal and normative at once.

Reference

Schueler, G. (2003), *Reasons and Purposes* (Oxford: Oxford University Press).

Further Reading

Raz, J. (2011), "On the Guise of the Good," in his *From Normativity to Responsibility* (Oxford: Oxford University Press), 59–84.

Stocker, M. (1976), "The Schizophrenia of Modern Ethical Theories," *Journal of Philosophy* 73 (14), 453–466.

25

Explanation in Science and in History §§1–3

Carl G. Hempel

1. Introduction

Among the diverse factors that have encouraged and sustained scientific inquiry through its long history are two pervasive human concerns which provide, I think, the basic motivation for all scientific research. One of these is man's persistent desire to improve his strategic position in the world by means of dependable methods for predicting and, whenever possible, controlling the events that occur in it. The extent to which science has been able to satisfy this urge is reflected impressively in the vast and steadily widening range of its technological applications. But besides this practical concern, there is a second basic motivation for the scientific quest, namely, man's insatiable intellectual curiosity, his deep concern to *know* the world he lives in, and to *explain*, and thus to *understand*, the unending flow of phenomena it presents to him.

In times past questions as to the *what* and the *why* of the empirical world were often answered by myths; and to some extent, this is so even in our time. But gradually, the myths are displaced by the concepts, hypotheses, and theories developed in the various branches of empirical science, including the natural sciences, psychology, and sociological as well as

historical inquiry. What is the general character of the understanding attainable by these means, and what is its potential scope? In this essay I will try to shed some light on these questions by examining what seem to me the two basic types of explanation offered by the natural sciences, and then comparing them with some modes of explanation and understanding that are found in historical studies.

First, then, a look at explanation in the natural sciences.

2. Two Basic Types of Scientific Explanation

2.1. Deductive-nomological explanation

In his book, *How We Think*,[1] John Dewey describes an observation he made one day when, washing dishes, he took some glass tumblers out of the hot soap suds and put them upside down on a plate: he noticed that soap bubbles emerged from under the tumblers' rims, grew for a while, came to a standstill, and finally receded inside the tumblers. Why did this happen? The explanation Dewey outlines comes to this: In transferring a tumbler to the plate, cool air is caught in it; this air is gradually warmed by the glass, which initially has the temperature of the hot suds. The warming of the air is accompanied by an increase in its pressure, which in turn produces an expansion of

Hempel, C. G. (1963), "Explanation in Science and in History §§1–3," in Robert G. Colodny (ed.), *Frontiers of Science and Philosophy* (Pittsburgh, Pa.: University of Pittsburgh Press), 276–284. Reprinted with permission of University of Pittsburgh Press.

Philosophy of Action: An Anthology, First Edition. Edited by Jonathan Dancy and Constantine Sandis.

the soap film between the plate and the rim. Gradually, the glass cools off, and so does the air inside, with the result that the soap bubbles recede.

This explanatory account may be regarded as an argument to the effect that the event to be explained (let me call it the explanandum-event) was to be expected by reason of certain explanatory facts. These may be divided into two groups: (i) particular facts and (ii) uniformities expressed by general laws. The first group includes facts such as these: the tumblers had been immersed, for some time, in soap suds of a temperature considerably higher than that of the surrounding air; they were put, upside down, on a plate on which a puddle of soapy water had formed, providing a connecting soap film, etc. The second group of items presupposed in the argument includes the gas laws and various other laws that have not been explicitly suggested concerning the exchange of heat between bodies of different temperature, the elastic behavior of soap bubbles, etc. If we imagine these various presuppositions explicitly spelled out, the idea suggests itself of construing the explanation as a deductive argument of this form:

$$\text{(D)} \quad \frac{\begin{array}{c} C_1, C_2, \ldots, C_k \\ L_1, L_2, \ldots, L_r \end{array}}{E}$$

Here, C_1, C_2, ..., C_k are statements describing the particular facts invoked; L_1, L_2, ..., L_r are general laws: jointly, these statements will be said to form the explanans. The conclusion E is a statement describing the explanandum-event; let me call it the explanandum-statement, and let me use the word "explanandum" to refer to either E or to the event described by it.

The kind of explanation thus characterized I will call *deductive-nomological explanation*; for it amounts to a deductive subsumption of the explanandum under principles which have the character of general laws: it answers the question "Why did the explanandum-event occur?" by showing that the event resulted from the particular circumstances specified in $C_1, C_2, \ldots, C_k$ in accordance with the laws $L_1, L_2, \ldots, L_r$. This conception of explanation, as exhibited in schema (D), has therefore been referred to as the covering-law model, or as the deductive model, of explanation.[2]

A good many scientific explanations can be regarded as deductive-nomological in character. Consider, for example, the explanation of mirror-images, of rainbows, or of the appearance that a spoon handle is bent at the point where it emerges from a glass of water: in all these cases, the explanandum is deductively subsumed under the laws of reflection and refraction. Similarly, certain aspects of free fall and of planetary motion can be accounted for by deductive subsumption under Galileo's or Kepler's laws.

In the illustrations given so far the explanatory laws had, by and large, the character of empirical generalizations connecting different observable aspects of the phenomena under scrutiny: angle of incidence with angle of reflection or refraction, distance covered with falling time, etc. But science raises the question "why?" also with respect to the uniformities expressed by such laws, and often answers it in basically the same manner, namely, by subsuming the uniformities under more inclusive laws, and eventually under comprehensive theories. For example, the question, "Why do Galileo's and Kepler's laws hold?" is answered by showing that these laws are but special consequences of the Newtonian laws of motion and of gravitation; and these, in turn, may be explained by subsumption under the more comprehensive general theory of relativity. Such subsumption under broader laws or theories usually increases both the breadth and the depth of our scientific understanding. There is an increase in breadth, or scope, because the new explanatory principles cover a broader range of phenomena; for example, Newton's principles govern free fall on the earth and on other celestial bodies, as well as the motions of planets, comets, and artificial satellites, the movements of pendulums, tidal changes, and various other phenomena. And the increase thus effected in the depth of our understanding is strikingly reflected in the fact that, in the light of more advanced explanatory principles, the original empirical laws are usually seen to hold only approximately, or within certain limits. For example, Newton's theory implies that the factor g in Galileo's law, $s = \frac{1}{2} gt^2$, is not strictly a constant for free fall near the surface of the earth; and that, since every planet undergoes gravitational attraction not only from the sun, but also from the other planets, the planetary orbits are not strictly ellipses, as stated in Kepler's laws.

One further point deserves brief mention here. An explanation of a particular event is often conceived as specifying its *cause*, or causes. Thus, the account outlined in our first illustration might be held to explain the growth and the recession of the soap bubbles by showing that the phenomenon was *caused* by a rise and a subsequent drop of the temperature of the air trapped in the tumblers. Clearly, however, these temperature changes provide the requisite explanation only in conjunction with certain other conditions, such as the presence of a soap film, practically constant pressure of the air surrounding the glasses, etc. Accordingly, in the context of explanation, a cause must be allowed to consist in a more or less complex set of particular circumstances; these might be described by a set of sentences: $C_1, C_2, ..., C_k$. And, as suggested by the principle "Same cause, same effect," the assertion that those circumstances jointly caused a given event – described, let us say, by a sentence E – implies that whenever and wherever circumstances of the kind in question occur, an event of the kind to be explained comes about. Hence, the given causal explanation implicitly claims that there are general laws – such as $L_1, L_2, ..., L_r$ in schema (D) – by virtue of which the occurrence of the causal antecedents mentioned in $C_1, C_2, ..., C_k$ is a sufficient condition for the occurrence of the event to be explained. Thus, the relation between causal factors and effect is reflected in schema (D): causal explanation is deductive-nomological in character. (However, the customary formulations of causal and other explanations often do not explicitly specify all the relevant laws and particular facts: to this point, we will return later.)

The converse does not hold: there are deductive-nomological explanations which would not normally be counted as causal. For one thing, the subsumption of laws, such as Galileo's or Kepler's laws, under more comprehensive principles is clearly not causal in character: we speak of causes only in reference to *particular facts* or events, and not in reference to *universal facts* as expressed by general laws. But not even all deductive-nomological explanations of particular facts or events will qualify as causal; for in a causal explanation some of the explanatory circumstances will temporally precede the effect to be explained: and there are explanations of type (D) which lack this characteristic. For example, the pressure which a gas of specified mass possesses at

a given time might be explained by reference to its temperature and its volume at the same time, in conjunction with the gas law which connects simultaneous values of the three parameters.[3]

In conclusion, let me stress once more the important role of laws in deductive-nomological explanation: the laws connect the explanandum-event with the particular conditions cited in the explanans, and this is what confers upon the latter the status of explanatory (and, in some cases, causal) factors in regard to the phenomenon to be explained.

2.2. Probabilistic Explanation

In deductive-nomological explanation as schematized in (D), the laws and theoretical principles involved are of *strictly universal form*: they assert that in *all* cases in which certain specified conditions are realized an occurrence of such and such a kind will result; the law that any metal, when heated under constant pressure, will increase in volume, is a typical example; Galileo's, Kepler's, Newton's, Boyle's, and Snell's laws, and many others, are of the same character.

Now let me turn next to a second basic type of scientific explanation. This kind of explanation, too, is nomological, i.e., it accounts for a given phenomenon by reference to general laws or theoretical principles; but some or all of these are of *probabilistic-statistical form*, i.e., they are, generally speaking, assertions to the effect that if certain specified conditions are realized, then an occurrence of such and such a kind will come about with such and such a statistical probability.

For example, the subsiding of a violent attack of hay fever in a given case might well be attributed to, and thus explained by reference to, the administration of 8 milligrams of chlortrimeton. But if we wish to connect this antecedent event with the explanandum, and thus to establish its explanatory significance for the latter, we cannot invoke a universal law to the effect that the administration of 8 milligrams of that antihistamine will invariably terminate a hay fever attack: this simply is not so. What can be asserted is only a generalization to the effect that administration of the drug will be followed by relief with high statistical probability, i.e., roughly speaking, with a high relative frequency in the long run. The resulting explanans will thus be of the following type:

John Doe had a hay fever attack and took 8 milligrams of chlortrimeton. The probability for subsidence of a hay fever attack upon administration of 8 milligrams of chlortrimeton is high.

Clearly, this explanans does not deductively imply the explanandum, "John Doe's hay fever attack subsided"; the truth of the explanans makes the truth of the explanandum not certain (as it does in a deductive-nomological explanation) but only more or less likely or, perhaps "practically" certain.

Reduced to its simplest essentials, a probabilistic explanation thus takes the following form:

(P) $\left. \begin{array}{l} \text{Fi} \\ p(O,F) \text{ is very high} \end{array} \right\}$ makes very likely : Oi.

The explanandum, expressed by the statement "Oi," consists in the fact that in the particular instance under consideration, here called i (e.g., John Doe's allergic attack), an outcome of kind O (subsidence) occurred. This is explained by means of two explanans-statements. The first of these, "Fi," corresponds to $C_1, C_2, \ldots, C_k$ in (D); it states that in case i, the factors F (which may be more or less complex) were realized. The second expresses a law of probabilistic form, to the effect that the statistical probability for outcome O to occur in cases where F is realized is very high (close to 1). [Because the law is probabilistic], the explanans does not logically imply the explanandum, but only confers a high likelihood upon it. The concept of likelihood here referred to must be clearly distinguished from that of statistical probability, symbolized by "p" in our schema. A statistical probability is, roughly speaking, the long-run relative frequency with which an occurrence of a given kind (say, F) is accompanied by an "outcome" of a specified kind (say, O). Our likelihood, on the other hand, is a relation (capable of gradations) not between kinds of occurrences, but between statements. The likelihood referred to in (P) may be characterized as the strength of the inductive support, or the degree of rational credibility, which the explanans confers upon the explanandum; or, in Carnap's terminology, as the *logical*, or *inductive* (in contrast to statistical), *probability* which the explanandum possesses relative to the explanans.

Thus, probabilistic explanation, just like explanation in the manner of schema (D), is nomological in that it presupposes general laws; but because these laws are of statistical rather than of strictly universal form, the resulting explanatory arguments are inductive rather than deductive in character. An inductive argument of this kind *explains* a given phenomenon by showing that, in view of certain particular events and certain statistical laws, its occurrence was to be expected with high logical, or inductive, probability.

By reason of its inductive character, probabilistic explanation differs from its deductive-nomological counterpart in several other important respects; for example, its explanans may confer upon the explanandum a more or less high degree of inductive support; in this sense, probabilistic explanation admits of degrees, whereas deductive-nomological explanation appears as an either-or affair: a given set of universal laws and particular statements either does or does not imply a given explanandum statement. A fuller examination of these differences, however, would lead us far afield and is not required for the purposes of this essay.[4]

One final point: the distinction here suggested between deductive-nomological and probabilistic explanation might be questioned on the ground that, after all, the universal laws invoked in a deductive explanation can have been established only on the basis of a finite body of evidence, which surely affords no exhaustive verification, but only more or less strong probability for it; and that, therefore, all scientific laws have to be regarded as probabilistic. This argument, however, confounds a logical issue with an epistemological one: it fails to distinguish properly between the *claim* made by a given law-statement and the *degree of confirmation*, or *probability*, which it possesses on the available evidence. It is quite true that statements expressing laws of either kind can be only incompletely confirmed by any given finite set – however large – of data about particular facts; but law-statements of the two different types make claims of different kind, which are reflected in their logical forms: roughly, a universal law-statement of the simplest kind asserts that *all* elements of an indefinitely large reference class (e.g., copper objects) have a certain characteristic (e.g., that of being good conductors of electricity); while statistical law-statements assert that in the long run, a specified proportion of the members of the reference class have some specified property. And our distinction of two types of law and, concomitantly, of two types of scientific explanation, is based on this difference in claim as reflected in the difference of form.

The great scientific importance of probabilistic explanation is eloquently attested to by the extensive and highly successful explanatory use that has been made of fundamental laws of statistical form in genetics, statistical mechanics, and quantum theory.

3. Elliptic and Partial Explanations: Explanation Sketches

As I mentioned earlier, the conception of deductive-nomological explanation reflected in our schema (D) is often referred to as the covering-law model, or the deductive model, of explanation: similarly, the conception underlying schema (P) might be called the probabilistic, or the inductive-statistical, model of explanation. The term "model" can serve as a useful reminder that the two types of explanation as characterized above constitute ideal types or theoretical idealizations and are not intended to reflect the manner in which working scientists actually formulate their explanatory accounts. Rather, they are meant to provide explications, or rational reconstructions, or theoretical models, of certain modes of scientific explanation.

In this respect our models might be compared to the concept of mathematical proof (within a given theory) as construed in metamathematics. This concept, too, may be regarded as a theoretical model: it is not intended to provide a descriptive account of how proofs are formulated in the writings of mathematicians: most of these actual formulations fall short of rigorous and, as it were, ideal, metamathematical standards. But the theoretical model has certain other functions: it exhibits the rationale of mathematical proofs by revealing the logical connections underlying the successive steps; it provides standards for a critical appraisal of any proposed proof constructed within the mathematical system to which the model refers; and it affords a basis for a precise and far-reaching theory of proof, provability, decidability, and related concepts. I think the two models of explanation can fulfill the same functions, if only on a much more modest scale. For example, the arguments presented in constructing the models give an indication of the sense in which the models exhibit the rationale and the logical structure of the explanations they are intended to represent.

I now want to add a few words concerning the second of the functions just mentioned; but I will have to forgo a discussion of the third.

When a mathematician proves a theorem, he will often omit mention of certain propositions which he presupposes in his argument and which he is in fact entitled to presuppose because, for example, they follow readily from the postulates of his system or from previously established theorems or perhaps from the hypothesis of his own theorem, if the latter is in hypothetical form; he then simply assumes that his readers or listeners will be able to supply the missing items if they so desire. If judged by ideal standards, the given formulation of the proof is elliptic or incomplete; but the departure from the ideal is harmless: the gaps can readily be filled in. Similarly, explanations put forward in everyday discourse and also in scientific contexts are often *elliptically formulated*. When we explain, for example, that a lump of butter melted because it was put into a hot frying pan, or that a small rainbow appeared in the spray of the lawn sprinkler because the sunlight was reflected and refracted by the water droplets, we may be said to offer elliptic formulations of deductive-nomological explanations; an account of this kind omits mention of certain laws or particular facts which it tacitly takes for granted, and whose explicit citation would yield a complete deductive-nomological argument.

In addition to elliptic formulation, there is another, quite important, respect in which many explanatory arguments deviate from the theoretical model. It often happens that the statement actually included in the explanans, together with those which may reasonably be assumed to have been taken for granted in the context at hand, explain the given explanandum only *partially*, in a sense which I will try to indicate by an example. In his *Psychopathology of Everyday Life*, Freud offers the following explanation of a slip of the pen that occurred to him: "On a sheet of paper containing principally short daily notes of business interest, I found, to my surprise, the incorrect date, 'Thursday,

October 20th,' bracketed under the correct date of the month of September. It was not difficult to explain this anticipation as the expression of a wish. A few days before I had returned fresh from my vacation and felt ready for any amount of professional work, but as yet there were few patients. On my arrival I had found a letter from a patient announcing her arrival on the 20th of October. As I wrote the same date in September I may certainly have thought 'X. ought to be here already; what a pity about the whole month!,' and with this thought I pushed the current date a month ahead."[5]

Clearly, the formulation of the intended explanation is *at least incomplete* in the sense considered a moment ago. In particular, it fails to mention any laws or theoretical principles in virtue of which the subconscious wish, and the other antecedent circumstances referred to, could be held to explain Freud's slip of the pen. However, the general theoretical considerations Freud presents here and elsewhere in his writings suggest strongly that his explanatory account relies on a hypothesis to the effect that when a person has a strong, though perhaps unconscious, desire, then if he commits a slip of pen, tongue, memory, or the like, the slip will take a form in which it expresses, and perhaps symbolically fulfills, the given desire.

Even this rather vague hypothesis is probably more definite than what Freud would have been willing to assert. But for the sake of the argument let us accept it and include it in the explanans, together with the particular statements that Freud did have the subconscious wish he mentions, and that he was going to commit a slip of the pen. Even then, the resulting explanans permits us to deduce only that the slip made by Freud would, *in some way or other*, express and perhaps symbolically fulfill Freud's subconscious wish. But clearly, such expression and fulfillment might have been achieved by many other kinds of slip of the pen than the one actually committed.

In other words, the explanans does not imply, and thus fully explain, that the particular slip, say s, which Freud committed on this occasion, would fall within the narrow class, say W, of acts which consist in writing the words "Thursday, October 20th"; rather, the explanans implies only that s would fall into a wider class, say F, which includes W as a proper subclass, and which consists of all acts which would express and

symbolically fulfill Freud's subconscious wish *in some way or other*.

The argument under consideration might be called a *partial explanation*: it provides complete, or conclusive, grounds for expecting s to be a member of F, and since W is a subclass of F, it thus shows that the explanandum, i.e., s falling within W, accords with, or bears out, what is to be expected in consideration of the explanans. By contrast, a deductive-nomological explanation of the form (D) might then be called *complete* since the explanans here does imply the explanandum.

Clearly, the question whether a given explanatory argument is complete or partial can be significantly raised only if the explanandum sentence is fully specified; only then can we ask whether the explanandum does or does not follow from the explanans. Completeness of explanation, in this sense, is relative to our explanandum sentence. Now, it might seem much more important and interesting to consider instead the notion of a complete explanation of some *concrete event*, such as the destruction of Pompeii, or the death of Adolf Hitler, or the launching of the first artificial satellite: we might want to regard a particular event as completely explained only if an explanatory account of deductive or of inductive form had been provided for all of its aspects. This notion, however, is self-defeating; for any particular event may be regarded as having infinitely many different aspects or characteristics, which cannot all be accounted for by a finite set, however large, of explanatory statements.

In some cases, what is intended as an explanatory account will depart even further from the standards reflected in the model schemata (D) and (P) above. An explanatory account, for example, which is not explicit and specific enough to be reasonably qualified as an elliptically formulated explanation or as a partial one, can often be viewed as an *explanation sketch*: it may suggest, perhaps quite vividly and persuasively, the general outlines of what, it is hoped, can eventually be supplemented so as to yield a more closely reasoned argument based on explanatory hypotheses which are indicated more fully, and which more readily permit of critical appraisal by reference to empirical evidence.

The decision whether a proposed explanatory account is to be qualified as an elliptically formulated deductive or probabilistic explanation, as a partial explanation, as an explanation sketch, or perhaps as none of these is a matter of judicious interpretation; it calls for an appraisal of the intent of the given argument and of the background assumptions that may be assumed to have been tacitly taken for granted, or at least to be available, in the given context. Unequivocal decision rules cannot be set down for this purpose any more than for determining whether a given informally stated inference which is not deductively valid by reasonably strict standards is to count nevertheless as valid but enthymematically formulated, or as fallacious, or as an instance of sound inductive reasoning, or perhaps, for lack of clarity, as none of these.

Notes

1. See Dewey, John. *How We Think*. Boston, New York, Chicago, 1910; Chapter VI.

2. For a fuller presentation of the model and for further references, see, for example, Hempel, C. G. and P. Oppenheim, "Studies in the Logic of Explanation," *Philosophy of Science* 15:135–175 (1948). (Secs. 1–7 of this article, which contain all the fundamentals of the presentation, are reprinted in Feigl, H. and M. Brodbeck (eds.), *Readings in the Philosophy of Science*. New York, 1953.) The suggestive term "covering law model" is W. Dray's; cf. his *Laws and Explanation in History*. Oxford, 1957; Chapter I. Dray characterizes this type of explanation as "subsuming what is to be explained under a general law" (p. 1), and then rightly urges, in the name of methodological realism, that "the requirement of a *single* law be dropped" (p. 24; italics, the author's): it should be noted, however, that, like the schema (D) above, several earlier publications on the subject (among them the article mentioned at the beginning of this note) make explicit provision for the inclusion of more laws than one in the explanans.

3. The relevance of the covering-law model to causal explanation is examined more fully in sec. 4 of Hempel, C. G., "Deductive-Nomological *vs.* Statistical Explanation." In Feigl, H., et al. (eds.), *Minnesota Studies in the Philosophy of Science*, vol. III. Minneapolis, 1962.

4. The concept of probabilistic explanation, and some of the peculiar logical and methodological problems engendered by it, are examined in some detail in Part II of the essay cited in note 3.

5. Freud, S. *Psychopathology of Everyday Life*. Translated by A. A. Brill. New York (Mentor Books), 1951; p. 64.

26

The Rationale of Actions

William Dray

1. Historical Understanding as 'Empathetic'

It will be my thesis in this chapter that the explanation of individual human behaviour as it is usually given in history has features which make the covering law model peculiarly inept. [*Editors' note:* see the first sentence of Chapter 25, Part III.] What I wish to say may be regarded as an attempt to rehabilitate to some extent a second traditional doctrine of idealist philosophers of history which Gardiner has attacked at length: the view that the objects of historical study are fundamentally different from those, for example, of the natural sciences, because they are the actions of beings like ourselves; and that even if (for the sake of argument) we allow that natural events may be explained by subsuming them under empirical laws, it would still be true that this procedure is inappropriate in history. Sometimes such a view will be supported by the belief that human actions – at any rate the ones we call 'free' – do not fall under law at all. Sometimes it will be alleged only that even if they do fall under law, discovery of the law would still not enable us to understand them in the sense proper to this special subject-matter. It is the second of these claims which I especially want to consider here.

Dray, W. (1957), "The Rationale of Action," in *Laws and Explanation in History* (Oxford: Oxford University Press), 118–137. Reprinted with permission of Oxford University Press.

The doctrine is commonly expressed with the aid of a characteristic set of terms. To understand a human action, it will be said, it is necessary for the inquirer somehow to discover its 'thought-side'; it is not sufficient merely to know the pattern of overt behaviour. The historian must *penetrate* behind appearances, achieve *insight* into the situation, *identify* himself sympathetically with the protagonist, *project* himself imaginatively into his situation. He must *revive, re-enact, re-think, re-experience* the hopes, fears, plans, desires, views, intentions, &c., of those he seeks to understand. To explain action in terms of covering law would be to achieve, at most, an external kind of understanding. The historian, by the very nature of his self-imposed task, seeks to do more than this.

It is worth noticing that historians themselves, and not just professional philosophers of history, often describe their task in these terms. Professor Butterfield is representative of a large group of his professional colleagues when he insists that "the only understanding we ever reach in history is but a refinement, more or less subtle and sensitive, of the difficult – and sometimes deceptive – process of imagining oneself in another person's place". And elsewhere in *History and Human Relations*, he writes:

Our traditional historical writing … has refused to be satisfied with any merely causal or stand-offish attitude towards the personalities of the past. It does not treat them as mere things, or just measure such features of them as the scientist might measure; and it does not

Philosophy of Action: An Anthology, First Edition. Edited by Jonathan Dancy and Constantine Sandis.
© 2015 John Wiley & Sons, Inc. Published 2015 by John Wiley & Sons, Inc.

content itself with merely reporting about them in the way an external observer would do. It insists that the story cannot be told correctly unless we see the personalities from the inside, feeling with them as an actor might feel the part he is playing – thinking their thoughts over again and sitting in the position not of the observer but of the doer of the action. If it is argued that this is impossible – as indeed it is – not merely does it still remain the thing to aspire to, but in any case the historian must put himself in the place of the historical personage, must feel his predicament, must think as though he were that man. Without this art not only is it impossible to tell the story correctly but it is impossible to interpret the very documents on which the reconstruction depends. Traditional historical writing emphasizes the importance of sympathetic imagination for the purpose of getting inside human beings. We may even say that this is part of the science of history for it produces communicable results – the insight of one historian may be ratified by scholars in general, who then give currency to the interpretation that is produced....[1]

Among covering law logicians there is an 'official' answer to philosophers or historians who talk in this way about the peculiarities of 'historical understanding'. The answer is that although there is something right about it, the element of truth in such an account is not a point of logic; it is a mixture of psychological description and methodological precept. As a psychological description of the historian's state of mind when he succeeds in explaining the action of one of his characters, the notion of 'empathy' or 'imaginative understanding', as it is often called, will be allowed some merit – although it will be represented as involving us all too easily in the philosophical error of thinking that merely having certain experiences, or thinking certain thoughts similar to those of the historical agents, itself constitutes understanding or explaining. Similarly, as a suggestion as to how to go about discovering what the agent's motives were, the 'empathy' theory will be admitted to have a certain methodological point – although the reservation will be made that the principle involved often leads the investigator astray. Professor Hempel puts the position succinctly in the following passage:

The historian, we are told, imagines himself in the place of the persons involved in the events which he wants to explain; he tries to realize as completely as possible the circumstances under which they acted, and the motives which influenced their actions; and by this imaginary self-identification with his heroes, he arrives at an understanding and thus at an adequate explanation of the events with which he is concerned.

This method of empathy is, no doubt, frequently applied by laymen and by experts in history. But it does not in itself constitute an explanation; it rather is essentially a heuristic device; its function is to suggest certain psychological hypotheses which might serve as explanatory principles in the case under consideration. Stated in crude terms, the idea underlying this function is the following: the historian tries to realize how he himself would act under the given conditions, and under the particular motivations of his heroes; he tentatively generalizes his findings into a general rule and uses the latter as an explanatory principle in accounting for the actions of the persons involved. Now, this procedure may sometimes prove heuristically helpful; but its use does not guarantee the soundness of the historical explanation to which it leads. The latter rather depends upon the factual correctness of the empirical generalizations which the method of understanding may have suggested.

Nor is the use of this method indispensable for historical explanation. A historian may, for example, be incapable of feeling himself into the role of a paranoiac historic personality, and yet be able to explain certain of his actions; notably by reference to the principles of abnormal psychology. Thus whether the historian is or is not in a position to identify himself with his historical hero, is irrelevant for the correctness of his explanation; what counts, is the soundness of the general hypotheses involved, no matter whether they were suggested by empathy, or by a strictly behaviouristic procedure.[2]

Now I do not wish to deny that there is any value at all in this sort of objection. But I think it important to show that the argument does not cut as deeply as covering law theorists commonly assume. For in recognizing the mixture of psychological and methodological elements in many statements of the idealist position, and in denying that these amount to an analysis of logical structure, these theorists fail to notice what it is about explanations of human actions in history which make the idealists want to say what they do – albeit in a quasi-psychological and quasi-methodological way. And what is left out, I wish to maintain, should properly be taken into account in a *logical* analysis of explanation as it is given in history. I shall argue that idealist theory partially, and perhaps defectively, formulates a certain pragmatic criterion operating in explanations of action given by historians, and that when this is ignored, we are quite properly puzzled as to why certain alleged explanations, which meet the covering law requirements, would be dismissed by historians as unsatisfactory – perhaps even as 'no explanation at all'.

The discussion to follow may be regarded in part as an attempt to 'make sense' of what Collingwood, in particular, has to say about historical understanding – and I make no apology for this. But although some reference will be made to dicta of his, I shall not offer any close textual discussion of his account. I shall try, rather, to bring out independently, by reference to examples, features which covering law theory seems to me to miss, going on thereafter to discuss likely misunderstandings of, and objections to, the logical point which appears to emerge out of such an examination.

2. Explaining and Justifying Actions

The following extract from G. M. Trevelyan's *The English Revolution* is typical of a wide range of explanations of individual actions to be found in ordinary historical writing. In the course of an account of the invasion of England by William of Orange, Trevelyan asks: "Why did Louis make the greatest mistake of his life in withdrawing military pressure from Holland in the summer of 1688?" His answer is:

> He was vexed with James, who unwisely chose this moment of all, to refuse the help and advice of his French patron, upon whose friendship he had based his whole policy. But Louis was not entirely passion's slave. No doubt he felt irritation with James, but he also calculated that, even if William landed in England, there would be civil war and long troubles, as always in that factious island. Meanwhile, he could conquer Europe at leisure. "For twenty years," says Lord Acton, "it had been his desire to neutralize England by internal broils, and he was glad to have the Dutch out of the way (in England) while he dealt a blow at the Emperor Leopold (in Germany)." He thought "it was impossible that the conflict between James and William should not yield him an opportunity." This calculation was not as absurd as it looks after the event. It was only defeated by the unexpected solidity of a new type of Revolution.[3]

What Trevelyan here makes quite explicit is that, when we ask for the explanation of an action, what we very often want is a reconstruction of the agent's *calculation* of means to be adopted toward his chosen end in the light of the circumstances in which he found himself. To explain the action we need to know what considerations convinced him that he should act as he did.

But the notion of discovering the agent's calculation, it must be admitted, takes us no more than one preliminary step towards a satisfactory analysis of such explanations; and it may in itself be misleading. It must not be assumed, for instance, that the agent 'calculated' in the sense of deriving by strict deductive reasoning the practical conclusion he drew – i.e. that the various considerations are elements in a calculus. Indeed, Trevelyan's explanation provides an obvious example to the contrary. Nor should we assume that the explanatory calculation must have been recited in propositional form, either aloud or silently – a notion which one might be forgiven for extracting out of Collingwood's discussion of the way thought must be re-enacted by historians in order to understand intelligent, purposive actions. Not all high-grade actions are performed deliberately in the sense that they are undertaken with a plan consciously preformulated.

Indeed, it is tempting to say that in such cases there is *no* calculation to be *re*constructed by the historian. But such an admission need not affect the main point; for in so far as we say an action is purposive at all, no matter at what level of conscious deliberation, there is a calculation which could be constructed for it: the one the agent would have gone through if he had had time, if he had not seen what to do in a flash, if he had been called upon to account for what he did after the event, &c. And it is by eliciting some such calculation that we explain the action. It might be added that if the agent is to understand his *own* actions, i.e. after the event, he may have to do so by constructing a calculation in exactly the same way, although at the time he recited no propositions to himself. No doubt there are special dangers involved in such construction after the fact. But although we may have to examine very critically any particular example, the point is that when we do consider ourselves justified in accepting an explanation of an individual action, it will most often assume the general *form* of an agent's calculation.

Since the calculation gives what we should normally call the agent's *reasons* for acting as he did, I shall refer hereafter to this broad class of explanations as 'rational'. It should be clear that this use of the expression 'rational explanation' is a narrower one than is often found in philosophical and semi-philosophical literature. It is sometimes said, for instance, that all science, all systematic inquiry, seeks a rational explanation for what is observed, where all that is meant is an explanation which takes account of all the facts considered puzzling, and which does not violate, say, the canons of coherence and induction. I intend something much more restricted than this: an explanation which displays the *rationale* of what was done.

The goal of such explanation is to show that what was done was the thing to have done for the reasons given, rather than merely the thing that is done on such occasions, perhaps in accordance with certain laws (loose or otherwise). The phrase 'thing to have done' betrays a crucially important feature of explanations in terms of agent calculations – a feature quite different from any we have noticed so far. For the infinitive 'to do' here functions as a value term. I wish to claim therefore that there is an element of *appraisal* of what was done in such explanations; that what we want to know when we ask to have the action explained is in what way it was *appropriate*. In the ordinary course of affairs, a demand for explanation is often recognized to be at the same time a challenge to the agent to produce either justification or excuse for what was done. In history, too, I want to argue, it will often be found impossible to bring out the point of what is offered as explanation unless the overlapping of these notions, when it is human actions we are interested in, is explicitly recognized.

Once again, however, I must be on guard against overstating the point; for I do not wish to imply that anything that is explained on the rational model is thereby certified *without qualification* as the right, or proper, or intelligent thing to have done. In saying that the explanation must exhibit what was done as appropriate or justified it is always necessary to add the philosopher's proviso: 'in a sense.'

The sense in question may be clarified if we note a scale along which rational explanations can be ranged. The scale falls away from the simple case in which we can say: 'I find his action perfectly intelligible; he did

exactly as I should have done.' It is a small step from such a case to one where we can understand an action when we see that it is what we should agree was the thing to do in view of the agent's peculiar circumstances. In such a case the explanation would consist of an account of these circumstances; they are the missing data which permit the construction of a calculation certifying the action as appropriate. Sometimes, of course, the agent is found to have been mistaken about the facts – including (as Trevelyan's example of Louis XIV shows) his views about what the results of certain lines of action will be. The agent is thus mistaken about the nature of his circumstances; yet his action can still be explained in the rational way so long as by bringing his erroneous beliefs to bear, the calculation can be satisfactorily constructed. It may also be necessary, at times, to take note explicitly of the agent's purposes, which may be quite different from the ones which the investigator would have had in the same circumstances, or even in the circumstances the agent envisaged. And the calculation may also have to take into account certain peculiar principles of the agent; for the action is rationally explained if it is in accordance with the agent's principles – no matter what we think of these.

There are thus gradations of rational explanation, depending on the amount of 'foreign' data which the investigator must bring in to complete the calculation: beliefs, purposes, principles, &c., of the agent which are different from those we might have assumed in absence of evidence to the contrary. Rational explanation may be regarded as an attempt to reach a kind of logical equilibrium at which point an action is *matched* with a calculation. A demand for explanation arises when the equilibrium is upset – when from the 'considerations' obvious to the investigator it is impossible to see the point of what was done. The function of the historian's explanatory story will in many cases be to sketch in the corrections to these 'obvious' considerations which require to be made if the reader is to be able to say: 'Now I understand what he was about.'

In the light of this account, it should be clear how restricted is the sense in which a rational explanation, as I use the term here, must show that what was done was the appropriate or right thing to have done. It is not necessary for the historian to show that the agent had reason for what he did; it is sufficient for explanation to show that he had reasons. But the element of appraisal remains in that what the historian declares to have been the agent's reasons must really *be* reasons (from the agent's point of view). To record what the agent *said* his reasons were would not be enough to provide a rational explanation unless the cogency of such reported reasons could be appreciated by the historian, when any peculiar beliefs, purposes, or principles of the agent were taken into account. Reported reasons, if they are to be explanatory in the rational way, must be *good* reasons at least in the sense that *if* the situation had been as the agent envisaged it (whether or not we, from our point of vantage, concur in his view of it), then what was done would have been the thing to have done. The historian must be able to 'work' the agent's calculation.

3. The Point of the 'Identification' Metaphor

If my account of rational explanation is correct, what should we say about the view that historical understanding is 'empathetic'? It seems to me that our being able to range rational explanations along a scale in the way described above gives a real point to the 'projection' metaphors used by empathy theorists. Perhaps it is because the scale has been either ignored or misunderstood that what such theorists have said has been so easily written off as obvious but uninteresting, or as interesting but dangerous.

Covering law logicians commonly speak of empathy as a 'methodological dodge'. And it might, I suppose, be claimed that if an old, practised historian were to say to a novice: 'You will never understand the way medieval knights behaved unless you drop your 20th century prejudices and try to see things from their point of view', he *may* be telling the novice how to get on with his job, and thus be making a point which might be called 'methodological'. But I cannot believe that what the old hand offers his young colleague is (in Hempel's words) "a heuristic device" whose function is "to suggest certain psychological hypotheses which might serve as explanatory principles in the case under consideration". As Hempel goes on to explain, by this he means that the historian, since he lacks empirically tested psychological laws

which fit, say, the behaviour of medieval knights, must do something about repairing the deficiency if he is ever to give an explanation of knightly activities; for according to the covering law theory there is no explanation without empirical laws. Clearly the historian, especially the novice, is in no position to work over the whole field himself in search of the required laws. So, according to Hempel, he takes a short cut ; he imagines himself in the knight's position, asks himself what *he* would have done, generalizes the answer as an empirical law covering knights (i.e. from a single imaginary case), and in this way satisfies the logical requirements of the model.

Hempel warns us, of course, that the use of the 'device' does not "guarantee the soundness of the historical explanation to which it leads", which depends rather "upon the factual correctness of the empirical generalizations which the method of understanding may have suggested". That is, we may presume, further empirical confirmation of the generalization must come in before we can regard the explanation as anything more than an inspired guess. In Hempel's terminology, the generalization is only a "hypothesis" until it has received the sort of empirical confirmation and testing that any respectable scientific law must undergo, losing in the process the marks of its Athena-like origin.

In the light of what was said in the previous section, it should be clear how misleading this is as an account of 'empathetic understanding'. No doubt there *is* a methodological side to the doctrine; and it might be formulated in some such way as: 'Only by putting yourself in the agent's position can you *find out* why he did what he did.' Here the suggestion is admittedly that by an imaginative technique we shall discover some *new information* – the agent's motives or reasons for acting. When Collingwood says that historical understanding consists of penetrating to the thought-side of actions – discovering the thought and nothing further – the temptation to interpret this in the methodological way is understandably strong. But there is another way in which the doctrine can be formulated: 'Only by putting yourself in the agent's position can you *understand* why he did what he did.' The point of the 'projection' metaphor is, in this case, more plausibly interpreted as a logical one. Its function is not to remind us of *how we come to know* certain facts, but to formulate, however tentatively, certain *conditions which must be satisfied* before a historian is prepared to say: 'Now I have the explanation.'

To dismiss 'empathy' as a mere 'methodological dodge' is to assume, falsely, that all there is to notice when rational explanations are given is a second-rate method of obtaining the same sort of result as can be obtained more reliably by direct attempts to subsume what is to be explained under an empirical covering law. But, as I have tried to show, at least part of what is meant by talking about the 'need to project', &c., is not achievable at all by the method recommended by covering law theorists. To accept Hempel's argument against 'empathy' is to obliterate a distinction between explanation types: a distinction between representing something as the thing generally done, and representing it as the appropriate thing to have done. Thus, when Hempel, after the passage quoted, goes on to say: "The kind of understanding thus conveyed must be clearly separated from scientific understanding", I have no objection to make, provided that by 'scientific understanding' is meant 'knowing to fall under an empirical law'. But Hempel's account of the alternative is quite unsatisfactory. For 'empathetic understanding', interpreted as 'rational explanation', is *not* a matter of "presenting the phenomena in question as somehow 'plausible' or 'natural' to us ... by means of attractively worded metaphors".

No doubt the widespread resistance to admitting the need to cite anything more than antecedent conditions and a general law in explaining actions owes something to the air of mystery surrounding the language in which 'empathy' theory is often framed: 'projection', 'identification', 'imagination', 'insight', 'intuition', &c. Such words arouse the suspicion that, if the conditions of the covering law theory are not met, it will be necessary to claim that the historian's explanation somehow goes beyond the limits of empirical inquiry into the realm of the unverifiable. As Gardiner puts it, historians often seem to be credited with "an additional power of knowing which allows them to 'penetrate into' the minds of the subjects of their study and take, as it were, psychological X-ray photographs".[4] And in the bulletin of the American Social Science Research Council already referred to, historians are warned against a view of 'historical understanding' supposed to be

"achieved not by introducing general laws or relevant antecedent events, but by an act of 'intuition', 'imaginative identification', 'empathy' or 'valuation' which makes the historical occurrence plausible or intelligible", and whose adequacy is determined by "a self-certifying insight".[5] To allow the legitimacy of empathy appears to many of its opponents as the granting of a licence to eke out scanty evidence with imaginative filler.

It is therefore worth my denying explicitly that what I have called rational explanation is in any damaging sense beyond empirical inquiry. As I have pointed out already, it has an inductive, empirical side, for we build up to explanatory equilibrium *from the evidence*. To get inside Disraeli's shoes the historian does not simply ask himself: 'What would I have done?'; he reads Disraeli's dispatches, his letters, his speeches, &c. – and not with the purpose of discovering antecedent conditions falling under some empirically validated law, but rather in the hope of appreciating the problem as Disraeli saw it. The attempt to provide rational explanation is thus – if you like the term – 'scientific' explanation in a broad sense; there is no question of the investigator letting his imagination run riot. Indeed, many 'empathy' theorists have expressly guarded against such a misinterpretation of their views. To Butterfield, for instance, historical understanding is not a deliberate commission of the sin of anachronism; it is a "process of emptying oneself in order to catch the outlook and feelings of men not like-minded with oneself".[6]

It is true, of course, that the *direction* of inquiry in the explanation of actions is generally from what the inquirer presumes the relevant agent calculation to be – using his own, or his society's conception of rational purposes and principles – to what he discovers to be the peculiar data of the historical agent: a direction suggested by the scale already indicated. In view of this, Butterfield's admonition to 'empty ourselves' is a little sweeping. In achieving rational explanation of an action we do project – but we project from our own point of view. In each case, the inclusion of 'foreign' data in the calculation requires positive evidence that the agent was *not* like-minded with us. The historian does not build up to explanatory equilibrium from scratch. But this is far from admitting the covering law objection that the whole direction of the inquiry amounts to a vicious methodology. The procedure is self-corrective.

There is thus no reason to think that what I am calling 'rational' explanations are put forward as self-evidently true, as some philosophers who talk of 'insight' may seem to imply. Collingwood has sometimes been thought to provide justification for those who attack empathy theory on this account – e.g. when he represents the understanding of an action as an immediate leap to the discovery of its 'inside', without the aid of any general laws, and (it may appear) without the use of any inductive reasoning at all.[7] But it is always possible that a mistake has been made in the inductive reasoning which provided the factual information for the calculation. It is always possible that further data may come in which will upset the logical equilibrium – perhaps evidence that the agent did not know something which it was at first thought he did. The ability of the historian to go through what he takes to be a relevant calculation does not guarantee the correctness of the explanation given; correct *form* is never a guarantee of correct *content*. But this is nothing more than the normal hazard of any empirical inquiry.

4. Generalizations and Principles of Action

Some exponents of the covering law model, while accepting the thesis of the two preceding sections, may object that this only amounts to recognizing an additional condition of a pragmatic sort which explanations must often satisfy in ordinary historical writing. It may be held, therefore, that what I say about rational explanation affects the claims of covering law theory only on its sufficient condition side. It seems to me, however, that in cases where we want to elicit the rationale of what was done, there are special reasons for regarding the model as false or misleading on its necessary condition side as well. For in an important sense, rational explanation falls short of, as well as goes beyond, subsuming a case under a general empirical law.

Any argument to the effect that a satisfactory or complete rational explanation must subsume what is explained under an empirically ascertainable 'regularity'

depends on treating the data of the agent's calculation as 'antecedent conditions' (no doubt a very complicated set). It will be said that no matter what *else* is said about these conditions, they must be data from which what was done could have been predicted; and that the only difficulties we should encounter in trying to formulate the implicit covering law linking these to actions of the kind performed would be the ones discussed in Chapter II above (which I propose to ignore here). If we say: 'Disraeli attacked Peel because Peel was ruining the landed class', we mean *inter alia* that anyone like Disraeli in certain respects would have done the same thing in a situation similar in certain respects – the respects in question being discovered by pressing for amplification of the single reason given.

Now this objection is an important one, because its plausibility arises out of a genuine characteristic of rational explanation which ought to be made clear. For it is quite true that 'reasons for acting' as well as 'conditions for predicting' have a kind of generality or universality. If y is a good reason for A to do x, then y would be a good reason for anyone sufficiently like A to do x under sufficiently similar circumstances. But this universality of reasons is unlike the generality of an empirically validated law in a way which makes it especially hazardous to say that by giving a rational explanation, an historian commits himself to the truth of a corresponding law. For if a negative instance is found for a general empirical law, the law itself must be modified or rejected, since it states that people *do* behave in a certain way under certain circumstances. But if a negative instance is found for the sort of general statement which might be extracted out of a rational explanation, the latter would not necessarily be falsified. For that statement would express a judgement of the form: 'When in a situation of type $C_1 \ldots C_n$ the thing to do is x.' The 'implicit law' in such explanation is better called a *principle of action* than a generalization (or even a principle of inference).[7]

It is true that finding a large number of negative instances – finding that people often do not act in accordance with it – would create a presumption against the claim of a given principle to universal validity. But it would not *compel* its withdrawal; and if it was not withdrawn, the explanatory value of the principle for those actions which *were* in accordance with it would remain. It is true, too, that if a particular person often acted at variance with a principle which he was said to hold, the statement that he held that principle would come into question. But that statement would not *necessarily* be falsified; and if it were retained, we could still explain in the rational way those of his actions which *were* in accordance with it. The connexion between a principle of action and the 'cases' falling under it is thus intentionally and peculiarly loose.

I do not deny, of course, that we often *can* predict successfully a person's response to a situation if we know, among other things, what his principles are (in so far as they are peculiar). In representing the action as the thing to have done, even in the extended sense required for rational explanation, we to some extent license the conclusion that it was the thing to have expected. Having said 'A did x because of y', where y is A's reason for doing x, we could also say that a bystander who knew the fact y, and also knew what A's purposes and principles were, should not be surprised at A's doing x. It is thus easy enough, under the guidance of a general theory of explanation which requires it, to slip into believing that the real force of the original explanation resides in alleviating such surprise; that its point is to show that this is the kind of thing we can expect to be done by such a person in such circumstances, and that the justification for the expectation must be found in experience of similar cases.

The widespread failure to distinguish between explanations which 'apply' empirical laws and those which 'apply' principles of action may owe something to the fact that the word 'because' is systematically ambiguous in this connexion. Taken in isolation, it is very seldom beyond all doubt whether a given explanatory statement of the form 'He did x because of y' is to be taken in the rational sense or not, i.e. whether the 'because' derives its explanatory force from an empirical law or a principle. The particular 'because' does not carry its language level on its face; this has to be determined by other means. It is thus often possible to interpret an explanation at the wrong level for a long time without committing any obvious logical errors. And this leaves plenty of room for manœuvring by philosophers who have a thesis to maintain which requires that only one level be recognized.

Whether an explanation of a piece of behaviour is to be interpreted rationally or not will often depend on the context of utterance; we may have to ask how the explanation would be argued for, what else would be said if it were expanded, &c. Take the following example from Trevelyan's discussion of the problem of the early eighteenth-century smog in London:

> On days when the north-east wind carried the smoke-cloud, even Chelsea became dangerous to the asthmatic, as the mild philosopher Earl of Shaftesbury had reason to complain. There is no wonder that King William with his weak lungs had lived at Hampton Court when he could, and at Kensington when he must.[8]

The explanation offered can easily be reduced to a 'because' statement. But what exactly does the historian mean to imply: does he mean that any person *would* have done so, circumstances being what they were? Or does he mean that any *sensible* person would have done so? The explanation could surely be pushed either way, depending on how we cared to read it. And the explanation may be satisfactory (in the sense of 'adequate for its type') no matter which way it is read. Butterfield would no doubt elect to defend it in the second, or rational, way, while Gardiner, in the interests of his thesis, could choose the regularity way without obvious logical error. We cannot settle the issue between them until the writer gives us a more definite indication of what he intends. It is worth noticing, in this connexion, that many of the examples used by Gardiner to support the covering law model could be plausibly re-analysed in the rational way. The force of the explanation of Louis XIV's unpopularity in terms of his policies being detrimental to French interests is very likely to be found in the detailed description of the aspirations, beliefs, and problems of Louis's subjects. Given these men and their situation, Louis and his policies, their dislike of the king was an *appropriate* response.

Nor is the ambiguity confined to the word 'because'; it can be traced through a wide variety of terms used to describe and explain actions. It can be found, for instance, in the terms 'natural' and 'humanly possible', which Mr. W. H. Walsh employs in *An Introduction to Philosophy of History*, when arguing that explanations of action in history are accomplished by means of basic non-technical generalizations.[9] "We are agreed", Walsh declares, "that to understand an historical situation we must bring some kind of general knowledge to bear on it, and the first question to ask here is clearly in what this general knowledge consists." Against the positivists he maintains that the most important generalizations used in an historian's explanations do not come from any of the sciences; they are fundamental judgements about human nature – "judgments about the characteristic responses human beings made to the various challenges set them in the course of their lives, whether by the natural conditions in which they live, or by their fellow beings". These constitute a 'science of human nature' distinguishable from scientific psychology; they provide the historian with a criterion of what is 'humanly possible', when he seeks to understand the past.

But the 'science of human nature' here described does not differ logically from scientific psychology; it is really just the common-sense psychology of the plain man. If left at that, Walsh's argument would make no other point against the positivists than Hempel's own admission that, because of the unfortunate backwardness of the science of psychology, historians must formulate many of the 'laws of human nature' required on the basis of their own experience. But the facts of historical writing which stimulate Walsh's sympathy with the idealists seem to me to require our drawing, not a distinction merely between different *sources* of empirical laws used, but between different *types* of explanation. For we sometimes want to explain actions not by representing them as instances of laws, but as the reasonable thing to have done; and when we do, if we appeal to 'general knowledge' at all, it is to principles of behaviour rather than empirical generalizations; to knowledge of what to do rather than of what is usually or always done.

Walsh does not put it this way, yet there are suggestions of the point in some of his remarks. For instance, in pointing out that the basic general knowledge which historians bring to their work differs from one historian to another, he includes both knowledge of how men *do* and (he adds 'perhaps') *should* behave.[10] And again, in a footnote, he considers favourably Ryle's term 'knowledge how' (i.e. practical knowledge of some kind) as a characterization of what is to be included in the envisaged 'science of human nature'.[11] There is a hint of the same view in his acceptance of the suggestion that the 'science' in question is continuous with common sense – which, it may be remarked, is generally taken to cover our knowledge of what to do, as well as of what is generally done.[12] And the use of 'challenge-response' terminology in describing the nature of the fundamental judgements concerned points roughly in the same direction.[13]

Walsh's terms 'humanly possible' and 'human nature' are located at the centre of the difficulty; they straddle the distinction between explanation types, or between the levels of language at which we talk about actions. Consider the following explanatory remark of Ramsey Muir about a political decision of George III. "The king", he writes, "... naturally chose Shelburne rather than the hated Whigs."[14] In a way, this word does, as Walsh might say, represent the action as a characteristic response, in that anyone with George III's political memories would have tried to keep the Whigs out. But there is a very strong suggestion, too, that this response was *appropriate* in a rational sense; to say the choice naturally went to Shelburne is to imply that this was obviously the right thing for the king to do – from his point of view. Similarly, saying that an historian has a keen appreciation of what is 'humanly possible' *may* refer to the sort of law-governed phenomenon Walsh cites, e.g. "that men who undergo great physical privations are for the most part lacking in mental energy". But I think it may just as well refer to the fundamental principles on which any man may be expected to order his activities.

Notes

1. *History and Human Relations* (London, 1951), pp. 145–6. See also pp. 116–17.
2. C. G. Hempel, "The Function of General Laws in History," in *Readings in Philosophical Analysis*, H. Feigl and W. Sellars, eds. (New York, 1949), p. 467. A similar argument is used by R. M. Crawford, "History as Science," *Historical Studies, Australia and New Zealand*, 1947, p. 157; R. S. Peters, "Motives and Causes,"

Proceedings of the Aristotelian Society, supp. vol., 1952, p. 143; P. L. Gardiner, *The Nature of Historical Explanation* (Oxford, 1952), p. 129; and A. Danto, "Mere Chronicles and History Proper," *Journal of Philosophy*, 1953, p. 176.

3. *The English Revolution* (London, 1938), pp. 105–6.
4. Op. cit., p. 128.
5. *Bulletin No. 54*, 1946, p. 128.
6. *History and Human Relations*, p. 146.
7. e.g. "When [the historian] knows what happened, he already knows why it happened" (*The Idea of History*, p. 214).

8. *English Social History* (London, 1946), p. 337.
9. *An Introduction to the Philosophy of History* (London, 1951), Chap. III, sections 4, 5.
10. p. 69.
11. p. 67.
12. p. 66.
13. p. 65.
14. *A Short History of the British Commonwealth* (London, 1922), vol. ii, p. 105.

27

Explanation in Science and in History §§4–7

Carl G. Hempel

So far, we have examined nomological explanation, both deductive and inductive, as found in the natural sciences; and we have considered certain characteristic ways in which actual explanatory accounts often depart from the ideal standards of our two basic models. Now it is time to ask what light the preceding inquiries can shed on the explanatory procedures used in historical research.

In examining this question, we will consider a number of specific explanatory arguments offered by a variety of writers. It should be understood from the beginning that we are here concerned, not to appraise the factual adequacy of these explanations, but only to attempt an explication of the claims they make and of the assumptions they presuppose.

Let us note first, then, that some historical explanations are surely nomological in character: they aim to show that the explanandum phenomenon resulted from certain antecedent, and perhaps, concomitant, conditions; and in arguing these, they rely more or less explicitly on relevant generalizations. These may concern, for example, psychological or sociological tendencies and may best be conceived as broadly probabilistic in character. This point is illustrated by the following argument, which might be called an attempt to explain Parkinson's Law by subsumption under broader psychological principles:

> As the activities of the government are enlarged, more people develop a vested interest in the continuation and expansion of governmental functions. People who have jobs do not like to lose them; those who are habituated to certain skills do not welcome change; those who have become accustomed to the exercise of a certain kind of power do not like to relinquish their control – if anything, they want to develop greater power and correspondingly greater prestige.... Thus, government offices and bureaus, once created, in turn institute drives, not only to fortify themselves against assault, but to enlarge the scope of their operations.[1]

The psychological generalizations here explicitly adduced will reasonably have to be understood as expressing, not strict uniformities, but strong *tendencies*, which might be formulated by means of rough probability statements; so that the explanation here suggested is probabilistic in character.

As a rule, however, the generalizations underlying a proposed historical explanation are largely left unspecified; and most concrete explanatory accounts have to be qualified as partial explanations or as explanation sketches. Consider, for example, F. J. Turner's essay "The Significance of the Frontier in

Hempel, C. G. (1963), "Explanation in Science and in History §§4–7," in Robert G. Colodny (ed.), *Frontiers of Science and Philosophy* (Pittsburgh, Pa.: University of Pittsburgh Press), 284–296. Reprinted with permission of University of Pittsburgh Press.

Philosophy of Action: An Anthology, First Edition. Edited by Jonathan Dancy and Constantine Sandis.

American History,"[2] which amplifies and defends the view that

> up to our own day American history has been in a large degree the history of the colonization of the Great West. The existence of an area of free land, its continuous recession, and the advance of American settlement westward explain American development.... The peculiarity of American institutions is the fact that they have been compelled to adapt themselves ... to the changes involved in crossing a continent, in winning a wilderness, and in developing at each area of this progress, out of the primitive economic and political conditions of the frontier, the complexity of city life.[3]

One of the phenomena Turner considers in developing his thesis is the rapid westward advance of what he calls the Indian trader's frontier. "Why was it," Turner asks, "that the Indian trader passed so rapidly across the continent?"; and he answers, "The explanation of the rapidity of this advance is bound up with the effects of the trader on the Indian. The trading post left the unarmed tribes at the mercy of those that had purchased firearms – a truth which the Iroquois Indians wrote in blood, and so the remote and unvisited tribes gave eager welcome to the trader.... This accounts for the trader's power and the rapidity of his advance."[4] There is no explicit mention here of any laws, but it is clear that this sketch of an explanation presupposes, first of all, various particular facts, such as that the remote and unvisited tribes had heard of the efficacy and availability of firearms, and that there were no culture patterns or institutions precluding their use by those tribes; but in addition, the account clearly rests also on certain assumptions as to how human beings will tend to behave in situations presenting the kinds of danger and of opportunity that Turner refers to.

Similar comments apply to Turner's account of the westward advance of what he calls the farmer's frontier:

> Omitting those of the pioneer farmers who move from the love of adventure, the advance of the more steady farmer is easy to understand. Obviously the immigrant was attracted by the cheap lands of the frontier, and even the native farmer felt their influence strongly. Year by year the farmers who lived on soil, whose returns were diminished by unrotated crops, were offered the virgin soil of the frontier at nominal prices. Their growing families demanded more lands, and these were dear. The competition of the unexhausted, cheap, and easily tilled prairie lands compelled the farmer either to go West ... or to adopt intensive culture.[5]

This passage is clearly intended to do more than describe a sequence of particular events: it is meant to afford an understanding of the farmers' westward advance by pointing to their interests and needs and by calling attention to the facts and the opportunities facing them. Again, this explanation takes it for granted that under such conditions normal human beings will tend to seize new opportunities in the manner in which the pioneer farmers did.

Examining the various consequences of this moving-frontier history, Turner states that "the most important effect of the frontier has been in the promotion of democracy here and in Europe,"[6] and he begins his elaboration of this theme with the remark that "the frontier is productive of individualism.... The tendency is anti-social. It produces antipathy to control, and particularly to any direct control":[7] and this is, of course, a sociological generalization in a nutshell.

Similarly, any explanation that accounts for a historical phenomenon by reference to economic factors or by means of general principles of social or cultural change is nomological in import, even if not in explicit formulation.

But if this be granted there still remains another question, to which we must now turn, namely, whether, in addition to explanations of a broadly nomological character, the historian also employs certain other distinctly historical ways of explaining and understanding whose import cannot be adequately characterized by means of our two models. The question has often been answered in the affirmative, and several kinds of historical explanation have been adduced in support of this affirmation. I will now consider what seem to me two especially interesting candidates for the role of specifically historical explanation; namely first, genetic explanation, and secondly, explanation of an action in terms of its underlying rationale.

1. Genetic Explanation in History

In order to make the occurrence of a historical phenomenon intelligible, a historian will frequently offer a "genetic explanation" aimed at exhibiting the principal stages in a sequence of events which led up to the given phenomenon.

Consider, for example, the practice of selling indulgences as it existed in Luther's time. H. Boehmer, in his work, *Luther and the Reformation*, points out that until about the end of the nineteenth century, "the indulgence was in fact still a great unknown quantity, at sight of which the scholar would ask himself with a sigh: 'Where did it come from?'"[8] An answer was provided by Adolf Gottlob,[9] who tackled the problem by asking himself what led the popes and bishops to offer indulgences. As a result, "... origin and development of the unknown quantity appeared clearly in the light, and doubts as to its original meaning came to an end. It revealed itself as a true descendant of the time of the great struggle between Christianity and Islam, and at the same time a highly characteristic product of Germanic Christianity."[10]

In brief outline,[11] the origins of the indulgence appear to go back to the ninth century, when the popes were strongly concerned with the fight against Islam. The Mohammedan fighter was assured by the teachings of his religion that if he were to be killed in battle his soul would immediately go to heaven; but the defender of the Christian faith had to fear that he might still be lost if he had not done the regular penance for his sins. To allay these doubts, John VII, in 877, promised absolution for their sins to crusaders who should be killed in battle. "Once the crusade was so highly thought of, it was an easy transition to regard participation in a crusade as equivalent to the performance of atonement ... and to promise remission of these penances in return for expeditions against the Church's enemies."[12] Thus, there was introduced the indulgence of the Cross, which granted complete remission of the penitential punishment to all those who participated in a religious war. "If it is remembered what inconveniences, what ecclesiastical and civil disadvantages the ecclesiastical penances entailed, it is easy to understand that the penitents flocked to obtain this indulgence."[13] A further strong incentive came from the belief that whoever obtained an indulgence secured liberation not only from the ecclesiastical penances, but also from the corresponding suffering in purgatory after death. The benefits of these indulgences were next extended to those who, being physically unfit to participate in a religious war, contributed the funds required to send a soldier on a crusade: in 1199, Pope Innocent III recognized the payment of money as adequate qualification for the benefits of a crusading indulgence.

When the crusades were on the decline, new ways were explored of raising funds through indulgences. Thus, there was instituted a "jubilee indulgence," to be celebrated every hundred years, for the benefit of pilgrims coming to Rome on that occasion. The first of these indulgences, in 1300, brought in huge sums of money; and the time interval between successive jubilee indulgences was therefore reduced to 50, 33, and even 25 years. And from 1393 on the jubilee indulgence was made available, not only in Rome, for the benefit of pilgrims, but everywhere in Europe, through special agents who were empowered to absolve the penitent of their sins upon payment of an appropriate amount. The development went even further: in 1477, a dogmatic declaration by Sixtus IV attributed to the indulgence the power of delivering even the dead from purgatory.

Undeniably, a genetic account of this kind can enhance our understanding of a historical phenomenon. But its explanatory role, far from being *sui generis*, seems to me basically nomological in character. For the successive stages singled out for consideration surely must be qualified for their function by more than the fact that they form a temporal sequence and that they all precede the final stage, which is to be explained: the mere enumeration in a yearbook of "the year's important events" in the order of their occurrence clearly is not a genetic explanation of the final event or of anything else. In a genetic explanation each stage must be shown to "lead to" the next, and thus to be linked to its successor by virtue of some general principle which makes the occurrence of the latter at least reasonably probable, given the former. But in this sense, even successive stages in a physical phenomenon such as the free fall of a stone may be regarded as forming a genetic sequence whose different stages – characterized, let us say, by the position and the velocity of the stone at different times – are interconnected by strictly universal laws; and the successive stages in the movement of a steel ball bouncing its zigzaggy way down a Galton pegboard may be regarded as forming a genetic sequence with probabilistic connections.

The genetic accounts given by historians are not, of course, of the purely nomological kind suggested by these examples from physics. Rather, they combine a certain measure of nomological interconnecting with more or less large amounts of straight description. For consider an intermediate stage mentioned in a genetic account: some aspects of it will be presented as having evolved from the preceding stages (in virtue of connecting laws, which often will be no more than hinted at); while other aspects, which are not accounted for by information about the preceding development, will be descriptively added because they are relevant to an understanding of subsequent stages in the genetic sequence. Thus, schematically speaking, a genetic explanation will begin with a pure description of an initial stage; thence, it will proceed to an account of a second stage, part of which is nomologically linked to, and explained by, the characteristic features of the initial stage; while the balance is simply described as relevant for a nomological account of some aspects of the third stage; and so forth.[14]

In our illustration the connecting laws are hinted at in the mention made of motivating factors: the explanatory claims made for the interest of the popes in securing a fighting force and in amassing ever larger funds clearly presuppose suitable psychological generalizations as to the manner in which an intelligent individual will act, in the light of his factual beliefs, when he seeks to attain a certain objective. Similarly, general assumptions underlie the reference to the fear of purgatory in explaining the eagerness with which indulgences were bought. And when, referring to the huge financial returns of the first jubilee indulgence, Schwiebert says "This success only whetted the insatiable appetite of the popes. The intervening period of time was variously reduced from 100 to 50, to 33, to 25 years …,"[15] the explanatory force here implied might be said to rest on some principle of reinforcement by rewards. As need hardly be added, even if

such a principle were explicitly introduced, the resulting account would provide at most a partial explanation; it could not be expected to show, for example, why the intervening intervals should have the particular lengths here mentioned.

In the genetic account of the indulgences, those factors which are simply described (or tacitly presupposed) rather than explained include, for example, the doctrines, the organization, and the power of the Church; the occurrence of the crusades and their eventual decline; and innumerable other factors which are not even explicitly mentioned, but which have to be understood as background conditions if the genetic survey is to serve its explanatory purpose.

The general conception here outlined of the logic of genetic explanation could also be illustrated by reference to Turner's studies of the American frontier; this will be clear even from the brief remarks made earlier on Turner's ideas.

Some analysts of historical development put special emphasis on the importance of the laws underlying a historical explanation; thus, e.g., A. Gerschenkron maintains, "Historical research consists essentially in application to empirical material of various sets of empirically derived hypothetical generalizations and in testing the closeness of the resulting fit, in the hope that in this way certain uniformities, certain typical situations, and certain typical relationships among individual factors in these situations can be ascertained,"[16] and his subsequent substantive observations include a brief genetic survey of patterns of industrial development in nineteenth-century Europe, in which some of the presumably relevant uniformities are made reasonably explicit.

2. Explanation by Motivating Reasons

Let us now turn to another kind of historical explanation that is often considered as *sui generis*, namely, the explanation of an action in terms of the underlying *rationale*, which will include, in particular, the ends the agent sought to attain, and the alternative courses of action he believed to be open to him. The following passage explaining the transition from the indulgence of the Cross to the institution of the jubilee indulgence illustrates this procedure:

> ... in the course of the thirteenth century the idea of a crusade more and more lost its power over men's spirits. If the Popes would keep open the important source of income which the indulgence represented, they must invent new motives to attract people to the purchase of indulgences. It is the merit of Boniface VIII to have recognized this clearly. By creating the jubilee indulgence in 1300 he assured the species a further long development most welcome to the Papal finances.[17]

This passage clearly seeks to explain the establishment of the first jubilee indulgence by suggesting the reasons for which Boniface VIII took this step. If properly spelled out, these reasons would include not only Boniface's objective of ensuring a continuation of the income so far derived from the indulgence of the Cross, but also his estimate of the relevant empirical circumstances, including the different courses of action open to him, and their probable efficacy as well as potential difficulties in pursuing them and adverse consequences to which they might lead.

The kind of explanation achieved by specifying the rationale underlying a given action is widely held to be fundamentally different from nomological explanation as found in the natural sciences. Various reasons have been adduced in support of this view; but I will limit my discussion largely to the stimulating ideas on the subjects that have been set forth by Dray.[18] According to Dray, there is an important type of historical explanation whose features "make the covering law model peculiarly inept"; he calls it "rational explanation," i.e., "explanation which displays the *rationale* of what was done," or, more fully, "a reconstruction of the agent's *calculation* of means to be adopted toward his chosen end in the light of the circumstances in which he found himself." The object of rational explanation is not to subsume the explanandum under general laws, but "to show that what was done was the thing to have done for the reasons given, rather than merely the thing that is done on such occasions, perhaps in accordance with certain laws." Hence, a rational explanation has "an element of *appraisal*" in it: it "must exhibit what was done as appropriate or justified." Accordingly, Dray conceives a rational explanation as being based on a standard of appropriateness or of

rationality of a special kind which he calls a "*principle of action*," i.e., "a judgment of the form 'When in a situation of type $C_1, C_2, \ldots C_n$ the thing to do is X.'"

Dray does not give a full account of the kind of "situation" here referred to; but to do justice to his intentions, these situations must evidently be taken to include, at least, items of the following three types: (i) the end the agent was seeking to attain; (ii) the empirical circumstances, as seen by the agent, in which he had to act; (iii) the moral standards or principles of conduct to which the agent was committed. For while this brief list requires considerable further scrutiny and elaboration, it seems clear that only if at least these items are specified does it make sense to raise the question of the appropriateness of what the agent did in the given "situation."

It seems fair to say, then, that according to Dray's conception a rational explanation answers a question of the form "Why did agent A do X?" by offering an explanans of the following type (our formulation replaces the notation "$C_1, C_2, \ldots C_n$" by the simpler "C", without, of course, precluding that the kind of situation thus referred to may be extremely complex):

(R)   A was in a situation of type C.
       In a situation of type C, the appropriate thing to do is X.

But can an explanans of this type possibly serve to explain A's having in fact done X? It seems to me beyond dispute that in any adequate explanation of an empirical phenomenon the explanans must provide good grounds for believing or asserting that the explanandum phenomenon did in fact occur. Yet this requirement, which is necessary though not sufficient[19] for an adequate explanation, is not met by a rational explanation as conceived by Dray. For the two statements included in the contemplated explanans (R) provide good reasons for believing that the appropriate thing for A to do was X, but not for believing that A did in fact do X. Thus, a rational explanation in the sense in which Dray appears to understand it does not explain what it is meant to explain. Indeed, the expression "the thing to do" in the standard formulation of a principle of action, "functions as a value term," as Dray himself points out: but then, it is unclear, on purely logical grounds, how the valuational principle expressed by the second sentence in (R), in conjunction with the plainly empirical, nonvaluational first sentence, should permit any inferences concerning empirical matters such as A's action, which could not be drawn from the first sentence alone.

To explain, in the general vein here under discussion, why A did in fact do X, we have to refer to the underlying rationale not by means of a normative principle of action, but by descriptive statements to the effect that, at the time in question A was a rational agent, or had the disposition to act rationally; and that a rational agent, when in circumstances of kind C, will always (or: with high probability) do X. Thus construed, the explanans takes on the following form:

(R′)   a. A was in a situation of type C
         b. A was disposed to act rationally
         c. Any person who is disposed to act rationally will, when in a situation of type C, invariably (with high probability) do X.

But by this explanans A's having done X is accounted for in the manner of a deductive or of a probabilistic nomological explanation. Thus, in so far as reference to the rationale of an agent does explain his action, the explanation conforms to one of our nomological models.

An analogous diagnosis applies, incidentally, also to explanations which attribute an agent's behavior in a given situation not to rationality and more or less explicit deliberation on his part, but to other dispositional features, such as his character and emotional make-up. The following comment on Luther illustrates this point:

> Even stranger to him than the sense of anxiety was the allied sense of fear. In 1527 and 1535, when the plague broke out in Wittenberg, he was the only professor besides Bugenhagen who remained calmly at his post to comfort and care for the sick and dying.... He had, indeed, so little sense as to take victims of the plague into his house and touch them with his own hand. Death, martyrdom, dishonor, contempt ... he feared just as little infectious disease.[20]

It may well be said that these observations give more than a description: that they shed some explanatory light on the particular occurrences mentioned. But in so far as they explain, they do so by presenting Luther's actions as manifestations of certain personality traits, such as fearlessness; thus, the particular acts are again subsumed under generalizations as to how a fearless person is likely to behave under certain circumstances.

It might seem that both in this case and in rational explanation as construed in (R′), the statements which we took to express general laws – namely, (c) in (R′), and the statement about the probable behavior of a fearless person in our last illustration – do not have the character of empirical laws at all, but rather that of analytic statements which simply express part of what is *meant* by a rational agent, a fearless person, or the like. Thus, in contrast to nomological explanations, these accounts in terms of certain dispositional characteristics of the agent appear to presuppose no general laws at all. Now, the idea of analyticity gives rise to considerable philosophical difficulties; but let us disregard these here and take the division of statements into analytic and synthetic to be reasonably clear. Even then, the objection just outlined cannot be upheld. For dispositional concepts of the kind invoked in our explanations have to be regarded as governed by entire clusters of general statements – we might call them symptom statements – which connect the given disposition with various specific manifestations, or symptoms, of its presence (each symptom will be a particular mode of "responding," or acting, under specified "stimulus" conditions); and the whole cluster of these symptom statements for a given disposition will have implications which are plainly not analytic (in the intuitive sense here assumed). Under these circumstances it would be arbitrary to attribute to some of the symptom statements the analytic character of partial definitions.

The logic of this situation has a precise representation in Carnap's theory of reduction sentences.[21] Here, the connections between a given disposition and its various manifest symptoms are assumed to be expressed by a set of so-called reduction sentences (these are characterized by their logical form). Some of these state, in terms of manifest characteristics, sufficient conditions for the presence of the given disposition; others similarly state necessary conditions. The reduction sentences for a given dispositional concept cannot, as a rule, all be qualified as analytic; for jointly they imply certain nonanalytic consequences which have the status of general laws connecting exclusively the manifest characteristics; the strongest of the laws so implied is the so-called *representative sentence*, which "represents, so to speak, the factual content of the set" of all the reduction sentences for the given disposition concept. This representative sentence asserts, in effect, that whenever at least one of the sufficient conditions specified by the given reduction sentences is satisfied, then so are all the necessary conditions laid down by the reduction sentences. And when A is one of the manifest criteria sufficient for the presence of a given disposition, and B is a necessary one, then the statement that whenever A is present so is B will normally turn out to be synthetic.

So far then, I have argued that Dray's construal of explanation by motivating reasons is untenable; that the normative principles of action envisaged by him have to be replaced by statements of a dispositional kind; and that, when this is done, explanations in terms of a motivating rationale, as well as those referring to other psychological factors, are seen to be basically nomological.

Let me add a few further remarks on the idea of rational explanation. First: in many cases of so-called purposive action, there is no conscious deliberation, no rational calculation that leads the agent to his decision. Dray is quite aware of this; but he holds that a rational explanation in his sense is still possible; for "in so far as we say an action is purposive at all, no matter at what level of conscious deliberation, there is a calculation which could be constructed for it: the one the agent would have gone through if he had had time, if he had not seen what to do in a flash, if he had been called upon to account for what he did after the event, etc. And it is by eliciting some such calculation that we explain the action."[22] But the explanatory significance of reasons or "calculations" which are "reconstructed" in this manner is certainly puzzling. If, to take Dray's example, an agent arrives at his decision "in a flash" rather than by deliberation, then it would seem to be simply false to say that the decision can be accounted for by some argument which the agent might have gone through under more propitious circumstances, or which he might produce later if

called upon to account for his action; for, by hypothesis, no such argument was in fact gone through by the agent at the crucial time; considerations of appropriateness or rationality played no part in shaping his decision; the rationale that Dray assumes to be adduced and appraised in the corresponding rational explanation is simply fictitious.

But, in fairness to Dray, these remarks call for a qualifying observation: in at least some of the cases Dray has in mind it might not be fictitious to ascribe the action under study to a disposition which the agent acquired through a learning process whose initial stages did involve conscious ratiocination. Consider, for example, the various complex maneuvers of accelerating, braking, signaling, dodging jaywalkers and animals, swerving into and out of traffic lanes, estimating the changes of traffic lights, etc., which are involved in driving a car through city traffic. A beginning driver will often perform these only upon some sort of conscious deliberation or even calculation; but gradually, he learns to do the appropriate thing automatically, "in a flash," without giving them any conscious thought. The habit pattern he has thus acquired may be viewed as consisting in a set of dispositions to react in certain appropriate ways in various situations; and a particular performance of such an appropriate action would then be explained, not by a "constructed" calculation which actually the agent did not perform but by reference to the disposition just mentioned and thus, again, in a nomological fashion.

The method of explaining a given action by "constructing," in Dray's sense, the agent's calculation of means faces yet another, though less fundamental, difficulty: it will frequently yield a rationalization rather than an explanation, especially when the reconstruction relies on the reasons the agent might produce when called upon to account for his action. As G. Watson remarks, "Motivation, as presented in the perspective of history, is often too simple and straightforward, reflecting the psychology of the Age of Reason.... Psychology has come ... to recognize the enormous weight of irrational and intimately personal impulses in conduct. In history, biography, and in autobiography, especially of public characters, the tendency is strong to present 'good' reasons instead of 'real' reasons."[23] Accordingly, as Watson goes on to point out, it is important, in examining the motivation of historical figures, to take into account the significance of such psychological mechanisms as reaction formation, "the dialectic dynamic by which stinginess cloaks itself in generosity, or rabid pacifism arises from the attempt to repress strong aggressive impulses."[24]

These remarks have a bearing also on an idea set forth by P. Gardiner in his illuminating book on historical explanation.[25] Commenting on the notion of the "real reason" for a man's action, Gardiner says: "In general, it appears safe to say that by a man's 'real reasons' we mean those reasons he would be prepared to give under circumstances where his confession would not entail adverse consequences to himself." And he adds, "An exception to this is the psychoanalyst's usage of the expression where different criteria are adopted."[26] This observation might be taken to imply that the explanation of human actions in terms of underlying motives is properly aimed at exhibiting the agent's "real reasons" in the ordinary sense of the phrase, as just described; and that, by implication, reasons in the psychoanalyst's sense require less or no consideration. But such a construal of explanation would give undue importance to considerations of ordinary language. Gardiner is entirely right when he reminds us that the "language in which history is written is for the most part the language of ordinary speech";[27] but the historian in search of reasons that will correctly explain human actions will obviously have to give up his reliance on the everyday conception of "real reasons" if psychological or other investigations show that real reasons, thus understood, do not yield as adequate an account of human actions as an analysis in terms of less familiar conceptions such as, perhaps, the idea of motivating factors which are kept out of the agent's normal awareness by processes of repression and reaction formation.

I would say, then, first of all, that historical explanation cannot be bound by conceptions that might be implicit in the way in which ordinary language deals with motivating reasons. But secondly, I would doubt that Gardiner's expressly tentative characterization does justice even to what we ordinarily mean when we speak of a man's "real reasons." For considerations of the kind that support the idea of

subconscious motives are quite familiar in our time, and we are therefore prepared to say in ordinary, nontechnical discourse that the reasons given by an agent may not be the "real reasons" behind his action, even if his statement was subjectively honest, and he had no grounds to expect that it would lead to any adverse consequences for him. For no matter whether an explanation of human actions is attempted in the language of ordinary speech or in the technical terms of some theory, the overriding criterion for what-if-anything should count as a "real," and thus explanatory, reason for a given action is surely not to be found by examining the way in which the term "real reason" has thus far been used, but by investigating what conception of real reason would yield the most satisfactory explanation of human conduct; and ordinary usage gradually changes accordingly.

3. Concluding Remarks

We have surveyed some of the most prominent candidates for the role of characteristically historical mode of explanation; and we have found that they conform essentially to one or the other of our two basic types of scientific explanation.

This result and the arguments that led to it do not in any way imply a mechanistic view of man, of society, and of historical processes; nor, of course, do they deny the importance of ideas and ideals for human decision and action. What the preceding considerations do suggest is, rather, that the nature of understanding, in the sense in which explanation is meant to give us an understanding of empirical phenomena, is basically the same in all areas of scientific inquiry; and that the deductive and the probabilistic model of nomological explanation accommodate vastly more than just the explanatory arguments of, say, classical mechanics: in particular, they accord well also with the character of explanations that deal with the influence of rational deliberation, of conscious and subconscious motives, and of ideas and ideals on the shaping of historical events. In so doing, our schemata exhibit, I think, one important aspect of the methodological unity of all empirical science.

Notes

1. McConnell, D. W., et al. *Economic Behavior*. New York, 1939; pp. 894–95.

2. First published in 1893, and reprinted in several publications, among them: Edwards, Everett E. (ed.), *The Early Writings of Frederick Jackson Turner*. Madison, Wisconsin, 1938. Page references given in the present article pertain to this book.

3. Ibid., pp. 185–86.

4. Ibid., pp. 200–201.

5. Ibid., p. 210.

6. Ibid., p. 219.

7. Ibid., p. 220.

8. Boehmer, H. *Luther and the Reformation*. Translated by E. S. G. Potter. London, 1930; p. 91.

9. Gottlob's study, *Kreuzablass und Almosenablass*, was published in 1906; cf. the references to the work of Gottlob and other investigators in Schwiebert, E. G., *Luther and His Times*. St. Louis, Missouri, 1950, notes to Chapter 10.

10. Boehmer, *Luther and the Reformation*, p. 91.

11. This outline follows the accounts given by Boehmer, ibid., Chapter III and by Schwiebert, *Luther and His Times*, Chapter 10.

12. Boehmer, *Luther and the Reformation*, p. 92.

13. Ibid., p. 93.

14. The logic of genetic explanations in history is examined in some detail in E. Nagel's recent book, *The Structure of Science*. New York, 1961; pp. 564–568. The conception outlined in the present essay, though arrived at without any knowledge of Nagel's work on this subject, accords well with the latter's results.

15. Schwiebert, *Luther and His Times*, p. 304.

16. Gerschenkron, A. "Economic Backwardness in Historical Perspective," in Hoselitz, B. F. (ed.), *The Progress of Underdeveloped Areas*. Chicago, 1952; pp. 3–29.

17. Boehmer, *Luther and the Reformation*, pp. 93–94.

18. Dray, W. *Laws and Explanation in History*. Oxford, 1957; Chapter V. All quotations are from this chapter; italics in the quoted passages are Dray's.

19. Empirical evidence supporting a given hypothesis may afford strong grounds for believing the latter without providing an explanation for it.

20. Boehmer, *Luther and the Reformation*, p. 234.

21. See especially Carnap's classical essay, "Testability and Meaning," *Philosophy of Science* 3: 419–71 (1936) and 4: 1–40 (1937); reprinted, with some omissions, in Feigl and Brodbeck, *Readings in the Philosophy of Science*. New York, 1953. On the point here under discussion, see sec. 9 and particularly sec. 10 of the original essay or sec. 7 of the reprinted version.

22. Dray, *Laws and Explanation in History*, p. 123.

23. Watson, G. "Clio and Psyche: Some Interrelations of Psychology and History," in Ware, C. F. (ed.), *The Cultural Approach to History*. New York, 1940; pp. 34–47, quotation from p. 36.

24. Watson, ibid.

25. Gardiner, P. *The Nature of Historical Explanation*. Oxford, 1952.

26. Ibid., p. 136.

27. Ibid., p. 63.

28

The Explanatory Role of Being Rational

Michael Smith

Humeans hold that actions are movements of an agent's body that are suitably caused by a desire that things be a certain way and a belief on the agent's behalf that something she can just do, namely perform a movement of her body of the kind to be explained, has some suitable chance of making things that way (Davidson 1963). Movements of the body that are caused in some other way are not actions, but are rather things that merely happen to agents.

Actions can, of course, be explained in other ways. Perhaps every action can be explained by neural activity, or by goings on at the sub-atomic level, and presumably many actions can be explained by the states of the world that make the beliefs that figure in Humean explanations true: that is, the states that make those beliefs knowledge. But Humeans insist that belief-desire explanations are distinctive because their availability is what makes our bodily movements into *actions* (Davidson 1971a). A belief-desire explanation of a bodily movement is thus, as we might put it, a *constitutive* explanation of an action (Smith 1998). Other explanations of actions may be available, but they

are all non-constitutive: their availability is not what makes our bodily movements into actions.

We can represent the Humean's view as in Figure 28.1.

Humeans may seem to hold that the constitutive explanation of an action has *four* basic elements: two psychological (a desire for an end and a means-end belief), one non-psychological (a bodily movement), and a relation that holds between them (a causal relation of the right kind). The main task of this essay is, however, to argue that this appearance is misleading. Humeans decompose actions into *five* basic elements, not four, as they posit *three* psychological elements, not two. An additional psychological element – the agent's possession and exercise of his rational capacities – is represented by the "→" sign.

So, at any rate, I shall argue (section 1). But once we acknowledge that an agent's possession and exercise of his rational capacities is part of the constitutive explanation of an action, a further question naturally suggests itself. To what extent can an agent's possession and exercise of his rational capacities be a part of a *non-constitutive* explanation of an action? As we shall see, the Humean's concession that an agent's possession and exercise of his rational capacities is part of the constitutive explanation of an action makes possible an answer to this question that is radically at odds with Hume's own strictures (section 2).

Smith, M. (2009), "The Explanatory Role of Being Rational," in D. Sobel and S. Wall (eds.), *Reasons for Action* (Cambridge: Cambridge University Press), 58–80. © Cambridge University Press 2009. Reprinted with permission.

Philosophy of Action: An Anthology, First Edition. Edited by Jonathan Dancy and Constantine Sandis.
© 2015 John Wiley & Sons, Inc. Published 2015 by John Wiley & Sons, Inc.

Means–ends
belief

    +   →   Bodily movement

Desire for
an end

Figure 28.1   Humean account of the constitutive explanation of an action

1. Hempel vs Davidson on the Explanation of Action

The idea that explanations of actions require an extra psychological element beyond desire and belief is not original to me. The idea emerged many years ago as a point of disagreement between two Humeans, Carl Hempel and Donald Davidson, over the proper form of a fully spelled-out action explanation (Hempel 1961, Davidson 1976).

According to Hempel, explanations of action must conform to the following schema:

A was in a situation of type C
A was a rational agent
In a situation of type C any rational agent will do x
Therefore A did x

                                        (Hempel 1961: 291)

a schema which he fills out as follows:

> When we call someone a rational agent, we assert by implication that he will behave in certain characteristic ways if he finds himself in certain kinds of situations; but ... those situations cannot be described simply in terms of certain environmental conditions and external stimuli; for characteristically they include the agent's having certain objectives and entertaining certain relevant beliefs. (Hempel 1961: 292–293)

We attribute certain desires and beliefs to an agent (this is what is captured in the first claim of the schema), and we also make the substantive claim that the agent is rational and hence will respond in certain characteristic ways to those desires and beliefs (this is what is said in the second claim of the schema). Given that actions are among the characteristic responses that rational agents have to their desires and beliefs (this is what is said in the third claim of the schema),

it follows that we are thereby in a position to derive a conclusion about how the agent in question will act.

There are various questions we might ask about Hempel's schema. In particular, we might ask how plausible it is to suppose, as Hempel does, that there are strict empirical generalizations of the kind he imagines there to be (see again the third claim of the schema), generalizations which in turn allow us to explain actions not just causally, but in terms of Hempel's own deductive–nomological model. For present purposes, however, we can be more relaxed about these empirical generalizations. What is to be at issue here is not the plausibility of fashioning such claims so that we can fit action explanations into Hempel's deductive nomological model, but rather his suggestion that an agent's being rational is a distinct psychological element in any such explanation.

Hempel puts the crucial point this way:

> [I]nformation to the effect that agent A was in a situation of kind C, and that in such a situation the rational thing to do is x, affords grounds for believing that it would have been *rational for A to do x*; but not for believing that A did *in fact* do x. To justify this latter belief, we clearly need a further explanatory assumption, namely that – at least at the time in question – A was a *rational agent* and thus was *disposed* to do whatever was rational under the circumstances. (Hempel 1961: 290)

We need such a further explanatory assumption, according to Hempel, because

> there are various kinds of circumstances in which we might well leave our belief- and goal-attributions unchanged and abandon instead the assumption of rationality. First of all, in deciding upon his action, a person may well overlook certain relevant items of information which he clearly knows or at least believes to be true and which, if properly taken into account, would have called for a different course of action. Second, the agent may overlook certain items in the total goal he is clearly seeking to attain, and may thus decide upon an action that is not rational as judged by his objectives and beliefs. Thirdly, even if the agent were to take into account all aspects of his total goal as well as all the relevant information at his disposal, and even if he should go through deliberate "calculation of means to be adopted toward his chosen end" ... the result may still

fail to be a rational decision because of some logical flaw in his calculation. It is quite clear that there could be strong evidence, in certain cases, that an agent had actually fallen short of rationality in one of the ways here suggested; and indeed, if his decision had been made under pressure of time or under emotional strain, fatigue, or other disturbing influences, such deviations from rationality would be regarded as quite likely. (Hempel 1961: 297)

Though rational agents respond in characteristic ways to their desires and beliefs, Hempel's idea thus seems to be that it is possible, and perhaps even likely, when agents are under certain sorts of pressure – "emotional strain, fatigue, or other disturbing influences" – that they do not respond in one of these ways. In such cases they will not be rational and so we won't be able to explain their doing what they do in the way characteristic of action.

Let's apply Hempel's ideas to a very simplified case. Imagine an agent, John, who has a non-instrumental desire to get healthier and the belief that something he can just do, namely flex his biceps, would make him healthier. Imagine further that, as a result, John flexes his biceps. If Hempel is right then the fully spelled-out explanation of his action must contain at least the following three elements:

1. John desires to get healthier
2. John believes that he can get healthier by flexing his biceps
3. John is instrumentally rational
∴ 4. John flexes his biceps

(3) is necessary, Hempel seems to be saying, because John may have a non-instrumental desire to get healthier and a belief that he can get healthier by flexing his biceps but, because he is instrumentally irrational, not form the instrumental desire to flex his biceps, and so not flex his biceps.

I take it that this possibility is either part of what Hempel had in mind, or is in any event a natural extension of what he had in mind, when he said that when an agent is set to act we need to allow for the possibility of a "logical flaw in his calculation." Since, in the circumstances, there is no way that John will flex his biceps if he doesn't have the instrumental desire to do so, it follows that if flexing his biceps is

something that John is to do then he must have more than the non-instrumental desire and means-end belief mentioned in (1) and (2). He must put these together in the way in which someone who is instrumentally rational would and actually desire the means. This is what (3) guarantees. Absent his putting them together he will not be instrumentally rational and so we won't be able to explain his doing anything in the way characteristic of action because he won't act.

Note, however, that we require a particular interpretation of (3) in order to secure this result. The claim that John is instrumentally rational is ambiguous between two readings. I will call the first of these the "pure-capacity" reading and the second the "capacity-plus-exercise" reading. On the pure-capacity reading, all that (3) says is that John *has the capacity* to be instrumentally rational in the circumstances. So understood, (3) is true even when John fails to exercise that capacity in the circumstances. This is plainly too weak to guarantee the truth of (4). For the truth of (4) requires at the very least that John has an instrumental desire to flex his muscles, something he won't have if he doesn't exercise his capacity. What Hempel must have had in mind, then, is a stronger reading of (3) than the pure-capacity reading.

On the alternative capacity-plus-exercise reading, (3) says that John *has and exercises the capacity* to be instrumentally rational. In so doing, it thereby guarantees that John has the instrumental desire to flex his biceps, because an exercise of a capacity for instrumental rationality, in the presence of a relevant non-instrumental desire and a means-end belief, is all it takes to bring an instrumental desire into existence. Indeed, we might well think that what it is for John's instrumental desire to flex his biceps to come into existence isn't for a separate entity above and beyond his non-instrumental desire and means-end belief to come into existence – an instrumental desire isn't like a new baby that is born to its non-instrumental desire and means-end belief parents – but is rather simply for John's non-instrumental desire and means-end belief to be brought together by the exercise of his capacity to be instrumentally rational in the circumstances (Smith 2004). So understood – perhaps together with some further plausible assumptions as well – (1)–(3) do indeed seem to entail (4).

My suggestion that there is an extra psychological element in a Humean constitutive explanation of an action can now be stated rather simply. Every constitutive explanation of an action, I want to suggest, comprises three basic psychological elements: a desire, a means-end belief, and the agent's exercise of her capacity to be instrumentally rational. This is what the "+" in Figure 28.1 represents. What makes a bodily movement into an action is the fact that these three elements combine to cause the bodily movement in the right way. In order to reach this conclusion, however, we must first address some problems with Hempel's own view. To anticipate, though the worries with Hempel's view are well founded, they point the way to a more nuanced view, where the more nuanced view is the one just stated: constitutive explanations of actions comprise three basic psychological elements: desire, means-end belief, and agents' exercise of their capacity to be instrumentally rational.

The problems with Hempel's own view are well brought out by Davidson in his commentary on "Rational Action." Davidson baulks at the suggestion that we need to make the substantive empirical assumption that an agent is rational – an assumption like the one we just made with respect to John's being instrumentally rational – and cite that fact about him as part of the explanation we give of any action:

> Hempel says rationality is a kind of character trait: some people have it and some don't, and it may come and go in the same individual. No doubt some people are more rational than others, and all of us have our bad moments. And perhaps we can propose some fairly objective criteria for testing when someone has the trait; if so, knowing whether someone is rational at a given time may help us to explain, and even predict, his behaviour, given his beliefs and desires. But reference to such a trait does not seem to me to provide the generality for reason explanations Hempel wants. For in the sense in which rationality is a trait that comes and goes, it can't be an assumption needed for every reason explanation. People who don't have the trait are still agents, have reasons and motives, and act on them. Their reasons are no doubt bad ones. But until we can say what their reasons are – that is, explain or characterize their actions in terms of their motives – we are in no position to say the reasons are bad. So being in a position to call a person rational, irrational, or nonrational in this sense presupposes that we have already

found it possible to give reason explanations of his actions … What is needed, if reason explanations are to be based on laws, is not a test of when a person is rational, but of when a person's reasons – his desires and beliefs – will result, in the right way, in an action. At this point the assumption of rationality seems in danger of losing empirical content. (Davidson 1976: 266–267)

We can discern several points here, points that it would be best to state and evaluate separately.

The first is that agents can only be assessed as being more or less rational against a background assumption that they have desires and beliefs and act, and hence against a background assumption of being rational. The idea here is, of course, the familiar Davidsonian one that being at least minimally rational is a precondition of a creature's having desires and beliefs at all (Davidson 1970, 1971b). Let's concede that this is so. Does that concession undermine the plausibility of the claim that every action explanation requires the substantive assumption that an agent is rational? Well, if when we say that an agent is rational all we mean is that she is minimally rational, in the familiar Davidsonian sense, then there would be nothing substantive added by the assumption of rationality, given that the agents in question are already being said to have certain desires and beliefs. In terms of Hempel's original schema, the second claim ("A was a rational agent") would follow *a priori* from the first ("A was in a situation of type C"). An agent's being minimally rational is, after all, a precondition of her having desires and beliefs. But being minimally rational plainly isn't what the assumption of instrumental rationality discussed earlier amounts to. It amounts rather to ruling out the possibility that an agent may desire some end and have a relevant means-end belief, but not desire the means. This kind of rationality is distinct from the minimal rationality that is required for a creature to have desires and beliefs at all, for, assuming that the creature has desires and beliefs, it simply amounts to the requirement that the desires and means-end beliefs are put together in such a way as to make it true that the agent has an instrumental desire. The first point that we can discern in the passage from Davidson is thus correct, but irrelevant.

The second point is, however, far more telling. Consider a case in which there is, as Hempel puts it, "strong evidence … that an agent ha[s] actually fallen short of rationality in one of the ways here suggested": A case in which an agent's decision is "made under pressure of time or under emotional strain, fatigue, or other disturbing influences," pressure of a kind that makes "deviations from rationality … quite likely." Suppose, for example, that John desires to get healthier and believes that he can get healthier by flexing his muscles – a regime of exercise is just what's needed – but fatigue makes him instrumentally irrational. He doesn't form an instrumental desire to flex his muscles. Instead, let's suppose, he relaxes and watches TV. The trouble is that, if this is what John does, *he still acts*. His relaxing on the couch and watching TV is an action, not something that merely happens to him. And, of course, to the extent that he acts, he also forms some instrumental desire: in this case, the instrumental desire to relax on the couch and watch TV. But if this is right then, in whatever sense it is true that John exhibits instrumental irrationality in such a case, it cannot be required that his being instrumentally rational, *in that very respect*, is an essential element of every action explanation. We will return to this point presently.

The third point builds on the second. Conceding now that agents do indeed display a kind of instrumental rationality every time they act, it focuses more squarely on whether being instrumentally rational in that sense could be a part of the explanation of every action. Davidson's suggestion is that it could not. For, his idea seems to be, being instrumentally rational in that sense is not conceptually distinct from the thing that it would have to explain, which is the agent's desires and means-end beliefs causing action in the right way. An agent's having and exercising his capacity to be instrumentally rational in the circumstances just is a matter of his acting on his desires and means-end beliefs in those circumstances, or so Davidson suggests. His having and exercising that capacity thus cannot be a distinct element in the explanation. (In terms of Figure 28.1, the element that I think is represented by "+" is, Davidson seems to think, already represented by the "→".)

There are two responses we might make to this third point. The first is that, since an agent's possession of an instrumental desire would appear to be one state of an agent, and the bodily movement that that instrumental desire may or may not cause is a distinct event, so, on the face of it at least, Davidson seems quite wrong to suppose that the agent's possession and exercise of the capacity to be instrumentally rational is not logically distinct from his desires and means-end beliefs causing his bodily movement in the right way. An agent's possession and exercise of his capacity to be instrumentally rational guarantees that his desires and means-end beliefs are put together in such a way as to make it true that he has the instrumental desire. It does not guarantee that that instrumental desire, in turn, causes a bodily movement.

In fact, however, this first response fails to appreciate the full force of Davidson's objection. In order to see why, we need to remember why Davidson introduced the idea that desires and beliefs must cause bodily movements *in the right way* for those bodily movements to count as actions. The problem, as he saw things, was that reflection on a range of examples shows that though causation by a desire and belief is a necessary condition for a bodily movement's being an action, it isn't clear what you need to add in order to provide a necessary and sufficient condition – or rather, it isn't clear what you need to add beyond the uninformative further requirement that the desire and belief must cause the bodily movement in the right way. The examples he had in mind were all cases of *internal wayward causal chains* (Davidson 1973). This is important, as the solution to the problem of internal wayward causal chains turns out to be very close to the issue at hand: very close to settling whether or not an agent's being rational is, or is not, conceptually distinct from his acting at all.

Imagine an actor playing a role that calls for her to shake as if extremely nervous. We can readily suppose that, despite the fact that she wants to play her role and believes that she can do so by shaking, once she gets on stage her desire and belief so unnerve her that she is overcome and rendered totally incapable of action. Instead of playing her role as required, she just stands there, shaking nervously. What examples like this suggest is that it is insufficient for an agent's bodily movements to be actions that she has relevant desires and beliefs that cause those movements. An agent may well have desires and beliefs that cause such movements, and yet, because they cause those movements in the wrong way, the movements aren't actions. In order to give necessary and sufficient conditions for an agent's bodily movements to be actions we therefore need to rule out the possibility of such wayward causal chains. In this particular case, we would need to rule out the possibility of the agent's desires and beliefs causing her to shake via causing her to become nervous.

Though Davidson is pessimistic about the possibility of doing this in anything other than the uninformative way – desires and beliefs must cause the bodily movements in the right way – others think it is plain what is needed (Peacocke 1979). The crucial feature in all such cases, they say, is that the match between what the agent does and the content of her desires and beliefs is entirely fluky. In the case just described, for example, it is entirely fluky that the actor wanted to make just the movements that her nerves subsequently caused. In order to state a sufficient condition for an agent's bodily movements being actions, we must therefore ensure that her movements are especially sensitive to the content of her desires and beliefs, as opposed to being sensitive to the operation of wayward factors like nerves. The movement of an agent's body is an action, the suggestion goes, only if, in addition to the other conditions, over a range of desires and beliefs that the agent might have had that differ ever so slightly in their content, she would still have performed an appropriate bodily movement. Suppose she had desired to act nervously and believed that she could do so making her teeth chatter. Then she would have made her teeth chatter. Or suppose she had desired to act nervously and believed that she could do so by walking around wringing her hands. Then she would have walked around wringing her hands. And so on. This further condition of non-flukiness is clearly violated in cases of internal wayward causal chains because, even if the actor had had such ever-so-slightly different desires and beliefs, her nerves would still have caused her to shake when she went on stage.

Whether or not this further requirement turns the necessary condition into a necessary and sufficient condition is a moot point (see Sehon 2005). But, for present purposes, that's not what's important. What's important is rather that everyone seems agreed that there is indeed some such requirement on the relationship between an agent's bodily movements and her desires and beliefs for those bodily movements to count as actions. But consider now the requirement itself. What does it amount to? It amounts to nothing less than the requirement that the agent has and exercises the capacity to be instrumentally rational *in a very local domain*. For a desire and belief to cause a bodily movement in the right way for that bodily movement to count as an action, is, *inter alia*, for the agent to have and exercise her capacity to be instrumentally rational in those circumstances. In the example just discussed, she mustn't just have the instrumental desire to shake, but must also be such that she would have had the instrumental desire to wring her hands if she had believed that wringing her hands was a way of acting nervous; that she would have had the instrumental desire to make her teeth chatter if she had believed that making her teeth chatter was a way of acting nervous; and so on. The requirement that desires and beliefs cause actions in the right way thus does indeed seem to entail that the agent has and exercises the capacity to be instrumentally rational, at least in a very local domain. So far, then, the main thrust of Davidson's third point would appear on the mark.

What I want to argue now, however, is that the capacity to be instrumentally rational whose exercise plays an explanatory role in the production of action need not be the exercise of the very localized capacity to be instrumentally rational that Davidson has in mind. In order to see that this is so, however, we will need to consider the various ways in which an agent's being more fully instrumentally rational in the circumstances in which he acts may and may not manifest itself, and how this differs from the manifestation conditions of the very localized capacity that Davidson has in mind. So let's begin by imagining a very simple example. Suppose that John has a non-instrumental desire to get healthier and that he believes there are two ways in which he could bring this about. He believes that his getting healthier would result from flexing his biceps or from flexing his triceps, but he does not believe that he could flex his biceps and his triceps at the same time. If John were fully instrumentally rational, what would he desire in this case?

The answer is that if John were fully instrumentally rational then he would put his non-instrumental desire to get healthier together with each of these beliefs. This is because his non-instrumental desire is already targeted, so to speak, on each of these ways the world could be. He desires the realization of the possibility that he is healthy, and he believes that this possibility partitions into two sub-possibilities: The possibility that he flexes his biceps and the possibility that he flexes his triceps. Putting at least one of his means-end beliefs together with his non-instrumental desire would allow him to be instrumentally rational to a certain degree – that would amount to a very local exercise of his capacity to be instrumentally rational – but he would be more instrumentally rational if he were to put his non-instrumental desire together with both his means-end beliefs. He would be more instrumentally rational because doing so prepares him for action in a modally strong sense: he is actually such that, had he believed himself unable to (say) flex his biceps, he would still have desired to flex his triceps, and vice versa. If, as seems plausible, being fully instrumentally rational is a matter of maximal preparedness to act in this modally strong sense, then being fully instrumentally rational would seem to require him to have both an instrumental desire to flex his biceps and an instrumental desire to flex his triceps.

Moreover, sticking with this case, being fully instrumentally rational would seem to have implications for the strengths of John's instrumental desires. If, for example, he is equally confident about the two causal claims just made – equally confident that flexing his biceps will cause him to get healthier and that flexing his triceps will cause him to get healthier – then, if he were fully instrumentally rational, he would be indifferent between the two options: his instrumental desires would be equally strong. But if he is more confident of one than the other, then it seems that, in order to satisfy all of the demands of instrumental rationality, his instrumental desire for the one about which he is more confident would have to be stronger. The effect of decreased confidence should be to dilute desire for that option. This, too, manifests itself modally. If John is fully instrumentally rational then he is actually such that he instrumentally desires more that about which he is more confident, but had he believed that to be impossible, he would have instrumentally desired that about which he is less confident. So even though agents might be instrumentally rational to the

extent that their non-instrumental desires are suitably related to two means-end beliefs they have, they might still fail to meet instrumental rationality's further demand on the strengths of their two instrumental desires.

Instrumental rationality would seem to make other more global demands on agent's instrumental desires, as well. Suppose this time that John has two desires, a non-instrumental desire to get healthier and a non-instrumental desire for knowledge, and that he believes all of the following: that flexing his biceps causes health, that reading causes knowledge, and that he cannot flex his biceps and read at the same time. Finally, just to keep things simple, suppose he is equally confident about each of these things and that he has no further desires or beliefs. If John were fully instrumentally rational, then the considerations adduced above would seem to apply equally to the two non-instrumental desires. Instrumental rationality requires that his two non-instrumental desires be suitably related to each of his means-end beliefs. If he were instrumentally rational then he would have both an instrumental desire to flex his biceps and an instrumental desire to read.

Moreover it once again seems that, though he might be instrumentally rational in this local sense, he might fail to meet a further demand that instrumental rationality makes on the strengths of these instrumental desires. If his non-instrumental desires for health and knowledge are equally strong then it seems that, if he were instrumentally rational, he would be indifferent between the two options: his instrumental desires to flex his biceps and to read would be equally strong. But if one of his non-instrumental desires is stronger than the other then it seems that, in order to satisfy the more global demands of instrumental rationality, his instrumental desire for the one which leads to the outcome that he desires more strongly would have to be stronger. The effect of having one desire greater than another in the face of equal confidence about the ways in which those desires can be satisfied should be to intensify the desire for the means to that which one desires more.

There are also cases that contain elements of both those discussed thus far. Suppose that John has a stronger non-instrumental desire to get healthier and a weaker non-instrumental desire for knowledge, and that he believes that flexing his biceps causes health, that reading causes knowledge, and that he cannot exercise and read at the same time, but that he is more confident of the connection between reading and knowledge than he is about the connection between flexing his biceps and health. What does instrumental rationality require in that case? Once again, it seems that if John were fully instrumentally rational then he would have instrumental desires both to exercise and to read, where the strengths of these instrumental desires would depend on the strengths of his two non-instrumental desires and the levels of confidence associated with his two means-end beliefs. Indeed, if his confidence is greater enough, then instrumental rationality may even require that the instrumental desire to read is stronger than the instrumental desire to flex his biceps, notwithstanding the fact that the non-instrumental desire for knowledge that partially constitutes it is weaker than the non-instrumental desire for health which partially constitutes the instrumental desire to flex his biceps.

Let's now return to Davidson's suggestion that there is nothing for an agent's being locally instrumentally rational in the circumstances to amount to beyond the fact that his desires and means-end beliefs issue in action. We can now see that, even when an agent's desires and means-end beliefs do issue in action, and hence the agent is instrumentally rational to some extent – the agent has and exercises his capacity for instrumental rationality in the very localized domain entailed by causation in the right way – there are at least two quite distinct ways the agent might be counterfactually. These two possibilities turn on the *extent* to which the agent is instrumentally rational in the circumstances.

Sticking with our very simple example, suppose that John has an intrinsic desire to get healthier and that he believes both that he could get healthy by flexing his biceps and by flexing his triceps, but that he is more confident of the former than the latter and hence, because he is instrumentally rational to a certain extent and has no other desires and means-end beliefs, he has a stronger instrumental desire to flex his biceps and so flexes his biceps. From this description of the case we cannot tell how strong John's instrumental desire to flex his biceps is. We know that it is stronger than his instrumental desire to flex his triceps,

but that doesn't entail it is as strong as it should be, if he were fully instrumentally rational, for that requires that the strength of his instrumental desire to flex his biceps reflects the strength of both his non-instrumental desire to get healthier and his confidence that flexing his biceps will lead to his getting healthier. So far, all we know is that it reflects his degrees of confidence. What does this further difference consist in?

The answer is that it consists in facts about what (say) John would have done if he had also had a weaker non-instrumental desire for knowledge, but had had the same level of confidence that reading a book would provide him with knowledge as that flexing his biceps would make him healthy. One answer to this counterfactual question is that, since John's instrumental desire to flex his biceps would have been stronger than his instrumental desire to read a book, he would still have flexed his biceps. Another is that, since his instrumental desire to flex his biceps would have been weaker than his instrumental desire to read a book, he would have read a book. If the answer is the first then, in the actual circumstances, it follows that John is instrumentally rational to a greater extent than he is if the answer is the second. For in that case the strength of his instrumental desire to flex his biceps reflects not just his confidence levels about the effect of flexing his biceps and triceps on his health, but also the strength of his non-instrumental desire to get healthier.

We are now in a position to see why Davidson is quite wrong to suggest that, since being instrumentally rational in a very local domain is entailed by an agent's desires and means-end beliefs causing his bodily movement in the right way, it follows that his being instrumentally rational cannot be a part of the explanation of his action. Different agents possess the capacity to be instrumentally rational to very different extents, and the extent to which they possess this capacity, and whether or not they exercise their capacity to whatever extent they have it, fixes not just what actually happens when they act – fixes not just that they do exercise their capacity to be instrumentally rational in the very local domain – but also what they would do in various counterfactual circumstances, circumstances in which they have very different non-instrumental desires, or in which their beliefs about their options are very different. It is thus an agent's possession and exercise of his capacity to be instrumentally rational *to the specific extent that he has it and exercises it* that figures in the explanation of his actions. To be sure, some agents may be so minimally instrumentally rational that, when they act, they thereby exercise all of the capacity to be instrumentally rational that they have. This is, if you like, the limit case of an agent. But not all agents are the limit case of an agent. Some are far more instrumentally rational than that and, when they act, they exercise their far more extensive capacity to be instrumentally rational. This more extensive capacity is what's involved in the explanation of their actions. This is evident from the very different counterfactuals that are true of them.

What is thus true, of course – and perhaps this is what misled Davidson – is that the *minimum required* for a bodily movement to be an action is that the agent possesses and exercises the very local capacity for instrumental rationality required for his desires and beliefs to cause his bodily movement in the right way. But it would be a fallacy to move from this to the conclusion that it is an agent's possession and exercise of the minimal capacity that figures in the explanation of his actions. It would be a fallacy on a par with supposing that, just because all that is strictly necessary for an agent to intentionally flip the switch (say) is that he has a very specific desire concerning the outcome of his flipping the switch, so the only desires that are ever part of the explanation of any agent's flippings of switches are desires with very specific contents.

Let me summarise. Hempel claimed, and Davidson denied, that an agent's being rational is a part of the explanation of every action. Davidson's argument against Hempel in effect takes the form of a dilemma. On the first horn, Hempel is committed to the conclusion that agents who are irrational never act. But that's plainly not true, even by Hempel's own lights. On the other horn, Hempel is claiming that the minimal exercise of instrumental rationality that is necessary whenever agents act on their desires and beliefs is itself a part of the explanation of those actions. But, while it is true that every agent who acts must possess and exercise the capacity for instrumental rationality in that very local domain, since this is entailed by the fact that their non-instrumental desires and means-end beliefs cause their bodily movements in the right

way, it cannot be a separate causal element in that explanation. It simply falls out of the account we give of what it is for desires and beliefs to cause actions in the right way.

Against this, I have argued that though a minimal exercise of instrumental rationality is indeed necessary whenever an agent acts, it does not follow from this that what agents exercise, when they act, is a minimal capacity to be instrumentally rational. Agents are instrumentally rational to different degrees and they exercise whatever capacities they have to different degrees. This is why very different counterfactuals are true of agents depending, first, on the extent to which they are instrumentally rational, and second, on whether their being instrumentally rational to that extent is or is not a part of the explanation of their bodily movements. This, it seems to me, is the crucial insight that we discover when we think through Davidson's disagreements with Hempel about the explanatory role of being rational. Hempel is essentially right. The Humean account of a constitutive explanation of an action posits three distinctive psychological elements, not two. Actions are bodily movements that are caused in the right way by desires, beliefs, and exercises of the capacity, which agents may have to a greater or a lesser extent, to be instrumentally rational.

2. Are There Any Distinctive Non-constitutive Explanations of Action?

Once we acknowledge that an agent's possession and exercise of his capacity to be instrumentally rational is part of the constitutive explanation of an action, a further question naturally suggests itself. To what extent can an agent's possession and exercise of his rational capacities be a part of a distinctive *non-constitutive* explanation?

Non-constitutive explanations, remember, are simply those explanations of actions which, even when available, are not explanations whose availability is what makes actions actions. Not all non-constitutive explanations are on a par, however, for, given the nature of the constitutive explanation of an action, the availability of certain non-constitutive explanations will be a mark of excellence in action, where the standard of excellence is internal to action itself. One such non-constitutive explanation is implicit in what's been said already. For when an agent does what he does not just because he is instrumentally rational to the extent that he is, but because, as it happens, the extent to which he is instrumentally rational is *fully*, then his action, though no more or less an action than it would have been if he had acted but been less than fully instrumentally rational, is better in a distinctive sense. It is better in the sense that it is the product of a better specimen of one of its constitutive causes.

What I want to argue now is that an agent's being fully rational – not just fully instrumentally rational, but fully rational both instrumentally and in such other departments of rationality as there are as well – can also figure in a non-constitutive explanation of his action. If this is right then it follows that the availability of an explanation of this kind will be the mark of an even better kind of action. For such an action will be the product of perhaps the very best specimen of one of its constitutive causes. In order to see that this is so, however, we must first remind ourselves about the argument that Hempel gave in favor of his schema for the explanation of action.

Hempel's argument, you'll recall, was that absent the assumption that an agent is rational there is no reason to expect him to respond in the way a rational agent would to the fact that he has certain desires and means-end beliefs. But note that a parallel line of argument shows that constitutive explanations of *rational beliefs* – these are explanations of beliefs in virtue of which they count as *rational beliefs* – must conform to a very similar schema:

A was in a situation of type D
A was a rational subject
In a situation of type D any rational subject will believe that p
Therefore A rationally believed that p

Imagine that A is in some type-D situation that makes the third premise of the schema come out true. At the most general level, perhaps we can describe this as a situation in which a conclusive reason to

believe that p is available, where a conclusive reason to believe that p may be some set of further facts – some facts that q and r – that bear evidentially on whether p. Absent the explicit assumption that A is a rational subject – this is the second premise in the schema – the most that we can derive from the fact that he was in a type-D situation, and that in such a situation any rational subject will believe that p, is that the rational thing for A to believe in that situation is p. In order to derive the conclusion that A in fact rationally believes that p we must add the further substantive claim that he is rational. By parity of reasoning from the case of action explanation, then, it follows that when subjects form rational beliefs, their being rational – that is to say, their possession and exercise of the capacity to revise their beliefs in a rational manner – plays a crucial causal role. And this in turn suggests that a further distinctive non-constitutive explanation of action is possible.

Imagine that some agent desires to (say) illuminate a room and that there is available a conclusive reason to believe that moving his finger against a switch will achieve that result. Imagine further that the agent forms the belief that moving his finger against a switch will illuminate the room precisely because of the availability of this conclusive reason – in other words, suppose he possesses and exercises the capacity to revise his beliefs in a rational manner – and that his desire and belief causes his finger to move against the switch in the right way. In that case we can explain his finger movement by citing not just his desire and belief – this is all that is required for a constitutive explanation of his action – but also by citing his desire and the fact that he *rationally believes* that moving his finger against the switch will illuminate the room. To be sure, this isn't a constitutive explanation. An agent's finger movement against a switch may be an action whether the belief that causes it is rational or irrational. But it is an explanation that may sometimes be available none the less.

We can represent this kind of non-constitutive explanation of an action in terms of a modified version of Figure 28.1 (Figure 28.2).

The "⇒" in Figure 28.2, like the "+", represents the agent's possession and exercise of a rational capacity. The only difference is that whereas the "+" represents the possession and exercise of the capacity

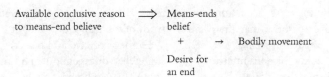

Figure 28.2 A Humean account of a distinctive non-constitutive explanation of action

to be instrumentally rational, the "⇒" represents the possession and exercise of the capacity to revise his beliefs in a rational manner. The "⇒" and the "+" thus represent the operation of different departments of rationality.

The non-constitutive explanation represented in Figure 28.2 is distinctive for much the same reason as a non-constitutive explanation of action in terms of the agent's being fully instrumentally rational is distinctive. It is distinctive because an action so explained is the product of a better specimen of one of its constitutive causes. An action caused not just by the agent's possession and exercise of the capacity to be instrumentally rational, but also by his possession and exercise of the capacity to revise his beliefs in a rational manner, is an action that is caused by an even better specimen of the underlying psychological state of being rational in all of its departments than is an action that cannot be so explained. The agent of such an action is, after all, more fully rational. This is what's reflected by the availability of the distinctive non-constitutive explanation represented in Figure 28.2.

At the beginning of this section I said that my aim is to argue that an agent's being fully rational – not just fully instrumentally rational, but fully rational both instrumentally and in such other departments of rationality as there are as well – can also figure in a distinctive non-constitutive explanation of his action. Is that argument now complete? In other words, is the non-constitutive explanation represented in figure 28.2 the only such distinctive non-constitutive explanation of an action that there can be? The issue that we must address in providing an answer to this question literally leaps off the page when we look at Figure 28.2. What about the desire for an end? Is it too susceptible to explanation in much the same way as the means-end belief?

Hume would of course insist that it is not. As he puts it:

'tis not contrary to reason to prefer the destruction of the whole world to the scratching of my finger. 'Tis not contrary to reason for me to chuse my total ruin, to prevent the least uneasiness of an Indian or person wholly unknown to me. 'Tis as little contrary to reason to prefer even my own acknowledg'd lesser good to my greater, and have a more ardent affection for the former than the latter ... In short, a passion must be accompany'd with some false judgement, in order to its being unreasonable; and even then 'tis not the passion, properly speaking, which is unreasonable, but the judgement. (Hume 1978: 416)

In other words, as Hume sees things the only kind of irrational desire is an irrational *instrumental* desire, where, as we have seen, an instrumental desire is simply a non-instrumental desire and means-end belief that have been brought together by an agent's exercise of his capacity to be instrumentally rational. The irrationality of an instrumental desire, according to Hume, resides in the irrationality of the means-end belief that partially constitutes it. He thus draws the radical conclusion that there is no such thing as a rational non-instrumental desire. Desires for ends cannot be either rational or irrational.

Hume seems to think that this radical conclusion follows from the fact that, whereas beliefs can be true or false – true beliefs are those whose contents represent the world as being the way it is, false beliefs are those whose contents fail to so represent the world – a desire "is an original existence ... and contains not any representative quality" (Hume 1978: 415). Desires for ends can be satisfied or unsatisfied, but not true or false. But it is hard to see why Hume should think that the conclusion follows from the premise. What is the connection supposed to be between a psychological state that can be true or false and a psychological state that can be rational or irrational? This question is somewhat urgent because, on the face of it, notwithstanding the fact that desires for ends cannot be true or false, it seems that a parallel line of argument to those already discussed in the case of action and rational belief would suffice to show that there are constitutive explanations of *rational desires for ends*. These are explanations of desires for ends in virtue of which, and contrary to Hume, they count as *rational* desires for ends.

The parallel line of argument I have in mind appeals to the following Hempelian schema:

> A was in a situation of type E
> A was a rational subject
> In a situation of type E any rational agent will desire the end that q
> Therefore A rationally desired the end that q

The crucial premise in this schema is of course the third. What exactly is a type-E situation? Borrowing from the Hempelian schema in the case of rational belief, we might suppose that a type-E situation is one in which a conclusive reason to desire the end that q is available. Here is where Hume would presumably dig in his heels. For, he might ask, what is it for there to be a conclusive reason to desire the end that q? We understand what conclusive reasons *to believe* are because reasons to believe are simply considerations that bear on the truth of the thing believed. But what are we to make of reasons *to desire some end*?

The trouble is, however, that there is an obvious answer to this question. To be sure, a reason *to believe* is a consideration that bears on the truth of the thing believed, but that's simply because what such a reason is is a reason *to believe*. Desires for ends cannot be true or false, rather they can be satisfied or unsatisfied. It therefore follows that reasons *to desire ends*, if such there be, will be considerations that bear not on truth or falsehood, but rather on the satisfaction of the desired ends. Thus, just as the question we must ask ourselves in figuring out what reasons there are to believe what we believe is whether there are considerations that bear on how we currently take it that things are, so the question that we ask ourselves in figuring out whether there are reasons to desire what we desire is whether there are considerations that bear on how we currently take it that things are to be. The mere fact that a reason to believe is a consideration that bears on the truth of the thing believed thus has no bearing on whether there is anything else for a

reason to be except a consideration that bears on the truth of the thing for which it is a reason.

Hume's argument also seems, to me at least, to be somewhat disingenuous. The first time we all heard about (say) Thomas Nagel's wonderful book *The Possibility of Altruism* (1970), we knew exactly what the point of the book was. It was supposed to lay out a number of considerations that provide reasons for desiring the end that people not suffer excruciating pain. The considerations were things like: that we each take ourselves to have a reason not to suffer excruciating pains when we have them; that the reason-giving feature of the pains that we suffer when we have them seem to be internal to the excruciating pains themselves, having to do with their intrinsic nature, not with the fact that the pains are present to us; that it follows from this that the intrinsic nature of our own future excruciating pains are reason-giving; and that it follows from this that the intrinsic nature of other people's pains are reason-giving, too. Whether we found Nagel's argument convincing once we read and thought about it is unimportant. What's important is rather that we immediately understood what his argument was supposed to be an argument for. Moreover I assume that when Hume wrote, he too had read books that attempted to do what Nagel attempts to do, and that he too understood what it was that they were attempting to do.

In terms of the Hempelian schema, what Nagel's book purports to provide is an elaborate specification of a type-E situation: a range of considerations which are such that any rational person who appreciates them will end up desiring the end that people not suffer excruciating pain. But of course, as the Hempelian schema makes plain, even if Nagel is right and an agent A is in such a type-E situation, absent the additional premise that A is a rational subject – this is the second premise in the schema – we will be unable to derive the conclusion that A rationally desires the end that people not suffer excruciating pain. Absent this premise, all we can conclude is that the end that people not suffer excruciating pain is the rational thing for the subject to desire as an end in such a type-E situation. By parity of reasoning from the cases of action explanation and rational belief explanation, then, we are forced to conclude that, if indeed it is possible for subjects to form rational desires for ends, as Nagel's book argues that it is, then their being rational – that is to say, their possession and exercise of the capacity to revise their desires in a rational manner – must play a crucial explanatory role.

This suggests that there may therefore be a distinctive anti-Humean kind of non-constitutive explanation of an action, a kind we can represent in terms of the following modified version of Figure 28.2 (Figure 28.3).

The "⇛" in Figure 28.3, like the "⇒", represents the agent's possession and exercise of a rational capacity. The difference between the "⇛" and the "⇒" is simply that, whereas the "⇒" represents the possession and exercise of the capacity to revise *beliefs* in a rational manner, the "⇛" represents the capacity to revise *desires for ends* in a rational manner. The "⇛", the "⇒", and the "+" each represent the operation of different departments of rationality.

What Figure 28.3 suggests is that we might explain (say) an agent's performing some bodily movement that he believes will cause the relief of some other person's excruciating pain by citing the fact that he *rationally desires* the end that people not suffer excruciating pain. Such would be the case if (say) Nagel were right and the agent in question came to desire the end that people not suffer after being convinced by what he says in *The Possibility of Altruism*. To be sure, such an explanation is non-constitutive. A bodily movement performed by an agent who desires the end that people not suffer excruciating pain and believes that that bodily movement will relieve someone else's excruciating pain may be an action whether the desire is rational or irrational. But, if Nagel is right, it is an explanation that may sometimes be available none the less.

Note that the non-constitutive explanation represented in Figure 28.3, if such there be, is distinctive in that an action that can be so explained is the product of an even better specimen of one of its constitutive causes than one that cannot be so explained. An action caused not just by the agent's possession and exercise of the capacity to be instrumentally rational and his possession and exercise of the capacity to revise his beliefs in a rational manner – this is what is represented in Figure 28.2 – but also by his possession and exercise of the capacity to revise his desires for ends in a rational manner, as in Figure 28.3, is an action that is caused by an *even better* specimen of the psychological state of being rational in all of its departments. The agent of such an action is more fully rational: indeed, it seems that he may be as fully rational as he can be, as there doesn't seem to be anything that is a further candidate for rational explanation.

Of course, nothing that I have said shows that Nagel is right, or that anyone else arguing for a similar conclusion is right, and hence nothing that I have said shows that there are non-constitutive explanations of the distinctive kind represented in Figure 28.3. What I have been concerned to show is simply that we can make sense of their possibility: the mere fact that beliefs can be true or false, whereas desires for ends cannot, goes no way towards showing that such explanations do not exist. The discussion has, however, been instructive, because it suggests how we might make progress on the more substantive issue of whether any such non-constitutive explanations do exist. What the discussion suggests is that believers and disbelievers in the possibility of non-constitutive explanations of the distinctive kind represented in Figure 28.3 should focus their attention on the crucial third premise of the final Hempelian schema: the claim that there is some type of situation, E, such that, in a situation of that type any fully rational agent will desire the end that q. What the believers desperately need to provide are concrete examples of Es and qs that make this claim seem credible, examples that

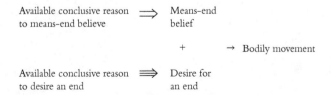

Figure 28.3   An anti-Humean account of a distinctive non-constitutive explanation of action

make it clear that it is *rationality* that is at issue, not some other form of evaluation. And what the disbelievers need to provide, if they want to argue against the very possibility of such explanations, is some argument, radically different from Hume's own, for supposing that the search for such examples is quixotic.

Speaking for myself, I am not sure that either side enters this debate with the upper hand. The substantive issue about the rational status of non-instrumental desires that divides those who follow Hume from those who oppose him seems to me to be wide open (though contrast the optimistic argument in Smith 1994, chapter 6, with the more pessimistic line of argument in Smith 2006). And this in turn means that it is wide open what exactly the scope is for providing non-constitutive explanations of actions in terms of agents' being rational.

References

Davidson, D. (1963) "Actions, Reasons, and Causes," reprinted here as Chapter 19.

Davidson, D. (1970) "Mental Events," reprinted in *Essays on Actions and Events*. Oxford: Oxford University Press, 1980: 207–228.

Davidson, D. (1971a) "Agency," reprinted here as Chapter 2.

Davidson, D. (1971b) "Psychology as Philosophy," reprinted in *Essays on Actions and Events*. Oxford: Oxford University Press, 1980: 229–245.

Davidson, D. (1973) "Freedom to Act," reprinted in *Essays on Actions and Events*. Oxford: Oxford University Press, 1980: 63–83.

Davidson, D. (1976) "Hempel on Explaining Action," reprinted in *Essays on Actions and Events*. Oxford: Oxford University Press, 1980: 261–277.

Hempel, Carl G. (1961) "Rational Action," reprinted in N.S. Care and C. Landesman, eds., *Readings in the Theory of Action*. Bloomington, IN: Indiana University Press, 1968: 285–286.

Hume, D. (1978) *A Treatise of Human Nature*, ed. L.A. Selby-Bigge and P.H. Nidditch. Oxford: Oxford University Press.

Nagel, T. (1970) *The Possibility of Altruism*. Oxford: Clarendon Press.

Peacocke, C. (1979) *Holistic Explanation: Action, Space, Interpretation*. Oxford: Oxford University Press.

Sehon, S. (2005) *Teleological Realism: Mind, Agency, and Explanation*. Cambridge, MA: MIT Press.

Smith, M. (1994), *The Moral Problem*. Oxford: Blackwell.

Smith, M. (1998) "The Possibility of Philosophy of Action," in J. Bransen and S. Cuypers, eds., *Human Action, Deliberation and Causation*. Dordrecht: Kluwer Academic, 17–41.

Smith, M. (2004) "Instrumental Desires, Instrumental Rationality," *Proceedings of the Aristotelian Society*, Supplementary Volume, 78: 93–109.

Smith, M. (2006), "Is that All there Is?", *The Journal of Ethics*, 10, Special Issue on Joel Feinberg: 75–106.

29

The Conceivability of Mechanism

Norman Malcolm

1. By "mechanism" I am going to understand a special application of physical determinism – namely, to all organisms with neurological systems, including human beings. The version of mechanism I wish to study assumes a neurophysiological theory which is adequate to explain and predict all movements of human bodies except those caused by outside forces. The human body is assumed to be as complete a causal system as is a gasoline engine. Neurological states and processes are conceived to be correlated by general laws with the mechanisms that produce movements. Chemical and electrical changes in the nervous tissue of the body are assumed to cause muscle contractions, which in turn cause movements such as blinking, breathing, and puckering of the lips, as well as movements of fingers, limbs, and head. Such movements are sometimes produced by forces (pushes and pulls) applied externally to the body. If someone forced my arm up over my head, the theory could not explain that movement of my arm. But it could explain any movement not due to an external push or pull. It could explain, and predict, the movements that occur when a person signals a taxi, plays chess, writes an essay, or walks to the store.[1]

It is assumed that the neurophysiological system of the human body is subject to various kinds of stimulation. Changes of temperature or pressure in the environment; sounds, odors; the ingestion of foods and liquids: all these will have an effect on the nerve pulses that turn on the movement-producing mechanisms of the body.

2. The neurophysiological theory we are envisaging would, as said, be rich enough to provide systematic causal explanations of all bodily movements not due to external physical causes. These explanations should be understood as stating *sufficient* conditions of movement and not merely necessary conditions. They would employ laws that connect neurophysiological states or processes with movements. The laws would be universal propositions of the following form: whenever an organism of structure S is in state q it will emit movement m. Having ascertained that a given organism is of structure S and is in state q, one could deduce the occurrence of movement m.

It should be emphasized that this theory makes no provision for desires, aims, goals, purposes, motives, or intentions. In explaining such an occurrence as a man's walking across a room, it will be a matter of indifference to the theory whether the man's purpose, intention, or desire was to open a window, or even whether his walking across the room was intentional. This aspect of the theory can be indicated by saying that it is a "nonpurposive" system of explanation.

The viewpoint of mechanism thus assumes a theory that would provide systematic, complete,

Malcolm, N. (1968), "The Conceivability of Mechanism," *Philosophical Review* 77 (1), 45–72 (omitting final section). *Philosophical Review* is published by Duke University Press, Durham, N.C.

Philosophy of Action: An Anthology, First Edition. Edited by Jonathan Dancy and Constantine Sandis.
© 2015 John Wiley & Sons, Inc. Published 2015 by John Wiley & Sons, Inc.

nonpurposive, causal explanations of all human movements not produced by external forces. Such a theory does not at present exist. But nowadays it is ever more widely held that in the not far distant future there will be such a theory – and that it will be true. I will raise the question of whether this is conceivable. The subject belongs to an age-old controversy. It would be unrealistic for me to hope to make any noteworthy contribution to its solution. But the problem itself is one of great human interest and worthy of repeated study.

3. To appreciate the significance of mechanism, one must be aware of the extent to which a comprehensive neurophysiological theory of human behavior would diverge from those everyday explanations of behavior with which all of us are familiar. These explanations refer to purposes, desires, goals, intentions. "He is running to catch the bus." "He is climbing the ladder in order to inspect the roof." "He is stopping at this store because he wants some cigars." Our daily discourse is filled with explanations of behavior in terms of the agent's purposes or intentions. The behavior is claimed to occur in order that some state of affairs should be brought about or avoided – that the bus should be caught, the roof inspected, cigars purchased. Let us say that these are "purposive" explanations.

We can note several differences between these common purposive explanations and the imagined neurophysiological explanations. First, the latter were conceived by us to be systematic – that is, to belong to a comprehensive theory – whereas the familiar purposive explanations are not organized into a theory. Second, the neurophysiological explanations do not employ the concept of purpose or intention. Third, the neurophysiological explanations embody contingent laws, but purposive explanations do not.

Let us dwell on this third point. A neurophysiological explanation of some behavior that has occurred is assumed to have the following form:

Whenever an organism of structure S is in neurophysiological state q it will emit movement m.
Organism O of structure S was in neurophysiological state q.
Therefore, O emitted m.[2]

The general form of purposive explanation is the following:

Whenever an organism O has goal G and believes that behavior B is required to bring about G, O will emit B.
O had G and believed B was required of G.
Therefore, O emitted B.

Let us compare the first premise of a neurophysiological explanation with the first premise of a purposive explanation. The first premise of a neurophysiological explanation is a contingent proposition, but the first premise of a purposive explanation is not a contingent proposition. This difference will appear more clearly if we consider how, in both cases, the first premise would have to be qualified in order to be actually true. In both cases a *ceteris paribus* clause must be added to the first premise, or at least be implicitly understood. (It will be more perspicuous to translate "*ceteris paribus*" as "provided there are no countervailing factors" rather than as "other things being equal.")

Let us consider what "*ceteris paribus*" will mean in concrete terms. Suppose a man climbed a ladder leading to a roof. An explanation is desired. The fact is that the wind blew his hat onto the roof and he wants it back. The explanation would be spelled out in detail as follows:

If a man wants to retrieve his hat and believes this requires him to climb a ladder, he will do so provided there are no countervailing factors.
This man wanted to retrieve his hat and believed that this required him to climb a ladder, and there were no countervailing factors.
Therefore, he climbed a ladder.

What sorts of things might be included under "countervailing factors" in such a case? The unavailability of a ladder, the fear of climbing one, the belief that someone would remove the ladder while he was on the roof, and so on. (The man's failure to climb a ladder would *not* be a countervailing factor.)

An important point emerging here is that the addition of the *ceteris paribus* clause to the first premise turns this premise into an a priori proposition. If there were no countervailing factors whatever (if the man knew a ladder was available, had no fear of ladders or high places, no belief that he might be marooned on the roof, and so on); if there were no hindrances or hazards, real or imagined, physical or psychological; then if the man did not climb a ladder it would not be true that he *wanted* his hat back, or *intended* to get it back.[3]

In his important recent book, *The Explanation of Behaviour*, Charles Taylor puts the point as follows:

> This is part of what we mean by "intending X," that, in the absence of interfering factors, it is followed by doing X. I could not be said to intend X if, even with no obstacles or other countervailing factors, I still didn't do it.[4]

This feature of the meaning of "intend" also holds true of "want," "purpose," and "goal."

Thus the universal premise of a purposive explanation is an a priori principle, not a contingent law. Some philosophers have made this a basis for saying that a purposive explanation is not a causal explanation.[5] But this is a stipulation (perhaps a useful one), rather than a description of how the word "cause" is actually used in ordinary language.

Let us consider the effect of adding a *ceteris paribus* clause to the universal premise of a neural explanation of behavior. Would a premise of this form be true a priori? Certainly not. Suppose it were believed that whenever a human being is in neural state q his right hand will move up above his head, provided there are no countervailing factors. What could be countervailing factors? That the subject's right arm is broken or that it is tied to his side, and so on. But the exclusion of such countervailing factors would have no tendency to make the premise true a priori. There is no connection of meaning, explicit or implicit, between the description of any neural state and the description of any movement of the hand. No matter how many countervailing factors are excluded, the proposition will not lose the character of a contingent law (unless, of course, we count the failure of the hand to move as itself a countervailing factor, in which case the premise becomes a tautology).

4. Making explicit the *ceteris paribus* conditions points up the different logical natures of the universal premises of the two kinds of explanation. Premises of the one sort express contingent correlations between neurological processes and behavior. Premises of the other sort express a priori connections between intentions (purposes, desires, goals) and behavior.

This difference is of the utmost importance. Some students of behavior have believed that purposive explanations of behavior will be found to be less basic than the explanations that will arise from a future neurophysiological theory. They think that the principles of purposive explanation will turn out to be dependent on the neurophysiological laws. On this view our ordinary explanations of behavior will often be true: but the neural explanations will also be true – and they will be *more fundamental*. Thus we could, theoretically, *by-pass* explanations of behavior in terms of purpose, and the day might come when they simply fall into disuse.

I wish to show that neurophysiological laws could not be more basic than purposive principles. I shall understand the statement that a law L_2 is "more basic" than a law L_1 to mean that L_1 is dependent on L_2 but L_2 is not dependent on L_1. To give an example, let us suppose there is a uniform connection between food abstinence and hunger: that is, going without food for n hours always results in hunger. This is L_1. Another law L_2 is discovered – namely, a uniform connection between a certain chemical condition of body tissue (called "cell-starvation") and hunger. Whenever cell-starvation occurs, hunger results. It is also discovered that L_2 is more basic than L_1. This would amount to the following fact: food abstinence for n hours will not result in hunger *unless* cell-starvation occurs; and if the latter occurs, hunger will result *regardless of whether* food abstinence occurs. Thus the L_1 regularity is contingently dependent on the L_2 regularity, and the converse is not true. Our knowledge of this dependency would reveal to us the conditions under which the L_1 regularity would no longer hold.

Our comparison of the differing logical natures of purposive principles and neurophysiological laws enables us to see that the former cannot be dependent on the latter. The a priori connection between intention or purpose and behavior cannot fail to hold. It cannot be contingently dependent on any contingent regularity. The neurophysiological explanations of behavior could not, in the sense explained, turn out to be more basic than our everyday purposive explanations.[6]

5. There is a second important consequence of the logical difference between neurophysiological laws and purposive principles. Someone might suppose

that although purposive explanations cannot be dependent on nonpurposive explanations, they would be refuted by the verification of a comprehensive neurophysiological theory of behavior. I think this view is correct: but it is necessary to understand what it *cannot* mean. It cannot mean that the principles (the universal premises) of purposive explanations would be proved false. They cannot be proved false. It could not fail to be true that if a person wanted X and believed Y was necessary for X, and there were absolutely no countervailing factors, he would do Y.[7] This purposive principle is true a priori, not because of its form but because of its meaning – that is, because of the connection of meaning between the words "He wanted X and he realized that Y was necessary for X" and the words "He did Y." The purposive principle is not a law of nature but a conceptual truth. It cannot be confirmed or refuted by experience. Since the verification of a neurophysiological theory could never *disprove* any purposive principles, the only possible outcome of such verification, logically speaking, would be to prove that the purposive principles have no application to the world. I shall return to this point later.

6. We must come to closer grips with the exact logical relationship between neural and purposive explanations of behavior. Can explanations of both types be true of the same bit of behavior on one and the same occasion? Is there any rivalry between them? Some philosophers would say not. They would say that, for one thing, the two kinds of explanation explain different things. Purposive explanations explain actions. Neurophysiological explanations explain movements. Both explain behavior: but we can say this only because we use the latter word ambiguously to cover both actions and movements. For a second point, it may be held that the two kinds of explanation belong to different "bodies of discourse" or to different "language games." They employ different concepts and assumptions. One kind of explanation relates behavior to causal laws and to concepts of biochemistry and physiology, to nerve pulses and chemical reactions. The other kind of explanation relates behavior to the desires, intentions, goals, and reasons of persons. The two forms of explanation can co-exist, because they are irrelevant to one another.[8]

It is true that the two kinds of explanation employ different concepts and, in a sense, explain different things: but are they really independent of one another? Take the example of the man climbing a ladder in order to retrieve his hat from the roof. This explanation relates his climbing to his intention. A neurophysiological explanation of his climbing would say nothing about his intention but would connect his movements on the ladder with chemical changes in body tissue or with the firing of neurons. Do the two accounts interfere with one another?

7. I believe there *would* be a collision between the two accounts if they were offered as explanations of one and the same occurrence of a man's climbing a ladder. We will recall that the envisaged neurophysiological theory was supposed to provide *sufficient* causal explanations of behavior. Thus the movements of the man on the ladder would be *completely* accounted for in terms of electrical, chemical, and mechanical processes in his body. This would surely imply that his desire or intention to retrieve his hat had nothing to do with his movement up the ladder. It would imply that on this same occasion he would have moved up the ladder in exactly this way even if he had had no intention to retrieve his hat, or even no intention to climb the ladder. To mention his intention or purpose would be no explanation, nor even part of an explanation, of his movements on the ladder. Given the antecedent neurological states of his bodily system together with general laws correlating those states with the contractions of muscles and movements of limbs, he would have moved as he did regardless of his desire or intention. If every movement of his was completely accounted for by his antecedent neurophysiological states (his "programming"), then it was not true that those movements occurred *because* he wanted or intended to get his hat.

8. I will briefly consider three possible objections to my claim that if mechanism were true the man would have moved up the ladder as he did even if he had not had any intention to climb the ladder. The first objection comes from a philosopher who espouses the currently popular psychophysical identity thesis. He holds that there is a neural condition that causes the man's movements up the ladder, and he further holds that the man's intention to climb the ladder (or, possibly, his having the intention) is contingently identical with

the neural condition that causes the movements. Thus, if the man had not intended to climb the ladder, the cause of his movements would not have existed, and so those movements would not have occurred. My reply would be that the view that there may be a contingent identity (and not merely an extensional equivalence) between an intention (or the having of the intention) and a neural condition is not a meaningful hypothesis. One version of the identity thesis is that A's intention to climb the ladder is contingently identical with some process in A's brain. Verifying this identity would require the meaningless step of trying to discover whether A's intention is located in his brain. One could give meaning to the notion of the location of A's intention in his brain by stipulating that it has the same location as does the correlated neural process. But the identity that arose from this stipulation would not be contingent.[9] Another version of the identity thesis is that the event of Smith's having the intention I is identical with the event of Smith's being in neural condition N. This version avoids the above "location problem": but it must take on the task (which seems hopeless) of explaining how the property "having intention I" and the property "being in neural condition N" could be contingently identical and not merely co-extensive.[10]

The second objection comes from an epiphenomenalist. He holds that the neurophysiological condition that contingently causes the behavior on the ladder also contingently causes the intention to climb the ladder, but that the intention stands in no causal relation to the behavior. If the intention had not existed, the cause of it and of the behavior would not have existed, and so the behavior would not have occurred. A decisive objection to epiphenomenalism is that, according to it, the relation between intention and behavior would be purely contingent. It would be conceivable that the neurophysiological condition that always causes ladder-climbing movements should also always cause the intention to *not* climb up a ladder. Epiphenomenalism would permit it to be universally true that whenever any person intended to *not* do any action, he did it, and that whenever any person intended to do any action, he did not do it. This is a conceptual absurdity.

The third objection springs from a philosopher who combines mechanism with logical behaviorism.

He holds that some condition of the neurophysiological system causes the preparatory movements, gestures, and utterances that are expressions of the man's intention to climb the ladder; and it also causes his movements up the ladder. The component of logical behaviorism in his over-all view is this: he holds that the man's having the intention to climb the ladder is simply a logical construction out of the occurrence of the expressions of intention and also the occurrence of the ladder-climbing movements. Having the intention is nothing other than the expressive behavior plus the subsequent climbing behavior. Having the intention is defined in terms of behavior-events that are contingently caused by a neurophysiological condition. The supposition that the man did not have the intention to climb the ladder would be identical with the supposition that either the expressive behavior or the climbing behavior, or both, did not occur. If either one did not occur, then neither occurred, since by hypothesis both of them have the same cause. Thus it would be false that the man would have moved up the ladder as he did even if he had not had an intention to climb the ladder.

I think that this third position gives an unsatisfactory account of the nature of intention. Actually climbing the ladder is not a necessary condition *simpliciter* for the existence of the intention to climb the ladder. It is a necessary condition *provided* there are no countervailing factors. But there is no definite number of countervailing factors, and so they cannot be exhaustively enumerated. In addition, some of them will themselves involve the concepts of desire, belief, or purpose. For example: a man intends to climb the ladder, but also he does not want to look ridiculous; as he is just about to start climbing he is struck by the thought that he will look ridiculous; so he does not climb the ladder, although he had intended to. An adequate logical behaviorism would have to analyze away not only the initial reference to intention, but also the reference to desire, belief, purpose, and all other psychological concepts, that would occur in the listing of possible countervailing factors. There is no reason for thinking that such a program of analysis could be carried out.

Thus a mechanist can hope to avoid the consequence that the man would have moved up the ladder as he did even if he had not had the intention of climbing the ladder, by combining his mechanist doctrine with the psychophysical identity thesis, or with epiphenomenalism, or with logical behaviorism. But these supplementary positions are so objectionable or implausible that the mechanist is not really saved from the above consequence.

9. Let us remember that the postulated neurophysiological theory is comprehensive. It is assumed to provide complete causal explanations for all bodily movements that are not produced by external physical forces. It is a closed system in the sense that it does not admit, as antecedent conditions, anything other than neurophysiological states and processes. Desires and intentions have no place in it.

If the neurophysiological theory were true, then in no cases would desires, intentions, purposes be necessary conditions of any human movements. It would never be true that a man would *not* have moved as he did if he had *not* had such and such an intention. Nor would it ever be true that a certain movement of his was due to, or brought about by, or caused by his having a certain intention or purpose. Purposive explanations of human bodily movements would *never* be true. Desires and intentions would not be even potential causes of human movements in the actual world (as contrasted with some possible world in which the neurophysiological theory did not hold true).

It might be thought that there could be two different systems of causal explanations of human movements, a purposive system and a neurophysiological system. The antecedent conditions in the one system would be the desires and intentions of human beings; in the other they would be the neurophysiological states and processes of those same human beings. Each system would provide adequate causal explanations of the same movements.

Generally speaking, it is possible for there to be a plurality of simultaneous sufficient causal conditions of an event. But if we bear in mind the comprehensive aspect of the neurophysiological theory – that is, the fact that it provides sufficient causal conditions for all movements – we shall see that desires and intentions could not be causes of movements. It has often been noted that to say *B causes C* does not mean merely that whenever *B* occurs, *C* occurs. Causation also has subjunctive and counterfactual implications: if *B* were to occur, *C* would occur; and if *B* had *not* occurred, *C*

would *not* have occurred. But the neurophysiological theory would provide sufficient causal conditions for every human movement, and so there would be no cases at all in which a certain movement would not have occurred if the person had not had this desire or intention. Since the counterfactual would be false in all cases, desires and intentions would not be causes of human movements. They would not ever be sufficient causal conditions nor would they ever be necessary causal conditions.

10. Let us tackle this immensely important point from a different angle. Many descriptions of behavior ascribe actions to persons: they say that someone *did* something – for example, "He signed the check," "You lifted the table," "She broke the vase." Two things are implied by an ascription of an "action" to a person:[11] first, that a certain state of affairs came into existence (his signature's being present on the check, the table's being lifted, the vase's being broken); second, that the person intended that this state of affairs should occur. If subsequently we learn that not both conditions were satisfied, either we qualify the ascription of action or reject it entirely. If the mentioned state of affairs did not come into existence (for example, the vase was not broken), then the ascription of action ("She broke the vase") must be withdrawn. If it did come into existence but without the person's intention, then the ascription of action to the person must be diminished by some such qualification as "unintentionally" or "accidentally" or "by mistake" or "inadvertently," it being a matter of the circumstances which qualification is more appropriate. A qualified ascription of action still implies that the person played some part in bringing about the state of affairs – for example, her hand struck the vase. If she played no part at all, then it cannot rightly be said, even with qualification, that she broke the vase.

Suppose a man intends to open the door in front of him. He turns the knob and the door opens. Since turning the knob is what normally causes the door to open, we should think it right to say that *he* opened the door. Then we learn that there is an electric mechanism concealed in the door which caused the door to open at the moment he turned the knob, and furthermore that there is no causal connection between the turning of the knob and the operation of the mechanism. So his act of turning the knob had nothing to do with the opening of the door. We can no longer say that *he* opened the door: nothing he did had any causal influence on that result. We might put the matter in this way: because of the operation of the electric mechanism he had no opportunity to open the door.

The man of our example could say that at least he turned the knob. He would have to surrender this claim, however, if it came to light that still another electrical mechanism caused the knob to turn when it did, independently of the motion of his hand. The man could assert that, in any case, he moved his hand. But now the neurophysiological theory enters the scene, providing a complete causal explanation of the motion of his hand, without regard to his intention.

The problem of what to say becomes acute. Should we deny that he moved his hand? Should we admit that he moved his hand, but with some qualification? Or should we say, without qualification, that he moved his hand?

11. There is an important similarity between our three examples and an important difference. The similarity is that in all three cases a mechanism produced the intended states of affairs, and nothing the agent did had any influence on the operation of the mechanism. But there is a difference between the cases. In each of the first two, we can specify something the man did (an action) which would normally cause the intended result to occur, but which did not have that effect on this occasion. The action in the first case was turning the knob, and in the second it was gripping the knob and making a turning motion of the hand. In each of these cases there was an action, the causal efficacy of which was nullified by the operation of a mechanism. Consequently, we can rightly say that the man's action *failed* to make a contribution to the intended occurrence, and so we can deny that *he* opened the door or turned the knob.

In the third case is there something the man did which normally causes that movement of the hand? What was it? When I move my hand in the normal way is there something else *I do* that causes my hand to move? No. Various events take place in my body (for example, nerve pulses) but they cannot be said to be *actions* of mine. They are not things I do.

But in this third case the man *intended* to make a turning motion of his hand. Is this a basis for a similarity between the third case and the first two? Can we say that one's intention to move one's hand is normally a cause of the motion of one's hand, but that in our third case the causal efficacy of the intention was nullified by the operation of the neurophysiological mechanism?

On the question of whether intentions are causes of actions, Taylor says something that is both interesting and puzzling. He declares that to call something an action, in an unqualified sense "means not just that the man who displayed this behaviour had framed the relevant intention or had this purpose, but also that *his intending it brought it about.*"[12] Now to say that *A* "brings about" *B* is to use the language of causation. "Brings about" is indeed a synonym for "causes."

12. Is there any sense at all in which a man's intention to do something can be a cause of his doing it? In dealing with this point I shall use the word "cause" in its widest sense, according to which anything that explains, or partly explains, the occurrence of some behavior is the cause, or part of the cause, of the behavior. To learn that a man intended to climb a ladder would not, in many cases, explain why he climbed it. It would not explain what he climbed it for, what his reason or purpose was in climbing it, whereas to say what his purpose was would, in our broad sense, give the cause or part of the cause of his climbing it.

In considering intention as a cause of behavior *X*, it is important to distinguish between the intention to do *X* (let us call this *simple intention*) and the intention to do something else *Y* in or by doing *X* (let us call this *further intention*). To say that a man intended to climb a ladder would not usually give a cause of his climbing it; but stating his purpose in climbing it would usually be giving the (or a) cause of the action. It is a natural use of language to ask, "What caused you to climb the ladder?"; and it is an appropriate answer to say, "I wanted to get my hat." (*Question:* "Good heavens, what caused you to vote a straight Republican ticket?" *Answer:* "I wanted to restore the two-party system.") Our use of the language of causation is not restricted to the cases in which cause and effect are assumed to be contingently related.

13. Can the simple intention to do *X* ever be a cause of the doing of *X*? Can it ever be said that a person's intention to climb a ladder caused him to climb it, or brought about his action of climbing it? It

is certainly true that whether a man does or does not intend to do *X* will make a difference in whether he will do *X*. This fact comes out strongly if we are concerned to predict whether he will do *X;* obviously, it would be important to find out whether he intends to do it. Does not this imply that his intention has "an effect on his behavior"?[13]

Commonly, we think of dispositions as causes of behavior. If with the same provocation one man loses his temper and another does not, this difference in their reactions might be explained by the fact that the one man, but not the other, is of an irritable disposition. If dispositions are causes, we can hardly deny the same role to intentions. Both are useful in predicting behavior. If I am trying to estimate the likelihood that this man is going to do so-and-so, the information that he has a disposition to do it in circumstances like these will be an affirmative consideration. I am entitled to give equal or possibly greater weight to the information that he intends to do it.

Not only do simple intentions have weight in predicting actions, but also they figure in the explanation of actions that have already occurred. If a man who has just been released from prison promptly climbs a flagpole, I may want an explanation of that occurrence. If I learn that he had previously made up his mind to do it, but had been prevented by his imprisonment, I have received a partial explanation of why he is climbing the flagpole, even if I do not yet know his further intention, if any, in climbing it. In general, if I am surprised at an action, it will help me to understand its occurrence if I find out that the agent had previously decided to do it but was prevented by an obstacle which has just been removed.

14. The simple intentions so far considered were formed in advance of the corresponding action. But many simple intentions are not formed in advance of the corresponding action. Driving a car, one suddenly (and intentionally) presses the brake pedal: but there was no time before this action occurred when one intended to do it. The intention existed only at the time of the action, or only *in* the action. Let us call this a merely concurrent simple intention. Can an intention of this kind be a causal factor in the corresponding action?

Here we have to remember that if the driver did not press the brake intentionally, his pressing of the brake was not unqualified action. The presence of simple intention in the action (that is, its being intentional) is an analytically necessary condition for its being unqualified action. This condition is not a cause but a defining condition of unqualified action. If this condition were not fulfilled, one would have to use some mitigating phrase – for example, that the driver pressed the brake by mistake. Thus, a simple intention that is merely concurrent cannot be a cause of the corresponding action.

15. Can we not avoid committing ourselves to the assumption that the pressing of the driver's foot on the brake was either intentional or not intentional? Can we not think of it, in a neutral way, as merely behavior? Yes, we can. But it *was* either intentional or not intentional. If the latter, then there was no simple intention to figure as a cause of the behavior. If the former, then the behavior was action, and the driver's merely concurrent simple intention was a defining condition and not a cause of the behavior. The "neutral way" of thinking about the behavior would be merely incomplete. It would be owing to ignorance and not to the existence of a third alternative. It is impossible, by the definition of "action," that the behavior of pressing the brake should be an action and yet not be intentional. Thus it is impossible that a merely concurrent simple intention should have caused the behavior of pressing the brake, whether the behavior was or was not action.

To summarize this discussion of intentions as causes: we need to distinguish between simple intentions and further intentions. If an agent does *X* with the further intention *Y*, then it is proper to speak of this further intention as the (or a) cause of the doing of *X*. Simple intentions may be divided into those that are formed prior to the corresponding actions, and those that are merely concurrent with the actions. By virtue of being previously formed, a simple intention can be a cause of action. But in so far as it is merely concurrent, a simple intention cannot be a cause of the corresponding action.

16. Let us try now to appraise Taylor's view as to the causal role of intention in behavior. He holds that it would not be true, without qualification, that one person stabbed another unless his intention to stab him "brought about" the stabbing (*ibid.*, p. 33). The example was meant to be of a previously formed

intention – for Taylor speaks of the agent's *deciding* to stab someone. But a majority of actions do not embody intentions formed in advance. They embody merely concurrent intentions. The latter cannot be said to cause (bring about) the corresponding actions. Possibly because he has fixed his attention too narrowly on cases of decision, Taylor errs in holding that, in general, the concept of action requires that the agent's intention should have brought about the behavior. When the action is merely intentional (without previous intention) the agent's intention cannot be said to bring about his behavior. In such cases his intention gives his behavior the character of *action*, but it does this by virtue of being a defining condition of action, not by virtue of being a cause of either behavior or action.

17. Our reflections on the relationship of intention to behavior arose from a consideration of three examples of supposed action – opening a door, turning a knob, making a turning motion of the hand. In the first two cases we imagined mechanisms that produced the intended results independently of the agent's intervention. Consequently, we had to deny that *he* opened the door or turned the knob. Then we imagined a neurophysiological cause of the motion of his hand, and we asked whether this would imply, in turn, that *he* did not move his hand.

Is the movement of his hand independent of his "intervention" by virtue of being independent of his intention? We saw previously (Section 8) that a comprehensive neurophysiological theory would leave no room for desires and intentions as causal factors. Consequently, neither the man's previously formed simple intention to move his hand nor his further intention (to open the door) could be causes of the movement of his hand.

18. We noticed before that it is true a priori that if a man wants Y, or has Y as a goal, and believes that X is required for Y, then in the absence of countervailing factors he will do X. It is also true a priori that if a man forms the intention (for example, decides) to do X, then in the absence of countervailing factors he will do X. These a priori principles of action are assumed in our everyday explanations of behavior.

We saw that mechanistic explanations could not be more basic than are explanations in terms of intentions or purposes.

We saw that the verification of mechanistic laws could not disprove the a priori principles of action.

Yet a mechanistic explanation of behavior rules out any explanation of it in terms of the agent's intentions. If a comprehensive neurophysiological theory is true, then people's intentions never are causal factors in behavior.

19. Thus if mechanism is true, the a priori principles of action do not apply to the world. This would have to mean one or the other of two alternatives. The first would be that people do not have intentions, purposes, or desires, or that they do not have beliefs as to what behavior is required for the fulfillment of their desires and purposes. The second alternative would be that although they have intentions, beliefs, and so forth, there always are countervailing factors – that is, factors that interfere with the operation of intentions, desires, and decisions.

The second alternative cannot be taken seriously. If a man wants to be on the opposite bank of a river and believes that swimming it is the only thing that will get him there, he will swim it unless there are countervailing factors, such as an inability to swim or a fear of drowning or a strong dislike of getting wet. In this sense it is not true that countervailing factors are present *whenever* someone has a goal. There are not *always* obstacles to the fulfillment of any purpose or desire.

It might be objected that mechanistic causation itself is a universal countervailing factor. Now if this were so it would imply that purposes, intentions, and desires never have any effect on behavior. But it is not a coherent position to hold that some creatures have purposes and so forth, yet that these have no effect on their behavior. Purposes and intentions are, in concept, so closely tied to behavioral effects that the total absence of behavioral effects would mean the total absence of purposes and intentions. Thus the only position open to the exponent of mechanism is the first alternative – namely, that people do not have intentions, purposes, or beliefs.

What I have called "a principle of action" is a conditional proposition, having an antecedent and a consequent. The whole conditional is true a priori, and therefore if the antecedent holds in a particular case, the consequent must also hold in that case. To say that the antecedent holds in a particular case means that it is true of some person (or animal). It means that the person has some desire or intention, and also has the requisite belief. If this were so, and if there were no countervailing factors, it would follow that the person would act in an appropriate manner. His intention or desire would, in our broad sense, be a cause of his action – that is, it would be a factor in the explanation of the occurrence of the action.

But this is incompatible with mechanism. A mechanist must hold, therefore, that the principles of action have no application to reality, in the sense that no one has intentions or desires or beliefs.

Some philosophers would regard this result as an adequate refutation of mechanism. But others would not. They would say that the confirmation of a comprehensive neurophysiological theory of behavior is a logical possibility, and therefore it is logically possible that there are no desires, intentions, and so forth, and that to deny these logical possibilities is to be dogmatic and antiscientific. I will avoid adopting this "dogmatic" and "antiscientific" position, and will formulate a criticism of mechanism from a more "internal" point of view.

20. I wish to make a closer approach to the question of the conceivability of mechanism. We have seen that mechanism is incompatible with purposive behavior, but we have not yet established that it is incompatible with the existence of merely intentional behavior. A man can do something intentionally but with no further intention: his behavior is intentional but not purposive. One possibility is that this behavior should embody a merely concurrent simple intention. Since such intentions are not causes of the behavior to which they belong, their existence does not appear to conflict with mechanistic causation. Mechanism's incompatibility with purposive behavior has not yet shown it to be incompatible with intentional behavior as such.

But could it be true that sometimes people acted intentionally although it was never true that they acted for any purpose? Could they do things intentionally but never with any further intention?

If some intentional actions are purposeless, it does not follow that all of them could be purposeless. And I do not think this is really a possibility. I will not attempt to deal with every kind of action. But consider that subclass of actions that are activities. Any physical activity is analyzable into components. If a man is painting a wall, he is grasping a brush, dipping the brush into the paint, moving his arm back and forth. He does these things in painting. They are parts of his activity of painting. If someone is rocking in a chair, he is pushing against the floor with his feet, and pressing his back against the back of the chair. These are subordinate activities in the activity of rocking. If the one who is painting is asked why he is dipping the brush into the paint, he can answer, "I am painting this wall." This is an explanation of what he is doing in dipping the brush, and also of what he is dipping it *for*. It is a purposive explanation. A person can put paint on a wall, or rock in a chair, or pace back and forth, without having any purpose in doing so. Still these activities could be intentional, although not for any purpose.

Whether intentional or not, these activities would be analyzable into component parts. If the activity is intentional, then at least some of its components will be intentional. If none of them were, the whole to which they belong would not be intentional. A man could not be intentionally putting paint on a wall if he did not intentionally have hold of a brush. Now this is not strictly true since he might not be aware that he was holding a *brush*, rather than a roller or a cloth. But there will have to be *some* description of what he is holding according to which it is true that he is intentionally holding it and intentionally dipping it in the paint.

Thus an intentional activity must have intentional components. The components will be purposive in relation to the whole activity. If X is an intentional component of Y, one can say with equal truth that in X-ing one is Y-ing, or that one is X-ing in order to Y. In moving the pencil on the paper one is drawing a figure: but also one is moving the pencil in order to draw a figure.

I conclude that if there could be no purposive behavior, there could be no intentional activities. Strictly speaking, this does not prove that there could be no intentional action, since many actions are not activities (for example, catching a ball or winning a race, as contrasted with playing ball or running in a race). But many of the actions that are not activities are stages in, or terminations of, activities and could not exist if the activities did not. Although I do not know how to prove the point for all cases, it seems to me highly plausible that if there could be no intentional activities there could be no intentional behavior of any sort – so plausible that I will assume it to be so. A life that was totally devoid of activities certainly could not be a human life. My conclusion is that since mechanism is incompatible with purposive behavior, it is incompatible with intentional activities, and consequently is incompatible with *all* intentional behavior.

21. The long-deferred question of whether the man of our example moved his hand on the door-knob will be answered as follows. The action of moving his hand cannot be rightly ascribed to him. It should not even be ascribed to him with some qualification such as "unintentionally" or "accidentally," for the use of these qualifications implies that there are cases in which it is right to say of a man that he did something "intentionally" or "purposely." But mechanism rules this out. On the other hand, to say "He did not move his hand" would be misleading, not only for the reason just stated, but also for the further reason that this statement would normally carry the implication that his hand did not move – which is false. Neither the sentence "He moved his hand" nor the sentence "He did not move his hand" would be appropriate. We would, of course, say "He moved his hand" if we understood this as merely equivalent to "His hand moved." (It is interesting that we do use these two sentences interchangeably when we are observing someone whom we know to be asleep or unconscious: we are equally ready to say either "He moved his hand" or "His hand moved.") But if we came to believe in mechanism we should, in consistency, give up the ascribing of action, even in a qualified way.

22. We can now proceed directly to the question of whether mechanism is conceivable. Sometimes when philosophers ask whether a proposition is conceivable, they mean to be asking whether it is self-contradictory. Nothing in our examination has indicated that mechanism is a self-contradictory theory, and I am sure it is not. Logically speaking, the earth and the whole universe might have been inhabited solely by organisms of such a nature that all of their movements could have been completely explained in terms of the neurophysiological theory we have envisaged. We can conceive that the world might have been such that mechanism was true. In this sense mechanism is conceivable.

But there is a respect in which mechanism is not conceivable. This is a consequence of the fact that mechanism is incompatible with the existence of any intentional behavior. The speech of human beings is, for the most part, intentional behavior. In particular, stating, asserting, or saying that so-and-so is true requires the intentional uttering of some sentence. If mechanism is true, therefore, no one can state or assert anything. In a sense, no one can *say* anything. Specifically, no one can assert or state that mechanism is true. If anyone were to assert this, the occurrence of his intentional "speech act" would imply that mechanism is false.

Thus there is a logical absurdity in asserting that mechanism is true. It is not that the doctrine of mechanism is self-contradictory. The absurdity lies in the human act of asserting the doctrine. The occurrence of this act of assertion is inconsistent with the content of the assertion. The mere proposition that mechanism is true is not self-contradictory. But the conjunctive proposition, "Mechanism is true and someone asserts it to be true," *is* self-contradictory. Thus anyone's assertion that mechanism is true is necessarily false. The assertion implies its own falsity by virtue of providing a counterexample to what is asserted.[14]

[…]

Notes

1. If you said "Get up!" and I got up, the theory would explain my movements in terms of neurophysiological events produced by the impact of sound waves on my auditory organs.

2. A neurophysiological *prediction* would be of the same form, with these differences: the second premise would say that O is or will be in state q (instead of *was*), and the conclusion would say that O *will* emit m (instead of *emitted*).

3. The correct diagnosis of such a failure will not be evident in all cases. Suppose a youth wants to be a trapeze performer in a circus, and he believes this requires daily exercise on the parallel bars. But he is lazy and frequently fails to exercise. Doesn't he really have the goal he professes to have: is it just talk? Or doesn't he really believe in the necessity of the daily exercise? Or is it that he has the goal and the belief and his laziness is a genuine countervailing factor? One might have to know him very well in order to give the right answer. In some cases there might be no definite right answer.

4. Charles Taylor, *The Explanation of Behaviour* (New York, 1964), p. 33.

5. E.g., Taylor says that the agent's intention is not a "causal antecedent" of his behavior, for intention and behavior "are not contingently connected in the normal way" (*ibid.*).

6. Taylor puts the point as follows:

Because explanation by intentions or purposes is like explanation by an "antecedent" which is non-contingently linked with its consequent, i.e., because the fact that the behaviour follows from the intention other things being equal is not a contingent fact, we cannot account for this fact by more basic laws. For to explain a fact by more basic laws is to give the regularities on which this fact causally depends. But not being contingent, the dependence of behaviour on intention is not contingent on anything, and hence not on any such regularities [*ibid.*, p. 44].

7. This is true if we use "wants X" to mean "is aiming at X." But sometimes we may mean no more than "would like to have X," which may represent a mere wish.

8. The following remarks by A. I. Melden present both of these points:

Where we are concerned with causal explanations, with events of which the happenings in question are effects in accordance with some law of causality, to that extent we are not concerned with human actions at all but, at best, with bodily movements or happenings; and where we are concerned with explanations of human action, there causal factors and causal laws in the sense in which, for example, these terms are employed in the biological sciences are wholly irrelevant to the understanding we seek. The reason is simple, namely, the radically different logical characteristics of the two bodies of discourse we employ in these distinct cases – the different concepts which are applicable to these different orders of inquiry [A. I. Melden, *Free Action* (New York, 1961), p. 184].

9. This point is argued in my "Scientific Materialism and The Identity Theory," *Dialogue*, 3 (1964); also in my *Problems of Mind* (New York, 1971), sec. 18.

10. For an exposition of this problem see Jaegwon Kim's "On the Psycho-Physical Identity Theory," *American Philosophical Quarterly*, 3 (1966).

11. I am following Charles Taylor here: *op. cit.*, pp. 27–32.

12. Taylor, *op. cit.*, p. 33 (my italics). Taylor says that an intention is *not* "a causal antecedent" of the intended behavior, for the reason that the intention and the behavior are not *contingently connected*. I think he may be fairly represented as holding that an intention does *cause* the intended behavior, although not in the sense of "cause" in which cause and effect are contingently correlated.

13. Taylor's phrase, *op. cit.*, p. 34. In my review of Taylor's book ("Explaining Behavior," *Philosophical Review*, LXXVI [1967], 97–104), I say that Taylor is wrong in holding that a simple intention *brings about* the corresponding behavior. But now I am holding that he is partly right and partly wrong: right about previously formed simple intentions, wrong about merely concurrent simple intentions.

14. [The final section of this article has been omitted here.]

30

Action, Causality, and Teleological Explanation

Arthur W. Collins

If, as Melden claims, causal explanations are "wholly irrelevant to the understanding we seek" of human actions then we are without an analysis of the "because" in "he did it because …," where we go on to name a reason.

Donald Davidson[1]

Introduction

In the fifties and sixties, many analytic philosophers argued that reason-giving explanations of human actions should not be interpreted as causal explanations. Some also thought that actions per se should not be thought caused at all. The concerns of this essay are limited to the first, that is, the lesser claim, that, whether or not actions are caused, reason-giving explanations do not appeal to the causes of the actions they explain. This once-popular view has been challenged, notably by Davidson as in the 1963 essay quoted above. What follows is an argument against views like that of Davidson. I support and explain a noncausal interpretation of reason-giving.

I will consider first teleological explanations of events that are not actions. Such explanations provide

a nonmysterious paradigm for explanations of occurrences that do not consist in picking out causes for what is explained. I do not know whether to say just this much is a controversial claim. In any case, the character of teleological explanations will be examined here with a view to securing agreement on the general proposition that a teleological explanation of phenomena in an organic system of a machine makes essential reference to the effect of the event explained and does not refer to causes. Correct teleological explanations can be given in cases where the causes of what is explained are unknown.

The further point of this discussion is the application of the concept of teleological explanation to the context of reason-giving explanations for actions. I mean to provide an analysis of the "because" in "He did it because …" that Davidson finds wanting. *Many reason-giving explanations fall under the general pattern of teleological explanation and are, as such, not to be interpreted causally.* I do not claim to have shown that all reason-giving explanations are teleological. Reason-giving is not a precise concept. Those

Collins, A. W. (1984), "Action, Causality, and Teleological Explanation," *Midwest Studies in Philosophy* 9 (1), 345–369. Reprinted with permission of John Wiley & Sons Ltd.

Philosophy of Action: An Anthology, First Edition. Edited by Jonathan Dancy and Constantine Sandis.
© 2015 John Wiley & Sons, Inc. Published 2015 by John Wiley & Sons, Inc.

explanations that Davidson called "rationalizations," the explanations for which he said that "primary reasons" can be given, appear to fit the pattern of tele-ological explanation quite readily.

1. The Standard View of Ends, Ends-in-View, and Causality

A provisional idea of the thesis to be defended here can be had by focusing on the role of reference to the objectives or goals of actions in reason-giving expla-nations. One line of thought is so commonly followed that it deserves to be called the *standard view*. Suppose a man explains his action as contributing to some future state of affairs. The standard view regards this as a condensed account wherein what is really intended is the assertion that, prior to acting, the agent had reaching that state of affairs as an objective, or that prior to acting he intended to reach that goal, or desired to reach it, or had reaching the objective as an end-in-view. What I call the standard view depends on the intuitive feeling that, if we fail to convert a reference to a future state into a reference to a prior aim, we will wind up explaining the present in terms of the future. This would be an unacceptable finalism that violates the temporal direction of causality and affronts firm convictions about nature. When we have deleted reference to the goal in favor of reference to *having that goal*, we have moved from the temporal framework later than the action to the temporal framework earlier than and up to the action. This pre-pares us to entertain the question, Could this item: 'His having such and such an objective,' be thought to have caused a man's action?

Much of the discussion of action and causality in the last few decades has been focused by following this standard line of thought. We are brought to think of having an intention, of wanting to accomplish something, or of setting an objective as eventlike items. We are to regard them as occurrences in the mental life of the agent. The debate centers on the appropriateness of thinking of these alleged prior occurrences as causes of what reason-giving explana-tions explain. Familiar debates have hinged on the conceptual independence that is required of causes and effects. Can intentions or desires be individuated

without essential reference to actions they are sup-posed to explain? This kind of question becomes rel-evant only if we accept the move from outcome to aim.

The standard line about reason-giving tends to make conscious functions a prominent element in the understanding of action. Our reason-giving abilities rely on matters such as planning, thinking about what will happen under various circumstances, realizing that particular steps will bring about a particular situ-ation, consciously making an effort, and conceiving of one's situation and prospects in a specific and articu-lated way. These conscious activities play a role in the standard line of thought about action because one can and one often does think about what one will do prior to acting, and one can decide to try to attain a goal before acting on that decision. Familiar prior conscious activities, therefore, provide illustrations that appear to encourage the view that it is always possible to restate reference to outcomes in terms that substitute prior ends-in-view, so that there is always an element in a reason-giving explanation about which the question, "But isn't this the cause?" is apt.

In what follows, I concede that these conscious functions are connected with the *giving* of explana-tions of one's own actions, but maintain that they are not a part of the *substance* of such explanations. The fact that a man can think in advance that he will act to attain a certain goal is another manifestation of the fact that he is able to say, having acted, what the goal of his action was, that is, to what outcome it contrib-uted. When a man thinks over things and forms an intention before acting, he knows what he will do and *he knows why*. He projects his action together with a teleological explanation for it. The fact that he knows the explanation in advance does not convert it into a causal explanation.

The standard view induces a double shift in focus in philosophical discussion of reason-giving explana-tion. The first shift is from one temporal frame to another. If we accept this shift we agree to consider matters that might, at any rate, be causes of what is explained in that they belong to the temporal frame appropriate for causes. The particular matters to which attention is directed are then such things as desires, intentions, decisions, and beliefs. So the second shift moves us from the question of the temporality of explanatory matters adduced in reason-giving to the question of the causal efficacy of mental things. The standard view thereby trades the problem of finalism for the quandaries of mind-body interaction.

Teleological explanation of organic and machine phenomena is unencumbered by the concept of consciousness. This is a great advantage for philosophical analysis. Isolation from unresolved issues in the philosophy of mind makes it possible to clarify a concept of explanation in terms of outcomes that is not causal explanation. When we have a good grasp of this concept, we are in a position to see the force of reason-giving explanations without being distracted by issues relating to consciousness. If we accept the view that I advance here, we are still entitled to the question, "How is it that men are able to give reasons for their actions?" I do not treat this important question here but rather try to distinguish it from the question, "What does a man say about his action when he gives a reason for having performed it?"

2. Teleology and Compensation

I call any explanation that derives its explanatory force from appeal to the outcome, goal, or objective of what is explained a teleological explanation. In physiological contexts where there is no question of intentions, desires, or beliefs, the validity of this type of explanation seems to be intuitively evident, although this appearance is often undermined by philosophical reflection and criticism. In the absence of subtleties, it seems obvious that some teleological explanations are true and others false. It is true to say that sweating occurs to cool the body and false to say that pumping it to the brain occurs to cool the blood. Teleological explanations can have different kinds of objects. Regularities are explained (sweating when it is hot), as are particular events (a rise in the rate of perspiration of an individual on an occasion) and the possession of organs (sweat glands). To further the analogy with explanations of particular actions, I will consider only teleological explanations of particular occurrences. Within this restricted domain, I will not present an analysis that tries to fit all cases but will confine attention to a single kind of illustration, namely, teleological explanation of instances of compensatory activity.

Any study of the human body reveals many compensatory physiological activities; among them (and most useful for our purposes) are instances of homeostasis, of which the maintenance of stable body temperature is an often-discussed example. I choose this illustration because it makes it particularly easy to separate the single issue of the outcome-orientation of explanations from other questions with which this single issue is often mixed up. The concept of compensation gets its footing from facts like these: Things happen in the environment of the human body that would, of themselves, cause significant changes in internal body temperature, but body temperature does not change much. Temperature stability is maintained in the face of destabilizing causal factors. How does this happen?

Although the full physiological story involves complex neural functions and is, as far as I know, not yet fully understood, there is no mystery here. Threats to the stability of body temperature are accompanied by offsetting changes in the body, such as changes in the rate of perspiration. Sweat on the skin evaporates and causes heat loss. The more sweat, the more heat loss. Perspiration is only one of the physiological resources for temperature control. Blood vessels dilate and contract. Various glands secrete various amounts of various substances. Under normal conditions, with the mediation of neural functions, perspiration together with other physiological responses combine to produce a joint causal influence that is precisely suited to the maintenance of stable temperature under the particular environmental conditions that happen to present themselves.

Homeostasis makes the fact of compensation obvious because environmental challenges and physiological responses can be extremely varied, whereas the outcome – stable temperature – remains the same. What is obvious is that a body reacts *in whatever way is required under the circumstances so as to produce the same outcome* vis-à-vis body temperature. To deny that this is what happens would be to suppose that the constancy of the outcome is somehow an accident or a coincidence. Such a denial would entail a refusal to predict that a given threat to stability will be accompanied by just the needed offsetting changes. The willingness to make that prediction, in turn, is equivalent to the acceptance of the idea of compensation. No one takes seriously the thought that the constant outcome might be an accident or coincidence, and everyone would predict offsetting changes to stability threats. Hence, it is right to say that the physiological changes do, indeed, compensate for environmental changes that would affect stability. The body is so structured that it produces whatever response is needed to secure the stability of internal temperature. The stability of the outcome is the foundation of our predictions and explanations of compensating activities.

This account is oversimplified in a number of ways. Some environmental changes are not offset. If it becomes too hot, temperature stability within the body will be lost. Some possible environmental temperatures, such as $1,000,000°$ F, are so great that they would destroy not only temperature stability but also the very circumstances under which talk of internal temperature is meaningful. But, where we can speak of compensation, there is a range of environmental changes for which compensation does succeed. Again, there are important differences among cases in which a given outcome is not preserved. Fevers sometimes have their own teleological explanation: to eliminate a heat-sensitive, invading microorganism. But fever can also result from the failure of temperature control mechanisms. The detailed structures required for these distinctions are complex but do not introduce anything that challenges the concept of compensation. The same is true of the fact that temperature-controlling responses of the body may compensate not only for environmental threats to temperature stability but also for changes originating within the body itself.

The concept of the outcome preserved by compensating changes may be more or less arbitrarily specified. Three outcomes with respect to which human bodies manifest compensatory activities are these:

O_1: Body temperature in the range 98.1–99.1° F
O_2: Body temperature in the range 98.0–100.0°F
O_3: Body temperature in the range 90.0–100.0°F

The degree of compensatory success ascribed to an organism will depend upon the choice of outcome and the range of environmental change for which that outcome is preserved. In actual investigations of organic systems, we think of outcomes preserved by compensation in terms of the normal functioning, health, and survival of organisms. These outcomes are easily thought of as goals related to the welfare of the system manifesting compensation. These understandings do not play any part in the concept of compensation and outcome-oriented explanations per se. We could readily identify compensatory behavior whether or not we possess any understanding at all of the outcome preserved and whether or not the preservation of that outcome does contribute anything whatever to the welfare of individuals or species. This point will be significant in discussions to come.

3. Compensation and Causality

In physiological illustrations of compensation, the event that compensates for environmental changes is a causal factor for the outcome adduced in a teleological explanation. That it will maintain normal temperature explains a change in perspiration rate, and that change, under the circumstances, causes the temperature to fall in the normal range. So the explanatory factor is the effect of the explained event. Teleological explanation would be finalistic if it represented the outcome as, somehow, the cause of the changes that produce it. But there is no reason to make such an implausible claim. The outcome is the effect in the ordinary sense and temporal order of things, but it is the effect that is explanatory. This is not at all, as is sometimes suggested, simply a way of bringing out the thought that the cause is a necessary condition for the effect. It is the compensatory structure of the behavior of the system generally that supports the teleological explanation, and not merely the fact that causes are necessary for their effects. It is only because we believe that just the right compensating change needed to cause *this* effect will be the one that occurs that we say of one such change that it occurs in order that the outcome be attained.

Causality bears on the concept of compensation at a second critical juncture. This fact can prompt scepticism about the distinctive character of teleological explanation. We have said that where compensation exists, environmental changes are accompanied by offsetting changes so as to bring about a given outcome. This accompaniment is itself a manifestation of causal relations. Let S be a system that reveals compensatory activity with respect to an outcome O, let F be a particular environmental change that threatens the attainment of O, and let E be the instance of compensatory activity that offsets F and, under the circumstances, causes O. What accounts for the fortunate occurrence of E just when F comes along and threatens the maintenance of the outcome O? No doubt, the occurrence of E is a consequence of a causal link between F and E. In other words, F threatens O and at the same time causes E, which removes the threat, again causally. A teleologically organized system is precisely one that works in a way that guarantees that this will happen for a range of environmental changes. There will be causal explanations for everything that happens in such compensatory mechanisms. Does teleology then reduce to causal explanation? I say that it does not.

Engineers are called upon to construct machines that exhibit compensatory activity, and that means activity that will be teleologically explicable. In building such a machine, an engineer has to exploit causal relationships between the machine, its environment, and possible outcomes. He is not called upon to go beyond such causal relationships nor to build in an occult device that anticipates the future. Outcome-oriented explanation is a feature of events in it because of the organization of his machine, given its environment, and not a further component or peculiar principle operating in it. It is for just this reason that teleological explanation in terms of compensation and outcome-orientation can be both successful and nonmysterious.

We can say that a fully understood compensating change is a causal link between an environmental change and the outcome. F causes E, which causes O. It would be entirely misleading, however, to say that the explanatory force of a teleological explanation comes from a tacit reference to the causes of the event explained. On the contrary, confidence that there is a causal relation between F and E is frequently engendered by acceptance of the teleological explanation itself. Our ideas about the causal history of a teleologically explained event may have

no support at all apart from the teleological explanation. We recognize that E compensates for F because E-like responses to F-like threats *actually do attain* O.

The example of homeostasis makes this particularly obvious. This much puts us in the position to assert, "Since E offsets F so that O is attained, there must be a causal connection between F and E, for we do not think that the compensatory activity is a miracle." In actual biological investigations, the discovery of homeostatic phenomena and other end-oriented organization raises the question of the causal relations that underlie compensation. Compensation can be identified and teleological explanations rightly given whether or not we have discovered anything about the causal history of the compensating events.

This point is brought with special force when the demand for teleological explanation includes some causal understanding of the puzzling event: "Why does working in hot weather make us sweat?" This is answered by: "To keep the body temperature from rising." The only causes of E (sweating) that we are familiar with are already incorporated in the explanation-seeking question. Surely they cannot also be presented as the answer. Here we are thinking of explanation for the layman. The conceptual point remains the same in the context of a technical explanation for E. We might know all there is to know about the cause of E but not know the teleological explanation for it. Teleological and causal explanations are independent. When we eat, enzymes are released in the saliva to trigger the secretion of hydrochloric acid in the stomach and facilitate digestion. Who knows what causes the release of the enzymes? Experts surely have a causal account and we could learn it. After reaching a complete causal understanding of E, we might discover that the teleological explanation was wrong to begin with. The enzymes may not be what causes secretion of the acid. Then too, the expert explanation we accept for E may prove to be wrong without threatening the teleological explanation.

It is the structure of the behavior of S in its environment that manifests compensation. This suffices for recognition of instances of compensation and, therefore, for teleological explanation. No causal account of what is teleologically explicable captures what is expressed in the teleological explanation.

4. Teleology and Behaviorism

I mean to use the pattern of teleological explanation considered so far as a paradigm for explanations of actions that state reasons for which they were done. A teleological explanation is never restatable as a causal explanation. Reference to an effect or outcome of what is explained is the crux of teleology. The standard view of reason-giving insists on a preliminary shift from outcomes to aims on the ground that appeals to outcomes are finalistic, if they are not heuristic shorthand for appeal to causes. The cases we have examined show that, as a general thesis, this is not true. There are plenty of correct explanations that advert to outcomes and not to causes. I plan to show that many reason-giving explanations of actions fit this pattern so that the preliminary shift is quite without justification.

In his book *Teleology*, Andrew Woodfield follows a line of thinking that is as opposed to what I will argue as is possible.[2] Whereas I argue that nonmentalistic teleological explanations of events that are not actions should be our model for reason-giving, Woodfield argues that mentalistic reason-giving explanations of actions should be our model for all teleological explanation. Woodfield's position is much influenced by his criticism of "the theory of goal-directedness" or of "directive correlation" that was developed by G. Sommerhof, E. Nagel, and others.[3] These accounts of teleology, like my own, which is much indebted to them, try to explicate teleological organization and teleological explanation without introducing anything either finalistic or mental in the contexts where teleological explanations have footing.

According to Woodfield's critique, these efforts to dispel mysteries employ a spurious conception of goals and goal-directedness, and this vitiates their account of teleology. He finds the theories of goal-directedness excessively *behavioristic*. Wherever explanations that invoke goals are legitimate, Woodfield contends, we must be able to say who it is that has the goal and we must be able to posit an inner state that constitutes *the having of that goal* by the organism. This, in turn, means that we must be able to think in terms of desirelike and belieflike states or events in organisms that have goals.[4] At least, Woodfield believes that all this is essential to the core concept of teleology from which usage has been extended more or less figuratively to other contexts that resemble but fall short of core cases. In other words, Woodfield accepts the standard view's reconstruction of reason-giving explanations of actions and then he extends that conception to teleological explanations generally. Apparently, even in contexts like temperature homeostasis, Woodfield will insist on one of three alternatives: (a) a posited framework of mental states and events, (b) an analogical similarity to cases where mental states and events are posited, or (c) the rejection of teleological explanations.

I cannot try to do justice to Woodfield's very full and subtle discussions of the problems of teleology in this essay. Some of the questions he raises are matters on which I do not have a view that is satisfactory. At the same time, I am quite confident that the mentalizing of all teleology is a big step in the wrong direction. I will consider only two themes here in the hope of making my antimentalism plausible. The first theme concerns the concept of a goal; the second is the claim that teleological organization and teleologically explicable behavior are manifest and, therefore, cannot be thought dependent upon posited, unobserved states.

In describing compensation and homeostasis in part 3, I intentionally avoided the expression "goal" and the expression "goal-directed behavior." I do not think that we should describe temperature stability as a goal of organisms that exhibit temperature homeostasis. This usage is worth avoiding just because it does give rise to the question, "Who or what is it that has this goal?" and the question, "In what does the possession of this goal by this organism consist?" When these questions go wholly unanswered, the very idea of outcome-oriented explanation comes to seem suspect. But that appearance is mostly the result of the ill-advised use of "goal" for the outcome for which compensation is exhibited in the behavior of the organism. We do not look for an owner of an outcome as we inevitably do look for the owner of a goal. So confinement to "outcome" deletes a mentalizing temptation.

We saw above that where there is compensation, the description of the outcome is arbitrary or, in any case, determined by understandings that are external to the fact of compensatory organization. Just what temperature is it that a human body maintains? There is nothing to be said against any of the three different outcomes formulated in part 3 or against other specifications. Woodfield thinks that, where teleological explanation is truly apt, we ought to be able to point to something answering to the idea of "having the goal G." But is it not extremely doubtful that we should ever find a reason for identifying one of the possible temperature ranges as the goal that the organism actually has? Notice that if we make the outcome range narrow – for example, 98.5–98.7 ° F – we will not be able to identify changes that keep temperature within wider limits as compensatory at all because they simply fail to maintain temperature in the chosen narrow range. Obviously, many compensatory events will be excluded since normal temperature so often strays from this range. A very wide range, such as 93.6–103.6 ° F, is no better. Though body temperature rarely escapes it, this range does not capture compensations that offset less extreme threats. With this huge outcome range, an environmental factor that would, by itself, cause a fever of 103 ° F would not even count as a threat to stability!

Our decision to think of some one range as "normal temperature" does not mean that this is the range the body really cares about. For every choice of ranges, wide, narrow, or medium, there will be compensatory activity that fails to be represented as such given that choice. The recognition that a system exhibits compensation is compatible with this variability in the description of the outcome. Thus the concept of compensation does not require that any outcome be identified as the real goal of the organism.

The fact that we can sometimes explain events teleologically even though they fail to attain the designated outcome is one of the reasons for which it seems tempting to think of the outcome as a goal. A goal, as Woodfield remarks, is an intentional object, and reference to it can explain even if it is not reached. Since this is sometimes true of outcome-explanations, outcomes seem goallike. But to speak of goals is to speak of what an agent has in mind, what he is trying to do, whether or not he succeeds. The concept of an

outcome does not support these ideas. We understand that sweating is explicable as producing normal temperature, in the first instance, because it succeeds in compensating for threats to normal temperature. On the basis of that understanding, we will explain an instance of sweating teleologically even though the outcome, normal temperature, is not produced. We may know, for example, that it would have been produced if the ambient temperature had not been so very high.

It is this sort of consideration and not analogies with conscious effort that accounts for teleological explanation in the face of goal-failure. Goals may be intentional objects, outcomes are certainly not. As Woodfield says, analysts of "goal-directedness" do not justify their use of the word "goal." But the concept of goals is simply not required at all for understanding compensation and, with it, teleological explanation.

I say that compensation is manifest in the behavior of an organism. In contrast Woodfield's requirement of an inner state of having goal G is intended as a condition for the legitimacy of teleological explanation. In the absence of such an inner state, we are supposed to withdraw the use of teleological language or, at best, to regard it as analogically extended usage. This is simply a mark of Woodfield's over-confidence in the standard view that recasts outcome-oriented explanations as causal explanations. It means, for example, that to the extent that we do not believe that the body contains a state roughly describable as "having the goal of keeping temperature normal," we should deny that the body does maintain normal temperature. No one, however, is going to deny this. Will Woodfield want to invoke unconscious mental items here, as he suggests elsewhere?[5] Does temperature homeostasis in lower animals go to show, as Woodfield says, that "Minds may be far *more* widespread than some philosophers have thought?"[6]

It seems clear that whatever scruples we feel about teleological explanations in physiology, nothing will be advanced by ascribing to ourselves unconscious ends-in-view, desires, and beliefs to go with every subtle manifestation of outcome orientation discovered in the body. The blood coagulates to minimize losses through bleeding. If we accept this explanation, it will not help us to express our understanding of the phenomenon to posit an unconscious desire to keep our blood from flowing out. Even if I have such a desire, it will be utterly ineffectual in the absence of the mechanism of coagulation. And with the mechanism of coagulation, blood loss through bleeding will be limited whether I desire it or not.

Woodfield's discussion of teleology is consistently sensitive to conceptual problems, but the direction in which he turns for solutions is faulty because of his reliance on the standard view of reason-giving as the ultimate pattern for all teleological explanation. The misuse of the word "goal" in the tradition that Woodfield calls behaviorist may be largely responsible for the inadequacies of his own thinking about teleology. Essentially, he believes that where one can properly speak of goals, one must be able to speak of the having of goals; goals will inevitably be the intentional objects of desirelike states and thus impose the general format of mentality on any context where goals play a part. A behaviorist analysis like that of Nagel uses the concept of goals but makes no room whatever for any of the required mental states or for any analogs to them. So behaviorism fails.

Woodfield is entirely right in this criticism. The proper response, however, is simply the deletion of the concept of goals from the behaviorist reconstruction of teleological explanation. We can thus retain the insight that teleological organization is something discoverable about a system and its environment that requires no behind-the-scenes functioning of any kind. As I have insisted above, compensatory structure is simply observable in behavior, and homeostasis makes this as obvious as it can be. Of course, it is correct to predict that the very organic changes that will maintain temperature stability are the ones that will occur. Compensation would be ascribable and prediction justified even if we had no idea whatever about either the utility of stable temperature for the organism or the causes of the bodily changes that ensure it.

Many philosophers reflecting on teleology have thought, "To be sure, this homeostasis is a good thing for the organism, but ought we say that changes are teleologically explicable unless we think that the organism, in some sense, wants and tries to secure homeostasis?" The fact is that compensatory behavior would authorize teleological explanation even if we could make out no advantage to the organism in the outcome and even if there were, in fact, no such advantage. Patent compensatory structure of behavior will always inspire speculations and research aimed at providing an understanding of the utility of the outcome and of the cause of the compensatory events. Recognition of the existence of compensation is in no way dependent on our actually attaining some understanding of the utility of the outcome or of the causal history of the events that we can explain teleologically.

5. Theology and Evolution

Compensatory behavior motivates investigation of the causal mechanisms that make compensation possible and also motivates the question, "How does the body come to possess these mechanisms?" Just as recognition of compensation does not depend on our understanding the causes of compensatory activity, so too the existence of compensation and its complete causal analysis do not depend on our success in explaining how systems exhibiting teleological organization come to exist.

Familiar theological arguments are relevant here. The body has features that are wonderfully suited to the welfare of the creature. It is as though bodies were designed as devices to secure that welfare. The body of a man, for example, is equipped with sweat glands as though its designer foresaw the need to control temperature in variable environments. Might not God be the designer here? If this were right, we could see through the phenomena to the goals and purposes of God. I am not interested in the merits of theological thinking here but rather in its assumptions concerning teleology and the goals and purposes of designers. Now that we have entered the age of genetic engineering, the format of the argument here is intelligible with or without the theology. We can plausibly, if incorrectly, discern the mentality of a designer through the structure and function of an organic body, just as we can discern the mentality of the designer through the structure and function of a machine made of springs and valves and gears.

There is something like the standard view at work again here in arguments that go from perceived organization to posited designer. Finding a subtly operating, outcome-oriented mechanism, we look for an agent designer to be the owner of the goals that the mechanism *automatically* attains. This way of putting the matter gives rise to the idea that the teleological discourse that comes into play rests on the mentality of the designer, and that the machine or organic body itself is only described in teleological language because it is the concrete embodiment of means to ends that are expressly desired by the designer. We can say that an automobile's carburetor exists in order to mix air with fuel only because this was the designer's reason for including a carburetor in his design. We can say that the human body maintains a constant internal temperature only because God has equipped it with sweat glands and other features so that its temperature should remain constant. This is the thought that teleology in mechanisms reduces to teleology in the goal-seeking actions of designers of them. The thought is based entirely on conflating explanations of events that occur in mechanisms with explanations of the existence of those mechanisms.

If the reduction in question here were not an error, we would be obliged to say that – in the absence of a designer – teleology in nature is only an illusion to be replaced by straightforward causal explanation. That is, we would say that, if the human body was not designed by God or by anyone else, then it is not a teleologically organized system at all, but only seems to be one. In the heyday of the debate between the mechanists and vitalists, I think that this principle was widely accepted by both sides. Entelechies and vital forces were like self-contained surrogates for a designer. Those who rejected these concepts and proposed a natural etiology for organisms of the sort suggested by the theory of evolution seemed to believe that the advocacy of such a view included opposition to teleological explanation in biology altogether. The hard-headed scientific school wanted to read teleology out of the organic world because science admits no designer for natural things and, therefore, no owner for any goals. Without an owner of goals, there can be no goals. With no goals, there can be no teleology.

I hope the appropriate refutation of this reduction of teleology to the goals of designers is by now familiar to the reader. Since compensation and teleological organization are manifest in behavior, failure to find a designer cannot possibly entail the absence of compensation and teleological organization. It is the irrev-

ocable recognition of compensation that generates the designer argument. The pattern here is, (a) *since there is compensation*, we need an explanation for this fact, and a designer would be a good explanation. The pattern is not, (b) *If there is compensation*, then there must be a designer. Only from the latter would it follow that there is no compensation if there is no designer.

Abandoning the theological designer argument does nothing to cloud our perception and study of compensatory mechanisms in the body. The very existence of evolutionary explanations of the existence of compensatory mechanisms (again, independent of the correctness of those explanations) should make this evident. The main point of evolution-based explanations is that they do not posit anything in the role of a designer, whereas they do accept the demand for some explanation of the existence of mechanisms whose operation is patently teleological.

If this point stands, we are entitled to a further conclusion. In the case of artifact machines where there is a designer, the outcome orientation of the structure of the behavior of the machine is conceptually independent of the thoughts, goals, and purposes of the designer. By hypothesis, a compensating mechanism in a man-made machine exists as a consequence of the purposes and foresight of designers and builders. But that they are compensating mechanisms is simply a fact about the structure of mechanisms in relation to their environment and not an allusion to the mental processes of their designers. A simple thermostat system compensates for changes in the temperature of a room by turning on and off a furnace: To say this is to remain at the level of the activity of the mechanism. Teleological explanation is fully authorized by the fact that these activities are compensatory. The system actually maintains a stable temperature. In the case of an artifact, we are entitled to infer designer goals from machine performance. We are not entitled to reduce teleological explanation to appeals to the goals of the designers of systems that exhibit teleological organization.

6. Teleology and Action

In "Teleological Explanation and Teleological Systems," Ernest Nagel does not address the question of the bearing of his analysis on human action and reason-giving explanation. In fact, he seems to adopt a conception of reason-giving explanation in passing that would rule out the possibility that teleological explanation might serve as a pattern for reason-giving. Although I do not follow Nagel in this connection at all, I do believe that attention to his apparent line of thought is instructive. Consider this passage:

> Quite apart from their association with the doctrine of final causes, teleological explanations are sometimes suspect in modern natural science because they are assumed to invoke purposes or ends-in-view *as causal factors* in natural processes. Purposes and *deliberate goals* admittedly play important roles in human activities; but there is no basis whatever for assuming them in the study of physico-chemical and most biological phenomena.[7]

Here Nagel is dismissing the charge that teleological explanations are anthropomorphic. (Curiously enough, Woodfield's criticism of Nagel is roughly the claim that they ought to be anthropomorphic.) Nagel thinks teleological explanations would be anthropomorphic if they ascribed "purposes and deliberate goals" to the nonhuman phenomena they explain, but, as his analysis shows, teleological explanations do not require any role for these concepts. In passing, Nagel makes it clear that he regards reason-giving explanations of human actions in much the same way as does Davidson. Purposes and ends-in-view are "causal factors." In its reference to ends-in-view, this passage illustrates what I have called the standard line of thought. A man has an end-in-view before he acts or when he acts, so that "having an end-in-view" could be a candidate causal factor for the explained behavior. A restatement of the explanation that adduced the end or outcome rather than the end-in-view would not make this candidate cause available.

Finally, Nagel's word "deliberate" in "deliberate goals" illustrates the pattern of thinking that appeals to conscious activities as a support for construing the purposiveness of actions in terms of antecedent events in the mind. In this case, the conscious activity would be the deliberate adoption of a goal or the adoption of a goal after conscious deliberation. Actually, the words "deliberate goals" are rather awkward. Why does not Nagel just say "purposes and goals?" The answer is surely that Nagel's account of teleological explanation of nonhuman organic and machine functioning will speak of "goals". He introduces "deliberate" in the context of human action out of the conviction that what is important in the human case is that people consciously think about what they are going to accomplish, weigh considerations, and so on. All this is true. If I am right, however, this is not what gives explanations of actions in terms of objectives and outcomes their force.

The prima facie case for regarding reason-giving as a kind of teleological explanation is strong. Whatever the bearing on action of the cluster of concepts – conscious deliberation, foresight, desire, understanding, planning, trying, and so on – reason-giving explanations obviously refer actions to objectives, outcomes, or end-states that are caused by the explained events. Consider an illustration of Davidson's: "I flipped the switch because I wanted to turn on the light." Ordinarily, in such cases, my flipping the switch certainly does cause the end-state: having the light on. Although Davidson's "I wanted to turn on the light" is perfectly natural, so too is simply "In order to turn on the light." Only the standard view of reason-giving explanation requires that the latter be considered a condensed version of the former.

The straightforward causality involved in the relationship between the switch flipping and the light going on contrasts with the murkiness of the supposed causal account of the act of flipping the switch. I say that, on the surface of it, it seems likely that the accessibility and intelligibility of the reason-giving explanation is a consequence of its reliance on the straightforward relationship between the act and the objective, and not on the precarious system of hypotheses converting reference to the outcome into reference to a prior state of *wanting*, together with the dark speculation that the wanting caused the relevant switch-flipping action.

To move beyond a primitive preference for the teleological interpretation of reason-giving, two analyses are relevant: (1) The context of reason-giving and action must be shown to exhibit structural similarities to the context of teleological explanations of events that are not actions. I believe that the similarities are so full and evident that they strengthen the credentials of the teleological interpretation to such a degree that the superimposition of a further causal claim about the explained action comes to seem entirely gratuitous. Contrary to Davidson's contention we do have a convincing and natural analysis of the "because" in "He did it because ...," that is not a causal analysis. Once we agree that the structure of a man's behavior in acting bears detailed similarities to the structure of teleologically explicable activities in organic systems and machines, it becomes very hard to avoid the conclusion that the made-to-order pattern of teleological explanation – outcome-oriented and noncausal – is just what we need in understanding the force of reason-giving.

(2) The standard line of thought must, at last, be expressly evaluated. The pull of the standard line is very strong. In construing reason-giving as teleological explanation, we seem to ignore the thought that the agent may experience pangs of desire before acting, that he may think it all out consciously beforehand, foresee the consequences of his action and deliberately set himself to realize those consequences. The resurgent standard view will insist on a role for these things in reason-giving explanations. Isn't it true that he only did it because he realized beforehand that ...? Didn't his gnawing desire finally drive him to do it? In short, the bare appeal to the attainment of an outcome seems to leave out something essential in reason-giving, however apt it may be for cases of compensation. It isn't just that the light is caused to go on by flipping the switch that makes it appropriate and true to say, "I flipped the switch in order to turn on the lights." Reason-giving involves my recognizing such causal relations and wanting to exploit them. Defense of the teleological interpretation requires either that this appearance of inadequate attention to these ingredients is an illusion or that giving the fullest play to these ingredients is compatible with the teleological interpretation of explanations of actions.

7. Action as Compensation

A satisfactory parallel between events in a teleologically organized system and actions depends upon finding something like compensation in ordinary action. The first thing to be noted on this head is that actions can be patently compensatory behavior for the maintenance of a homeostatic outcome. Given a

man in a room with a thermometer, a heater, and an air conditioner, we can construct a perfect analogy for the control of body temperature where the compensating events are not the operations of automatic mechanisms but the actions of the man. A man steering a boat with the help of a compass is a naturally occurring illustration of the same type. The homeostatic outcome is the coincidence of the direction of the motion of the boat and a point of the compass. Whenever currents, swells, or wind would move the boat from the given heading, the helmsman acts so as to maintain the constant outcome-state. Here we find exactly the relationships that obtain in a physiological system with homeostatic compensatory activities, except for one point. In the exposition of physiologically based homeostasis, we required that the environmental event needing to be offset be causally related to the compensating event, which is then explained teleologically as occurring in order that homeostasis be maintained.

In the context of action-based homeostasis, this relationship between the outcome-threat and the compensating occurrence is uncertain. It is an action that does the compensating, and we cannot baldly assert that the helmsman's action is *caused* by the shift in the wind that tends to move the boat off course and thus threatens the heading in a manner for which the helmsman compensates. Insofar as we are in doubt about the relationship of action and causality, we cannot simply claim a causal relationship here. This uncertainty is a significant issue for the teleological interpretation of reason-giving. But uncertainty here does not tell in favor of accounts like that of Davidson.

In this kind of illustration, a man's action is fitted into a context that has exactly the same broad organizational features as a teleologically explicable instance of compensation in a physiological context. We cannot draw the unqualified conclusion that reason-giving (in this kind of case, at least) is teleological explanation because the causal relationship between outcome-threats from the environment and compensatory events is essential to our account of teleology, and it is not clear that it is to be found where compensations are actions. However, if the relationship between outcome-threats and compensating actions were found to be causal, that would tell *against* a causal interpretation of reason-giving, *against* the standard view, and *against* Davidson's account. The discovery (or decision to say) that actions are caused by the events that threaten homeostasis would remove the only scruple standing in the way of saying that the helmsman with compass and boat *constitutes* a teleologically organized system and does not merely resemble such a system. It is precisely in teleological systems, where the relationship in question is certainly causal, that one can give teleological explanations that do not adduce causes of what they explain. We know that it is the heat that somehow causes sweating that offsets it and keeps temperature within the body stable. But the teleological explanation cites the outcome and not the cause of the sweating. Were we satisfied that the shifting wind somehow caused the compensating adjustment at the helm, we would be in a position to say with confidence that the explanation "He moved the wheel in order to stay on course" is teleological and not causal.

Doubts about this causal relationship are not a serious threat to the teleological interpretation of reason-giving in any case. We required a causal relationship in the case of physiological compensatory activity in order to understand how the right compensating event manages to accompany the right threat. Without a causal relation, compensatory behavior would appear either miraculous or coincidental and, in that case, not really compensation at all. That is why we posit a causal connection between environmental changes and compensatory responses though we are ignorant of the details. In the context of action, doubts about the causal character of the relation between environmental changes and compensating actions do not have the same basis at all.

We do not suspect that if a compensating action was not caused by events threatening a goal then it is not compensation. Those who hold that actions are uncaused do not mean that actions do not help to bring about objectives. Whatever the relationship between environmental change and compensating act, that relationship will support counterfactuals such as "Had the wind not shifted as it did, the helmsman would not have done what he did." Even in the setting of physiology it is the support of counterfactuals like this and not an actual causal story that is crucial for the recognition of homeostasis. All we really need know about rises in environmental temperature and

sweating is that, had the environment not become hotter, the sweating would not have occurred. Compensation and teleology could be systematically characterized by substituting supporting counterfactuals for causal connection between threat and compensation. We could then distinguish two ways in which this condition could be satisfied, since both activities *caused by* threats to homeostasis and actions *prompted by* threats to homeostasis offer the needed counterfactual support.

We have considered only very special examples of explanation of actions constructed in order to create a systematic resemblance to physiological homeostasis, that is, examples wherein actions plainly compensate for outer influences for the sake of the maintenance of a constant outcome-state. Within the framework of this narrowly conceived set of examples, the basis for rejecting a teleological interpretation for reason-giving explanation seems to shrink to dogmatism. But most human actions do not offer such good analogies to physiological compensatory activities. For the most part, actions are not compensations prompted by the presence of some particular factor that threatens homeostasis. The difficulty, however, in seeing actions as similar to compensation stems largely from the fact that there is nothing in particular to pick out as environmental menace to a given objective and, therefore, nothing for which the action could be viewed as compensating.

The maintenance of body temperature and the steering of a boat are both examples of homeostasis, and homeostasis puts the concept of compensation in high relief just because it draws attention to specific influences that threaten the homeostatic goal. The control mechanism is structured in relation to these influences so as to prevent their having their normal effect and thus protect the "goal." It is not the case that all organic and machine activity that is teleologically explicable is homeostatic. Enzymes are released in the saliva to bring about the secretion of hydrochloric acid, but the release of enzymes does not keep the value of some organic parameter in a constant normal range on the analogy of temperature control.

I have directed attention to homeostasis not because it is essential to teleological explanation, but only because the constancy of the outcome makes the outcome-orientation of our explanations most obvious.

For the most part, actions pursue short-term goals that cannot be represented as homeostasis; however, this does not tend to show that reason-giving explanations for actions are not generally teleological.

One might say that any action that is done to bring about something or to reach some objective compensates for the fact that the ordinary course of events does not bring about that something without help. A man wants to see in a dark room. The world being what it is, the light is not going to go on by itself. So a man compensates for this general feature of the world by flipping the switch that turns it on. Looked at in this way, the compensatory character of most actions is masked by the fact that nothing usually stands to bring about the objective except the action itself, and nothing stands to impede the objective if the action is done. Action is a kind of limiting case of compensation. The action compensates for the general failure of the world to produce the objective without intervention from the agent.

Somewhat more naturally, a kind of compensatory character is detectable in the fact that circumstances sometimes do block the success of the undertaken and ordinarily effective action. Reason-giving explanations carry the implication that the failure of the explained action to reach its goal would have prompted other actions as explicit compensation for whatever obstacles it is that have prevented attainment of the objective. A man who wants a lighted room will do various things besides flipping a switch in order to turn on a light, if other actions are needed. He will pull chains, test bulbs, run extension cords, check fuse boxes, and pay overdue electric bills. There is no particular limit to the things that might be relevant and that might be done. The explanation "in order to turn on the light" does not define the lengths to which a man would go rather than let this objective remain unattained. This parallels the fact that the correctness of teleological explanations outside the context of action also implies nothing about the range of variations for which the teleologically organized system will provide compensation, although it does imply that there is such a range.

Intuitively, if we accept a certain reason-giving explanation, we will certainly expect that the agent was prepared to do other things that he recognized as alternative routes to his objective, especially if those alternatives are of equal simplicity and without deterrent side effects. To establish that action is essentially compensatory, however, we have to go beyond appeal to customary expectations. We have to show that reason-giving actually carries the implication that compensatory actions would have been undertaken had the explained action failed.

The required allusion to alternatives and consequent compensatory structure is tacitly incorporated in Davidson's account of reason-giving. According to Davidson, "a primary reason" always involves two elements: "a pro attitude toward actions of a certain kind" and a belief "that [the performed action] is of that kind."[8] The appeal to a class of actions of a certain kind is needed because "we cannot explain why someone did what he did simply by saying that the particular action appealed to him; we must indicate what it was in the action that appealed."[9] This leads us to a general class of actions since any appropriate characterization of the explained action will impute to it something that other actions will also possess. Davidson shows that the particularity of the action: "I turned on the light," is not shared by the pro attitude: "I wanted to turn on the light." The latter does indicate a pro attitude toward a general class of actions, although grammatical similarities mask the generality:

> If I turned on the light, then I must have done it at a precise moment in a particular way – every detail is fixed. But it makes no sense to demand that my want be directed at an action performed at any one moment in some unique manner. Any one of an indefinitely large number of actions would satisfy the want, and can be considered equally eligible as its object.[10]

Davidson does not say that the members of the class of actions alluded to in a primary reason include alternative actions that would compensate for obstacles to the attainment of an objective. It is certain, however, that the principle of similarity in terms of which actions are "of a certain kind" has to be the fact that they are all thought by the agent to be ways of bringing about the objective. In the quoted passage, Davidson seems to have in mind only trivial differences between actions having the same outcome, such as flipping the switch with my right index finger, flipping the switch with my left index finger, etc. This is all that is needed to show that a general class of actions is involved. But true alternative actions emerge as constituents of the class toward the members of which the agent has a pro attitude in a further example Davidson offers: "If I say I am pulling weeds because I want a beautiful lawn, it would be fatuous to eke out the account with, 'And so I see something desirable in any action that does [make], or has a good chance of making, the lawn beautiful.'"[11] Davidson means that it would be fatuous just because this general assertion is obviously implied by the reason-giving explanation.

What is common, then, to all the actions that are equally objects of a pro attitude involved in reason-giving is that they are all causally relevant to the same outcome, namely, to the objective of the explained action. Upon reflection, we are entitled to say that compensatory actions will be found in any such class of actions, even those that appear to differ only trivially. After all, if my left index finger proves to be too weak, will I not try to flip the switch with another finger, that is, if I really do want to turn on the light? In saying that the generality involved in pro attitudes is equivalent to the ascription of compensatory status to actions, I mean to assert that a man who explains performing one action by saying that it belonged to a class of actions toward each of which he had a pro attitude is, at the same time, committing himself to the assertion that, had the performed action been inefficacious in attaining the goal that defines the class in question, then (in the absence of countervailing reasons) he would have performed one or more other such actions in order to secure the goal.

The number of alternatives that stand to compensate for the failure of an action may be limited, and a man can fend off challenges for failing to employ recognized alternatives rather easily, saying, for example, "I just didn't care about it that much," or "I decided not to bother." He may be ignorant of available alternatives, and he may reject otherwise viable alternatives that he does recognize for countless reasons. But reference to the limited urgency of the objective, or ignorance of alternative means to it, or countervailing reasons against their adoption are all of them pertinent only because of the general implication that alternative courses would be pursued if the one adopted did not produce the objective. Were this

implication to fail utterly, were the agent to wholly reject liability for this implication, or to have no explanation at all for not satisfying it, then the reason-giving explanation would itself fail.

Thus, the concept of reason-giving explanations of actions reproduces the essential features of teleological organization that we found to account for the intelligibility of explanations that cite effects rather than causes. An explained action is referred to its objective or goal, and reason-giving explanation implies the kind of compensatory plasticity upon which the analysis of teleology was found to depend. Therefore, noncausal teleological explanation constitutes a natural interpretation for reason-giving. The premise that no noncausal interpretation of the "because" in a reason-giving explanation is available, the premise that motivates Davidson and other causal theorists, is overthrown. As Davidson himself expressed this premise, "Failing a satisfactory alternative the best argument for a [causal] scheme like Aristotle's is that it alone promises to give an account of the mysterious connection between reasons and causes."[12]

This connection is no longer mysterious. Reasons explain actions by referring them to their effects and to the compensatory character of behavior vis-à-vis those effects. In light of the availability of this interpretation, there is no foundation at all for the expectation that reason-giving explanations may *also* refer to the causes of what they explain. We have seen that, in connection with organic or mechanical outcome-oriented explanation, the question of the causal history of teleologically explained events is always raisable. No answers to this question, however, are contained in teleological explanations themselves.

8. Pro Attitudes and Causality

In the interpretation of reason-giving put forward here, I press for the elimination of any role for the fact (where it is a fact) that the agent wanted to attain the objective reference to which explains his action. Of course, I do not deny that agents commonly do want to reach the objectives that their actions do reach. The teleological interpretation removes reference to this antecedent desire in favor of reference to the outcome itself. The thesis that I called the standard view of reason-giving earlier in this essay regards antecedent desires and beliefs about their possible satisfaction as the very crux of reason-giving. Can I really mean to assert that the mere outcome of the action can be explanatory without the mental processes of the agent who desired and tried to produce that outcome? I do not assert that the mere fact that an action has a certain outcome will validate an explanation adverting to that outcome. We must believe that the agent was disposed to compensate for some obstacles, at least, had the outcome not occurred. Action has a compensatory aspect that is entailed by reason-giving explanations but is not legible from the outcome alone.

This parallels organic cases closely. Suppose that we know about a creature S that its environment changed in temperature from T_1 to T_2 and that the effect of this on constitution of S produced an internal temperature of T_0. By itself, this outcome does not vouch for any teleological explanation. We have to know about the structure of S and, in particular, its compensatory organization. This means that we have to know what would have happened in other circumstances before we can offer "in order to reach or retain T_0" as an explanation for anything. In the same way, desires and beliefs are relevant to explanations of actions because they are the source of our confidence in the compensatory dispositions of the agent, and not because desires and beliefs cause his actions.

It is worth emphasizing that the teleological structure of reason-giving explanations is independent of the resolution of the question, "Do desires and beliefs cause actions?" We have seen in the setting of organic homeostasis that compensation involves two causal relations. The compensating event in the organism causes the homeostatic outcome (under the threatening environmental conditions), and the threatening environmental conditions cause the compensating event in the organism. We saw that the existence of these two causal relationships cannot be constructed as implying a causal reading for teleological explanation. This is brought out by the independence of the teleological and causal explanations of the compensating event. The causal account may be utterly unspelled out, or may be in error and rejected, or may be corrected, without affecting the teleological explanation at all. The causal account may be correct, and the teleological explanation may turn out to be

mistaken (in case we are right about what causes perspiration and wrong about what perspiration causes). If we have complete knowledge of the relationships, the causal account of the compensating event cannot be substituted for the teleological explanation.

When we compare these relations with the context of explanations of actions, the question of the causal powers of desires and beliefs is analogous to the question of a causal account for a compensating event in an organic system. We said that the compensatory element in action must support counterfactuals with the form, "Had such and such obstacle arisen, the agent would have taken such and such compensatory course." The thought that desires and beliefs cause actions would show up as part of the background of the truth of such counterfactuals. Roughly, the perception of the obstacle would be presumed to engender a belief about the prospects of various courses of action. The desire together with this obstacle-appreciative belief will cause an action that compensates for the obstacle.

I do not endorse any such account of desire, belief, and causality. But that is not at issue. If this causal theory of mental items were fully acceptable, its contribution to the understanding of reason-giving explanations would be limited to the auxiliary question "What caused the compensating action?" Insofar as we see compensation in action, we cannot substitute the successful account of this auxiliary matter for the teleological explanation of action. By the same token, uncertainty, both empirical and philosophical, about the status of desires and beliefs vis-à-vis the causes of actions is no more relevant to teleological explanation offered in giving reasons than uncertainty about the causal account of sweating is relevant to the fact that sweating occurs to keep body temperature normal. In sum, whether the claim that certain desires and beliefs caused a given action turns out to be true or false, that causal explanation is not even in the running in the search for the character of objective-oriented explanations of actions.

This contention faces a formidable objection. I say that prior desires and beliefs are strictly irrelevant to reason-giving, which should be interpreted teleologically and not in terms of antecedent matters at all. The objection is the plain fact that reason-giving explanations are commonly formulated by simply stating the desires and beliefs that might or might not be causes. "Why did you flip that switch?" Natural answers will include, "Because I wanted the light on" and "Because I thought that would turn the light on." The availability of these formulations undermines the credibility of the analogy of action and compensatory physiological activities. In the physiological framework, "To maintain stable temperature" does not name the cause of sweating on the surface of it. In consequence, it is conceivable that the teleological explanation is not an appeal to causes. But reason-giving explanations explicitly mention desires and beliefs. If these are the causes of the action explained, how can one possibly argue that the explanation that is offered by mentioning these desires and beliefs does not really invoke their causal efficacy?

Part of the difficulty here stems from the use of the verb "want" and its connection with desires. There is no denying that, if I flipped the switch in order to turn on the light, it will be proper for me to say, in a sense, "I wanted to turn on the light." "He wanted to …" is available in the context of any action that could conceivably be explained by adverting to an outcome or objective. The formula with "want" will always be constructible out of the outcome or objective mentioned. The universal feasibility of "want" formulas is, however, misconstrued as an expression of the presence of something like a prior state of desire for the outcome. On the evidence provided by this misconstruction, the causal picture of reason-giving is encouraged to regard behavior that tries to satisfy a desire as behavior caused by that desire. People do sometimes act in an effort to satisfy desires that they had prior to acting. But I say that the phrase "I wanted to …" does not classify an action as one of those to be understood as an effort to satisfy an antecedent desire. The universal availability of "I wanted to …" should be evidence against the idea that it alludes to a prior desire, since satisfaction of a desire is one among many alternative backgrounds for action.

There is a sense in which "I wanted the light on" follows immediately from the fact that I acted so as to put it on. In the same way, "I thought that would get the light to go on" will always be feasible if I have acted so as to put on the light. But there is another sense in which the assertions "I wanted the light on" and "I thought that would get the light to go on"

contrast with "She wanted the light on" and "She thought that would get the light to go on." I flip the switch and I am asked, "Why did you want the light on?" Cannot I say, "I didn't want it on, she did?" Or, to, "Why did you think that switch would turn on the light?" Cannot I answer, "I didn't think so. I rather doubted it. She thought so." In other words, it seems that, if desires or states of that genre do have a role here, they need not be the desires of the agent. And the same for beliefs. But the desires of others, though they may motivate my switch-flipping, will not seem as plausible as causes of my switch-flipping as my own desires and beliefs. In fact, even in these contexts, we would be ill-advised to move at once to a desire-interpretation of wanting. In placing my action in the setting of what someone else wants, I need not be asserting that the sense in which she wants the light on has anything to do with her desires. I can speak of her wanting the light on, as opposed to my wanting it on, whenever I have turned it on because she was in favor of it, asked me to turn it on, or the like. I am asked, "Would you please turn on the light?" I flip the switch. I am entitled to say, "She wanted the light on." But do I know anything at all about her desires? Maybe a third party asked her. Talk about "wanting" bodes nothing for desire.

The fact that the wants, desires, and beliefs of another can appear in explanatory discourse about my actions helps to dispel the illusion that references to desire and beliefs are especially strong candidates for causes of my actions. Being an agent, if a man has a desire that really is a desire (a state of desire that might exist and be appreciated prior to a satisfaction-seeking act), he can try to gratify that desire. This only manifests the same ability he has to gratify the desire of another. Mention of an agent's desire is explanatory not because the desire caused anything, but simply because it leads us to see what objective the action had, namely, the satisfaction of the desire. When an agent explains his action saying, "She wanted …," he leads us to the goal of his action, namely, the satisfaction of her desire, if the "wanted" really alludes to a desire. Whether the desire was his or hers, reference to it furthers the intelligibility of an action only on the assumption that he acted so as to bring about the satisfaction of a desire. In other words, it is not the case that reference to an outcome in explaining an action presupposes a tacit reference to a desire, but it is the case that reference to a desire in explaining action presupposes tacit reference to an outcome.

Desires play a role in the explanation of actions that parallels reference to contractual obligations, moral principles, promises, the expectations of others, orders, requests, rules, laws, and so on. All these generate reason-giving explanations because reference to them enables us to see the goal of the explained action. Being able to act means being able to bring it about that contractual obligations are met, or to bring it about that a promise is kept, or the expectation of another fulfilled, or an order obeyed, a request acceded to, a rule followed. In just this way, an agent can bring it about that a desire (whether his or not) is satisfied. We are wrong to try to generate a desire to go with every sort of reason: a desire to obey the law, a desire to follow a rule, or a desire to meet a contractual obligation. We are wrong if we say that "in order to turn on the light" only explains in virtue of a tacit "I wanted to turn on the light." In the sense in which "I wanted to …" is always available, it is merely another way of saying "In order to …" and not a further premise about prior states. In the sense in which "I wanted to …" can refer to something like a prior state of desire for something, *wanting* will not enter into all reason-giving explanations, and it will enter only when I have acted so as to satisfy a desire as opposed to acting because it is my job, because I promised, in order to please her, etc.

The thought that there is always a desire or something like a desire involved in actions, as a candidate causal factor, is not suggested in the least by the phenomenology of action. It originates in the requirements of a causal theory of action together with the hope that desires are more plausible as causes than other matters that are equally natural as reasons. Whatever the foundation of this theory of desire and causality, it does not even make much sense when we try to project it into the realities of desire and reason-giving.

Imagine a setting in which a man does have a desire to have a light on. "Oh, if only the light were on," he says, by way of expressing this desire. Then he sees a switch and he forms the belief that flipping that switch would turn the light on. He flips the switch. What does the agent himself understand about his action

here, so that he might try to convey that understanding to us by giving a reason for his action? Does he seem to know something about how he brought about his own action? Does he seem to be able to tell us how he got himself to flip the switch? Does he know what caused switch-flipping to take place?

It is hard to assign a clear sense to these questions, much less to suppose that in offering the explanation "I wanted to turn on the light," an agent is relying on an affirmative answer for these questions. In contrast, is it not obvious that what he understands is the end state that his action was chosen to bring about? Flipping a switch is something that a man is able to do, and, in consequence, he is able to bring about whatever can be brought about by flipping switches accessible to him. A man who knows what is caused by flipping switches accessible to him has a range of potential goals. He knows that he can have the light on if he wants (or someone else does), not because he understands that wanting the light on will somehow cause him to move the switch, but because he knows that the switch turns on the light and that he can flip it.

Finally, there are contexts where causal factors are the point of explanatory discussions of actions, and these contexts offer sharp contrasts with reason-giving explanation. We can describe actions in terms of their effects in ways that provoke curiosity satisfiable only by explaining how causal factors were deployed so as to bring about an objective. I tell you that I put the engine block on the workbench and you wonder how I managed to get that state of affairs to come about, because the engine block weighs 900 pounds. Then I explain how I deployed causal factors such as jacks or pulleys in raising the object. Prior to this explanation, you know the goal of my action, but you are left with a question of the form, "That was the goal alright, but how did he get it to come about?"

Causal theorists of pro attitudes construe the explanatory function of wants and desires as though they answer to this kind of curiosity. The standard line about reason-giving insists that it is well and good to say that an action brought about such and such an outcome, but, without reference to a want or other pro attitude, we are entitled to ask, "That was the outcome, but how did he get something with that outcome to come about?" If this were a feasible interpretation for the role of pro attitudes, then "He wanted to turn on the light" would parallel "He put a jack under it." They would be offered as the causes of the motion of the engine and the switch-flipping, respectively. Where an understanding of causes is involved an agent can say, "If I could put a jack under that, I could get it up on the bench." If pro-attitude reasons were offered as causal illumination, they would also generate "I could have the switch flipped in no time, if only I had a cause like wanting the light on." It seems reasonably certain that "I wanted the light on" is never offered as a causal explanation for switch-flipping. If this is so, then there is really no serious competition for the teleological interpretation of reason-giving explanation.

Notes

1. "Actions, Reasons, and Causes," Chapter 19 in this volume, 187. The phrase Davidson quotes is from A. I. Melden, *Free Action* (London, 1961), 184.
2. A. Woodfield, *Teleology* (Cambridge, 1976).
3. G. Sommerhof, *Analytical Biology* (London, 1950); and E. Nagel, "Teleological Explanation and Teleological Systems," in *Vision and Action*, edited by S. Ratner (New Brunswick, N. J., 1953).
4. Thus, for example, plants cannot be said to have goals according to Woodfield (*Teleology*, 33). Chap. 10 of *Teleology* presents Woodfield's frankly mentalist theory of teleology.

5. *Teleology*, 171.
6. *Teleology*, 172.
7. Quoted as reprinted in H. Feigl and M. Brodbeck, *Readings in the Philosophy of Science* (New York, 1953), 540. Emphasis added.
8. Davidson, op. cit., 183.
9. Ibid., 183.
10. Ibid., 184.
11. Ibid., 185.
12. Ibid., 187.

31

Psychological vs. Biological Explanations of Behavior

Fred Dretske

Causal explanations are context-sensitive. What we pick out as the cause of E depends on our interests, our purposes, and our prior knowledge. Almost any event, E, depends on a great variety of other events in such a way that makes any one of them eligible, given the right context, for selection as the cause in a causal explanation of E. The multiplicity of conditions on which the effect depends has both a synchronic and a diachronic dimension. At any given time there are a variety of synchronous events and conditions without which E would not occur. Any one of these can be singled out as the cause of E. Furthermore, because any cause of a cause of E is also a cause of E, a more remote cause, there is a diachronic aspect to this multiple dependency. Temporal chaining of causes gives rise to proximal as opposed to ultimate (or more distal) causes, and, once again, any one of these events can be featured in a causal explanation of E. There is no privileged vantage point, no such thing as *the* causal explanation of E.

I think these facts are reasonably well understood. When the event being explained is a piece of animal behavior, no one thinks that there is only one correct causal explanation of it. Functional explanations, the sort we get from evolutionary biology, are surely consistent with the more proximal explanations of

neurophysiology. Both can be correct, and both reveal part of the truth. They do not compete with but complement one another. They merely deal with different sets of causally relevant factors.

Nonetheless, there seems to be a widespread feeling that such harmonious coexistence is not possible between neurophysiological and commonsense psychological explanations of behavior (in speaking of "psychological" explanations of behavior I will always mean *commonsense* psychological explanations of behavior – those that appeal to what the subject believes, desires, fears, expects, etc). Here, it seems, is a tension, perhaps even a conflict arising from the fact that both explanations appear to describe proximal events and conditions. Beliefs, desires, expectations, and fears – the sorts of factors mentioned in commonsense psychological explanations of behavior – operate alongside and are concurrent with the neuronal activities featured in biological explanations of bodily movement and change. Hence, the apparent competition between these explanations cannot be relieved, as it is in other cases, by appealing to a proximal-remote difference. Nor is it much help to think of psychological explanations as describing causally relevant conditions that are synchronous with the biological processes controlling muscles and glands but that can be ignored in neuroscientific explanations of behavior, because if the psychological factors are causally relevant they cannot be ignored with impunity. If they are relevant, *qua* psychological, then the explanatory

Dretske, F. (2004), "Psychological vs. Biological Explanations of Behavior," *Behavior and Philosophy* 32 (1), 167–177. *Behavior and Philosophy* is published by the Cambridge Center for Behavioral Studies. Reprinted with permission.

resources of physics, chemistry, and biology must be essentially incomplete. Dualists may welcome that conclusion, but it is not likely to gain much favor in the naturalistic framework of contemporary cognitive science.

My purpose in this paper is to describe a difference between two types of causes – triggering and structuring causes – that I think is useful for understanding the difference between biological and psychological explanations of behavior. The difference might, at first, appear to be an instance of the familiar distinction between a proximal and a remote cause, merely a difference in the temporal location of the causal factors featured in the explanation, but the differences, I think, run much deeper. They run deeply enough to show promise of reconciling, within a naturalistic framework, the apparent conflict between explanations of behavior that invoke and those that ignore an agent's beliefs and desires. My ultimate purpose is to show that psychological and neuroscientific explanations of behavior are not only compatible but complementary.

Triggering and Structuring Causes

An operator moves the cursor on a screen by pressing a key on the keyboard. Pressure on this key causes or (as we sometimes say) *makes* the cursor move. Though other events can make the cursor move, pressure on this key causes the cursor to move if, given existing conditions, the cursor would not have moved without the key press.[1] It is this kind of causal relationship that allows us to speak of the operator as moving the cursor *by* pressing the key, and I shall speak of such causes as triggering causes of their effect.

As opposed to this kind of cause, we sometimes speak of events that produced hardware conditions (actual electrical connections in the computer) and programming (software) as the causes of movement. This is especially evident when cursor movement in response to pressure on a certain key is unexpected or unusual. Imagine a puzzled operator, watching the cursor move as he pokes the key, asking "Why is the cursor moving?" Because the operator knows that pressure on the key is making the cursor move (that, in fact, is what he finds puzzling), a different explanation of cursor movement is being sought. The operator is

looking for what I will call a structuring cause (C_s).[2] He wants to know what brought about or caused the machine to occupy a state or to be in a condition in which pressure on the key has this effect. He knows, or can easily be assumed to know (after a few presses of the key) that E (cursor movement) is being caused by the triggering cause C_T (pressure on the key). What he wants to know is *why* it is. Who or what made E depend on C_T in this way?

A terrorist plants a bomb in the general's car. The bomb sits there for days until the general gets in his car and turns the key to start the engine. The bomb is detonated (triggered by turning the key in the ignition) and the general is killed. Who killed him? The terrorist, of course. How? By planting a bomb in his car. Although the general's own action (turning on the engine) was the triggering cause, the terrorist's action, wiring the bomb to the ignition, is the structuring cause, and it will surely be the terrorist's action, something that happened a week ago, that will be singled out, in both legal and moral inquiries, as the cause of the explosion that resulted in the general's death.[3]

Specifying the structuring cause of an event yields quite a different *kind* of causal explanation than does specification of its triggering cause. The two causes exhibit a much different relation to their effect. For those who think of causal relationships in a Humean way, in terms of constant conjunction, the triggering cause, C_T, produces E in a familiar way: in the circumstances that exist at the time of its $(C_T$'s) occurrence, events of type C_T are regularly followed by events of type E. A triggering cause of E merely tops up[4] a preexisting set of conditions, a set of conditions that, together with C_T (but not without it) are sufficient for E. Because these conditions exist at the time of C_T's occurrence, triggering causes of E give rise to causal regularities of the following sort: whenever C_T occurs in *these* conditions (i.e., the conditions existing at the time of C_T's occurrence), E occurs. Structuring causes, however, occur in conditions that, generally speaking, are (even together with C_s) in no way sufficient for E. Later events, events that are independent of C_s, must conspire to promote C_s into a structuring cause of E, and these later events might or might not occur. If the general never gets in his car and turns on the ignition, then the plot fizzles. But if the general does behave in the way expected, then the terrorist succeeds in killing him – succeeds, that is, in causing his death. Unlike a triggering cause, therefore, there are no regularities between a structuring cause and its effect of the form. When events of type C_S occur in *these* conditions (i.e., conditions existing at the time of C_S), events of type E also occur. Tom can wire the computer so that pressure on a certain key will move the cursor, but if no one ever presses that key then Tom's activities will never explain why the cursor moves. Nonetheless, if someone, by chance, presses the key, then Tom's action becomes a structuring cause of cursor movement.

There is another important difference between structuring and triggering causes. The structuring causal relationship is a one–many relation, whereas the triggering causal relationship is one–one. Each movement of the cursor is produced by a distinct (token) press of the key. With triggering causes, distinct effects are produced by distinct causes, and distinct causes produce distinct effects. This is not so with structuring causes; distinct effects might have the same cause. Our terrorist example is unsuitable for illustrating this point because the explosion of the bomb destroys the condition the terrorist created, the condition that made the explosion depend on turning on the ignition. But consider a similar case in which this condition persists. I wire a switch to a light so that I can – again and again – turn on the light by throwing the switch. The structuring cause of the light going on *Saturday* is the same as it going on *Sunday* – viz., my wiring the switch to the light on *Friday*. The triggering causes are different each time the light goes on because the movement of the switch on Saturday is different than its movement on Sunday, but the structuring cause of each lighting is the same: my activities on Friday.

Some might object to this way of describing things. They might prefer to say that what I am calling the structuring cause of E is not a cause of E at all. It is, rather, a good, old-fashioned cause of those background or standing conditions (call them B) in which C_T causes E. So instead of having two different types of cause for E, a triggering and a structuring cause, we have one sort of cause, a triggering cause, for different effects. C_T (what I am calling the triggering cause of E) causes E, but C_S (what I am calling the structuring cause of E) causes B, the conditions (or one of the conditions) in which C_T causes E. C_S, if you like, is the

cause, not of E, but of C_T's causing E or, if you prefer, the conditions that enable C_T to cause E.

I have no objection to this way of putting things. Quite the contrary. For certain purposes this is the way I prefer to think about matters. For these special purposes, structuring causes of E are best thought of as causes, not of E, but of conditions, B, in which certain other events (what I am calling a triggering cause) cause E. From this vantage point, the designers, builders, and programmers of word processors do not cause individual (i.e., token) movements of the cursor. Keyboard operators do that. Instead, as designers, builders, and programmers they cause the machine to be in a condition that allows, or enables, an operator to move the cursor by pressing a key. Structuring causes of E are, in reality, causes of more or less persisting conditions (B) that make (events of type) E depend on (events of type) C_T in such a way that tokens of C_T (if and when they occur) cause tokens of E.[5]

Nonetheless, although I think that, for certain purposes, this is a better way to describe the relation of a structuring cause to its effect, I will continue to speak of these causes as causes of E out of deference for those (and I think this is most of us most of the time) who think that a cause of E is an earlier event on which E is counterfactually dependent in the right way,[6] a way that allows us (given a suitable context) to single it out as the cause of E in causal explanations of E, for (as the above examples are meant to show) it seems clear that structuring causes of E are earlier events on which E depends and which are often singled out in causal explanations of E. The cursor would not have moved (just now, when the operator pressed the key) if the wires had not been changed earlier. The terrorist killed the general by planting a bomb in his car. The light came on because Tom fixed the wiring. So, in deference to these facts, I propose to continue speaking of events that "configure" circumstances so as to make (tokens of) C_T, when (and if) they occur, cause (tokens of) E, events which (in this sense) cause C_T to cause E, as themselves causes of E. There is some danger in speaking this way, a danger of confusing causes of different (sorts of) things with different (sorts of) causes of the same thing, but as long as one is aware of just what I am calling a structuring cause of E and just how it differs from a triggering cause, this way of talking will, I hope, do no harm.[7]

One final point about the distinction before we attempt to apply it. Triggering and structuring causes, although always distinct, might sometimes appear to "fuse." Suppose a dim-witted terrorist forgets that he planted a bomb, or he forgets in *which* car he planted a bomb. A few days later, needing a car, he steals the wired car and blows himself up. Is the terrorist both the triggering and structuring cause of his death? He created the conditions that enabled him to (unintentionally) blow himself up, yes, but that only means that one and the same individual was involved in both causes. It does not show that the causes are the same. *What he did* to trigger this outcome is different than *what he did* to structure it. It was his *turning on the ignition* that triggered the explosion; it is was his *wiring the bomb to the ignition* (a week ago) that structured it. Though both events (actions) *involved* the terrorist, they were quite different. One and the same object figures in both triggering and structuring causes, but it is its having one property that triggers the effect and its having another property that structures it.

External Structuring Causes

I will use a botanical example to illustrate the way triggering and structuring explanations exist comfortably alongside one another in the explanation of an organism's behavior. In the case of plants, the structuring causes, unlike those with which I will eventually be concerned, are external, temporally remote, *extrinsic* to the system whose behavior we seek to explain. Though this is not what we are after in the case of psychological explanations of behavior (beliefs and desires, if they act as causes at all, are presumably internal causes), it will, I think, serve to clarify the differing explanatory roles of structuring and triggering causes. I return to *internal* structuring causes, psychological causes, in the next section.

A plant, the Scarlet Gilia, changes color during the summer. This is something the plant does, a piece of plant behavior. A plant does not have thoughts and desires or intentions and plans, but it does things, sometimes very interesting things, and botanists are interested in explaining why plants behave in the way they do. Why does the Scarlet Gilia do that – change from red to white in the middle of June?

One explanation is that the plant changes color to attract pollinators.[8] Early in the flowering season hummingbirds are the pollinators, and hummingbirds are attracted to red blossoms. Later in the season the hummingbirds migrate and hawkmoths, preferring whiter blossoms, become the principal pollinators. The flower changes color "in order to" exploit this seasonal alteration in its circumstances. It sets more fruit by changing color, and this, in the words of the botanists from whom I take the example, is why it does it.

This explanation of the plant's behavior appeals to factors in the evolutionary history of the plant, to events and circumstances that existed long ago and probably far away.[9] It is, nonetheless, a perfectly respectable explanation of why the plant changes color – at least evolutionary biologists and botanists will regard it as a perfectly acceptable explanation, an example of a functional or teleological, an ultimate as opposed to a proximal, account of the plant's behavior.

Suppose, then, someone observes the plant changing color in, say, June of 2001. She wants to know why it is changing color. At least two causal explanations are available. Which one we give will depend on a variety of factors, the most important of which is, perhaps, what the questioner is presumed to already know. One answer we might give is in terms of the events, whatever they are, that induce the chemical changes that produce a change in pigment. These events – let us suppose they have to do with longer daylight hours – trigger a change in color. Let us suppose, however, that our observer already knows (or thinks she knows) what triggers the behavior. Her question about why the plant is changing color is then a different question. It is like the question I ask when I ask why certain trees shed their leaves each fall. What I want to know is not what makes them shed their leaves – I already know that – it is, or so I believe, the colder weather. What I want to be told is not that winter is approaching but why trees do that – shed their leaves – at the approach of winter. If that is the kind of question our hypothetical observer is asking about the Scarlet Gilia, then she is looking for a structuring, not a triggering, cause of color change, and she has to be told what (if any) adaptive benefits are secured by such behavior.

Imagine that a molecular twin of Scarlet Gilia, Twin Plant, evolved in quite a different environment, an environment in which, in the midst of its flowering season, rapacious beetles arrived that were attracted by red blossoms. As a result of this selection pressure a slow change occurred. The plant evolved into a form in which it changed color, from red to white, in the midst of every flowering season. The beetles hate white blossoms, and thereafter they avoided Twin Plant and it flourished.

Twin Plant, let us suppose, is physically indistinguishable from the Scarlet Gilia. It therefore behaves in exactly the same way. Furthermore, the triggering cause of this behavior is exactly the same. Nonetheless, the structuring cause is much different in the two cases. This makes a difference in why these plants behave the way they do. Scarlet Gilia changes color to attract hawkmoths; Twin Plant changes color to repel beetles. Examining today's plants would never tell you that they had much different reasons for behaving the way they do. Their behavior is a physical event, to be sure, and it is produced by well-understood chemical changes inside the plant, but the explanation of the plant's behavior nonetheless requires going outside the plant to something that happened in the history of the plant (or the history of this *kind* of plant).

This illustrates something very important: even if you know what physical events inside the plant produced the change in color, even if you also know what events outside the plant triggered these internal changes, you do not necessarily know why the plant changes color. The changes in the Scarlet Gilia and the Twin Plant were produced by exactly the same chemical changes, and these chemical changes were induced by exactly the same triggering cause – the lengthening days of summer – yet these plants did not change color for the same reason.[10]

I have taken great liberties in describing these plants. I have, for dramatic effect, spoken of them as having reasons for behaving the way they did, as having some purpose for changing color. The plants, of course, do not have reasons in the sense in which humans have reasons for behaving the way they do. The plants do not have purposes, thoughts, desires, and intentions. None of them have a mind. Although misleading, I nonetheless used a figurative way of speaking to make a point about the explanation of behavior. In explaining a system's behavior we are often looking not *inside* for the physical cause of

external change but *outside* for the events that shaped that internal structure, that made the system into what it is today. We are looking for what I am calling structuring causes of behavior, not the events, either internal or external, neither proximal nor remote, in the sequence of causes that trigger that behavior.

When we turn from plants to animals an important difference appears. Structuring causes are sometimes, in the case of the intentional behavior, *internal*. Let me turn to animal behavior and that special subclass of animal behavior, intentional behavior, which is explicable in terms of the animal's beliefs and desires.

Internal Structuring Causes

A bird I will call Robin, as a result of a few taste tests, learns to avoid a noxious type of bug Nox. It not only avoids Nox, but, understandably enough (what else does it have to go on?), everything that looks like a Nox. Knowing none of this, you observe Robin foraging. Robin spots a tasty Benny bug, a bug on which it used to feast, but then, to your surprise, Robin ignores it. Why? Robin is obviously hungry. Why didn't he eat the Benny bug?

Benny bugs look just like Nox bugs, of course, but we cannot explain Robin's behavior by saying that the Benny bug looks like a Nox bug. That is true, and surely part of the right explanation, but Benny bugs have always looked that way, and a few days ago, before his unpleasant encounter with a Nox bug, Robin ate them with great relish. The fact that Benny bugs look like Nox bugs cannot therefore be the explanation you are looking for because this fact was true, and you might even have known it to be true, before, when Robin ate the Benny bugs.

Seeing a bug that looks like a Nox bug is the type of event that triggers the behavior we are trying to explain. You can convince yourself of this by a little patient observation. That, though, would not tell you what you want to know. What you want to know is why Robin ignores the bugs, especially the tasty Benny bugs that look like Nox bugs. He ate them before. Why doesn't he eat them now? In seeking an explanation of Robin's behavior, what we are seeking is an explanation of the triggering potential of various stimuli. We did the same thing with the plant. Before it evolved the Scarlet Gilia ignored the longer days of June. Now it responds to them by changing color. When we seek an explanation of its behavior, we seek an explanation of why this event triggers this reaction.

As I said, it is clear that at least part of the explanation for this behavior is Robin's past encounters with Nox bugs, bugs that look exactly like Benny bugs. Robin learned something in his encounters with Nox, something that, together with the perceived resemblance between Nox and Benny bugs, explains Robin's present reaction to Benny bugs. This sort of explanation is, once again, an appeal to Robin's history, to events that helped configure the motor circuitry responsible for Robin's current response to Nox-looking bugs. By talking about this learning process we are, just as with Scarlet Gilia, explaining a system's behavior by describing the historical events that helped structure it. There is an important difference between these two cases, however. Unlike the plant, there is something in Robin, the organism whose behavior we are trying to explain, that helps structure the behavior. The plant's behavior is structured by an evolutionary process in which the individual organism whose behavior we are trying to explain played no part. This is not true of Robin. In Robin's case not only is the triggering cause internal (the most proximal triggering cause of behavior is *always* internal), a structuring cause is also internal.

To see why this is so, why Robin's own internal states, unlike those of a plant, figure in the restructuring process, consider Robin before learning occurs. Robin can see Benny bugs; when hungry, he is relentless and unerring in his pursuit of them. Because Robin can see Benny bugs, we must suppose that there is, inside Robin, some internal state that represents, indicates, or somehow signals (use whatever word best suits you) the presence of Benny bugs in Robin's immediate environment. Call this internal state R_B (representation of a Benny-looking bug). R_B is some state (think of it as a sensory state) in Robin that is caused by and (normally) only by Benny-looking bugs (this includes Nox bugs). If we let E stand for Robin's behavior after his unpleasant encounter with Nox bugs, then what has happened during this brief learning episode is that Robin has been rewired in such a way that R_B now produces E. R_B (and, of course, anything capable of

Before learning: Benny bugs → RB

Robin's unpleasant interaction with Nox bugs

After learning: Benny bugs → RB → E (avoidance behavior)
                                          ▲

Figure 31.1   Change brought about by learning.

causing R_B – e.g., Benny and Nox bugs) has become a triggering cause of E.

This situation is depicted in Figure 31.1. The change recorded in this figure is a change brought about by Robin's experience with Nox bugs. In looking for the structuring cause of Robin's behavior, why he is reacting in this way to Benny bugs, we are looking for the cause of RB's (his perception of a Benny bug) causing E, something it did not cause before.

As noted earlier, for any event there are a great many other events that might be singled out as its cause. This case is no different. Nonetheless, it does seem clear that an important factor in the restructuring of Robin, an important contributing cause in the transformation of R_B into a cause of E, was a fact about R_B itself, the fact that it signaled the presence of (represented or indicated) a bug of a certain kind. If R_B did not represent or somehow indicate the presence of a Benny-looking bug, there would be no point in modifying its causal role, no point in making it into a cause of E. If Robin is to change the way he reacts to Benny-looking bugs, what is required to implement this change is the way the internal state that signals the presence of a Benny-looking bug functions in Robin's control circuits. Hence, if Robin is to avoid Benny bugs (and Benny-looking bugs) successfully (something we observe him doing), what must change is the causal role of whatever it is *in* Robin that signals the presence of Benny-looking bugs. This, of course, is R_B. The causal role of R_B was changed precisely because it was a representation (indicator) of Benny-looking bugs.

What this means is that R_B comes to be a cause, a triggering cause of behavior E because of some fact about it, the fact that it is a representation of the kind of environmental condition with which behavior E must be coordinated. Hence, this fact about R_B, the fact that it is a representation of Benny-looking bugs, plays the role of a structuring cause. The same internal condition, R_B, is involved in both the triggering and structuring causes of behavior E, but as we saw in our terrorist example (when a dim-witted terrorist blew himself up), the causes, though involving the same element, are different. It is R_B's possession of one set of properties, the intrinsic electrical–chemical properties that triggers the behavior. It is R_B's possession of quite a different property, a representational property, the fact that it indicates the presence of a certain environmental condition (the presence of a Benny-looking bug) that structures this behavior. That, I submit, is precisely the difference between a biological and a psychological explanation of behavior. Unlike biological explanations of behavior, commonsense psychological explanations appeal to extrinsic, representational facts about the internal causes of bodily movements.

Notes

1. I will not go much beyond this in my general statement of what it means for one event to cause another, though I rely on David Lewis's account in "Causation" (and postscripts) in Vol. 2 of his *Philosophical Papers* (1986) and J. L. Mackie (1974). My purpose in this paper is not to analyze the general notion of cause, but, assuming we already have a workable notion of cause, to make a distinction between different types of causes hence types of causal explanation. For this reason I also ignore complications having to do with overdetermination and causal preemption, probabilistic causal relations, etc. These complications, though relevant to clarifying the general idea, are not relevant to the distinction I seek to make because they apply equally to both sorts of causes I distinguish.

2. Mackie (1974, p. 36) uses the term "triggering cause" and contrasts it with what he calls a "predisposing cause." This is close, but not quite the same, as my own distinction. For Mackie the predisposing cause is part of what he calls the "field" for the triggering cause, part of the existing background (standing) conditions relative to which the trigger becomes necessary (and often sufficient) for its effect. The spark is a triggering cause, whereas the presence of flammable material is a predisposing cause of the explosion. A shift in interest and purposes could promote the standing condition, the presence of flammable material, to a triggering cause. A structuring cause, as I use the term, is best understood as a triggering cause of one of Mackie's predisposing causes (i.e., one of the standing conditions).

3. By changing the constellation of intentions and knowledge on the part of the bomber and bombee we can, without changing any of the causal dependency relations, change the context in such a way that the victim's actions become the cause of death. Imagine an unsuspecting mechanic wiring what he takes to be an emission control device to a car's engine. Unknown to the mechanic, but known to the car's owner, the device is actually a bomb. The suicidal owner, pleased by this convenient development, waits until the bomb is wired, climbs in the car, starts the engine, and blows himself up. In this case the owner causes his own death – kills himself. In this case the triggering cause, not the structuring cause, is *the* cause of death.

4. This is Jonathan Bennett's language (Bennett, 1988).

5. One can think of a structuring cause as producing a certain disposition in a system, a disposition to do E when C_T. However, this way of thinking about them should not prevent one from thinking of them as causes of particular behaviors, those that realize the disposition. If C_S makes X soluble, then C_S causes X to dissolve when it is put into water.

6. *In the right way* because we want to rule out "backtracking" counterfactuals that make two events "depend" on each other (counterfactually) when they are related, not as cause to effect, but as common effects of a single cause. When B and C (slightly later than B) have a common cause, A, and we allow a backtracking interpretation of the counterfactual (expressing the dependency between B and C), we can say that if B had not happened, then (because that would mean – and here we are backtracking – that its cause, A, did not occur), C would not have happened. Once again, I ignore these complications as irrelevant to the point I am making. Both triggering and structuring causes are causes, so we need to understand or assume that in both cases the dependency relations (whatever they are) are right.

7. In *Explaining Behavior* (Dretske, 1988) I identified behavior with a causal process (some internal event, C_T, causing bodily movement, M). A causal explanation of behavior was then a description of (what I am now calling) the structuring cause of M: the earlier event or state that caused the system to be in the condition in

which tokens of C_T cause tokens of M. I still think this is the right and proper way to proceed, but I have changed the way I express the point to avoid unnecessary complications.

8. This is the explanation given by the botanists from whom I take the example: Paige & Whitham (1985).

9. I do not think that these evolutionary explanations are explanations of *individual* (plant or animal) behavior, but this is a technical point that I skip over here. The analogy is useful, I think, even if selectional explanations are not quite the same as developmental explanations of behavior.

10. For those familiar with Hilary Putnam's Twin Earth (Putnam, 1975) example, this is reminiscent – and I deliberately made it so – of a situation in which molecular duplicates with different histories have different beliefs and, therefore, potentially different reasons for doing the things they do.

References

Bennett, J. (1988). *Events and their names*. Indianapolis, IN: Hackett.

Dretske, F. (1988). *Explaining behavior: Reasons in a world of causes*. Cambridge, MA: MIT Press.

Lewis, D. (1986). *Philosophical papers: Vol. II*. Oxford: Oxford University Press.

Mackie, J. L. (1974). *The cement of the universe: A study of causation*. Oxford: Oxford University Press.

Paige, K. N., & Whitham, T. G. (1985). [Report of research published in *Science*]. *Scientific American, 252*(4), 74.

Putnam, H. (1975). The meaning of meaning. In K. Gunderson (Ed.), *Language, mind and knowledge: Minnesota studies in the philosophy of science VII*. Minneapolis, MN: University of Minnesota Press.

Part VI

Free Agency and Responsibility

Introduction to Part VI

1.

As a topic in philosophy, the so-called 'question' of free will ranges far wider than any set of concerns pertaining to the philosophy of action proper. Aspects of it, for example, relate to issues belonging to the philosophy of science and metaphysics, such as those of about causal determinism and indeterminism, the alleged causal closure of the physical, and so on. We shall not be concerned with such questions here, there being entire anthologies dedicated specifically to them. Instead, the articles we have included represent a narrower range of concerns, ones more closely attached to the sort of issues related to agency and reasons discussed in Part I and Part IV respectively.

It is one thing to ask what it is to act, another to ask what it is to act intentionally and yet another what it is to act freely. But even if we knew the answers to these questions, they might not yet tell us what it is to be responsible for what one has done (or for what someone else has done). Can we perhaps say that we are responsible for all and only those acts that we freely chose to do? Responsibility seems to come in degrees; we might say that he is more responsible for this mess than she is. This does not exactly require that freedom comes in degrees, since there need be no suggestion that he was acting more freely than she was. It might be merely that all responsibility requires the agent to have been free to act or to refrain, but that such freedom is an all or nothing matter, and

merely a necessary condition for responsibility rather than identical with it. On this account, that responsibility comes in degrees would not establish that freedom comes in degrees.

2.

According to Chisholm (Chapter 32) a person is responsible for her actions if she could have done otherwise. This conception of responsibility can be traced back to the Aristotelian view that some agents (for Aristotle these are limited to fully functional adults) have a two-way power of either doing or refraining from doing some specific thing, whereas by contrast, agents not responsible for their actions have no choice but to act as they (are causally or otherwise necessitated to) do. On such a conception, a two-way power would be the bare minimum to get responsibility going. Once we allow such powers (but see Strawson, Chapter 35), it seems conceivable that one might have multi-way powers, not only either to do or not to do x but, say, to do x instead of y, to do x and y (instead of z) at time $t1$ (rather than $t2$), and so on.

Chisholm's conception of responsibility seems highly intuitive. If we are unable to do otherwise than we do, how could we be held responsible for our actions? *Equally*, if we *could* have done otherwise than we did, it seems (questions of mitigation aside) that we can, at least *prima facie*, be held responsible for our

Philosophy of Action: An Anthology, First Edition. Edited by Jonathan Dancy and Constantine Sandis.
© 2015 John Wiley & Sons, Inc. Published 2015 by John Wiley & Sons, Inc.

actions. But this intuition has been challenged by Frankfurt (Chapter 33). He offers two ingenious counter-examples. The first of these considers the case of someone who sets out to perform a certain action only to find herself threatened with death (by someone who is unaware of her intentions) if she fails to perform the very act that she has set out to do. While she could still do otherwise in the existentialist sense (defended by Sartre) of being free to decide to take the risk of being shot for disobedience, people acting under duress, coercion, threat, etc. are typically excused for their actions, and held not to have acted freely. Yet Frankfurt's example suggests that this need not always be appropriate. If someone freely sets out to commit murder, their being subsequently threatened with death if they fail to go through with it doesn't diminish their moral (as opposed to legal) responsibility, regardless of whether or not we should think of them as coerced. This is because they end up doing something that they would have done anyway. On Frankfurt's view, whether or not we hold them morally responsible depends on why they go ahead with their original plan. If they do so *because* they are being threatened we may not hold them responsible. But if they continue to act on their original reason (whatever it was) it would be wrong to absolve them from moral guilt simply because if they had not done it for this reason they would have done it for that one (the threat). The additional information just seems irrelevant.

In Frankfurt's second example, we are asked to imagine an evil and omniscient scientist (Black) who wants Jones to perform a certain action but will not interfere with Jones unless he has to. If Jones decides to perform this action then Black won't interfere. But if he changes his mind, Black will trigger Jones' neurons in such a way that Jones is caused to act as he originally intended anyway – against his will, so to speak. Whether or not Jones chooses to act as Black wishes him to, the resulting behavior will be the same. This implies that he cannot do otherwise than he does, even if he freely chooses to act as he does. And yet, assuming people are at least sometimes responsible for their actions (but see again Strawson, Chapter 35), we would hold Jones responsible in the former case, but not the latter. What makes the difference then, Frankfurt maintains, cannot be whether or not Jones is able to do otherwise, since he isn't able to

do otherwise even in the case in which Black has not interfered (for Black would have interfered had Jones chosen differently).

So if Frankfurt is right, the question of whether or not we are able to do otherwise is irrelevant to that of responsibility. This is Frankfurt's negative claim. His positive claim is to locate the feature making the relevant difference. As already anticipated in our discussion of the first example, Frankfurt's view is that what really matters (what we should care about, to use his language) is the reason *why* we act. If I do *x* because I cannot do otherwise, then I should not be held responsible for my action (notwithstanding Sartre's existentialist sense of freedom). But if I do *x* for some independent reason, entirely unaware that Black will interfere with my mind if I change it, any additional information about whether or not I possessed a two-way power in this situation just seems irrelevant. Responsibility, then, is tied to our reasons, whether or not it was in our power to do otherwise. Frankfurt does not offer an account of the nature of these reasons, but it is worth noting in this connection that 'because I cannot do otherwise' does not sound like the sort of reason one might typically act *for*.

This is one of the ways in which the questions of free agency and responsibility differ from more traditional worries about free will and determinism. Many take Frankfurt to be offering a new argument for the old compatibilist view that determinism is compatible with free will. While Frankfurt remains sympathetic to such approaches, his argument here might be taken to be about the irrelevance of free will to at least *some* cases of responsibility. Responsibility depends on our reasons for acting and not on whether we were free to act as we did. As Frankfurt himself writes in his later paper "Freedom of the Will and the Concept of a Person":

> It is not true that a person is morally responsible for what he has done only if his will was free when he did it. He may be morally responsible for having done it even if his will was not free at all. (1971: 22–24; note the phrase "free *when* he did it")

Frankfurt's view here seems to be that not all cases of responsibility require free will (at least not in the sense of the ability to act otherwise). Fischer (Chapter 34) has built on this account the 'semi-compatibilist' view that we can still have responsibility even if determinism is universally true. The compatibilism in question here, though, is not compatibilism of free will and determinism, but of responsibility and the lack of free will. Fischer's semi-compatibilism rests on his notion of a 'guidance control', which we can have even when we don't have the ability to do otherwise. In the case of actions – which Fischer calls 'positive agency' – I exhibit guidance control over the movements of a body (be it my own or that of my car, etc.) so long as I have the ability to align such movements to my intentions. Crucially, Fischer maintains, this ability does not require me to have control over any movements other than the ones I choose to make happen. In Fischer's terminology, I thereby have guidance control over a body even if I lack the 'regulative control' of being able to make it do something other than what I choose. In the article reprinted below, Fischer extends his position to cover guidance control of omissions ('negative agency'). He argues that just as I can be responsible for *doing* X even if I cannot *not* do X, so I can also be responsible for *not doing* X, even if I cannot *do* X.

3.

One can of course defend the view that strictly speaking we are never responsible for our own actions. P. F. Strawson's famous claim (1962) that moral responsibility is closely connected to our reactive attitudes towards people's actions (rather than vice versa) appears still to leave room for the claim that we are not responsible in the stronger sense of 'ultimate responsibility' which some philosophers, and perhaps laypeople as well, may on occasion have in mind. This notion is the central focus of G. Strawson's chapter (Chapter 35). Strawson builds on Nietzsche's brief *causa sui* argument as it appears in *Beyond Good and Evil* (1973: §21), though the latter concludes that unfree will is as much a chimera as free will (there being only strong and weak wills).

According to this argument, one can only be truly (or absolutely) free if one is a self-cause, and yet there could never be such a thing as a self-cause, since the characteristics of whatever does the causing in

question must be logically prior to those of the self which has been caused. This argument is *a priori*, functioning independently of any empirical discoveries about whether or not the universe is causally determined. Strawson's main point is that ultimate responsibility for actions requires that agents are fully responsible for their characters, since the latter influence our actions. While it may be argued that our characters are determined by our past actions, there is a serious worry of an infinite regress here since we can always ask about the character behind the earlier act. Ultimately, we will reach genetic and societal factors that lie beyond our control and for which we therefore cannot be said to be responsible. According to Sartre, this 'facticity' is the necessary background without which action (free or otherwise) could not occur. Strawson, by contrast, sees these enabling conditions of action as an insurmountable obstacle to ultimate responsibility. So, while we may be responsible in some weak sense (in tune with one strand of our ordinary discourse) we can only be ultimately responsible for our characters if being the persons we are is *completely* up to us (and not even partly determined by nature and/or nurture); but this is logically and/or metaphysically impossible. Even if we reject such up-to-us-ness for Frankfurtian reasons, it remains the case that we do not become who we are (to use Nietzsche's phrase) purely via responses to reasons. This is because every choice we make is framed within a prior background for which we are ultimately not responsible.

Strawson's incompatibilist assumptions are shared by Steward (Chapter 36), but she doesn't take their threat to free agency to be successful. Steward argues that Frankfurt's counter-examples fail to show that moral responsibility is consistent with determinism. Rather, they show that we need to disambiguate between two senses of the power to do otherwise. The first is the wide-scope one which Frankfurt focuses on. But lacking alternate possibilities in this sense is compatible with having the *agential* power to decide whether or not to do X. According to Steward, decisions are 'essentially actions'. In the case of Jones, the decisions that are 'up to him' are actions (or refrainings) which have the power to trigger Black's interference. Accordingly, whether or not this interference takes place is up to Jones. Responsibility, on her view, depends on the possibility of such exercises of agency. Agency, on this view, requires more than just guidance control over our actions. It also requires regulative control over those actions of ours that are decisions.

A very different sort of worry about free agency has sprung from neuro-scientific challenges to the view that we can freely decide what to do (or not do) prior to (or somehow 'in') acting (for the notion of an intention *in* action see Part III). The best-known experiments thought to threaten this assumption are those of Libet (1985, 1999) and Wegner (2002). Libet maintains that his experiments (in which subjects are, for example, encouraged to flex their wrists whenever they wish, while reporting any 'preplanning') reveal that the brain 'decides' to initiate action before we are aware of any intention to act and that we can only exercise free will by vetoing such decisions once we have become 'consciously aware' of their 'readiness potentials', which are said to begin 550 milliseconds before any relevant muscle contraction takes place. Wegner goes even further, arguing that 'conscious

intentions' are epiphenomenal in that they do not make any causal difference to what we do. He first attempts to demonstrate that we often act without the presence of conscious 'proximal' intentions and then infers from this that such intentions can never be causally efficacious, since it makes sense to assume that actions are caused in 'basically the same way' across all scenarios. From this he concludes that the 'experience of free will' is illusory.

Mele (who has been a subject of Libet-style experiments) emphasizes in Chapter 37 some of the conceptual worries that the philosopher might have with such experiments, e.g. what exactly is meant in these contexts by 'decision', 'conscious', 'basically', and 'free'. He also asks methodological questions relating to the timing and nature of verbal reports and the practice of generalizing from domain-specific results. Overall, Mele makes the case for taking these experiments seriously whilst pausing to consider how the experimenters' interpretations of their own results relate to grand philosophical questions that are not *obviously* empirical.

References

Frankfurt, H. G. (1971), "Freedom of the Will and the Concept of a Person," *Journal of Philosophy* 68 (1), 5–20; reprinted in his *The Importance of What We Care About* (Cambridge: Cambridge University Press, 1988), 11–25, to which any page numbers given refer.

Libet, B. (1985), "Unconscious Cerebral Initiative and the Role of Conscious Will in Voluntary Action," *Behavioral and Brain Sciences* 8 (4), 529–566.

Libet, B. (1999), "Do We Have Free Will?," *Journal of Consciousness Studies* 6 (8–9), 47–57.

Nietzsche, F. (1973), *Beyond Good and Evil*, trans. R. J. Hollingdale (London: Penguin).

Strawson, P. F. (1962), "Freedom and Resentment," *Proceedings of the British Academy* 48, 1–25.

Wegner, D. (2002), *The Illusion of Conscious Will* (Cambridge, Mass.: MIT Press).

Further Reading

Bennett, M. R., and Hacker, P. M. S. (2003), *Philosophical Foundations of Neuroscience* (Oxford: Blackwell).

Davidson, D. (1973), "Freedom to Act"; reprinted in his *Essays on Actions and Events* (Oxford: Clarendon Press, 1980), 63–82.

Searle, J. (2007), *Freedom and Neurobiology: Reflections on Free Will, Language, and Political Power* (New York: Columbia University Press).

32

Human Freedom and the Self

Roderick Chisholm

A staff moves a stone, and is moved by a hand, which is moved by a man.
Aristotle, *Physics*, 256a

1. The metaphysical problem of human freedom might be summarized in the following way: Human beings are responsible agents; but this fact appears to conflict with a deterministic view of human action (the view that every event that is involved in an act is caused by some other event); and it *also* appears to conflict with an indeterministic view of human action (the view that the act, or some event that is essential to the act, is not caused at all). To solve the problem, I believe, we must make somewhat far-reaching assumptions about the self or the agent – about the man who performs the act.

Perhaps it is needless to remark that, in all likelihood, it is impossible to say anything significant about this ancient problem that has not been said before.[1]

2. Let us consider some deed, or misdeed, that may be attributed to a responsible agent: one man, say, shot another. If the man *was* responsible for what he did, then, I would urge, what was to happen at the time of the shooting was something that was entirely up to the man himself. There was a moment at which it was true, both that he could have fired the shot and also

that he could have refrained from firing it. And if this is so, then, even though he did fire it, he could have done something else instead. (He didn't find himself firing the shot "against his will," as we say.) I think we can say, more generally, then, that if a man is responsible for a certain event or a certain state of affairs (in our example, the shooting of another man), then that event or state of affairs was brought about by some act of his, and the act was something that was in his power either to perform or not to perform.

But now if the act which he *did* perform was an act that was also in his power *not* to perform, then it could not have been caused or determined by any event that was not itself within his power either to bring about or not to bring about. For example, if what we say he did was really something that was brought about by a second man, one who forced his hand upon the trigger, say, or who, by means of hypnosis, compelled him to perform the act, then since the act was caused by the *second* man it was nothing that was within the power of the *first* man to prevent. And precisely the same thing is true, I think, if instead of referring to a second man who compelled the first one, we speak instead of the *desires* and *beliefs* which the first man happens to have had. For if what we say he did was really something that was brought about by his own beliefs and desires, if these beliefs and desires in the

Chisholm, R. (1964), "Human Freedom and the Self," in *The Lindley Lectures* (Lawrence, Kans.: University of Kansas), 3–15. Reprinted with permission of The University of Kansas.

Philosophy of Action: An Anthology, First Edition. Edited by Jonathan Dancy and Constantine Sandis.
© 2015 John Wiley & Sons, Inc. Published 2015 by John Wiley & Sons, Inc.

particular situation in which he happened to have found himself caused him to do just what it was that we say he did do, then since *they* caused it, *he* was unable to do anything other than just what it was that he did do. It makes no difference whether the cause of the deed was internal or external; if the cause was some state or event for which the man himself was not responsible, then he was not responsible for what we have been mistakenly calling his act. If a flood caused the poorly constructed dam to break, then, given the flood and the constitution of the dam, the break, we may say, *had* to occur and nothing could have happened in its place. And if the flood of desire caused the weak-willed man to give in, then he, too, had to do just what it was that he did do and he was no more responsible than was the dam for the results that followed. (It is true, of course, that if the man is responsible for the beliefs and desires that he happens to have, then he may also be responsible for the things they lead him to do. But the question now becomes: *is* he responsible for the beliefs and desires he happens to have? If he is, then there was a time when they were within his power either to acquire or not to acquire, and we are left, therefore, with our general point.)

One may object: But surely if there were such a thing as a man who is really *good*, then he would be responsible for things that he would do; yet, he would be unable to do anything other than just what it is that he does do, since, being good, he will always choose to do what is best. The answer, I think, is suggested by a comment that Thomas Reid makes on an ancient author. The author had said of Cato, "He was good because he could not be otherwise," and Reid observes: "But this saying, if understood literally and strictly, is not the praise of Cato, but of his constitution, which was no more the work of Cato, than his existence."[2] If Cato was himself responsible for the good things that he did, then Cato, as Reid suggests, was such that, although he had the power to do what was not good, he exercised his power only for that which was good.

All of this, if it is true, may give a certain amount of comfort to those who are tender-minded. But we should remind them that it also conflicts with a familiar view about the nature of God – with the view that St Thomas Aquinas expresses by saying that "every

movement both of the will and of nature proceeds from God as the Prime Mover."[3] If the act of the sinner *did* proceed from God as the Prime Mover, then God was in the position of the second agent we just discussed – the man who forced the trigger finger, or the hypnotist – and the sinner, so-called, was *not* responsible for what he did. (This may be a bold assertion, in view of the history of western theology, but I must say that I have never encountered a single good reason for denying it.)

There is one standard objection to all of this and we should consider it briefly.

3. The objection takes the form of a stratagem – one designed to show that determinism (and divine providence) is consistent with human responsibility. The stratagem is one that was used by Jonathan Edwards and by many philosophers in the present century, most notably, G. E. Moore.[4]

One proceeds as follows: The expression

a. He could have done otherwise,

it is argued, means no more nor less than

b. If he had chosen to do otherwise, then he would have done otherwise.

(In place of "chosen," one might say "tried," "set out," "decided," "undertaken," or "willed.") The truth of statement (b), it is then pointed out, is consistent with determinism (and with divine providence); for even if all of the man's actions were causally determined, the man could still be such that, *if* he had chosen otherwise, then he would have done otherwise. What the murderer saw, let us suppose, along with his beliefs and desires, *caused* him to fire the shot; yet he was such that *if*, just then, he had chosen or decided *not* to fire the shot, then he would not have fired it. All of this is certainly possible. Similarly, we could say, of the dam, that the flood caused it to break and also that the dam was such that, *if* there had been no flood or any similar pressure, then the dam would have remained intact. And therefore, the argument proceeds, if (b) is consistent with determinism, and if (a) and (b) say the same thing, then (a) is also consistent with determinism; hence we can say that the agent *could* have done otherwise even though he was caused to do what he did do; and therefore determinism and moral responsibility are compatible.

Is the argument sound? The conclusion follows from the premises, but the catch, I think, lies in the first premise – the one saying that statement (a) tells us no more nor less than what statement (b) tells us. For (b), it would seem, could be true while (a) is false. That is to say, our man might be such that, if he had chosen to do otherwise, then he would have done otherwise, and yet *also* such that he could not have done otherwise. Suppose, after all, that our murderer could not have *chosen*, or could not have *decided*, to do otherwise. Then the fact that he happens also to be a man such that, if he had chosen not to shoot he would not have shot, would make no difference. For if he could *not* have chosen *not* to shoot, then he could not have done anything other than just what it was that he did do. In a word: from our statement (b) above ("If he had chosen to do otherwise, then he would have done otherwise"), we cannot make an inference to (a) above ("He could have done otherwise") unless we can *also* assert:

c. He could have chosen to do otherwise.

And therefore, if we must reject this third statement (c), then, even though we may be justified in asserting (b), we are not justified in asserting (a). If the man could not have chosen to do otherwise, then he would not have done otherwise – *even if* he was such that, if he *had* chosen to do otherwise, then he would have done otherwise.

The stratagem in question, then, seems to me not to work, and I would say, therefore, that the ascription of responsibility conflicts with a deterministic view of action.

4.   Perhaps there is less need to argue that the ascription of responsibility also conflicts with an indeterministic view of action – with the view that the act, or some event that is essential to the act, is not caused at all. If the act – the firing of the shot – was not caused at all, if it was fortuitous or capricious, happening so to speak out of the blue, then, presumably, no one – and nothing – was responsible for the act. Our conception of action, therefore, should be neither deterministic nor indeterministic. Is there any other possibility?

5.   We must not say that every event involved in the act is caused by some other event; and we must not say that the act is something that is not caused at all. The possibility that remains, therefore, is this: We should say that at least one of the events that are involved in the act is caused, not by any other events, but by something else instead. And this something else can only be the agent – the man. If there is an event that is caused, not by other events, but by the man, then there are some events involved in the act that are not caused by other events. But if the event in question is caused by the man then it *is* caused and we are not committed to saying that there is something involved in the act that is not caused at all.

But this, of course, is a large consequence, implying something of considerable importance about the nature of the agent or the man.

6.   If we consider only inanimate natural objects, we may say that causation, if it occurs, is a relation between *events* or *states of affairs*. The dam's breaking was an event that was caused by a set of other events – the dam being weak, the flood being strong, and so on. But if a man is responsible for a particular deed, then, if what I have said is true, there is some event, or set of events, that is caused, *not* by other events or states of affairs, but by the agent, whatever he may be.

I shall borrow a pair of medieval terms, using them, perhaps, in a way that is slightly different from that for which they were originally intended. I shall say that when one event or state of affairs (or set of events or states of affairs) causes some other event or state of affairs, then we have an instance of *transeunt* causation. And I shall say that when an *agent*, as distinguished from an event, causes an event or state of affairs, then we have an instance of *immanent* causation.

The nature of what is intended by the expression "immanent causation" may be illustrated by this sentence from Aristotle's *Physics*. "Thus, a staff moves a stone, and is moved by a hand, which is moved by a man" (Book VII, Chap. 5, 256a, 6–8). If the man was responsible, then we have in this illustration a number of instances of causation – most of them transeunt but at least one of them immanent. What the staff did to the stone was an instance of transeunt causation, and thus we may describe it as a relation between events:

"the motion of the staff caused the motion of the stone." And similarly for what the hand did to the staff: "the motion of the hand caused the motion of the staff." And, as we know from physiology, there are still other events which caused the motion of the hand. Hence we need not introduce the agent at this particular point, as Aristotle does – we *need* not, though we *may*. We *may* say that the hand was moved by the man, but we may *also* say that the motion of the hand was caused by the motion of certain muscles; and we may say that the motion of the muscles was caused by certain events that took place within the brain. But some event, and presumably one of those that took place within the brain, was caused by the agent and not by any other events.

There are, of course, objections to this way of putting the matter; I shall consider the two that seem to me to be most important.

7.   One may object, firstly: "If the *man* does anything, then, as Aristotle's remark suggests, what he does is to move the *hand*. But he certainly does not *do* anything to his brain – he may not even know that he *has* a brain. And if he doesn't do anything to the brain, and if the motion of the hand was caused by something that happened within the brain, then there is no point in appealing to 'immanent causation' as being something incompatible with 'transeunt causation' – for the whole thing, after all, is a matter of causal relations among events or states of affairs."

The answer to this objection, I think, is this: It is true that the agent does not *do* anything with his brain, or to his brain, in the sense in which he *does* something with his hand and does something to the staff. But from this it does not follow that the agent was not the immanent cause of something that happened within his brain.

We should note a useful distinction that has been proposed by Professor A. I. Melden – namely, the distinction between "making something A happen" and "doing A."[5] If I reach for the staff and pick it up, then one of the things that I *do* is just that – reach for the staff and pick it up. And if it is something that I do, then there is a very clear sense in which it may be said to be something that I know that I do. If you ask me, "Are you doing something, or trying to do something, with the staff?", I will have no difficulty in

finding an answer. But in doing something with the staff, I also make various things happen which are not in this same sense things that I do: I will make various air-particles move; I will free a number of blades of grass from the pressure that had been upon them; and I may cause a shadow to move from one place to another. If these are merely things that I make happen, as distinguished from things that I do, then I may know nothing whatever about them; I may not have the slightest idea that, in moving the staff, I am bringing about any such thing as the motion of air-particles, shadows, and blades of grass.

We may say, in answer to the first objection, therefore, that it is true that our agent does nothing to his brain or with his brain; but from this it does not follow that the agent is not the immanent cause of some event within his brain; for the brain event may be something which, like the motion of the air-particles, he made happen in picking up the staff. The only difference between the two cases is this: in each case, he made something happen when he picked up the staff; but in the one case – the motion of the air-particles or of the shadows – it was the motion of the staff that caused the event to happen; and in the other case – the event that took place in the brain – it was this event that caused the motion of the staff.

The point is, in a word, that whenever a man does something A, then (by "immanent causation") he makes a certain cerebral event happen, and this cerebral event (by "transeunt causation") makes A happen.

8.   The second objection is more difficult and concerns the very concept of "immanent causation," or causation by an agent, as this concept is to be interpreted here. The concept is subject to a difficulty which has long been associated with that of the prime mover unmoved. We have said that there must be some event A, presumably some cerebral event, which is caused not by any other event, but by the agent. Since A was not caused by any other event, then the agent himself cannot be said to have undergone any change or produced any other event (such as "an act of will" or the like) which brought A about. But if, when the agent made A happen, there was no event involved other than A itself, no event which could be described as *making* A happen, what did the agent's causation consist of? What, for example, is the difference

between A's just happening, and the agent's *causing* A to happen? We cannot attribute the difference to any event that took place within the agent. And so far as the event A itself is concerned, there would seem to be no discernible difference. Thus Aristotle said that the activity of the prime mover is nothing in addition to the motion that it produces, and Suarez said that "the action is in reality nothing but the effect as it flows from the agent."[6] Must we conclude, then, that there is no more to the man's action in causing event A than there is to the event A's happening by itself? Here we would seem to have a distinction without a difference – in which case we have failed to find a *via media* between a deterministic and an indeterministic view of action.

The only answer, I think, can be this: that the difference between the man's causing A, on the one hand, and the event A just happening, on the other, lies in the fact that, in the first case but not the second, the event A *was* caused and was caused by the man. There was a brain event A; the agent did, in fact, cause the brain event; but there was nothing that he did to cause it.

This answer may not entirely satisfy and it will be likely to provoke the following question: "But what are you really *adding* to the assertion that A happened when you utter the words 'The agent *caused* A to happen'?" As soon as we have put the question this way, we see, I think, that whatever difficulty we may have encountered is one that may be traced to the concept of causation generally – whether "immanent" or "transeunt." The problem, in other words, is not a problem that is peculiar to our conception of human action. It is a problem that must be faced by anyone who makes use of the concept of causation at all; and therefore, I would say, it is a problem for everyone but the complete indeterminist.

For the problem, as we put it, referring just to "immanent causation," or causation by an agent, was this: "What is the difference between saying, of an event A, that A just happened and saying that someone caused A to happen?" The analogous problem, which holds for "transeunt causation," or causation by an event, is this: "What is the difference between saying, of two events A and B, that B happened and then A happened, and saying that B's happening was the *cause* of A's happening?" And the only answer that one can give is this – that in the one case the agent was the

cause of A's happening and in the other case event B was the cause of A's happening. The nature of transeunt causation is no more clear than is that of immanent causation.

9. But we may plausibly say – and there is a respectable philosophical tradition to which we may appeal – that the notion of immanent causation, or causation by an agent, is in fact more clear than that of transeunt causation, or causation by an event; and that it is only by understanding our own causal efficacy, as agents, that we can grasp the concept of *cause* at all. Hume may be said to have shown that we do not derive the concept of *cause* from what we perceive of external things. How, then, do we derive it? The most plausible suggestion, it seems to me, is that of Reid, once again: namely that "the conception of an efficient cause may very probably be derived from the experience we have had … of our own power to produce certain effects."[7] If we did not understand the concept of immanent causation, we would not understand that of transeunt causation.

10. It may have been noted that I have avoided the term "free will" in all of this. For even if there is such a faculty as "the will," which somehow sets our acts agoing, the question of freedom, as John Locke said, is not the question "*whether the will be free*"; it is the question "*whether a man be free*."[8] For if there is a "will," as a moving faculty, the question is whether the man is free to will to do these things that he does will to do – and also whether the man is free *not* to will any of those things that he does will to do, and, again, whether he is free to will any of those things that he does not will to do. Jonathan Edwards tried to restrict himself to the question – "Is the man free to do what it is that he wills?" – but the answer to the question will not tell us whether the man is responsible for what it is that he *does* will to do. Using still another pair of medieval terms, we may say that the metaphysical problem of freedom does not concern the *actus imperatus*, it does not concern the question whether we are free to accomplish whatever it is that we will or set out to do; it concerns the *actus elicitus*, the question whether we are free to will or to set out to do those things that we do will or set out to do.

11.   If we are responsible, and if what I have been trying to say is true, then we have a prerogative which some would attribute only to God: each of us, when we act, is a prime mover unmoved. In doing what we do, we cause certain events to happen, and nothing – or no one – causes us to cause those events to happen.

12.   If we are thus prime movers unmoved and if our actions, or those for which we are responsible, are not causally determined, then they are not causally determined by our *desires*. And this means that the relation between what we want or what we desire, on the one hand, and what it is that we do, on the other, is not as simple as most philosophers would have it.

We may distinguish between what we might call the "Hobbist approach" and what we might call the "Kantian approach" to this question. The Hobbist approach is the one that is generally accepted at the present time, but the Kantian approach, I believe, is the one that is true. According to Hobbism, if we *know*, of some man, what his beliefs and desires happen to be and how strong they are, if we know what he feels certain of, what he desires more than anything else, and if we know the state of his body and what stimuli he is being subjected to, then we may *deduce*, logically, just what it is that he will do – or, more accurately, just what it is that he will try, set out, or undertake to do. Thus Professor Melden has said

that "the connection between wanting and doing is logical."[9] But according to the Kantian approach to our problem, and this is the one that I would take, there is no such logical connection. No set of statements about a man's desires, beliefs, and stimulus situation at any time implies any statement telling us what the man will try, set out, or undertake to do at that time. As Reid put it, though we may "reason from men's motives to their actions and, in many cases, with great probability," we can never do so "with absolute certainty."[10]

This means that, in one very strict sense of the terms, there can be no science of man. If we think of science as a matter of finding out what laws happen to hold, and if the statement of a law tells us what kinds of events are caused by what other kinds of events, then there will be human actions which we cannot explain by subsuming them under any laws. We cannot say, "It is causally necessary that, given such and such desires and beliefs, and being subject to such and such stimuli, the agent will do so and so." For at times the agent, if he chooses, may rise above his desires and do something else instead.

But all of this is consistent with saying that, perhaps more often than not, our desires do exist under conditions such that those conditions necessitate us to act. And we may also say, with Leibniz, that at other times our desires may "incline without necessitating." [...]

Notes

1.   The general position to be presented here is suggested in the following writings, among others: Aristotle, *Eudemian Ethics*, book II, ch. 6; *Nicomachean Ethics*, book III, chs 1–5; Thomas Reid, *Essays on the Active Powers of Man*; C. A. Campbell, "Is 'Free Will' a Pseudo-Problem?" *Mind*, n.s. 60 (1951), pp. 441–65; Roderick M. Chisholm, "Responsibility and Avoidability," and Richard Taylor, "Determination and the Theory of Agency," in Sidney Hook, ed., *Determinism and Freedom in the Age of Modern Science* (New York: New York University Press, 1958).

2.   Thomas Reid, *Essays on the Intellectual Powers of Man* (Cambridge, Mass.: MIT Press, 1969; first published 1788), p. 261.

3.   *Summa Theologia*, First Part of the Second Part, Question VI: "On the Voluntary and Involuntary."

4.   Jonathan Edwards, *Freedom of the Will* (New Haven, Conn.: Yale University Press, 1957); G. E. Moore, *Ethics* (Home University Library, 1912), ch. 6.

5.   A. I. Melden, *Free Action* (Oxford: Blackwell, 1961), especially ch. 3. Mr Melden's own views, however, are quite the contrary of those proposed here.

6.   Aristotle, *Physics*, book III, ch. 3; Suarez, *Disputationes Metaphysicae*, Disputation 18, Section 10.

7.   Reid, *Essays on the Active Powers*, p. 39.

8.   John Locke, *Essay Concerning Human Understanding*, book II, ch. 21.

9.   Melden, *Free Action*, p. 166.

10.   Reid, *Essays on the Active Powers*, p. 291.

33

Alternate Possibilities and Moral Responsibility

Harry G. Frankfurt

A DOMINANT role in nearly all recent inquiries into the free-will problem has been played by a principle which I shall call "the principle of alternate possibilities." This principle states that a person is morally responsible for what he has done only if he could have done otherwise. Its exact meaning is a subject of controversy, particularly concerning whether someone who accepts it is thereby committed to believing that moral responsibility and determinism are incompatible. Practically no one, however, seems inclined to deny or even to question that the principle of alternate possibilities (construed in some way or other) is true. It has generally seemed so overwhelmingly plausible that some philosophers have even characterized it as an *a priori* truth. People whose accounts of free will or of moral responsibility are radically at odds evidently find in it a firm and convenient common ground upon which they can profitably take their opposing stands.

But the principle of alternate possibilities is false. A person may well be morally responsible for what he has done even though he could not have done otherwise. The principle's plausibility is an illusion, which can be made to vanish by bringing the relevant moral phenomena into sharper focus.

Frankfurt, H. G. (1969), "Alternate Possibilities and Moral Responsibility," *Journal of Philosophy* 66 (23), 829–839. Reprinted with permission of Harry Frankfurt and The Journal of Philosophy.

I

In seeking illustrations of the principle of alternate possibilities, it is most natural to think of situations in which the same circumstances both bring it about that a person does something and make it impossible for him to avoid doing it. These include, for example, situations in which a person is coerced into doing something, or in which he is impelled to act by a hypnotic suggestion, or in which some inner compulsion drives him to do what he does. In situations of these kinds there are circumstances that make it impossible for the person to do otherwise, and these very circumstances also serve to bring it about that he does whatever it is that he does.

However, there may be circumstances that constitute sufficient conditions for a certain action to be performed by someone and that therefore make it impossible for the person to do otherwise, but that do not actually impel the person to act or in any way produce his action. A person may do something in circumstances that leave him no alternative to doing it, without these circumstances actually moving him or leading him to do it – without them playing any role, indeed, in bringing it about that he does what he does.

An examination of situations characterized by circumstances of this sort casts doubt, I believe, on the relevance to questions of moral responsibility of the fact that a person who has done something could not have done otherwise. I propose to develop some examples of this kind in the context of a discussion of coercion and to suggest that our moral intuitions concerning these examples tend to disconfirm the principle of alternate possibilities. Then I will discuss the principle in more general terms, explain what I think is wrong with it, and describe briefly and without argument how it might appropriately be revised.

II

It is generally agreed that a person who has been coerced to do something did not do it freely and is not morally responsible for having done it. Now the doctrine that coercion and moral responsibility are mutually exclusive may appear to be no more than a somewhat particularized version of the principle of alternate possibilities. It is natural enough to say of a person who has been coerced to do something that he could not have done otherwise. And it may easily seem that being coerced deprives a person of freedom and of moral responsibility simply because it is a special case of being unable to do otherwise. The principle of alternate possibilities may in this way derive some credibility from its association with the very plausible proposition that moral responsibility is excluded by coercion.

It is not right, however, that it should do so. The fact that a person was coerced to act as he did may entail both that he could not have done otherwise and that he bears no moral responsibility for his action. But his lack of moral responsibility is not entailed by his having been unable to do otherwise. The doctrine that coercion excludes moral responsibility is not correctly understood, in other words, as a particularized version of the principle of alternate possibilities.

Let us suppose that someone is threatened convincingly with a penalty he finds unacceptable and that he then does what is required of him by the issuer of the threat. We can imagine details that would make it reasonable for us to think that the person was coerced to perform the action in question, that he could not have done otherwise, and that he bears no moral responsibility for having

done what he did. But just what is it about situations of this kind that warrants the judgment that the threatened person is not morally responsible for his act?

This question may be approached by considering situations of the following kind. Jones decides for reasons of his own to do something, then someone threatens him with a very harsh penalty (so harsh that any reasonable person would submit to the threat) unless he does precisely that, and Jones does it. Will we hold Jones morally responsible for what he has done? I think this will depend on the roles we think were played, in leading him to act, by his original decision and by the threat.

One possibility is that $Jones_1$ is not a reasonable man: he is, rather, a man who does what he has once decided to do no matter what happens next and no matter what the cost. In that case, the threat actually exerted no effective force upon him. He acted without any regard to it, very much as if he were not aware that it had been made. If this is indeed the way it was, the situation did not involve coercion at all. The threat did not lead $Jones_1$ to do what he did. Nor was it in fact sufficient to have prevented him from doing otherwise: if his earlier decision had been to do something else, the threat would not have deterred him in the slightest. It seems evident that in these circumstances the fact that $Jones_1$ was threatened in no way reduces the moral responsibility he would otherwise bear for his act. This example, however, is not a counterexample either to the doctrine that coercion excuses or to the principle of alternate possibilities. For we have supposed that $Jones_1$ is a man upon whom the threat had no coercive effect and, hence, that it did not actually deprive him of alternatives to doing what he did.

Another possibility is that $Jones_2$ was stampeded by the threat. Given that threat, he would have performed that action regardless of what decision he had already made. The threat upset him so profoundly, moreover, that he completely forgot his own earlier decision and did what was demanded of him entirely because he was terrified of the penalty with which he was threatened. In this case, it is not relevant to his having performed the action that he had already decided on his own to perform it. When the chips were down he thought of nothing but the threat, and fear alone led him to act. The fact that at an earlier time Jones$_2$ had decided for his own reasons to act in just that way may be relevant to an evaluation of his character; he may bear full moral responsibility for having made *that* decision. But he can hardly be said to be morally responsible for his action. For he performed the action simply as a result of the coercion to which he was subjected. His earlier decision played no role in bringing it about that he did what he did, and it would therefore be gratuitous to assign it a role in the moral evaluation of his action.

Now consider a third possibility. Jones$_3$ was neither stampeded by the threat nor indifferent to it. The threat impressed him, as it would impress any reasonable man, and he would have submitted to it wholeheartedly if he had not already made a decision that coincided with the one demanded of him. In fact, however, he performed the action in question on the basis of the decision he had made before the threat was issued. When he acted, he was not actually motivated by the threat but solely by the considerations that had originally commended the action to him. It was not the threat that led him to act, though it would have done so if he had not already provided himself with a sufficient motive for performing the action in question.

No doubt it will be very difficult for anyone to know, in a case like this one, exactly what happened. Did Jones$_3$ perform the action because of the threat, or were his reasons for acting simply those which had already persuaded him to do so? Or did he act on the basis of two motives, each of which was sufficient for his action? It is not impossible, however, that the situation should be clearer than situations of this kind usually are. And suppose it is apparent to us that Jones$_3$ acted on the basis of his own decision and not because of the threat. Then I think we would be justified in regarding his moral responsibility for what he did as unaffected by the threat even though, since he would in any case have submitted to the threat, he could not have avoided doing what he did. It would be entirely reasonable for us to make the same judgment concerning his moral responsibility that we would have made if we had not known of the threat. For the threat did not in fact influence his performance of the action. He did what he did just as if the threat had not been made at all.

III

The case of Jones$_3$ may appear at first glance to combine coercion and moral responsibility, and thus to provide a counterexample to the doctrine that coercion excuses. It is not really so certain that it does so, however, because it is unclear whether the example constitutes a genuine instance of coercion. Can we say of Jones$_3$ that he was coerced to do something, when he had already decided on his own to do it and when he did it entirely on the basis of that decision? Or would it be more correct to say that Jones$_3$ was not coerced to do what he did, even though he himself recognized that there was an irresistible force at work in virtue of which he had to do it? My own linguistic intuitions lead me toward the second alternative, but they are somewhat equivocal. Perhaps we can say either of these things, or perhaps we must add a qualifying explanation to whichever of them we say.

This murkiness, however, does not interfere with our drawing an important moral from an examination of the example. Suppose we decide to say that Jones$_3$ was *not* coerced. Our basis for saying this will clearly be that it is incorrect to regard a man as being coerced to do something unless he does it *because of* the coercive force exerted against him. The fact that an irresistible threat is made will not, then, entail that the person who receives it is coerced to do what he does. It will also be necessary that the threat is what actually accounts for his doing it. On the other hand, suppose we decide to say that Jones$_3$ *was* coerced. Then we will be bound to admit that being coerced does not exclude being morally responsible. And we will also surely be led to the view that coercion affects the judgment of a person's moral responsibility only when the person acts as he does because he is coerced to do so — i.e., when the fact that he is coerced is what accounts for his action.

Whichever we decide to say, then, we will recognize that the doctrine that coercion excludes moral responsibility is not a particularized version of the principle of alternate possibilities. Situations in which a person who does something cannot do otherwise because he is subject to coercive power are either not instances of coercion at all, or they are situations in which the person may still be morally responsible for what he does if it is not because of the coercion that he does it. When we excuse a person who has been coerced, we do not excuse him because he was unable to do otherwise. Even though a person is subject to a coercive force that precludes his performing any action but one, he may nonetheless bear full moral responsibility for performing that action.

IV

To the extent that the principle of alternate possibilities derives its plausibility from association with the doctrine that coercion excludes moral responsibility, a clear understanding of the latter diminishes the appeal of the former. Indeed the case of $Jones_3$ may appear to do more than illuminate the relationship between the two doctrines. It may well seem to provide a decisive counterexample to the principle of alternate possibilities and thus to show that this principle is false. For the irresistibility of the threat to which $Jones_3$ is subjected might well be taken to mean that he cannot but perform the action he performs. And yet the threat, since $Jones_3$ performs the action without regard to it, does not reduce his moral responsibility for what he does.

The following objection will doubtless be raised against the suggestion that the case of $Jones_3$ is a counterexample to the principle of alternate possibilities. There is perhaps a sense in which $Jones_3$ cannot do otherwise than perform the action he performs, since he is a reasonable man and the threat he encounters is sufficient to move any reasonable man. But it is not this sense that is germane to the principle of alternate possibilities. His knowledge that he stands to suffer an intolerably harsh penalty does not mean that $Jones_3$, strictly speaking, *cannot* perform any action but the one he does perform. After all it is still open to him, and this is crucial, to defy the threat if he wishes to do so and to accept the penalty his action would bring down upon him. In the sense in which the principle of alternate possibilities employs the concept of "could have done otherwise," $Jones_3$'s inability to resist the threat does not mean that he cannot do otherwise than perform the action he performs. Hence the case of $Jones_3$ does not constitute an instance contrary to the principle.

I do not propose to consider in what sense the concept of "could have done otherwise" figures in the principle of alternate possibilities, nor will I attempt to measure the force of the objection I have just described.[1] For I believe that whatever force this objection may be thought to have can be deflected by altering the example in the following way.[2] Suppose someone – Black, let us say – wants $Jones_4$ to perform a certain action. Black is prepared to go to considerable lengths to get his way, but he prefers to avoid showing his hand unnecessarily. So he waits until $Jones_4$ is about to make up his mind what to do, and he does nothing unless it is clear to him (Black is an excellent judge of such things) that $Jones_4$ is going to decide to do something *other* than what he wants him to do. If it does become clear that $Jones_4$ is going to decide to do something else, Black takes effective steps to ensure that $Jones_4$ decides to do, and that he does do, what he wants him to do.[3] Whatever $Jones_4$'s initial preferences and inclinations, then, Black will have his way.

What steps will Black take, if he believes he must take steps, in order to ensure that $Jones_4$ decides and acts as he wishes? Anyone with a theory concerning what "could have done otherwise" means may answer this question for himself by describing whatever measures he would regard as sufficient to guarantee that, in the relevant sense, $Jones_4$ cannot do otherwise. Let Black pronounce a terrible threat, and in this way both force $Jones_4$ to perform the desired action and prevent him from performing a forbidden one. Let Black give $Jones_4$ a potion, or put him under hypnosis, and in some such way as these generate in $Jones_4$ an irresistible inner compulsion to perform the act Black wants performed and to avoid others. Or let Black manipulate the minute processes of $Jones_4$'s brain and nervous system in some more direct way, so that causal forces running in and out of his synapses and along the poor man's nerves determine that he chooses to act and that he does act in the one way and not in any other. Given any conditions under which it will be maintained that $Jones_4$ cannot do otherwise, in other words, let Black bring it about that those conditions prevail. The structure of the example is flexible enough, I think, to find a way around any charge of irrelevance by accommodating the doctrine on which the charge is based.[4]

Now suppose that Black never has to show his hand because Jones$_4$, for reasons of his own, decides to perform and does perform the very action Black wants him to perform. In that case, it seems clear, Jones$_4$ will bear precisely the same moral responsibility for what he does as he would have borne if Black had not been ready to take steps to ensure that he do it. It would be quite unreasonable to excuse Jones$_4$ for his action, or to withhold the praise to which it would normally entitle him, on the basis of the fact that he could not have done otherwise. This fact played no role at all in leading him to act as he did. He would have acted the same even if it had not been a fact. Indeed, everything happened just as it would have happened without Black's presence in the situation and without his readiness to intrude into it.

In this example there are sufficient conditions for Jones$_4$'s performing the action in question. What action he performs is not up to him. Of course it is in a way up to him whether he acts on his own or as a result of Black's intervention. That depends upon what action he himself is inclined to perform. But whether he finally acts on his own or as a result of Black's intervention, he performs the same action. He has no alternative but to do what Black wants him to do. If he does it on his own, however, his moral responsibility for doing it is not affected by the fact that Black was lurking in the background with sinister intent, since this intent never comes into play.

V

The fact that a person could not have avoided doing something is a sufficient condition of his having done it. But, as some of my examples show, this fact may play no role whatever in the explanation of why he did it. It may not figure at all among the circumstances that actually brought it about that he did what he did, so that his action is to be accounted for on another basis entirely. Even though the person was unable to do otherwise, that is to say, it may not be the case that he acted as he did *because* he could not have done otherwise. Now if someone had no alternative to performing a certain action but did not perform it because he was unable to do otherwise, then he would have performed exactly the same action even if he *could* have done otherwise. The circumstances that made it impossible for him to do otherwise could have been subtracted from the situation without affecting what happened or why it happened in any way. Whatever it was that actually led the person to do what he did, or that made him do it, would have led him to do it or made him do it even if it had been possible for him to do something else instead.

Thus it would have made no difference, so far as concerns his action or how he came to perform it, if the circumstances that made it impossible for him to avoid performing it had not prevailed. The fact that he could not have done otherwise clearly provides no basis for supposing that he *might* have done otherwise if he had been able to do so. When a fact is in this way irrelevant to the problem of accounting for a person's action it seems quite gratuitous to assign it any weight in the assessment of his moral responsibility. Why should the fact be considered in reaching a moral judgment concerning the person when it does not help in any way to understand either what made him act as he did or what, in other circumstances, he might have done?

This, then, is why the principle of alternate possibilities is mistaken. It asserts that a person bears no moral responsibility – that is, he is to be excused – for having performed an action if there were circumstances that made it impossible for him to avoid performing it. But there may be circumstances that make it impossible for a person to avoid performing some action without those circumstances in any way bringing it about that he performs that action. It would surely be no good for the person to refer to circumstances of this sort in an effort to absolve himself of moral responsibility for performing the action in question. For those circumstances, by hypothesis, actually had nothing to do with his having done what he did. He would have done precisely the same thing, and he would have been led or made in precisely the same way to do it, even if they had not prevailed.

We often do, to be sure, excuse people for what they have done when they tell us (and we believe them) that they could not have done otherwise. But this is because we assume that what they tell us serves to explain why they did what they did. We take it for granted that they are not being disingenuous, as a person would be who cited as an excuse the fact that he could not have avoided doing what he did but who knew full well that it was not at all because of this that he did it.

What I have said may suggest that the principle of alternate possibilities should be revised so as to assert that a person is not morally responsible for what he has done if he did it because he could not have done otherwise. It may be noted that this revision of the principle does not seriously affect the arguments of those who have relied on the original principle in their efforts to maintain that moral responsibility and determinism are incompatible. For if it was causally determined that a person perform a certain action, then it will be true that the person performed it because of those causal determinants. And if the fact that it was causally determined that a person perform a certain action means that the person could not have done otherwise, as philosophers who argue for the incompatibility thesis characteristically suppose, then the fact that it was causally determined that a person perform a certain action will mean that the person performed it because he could not have done otherwise. The revised principle of alternate possibilities will entail, on this assumption concerning the meaning of 'could have done otherwise', that a person is not morally responsible for what he has done if it was causally determined that he do it. I do not believe, however, that this revision of the principle is acceptable.

Suppose a person tells us that he did what he did because he was unable to do otherwise; or suppose he makes the similar statement that he did what he did because he had to do it. We do often accept statements

like these (if we believe them) as valid excuses, and such statements may well seem at first glance to invoke the revised principle of alternate possibilities. But I think that when we accept such statements as valid excuses it is because we assume that we are being told more than the statements strictly and literally convey. We understand the person who offers the excuse to mean that he did what he did *only because* he was unable to do otherwise, or *only because* he had to do it. And we understand him to mean, more particularly, that when he did what he did it was not because that was what he really wanted to do. The principle of alternate possibilities should thus be replaced, in my opinion, by the following principle: a person is not morally responsible for what he has done if he did it only because he could not have done otherwise. This principle does not appear to conflict with the view that moral responsibility is compatible with determinism.

The following may all be true: there were circumstances that made it impossible for a person to avoid doing something; these circumstances actually played a role in bringing it about that he did it, so that it is correct to say that he did it because he could not have done otherwise; the person really wanted to do what he did; he did it because it was what he really wanted to do, so that it is not correct to say that he did what he did only because he could not have done otherwise. Under these conditions, the person may well be morally responsible for what he has done. On the other hand, he will not be morally responsible for what he has done if he did it only because he could not have done otherwise, even if what he did was something he really wanted to do.

Notes

1. The two main concepts employed in the principle of alternate possibilities are "morally responsible" and "could have done otherwise." To discuss the principle without analyzing either of these concepts may well seem like an attempt at piracy. The reader should take notice that my Jolly Roger is now unfurled.
2. After thinking up the example that I am about to develop I learned that Robert Nozick, in lectures given several years ago, had formulated an example of the same general type and had proposed it as a counterexample to the principle of alternate possibilities.

3. The assumption that Black can predict what $Jones_4$ will decide to do does not beg the question of determinism. We can imagine that $Jones_4$ has often confronted the alternatives – A and B – that he now confronts, and that his face has invariably twitched when he was about to decide to do A and never when he was about to decide to do B. Knowing this, and observing the twitch, Black would have a basis for prediction. This does, to be sure, suppose that there is some sort of causal relation between $Jones_4$'s state at the time of the twitch and his subsequent states.

But any plausible view of decision or of action will allow that reaching a decision and performing an action both involve earlier and later phases, with causal relations between them, and such that the earlier phases are not themselves part of the decision or of the action. The example does not require that these earlier phases be deterministically related to still earlier events.

4. The example is also flexible enough to allow for the elimination of Black altogether. Anyone who thinks that the effectiveness of the example is undermined by its reliance on a human manipulator, who imposes his will on Jones$_4$, can substitute for Black a machine programmed to do what Black does. If this is still not good enough, forget both Black and the machine and suppose that their role is played by natural forces involving no will or design at all.

34

Responsibility, Control, and Omissions

John Martin Fischer

I. Omissions and Alternative Possibilities

I believe that an individual can be held morally responsible for an action, even though he could not have done otherwise. (Also, I believe that there are examples in which one can be held morally responsible for a consequence, in which the agent could not have prevented the consequence from obtaining.) Actions and consequences are instances of what might be called "positive agency." It will be useful to have before us here an example involving positive agency.

Matthew is walking along a beach, looking at the water. He sees a child struggling in the water, and he quickly deliberates about the matter, jumps into the water, and rescues the child. We can imagine that Matthew does not give any thought to not trying to rescue the child, but that if he had considered not trying to save the child, he would have been overwhelmed by literally irresistible guilt feelings which would have caused him to jump into the water and save the child anyway. I simply stipulate that in the alternative sequence the urge to save the child would be genuinely irresistible.

Apparently, Matthew is morally responsible – indeed, praiseworthy – for his action, although he

Fischer, J. M. (1997), "Responsibility, Control, and Omissions," *Journal of Ethics* 1 (1), 45–64. Reprinted with permission of Springer.

could not have done otherwise. Matthew acts freely in saving the child; he acts exactly as he would have acted, if he had lacked the propensity toward strong feelings of guilt. Here is a case in which no responsibility-undermining factor operates in the actual sequence and thus Matthew is morally responsible for what he does. (A "responsibility-undermining factor" rules out moral responsibility; intuitively, one tends to think of certain kinds of brainwashing, hypnosis, subliminal advertising, coercion, and direct manipulation of the brain as such factors.) And yet the presence of Matthew's propensity toward very strong feelings of guilt renders it true that Matthew could not have done otherwise. Call the case of Matthew, "Hero."[1] (Of course, one could alter the case so that there would be a "counterfactual intervener" – such as a nefarious or even nifty and nice neurologist – associated with Matthew, as in the typical Frankfurt-type examples.)

Hero is just one example of many cases of moral responsibility for positive agency in which the agent does not have alternative possibilities. Are there such cases – in which the agent does not have alternative possibilities – of moral responsibility for negative agency (i.e., for omissions)?

Before considering some examples, let me pause to say a few words about the admittedly very problematic notion of "omissions." There are various different conceptions of omissions. One way

Philosophy of Action: An Anthology, First Edition. Edited by Jonathan Dancy and Constantine Sandis.
© 2015 John Wiley & Sons, Inc. Published 2015 by John Wiley & Sons, Inc.

of classifying them distinguishes wider and narrower conceptions of omissions. On the wider conception (which may not link up closely with ordinary usage), whenever a person does not do something, X, he fails in the relevant sense to do it, and he omits to do it. Thus, we are all now failing to stop the Earth's rotation (and omitting to stop the Earth's rotation). Omission to do X (according to the wide conception) need not require explicit deliberation about X, and it need not require the ability to do X. I shall, in part for the sake of simplicity, adopt this wide conception of omissions. My views, however, are compatible with various ways of narrowing the notion of omissions. And even if one takes a rather narrow view of what an omission is, it still is important to have an account of moral responsibility for failures which don't count as omissions (narrowly construed); after all, in ordinary usage we do talk of moral responsibilty for not doing X (where this not-doing may not count as an omission, narrowly construed).

Consider, now, an example I shall call "Sloth."[2] In "Sloth," John is walking along a beach, and he sees a child struggling in the water. John believes that he could save the child with very little effort, but he is disinclined to expend any energy to help anyone else. He decides not to try to save the child, and he continues to walk along the beach.

Is John morally responsible for failing to save the child? Unbeknownst to John, the child was about to drown when John glimpsed him, and the child drowned one second after John decided not to jump into the water. I believe that the facts of the case exert pressure to say that John is not morally responsible for failing to save the child: after all, the child would have drowned, even if John had tried to save it. John could not have saved the child. John may well be morally responsible for deciding not to try to save the child and even for not trying to save the child, but he is *not* morally responsible for not saving the child. "Sloth" is no different in this respect from a case ("Shark") exactly like it except that the child would not have drowned immediately; rather, a patrol of sharks which (unbeknownst to John) infested the water between the beach and the struggling child would have eaten John, had he jumped in.

In Sloth and Shark, it seems clear that John cannot fairly be held morally responsible for failing to save the child. This of course is compatible with John's being appropriately held responsible for deciding not to try to save the child, for not trying to save the child, and so forth. It's just that he cannot appropriately be held morally responsible for *not saving the child*.

Imagine, similarly, that Sue thinks that she can end a terrible drought by doing a rain dance. Of course, we would say that Sue (although quite sincere in her convictions) does not in fact have the power to affect the weather. Suppose, also, that there are no clouds in sight (and no clouds within hundreds of miles); atmospheric conditions imply that it will not rain for weeks. Now Sue happens to hate the local farmers, and she would like to hurt them in any way possible. While falsely believing that she could easily end the drought immediately, she deliberately refrains from doing her rain dance.[3] Let us call this example, "Rain Dance."

Is Sue morally responsible for failing to cause it to rain (i.e., for not ending the drought) in "Rain Dance"? Again, there is pressure to say that, whereas Sue might be morally responsible for not doing the rain dance and for not trying to end the drought, she is *not* morally responsible for not ending the drought. After all, Sue could not have ended the drought.

The cases presented above are cases in which an agent omits to do something *good*. I now turn to a similar case in which an agent omits to do something *bad*. Imagine that you are a small-time thug strolling along a dimly-lit street in a deserted part of town. Suddenly you spy a shiny, new Mercedes with a flat tire stranded by the side of the road. The driver of the car is a well-dressed, elderly gentleman with a bulging billfold in his breast pocket. You are tempted to hurry over to the car, assault the old man, and steal his money. Fortunately, you decide against this, and you continue along your way.

Are you morally responsible for failing to rob the driver? Well, unbeknownst to you (and the driver of the car), the Mafia has put drugs into the trunk of the car. Five Mafioso thugs are watching the car from five other cars in the neighborhood. They have strict instructions: if anyone threatens the driver of the car, they are to shoot him with their "Uzis." In these circumstances, we can safely imagine that, if you had attempted to rob the driver, you would have been killed.

I believe that you are *not* morally responsible for failing to rob the driver. You might be morally responsible for deciding not to rob the driver, for not deciding to rob the driver, and for not trying to rob the driver. But there is strong pressure to say that you are simply *not* morally responsible for not robbing the driver, and this pressure seems to come from the fact that you *could not* rob the driver.

These cases suggest that an agent cannot be held morally responsible for not performing an action which he cannot perform. Thus, these cases in conjunction with "Hero" (and a whole array of cases of positive agency) suggest that actions and omissions are asymmetric with respect to the requirement of alternative possibilities. That is, it seems that moral responsibility for an action does not require the freedom to refrain from performing the action, whereas moral responsibility for failure to perform an action requires the freedom to perform the action. A similar asymmetry is suggested for moral responsibility for consequences and moral responsibility for omissions: moral responsibility for a consequence does not require the freedom to prevent the consequence from occurring, whereas moral responsibility for failure to perform an action requires the freedom to perform the action. Although the "asymmetry thesis" holds that positive agency in general – actions and their consequences – is relevantly different from omissions with respect to the requirement of alternative possibilities, it will be simpler, especially at first, to focus on the asymmetry between actions and omissions.

II. Omissions and Frankfurt-type Cases

The cases of omissions presented in the previous section suggest that moral responsibility for the failure to do X requires the ability to do X. But there are other cases which suggest precisely the opposite. Here are some.

Consider the following remarks by Harry Frankfurt:

In "Sloth" ["Shark"] John decides against saving a drowning child who (because there are sharks nearby) would have drowned even if John had tried to save him. Fischer and Ravizza suggest that it is discordant to insist that in these circumstances John is morally responsible

for not saving the child. They are right about this. But what explains the discordance is not, as they suppose, the fact that it was impossible for John to save the child.

This fact might have been due to circumstances of quite a different sort than those that they describe. Thus, imagine that if John had even started to consider saving the child, he would have been overwhelmed by a literally irresistible desire to do something else; and imagine that this would have caused him to discard all thought of saving the child. With this change, the case of John exactly parallels another of Fischer's and Ravizza's examples – that of Matthew ("Hero").[4]

In virtue of the apparent parallel status of Hero and the Frankfurt-style version of Sloth, Frankfurt holds that John should be considered morally responsible for failing to save the child (in his version of Sloth). If so, this is a case in which an individual is morally responsible for failing to do X even though he *cannot* do X.

Other philosophers have presented similar "Frankfurt-type" omissions cases.[5] Clearly, the Frankfurt-type version of Sloth could be developed with a counterfactual intervener. Here is just this sort of case (developed by Randolph Clarke):

Sam promises to babysit little Freddy. But Sam forgets. No one makes Sam forget; it just slips his mind. Consequently, he fails to show up to babysit little Freddy. Unbeknownst to Sam, a mad scientist is monitoring his thoughts. Had Sam been going to remember his promise, the scientist would have intervened and prevented him from remembering it. The scientist would not have intervened in any other way. As it happened, the scientist did not intervene at all; there was no need to.[6]

Clarke's analysis of this case, call it "Babysitter," is as follows:

Here … Sam's not showing up depends on his forgetting; had Sam remembered, nothing would have prevented him from keeping his promise. He would have done so. And Sam is responsible for forgetting. Since his not showing up *depends* in this way on something for which he is responsible, it seems to me that he is responsible for not showing up.[7]

Clarke goes on to suggest a principle according to which an agent is morally responsible for an omission to perform a certain action only if: had she intended to perform that action, and had she tried to carry out that intention, then she would have performed the omitted action.

A very similar view about moral responsibility for omissions is defended by Alison McIntyre.[8] She first presents the following case, which appears to confirm the idea (of the previous section) that moral responsibility for omissions requires the ability to do the relevant action:

> You are a forest ranger and a large forest fire is approaching from the north. You believe that you could start a backfire heading north which would burn the timber in the fire's path and thereby prevent the forest fire from continuing southward. More specifically, you believe that you could use the gasoline in your truck's fuel tank and some dry matches in your kitchen to do this. But you decide not to start a backfire, the forest fire sweeps onward, and a large area of forest to the south is destroyed. Unbeknownst to you, the truck's fuel tank has sprung a leak and is now empty, and your matches are sitting in a puddle of water. You couldn't have started a backfire if you had tried. If we suppose that there was no other method of stopping the fire available to you, it follows that you could not have prevented the fire from continuing southward if you had tried.[9]

McIntyre goes on to give this version of the case:

> *Case 1.* It is your duty as a forest ranger to start a backfire and you believe that you should do so, but out of laziness rationalized with the vain hope that the fire will burn itself out, you do nothing to stop the fire. When you come to be aware of what you believe to be the full consequences of your omission you feel terrible.[10]

Here, in "Forest Ranger 1," it seems that you are not morally responsible for failing to start a backfire or for failing to stop the forest fire. McIntyre agrees with this view, but she now presents a Frankfurt-type version of her case; in this version of the case, she assumes that the fuel tank has *not* sprung a leak and the matches are *not* wet, and she says:

> You, the forest ranger, decide not to start a backfire to prevent the forest fire from advancing southward. A group of fanatical environmentalists who are zealous opponents of forest fire prevention efforts have hired a super-skilled neurologist to monitor your deliberations.

> If you had shown any sign of seriously considering the option of starting a backfire, the neurologist would have intervened and caused you to decide not to take any preventive action. As things turned out, you decided 'under your own steam' not to act, but because of the neurologist's monitoring, you could not have decided to start a backfire if you had believed that there was reason to do so, and because of this fact, you could not have started a backfire.[11]

As McIntyre points out, in contrast to her first case, in this case (which I shall call "Forest Ranger 2"), you seem to be morally responsible for failing to start the backfire and thus for failing to stop the forest fire. And this is so, even though you could not have started a backfire and you could not have stopped the forest fire. You are responsible for your failures here, on her view, because in the Frankfurt-type version of the case, "you could have started a backfire [and thus stopped the forest fire] if you had decided to do so and had tried."[12] This fact highlights the difference between Forest Ranger 1 and 2: in Forest Ranger 1 you would not have started a backfire if you had tried (because of the leaking fuel tank and wet matches); but in Forest Ranger 2, you would have succeeded in starting a backfire, if you had tried.

McIntyre and Clarke thus hold a similar view: they contend that in cases in which one could have performed the relevant action, if one had decided (and/or tried), one can be morally responsible for the omission. That is, McIntyre and Clarke hold that when one's ability to do the act in question is dependent upon one's decision (and/or efforts), then one may be morally responsible for failing to do X, even if one cannot do X.

Reflection on the cases of omissions presented in this and the previous section leads to a puzzle. Cases such as Sloth, Shark, Rain Dance, and Flat Tire render it plausible that in order to be morally responsible for failing to do X, one must be able to do X. However, cases such as the Frankfurt-style Sloth case, Babysitter, and Forest Ranger 2 suggest precisely the opposite. If one wants to say what seems plausible about the Frankfurt-style omissions cases, how can one also say what is plausible about the first range of cases?

There are cases of positive agency – performing actions and bringing about consequences of those actions – in which moral responsibility does not require alternative possibilities. But in the realm of negative agency – omissions – we have a puzzle: in part of the realm it seems that there is a requirement of alternative possibilities for moral responsibility, but in another part of the realm it seems that there is no such requirement.

I believe the puzzle can be solved by appeal to an association of moral responsibility with control. In the following section, I shall present (in an admittedly very sketchy fashion) some tools that will be helpful in seeking to solve the puzzle. Then I shall employ these tools to argue that the conditions for moral responsibility for positive and negative agency are *symmetric*; in neither case does moral responsibility require alternative possibilities. I shall maintain that there *is indeed* an interesting difference between the two groups of omissions cases described above; but I shall show how this difference can be acknowledged compatibly with the view that moral responsibility for neither positive nor negative agency requires alternative possibilities.

III. Some Tools to Solve the Puzzle

1. Two kinds of control

It seems to me that the conclusion tentatively adopted above about positive agency is correct: moral responsibility for positive agency does not require the sort of control which involves the existence of genuinely open alternative possibilities. But this is not to say that moral responsibility in the context of positive agency does not require control of *any* sort. Indeed, it is important to distinguish two sorts of control, and it will emerge that moral responsibility for positive agency is associated with one (but not the other) kind of control.[13]

Let us suppose that I am driving my car.[14] It is functioning well, and I wish to make a right turn. As a result of my intention to turn right, I signal, turn the steering wheel, and carefully guide the car to the right. Further, I here assume that I was able to form the intention *not* to turn the car to the right but to turn the car to the left instead. Also, I assume that had I formed such an intention, I would have turned the steering wheel to the left and the car would have

gone to the left. In this ordinary case, I guide the car to the right, but I could have guided it to the left. I control the car, and also I have a certain sort of control *over* the car's movements. Insofar as I actually guide the car in a certain way, I shall say that I have "guidance control." Further, insofar as I have the power to guide the car in a different way, I shall say that I have "regulative control" (of course, here I am not making any special assumptions, such as that causal determinism obtains or God exists).

To develop these notions of control (and their relationship), imagine a second case. In this analogue of the Frankfurt-type case presented above, I again guide my car in the normal way to the right. The car's steering apparatus *works properly* when I steer the car to the right. But unbeknownst to me, the car's steering apparatus is broken in such a way that, if I were to try to turn it in some other direction, the car would veer off to the right in precisely the way it actually goes to the right.[15] Since I actually do not try to do anything but turn to the right, the apparatus functions normally and the car's movements are precisely as they would have been, if there had been no problem with the steering apparatus. Indeed, my guidance of the car to the right is precisely the same in this case and the first car case.

Here, as in the first car case, it appears that I control the movement of the car in the sense of guiding it (in a certain way) to the right. Thus, I have guidance control of the car. But I cannot cause it to go anywhere other than where it actually goes. Thus, I lack regulative control of the car. I control the car, but I do not have control *over* the car (or the car's movements). Generally, we assume that guidance control and regulative control go together. But this Frankfurt-type case shows how they can at least in principle pull apart: one can have guidance control without regulative control. That is, one can have a certain sort of control without having the sort of control that involves alternative possibilities. (The Frankfurt-type cases of actions and omisisons presented above have this structure. For example, in Hero Matthew has guidance control of his saving the child, even though he lacks regulative control over his saving the child. And so on.)

The Frankfurt-type cases (involving actions), unusual as they are, may well point us to something as significant as it is mundane. When we are morally responsible for our actions, we *do* possess a kind of control. So the traditional assumption of the association of moral responsibility (and personhood) with control is quite correct. But it need not be the sort of control that involves alternative possibilities. The suggestion, derived from the Frankfurt-type cases, is that the sort of control necessarily associated with moral responsibility for action is *guidance control*. Whereas we may intuitively suppose that regulative control always comes with guidance control, it is not, at a deep level, regulative control that grounds moral responsibility.

I have not sought to give a precise (or even very informative) account of the two sorts of control. Rather, I have relied on the intuitive idea that there is a sense of control in which I control the car when I guide it (in the normal way) to the right. Further, I have employed the Frankfurt-type example to argue that this sense of control need not involve any alternative possibilities. Then, I have simply contrasted this sort of control with a kind of control which does indeed require alternative possibilities. Now I shall attempt to say more (just a bit more!) about the first sort of control – guidance control. It is this sort of control which, I have claimed, is associated with moral responsibility for actions.

2. Guidance control of actions

The basic idea is that an agent has guidance control of an action insofar as the action issues from the agent's own moderately reasons-responsive mechanism. Although what it is for a mechanism to be an "agent's own" is a difficult and important issue, I shall not be addressing it here; here I shall simply assume an intuitive understanding of this notion.[16] Further, I shall here give a only the skimpiest sketch of moderate reasons-responsiveness.[17] To say whether an action issues from a moderately reasons-responsive mechanism, we first need to identify the kind of mechanism that actually issues in action. It is important to see that, in some cases, intuitively different kinds of mechanisms operate in the actual sequence and the alternative sequence. So, for instance, in "Hero," Matthew's actual-sequence mechanism is of a different sort from his alternative-sequence mechanism; in the actual sequence, he quickly deliberates and decides to save the struggling child, and his reasoning is uninfluenced

by any overwhelming urge. However, in the alternative sequence, his deliberations are influenced by an overwhelming and irresistible urge to save the swimmer. Whereas it is difficult to produce an explicit criterion of mechanism-individuation, I believe that it is natural to say that in Frankfurt-type cases different sorts of mechanisms issue in the actions in the actual and alternative sequences; indeed, this seems to be definitive of Frankfurt-type cases.

For a mechanism to be moderately responsive to reasons, it must at least be weakly reasons-responsive. In order to determine whether a mechanism of a certain type is weakly reasons-responsive, one asks whether there exists some possible scenario (with the same natural laws as the actual world) in which that type of mechanism operates, the agent has reason to do otherwise, and the agent does otherwise (for that reason). That is, we hold fixed the actual type of mechanism (and natural laws), and we ask whether the agent would respond to *some* possible incentive to do otherwise. Now moderate responsiveness differs from mere weak responsivness in that it demands not only that the agent would respond to at least one possible incentive to do otherwise; the agent must also exhibit a minimally coherent pattern of *recognition* of reasons. If (under the envisaged circumstances) the agent would so respond, then the actually operative mechanism is moderately reasons-responsive. In contrast, strong reasons-responsiveness obtains when a certain kind of mechanism (K) actually issues in an action and if there were sufficient reason to do otherwise and K were to operate, the agent would recognize the sufficient reason to do otherwise and thus choose to do otherwise and do otherwise.

Let me say a little more about strong, weak, and moderate reasons-responsiveness. Under the requirement of strong reasons-responsiveness, we ask what would happen if there were a sufficient reason to do otherwise (holding fixed the actual kind of mechanism). Strong reasons-responsiveness points us to the alternative scenario in which the actual kind of mechanism operates and there is a sufficient reason to do otherwise which is most similar to the actual situation. Strong reasons-responsiveness is similar to Robert Nozick's notion of "tracking value" or "tracking bestness."[18] In contrast, under weak reasons-responsiveness, there must simply exist *some* possible scenario in which the agent's actual kind of mechanism operates, the natural laws are held fixed, there is a sufficient reason to do otherwise, and the agent does otherwise. A weak-willed agent may exhibit weak-reasons responsiveness, even though he does not exhibit strong-reasons responsiveness (similarly for a morally bad agent). Finally, moderate reasons-responsiveness is stronger than weak reasons-responsiveness, and weaker than strong reasons-responsiveness. Whereas it demands only the sort of reactivity to reasons posited by weak reasons-responsiveness, it demands more in the way of reasons-recognition. It thus demands a certain sort of "normative competence."[19]

3. Guidance control of consequences

The account of guidance control of consequences is in certain respects parallel to (and also an extension of) the account of guidance control of actions. The leading idea is that the agent displays guidance control of a consequence insofar as the consequence emanates from a responsive *sequence*. It is necessary, in the context of a consequence that is more than simply a bodily movement, to distinguish *two components* of the sequence leading to the consequence. The first component is the mechanism leading to the bodily movement, and the second component is the process leading from the bodily movement to the event in the external world. I shall say that, in order for the sequence leading to a consequence to be responsive, both the mechanism leading to the bodily movement must be moderately reasons-responsive and the process leading from the bodily movement to the event in the external world must be "sensitive to the bodily movement."

Before proceeding, it is important to note that the counterfactual intervener in a Frankfurt-type case need not be another agent (whose action in the alternative sequence would bring about the consequence in question). As Frankfurt points out, the role of counterfactual intervener may be played "by natural forces involving no will or design at all."[20] It seems, then, that in evaluating the sensitivity of a process one wants to hold fixed not only the actions of other agents in the actual sequence, but also any natural events which play no role in the actual sequence but which would, in the alternative sequence, *trigger* causal chains leading to the consequence in question. For convenience we can group *both* other actions that would trigger causal chains leading to the consequence *and* natural events that would do so under the heading, "triggering events." Let us think of a triggering event (relative to some consequence *C*) as an event which is such that if it were to occur, it would *initiate* a causal sequence leading to *C*.

Now I can present the account of guidance control of consequences as follows. As I have said above, the bodily movement must be moderately reasons-responsive. Further, the process leading from the bodily movement to the event in the external world must be "sensitive to bodily movement" in roughly the following sense: if the actual type of process were to occur and all triggering events which do not actually occur were not to occur, then a different bodily movement would result in a different upshot. Guidance control of a consequence then involves two interlocked – and linked – sensitivities.

Here is a bit more explicit statement of the account. Suppose that in the actual world an agent *S* moves his body in way *B* via a type of mechanism *M*, and *S*'s moving his body in way *B* causes some consequence *C* via a type of process *P*.[21] I shall say that the sequence leading to the consequence *C* is responsive if and only if there exists some way of moving *S*'s body *B** (other than *B*) such that: (i) there exists some possible scenario in which an *M*-type mechanism operates, the agent has reason to move his body in way *B**, and the agent does move his body in *B**; and (ii) if *S* were to move his body in way *B**, all triggering events which do not actually occur were not to occur, and a *P*-type process were to occur, then *C* would not occur.

Let me now take a moment to discuss a few points which should help both to clarify and to illustrate the principle. (1) In formulating the definition of a responsive sequence, I make use of the intuitive notion of a "type of process" leading from the bodily movement to the event in the external world. This is parallel to the notion of a kind of mechanism issuing in action. I concede both that process-individuation is problematic and that I do not have an explicit theory of process-individuation. But I believe that there is a relatively clear intuitive distinction between different types of processes, just as there is a relatively clear intuitive distinction between different kinds of mechanisms leading to bodily movements.

I do not deny that there will be difficult questions about process-individuation. Nevertheless, all that is required for my purposes here is that there be agreement about some fairly clear cases. If we are unsure about an agent's moral responsibility for a consequence in precisely those cases in which we are unsure about process-individuation, then at least the vagueness in our theory will match the vagueness of the phenomena it purports to analyze.

(2) In ascertaining the responsiveness of a particular sequence involving a mechanism issuing in a bodily movement, a bodily movement, and a process leading from that bodily movement to a consequence, we "hold fixed" the actual type of mechanism and the actual type of process. If it is the case that a different mechanism or process would have taken place if things had been different (i.e., if the case is a Frankfurt-type case), this is irrelevant to the responsiveness of the *actual* sequence.

Further, imagine that we are testing the sensitivity of a particular process leading from a bodily movement to a consequence. Suppose that the agent actually moves his body in a certain way thus causing some consequence, and that no one else actually performs that type of action. Under these conditions, we "hold fixed" others' behavior when we test for the sensitivity of the process leading from action to consequence. The point is that, when we are interested in the sensitivity of the process to action, we are interested in whether there would have been a different outcome, if the agent had not performed a certain sort of action *and all non-occurring triggering events were not to occur.*

The sequence leading to a consequence (of a certain sort) includes more than just the mechanism issuing in bodily movement. Thus, both components – i.e., the mechanism leading to the bodily movement and the process leading from the bodily movement to the event in the external world – are relevant to guidance control of a consequence. The account of guidance control of a consequence involves what might be called "two stages."

(3) The notion of a "triggering event" is – like the notions of "mechanism" and "process" – fuzzy around the edges. But, again, I believe that it is tolerably clear for the present purposes. Note that a triggering event is an event which would "inititate" a causal chain

leading to a certain consequence. Although the concept of "initiation" is difficult to articulate crisply, we rely on the fact that there are some fairly uncontroversial instances of the concept. So, for example, if a lightning bolt hits a house and there is a resulting fire, the event of the lightning's hitting the house could be said to initiate the sequence leading to the destruction of the house. And this is so even if there were certain atmospheric events which antedated the lightning bolt and which led to it. Of course, the notion of "initiation" is highly context-dependent, and the truth of claims about purported initiations will depend on the purposes and goals of the individuals making (and considering) the claims. But I believe that the notion of initiation issues in tolerably clear intuitive judgments about the cases relevant to our purposes.

IV. The Symmetric Principle of Moral Responsibility

Now the tools for resolving the puzzle about moral responsibility for omissions are at hand. I have suggested that in cases of positive agency, moral responsibility is associated with control in a certain way. More specifically, I have claimed that guidance control is the kind of control associated with moral responsibility in cases of positive agency. I started with actions, and developed an account of guidance control of actions. This account employs the notion of moderate reasons-responsiveness. I then built on this model to develop an account of guidance control of consequences. On this account, there may be two steps: the bodily movement and then some event in the external world. In order for the sequence (involving both steps) to be appropriately responsive to reason, the bodily movement must be moderately reasons-responsive, and the event in the external world must be sensitive to the bodily movement.

The key to resolving the puzzle about omissions is to develop an analogous account of guidance control for omissions. If guidance control is all the control required for moral responsibility for omissions, then perhaps one can say just the right thing about the entire array of cases presented in the first two sections of this paper. On this approach, it is *not* the case that alternative possibilities are required for any part of the realm of omissions. Whereas it may seem that the only way to explain why an agent is not morally responsible for certain omissions is to cite his inability to perform the relevant action, another explanation is available: the agent may lack guidance control of the omission. Further, on this approach positive and negative agency are symmetric with respect to the requirement of alternative possibilities: guidance control (and not regulative control) is the kind of control associated with moral responsibility for positive and negative agency. Let us call this the "Symmetric Principle of Moral Responsibility" (in the rest of this paper, I shall be focusing primarily on the negative-agency component of the Symmetric Principle; thus, when I speak of the Symmetric Principle, I shall be speaking about the component of it which claims that guidance control is the sort of control necessary and sufficient for moral responsibility for omissions).

Like actions (and their consequences), omissions may be relatively simple or complex. A simple omission would be the failure to move one's body in a certain way. (Let us call these "bodily omissions.") In these cases, the failure to move one's body in a certain way "fully constitutes" the omission.[22] Here the application of the notion of guidance control is also relatively simple: it is natural to say that one has guidance control of one's failure to do X (in a case of a bodily omission) just in case one's failure to do X issues from one's own, moderately reasons-responsive mechanism. As with the case of actions, one here holds fixed the actual-sequence mechanism that issues in the failure to move one's body in a certain way, and asks what would happen in a relevant range of alternative scenarios. The account is parallel to the account in the case of action.

A bit more specifically, let us suppose that the failure to do X here is the failure to move one's body in a certain way B^* which actually occurs via mechanism M. What is it for one's failure to move one's body in way B^* to issue from a moderately reasons-responsive mechanism? It must be the case that, if M were to operate and the natural laws were held fixed, there is at least some scenario in which one has reason to move in way B^* and one does so (for that reason).

The treatment of moral responsibility for more complex omissions – omissions that are not simply bodily omissions – is analogous to the treatment of moral responsibility for the consequences of one's actions. As I pointed out above, in the context of assessing moral responsibility for the consequences of one's actions, there are typically two steps or stages: the bodily movement must be moderately responsive to reasons, and the event in the "external world" must be appropriately sensitive to one's action. Just as one holds fixed the actual-sequence mechanism when assessing the moderate reasons-responsiveness of the bodily movement, one holds fixed the actual conditions in the world when assessing the sensitivity of the external event to the bodily movement. That is, at both stages one holds fixed the relevant features of the actual sequence; and at both stages one looks for a certain sort of responsiveness or sensitivity.

In the context of complex omissions, the account of guidance control is parallel to the account of guidance control of consequences of actions. It is natural to say that an agent has guidance control of his failure to do X (where X is not simply a bodily movement) just in case there exists a way of moving his body (different from the way he actually moves it) such that: (1) his failure to move his body in this way issues from his own, moderately reasons-responsive mechanism, and (2) the relevant event in the external world is suitably sensitive to that failure to move his body. The details of the analyses are understood to be parallel to those in the context of positive agency.

More specifically, what is it for one's failure to do X here to issue from a sequence in which the agent has guidance control? Let us suppose that the agent fails to move his body in way B^*, and this issues in some result in the world C via process P. (This counts as the agent's not doing X.) It must be the case that i) there exists a way of moving his body B^* (different from how he actually moves it) such that, if the actual type of mechanism M were to occur and the natural laws were held fixed, then there is some scenario in which there is a reason for the agent to move in way B^* and he does so (for that reason); and ii) if he were to move in way B^*, process P were to occur, and all non-occurring triggering events were not to occur, then some different result C^* would occur.

It should be noted that the notion of a mechanism leading to a *failure* (a failure to move one's body, or an omission) is not as clear as the notion of a mechanism leading to an action. To make this notion as clear as possible, I shall say that the mechanism leading to an omission is the mechanism leading to *what the agent does instead*. So, for example, in "Sloth," John walks along the beach instead of jumping in to save the child; thus, I shall say that the mechanism leading to his not jumping in to save the child is the mechanism that leads to his action of walking along the beach.[23]

Let us now apply this account to the range of examples presented above. In "Sloth," "Shark," "Rain Dance," and "Flat Tire," the agents all actually move their bodies in certain ways; thus, they all fail to move their bodies in certain other ways. These failures are plausibly taken to be moderately responsive to reasons. In all these cases, however, there is a problem at the second stage: the relevant events in the external world are not suitably sensitive to the agents' bodily movements (or failures to move their bodies in certain ways). So, in "Shark," John's failure to jump into the water and head toward the struggling child is moderately responsive to reason (he is thus morally responsible for his bodily omission). But even if John had moved his body in this alternative way, the child would have drowned – the sharks would have eaten him (so John is not morally responsible for the complex omission). Similarly, although Sue's failure to do the rain dance is moderately responsive to reason, the drought would not have ended (presumably), even if she had done it. Whereas Sue is responsible for the bodily omission, she is not responsible for the complex omission.

The same sort of analysis applies to all the cases in the first group. In all of these cases the agents are not morally responsible for the relevant complex omissions because they lack guidance control of the omissions. And they lack such control in virtue of their failure to meet the conditions that pertain to the second stage: sensitivity of the external event to one's bodily movements.

Now consider the second group of cases: Frankfurt-type omissions (the Frankfurt-type "Sloth" case, "Babysitter," and "Forest Ranger 2"). In all of these cases the agents lack the ability to do the relevant action. But in all of these cases the agents have guidance control of the relevant omissions, and thus are appropriately considered morally responsible for those omissions.

Take, for example, the Frankfurt-type "Sloth" case. Here, in virtue of his propensity toward strong feelings

of guilt, John cannot move his body in any way other than the way he actually does, and thus he cannot save the child. But nevertheless his actual bodily movements issue from a moderately reasons-responsive mechanism. After all, the guilt feelings play no role in the actual sequence – they are not a part of the mechanism that actually issues in action. Further, the child would have been saved (presumably), if John had moved his body in certain different ways. Thus, John's failure to move his body in the relevant way is moderately responsive to reason, and the child's not being saved is sensitive to that failure to move his body. So John has guidance control of his failure to save the child, and is morally responsible for it. And the same sort of analysis applies to all the Frankfurt-type omissions cases.

V. An Objection

The Symmetric Principle, then, seems to imply all the right judgments about the cases assembled above. But I shall now turn to an objection to it. McIntyre objects with an example and a set of ancillary considerations. First the example:

> A meeting of the New York Entomological Society features an international array of dishes prepared using insects. [McIntyre here refers to Maialisa Calta, "Bug Seasoning: When Insect Experts Go in Search of Six-Legged Hors d'oeuvres," *Eating Well* 3 (1992), pp. 22–24.] You, a guest, are invited to sample a tempura dish made of fried crickets. You don't find the prospect of eating insects appealing, though you don't find it disgusting either, and you decline the offer. Suppose that in order to have decided to accept the offer, you would have had to look more closely at the fried crickets. But if you had looked more closely you would have been overwhelmed with revulsion and would have been incapable of deciding to eat some. Since you never do look more closely at the crickets, you decide not to have any without experiencing any feelings of revulsion, and without even suspecting that you would feel revulsion if you examined the dish more closely.[24]

McIntyre employs this example, call it "Insects," as part of a critique of the Symmetric Principle. She says:

... this approach, when applied to omissions, would yield too liberal a condition of moral responsibility. It will turn out that you are morally responsible for omitting to eat the crickets even if there is no possible situation in which you, as you actually are disposed and constituted, could have eaten them.[25]

McIntyre's point is that, in the story, you are actually so constituted that you would have been overwhelmed with revulsion if you looked more closely at the fried crickets, and if we assume that this revulsion is so strong that there is no possible situation in which you could have decided to eat the crickets (given this revulsion), it seems implausible to say that you are morally responsible for your failing to eat the crickets.

But recall that as things actually went, the revulsion played absolutely no role in your deliberations and your decision not to eat the crickets. And note that McIntyre's "Insects" case, in the version which she employs to criticize the Symmetric Principle, seems to be precisely parallel to the Frankfurt-style "Sloth" case. Recall that in the Frankfurt-style Sloth case, John fails to save the child and indeed fails to even consider doing so; but if he were to start to consider saving the child, he would have been overwhelmed by a literally irresistible desire to do something else. Here it is Frankfurt's view (and mine) that John is morally responsible for failing to save the child. Since I agree with Frankfurt about his version of "Sloth," and the two cases appear to be parallel, I am inclined to disagree with McIntyre about "Insects." That is, just as John is morally responsible for failing to save the child in Frankfurt's version of "Sloth," so you are morally responsible for failing to eat the crickets in "Insects."

Further support for my position comes from reflection on the theoretical considerations McIntyre invokes as part of her critique of the Symmetric Principle. She says:

... According to that approach [of Fischer and Ravizza], even if *you* could not have decided to eat some crickets because of your propensity to revulsion, *the mechanism* that actually produced your decision could have done so, and, as a result, you can be morally responsible for your omission. Of course, if we can stipulate that you do not have, or are not affected by, your propensity to feel revulsion, then there would be no obstacle to identifying some possible situation in which you eat some crickets.

But what justifies this stipulation? It seems that one could quite reasonably object that this is suspiciously similar to inferring that *you could have done otherwise* from the fact that *you could have done otherwise if what would have prevented you from doing otherwise hadn't existed!*[26]

I believe McIntyre's criticism here is unfair. On my approach to both actions and omissions, freedom to do otherwise is not required for moral responsibility; rather, what is relevant are features of the actual sequence that leads to the action or the omission. I certainly agree that someone who actually faces some insuperable obstacle to doing otherwise cannot do otherwise, and it would simply be irrelevant, for most purposes, to point out (what might, in any case, be true) that the agent would be able to do otherwise, if the obstacle were subtracted. Since my approach to moral responsibility does not require alternative possibilities, I am not here in the business of assessing an agent's freedom to do otherwise.

Rather, I am interested in evaluating the mechanisms and processes that actually lead to actions, consequences, and omissions. Since in "Insects" the propensity toward revulsion played no role in your decision or bodily movements, it is not part of the mechanism that actually issues in that decision and those bodily movements. Thus, it is irrelevant to the issue of whether that actual-sequence mechanism is responsive to reasons, and thus also to the issue of whether you are morally responsible for your actions. Clearly, it would be inappropriate to subtract the propensity toward revulsion in considering whether you could have done otherwise; but it is not inappropriate to subtract it when considering whether the actual-sequence mechanism that issues in your omission has a certain feature-responsiveness to reasons.

In focusing on the properties of the actual mechanisms and processes that lead to actions, consequences, and omissions, I am seeking to develop what might be dubbed an "actual-sequence" approach to moral responsibility. But notice that the "actual-sequence" properties fixed on by such an approach may indeed be dispositional properties; as such, their proper analysis may involve (for example) other possible worlds. In the context of an actual-sequence approach to moral responsibility, I have argued that it is required that a reasons-responsive mechanism actually operate; then,

I have analyzed reasons-responsiveness in terms of other possible worlds. Whereas other possible worlds are relevant to ascertaining whether there is some actually operative dispositional feature (such as reasons-responsiveness), such worlds are *not* relevant in virtue of bearing on the question of whether some alternative sequence is genuinely accessible to the agent.

VI. Conclusion

I started with a puzzle about moral responsibility for failures. Some cases suggest that in order to be morally responsible for failing to do X, you must have the ability to do X. But other cases suggest exactly the opposite. In response to this puzzle, I have argued that moral responsibility for failing to do X does not in fact require the ability to do X; rather, it simply requires that the agent have guidance control of his failure to do X.

This suggestion has the virtue of treating positive and negative agency *symmetrically*. Further, I can respect the intuitive view that the first group of cases is interestingly different from the second; but the explanation of the difference is not in terms of freedom to do otherwise (or alternative possibilities). The account of guidance control implies that the two groups are different while nevertheless offering a unified account of moral responsibility for omissions. Further, it helps to exhibit a unified, systematic view of moral responsibility for actions, consequences, and omissions. That is, it helps to show how the association of moral responsibility with control – and more specifically, with guidance control – can begin to systematize and illuminate our considered judgments about the *full content* of moral responsibility, which must include responsibility for actions, consequences, and omissions. Finally, the Symmetric Principle helps to establish semicompatibilism; as with positive agency, there is no reason to think guidance control is incompatible with causal determinism, and thus there is no reason to think moral responsibility for omissions is incompatible with causal determinism.

Notes

1. The case is presented and discussed in J.M. Fischer and M. Ravizza, "Responsibility and Inevitability," *Ethics* 101 (1991), pp. 258–278.
2. The examples presented in this section are from Fischer and Ravizza, 1991.
3. This kind of example is due to C. Ginet.
4. H. Frankfurt, "An Alleged Asymmetry between Actions and Omissions," *Ethics* 104 (1994), pp. 620–623, esp. p. 620.
5. For interesting and useful discussions of moral responsibility for omissions, including Frankfurt-type omissions cases, see: I. Haji, "A Riddle Regarding Omissions," *Canadian Journal of Philosophy* 22 (1992), pp. 485–502; R. Clarke, "Ability and Responsibility for Omissions," *Philosophical Studies* 73 (1994), pp. 195–208; D. Zimmerman, "Acts, Omissions and 'Semi-compatibilism'," *Philosophical Studies* 73 (1994), pp. 209–223; A. McIntyre, "Compatibilists Could Have Done Otherwise: Responsibility and Negative Agency," *Philosophical Review* 103 (1994), pp. 453–488; and W. Glannon, "Symmetrical Responsibility," *Journal of Philosophy* 92 (1995), pp. 261–274.
6. Clarke, p. 203.
7. Clarke, pp. 203–204.
8. McIntyre, 1994.
9. McIntyre, p. 458.
10. McIntyre, p. 458.
11. McIntyre, pp. 465–466.
12. McIntyre, p. 466.
13. For a parallel distinction between two kinds of control, see M.J. Zimmerman, *An Essay on Moral Responsibility* (Totowa, NJ: Rowman and Littlefield, 1988), pp. 32–34.
14. For this following discussion, see J.M. Fischer, *The Metaphysics of Free Will: An Essay on Control* (Cambridge, MA: Blackwell, 1994), pp. 132–134.
15. Note that the example would have precisely the same implications if alternative possibilities were ruled out by virtue of the existence of *another agent*. So imagine that the car is a "driver instruction" automobile with dual controls. Although I actually guide the car to the right, we can imagine that the instructor could have intervened and caused the car to go to the right, if I had shown any inclination to cause it to go in some other direction.
16. For an attempt to say what it is for a mechanism to be "the agent's own," see J.M. Fischer and M. Ravizza, *Responsibility and Control: A Theory of Moral Responsibility* (Cambridge: Cambridge University Press, 2000).

17. For further details, see Fischer and Ravizza, 2000.

18. R. Nozick, *Philosophical Explanations* (Cambridge, MA: Harvard University Press, 1981).

19. For a development of the relevant notion of normative competence. see Fischer and Ravizza, 2000.

20. H. Frankfurt, "Alternate Possibilities and Moral Responsibility," *Journal of Philosophy* 66 (1969), pp. 829–839, note 4; p. 359 in this volume.

21. This is still only an approximation to an adequate account. For example, it assumes that there is an appropriate range of scenarios in which S recognizes reasons to move his body in way B^*. It also assumes that in the alternative possible scenario the agent moves his body in way B^* for the relevant reason *qua* reason, and so forth.

   I shall here also assume that there is just one causal sequence leading to the consequence; thus, in this paper I am concerned with cases of "pre-emptive overdetermination" rather than "simultaneous overdetermination." Further, the focus here is on what might be called "action-triggered" consequences. There might also be "omission-triggered" consequences for which an agent might be morally responsible. A more complete theory of responsibility – one which attends to the full range of possible cases – is presented in Fischer and Ravizza, 2000.

22. These omissions are like Frankfurt's "personal" failures; see H. Frankfurt, "What We Are Morally Responsible For," in L.S. Cauman, I. Levi, C. Parsons, and R. Schwartz (eds.), *How Many Questions? Essays in Honor of Sidney Morgenbesser* (Indianapolis, IN: Hackett, 1982), pp. 321–335.

23. I am indebted to C. Ginet for this suggestion.

24. McIntyre, pp. 485–486.

25. McIntyre, pp. 486–487.

26. McIntyre, p. 486.

35

The Impossibility of Ultimate Responsibility?

Galen Strawson

1. The Basic Argument

You set off for a shop on the evening of a national holiday, intending to buy a cake with your last five-pound note to supplement the preparations you've already made. There's one cake left in the shop and it costs five pounds; everything is closing down. On the steps of the shop someone is shaking a box, collecting money for Oxfam. You stop, and it seems clear to you that it is *entirely up to you* what you do next. It seems clear to you that you are truly, radically free to choose, in such a way that you will be ultimately morally responsible for whatever you do choose.

There is, however, an argument, which I will call the Basic Argument, which appears to show that we can never be truly or ultimately morally responsible for our actions. According to the Basic Argument, it makes no difference whether determinism is true or false.

The central idea can be quickly conveyed:

A. Nothing can be *causa sui* – nothing can be the cause of itself.
B. In order to be truly or ultimately morally responsible for one's actions one would have to be *causa sui*, at least in certain crucial mental respects.

C. Therefore no one can be truly or ultimately morally responsible.

We can expand the argument as follows:

1. Interested in free action, we're particularly interested in actions performed for a reason (as opposed to reflex actions or mindlessly habitual actions).
2. When one acts for a reason, what one does is a function of how one is, mentally speaking. (It's also a function of one's height, one's strength, one's place and time, and so on; but it's the mental factors that are crucial when moral responsibility is in question.)
3. So if one is to be truly responsible for how one acts, one must be truly responsible for how one is, mentally speaking – at least in certain respects.
4. But to be truly responsible for how one is, in any mental respect, one must have brought it about that one is the way one is, in that respect. And it's not merely that one must have caused oneself to be the way one is, in that respect. One must also have consciously and explicitly chosen to be the way one is, in that respect, and one must have succeeded in bringing it about that one is that way.
5. But one can't really be said to choose, in a conscious, reasoned, fashion, to be the way one is in any respect at all, unless one already exists, mentally speaking, already equipped with some principles of choice, 'P1' – preferences, values, ideals – in the light of which one chooses how to be.

Strawson, G. (2011), "The Impossibility of Ultimate Responsibility?," in R. Swinburne (ed.), *Free Will and Modern Science* (Oxford: Oxford University Press), 126–140. Reprinted with permission of Oxford University Press.

Philosophy of Action: An Anthology, First Edition. Edited by Jonathan Dancy and Constantine Sandis.

6. But then to be truly responsible, on account of having chosen to be the way one is, in certain mental respects, one must be truly responsible for one's having the principles of choice P1 in the light of which one chose how to be.

7. But for this to be so one must have chosen P1, in a reasoned, conscious, intentional fashion.

8. But for this to be so one must already have had some principles of choice P2, in the light of which one chose P1.

9. And so on. Here we are setting out on a regress that we cannot stop. True self-determination is impossible because it requires the actual completion of an infinite series of choices of principles of choice.

10. So true moral responsibility is impossible, because it requires true self-determination, as noted in (3).[1]

This may seem contrived, but essentially the same argument can be given in a more natural form.

1. It's undeniable that one is the way one is, initially, as a result of heredity and early experience, and it's undeniable that these are things for which one can't be held to be in any way responsible (morally or otherwise).

2. One can't at any later stage of life hope to accede to true or ultimate moral responsibility for the way one is by trying to change the way one already is as a result of one's genetic inheritance and previous experience.

For

3. Both the particular way in which one is moved to try to change oneself, and the degree of one's success in one's attempt to change, will be determined by how one already is as a result of one's genetic inheritance and previous experience.

And

4. Any further changes that one can bring about only after one has brought about certain initial changes will in turn be determined, via the initial changes, by one's genetic inheritance and previous experience.

5. This may not be the whole story, and there may be changes in the way one is that can't be traced to one's genetic inheritance and experience but rather to the influence of indeterministic factors. It is, however, absurd to suppose that indeterministic factors, for which one is obviously not responsible, can contribute in any way to one's being truly morally responsible for how one is.

2. Ultimate Moral Responsibility

But what is this supposed 'true' or 'ultimate' moral responsibility? An old story may be helpful. As I understand it, it's responsibility of such a kind that, if we have it, then it *makes sense* to suppose that it could be just to punish some of us with (eternal) torment in hell and reward others with (eternal) bliss in heaven. The stress on the words 'makes sense' is important, because one certainly doesn't have to believe in any version of the story of heaven and hell in order to understand, or indeed believe in, the kind of true or ultimate moral responsibility that I'm using the story to illustrate. A less colourful way to convey the point, perhaps, is to say that true or ultimate responsibility exists if punishment and reward can be fair without having any sort of pragmatic justification whatever.

One certainly doesn't have to refer to religious faith in order to describe the sorts of everyday situation that give rise to our belief in such responsibility. Choices like the one with which I began (the cake or the collection box) arise all the time, and constantly refresh our conviction about our responsibility. Even if one believes that determinism is true, in such a situation, and that one will in five minutes' time be able to look back and say that what one did was determined, this doesn't seem to undermine one's sense of the absoluteness and inescapability of one's freedom, and of one's moral responsibility for one's choice. Even if one accepts the validity of the Basic Argument, which concludes that one can't be in any way ultimately responsible for the way one is and decides, one's freedom and true moral responsibility seem, in the moment, as one stands there, obvious and absolute.

Large and small, morally significant or morally neutral, such situations of choice occur regularly in human life. I think they lie at the heart of the experience of freedom and moral responsibility. They're the fundamental source of our inability to give up belief in true or ultimate moral responsibility. We may wonder why human beings experience these situations of choice as they do; it's an interesting question whether any possible cognitively sophisticated, rational, self-conscious agent must experience situations of choice in this way.[2] But these situations of choice are the experiential rock on which the belief in ultimate moral responsibility is founded.

Most people who believe in ultimate moral responsibility take its existence for granted, and don't ever entertain the thought that one needs to be ultimately responsible for the way one *is* in order to be ultimately responsible for the way one *acts*. Some, however, reveal that they see its force. E.H. Carr states that 'normal adult human beings are morally responsible for their own personality' (Carr 1961: 89). Sartre holds that 'man is responsible for what he is' (Sartre 1946: 29) and seeks to give an account of how we 'choose ourselves' (Sartre 1943: 440, 468, 503). In a later interview he judges his earlier assertions about freedom to be incautious – 'When I read this, I said to myself: it's incredible, I actually believed that!' – but he still holds that 'in the end one is always responsible for what is made of one' (Sartre 1970: 22). Kant puts it clearly when he claims that

> man *himself* must make or have made himself into whatever, in a moral sense, whether good or evil, he is to become. Either condition must be an effect of his free choice; for otherwise he could not be held responsible for it and could therefore be *morally* neither good nor evil. (Kant 1793: 40)

Since he is committed to belief in radical moral responsibility, Kant holds that such self-creation does indeed take place, and writes accordingly of 'man's character, which he himself creates' (Kant 1788: 101), and of 'knowledge of oneself as a person who ... is his own originator' (Kant 1800: 213). John Patten, a former British Secretary of State for Education, claims that 'it is ... self-evident that as we grow up each individual chooses whether to be good or bad' (Patten

1992).[3] Robert Kane, an eloquent recent defender of this view, writes as follows:

> if ... a choice issues from, and can be sufficiently explained by, an agent's character and motives (together with background conditions), then to be ultimately responsible for the choice, the agent must be at least in part responsible by virtue of choices or actions voluntarily performed in the past for having the character and motives he or she now has. (Kane 2000: 317–18)

Christine Korsgaard agrees: 'judgements of responsibility don't really make sense unless people create themselves' (Korsgaard 2009: 20).

Most of us, as remarked, never actually follow this line of thought. It seems, though, that we do tend, in some vague and unexamined fashion, to think of ourselves as responsible for – answerable for – how we are. The point is somewhat delicate, for we don't ordinarily suppose that we have gone through some sort of active process of self-determination at some past time. It seems nevertheless that we do unreflectively experience ourselves, in many respects, rather as we might experience ourselves if we did believe that we had engaged in some such activity of self-determination; and we may well also think of others in this way.

Sometimes a part of one's character – a desire or tendency – may strike one as foreign or alien. But it can do this only against a background of character traits that aren't experienced as foreign, but are rather 'identified' with. (It's only relative to such a background that a character trait can stand out as alien.) Some feel tormented by impulses that they experience as alien, but in many a sense of general identification with their character predominates, and this identification seems to carry within itself an implicit sense that one is generally speaking in control of, or at least answerable for, how one is (even, perhaps, for aspects of one's character that one doesn't like). So it seems that we find, semi-dormant in common thought, an implicit recognition of the idea that true or ultimate moral responsibility for one's actions (for what one does) does somehow involve responsibility for how one is: it seems that ordinary thought is ready to move this way under pressure.

There are also many aspects of our ordinary sense of ourselves as morally responsible free agents that we don't feel to be threatened in any way by the fact that we can't be ultimately responsible for how we are. We readily accept that we are products of our heredity and environment without feeling that this poses any threat to our freedom and moral responsibility at the time of action. It's natural to feel that if one is fully consciously aware of oneself as able to choose in a situation of choice, then this is already entirely sufficient for one's radical freedom of choice – whatever else is or is not the case (see further the penultimate paragraph of this chapter). It seems, then, that our ordinary conception of moral responsibility may contain mutually inconsistent elements. If this is so, it is a profoundly important fact (it would explain a great deal about the character of the philosophical debate about free will). But these other elements in our ordinary notion of moral responsibility, important as they are, are not my present subject.[4]

3. Restatement of the Basic Argument

I want now to restate the Basic Argument in very loose – as it were conversational – terms. New forms of words allow for new forms of objection, but they may be helpful nonetheless – or for that reason.

1. You do what you do, in any situation in which you find yourself, because of the way you are.

So

2. To be truly morally responsible for what you do you must be truly responsible for the way you are – at least in certain crucial mental respects.

Or:

1. When you act, what you do is a function of how you are (what you do won't count as an action at all unless it flows appropriately from your beliefs, preferences, and so on).

Hence

2. You have to get to have some responsibility for how you are in order to get to have some responsibility for what you intentionally do.

Once again I take the qualification about 'certain mental respects' for granted. Obviously one isn't responsible for one's sex, basic body pattern, height, and so on. But if one weren't responsible for anything about oneself, how could one be responsible for what one did, given the truth of (1)? This is the fundamental question, and it seems clear that if one is going to be responsible for any aspect of oneself, it had better be some aspect of one's mental nature.

I take it that (1) is incontrovertible, and that it is (2) that must be resisted. For if (1) and (2) are conceded the case seems lost, because the full argument runs as follows:

1. You do what you do because of the way you are.[5]

So

2. To be truly morally responsible for what you do you must be truly responsible for the way you are – at least in certain crucial mental respects.

But

3. You can't be truly responsible for the way you are, so you can't be truly responsible for what you do.

Why can't you be truly responsible for the way you are? Because

4. To be truly responsible for the way you are, you must have intentionally brought it about that you are the way you are, and this is impossible.

Why is it impossible? Well, suppose it isn't. Suppose

5. You have somehow intentionally brought it about that you are the way you now are, and that you have brought this about in such a way that you can now be said to be truly responsible for being the way you are now.

For this to be true

6. You must already have had a certain nature N in the light of which you intentionally brought it about that you are as you now are.

But then

7. For it to be true that you are truly responsible for how you now are, you must be truly responsible for having had the nature N in the light of which you intentionally brought it about that you are the way you now are.

So

8. You must have intentionally brought it about that you had that nature N, in which case you must have existed already with a prior nature in the light of which you intentionally brought it about that you had the nature N in the light of which you intentionally brought it about that you are the way you now are …

Here one is setting off on the regress again. Nothing can be *causa sui* in the required way. Even if this attribute is allowed to belong (unintelligibly) to God, it can't plausibly be supposed to be possessed by ordinary finite human beings. 'The *causa sui* is the best self-contradiction that has been conceived so far', as Nietzsche remarked in 1886:

> it is a sort of rape and perversion of logic. But the extravagant pride of man has managed to entangle itself profoundly and frightfully with just this nonsense. The desire for 'freedom of the will' in the superlative metaphysical sense, which still holds sway, unfortunately, in the minds of the half-educated; the desire to bear the entire and ultimate responsibility for one's actions oneself, and to absolve God, the world, ancestors, chance, and society involves nothing less than to be precisely this *causa sui* and, with more than Baron Münchhausen's audacity, to pull oneself up into existence by the hair, out of the swamps of nothingness … (Nietzsche 1886, §21)

The rephrased argument is essentially exactly the same as before, although the first two steps are now more simply stated. Can the Basic Argument simply be dismissed? Is it really of no importance in the discussion of free will and moral responsibility, as some have claimed? (No and No.) Shouldn't any serious defence of free will and moral responsibility thoroughly acknowledge the respect in which the Basic Argument is valid before going on to try to give its own positive account of the nature of free will and moral responsibility? Doesn't the argument go to the heart of things if the heart of the free will debate is a concern about whether we can be truly morally responsible in the absolute way that we ordinarily suppose? (Yes and Yes.)

We are what we are, and we can't be thought to have made ourselves *in such a way* that we can be held to be free in our actions *in such a way* that we can be held to be morally responsible for our actions *in such a way* that any punishment or reward for our actions is ultimately just or fair. Punishments and rewards may seem deeply appropriate or intrinsically 'fitting' to us; many of the various institutions of punishment and reward in human society appear to be practically indispensable in both their legal and non-legal forms. But if one takes the notion of justice that is central to our intellectual and cultural tradition seriously, then the consequence of the Basic Argument is that there is a fundamental sense in which no punishment or reward is ever just. It is exactly as just to punish or reward people for their actions as it is to punish or reward them for the (natural) colour of their hair or the (natural) shape of their faces. The conclusion seems intolerable, but inescapable.

Darwin develops the point as follows in a notebook entry for 6 September 1838:

> The general delusion about free will obvious … One must view a [wicked] man like a sickly one – We cannot help loathing a diseased offensive object, so we view wickedness. – it would however be more proper to pity than to hate & be disgusted with them. Yet it is right to punish criminals; but solely to *deter* others … This view should teach one profound humility, one deserves no credit for anything. (yet one takes it for beauty and good temper), nor ought one to blame others. – This view will do no harm, because no one can be really *fully* convinced of its truth except man who has thought very much, & he will know his happiness lays in doing good & being perfect, & therefore will not be tempted, from knowing every thing he does is independent of himself[,] to do harm.[6]

4. Response to the Basic Argument

I've suggested that it is step (2) of the restated Basic Argument that must be rejected, and of course it can be rejected, because the phrases 'truly responsible' and 'truly morally responsible' can be defined in many ways. I'll sketch three sorts of response.

(I) The first response is *compatibilist*. Compatibilists say that one can be a free and morally responsible agent even if determinism is true. They claim that one can correctly be said to be truly responsible for what one does, when one acts, just so long as one is in control of one's action in the way that we take an ordinary person to be in ordinary circumstances: one isn't, for example, caused to do what one does by any of a certain set of constraints (kleptomaniac impulses, obsessional neuroses, desires that are experienced as alien, post-hypnotic commands, threats, instances of *force majeure*, and so on). Compatibilists don't impose any requirement that one should be truly responsible for how one is, so step (2) of the Basic Argument comes out as false, on their view. They think one can be fully morally responsible even if the way one is is entirely determined by factors entirely outside one's control. They simply reject the Basic Argument. They know that the kind of responsibility ruled out by the Basic Argument is impossible, and conclude that it can't be the kind of responsibility that is really in question in human life, because (they insist) we are indeed genuinely morally responsible agents. No theory that concludes otherwise can possibly be right, on their view.

(II) The second response is *libertarian*. Incompatibilists believe that freedom and moral responsibility are incompatible with determinism, and some incompatibilists are libertarians, who believe that we are free and morally responsible agents, and that determinism is therefore false. Robert Kane, for example, allows that we may act responsibility from a will already formed, but argues that the will must in this case be

> 'our own' free will by virtue of other past 'self-forming' choices or other actions that were undetermined and by which we made ourselves into the kinds of persons we are … [T]hese undetermined self-forming actions (SFAs) occur at those difficult times of life when we are torn between competing visions of what we should do or become. (Kane 2000: 318–19)

They paradigmatically involve a conflict between moral duty and non-moral desire, and it is essential that they involve indeterminism, on Kane's view, for this 'screens off complete determination by influences

of the past' (Kane 2000: 319). He proposes that we are in such cases of 'moral, prudential and practical struggle … truly "making ourselves" in such a way that we are ultimately responsible for the outcome', and that this 'making of ourselves' means that 'we can be ultimately responsible for our present motives and character by virtue of past choices which helped to form them and for which we were ultimately responsible' (Kane 1989: 252).

Kane, then, accepts step (2) of the Basic Argument, and challenges step (3) instead. He accepts that we have to 'make ourselves', and so be ultimately responsible for ourselves, in order to be morally responsible for what we do; and he thinks that this requires indeterminism. But the old, general objection to libertarianism recurs. How can indeterminism possibly help with moral responsibility? How can the occurrence of indeterministic or partly random events contribute to my being truly or ultimately morally responsible either for my actions or for my character? If my efforts of will shape my character in a positive way, and are in so doing essentially partly indeterministic in nature, while also being shaped (as Kane grants) by my already existing character, why am I not merely *lucky*?

This seems to be a very strong general objection to any libertarian account of free will. Suppose, in the light of this, that we put aside the Basic Argument for a moment, and take it as given that there is – that there must be – some respectable sense in which human beings are or can be genuinely morally responsible for their actions. If we then ask what sort of account of moral responsibility this will be, compatibilist or incompatibilist, I think we can safely reply that it will have to be compatibilist. This is because it seems so clear that nothing can ever be gained, in an attempt to defend moral responsibility, by assuming that determinism is false.

(III) The third response begins by accepting that one can't be held to be ultimately responsible for one's character or personality or motivational structure. It accepts that this is so whether determinism is true or false. It then directly challenges step (2) of the Basic Argument. It appeals to a certain picture of the *self* in order to argue that one can be truly free and morally responsible in spite of the fact that one can't be held to be ultimately responsible for one's character or personality or motivational structure.

It can be set out as follows. One is free and truly morally responsible because one's self is, in a crucial sense, independent of one's character or personality or motivational structure – one's CPM, for short. Suppose one is in a situation which one experiences as a difficult choice between A, doing one's duty, and B, following one's non-moral desires. Given one's CPM, one responds in a certain way. One's desires and beliefs develop and interact and constitute reasons in favour both of A and of B, and one's CPM makes one tend towards either A or B. So far, the problem is the same as ever: whatever one does, one will do what one does because of the way one's CPM is, and since one neither is nor can be ultimately responsible for the way one's CPM is, one can't be ultimately responsible for what one does.

Enter one's self, S. S is imagined to be in some way independent of one's CPM. S (i.e. one) considers the deliverances of one's CPM and decides in the light of them, but it – S – incorporates a power of decision that is independent of one's CPM in such a way that one can after all count as truly and ultimately morally responsible in one's decisions and actions, even though one isn't ultimately responsible for one's CPM. The idea is that step (2) of the Basic Argument is false because of the existence of S (for a development of this view see, for example, Campbell 1957).

The trouble with the picture is obvious. S (i.e. one) decides on the basis of the deliverances of one's CPM. But whatever S decides, it decides as it does because of the way it is (or because of the occurrence in the decision process of indeterministic factors for which it – i.e. one – can't be responsible, and which can't plausibly be thought to contribute to its ultimate moral responsibility). And this brings us back to where we started. To be a source of ultimate responsibility, S must be responsible for being the way it is. But this is impossible, for the reasons given in the Basic Argument. So while the story of S and CPM adds another layer to the description of the human decision process, it can't change the fact that human beings cannot be ultimately self-determining in such a way as to be ultimately morally responsible for how they are, and thus for how they decide and act.

In spite of all these difficulties, many of us (nearly all of us) continue to believe that we are truly morally responsible agents in the strongest possible sense. Many of us, for example, feel that our capacity for fully explicit self-conscious deliberation in a situation of choice suffices – all by itself – to constitute us as such. All that is needed for true or ultimate responsibility, on this view, is that one is in the moment of action *fully self-consciously aware of oneself as an agent facing choices*. The idea is that such full self-conscious awareness somehow renders irrelevant the fact that one neither is nor can be ultimately responsible for any aspect of one's mental nature: the mere fact of one's self-conscious presence in the situation of choice can confer true moral responsibility. It may be undeniable that one is, in the final analysis, wholly constituted as the sort of person one is by factors for which one cannot be in any way ultimately responsible, but the threat that this fact appears to pose to one's claim to true moral responsibility is, on this view, simply annihilated by one's self-conscious awareness of one's situation.

This is an extremely natural intuition; but the Basic Argument appears to show that it is a mistake. For however self-consciously aware we are as we deliberate and reason, every act and operation of our mind happens as it does as a result of features for which we are ultimately in no way responsible. And yet the conviction that self-conscious awareness of one's situation can be a sufficient foundation of strong free will is extremely powerful. It runs deeper than rational argument, and it survives untouched, in the everyday conduct of life, even after the validity of the Basic Argument has been admitted. Nor, probably, should we wish it otherwise.[7]

Notes

1. Wouldn't it be enough if one simply endorsed the way one found oneself to be, mentally, in the relevant respects, without actually changing anything? Yes, if one were ultimately responsible for having the principles in the light of which one endorsed the way one found oneself to be. But how could this be?

2. See, e.g., MacKay (1960); Strawson (2010: 246–50; 1986: 281–6).
3. Nussbaum has something much less dramatic in mind, I think, when she writes that 'one's own character is one's own responsibility and not that of others' (Nussbaum 2004).
4. For some discussion of the deep ways in which we're naturally compatibilist in our thinking about free will or moral responsibility, and don't feel that it is threatened either by determinism or by our inability to be self-determining, see Strawson 2010: §6.4 ('Natural compatibilism'). Clarke and Fischer are prominent among those who misrepresent my position on free will to the extent that they focus only on the line of thought set out in the current paper. See, e.g., Clarke (2005), Fischer (2006).
5. During the symposium on free will at the British Academy in July 2010, J.R. Lucas objected that this claim involved an equivocation. He suggested that it operated simultaneously as a conceptual claim and as a causal claim, in a way which vitiated it. I agree that it is both a conceptual claim and a causal claim, but not that this vitiates it. The following is a *conceptual* truth about the *causation* of intentional action: that with regard to the respect in which it is true to say that the action is intentional, it must be true to say that the agent does what he does – given, as always, the situation in which he finds himself or takes himself to be – because (this is a causal 'because') of the way he is; and indeed because of the way he is in some mental respect; whatever else is true, and whatever else may be going on. The truth of this claim is wholly compatible with the fact that the way you are when you act is a function of many things, including of course your experience of your situation – which is part of the way you are mentally speaking. Certainly the way

you are mentally speaking isn't just a matter of your overall character or personality, and the present argument has its full force even for those who question or reject the explanatory viability of the notion of character when it comes to the explanation of action (see, e.g., Harman (1999, 2000); Doris (2002); see also Note 7 below).
6. Darwin (1838: 608). For 'wicked' in the first line Darwin has 'wrecked' (a characteristic slip).
7. On this last point, see, e.g., P.F. Strawson (1962); for a doubt, see Smilansky (1994). It will be interesting to see how the conviction of free will stands up to increasing public awareness of results in experimental and social psychology, which show that our actions are often strongly influenced by factors, situational or otherwise, of which we are completely unaware (see, e.g., Doris (2002), Wilson (2002), Nahmias (2007), Knobe and Nichols (2008). The general effect of this 'situationist' line of enquiry is to cast increasing doubt on our everyday picture of ordinary adult human agents as consciously aware of, and in control of, themselves and their motivations and subsequent actions in such a way that they are, generally speaking, fully morally responsible for what they do. Situationism finds a natural ally in Freudian theory, while considerably extending the range of factors that threaten to undermine our everyday picture of responsibility. It tells us that we are far more 'puppets of circumstances' than we realize; it questions our conception of ordinary human beings as genuinely free agents in a way that is independent of any considerations about determinism or the impossibility of self-origination. At the same time (again in line with Freudian theory) it grounds a sense in which greater self-knowledge, a better understanding of what motivates one, can increase one's control of and responsibility for one's actions.

References

Campbell, C.A. (1957) Has the self free will'? In C.A. Campbell, *On Selfhood and Godhood*, London: Allen & Unwin.
Carr, E.H. (1961) *What Is History?*, London: Macmillan.
Clarke, R. (2005) On an argument for the impossibility of moral responsibility, *Midwest Studies in Philosophy*, 19: 13–24.
Darwin, C. (1987 [1838]) *Charles Darwin's Notebooks, 1836–44*, Cambridge: Cambridge University Press.
Doris, J. (2002) *Lack of Character: Personality and Moral Behavior*, Cambridge: Cambridge University Press.
Fischer, J. (2006) The cards that are dealt you, *The Journal of Ethics*, 10: 107–29.

Harman, G. (1999) Moral philosophy meets social psychology: virtue ethics and the fundamental attribution error, *Proceedings of the Aristotelian Society*, 99: 315–31.
Harman, G. (2000) The nonexistence of character traits, *Proceedings of the Aristotelian Society*, 100: 223–6.
Kane, R. (1989) Two kinds of incompatibilism, *Philosophy and Phenomenological Research*, 50: 219–54.
Kane, R. (2000) Free will and responsibility: ancient dispute, new themes, *The Journal of Ethics*, 4: 315–22.
Kant, I. (1956 [1788]) *Critique of Practical Reason*, trans. L.W. Beck, Indianapolis: Bobbs-Merrill.

Kant, I. (1960 [1793]) *Religion within the Limits of Reason Alone*, trans. T.M. Greene and H.H. Hudson, New York: Harper & Row.

Kant, I. (1993 [1800]) *Opus postumum*, trans. E. Förster and M. Rosen, Cambridge: Cambridge University Press.

Knobe, J. and Nichols, S. (2008), *Experimental Philosophy*, New York: Oxford University Press.

Korsgaard, C. (2009) *Self-Constitution: Agency, Identity, and Integrity*, Oxford: Oxford University Press.

MacKay, D.M. (1960) On the logical indeterminacy of free choice, *Mind*, 69: 31–40.

Nahmias, E. (2007) Autonomous agency and social psychology. In M. Marraffa *et al.* (eds), *Cartographies of the Mind: Philosophy and Psychology in Intersection*, Dordrecht: Springer.

Nietzsche, F. (1966 [1886]) *Beyond Good and Evil*, trans. Walter Kaufmann, New York: Random House.

Nussbaum, M. (2004) Discussing disgust: on the folly of gross-out public policy: an interview with Martha Nussbaum, *Reason*, 15 July 2004.

Patten, J. (1992) article in *The Spectator*, 16 April 1992.

Sartre, J.-P. (1969 [1943]) *Being and Nothingness*, trans. Hazel E. Barnes, London: Methuen.

Sartre, J.-P. (1970) interview in *New Left Review*, 58, reprinted in *New York Review of Books*, 26 March 1970, 22.

Sartre, J.-P. (1989 [1946]) *Existentialism and Humanism*, trans. Philip Mairet, London: Methuen.

Smilansky, S. (1994) The ethical advantages of hard determinism, *Philosophy and Phenomenological Research*, 54: 355–63.

Strawson, G. (1986) *Freedom and Belief*, Oxford: Clarendon.

Strawson, G. (2010) *Freedom and Belief*, Second edition, Oxford: Clarendon.

Strawson, P.F. (1974 [1962]) Freedom and resentment. In P.F. Strawson, *Freedom and Resentment*, London: Methuen.

Wilson, T. (2002) *Strangers to Ourselves: Discovering the Adaptive Unconscious*, Cambridge, MA: Harvard University Press.

36

Moral Responsibility and the Concept of Agency

Helen Steward

It is strange that philosophers have been able to argue endlessly about determinism and free-will, to cite examples in favour of one or the other thesis without ever attempting first to make explicit the structures contained in the very idea of action.

(Sartre 1958: 433)

There is a long tradition of supposing that moral responsibility must be inconsistent with a deterministic view of the universe. In this chapter, I shall follow in that long libertarian tradition, and insist, as many others have done, on the incompatibility of moral responsibility and determinism. But if libertarianism is not to be too easily vanquished, I think it is crucially important to be clear about exactly where the source of the incompatibility really lies. Traditionally, the argument for incompatibility has gone by way of the principle that an agent cannot be morally responsible for what she has done unless she could have done otherwise, incompatibilists believing that determinism would be inconsistent with agents possessing this essential power of having done something different. But in recent years, this principle – usually dubbed the Principle of Alternate Possibilities, or PAP – has fallen into widespread disfavour. Harry Frankfurt, in particular, is supposed by many to have shown conclusively, by means of an ingenious counterexample, that the principle is simply not true (Frankfurt

1969). In this paper, though, I shall try to explain why I think the real lesson of Frankfurt's example lies elsewhere. What it shows us is not that moral responsibility is consistent with determinism after all. What it shows is rather that the power to do otherwise which moral responsibility depends upon is not quite the power it has usually been taken to be, and moreover is important for a reason quite different from the one which is usually emphasized. The reason usually emphasized is a moral reason – that it is unfair to hold an agent morally responsible for what she cannot help.[1] But the real reason why determinism and moral responsibility are inconsistent is, I shall argue, not moral, but metaphysical. The real reason is that determinism is inconsistent with *agency*, which is a necessary (though not, of course, a sufficient) condition of moral responsibility.

1. Frankfurt and the Principle of Alternate Possibilities

Let me begin with a quick reminder of Frankfurt's counterexample. We are supposed to imagine an agent, Jones, who is considering doing something – say,

Steward, H. (2011), "Moral Responsibility and the Concept of Agency," in R. Swinburne (ed.), *Free Will and Modern Science* (Oxford: Oxford University Press), 141–157. Reprinted with permission of Oxford University Press.

voting Labour in the forthcoming election. Black, a second agent, would very much like Jones to vote Labour in the election – and, Frankfurt tells us, 'is prepared to go to considerable lengths to get his way' (Frankfurt 1969: p. 356 in this volume). In what has become the most popular version of the case, we are to imagine that Black is an exceedingly clever neurosurgeon who has implanted a device in Jones's brain by which he can monitor Jones's thought processes, and by means of which (we are told) he would also be able to ensure, if necessary, that Jones will decide to vote, and then will vote, as he, Black, wishes.[2] However, Black would also greatly prefer *not* to intervene if there is any hope of avoiding it. He waits, therefore, until Jones is about to make up his mind what to do, scanning Jones's brainwaves by means of his clever device, for signs of the impending decision. If there is any sign that Jones is about to form an intention to vote for anyone else, or to form an intention not to vote at all, Black will intervene at that moment to ensure that Jones instead forms the intention to vote Labour – and will then continue to monitor Jones's thought processes to ensure that he actually follows through in the polling booth. But in fact, in the event, there is no such sign. Jones simply makes up his mind to vote Labour, and then does so unhesitatingly, without Black having had to intervene at all. In this circumstance, Frankfurt argues, we would surely regard Jones as morally responsible for having voted the way he did. After all, in the event, Black did nothing whatever. But it is also true, according to Frankfurt, that Jones could not have done other than vote Labour. For if he had shown any inclination to do anything other than vote Labour, Black would have intervened, and Jones would have ended up voting Labour in any case. The Principle of Alternate Possibilities, then, which says that an agent can be morally responsible for what she has done only if she could have done otherwise, must be false. The power to do otherwise cannot be a necessary condition of moral responsibility.

I will not attempt to offer any kind of comprehensive overview of the vast number of different responses that this purported counterexample to PAP has generated. The provision of such an overview would be too large a task to be confined within the limits of a volume such as this. I want instead to concentrate on developing what I take to be the moral of Frankfurt's story; and though I think my view has certain things in common with various responses which have been made before to Frankfurt's example, it is not quite the same as any of them. Moreover the view I shall outline brings to the surface an important intuition which I think is present, but has often been left submerged in the views of others. I should perhaps say that what I shall offer here is the briefest of brief overviews of a position on free will each of whose parts really needs much more in the way of defence than I am able to provide here. But I hope I shall be able to say enough, at any rate, to make it persuasive that a position with the shape I shall characterize is possible – and that it provides a path worthy of further exploration for the libertarian.

Let us begin, then, by asking why anyone would ever have thought that moral responsibility should require the ability to do otherwise. Here is what I think is a very common line of thought: it would be simply *unfair* to hold anyone responsible for what they cannot help, for doing something they could not have avoided doing. 'I couldn't help it', 'there was no alternative', 'I was forced', etc. are common excuses – and a generalization from these practices of exculpation might make us think that the general principle that a person cannot be held responsible for what they cannot help, for reasons of fairness, was highly plausible. But Frankfurt's argument casts considerable doubt on this line of thinking, as Frankfurt himself was at pains to emphasize in his original article. Jones had (unbeknownst to him) no alternative to voting Labour – there is a sense, then, in which it would be right to say that he could not help doing so – or at any rate, that he could not avoid it.[3] But it does not follow, it seems, that it would not be fair to hold him morally responsible for what he did. For in fact, nothing interfered with his normal processes of deliberation and decision-making. Jones's lack of alternatives in this case seems to have nothing whatever to do with the question whether or not he is responsible for what he does. If the Principle of Alternative Possibilities is to be thought of as based upon these ideas concerning fairness, then, it seems we must reject it. Frankfurt himself claims that 'The doctrine that coercion excludes moral responsibility is not correctly understood … as a particularized version of the principle of alternate possibilities'.[4] That is right – but for my purposes, it is better to put things the other way around. The Principle of Alternate Possibilities is not correctly understood as a generalized version of our principles concerning the unfairness of blame in cases of coercion, psychological compulsion, etc.

How, then, is it to be understood? The suggestion of many writing in the wake of Frankfurt's work, of course, is that it is to be understood simply as a mistaken *over*-generalization from plausible principles of exculpation – an over-generalization which we ought now to reject, having seen that it cannot be maintained – and that with its rejection, compatibilism about moral responsibility and determinism is set fair to triumph, since the condition with which determinism was judged by some to be inconsistent has turned out not to be a necessary condition of moral responsibility after all. But I want here to make a rather different suggestion. In my view, Frankfurt's example merely highlights rather neatly that the Principle of Alternate Possibilities as usually formulated (i.e. as the principle that an agent S is morally responsible for what she has done only if she could have done otherwise) does not properly and unambiguously capture the premise from which the best argument for libertarianism ought to begin. I suggest that in order to arrive at a preferable formulation, rather than beginning with a thought about what fairness demands, we should begin the libertarian argument with a thought about what *agency* requires.

2. Agency and Determinism

To understand how this thought might arise, and to see the intuitions from which it flows, consider for a moment the world as it is supposed to be according to the determinist, a series of events and states of affairs, inexorably superseded by other events and states of affairs, according to ineluctable laws of nature. I suggest that one might well feel that this kind of world is not correctly characterized as a world in which there are agents doing things they could not have avoided doing (as traditional versions of libertarianism tend to suggest). I suggest that this world is best characterized as a world in which there are *no agents at all* – in which there is simply no space whatever for the entities we

think of as agents, entities that things can be *up to*, entities which can hold portions of the fate of the universe in their hands.[5] How can anything be up to an entity in a world where everything is settled by initial conditions and the laws of nature? The compatibilist will attempt to insist that the notion of something's being 'up to' an agent can be reduced to the idea of that thing's being the causal consequence of an (appropriately formed) decision on the part of that agent – one which flows in the right sort of way, say, from her beliefs and desires. But the 'decision' itself, of course, (and the preceding beliefs and desires) are themselves simply further inevitable consequences of initial conditions and laws of nature, which will make someone who is persuaded by the sort of intuitions I am attempting to elicit ask by what right we are to call these things 'decisions' in the first place. What has the *decision-maker* to do with anything, given this picture? What is she able to settle at the time of decision, given that everything is settled already by the initial conditions and the laws? The agent herself as a genuine source of settling seems to vanish from the picture of causality that we are offered, turned into a mere place or vessel where events bring others about.[6] And for this reason, one might well think that in a deterministic world there can be no actions and there can be no agents – and so a fortiori, that there could be nothing that was morally responsible for anything. Moral responsibility is reserved to agents – and so a world which excludes agency is also a world which excludes moral responsibility. In the rest of this chapter, I want to defend this line of thinking – by showing how it is perfectly consistent with our intuitions in the Frankfurt case, by developing a little the conception of agency in question, and finally, by answering what I expect will be the main line of objection to the claim – namely that since we do not know for sure whether or not determinism is true, my view must raise absurd doubts about the very existence of agents.

Let us begin then, by returning to Frankfurt's own example, armed with this new thought about why we might think that moral responsibility is inconsistent with determinism. Why are we so ready to concede that Jones is morally responsible for what he does? Because it is obvious that his actual decision to vote Labour is an exercise of agency.[7] Nothing is lacking to that decision and its mode of formation that would not be a feature of any perfectly ordinary and utterly unfettered instance of decision-making. And since there are no further special responsibility-undermining features in this case, if we are ever morally responsible for making decisions, Jones is responsible for this one. And equally, in the counterfactual situation in which Black is forced to intervene, it is obvious that Jones would not have been responsible for his 'decision'. Why not? Well, because this so-called decision would not have been, in that case, an exercise of agency on his part. It would have been the result of an exercise of agency, rather, on *Black's* part, a fact which makes it, I suggest, problematic to speak, in this case, of Jones's having made a decision at all, even one which was somehow brought about by Black. A decision is a variety of mental action – one which normally consists in putting oneself into a state of intention. But Jones did not put himself into a state of intention in the counterfactual scenario. Black put him (Jones) into a state of intention. It seems to me a mistake, therefore, to say that *Jones* decided anything under these circumstances. And if this is a mistake, that has a bearing on what we ought to say about the *actual* situation. If the counterfactual situation is not one in which Jones decides to vote Labour, then we need to re-evaluate the suggestion that he could not have done other than decide to do this. Had he not thus decided, what would have happened would not have been that Black would have made him decide. What would have happened would have been that Black would have put him into the state of intention that decisions normally effect. But in that case, surely Jones could have refrained from deciding to vote Labour simply by not thus deciding and thereby triggering an intervention by Black. And if he could have thus refrained, then the Frankfurt example is not a counterexample to PAP after all.

This particular way of dealing with alleged Frankfurtian counterexamples to the Principle of Alternate Possibilities will not work quite so neatly as this, unfortunately, in every kind of case. The strategy I have adopted here is dependent on the thing which Jones cannot do other than being a decision. For it is quite plausible that decisions are *essentially* actions (one cannot decide involuntarily or accidentally, for instance)[8] – and hence that nothing can count as A's decision which does not also count as A's action. This is what makes it possible to insist that

the counterfactual scenario is not in fact one in which Jones decides anything at all – and hence, in turn, that the actual situation is not one in which Jones could not have refrained from thus deciding. But many Frankfurt cases relate not to such mental acts as decisions but rather to overt actions like shooting a President, say. And one cannot maintain the principle that one is morally responsible for shooting a President, only if one could have done otherwise in the face of a Frankfurt-style example – for there is no reason to deny that Black *can* make Jones shoot the President. It is not possible to insist that all shootings are essentially actions – for shootings may perfectly well be accidental or involuntary. But though Black can make Jones shoot the President, there remains, I insist, something that Black cannot do. What he cannot do is make Jones shoot the President by directly producing an event that nevertheless still counts as an exercise of agency – as an action – on Jones's part. To coin a bit of terminology – he cannot make Jones shoot$_A$ the President – where to shoot$_A$ is to shoot in such a way that that shooting is *one's own action*.[9]

Why not? On a certain conception of what actions *are*, this might seem puzzling. Actions, it might be said, are just physical events of certain sorts – either bodily movements, or perhaps prior neural events, or perhaps composites of the two. But whatever sort of physical event we decide actions are, there seems no reason to suppose that Black cannot organize for the occurrence of a physical event of that sort. So why can't Black's intervention make it the case that Jones has acted? The answer, I think, is that even if actions are physical events – as I agree, in some sense, they must be – their categorization as *actions on the part of a certain agent* depends not on this physical characterization, but on the relation borne by that agent to the event in question – actions are events that only exist in virtue of the fact that their *agent* has been the source of some input into the world. Actions are the beginnings of causal chains which are initiated by their agents – and so where the initiation of such a chain lies elsewhere than with a given agent, what has occurred cannot be an action *of* that agent. There are therefore conceptual conditions on the classification of any event as an action which are flouted in the case we are asked to imagine by Frankfurt. If an action is essentially an input into the course of nature *by its agent*, then the agent must possess and retain certain capacities in respect of the processes that constitute it – in particular, the bodily systems in question must be ones which are under her control to exert or not exert at the time of action – otherwise, it is not up to her whether or not the action occurs, or how, precisely, it does so; and hence she settles nothing at the time of action. There is a sense, therefore, in which we simply cannot be *directly* manipulated to act, because the manipulation itself contravenes the conditions of agency. Where action is concerned, manipulation is of course possible – but it has to go by way of our motivational systems – we have to be persuaded, cajoled, bribed, guilt-tripped, made offers we can't refuse, etc. But my actions, I suggest, simply cannot be *directly* brought about by others. For no event that is directly brought about by another's action could be an action *of mine*.[10] Though it is not right, then, to uphold the Principle of Alternate Possibilities in its original form – i.e. that an agent is morally responsible for what she has done only if she could have done otherwise – we ought to be able to uphold some version of the following thought, even in the teeth of Frankfurt-style examples – that the existence of an action is always dependent upon the simultaneous possession by the agent of a certain power of refrainment in respect of that action – since nothing in respect of which I do not possess this power of refrainment could count as my action in the first place.

In a moment, I shall move on to say something about this power of refrainment and how it ought to be specified. Before that, though, it will be necessary to address, albeit briefly, a worry many will feel about what I have just said about the concept of an action. I have characterized actions as the beginnings of causal chains which are initiated by their agents. But it will be said that apart from random occurrences, such as, for example, the individual emissions involved in radioactive decay, which surely cannot serve as a model for actions, there are no such things as the beginnings of causal chains – that everything that ever happens in our universe can be traced back to antecedents which produce and explain it. In the next section, I shall question what reason there is to hold this view.

3. Causality, Determinism and the 'Beginnings' of Chains

There will not be space here to say everything I should like to say about the view that there are no such things as the 'beginnings' of causal chains at the macroscopic level, much less adequately to defend what I should like to say.[11] But since it is, I suspect, likely to be the source of much scepticism about the type of view I want to defend, I must say *something*. Suffice it to say, then, that I believe the widespread conviction that (whatever may be the case in the realms of microphysics) at any rate *macrophysical* determinism must be true, is an outdated hangover from Newtonian visions of the universe that we philosophers mostly still remain entranced by, because we have not properly escaped the worldviews encouraged by our school-level maths and physics lessons; and I do not think that we shall ever have an acceptable metaphysics of action until we give it up. Some substances, I should like to insist – the higher animals – have powers to make certain things happen – in particular, changes to the distribution and arrangement of their own bodily parts – in ways not merely dictated by the past and the laws. Perhaps this amounts to a denial of Galen Strawson's claim that nothing can be *causa sui*;[12] though I confess I am not sure about that, because I am not exactly sure what that claim is supposed to imply. That nothing can be the cause of itself seems a reasonable enough claim – but what Strawson's argument seems to need is the stronger claim that nothing can be the cause of that same thing's coming to have a certain property – which seems a much more dubious proposition. At any rate, the idea that animals can make changes happen in the parts of their own bodies is, I think, an ancient and utterly natural view which I believe we have been encouraged to give up by a range of principles which are thought to be in conflict with it: some physical; some metaphysical; some false, like the claim that causal relations are always relations between events; some whose consequences are merely poorly understood, like the conservation laws. None of these principles, though, I believe, is truly justificatory of the idea that there cannot be what I have elsewhere called 'fresh starts'[13] – places in the structure of time and space where things occur which are not wholly attributable to what has gone before.[14] The general idea that perhaps there are some *microphysical* fresh starts is generally accepted by philosophers, inclined to believe that physics requires them because they have been told so. But what philosophers seem to find it very difficult to permit is the idea that there might be such top-down fresh starts as it is pre-theoretically natural to suppose animal actions might be – macroscopic events whereby macroscopic individuals exercise powers to make things happen in their own parts. We are used to supposing that the powers of large things are merely epiphenomenal products of the powers of their small components – as seems broadly to be the case for the mechanical systems we know how to produce. But the idea that this is so is so manifestly at odds, I believe, with the structure of the phenomenon of action that we need to seek a non-mechanistic, though not, for all that, *non-naturalistic* understanding of what biology has managed to accomplish by means of the evolution of animals. An unprejudiced assessment of the facts, it seems to me, suggests that evolution has produced some entities which are able themselves to be the source of outcomes that are not fully determined in all their details by what has gone before, but which are up to the animal to settle at the time of action. I do not say it is easy to come by the emergentist-style metaphysics which might enable us to make sense of this idea. But I do say that it is far more reasonable to suppose that such a metaphysics must be available for the formulating, than to deny the things that would have to be denied were it to be true that the exercise of our agential powers were only epiphenomenal by-products of the hum and buzz of chemical processes taking place amongst our neurons and synapses.

4. The Relevant Power of Refrainment

Let me return, now, though, to the business I left off above, which is the elaboration of my assertion that a certain power of refrainment attends all genuine actions. I think it needs to be admitted straightaway that it is not a simple matter to say what this relevant power of refrainment *is* – what it is that the agent needs to be able to refrain *from*, as it were, if she is genuinely to act. The simple and tempting idea that

in the case of a φ-ing which is an action – i.e. a φ_A-ing – the agent must have been able to refrain *from* φ_A-ing, is clearly wrong, I believe. Counterexamples seem to me to be provided by instances of so-called 'volitional necessity' (Frankfurt 1982: 86). Consider, for instance, a case in which I know that my children are inside a burning house and that there is no hope of their being rescued unless I go in to save them. It might seem right to say that under these circumstances, I am simply not able not to do so – I cannot refrain. But surely, if I do rush in to rescue them, then that is an action of mine – and one, moreover, for which I would clearly be morally responsible.

It might be retorted at this point that the capacity to do otherwise that is relevant to moral responsibility cannot be the kind of capacity that can be rendered ineffectual by the mere strength of an opposing motivation. Thus, for example, one might be inclined to insist that I could (in the relevant sense) have done other than have run into the burning house, even though it might be admitted that there was no realistic possibility whatever, my motivations being what they were, that anything else should have happened. This tends to be what compatibilists sympathetic to some form of the Principle of Alternate Possibilities are wont to say – that the capacity to do otherwise that is relevant to moral responsibility does not depend on the bare possibility that another thing should have happened in the precise circumstances in question, but rather on the agent's abilities thought of in some rather more general way. And thought of in this more general way, it might be said, I continue to possess those capacities – for instance, it might be insisted that I could have stayed put instead of running into the house, on the grounds that there was no one forcing my limbs to move, no external force pulling me along, etc. But though I have some sympathy with this line of thinking, ultimately I think it will not do. It is a rejoinder that underestimates the threat that determinism poses to the very idea of agency – that underestimates the power of the idea that as agents, open possibilities must exist for us at the very moment of action, t – and throughout any period t_j to t_n for which the action persists. Compatibilists are apt to scoff at the suggestion that we might require for freedom the capacity to do something other than what we in fact go on to do, *even given* the set of motivations, reasons, emotions, etc. which attend us at the moment just prior to our action – how could it be important or valuable to us, they ask, to have the capacity to go on to do something that might, in the light of those motivations, reasons, emotions, etc. appear simply insane? It is a powerful point, and I think it ought to be conceded that the libertarian should not insist on this requirement in the form in which it is usually offered. Given alternative courses of action A and B and a set of reasons and motivations clearly favouring A, that is, we ought not to insist that there need be any possibility at the time of action that the free agent undertake course of action B instead. But it does not follow from this concession that no possibilities at all need exist at t of the sort that might make trouble for the compatibilist. A bit of terminology will prove useful here to formulate the claim I want to make. Let us say that an event or state of affairs whose occurrence or obtaining at a given time t is necessitated by certain events and states of affairs prior to t together with the laws of nature is 'historically inevitable'. The claim I want to make is that it is impossible that an event that was historically inevitable could be an action.

Note that the proposition I want to defend is not simply the claim that *facts about what we will do* cannot be historically inevitable, given our motivations and other circumstances. What I have already said implies that such facts may indeed be historically inevitable. It might, for example, be historically inevitable that I will run into the house to rescue my children – that given the way things are with me motivationally speaking at t-1, and given my children's predicament, for example, there is simply no possibility whatever that I will not run in and attempt to rescue them at some time in the vicinity of t. But suppose it were also true that given the way things are at t-1, there is also no possibility that I shall not run in at precisely 10 mph, along precisely the trajectory I in fact take, through the precise door and at the precise time that I do in fact enter the house, making all the precise individual movements that I do in fact make, at precisely the times that I do in fact make them, etc. Then my suggestion is, we would not be able properly to conceive of what had occurred as a sequence which was truly a sequence of *activity* on my part. The concept of an agent is the concept of something that certain things can be *up to*; the concept of a being which can *settle*, at the time of action, how

certain things in the world are to be, in particular, in the first instance, certain things which concern the disposition and movement of parts of her own body. And the concept of an action, I would maintain, is just the concept of a settling of some of these settleable questions by an agent. Not everything about the action has to be up for settling at the time of action – there may be respects in which what will happen is already settled by the time of action – for example, given my motivations and the fact that my children are in a burning house at t-1, it may already be settled that some sort of running-into-the-house on my part is going to happen shortly. But *some* things have to remain unsettled, I claim, if what is to occur is to be an exercise of agency on my part at all. Some of the following sorts of question, for example, have to be not yet settled: precisely which movements I shall make; whether I shall go through the window or the door; whether I shall call out as I run from room to room; whether I shall search the kitchen before or after I search the living room; when precisely the action will occur, etc. For if the precise description of the entirety of a course of action is all settled in advance by the past and the laws, there seems no sense in which its agent can count as the true source of any of that action's outcomes, and hence, no possibility that what brings about those outcomes should be an agent's *acting*. The agent would simply dissolve, under such circumstances, into a location, a place where the relevant inexorable events occur. What we can say, then, is this: that any φ-ing which is an agent's action must have some detailed and specific description as a D-ing, say, such that the agent could have refrained from D-ing. For unless this is the case, there is nothing left for the agent to settle at the time of action, and hence no possibility that what occurred at that time should have been an action at all. It is this, I believe, that constitutes the legitimate truth lurking behind the Principle of Alternate Possibilities. Actions being settlings, some of their features and characteristics must be left for the agent to settle at the time of action. And that is as much as to say that actions cannot be determined events. The reason why moral responsibility is inconsistent with determinism, then, is this: the existence of moral responsibility (for anything) requires the existence of agents who may be held responsible; and the existence of agents requires the falsity of determinism.

5. The Objection from Ignorance

Does this view not imply, though, quite absurdly, that we do not know whether there are any agents? Only if we accept the premise that we do not know whether or not determinism is true. There is a tendency in much recent literature for philosophers to accept that the question whether determinism is true is a scientific question, and that it behoves us to maintain with respect to it that openness of mind that one ought to maintain about questions which it is the job of science to settle. But I should insist rather that the question whether determinism is true is quite plainly a *metaphysical* question, and that philosophical reflection, including, of course, philosophical reflection on the biological phenomenon that is agency, is therefore needed to settle it. In particular, it is not, as many suggest, merely a question for *physicists*, since determinism is a doctrine not merely about the events that come within the purview of physics, but about *all* events, and so one must, at the very least, take a metaphysical view about the dependence of all events on those that belong to physics before the question whether or not determinism is true could even begin to seem as though it might be up for decision within physics. For instance, Fischer claims in a recent work that the doctrine of causal determinism states that:

> for any given time, a complete statement of the (temporally genuine or nonrelational) facts about that time, together with a complete statement of the laws of nature, entails every truth as to what happens after that time. (Fischer 2006: 5)

But a complete statement of the facts about any time must presumably include the biological, psychological, sociological and economic facts, as well as the physical ones – and so it is not *immediately* clear why the truth or otherwise of determinism should be a matter only for physicists to decide. Many believe, of course, that facts of all these various sorts supervene on the physical facts. But first, that is not, in itself, a doctrine of physics, but of metaphysics; and second, even if it is true, it is not clear what follows from it, so far as the claim that the question of determinism is a matter for physicists to decide is concerned. It would seem to follow, admittedly, from supervenience that the truth

or otherwise of determinism generally rests on the truth or otherwise of *physical* determinism. But it is not clear what our intellectual attitude ought to be to this fact. One view might be that we must await the verdict of physicists before we can hope to decide whether or not the universe is deterministic. But one person's modus ponens is another's modus tollens, and so another view might be this: that since we know from reflecting on what we know of the world in general (including the fact, for example, that it contains agents like ourselves) that determinism quite generally is not true, we know *already* that physical determinism cannot be true. And in case this seems like sheer hubris, just reflect for a moment on how much hubris is implicit in the idea that *physics* alone might be what determines the occurrence and precise nature of such things as wars, political decisions, banking crises, epidemics, the distribution of poverty in a society, the reach of democracy on a continent, the composition of individual works of art and literature. If we were not already mesmerized by a Laplacian picture of reality, the claim that this is so would surely strike us as the height of absurdity.

Of course, it cannot be denied that we cannot rule out for certain that physicists might one day show that physical determinism is true – that each physically characterized state of the world necessitates the next. But it does not follow from this that it is absurd to maintain a view according to which, if physical determinism should turn out to be true, agency would be found not to exist. Instead of this, we might surely say the following: that since we are in fact entitled to a very high degree of assurance about the fact that there are agents, we are entitled to a similarly high degree of assurance that determinism is false. Agency refutes it. It is an absolutely basic part of our worldview that by means of their actions, agents settle a range of matters that were hitherto not settled – and how could this be unless determinism were false? We know, then, with a perfectly reasonable degree of assurance that it *is* false. Of course, here as elsewhere in philosophy, the possibility of radical scepticism remains – perhaps it might be maintained that we cannot know for certain that determinism will not turn out to be true, and so that we cannot know for certain that there are any agents. But the scepticism implied here is radical indeed – as radical as wondering about the existence of the external world, or of other minds, say. Agency is part of our fundamental conceptual scheme. It cannot be ruled out that our fundamental conceptual scheme is mistaken, of course.

But how much more likely it should seem to the unprejudiced that we might have made a mistake in formulating the metaphysics that seems to rule it out.

Notes

1. Though people's intuitions that this is so are usually much stronger in the case of blame than they are in the case of praise – one sign, perhaps, that all is not quite right with the traditional line of argument.

2. Later I shall question whether this description of the extent of Black's power over Jones is really coherent.

3. In fact, I think, the much greater naturalness of the latter over the former locution may tell us something. It would be odd, I suggest, to say of Jones, who went ahead and voted Labour in a perfectly ordinary way that he 'couldn't help it'. 'He couldn't help it' is most naturally understood to be a comment on a person's actual action – not a remark concerning their overall modal situation – and thus understood, it seems inappropriate to use it of Jones, whose actual action was (we may suppose for the sake of argument) fully deliberate and entirely voluntary. What this fact usefully reveals is that – *pace* Frankfurt – we sometimes want to speak of a person's powers in relation to something *particular* – the event which is their action or movement itself – not merely in respect of something general – their act considered as a *type*. Jones could not have avoided voting Labour (the 'act type'). But *this* act of voting (it) was arguably something he could have helped. This distinction between types of action and particular doings is a distinction which my view exploits – as will shortly be seen.

4. Frankfurt (1969: p. 354 in this volume).

5. It has been suggested to me that perhaps the claim that an agent must be the sort of thing that various matters can be 'up to' already begs the question against the compatibilist – and that it would be less tendentious merely to say that an agent is something that can act. But to say that an agent is something that can act does nothing other than to connect a noun to an associated verb, and merely raises the question which things may be said to *act*. Can a wave act? Or a computer? If not, why not? It might perhaps be said that actions are events which are caused by appropriate types of mental event or state – things like decisions and intentions. But this merely pushes the question back. We now need to know to which things we are genuinely entitled to take what Dennett (1971, 1987) has called the intentional stance – to which things we may apply various of the psychological concepts by means of which we organize our understanding of certain of the entities we come across in the world. I should want to claim that the answer to this question is that we are truly entitled to take the stance – and to construe it realistically – towards all and only entities which are such that things can be up to them, because this sort of representational psychology is only truly essential to the explanation of a thing's activity if things may conceivably be settled *by* that entity in the light of what it thinks and wants – and thus that we have come full circle to the principle that agents are entities that certain matters can be up to.

   These claims about the connections that exist between folk psychology, agency and the power to settle things (to have things be 'up to' one) are controversial, of course, and I cannot properly defend them here against all comers. But the charge specifically of begging the question against the compatibilist must be refuted. The best way to refute it, I believe, is to argue that even if it is thought that the conception of agency which is in play here is implausibly rich, there can be nothing implausible about the idea that various matters have to be up to beings which possess those powers constitutive of a much more traditional candidate for compatibilist rescue – *free will*. If compatibilism is to be worthy of its name, then what it finds to be compatible with determinism must be something worth having. Free will of a sort which is consistent with things *not* being up to me seems scarcely worth wanting – it certainly seems most unlikely that any such power could underpin moral responsibility. The issue, then, is not (as the charge of question-begging suggests) whether the compatibilist should want her compatibilism to validate the claim that (certain) things are up to us; clearly, she should want this. The issue is whether the compatibilist *can* validate the claim. Any compatibilist worth her salt, I believe, will think she can do so. I shall be claiming below, of course, that she cannot – but *this* is the issue and no question has been begged against compatibilism by the assumption that 'up-to-usness' is part of what it needs to save.

6. It might be said that it is not the determinism as such that makes for the difficulty here – and in a sense that is

right, since certain sorts of *in*deterministic picture would certainly not help to solve the problem. But as I see it, there are varieties of indeterministic picture that *do* solve it; but no varieties of deterministic picture that do. When it is said that indeterminism is of no help to those in search of free will, that is because only the unhelpful pictures (involving, e.g., mere microphysical randomness) are in view.

7. Of course, we can be morally responsible for all sorts of things which are not *themselves* exercises of agency – such as beliefs, states of affairs, character traits, etc. But I think we can only coherently be held responsible for these other things if we can be held to have powers of agency which relate to them – for instance, that I can *examine* my beliefs and subject them to scrutiny; I can *alter* certain states of affairs; I can *transform* my character in various respects. Where such powers as these are imagined to be entirely lacking, it does not seem plausible any longer to hold an agent responsible for the things in question.

8. Matters pertaining to the *content* of the decision can be accidental, of course. For instance, I could decide accidentally to shoot my mother, by deciding to shoot the person who has just knocked at my door (not realizing that the person who has just knocked at my door is my mother). But the occurrence of the decision itself cannot be something that is accidental. That I have decided (something) cannot be an accident. That I have shot someone can be.

9. Might it be said that the alternate possibility which I have alleged remains available to Jones – the power not to *act* in the way in which he did in fact act – is insufficiently 'robust' to do the work required of it here? (See Fischer (1994) for the original 'robustness' objection.) Full details of my response to this challenge can be found in Steward (2009), but in brief, my claims there are as follows. A number of quite separate demands on the wielder of PAP have been made in the name of 'robustness', some more readily justifiable

than others, and it is essential to be clear about which of these demands is truly legitimate. I recognize two valid concerns: (i) whatever Principle of Alternate Possibilities is endorsed by the libertarian, it should be a principle which there is at least some *prima facie* temptation to endorse, whether one is a libertarian or not; and (ii) whatever alternate possibility is alleged to exist in a Frankfurt case, it must be an alternate possibility which it is within the power of the agent to bring about, not merely an alternative outcome which might have happened. Both these concerns are met by my view. The principle on which I rely below is one which says that an agent S is morally responsible for φ-ing only if her actual φ-ing has some detailed and specific description as a D-ing, say, such that the agent could have refrained from D-ing (because only thus could her φ-ing have been an action in the first place). I believe (and argue in the chapter) that this admittedly unwieldy formulation relies in fact on a very intuitive conception of action which compatibilists as well as libertarians might have reason to want to endorse; a conception which insists that the power to act involves the power to refrain. There is evidence in the work of such classical compatibilists as Hobbes and Hume of an acceptance of this conception of action; thus concern (i) is met. And in the case described above, Jones genuinely has it within his power to refrain from *acting* in the way he does – which demonstrates that concern (ii) is also met.

10. See Alvarez (2009) for a similar view.

11. I have made a start on the defence elsewhere – see Steward (2008).

12. See Chapter 35 in this volume.

13. Following Ross (1924: lxxxi).

14. The word 'wholly' is important here. Causal *influence* is perfectly consistent with the existence of what I am here calling 'fresh starts'. What is necessary for a fresh start is only that what happens should not be *wholly* settled by what has gone before.

References

Alvarez, Maria (2009) Actions, thought experiments and the 'Principle of Alternate Possibilities', *Australasian Journal of Philosophy*, 87: 61–82.

Dennett, Daniel (1971) Intentional systems, *Journal of Philosophy*, 8: 87–106.

Dennett, Daniel (1987) *The Intentional Stance*, Cambridge, MA: MIT Press.

Fischer, John Martin (1994) *The Metaphysics of Free Will*, Oxford: Blackwell.

Fischer, John Martin (2006) *My Way*, Oxford: Oxford University Press.

Frankfurt, H. (1969) Alternate possibilities and moral responsibility, Chapter 33 in this volume.

Frankfurt, H. (1982) 'The importance of what we care about, *Synthese*, 53: 257–72, reprinted in Frankfurt (1988): 80–94.

Frankfurt, Harry (1988) *The Importance of What We Care About: Philosophical Essays*, Cambridge and New York: Cambridge University Press.

Ross, W.D. (1924) Introduction to *Aristotle's Metaphysics* Vol. 1, Oxford: Clarendon.

Sartre, J.-P. (1958) *Being and Nothingness*, trans. Hazel E. Barnes, London: Methuen.

Steward, Helen (2008) Fresh starts, *Proceedings of the Aristotelian Society*, 108: 197–217.

Steward, Helen (2009) Fairness, agency and the flicker of freedom, *Nous*, 43: 64–93.

37

Free Will and Science

Alfred R. Mele

ONE argument for skepticism about free will features the belief – defended by Daniel Wegner (2002, 2008) and Benjamin Libet (1985, 2004), among others – that conscious intentions (and their physical correlates) never play a role in producing corresponding overt actions.[1] This chapter examines alleged scientific evidence for the truth of this belief and reviews some recent philosophical work on this alleged evidence.

Because the expression "neural correlate" is used in various distinct senses in the literature, I avoid it here. "Physical correlate" is, I hope, a relatively innocuous technical term. From a physicalist, neuroscientific point of view, proof that the physical correlates of, for example, a particular intention were among the causes of a particular action constitutes proof that the intention was among the causes of the action. It is primarily philosophers who would worry about the metaphysical intricacies of the mind-body problem despite accepting the imagined proof about physical correlates, and the relevant argumentation would be distinctly philosophical.[2] In this chapter, I focus on empirical work at the expense of metaphysics.

Mele, A. R. (2011), "Free Will and Science," in R. Kane (ed.), *The Oxford Handbook of Free Will*, 2nd edn. (Oxford: Oxford University Press), 499–514. Reprinted with permission of Oxford University Press.

Libet's Work: Introduction

Libet (1985, 536) contends both that "the brain 'decides' to initiate or, at least, prepare to initiate [certain actions] before there is any reportable subjective awareness that such a decision has taken place"[3] and that "If the 'act now' process is initiated unconsciously, then conscious free will is not doing it" (Libet 2001, 62; also see 2004, 136). He also contends that once we become aware of these decisions, we can exercise free will in vetoing them (Libet 2004, 137–49). Libet has many critics and many supporters. Some people follow him part of the way: They accept the thesis about when and how decisions are made but reject the window of opportunity for free will as illusory (Wegner 2002, 55; Hallett 2007).

In some of Libet's studies, subjects are regularly encouraged to flex their right wrists whenever they wish. In subjects who do not report any "preplanning" of flexings, electrical readings from the scalp (EEGs) – averaging over at least forty flexings for each subject – show a shift in "readiness potentials" (RPs) that begins about 550 milliseconds (ms) before the time at which an electromyogram (EMG) shows relevant muscular motion to begin (Libet 1985, 529–30). These are "type II RPs" (531). Subjects who are not regularly encouraged to act spontaneously or who report some preplanning produce RPs that begin about half a second earlier – "type I RPs." The same is true of subjects instructed to flex at a "preset" time

(Libet, Wright, and Gleason 1982, 325). (According to a common use of "readiness potential" [RP], it is a measure of activity in the motor cortex that precedes voluntary muscle motion and, by definition, EEGs generated in situations in which there is no muscle burst do not count as RPs. Libet's use of the term is broader. For example, because there is no muscle burst in the veto experiment described later, some scientists would not refer to what Libet calls "the 'veto' RP" [538] as an RP.)

Subjects are also instructed to "recall ... the spatial clock position of a revolving spot at the time of [their] initial awareness" (Libet 1985, 529) of something (x) that Libet variously describes as a decision, intention, urge, wanting, will, or wish to move.[4] (The spot makes a complete revolution in under three seconds.) On average, in the case of type II RPs, "RP onset" precedes what subjects report to be the time of their initial awareness of x (time W) by 350 ms. Reported time W, therefore, precedes the beginning of muscle motion by about 200 ms. The results may be represented as follows:

Libet's results for type II RPs

time:	−550 ms	−200 ms	0 ms
	RP onset	reported time W	muscle begins to move

(Libet [1985, 531, 534] finds evidence of what he regards as an error in subjects' recall of the times at which they first become aware of sensations. Correcting for it, time W is −150 ms.)

Again, in Libet's view, consciousness opens a tiny window of opportunity for free will in his subjects. If a subject becomes aware of his decision or intention at −150 ms, and if by −50 ms his condition is such that "the act goes to completion with no possibility of its being stopped by the rest of the cerebral cortex" (Libet 2004, 138), his window is open for 100 ms. Libet (1999, 54) writes: "The role of conscious free will [is] not to initiate a voluntary act, but rather to control whether the act takes place. We may view the unconscious initiatives as 'bubbling up' in the brain. The conscious-will then selects which of these initiatives may go forward to an action or which ones to

veto and abort." His position on vetoing is discussed below ("Vetoing and Free Will").

Some Conceptual Background

A sketch of some conceptual background will facilitate an assessment of Libet's work. I start with the concept of deciding to do something (i.e., "practical deciding"). (Deciding that something is true [i.e., "propositional deciding"] is a distinct phenomenon.) Like many philosophers, I take "deciding to A" to be an action – as I see it, a momentary action of forming an intention to A (Mele 2003, ch. 9). The momentary action is, more fully, a mental action of "executive assent to a first-person plan of action" (210), in which the plan may be as simple as a prospective representation of flexing one's right wrist. Deliberating about what to do is not a momentary action, but it must be distinguished from an act of deciding that is based on deliberation.

This conception of practical deciding does not entail that all intentions are formed in acts of deciding. In fact, many intentions seem to be acquired without being so formed. For example, when Al unlocked his office door this morning, he intended to unlock it. But because he is in the habit of unlocking his door in the morning and conditions were normal, nothing called for a decision to unlock it. If Al had heard a fight in his office, he might have paused to consider whether to unlock the door or walk away, and he might have decided to unlock it. But given the routine nature of his conduct, there is no need to posit an action of intention formation in this case. His intention to unlock the door may have arisen without having been actively formed. If, as I believe, all decisions about what to do are prompted partly by uncertainty about what to do (Mele 2003, ch. 9), in situations in which there is no such uncertainty, no decisions will be made. Even so, intentions may be acquired in these situations.

Some decisions and intentions are about things to do straightaway. They are "proximal" decisions and intentions. Others – "distal" decisions and intentions – are about things to do later. Al's decision to phone Bob now is a proximal decision; his decision to phone Beth tomorrow evening is a distal decision. The scientific work on decisions and intentions to be discussed here focuses on the proximal variety.

Deciding to do something should be distinguished from wanting (or having an urge) to do it. Sometimes people want to do things that they decide not to do. And often, when people want to do each of two incompatible things – for example, meet some friends for lunch at noon and go to class at noon – they settle matters by deciding which one to do. Just as deciding should be distinguished from wanting, so should intending. Intending to do something is more tightly connected to action than is merely wanting to do it.

The account of practical deciding sketched here is not the only one in the philosophical literature. (For critical discussion of alternative accounts, see Mele [2003, ch. 9].) For present purposes, a virtue of the account just sketched is that it is consonant with Libet's apparent conception of practical deciding.

Type II RPs, Conscious Decisions, and Actions

A brief description of my own experience as a subject in a Libet-style experiment will give readers a better feel for the subjects' task. I wanted to conduct myself as a naïve subject might. My plan included waiting for something like a conscious proximal urge to flex to emerge and flexing in response to it. Of course, I also planned to attend to the clock and to report, after flexing, where I believed the revolving spot was when my conscious urge emerged. However, because conscious proximal urges to flex did not emerge in me, I altered my plan. My new plan was to say "now!" silently to myself, to flex straightaway in response to that silent speech act, and then, after flexing, to report where I thought the spot was when I said "now!" (I reported on this by moving a cursor to a point on the clock.)

I thought of the "now!" as being in the imperative mood. I thought of my conscious "now!"-sayings as conscious self-commands and as expressions of conscious proximal decisions to flex. *Must* I have been wrong about that? If I proximally decided to flex, must I have done that unconsciously? Here one must be careful not to confuse unconsciousness of *causes* of a decision with unconsciousness of the decision. As it

happens, I believe that all actions – including decisions – are caused (Mele 2003). If I had been asked what caused my proximal decisions to flex, I would not have said "nothing." I might have mentioned some relevant factors: for example, my desire to have a relevant conscious event to report after each flexing and my desire to wait only a few seconds between flexings. But I certainly would have admitted that I did not experience anything as a proximal cause of any of my "now!"-sayings (or conscious proximal decisions to flex, if that is what my "now!"-sayings expressed). The point to be emphasized is that this is compatible with my having consciously proximally decided to flex. I consciously said "now!" to myself (many times); and my not being conscious of the proximal causes of those silent speech acts does not prevent those speech acts from expressing decisions I was consciously making at the time. (For a model of conscious deciding, see Mele [2009, 40–44].)

As Daniel Dennett (2003, 228–42) observes, Libet's subjects must deal with pairs of conscious experiences in their reporting task. In my case, for example, the pairs were composed of conscious experiences of saying "now!" and conscious experiences of clock positions of the revolving spot. Dennett believes that the type II RP "is a highly reliable predictor" of flexing (229), and he contends that it is possible that Libet's subjects were conscious at −550 ms of their decisions to flex and that, owing partly to their having to keep track of and compare a pair of experiences, it seemed to them as though they were first conscious of the decisions around −200 ms (234–36). (For reply to an earlier suggestion by Dennett along these lines, see Libet [2004, 59–67]. For a discussion of grounds for skepticism about the accuracy of subjects reports about when they became conscious of their proximal decisions or intentions, see Mele [2009, ch. 6].)

Even if, as Dennett (2003, 229) says, the type II RP, which begins at −550 ms, is "a highly reliable predictor" of flexing, is the brain activity registered by, say, the first 300 ms of this RP – call it "type 300 activity" – a highly reliable predictor of a flexing action or even a muscle burst? In fact, this is not known. In the experiments that yield Libet's type II RPs, it is the muscle burst that triggers a computer to make a record of the preceding brain activity. In the absence of a muscle burst, there is no record of that activity.

So, for all anyone knows, there were many occasions on which type 300 activity occurred in Libet's subjects and there was no associated muscle burst. Some of his subjects reported spontaneously suppressing or aborting (i.e., vetoing, in his terminology) conscious urges to flex. As Libet (2004, 141) points out, "In the absence of the muscle's electrical signal when being activated, there was no trigger to initiate the computer's recording of any RP that may have preceded the veto." So, for all anyone knows, type 300 activity was present before the urges were suppressed.

Notice that it is *urges* that these subjects are said to report and suppress. Might it be that type 300 activity is a potential cause of conscious urges to flex in Libet's subjects and some subjects make no decision about when to flex – unconsciously or otherwise – until after the conscious urge emerges? And might it be that prior to the emergence of the conscious urge, these subjects have no proximal intention to flex – not even an unconscious one? That our urges often are generated by processes of which we are not conscious is not surprising. And if we sometimes make effective decisions about whether or not to act on a conscious urge, so much the better for free will.

Someone who is confident that the brain events indicated by the first few milliseconds of a type II RP or by type 300 activity are reliably associated with a muscle burst at 0 ms might be attracted to Libet's claim that unconscious decisions to flex are made at −550 ms or to Dennett's (2003) suggestion that decisions are made consciously at that time. However, in light of the point just made about how the EEG data are gathered, this confidence obviously is misplaced.

How might one get evidence about whether the onset of the type II RPs at −550 ms is correlated with (unconscious) proximal decisions to flex or instead, for example, with potential causes of proximal decisions or intentions to flex (as suggested in Mele [2009, chs. 3,4])? An apt question to ask in this connection is how long it takes a proximal intention to flex to generate a muscle burst. If, in fact, the brain produces proximal decisions or intentions in Libet's study about 550 ms before the muscle burst, then in his subjects it takes those decisions or intentions about 550 ms to produce a muscle burst. Is this a realistic figure?

Some reaction time studies provide relevant evidence. In one study in which subjects are watching a

Libet clock, the mean time between the sounding of the "go signal" and the muscle burst is 231 ms (Haggard and Magno 1999, 104). The subjects are instructed to respond as rapidly as possible to the "go signal" by pressing a button. If detection of the "go signal" produces a proximal intention to press the button, then the mean time between a subject's acquiring a proximal intention to press and the muscle burst is less than 231 ms. (Detecting a "go signal" takes time.) Notice how close this is to Libet's time W – his subjects' reported time of their initial awareness of something he variously describes as an intention, urge, wanting, decision, will, or wish to move (−200 ms). Even without putting much weight on the exact number (231 ms), one can fairly observe that if proximal intentions to flex are acquired in Libet's studies, the finding just reported makes it look like a much better bet that they are acquired around time W than that they are acquired around −550 ms.

Someone might object that in reaction time studies, muscle bursts and actions are not produced by proximal intentions but by something else. It may be claimed, for example, that the combination of subjects' "conditional intentions" to press whenever they detect the "go signal" together with their detecting it produces muscle bursts and pressings without the assistance of proximal intentions to press. But if this claim is accepted, a parallel claim about Libet's studies should be taken seriously. The parallel claim is that, in Libet's studies, muscle bursts and actions are not produced by proximal intentions but by the combination of subjects' conditional intentions to flex whenever they detect a conscious proximal urge to flex together with their detecting such an urge. (In my case, the operative conditional intention might have been to flex whenever I said "now!") Someone who makes this claim may hypothesize that the onset of the type II RPs at −550 ms is correlated with a potential cause of a conscious proximal urge to flex (or of a conscious "now" -saying, in my case). Libet's findings do not contradict this hypothesis.

Someone may contend that even if type 300 activity is a potential cause of a conscious proximal decision to flex and such a decision precedes a muscle burst by, say, 150 to 200 ms, that decision is not among the causes of the flexing. Some ways of defending this contention definitely fail. Roediger, Goode, and

Zaromb (2008, 208) write: "Clearly conscious intention cannot cause an action if a neural event that precedes and correlates with the action comes before conscious intention." This claim is surprising. Consider the following claim: Clearly, the burning of a fuse cannot cause an explosion of a firecracker if a lighting of a fuse that precedes and correlates with the explosion comes before the burning of the fuse. Obviously, both the lighting of the fuse and the burning of the fuse are among the causes of the explosion. Other things being equal, if the fuse had not been lit – or if the lit fuse had stopped burning early – there would have been no explosion. The surprising claim by Roediger, Goode, and Zaromb cannot undermine the hypothesis (Pacherie 2006, 162) that conscious proximal intentions to flex are part of the causal chain leading to the flexings of Libet's subjects.

Even if the claim that Libet's subjects have proximal intentions to flex before they think they do is not warranted by Libet's data, his idea that people have unconscious proximal intentions merits attention. Some psychologists view unconscious intentions as conceptually impossible (Wegner 2002, 18), and others disagree (Marcel 2003). I myself accept the existence of unconscious proximal intentions (Mele 2009; also see Nahmias 2005, 782). Unconscious proximal intentions may be at work when, for example, experienced drivers flip their turn indicators to signal for turns they are about to make. In a study in which subjects are instructed to flex whenever they feel like it *without also being instructed* to report after flexing on when they first became aware of a relevant intention, urge, or whatever, would they often be conscious of proximal intentions (or urges) to flex? Might unconscious proximal intentions to flex – and, more specifically, proximal intentions of which they are never conscious – be at work in producing flexings in the imagined scenario?

Imagine that the experiment just sketched is conducted and it is discovered (somehow) that the subjects were never or rarely conscious of proximal urges or intentions to flex.[5] Could one legitimately infer that, in Libet's own experiment, conscious urges, decisions, and intentions never or rarely had an effect on the flexings? No. One possibility is that some of Libet's subjects treat their initial consciousness of an urge to flex as a "go signal" (as suggested in Keller and

Heckhausen 1990, 352). If they do, the conscious urge seemingly has a place in the causal process that issues in the flexing. Another possibility is that some subjects treat the conscious urge as what may be called a "decide signal" – a signal calling for them consciously to decide right then whether to flex right away or to wait a while. If that is so, and if they consciously decide to flex and execute that decision, the conscious urge again seemingly has a place in the causal process, as does the conscious decision.

Perhaps it will be suggested that even if a subject treats a conscious urge to flex as a "go" or "decide signal," that urge has no place in the causal process that issues in a flexing because "a neural event that precedes and correlates with the action comes before" the conscious urge (Roediger, Goode, and Zaromb 2008, 208). But the suggestion here suffers from the same problem as the surprising claim about "conscious intention" discussed earlier. Possibly, it will be claimed that by the time the conscious urge emerges it is too late for the subject to refrain from acting on it (something that Libet denies) and that is why the conscious urge should not be seen as part of the process at issue, even if subjects think they are treating the urge as a "go" or "decide signal." One way to get evidence about this (suggested in Mele 2009, 75–76) is to conduct an experiment in which subjects are instructed to flex at time *t unless* they detect a "stop signal." (On "stop signal" experiments, see Logan 1994.) By varying the interval between the "stop signal" and the mean time of the completion of a full flex when there is no "stop signal" experimenters can try to ascertain when subjects reach the point of no return.[6]

Vetoing and Free Will

This section begins with a discussion of some of Libet's ideas about vetoing and ends with a discussion of the bearing of his data on the question whether people ever act freely. Along the way, another problem emerges for Libet's contention that unconscious decisions are made or unconscious intentions acquired at around −550 ms in studies that yield type II RPs.

Libet (1999, 52) discusses "the possibility that the conscious veto itself may have its origin in preceding unconscious processes, just as is the case for the development and appearance of the conscious will." If having such an origin renders the proximal decision to flex unfree and the (decision to) veto has an origin of the same kind, its origin would seem to render it unfree. Libet contends that although "factors on which the decision to veto … is *based*" may "develop by unconscious processes that precede the veto … the *conscious decision to veto* could still be made without direct specification for that decision by the preceding unconscious processes" (53, emphasis in original). He also asserts that the "decision to veto" might not "require preceding unconscious processes." Libet seems to be making two suggestions: first, although free decisions to veto have unconscious processes among their causes, these decisions are *not deterministically caused;* second, free decisions to veto are *not causally dependent* on "preceding unconscious processes."

Libet (1985) mentions what he regards as two sources of evidence for veto power. The first is an experiment in which subjects are instructed to prepare to flex their fingers at a prearranged clock time but to refrain from actually flexing and "to veto the developing intention/preparation to act … about 100 to 200 ms before [that] time" (538). The second is subjects' reports about unsolicited vetoing. Subjects encouraged to flex spontaneously (in nonveto experiments) "reported that during some of the trials a recallable conscious urge to act appeared but was 'aborted' or somehow suppressed before any actual movement occurred; in such cases the subject simply waited for another urge to appear, which, when consummated, constituted the actual event whose RP was recorded" (538). No record was made of brain activity associated with suppressed urges for a reason explained above.

The results of Libet's (1985) veto study suggest an interpretation of type I and type II RPs that is contrary to his own interpretation of them. As a first step toward seeing why, notice that Libet's claim that the subjects in this study veto "*intended* motor action" (38; emphasis added) is implausible (see Mele 1997, 322; 2009, 52–53). These subjects were instructed in advance *not* to flex, but to prepare to flex at the prearranged time and to "veto" this. The subjects intentionally complied with the request. They intended from the beginning not to flex at the appointed time. So what is indicated by what Libet

refers to as "the 'veto' RP" before "about 150–250 ms before the preset time" (Libet 1985, 538)? Presumably, not the acquisition or presence of an *intention* to flex; for then, at some point in time, the subjects would have both an intention to flex at the prearranged time and an intention not to flex at that time. And how can a normal agent simultaneously be settled on A-ing at t and settled on not A-ing at t?[7]

A segment of "the 'veto' RP" resembles segments of type I RPs in cases in which subjects do flex, as Libet (1985, 538) observes. Given that this segment of "the 'veto' RP" is not correlated with a proximal intention to flex, perhaps the similar segments of type I RPs (and of type II RPs) also are not correlated with proximal intentions to flex. Even so, they might be correlated with potential causes of such intentions.

This idea is developed in Mele (2006, 2009). The shape the idea takes there is based partly on the following possibilities about subjects in the veto experiment:

> perhaps a subject's wanting to comply with the instructions – including the instruction to prepare to flex at the appointed time – together with his recognition that the time is approaching produces an unconscious urge to flex soon, a pretty reliable causal contributor to an urge to flex soon, or the motor preparedness typically associated with such an urge. Things of these kinds are potential causal contributors to the acquisition of proximal intentions to flex. A related possibility is suggested by the observation that "the pattern of brain activity associated with imagining making a movement is very similar to the pattern of activity associated with preparing to make a movement" (Spence and Frith 1999, 27).[8] The instructions given to [the subjects in the veto experiment] would naturally elicit imagining flexing very soon, an event of a kind suitable, in the circumstances, for making a causal contribution to the emergence of a proximal urge to flex. (Mele 2009, 55)

The suggestion is that these same items – as opposed to proximal intentions to flex – are candidates for what the pertinent segments of type I RPs signify and that proximal intentions to flex emerge later, both in the case of flexings associated with type I RPs and in the case of flexings associated with type II RPs (Mele 2009, ch. 3). And again, the reaction time study discussed earlier provides independent evidence about when proximal intentions emerge that places their emergence much closer to the muscle burst than −550 ms. (For new evidence, see Trevena and Miller [2010].)

How might Libet's studies bear on free will? In instances of what has been termed "the liberty of indifference," agents are, in Kane's (1996, 108) words, "equally attracted to more than one option." For example, Ann may be equally attracted to the corn flakes and the wheat flakes on her breakfast menu. Arguably, she may freely choose one of the two items even though nothing important hinges on her choice. The choice of a moment to begin flexing from among an array of similar moments may be similar enough to a choice of cereal in an instance of the liberty of indifference that theorists who see the latter choice as possibly free may take the same view about the former choice. On a latitudinarian conception of free will, Libet's studies may have some bearing on free will. Of course, even if they do, their bearing may be restricted to a relatively unimpressive range of free decisions − free proximal decisions in the sphere of the liberty of indifference (see Mele 2009, ch. 4). Generalizing from results obtained in this domain to, for example, a view about distal decisions made about important issues in situations of a very different kind would be extremely bold, to say the least. Even so, Libet (1985) is inclined to generalize: "our overall findings do suggest some fundamental characteristics of the simpler acts that may be applicable to all consciously intended acts and even to responsibility and free will" (563).

Wegner's Work: Introduction

Daniel Wegner attempts to support his claim that conscious intentions are not among the causes of corresponding actions in two general ways. One line of argument features Libet's studies. The other, as Richard Holton (2004, 219) interprets it, "is a version of the argument from illusion." Because I discussed Libet's work at length in previous sections, I focus on Wegner's second line of argument here. If Wegner is right about conscious intentions, then if only beings whose conscious intentions sometimes are among the causes of corresponding actions are capable of acting freely, free will is an illusion.

A variety of studies provide evidence that, in some circumstances, people are not conscious of some of their actions; in others, people believe they intentionally did things that, in fact, they did not do; and in yet others, people do things "automatically" and for no good reason. This section reviews some such findings. Assessment of their implications is reserved for subsequent sections. Some background on epiphenomenalism sets the stage.

The thesis that although all mental events are caused by physical events, no mental events are among the causes of any physical events may be termed "philosophical epiphenomenalism." Some scientists appeal to findings of the sort to be reviewed here to support what they call "epiphenomenalism" about intentions. However, what they mean by this word in this connection is not what philosophers mean by it (see Bayne 2006, 182; Hohwy 2004, 395–96; Holton 2004, 219; Nahmias 2002, 530, 537). Attention to the difference helps forestall confusion.

Let "proximal intentions★" name a collection composed of proximal intentions, their acquisition, and their persistence. Suppose that all proximal intentions★ are caused by physical events but no proximal intentions★ are among the causes of any physical events. Suppose also that physical correlates of proximal intentions★ sometimes are among the causes of physical events − for example, bodily motions involved in overt intentional actions. Although this pair of suppositions does not contradict philosophical epiphenomenalism, it does contradict a scientific epiphenomenalism according to which neither proximal intentions★ nor their physical correlates are among the causes of bodily motions. The scientific epiphenomenalism at issue here extends to the physical correlates of proximal intentions★: The claim at issue is that neither proximal intentions★ nor their physical correlates are among the causes of physical events that proximal intentions★ are thought to cause − those involved in corresponding overt intentional actions.

I turn to data. Wegner (2002, 195) discusses the practice of "facilitated communication," in which a "trained facilitator" holds the hand of "an impaired client … at a computer keyboard." The clients are people with disorders that hamper speech, such as autism or cerebral palsy. Facilitators are supposed to help clients express themselves without influencing which keys they press or touch, and there is considerable evidence that this is what many of the facilitators intended to do and believed they were doing. "It was often [apparently] found that individuals who had never said a word in their lives were quickly able to communicate, typing out meaningful sentences and even lengthy reports" (196). But it was discovered that the clients' "responses actually originate with the facilitators themselves" (197). The facilitators controlled what was typed – without realizing that.

Some actions that people do not realize they are performing are detectable with sensitive devices. Wegner (2002, 122) mentions studies done in the late nineteenth century with an automatograph, a device consisting of "a piece of plate glass resting in a wooden frame, topped by three brass balls, upon which rested another glass plate." There also is a screen between the participant and a recording device that is attached to the automatograph. Wegner reports "some remarkable regularities" (123). "Asked to count the clicks of a metronome, ... one person showed small hand movements to and fro in time with the rhythm." Someone "asked to think of a building to his left ... slowly moved his hand in that direction." A man who was invited to hide a knife in the room and then told to think about the object moved his hand in the knife's direction "over the course of some 30 seconds."

People suffering from a certain kind of damage to the frontal lobes display "utilization behavior" (Lhermitte 1983). An examiner touches a brain-damaged patient's hands with an empty glass and a pitcher of water or a pack of cigarettes and a lighter (Wegner 2002, 122). "The frontal-damage patients may grasp the glass and pour it full from the carafe" or light a cigarette. "One patient given three pairs of eyeglasses donned them in sequence and ended up wearing all three." Wegner writes: "it is as though ... the idea of the act that is suggested by the object is enough to instigate the action." The actions at least resemble automatisms.

In some experimental situations, people are caused to believe that they intentionally did things they did not in fact do. In one study (Wegner and Wheatley 1999), a confederate and a subject, both of whom are wearing headphones, jointly operate a computer mouse on which "a 12-centimeter square board" is mounted (487). About fifty tiny objects are displayed

on a computer monitor, and the mouse controls the movement of a cursor over the display. Subjects are asked how much they "intended" to make a stop of the cursor on an image (488). When subjects hear the name of an image in the display (e.g., "swan") very shortly before the cursor stops on that image, they give, on average, a higher "intended" rating to the stop than they do under other conditions, even though, in fact, the confederate is stopping the cursor on that image. (For an instructive critique of this study, see Malle 2006, 223–24.)

Studies and findings such as the ones described here are sometimes taken to support the claim that actions never have conscious proximal intentions⋆ or their physical correlates among their causes. This is the thesis of "scientific epiphenomenalism" about conscious proximal intentions⋆. Now, it is true that the studies and findings indicate that people sometimes perform actions of which they are not conscious, sometimes do things for no good reason, and sometimes believe they intentionally did things they did not actually do. But how are these truths supposed to lead to scientific epiphenomenalism about conscious proximal intentions⋆?

One route that Wegner (2002, 144) maps features the proposition that all actions are caused in basically the same way. If some actions are performed in the absence of conscious intentions to perform them and all actions are caused in basically the same way, that basic way includes neither conscious intentions to perform the actions at issue nor the physical correlates of such intentions. (Only existing conscious intentions have existing physical correlates.) Why then do we even have conscious intentions? Why did we evolve in such a way as to have them? Wegner's (341) reply is that we have conscious intentions because they give us a sense of which of the things we do we are responsible for.

Whether all actions are caused in basically the same way depends on how "basically the same way" is to be read. For example, if what is meant is simply that all actions have brain events among their causes, the claim is true (in my opinion). But, of course, this leaves it open that some of the brain events that are among the causes of some actions are physical correlates of conscious intentions to perform actions of those kinds. Wegner means something much more specific – that just as people who unknowingly move a hand slowly in the direction of an object they are thinking about are caused to do so by automatic processes of which they are unaware, all actions are caused by, and only by, such processes. Wegner (2002, 97) reports that his "analysis suggests that the real causal mechanisms underlying behavior are never present in consciousness." As usual, he has the relatively proximal causes of behavior in mind (see Nahmias 2002, 537–38). In the following passage, Wegner goes well beyond merely *suggesting:* "it has to be one way or the other. Either the automatisms are oddities against the general backdrop of conscious behavior causation in everyday life, or we must turn everything around quite radically and begin to think that behavior that occurs *with* a sense of will is somehow the odd case, an add-on to a more basic underlying system" (144).

Conscious Will and Scientific Epiphenomenalism

As Eddy Nahmias (2002, 536) observes, Wegner's defense of his "illusion" thesis about "conscious will" is focused on *proximal* intentions. This is not surprising given Wegner's assertion that "*Intention* is normally understood as an idea of what one is going to do that appears in consciousness just before one does it" (18, emphasis in original). This assertion plainly does not apply to distal intentions. (Nor does it identify a sufficient condition for something's being an intention. As you are driving, another driver cuts you off. The following idea of what you are "going to do … appears in consciousness just before" you hit his car: "Oh no! I'm going to hit that car." The idea expresses a prediction, not an intention; and "intention" definitely is not normally understood in such a way that this idea is an intention.) If Wegner intends his "illusion" thesis to apply even to distal intentions, he has done little to support that application. In this section, the spotlight remains where Wegner shines it – on proximal intentions.[9]

Some philosophers express puzzlement about what Wegner means by "will," "conscious will," and "the experience of conscious will," and they float various interpretations (Bayne 2006; Holton 2004; Mele 2004). As Bayne (2006, 170) observes, the

distinction between willing and the experience of willing sometimes seems to disappear in Wegner's work. Holton (2004, 220) points out that even if "conscious willings [to *A*] … contain an element that is extrinsic to the causal process" that issues in *A*-ing, the extrinsic element may be "the element that makes the willing conscious, rather than being the willing itself" (also see Mele 2004, 206, 209–10). Holton's point harks back to the discussion in "Type II RPs, Conscious Decisions, and Actions" (above) of work that may be done by unconscious proximal intentions. If, for example, conscious proximal intentions are understood, straightforwardly, as proximal intentions of which the agent is conscious, proximal intentions★ (or their physical correlates) may, in some cases, do action-producing work in which consciousness of the intentions (or the physical correlate of the consciousness) is not involved. (For a modest reading of "conscious intention" designed to accommodate various things Wegner may mean by that expression, see Mele 2009, ch. 2.)

Several philosophers criticize Wegner's moving from the data he reports to the thesis that scientific epiphenomenalism about conscious intentions is true (Bayne 2006, 178; Nahmias 2002, 533; Pacherie 2006, 163; Ross 2006, 139). Elisabeth Pacherie (2006) voices a common complaint: "Some authors, including Wegner himself on occasion, seem to think that the fact that the experience of conscious will can be nonveridical is evidence for the claim that conscious mental causation is an illusion. This inference [is not] compelling. To show that the experience of willing is not always errorless is certainly not to show that it is always in error" (163). Bayne criticizes both this inference and an alternative route to Wegner's thesis that is similar to the one highlighted in "Wegner's Work: Introduction" (above), which features the idea that "it has to be one way or the other" (Wegner 2002, 144) – either unconscious automatic processes are what produce all of our actions or "conscious will" does it all.

This stark formulation of the idea raises some of questions. Does it really have to be one way or the other? Do conscious proximal intentions★ or decisions (or their physical correlates) sometimes benefit from automatic mechanisms in the causation of actions? What might count as evidence that conscious proximal intentions★ or decisions (or their physical correlates) play a role in producing some actions?

Return to Libet's studies. Imagine a study of this kind in which subjects are explicitly instructed to make a *conscious decision* about when to flex a wrist and to flex in response to it. Can they comply with this instruction, literally interpreted? If they do comply, then it would seem that their conscious decisions (or their physical correlates) are among the causes of their flexing actions.

A scientific epiphenomenalist about conscious decisions, may reply that these subjects would have flexed even if they had unconsciously decided (or intended) to flex and, therefore, that the conscious decisions (and their physical correlates) played no causal role in producing the flexing actions. (Wegner cannot offer this reply if he is committed to the view that intentions and decisions are essentially conscious.) There is a serious problem with this reply. The reply implicitly appeals to the following principle: If *y* would have happened even if *x* had not happened, then *x* is not among the causes of *y*. And this principle is false. For example: Sally's mother drove her to school, and Sally arrived there at 8:00 A.M. What Sally's mother did was a cause of Sally's arriving at school when she did. This is true, even though, if Sally's mother had not driven her to school, Sally's father would have done so and delivered her there at the same time.

Might a scientific epiphenomenalist about conscious decisions claim that, in the imagined experiment, the subjects' conscious decisions were not among the causes of their flexing actions because the decisions themselves were caused by unconscious processes? A reader who is tempted to accept this claim has failed to absorb the moral of the firecracker analogy in an earlier section. The fact that *x* has a cause does not entail that *x* is not among the causes of *y*.

Wegner on Free Will

In Wegner's (2004) view, conscious will is intimately related to free will. He reports that his discussion of conscious will "has actually been *about* the experience of free will, examining at length when people feel it and when they do not. The special idea we have been exploring is to explain the experience of free will in terms of deterministic or mechanistic processes" (656, emphasis in original).

In a discussion of Wegner's work, Dennett (2003, 222) writes:

> If you are one of those who think that free will is only *really* free will if it springs from an immaterial soul that hovers happily in your brain, shooting arrows of decision into your motor cortex, then, given what *you* mean by free will, my view is that there is no free will at all. If, on the other hand, you think free will might be morally important without being supernatural, then my view is that free will is indeed real, but just not quite what you probably thought it was.

Dennett adds that, despite his admiration for Wegner's work, he sees Wegner as "the killjoy scientist who shows that Cupid doesn't shoot arrows and then insists on entitling his book *The Illusion of Romantic Love*" (224). One moral to take away from this is that if one sets the bar for free will (that is, for the power or ability to act freely) ridiculously high, the thesis that people sometimes act freely should strike one as ridiculous.

Wegner (2008, 234) writes:

> Experience of apparent mental causation renders the self magical because it does not draw on all the evidence. We don't have access to the myriad neural, cognitive, dispositional, biological, or social causes that have contributed to the action – nor do we have access to the similar array of causes that underlie the production of the thoughts we have about the action. Instead, we look at the two items our magic selves render visible to us – our conscious thought and our conscious perception of our act – and believe that these are magically connected by our will. In making this link, we take a mental leap over the demonstrable power of the unconscious to guide action … and conclude that the conscious mind is the sole player.

Obviously, even people who believe that some of their conscious intentions play a role in causing some of their behavior should not believe that "the conscious mind is the sole player." After all, among the things that play a role in causing our intentions are events in the external world. And if, for example, conscious proximal intentions★ play a role in causing overt actions, causal processes of which we are not conscious link them to bodily motions.

So one should set aside the magical idea that the conscious mind or self is not itself causally influenced by anything and is a direct and complete cause of some of our actions. More realistic ideas are more worthy of attention: for example, the hypothesis that conscious intentions* or their physical correlates make a causal contribution to some behavior. Again, Wegner marshals evidence that, in some circumstances, people believe they did things that, in fact, they did not do and, in others, people believe they did not do things that they actually did. But, of course, it is a long way from these findings to the conclusion that the hypothesis just formulated is false.

Some readers who believe that our intentions to A sometimes make causal contributions to our A-ings may think that if all of our decisions and intentions have causes, then we never act *freely*. Such readers should try to explain why compatibilists and event-causal libertarians are wrong about what free action is: Theorists of these kinds regard all free actions as caused, and they regard the causes of free actions as caused. (In Mele [2006], causal theories of free action are reviewed and two such theories are developed in some detail.) Wegner (2008, 228) asks: "Why do we experience our actions as freely willed, arising mysteriously from the self, and why too do we resist attempts to explain those actions in terms of real causal sequences, events that are going on behind the curtain of our minds?" But why think of free will in terms of a magical self? Why not side with compatibilists or event-causal libertarians?

Do we ever act freely? That depends on how free action is to be understood. If (quoting Dennett 2003, 222 again) "free will might be morally important without being supernatural," then maybe we sometimes act freely. If acting freely requires the existence of something that does not exist – a supernatural, magical self – then we never act freely. But I know of no good reason to understand free action in the latter way.

I have not offered an account of free will here. My presumed audience is primarily philosophers, and most philosophers are familiar with most of the live options about how to understand free will. In my opinion, it is fair to conclude that, on any reasonable conception of free will, the studies and data reviewed here leave it open both that we sometimes exhibit it and that we never do. For a discussion of imaginary experimental results that would show that no one ever acts freely, see Mele (2009, ch. 8).[10]

Notes

1. Overt actions are actions that essentially involve peripheral bodily motion. Libet (1985; 1999; 2004, 137–49) maintains that once we become conscious of a decision to perform an overt action, we can exercise free will in "vetoing" it. Neither the veto nor the associated refraining from acting on the vetoed decision is an overt action.

2. For an excellent brief critical review of various relevant philosophical positions that highlights the metaphysical nature of the debate, see Jackson (2000).

3. Elsewhere, Libet (1992, 263) writes: "the brain has begun the specific preparatory processes for the voluntary act well before the subject is even aware of any wish or intention to act."

4. Libet, Gleason, Wright, and Pearl (1983, 627) report that "the subject was asked to note and later report the time of appearance of his conscious *awareness of 'wanting'* *to perform* a given self-initiated movement. The experience was also described as an 'urge' or 'intention' or 'decision' to move, though subjects usually settled for the words 'wanting' or 'urge.'"

5. At the end of the experiment, subjects can be asked how often (if ever) they were aware of proximal intentions to flex. Of course, researchers may worry about the accuracy of their reports.

6. Time t can be a designated point on a Libet clock, and brain activity can be measured backward from t. My guess is that in trials in which there is no stop signal and in trials in which the stop signal does not inhibit a flexing, subjects will produce something resembling a type I RP. In trials in which the stop signal inhibits the onset of EMG activity, subjects might produce EEGs that resemble what Libet calls "the 'veto' RP."

7. Try to imagine that you intend to eat some pie now while also intending not to eat it now. What would you do? Would you reach for it with one hand and grab the reaching hand with your other hand? People who suffer from anarchic hand syndrome sometimes display behavior of this kind (see Marcel 2003, 76–81). Sean Spence and Chris Frith (1999, 24) suggest that these people "have conscious 'intentions to act' [that] are thwarted by … 'intentions' to which the patient does not experience conscious access."

8. Kilner, Vargas, Duval, Blakemore, and Sirigu (2004, 1299) produce evidence that, as they put it, "the readiness potential (RP) – an electrophysiological marker of motor preparation – is present when one is observing someone else's action."

9. Powerful evidence that some conscious distal intentions play a role in producing corresponding intentional actions is discussed in Mele (2009, ch. 7).

10. Parts of this chapter derive from Mele (2008; 2009).

References

Bayne, T. (2006), "Phenomenology and the feeling of doing." In *Does consciousness cause behavior?* ed. S. Pockett, W. Banks, and S. Gallagher, 169–85. Cambridge, Mass.: MIT Press.

Dennett, D. (2003), *Freedom evolves*. New York: Viking.

Haggard, P. and Magno, E. (1999), "Localising awareness of action with transcranial magnetic stimulation." *Experimental Brain Research* 127: 102–107.

Hallett, M. (2007), "Volitional control of movement: The physiology of free will." *Clinical Neurophysiology* 118: 1179–92.

Hohwy, J. (2004), "The experience of mental causation." *Behavior and Philosophy* 32: 377–400.

Holton, R. (2004), "Review of Wegner 2002." *Mind* 113: 218–21.

Jackson, F. (2000), "Psychological explanation and implicit theory." *Philosophical Explorations* 3: 83–95.

Kane, R. (1996), *The significance of free will*. New York: Oxford University Press.

Keller, I. and Heckhausen, H. (1990), "Readiness potentials preceding spontaneous motor acts: Voluntary vs. involuntary control." *Electroencephalography and Clinical Neurophysiology* 76: 351–61.

Kilner, J., Vargas, C., Duval, S., Blakemore, S., and Sirigu, A. (2004), "Motor activation prior to observation of a predicted movement." *Nature Neuroscience* 7: 1299–301.

Lhermitte, F. (1983), "Utilization behavior and its relation to lesions of the frontal lobes." *Brain* 106: 237–55.

Libet, B. (1985), "Unconscious celebral initiative and the role of conscious will in voluntary action." *Behavioral and Brain Sciences* 8: 529–66.

Libet, B. (1992), "The neural time-factor in perception, volition and free will." *Revue de Métaphysique et de Morale* 2: 255–72.

Libet, B. (1999), "Do we have free will?" *Journal of Consciousness Studies* 6: 47–57.

Libet, B. (2001), "Consciousness, free action and the brain." *Journal of Consciousness Studies* 8: 59–65.

Libet, B. (2004), *Mind time*. Cambridge, Mass.: Harvard University Press.

Libet, B., Gleason, C., Wright, E., and Pearl, D. (1983), "Time of unconscious intention to act in relation to onset of cerebral activity (readiness potential)." *Brain* 106: 623–42.

Libet, B., Wright, E., and Gleason, C. (1982), "Readiness potentials preceding unrestricted 'spontaneous' vs. pre-planned voluntary acts." *Electroencephalography and Clinical Neurophysiology* 54: 322–35.

Logan, G. (1994), "On the ability to inhibit thought and action: A users' guide to the stop signal paradigm." In *Inhibitory process in attention, memory, and language*, ed. E. Dagenbach and T. Carr, 142–63. San Diego: Academic Press.

Malle, B. (2006), "Of windmills and straw men: Folk assumptions of mind and action." In *Does consciousness cause behavior?* ed. S. Pockett, W. Banks, and S. Gallagher, 207–31. Cambridge, Mass.: MIT Press.

Marcel, A. (2003), "The sense of agency: Awareness and ownership of action." In *Agency and self-awareness*, ed. J. Roessler and N. Eilan, 48–93. Oxford: Clarendon Press.

Mele, A.R. (1997), "Strength of motivation and being in control: Learning from Libet." *American Philosophical Quarterly* 34: 319–32.

Mele, A.R. (2003), *Motivation and agency*. New York: Oxford University Press.

Mele, A.R. (2004), "The illusion of conscious will and the causation of intentional actions." *Philosophical Topics* 32: 193–213.

Mele, A.R. (2006), *Free will and luck*. New York: Oxford University Press.

Mele, A.R. (2008), "Recent work on free will and science." *American Philosophical Quarterly* 45: 107–29.

Mele, A.R. (2009), *Effective intentions: The power of the conscious will*. New York: Oxford University Press.

Nahmias, E. (2002), "When consciousness matters: A critical review of Daniel Wegner's *The illusion of conscious will.*" *Philosophical Psychology* 15: 527–41.

Nahmias, E. (2005), "Scientific challenges to free will." In *A companion to the philosophy of action*, ed. T. O'Connor and C. Sandis, 167–84. Oxford: Blackwell.

Pacherie, E. (2006), "Toward a dynamic theory of intentions." In *Does consciousness cause behavior?* ed. S. Pockett, W. Banks, and S. Gallagher, 145–67. Cambridge, Mass.: MIT Press.

Roediger, H., Goode, M., and Zaromb, F. (2008), "Free will and the control of action." In *Are we free? Psychology and free will*, ed. J. Baer, J.C. Kaufman, and R.F. Baumeister, 205–25. New York: Oxford University Press.

Ross, P. (2006), "Empirical constraints on the problem of free will." In *Does consciousness cause behavior?* ed. S. Pockett, W. Banks, and S. Gallagher, 125–44. Cambridge, Mass.: MIT Press.

Spence, S. and Frith, C. (1999), "Towards a functional anatomy of volition." *Journal of Consciousness Studies* 6: 11–29.

Trevena, J. and Millner, M. (2010), "Brain preparation before a voluntary action: Evidence against unconscious movement initiation." *Consciousness and Cognition* 19: 447–57.

Wegner, D. (2002), *The illusion of conscious will*. Cambridge, Mass.: MIT Press.

Wegner, D. (2004), "Précis of *The illusion of conscious will*." *Behavioral and Brain Sciences* 27: 649–59.

Wegner, D. (2008), "Self is magic." In *Are we free? Psychology and free will*, ed. J. Baer, J.C. Kaufman, and R.F. Baumeister, 52–69. New York: Oxford University Press.

Wegner, D. and Wheatley (1999), "Apparent mental causation: Sources of the experience of will." *American Psychologist* 54: 480–91.

CPSIA information can be obtained
at www.ICGtesting.com
Printed in the USA
JSHW011811190822
29491JS00004B/49